Behavioral Finance and AI Tools for Sustainability

Fouad Daidai
University Chouaib Doukkali, Morocco

Mimoun Benali
Sidi Mohamed Ben Abdellah University, Morocco

Larbi Tamnine
Sidi Mohamed Ben Abdellah University, Morocco

IGI Global
Scientific Publishing
Publishing Tomorrow's Research Today

Vice President of Editorial	Melissa Wagner
Director of Acquisitions	Mikaela Felty
Director of Book Development	Jocelynn Hessler
Production Manager	Mike Brehm
Cover Design	Phillip Shickler

Published in the United States of America by
IGI Global Scientific Publishing
701 East Chocolate Avenue
Hershey, PA, 17033, USA
Tel: 717-533-8845
Fax: 717-533-7115
Website: https://www.igi-global.com E-mail: cust@igi-global.com

Library of Congress Cataloging-in-Publication Data

Names: Daidai, Fouad, 1986- editor. | Benali, Mimoun, 1970- editor. | Tamnine, Larbi, 1969- editor.
Title: Behavioral finance and AI tools for sustainability / edited by: Fouad Daidai, Mimoun Benali, Larbi Tamnine.
Other titles: Behavioral finance and artifical intelligence tools for sustainability
Description: Hershey, PA : IGI Global Scientific Publishing, [2025] | Includes bibliographical references and index. | Summary: "This book examines the integration of behavioral finance principles and artificial intelligence (AI) tools to support economic, social, and environmental sustainability"-- Provided by publisher.
Identifiers: LCCN 2024055471 (print) | LCCN 2024055472 (ebook) | ISBN 9798369396841 (hardcover) | ISBN 9798369396858 (paperback) | ISBN 9798369396865 (ebook)
Subjects: LCSH: Artificial intelligence--Financial applications. | Finance--Data processing.
Classification: LCC HG4515.5 .B39 2025 (print) | LCC HG4515.5 (ebook) | DDC 332.640285--dc23/eng/20250214
LC record available at https://lccn.loc.gov/2024055471
LC ebook record available at https://lccn.loc.gov/2024055472
British Cataloguing in Publication Data
A Cataloguing in Publication record for this book is available from the British Library.

Table of Contents

Detailed Table of Contents

Artificial intelligence (AI) has made its way through sustainable finance to make it more efficient in data-driven decision-making with machine learning (ML) and data analytics while evaluating sustainability risks, optimize resource allocation, and ensuring ensure informed investment decisions. All these are crucial for long-term economic growth, staying within the boundaries of the Environmental, Social, and Governance (ESG) framework that opens a future scope for technology-driven financial practices along with global sustainability goals. However, along with the profound blessings, AI has brought many systematic risks like bias, lack of ethical governance, data privacy, regulatory issues, exploitation of developing countries, etc. AI is still developing and should be observed and regulated correctly. These unregulated AI systems in finance pose significant risks to Sustainable Development Goals (SDGs). Hence, this chapter stresses the significance of ethical governance with competent regulation, which promotes sustainability without impeding growth.

This study examines the potential of ChatGPT v4.0 for stock market analysis, particularly within the Indian stock market. The research uses prompt engineering to assess ChatGPT's ability to recommend stocks, construct portfolios, provide fundamental analysis, and understand price movements. The study combines sentiment analysis of news data with historical price data to forecast future price movements. Results demonstrate ChatGPT's effectiveness in identifying investment opportunities and providing insights for decision-making. The study also evaluates the accuracy of ChatGPT's predictions, finding an 88.89% accuracy rate based on news sentiment analysis and a 94% accuracy rate when integrating sentiment analysis with historical price data. Despite limitations, including constraints in handling large datasets, ChatGPT exhibits promise for supporting investors in the Indian stock market. Future research should focus on refining models and addressing ethical considerations to ensure responsible AI integration in finance.

The paper explores how corporate governance practices influence non-financial performance, particularly sustainability. Strong governance ensures that ESG principles are integrated into business operations, promoting long-term sustainability. The study examines the effectiveness of AI-assisted behavioral interventions in advancing sustainable practices. AI can mitigate cognitive biases and irrational decisions,

This chapter explores how the integration of Artificial Intelligence (AI) is redefining the governance and regulation of global financial markets in the era of technological transformation. It examines AI's impacts on regulatory frameworks and practices, focusing on its potential to enhance financial stability, transparency, and efficiency while addressing the specific challenges faced by developing countries. Through a qualitative approach, the study highlights key opportunities, including improved risk detection, optimized regulatory policies, and greater financial inclusivity in less developed regions. However, it also emphasizes challenges such as cybersecurity risks, the need for regulatory adaptation, and the inequalities that AI may exacerbate. The findings underline AI's pivotal role in modernizing financial regulatory practices and fostering international cooperation, offering critical insights into how AI is shaping the future of financial governance and regulation.

This chapter examines the interdependencies among financial sustainability, governance by community-based corporates, and the economics of green ecosystem. Through the use of a quantitative investigation approach, the results show that good governance by community-based corporates has a major positive impact on sustainable financing activities, which in turn helps to advance the development of a strong economics of green ecosystem. Regression analysis reveals that financial sustainability plays a key role in promoting environmental sustainability and governance by community-based corporates. It also delivers convincing experiential indications in support of including ecological, communal, and authority deliberations into in commercial decision-making. This chapter highlights the need for companies to create comprehensive governance structures that link their financial plans to their sustainability goals. It also offers executives and policymakers practical guidance on collaborative initiatives that can foster and support sustainable practices.

This paper aims to analyze the intellectual structure and research directions pertaining to about the impacts of AI on financial decision-making. A systematic bibliometric review was conducted, in which

Preface

OVERVIEW OF THE TOPIC

Integrating behavioral finance and artificial intelligence (AI) is revolutionizing financial decision-making, particularly in the context of sustainability. Behavioral finance, which explores how psychological biases influence investors' choices, has traditionally analyzed cognitive distortions such as overconfidence, loss aversion, and herd behavior (Mohammadi, 2024). However, recent developments in AI allow for real-time detection and correction of these biases, improving investment efficiency and promoting sustainable financial practices (Rane et al., 2024).

Moreover, AI transforms sustainable finance by aligning investment strategies with Environmental, Social, and Governance (ESG) criteria. Advanced machine learning models assess corporate sustainability efforts, identify greenwashing risks, and ensure data-driven responsible investing. These innovations are crucial as investors demand greater transparency and accountability in ESG investing, ensuring long-term financial and environmental stability (Matos, 2020).

These publications offer valuable insights into the potential of AI and big data to enhance the efficiency of sustainable investment strategies. They emphasize the importance of data analytics in understanding investor behavior, identifying irrational financial decisions, and promoting more responsible market practices. Scholars have also highlighted the challenges of implementing AI-driven financial models, including data biases, ethical concerns, and the need for robust regulatory oversight (Barocas, Hardt, & Narayanan, 2019).

Finally, AI and data engineering provide new opportunities for improving investment decision-making and risk management. Financial institutions that leverage these technologies innovatively will be better positioned to address sustainability challenges, manage risks proactively, and meet the evolving expectations of investors. As AI models become more sophisticated and transparent, they will play a crucial role in bridging the gap between sustainable finance theories and practical applications, shaping the future of ethical and responsible investing.

OBJECTIVES OF THE BOOK

The primary goal of this book is to explore the intersection of Artificial Intelligence (AI) and Behavioral Finance, particularly in the context of sustainability and responsible investing. By breaking down complex financial behaviors and demonstrating how AI can be leveraged to understand, predict, and mitigate irrational decision-making, this book aims to provide a comprehensive yet accessible overview for a diverse audience. Whether readers come from finance, technology, policymaking, or academia, they will gain a foundational understanding of how AI-driven behavioral finance can influence sustainable financial strategies. This objective seeks to empower individuals to engage with and contribute to discussions on the evolving role of AI in shaping responsible investment practices.

Another key objective is to offer practical, actionable insights for financial professionals, data scientists, and policymakers looking to integrate AI into behavioral finance models. The book will include real-world case studies, best practices, and examples of successful AI applications in market sentiment analysis, investment behavior modeling, and ESG-focused investment strategies. Financial analysts and investment managers will learn how to leverage AI to design behaviorally informed, sustainable portfolios, while technologists will gain insights into building AI models that reduce market inefficiencies and investor biases. This objective serves to bridge the gap between theoretical knowledge and practical implementation, ensuring that AI-driven behavioral finance is not just an academic concept, but a transformative tool in the financial industry.

In addition to practical applications, the book aims to equip readers with the critical knowledge needed for informed decision-making in an AI-powered financial landscape. By analyzing regulatory challenges, ethical considerations, and future trends, the book will provide a holistic view of how AI is reshaping finance while ensuring compliance with global regulations and ethical investment standards. Readers will develop the ability to navigate AI's risks and limitations, address concerns related to algorithmic bias, data privacy, and transparency, and anticipate emerging trends in AI-driven behavioral finance. This objective contributes to shaping a new generation of finance professionals and policymakers who can make strategic, ethical, and well-informed financial decisions in an increasingly AI-driven world.

By integrating behavioral finance, AI technologies, and sustainability principles, this book seeks to empower professionals, academics, and decision-makers with the tools needed to navigate and influence the future of AI-enhanced financial decision-making.

TARGET AUDIENCE AND POTENTIAL USES

This book is intended for researchers, academics, and students in finance, behavioral economics, AI, and sustainability, providing theoretical insights and empirical studies on AI-driven financial decision-making. It also serves finance professionals, investment managers, and policymakers, offering practical applications of AI in portfolio management, risk mitigation, and ESG investing. Entrepreneurs and technology developers will find valuable strategies for leveraging AI in sustainable finance. By bridging theory and practice, this book equips readers with actionable knowledge to navigate and shape the evolving landscape of AI-powered financial markets.

OVERALL DESCRIPTION OF CONTRIBUTIONS

This book presents a carefully curated selection of advanced and relevant scientific research conducted by renowned researchers and experts in the field. It aims to offer precise and insightful answers to key questions at the intersection of generative artificial intelligence and behavioral finance. By exploring the integration of AI-driven innovations into financial decision-making, this work examines how generative AI enhances market analysis, models cognitive biases, and refines investment strategies. Additionally, it delves into the practical challenges of implementing these technologies, the regulatory and ethical considerations to be addressed, and their overall impact on financial markets and investor behavior. Through a comprehensive approach, this book provides valuable insights into the evolving role of AI in shaping modern financial ecosystems.

The 1st chapter "Technological Options For Implementing Central Bank Digital Currency And Its Potential Impacts On Financial And Monetary Stability: A Prospective Analysis", reviews the main technical and regulatory issues that would need to be faced in the event of a Central Bank's decision to operate a public digital currency scheme, also called a 'central bank digital currency' (CBDC). It reviews in particular the conditions and motivations that might warrant such monetary innovation; its modalities of implementation; the effects of the CBDC issue on the financial stability and its consequences for monetary policy. In so doing, it addresses a gap in digital currency literature, thus far overly focused on private schemes, whilst neglecting the opportunities and challenges involved in a central bank-issued scheme.

The second chapter, "Deep Learning Approaches to Market Sentiment and Stock Returns: A Cross-Country Analysis in Africa in the Time of the COVID-19 Pandemic", explores the intersection of behavioral finance and artificial intelligence through an analysis of market sentiment and stock returns in three African financial markets: the Casablanca Stock Exchange (MASI), the Tunisian Stock Exchange (TUNINDEX), and the Regional African Stock Exchange (BRVM Composite). Using advanced natural language processing techniques, particularly BERT, the study analyzes sentiment from news articles to evaluate its influence on stock performance during the COVID-19 pandemic. The findings reveal diverse dynamics: the BRVM Composite exhibited a significant causal relationship between sentiment and returns, while the MASI and TUNINDEX showed weaker correlations, highlighting the complexity of sentiment-driven behavior. Structural factors, policy interventions, and market-specific dynamics emerged as key influences. This research contributes to behavioral finance by deepening our understanding of sentiment's impact in emerging markets and offering actionable insights for investors and policymakers during crises.

The third chapter "Behavioral And Financial Barriers To The Integration Of Artificial Intelligence In The Tourism And Hospitality Industry", examines the behavioral and financial barriers to its adoption. The study highlights major challenges such as resistance to change, high implementation costs, and lack of resources. A systematic analysis of key themes from 29 recent articles, carried out with IRaMuTeQ, reveals that these barriers are holding back technology adoption. The results underline the need for inclusive strategies, including incentive policies and training programs, to ensure an equitable and sustainable digital transition.

The fourth chapter "Investor Sentiment Contagion-An Industry Perspective of Investors' Heterogeneity Presented by "Informational Cycle Cascade" with AI's Algorithm", uses the FEM algorithm of artificial intelligence (AI) to analyze the rule of investor sentiment contagion under "informational cycle cascade". There are five big up or down phases of investor sentiment contagion for the industry average at the whole period. Bad information contagion under the influence of the global finance crisis and good information contagion under the influence of an economic stimulating plan on big scale indicate that investor sentiment contagion differentiates between the up phase and down phase. The FEM coupling model of investor sentiment is created to compute and analyze investor sentiment contagion among the industries. Cloud picture presents the average space distribution of investor sentiment contagion. In the real capital market, some investors often adjust their investment decisions, and the informational cycle cascade can well explain this phenomenon.

The fifth chapter "Enhancing Portfolio Optimization with Deep Learning Evidence from African Stock Markets", explores the potential of deep learning models, specifically Long Short-Term Memory (LSTM), Deep Multilayer Perceptron (DMLP), and Convolutional Neural Networks (CNN), to predict the movements of three key African stock indices: MASI (Morocco), BRVM Composite (West Africa) and TUNINDEX (Tunisia). By comparing the performance of these architectures, this research aims to identify the models most suitable for prediction in the context of limited data and high volatility. The results of this study will provide crucial insights for investors, portfolio managers, and researchers, thereby contributing to the development of more robust and effective portfolio optimization strategies for African markets, often overlooked by traditional methods.

The sixth chapter "Ethics in AI-Driven Sustainable Finance: Balancing Innovation with Integrity" aims to evaluate sustainability risks, optimize resource allocation, and ensuring ensure informed investment decisions. All these are crucial for long-term economic growth, staying within the boundaries of the Environmental, Social, and Governance (ESG) framework that opens a future scope for technology-driven financial practices along with global sustainability goals. However, along with the profound blessings, AI has brought many systematic risks like bias, lack of ethical governance, data privacy, regulatory issues, exploitation of developing countries, etc. AI is still developing and should be observed and regulated correctly. These unregulated AI systems in finance pose significant risks to Sustainable Development Goals (SDGs). Hence, this chapter stresses the significance of ethical governance with competent regulation, which promotes sustainability without impeding growth.

The seventh chapter "AI Chatbots and Market Dynamics-Analyzing the Impact of AI on the Indian Stock Market", examines the potential of ChatGPT v4.0 for stock market analysis, particularly within the Indian stock market. The research uses prompt engineering to assess ChatGPT's ability to recommend stocks, construct portfolios, provide fundamental analysis, and understand price movements. The study combines sentiment analysis of news data with historical price data to forecast future price movements. Results demonstrate ChatGPT's effectiveness in identifying investment opportunities and providing insights for decision-making. The study also evaluates the accuracy of ChatGPT's predictions, finding an 88.89% accuracy rate based on news sentiment analysis and a 94% accuracy rate when integrating sentiment analysis with historical price data. Despite limitations, including constraints in handling large datasets, ChatGPT exhibits promise for supporting investors in the Indian stock market. Future research should focus on refining models and addressing ethical considerations to ensure responsible AI integration in finance.

The eighth chapter "Navigating towards Sustainability: The role of Corporate governance and AI-driven behavioral interventions" explores how corporate governance practices influence non-financial performance, particularly sustainability. Strong governance ensures that ESG principles are integrated into business operations, promoting long-term sustainability. The study examines the effectiveness of AI-assisted behavioral interventions in advancing sustainable practices. AI can mitigate cognitive biases and irrational decisions, pushing individuals and organizations toward sustainability. AI-driven governance frameworks can enhance non-financial performance, including environmental stewardship, social responsibility, and ethical governance. Through case studies and analysis, the paper provides insights into how AI and corporate governance can optimize sustainability strategies beyond traditional financial metrics.

The ninth chapter "Impact of ESG Factors on the Financial Performance of Corporates in India", investigates the connection between Indian companies' financial results and Environmental, Social, and Governance (ESG) performance, with a focus on socially and environmentally sensitive industries. There is little data on the financial effects of ESG integration in developing nations like India, even though it is becoming more crucial for long-term value development. Using a quantitative approach involving ESG ratings and financial indicators (Return on Equity [ROE], Return on Assets [ROA], and Return on Capital Employed [ROCE]) we analyze the performance of firms from 2021 to 2023 in five different sectors. Among the pillars, environmental issues had the most significant effect on material financial success, showing a positive but weak correlation with ESG scores. However, the study also investigates into sectoral distinctions, pointing to differential financial outcomes associated with ESG across industries.

The tenth chapter "Artificial Intelligence, Open Innovation and Financial Sustainability: Trends, Perspectives and Future Research Directions", examines the intersection of finance, AI and open innovation, emphasizing decision-making, operational efficiency and financial inclusion. Using bibliometric methods on 420 Wos publications and co-author network analysis with VOSviewer, we identified key contributors and thematic clusters. It is found that research grew exponentially from 2016, peaking in 2023, with strong AI and OI synergies in finance's digital transformation. Co-authorship analysis highlighted core themes: AI applications, innovation management and financial sustainability. The co-author network shows three principal collaborative clusters knew centers of these networks included the National University of Singapore. There is, however, very little cross cluster collaboration and the regions of Africa and MENA are largely absent. Achieving a greater degree of multi-regional collaboration will make it possible to support the development of more sustainable financial practices. This study contributes to understanding the impact of AIs and OI on the creation of inclusive financial ecosystems.

The eleventh chapter "Artificial Intelligence Shaping Financial Governance and Global Regulation Through the IMF and World Bank" explores how the integration of Artificial Intelligence (AI) is redefining the governance and regulation of global financial markets in the era of technological transformation. It examines AI's impacts on regulatory frameworks and practices, focusing on its potential to enhance financial stability, transparency, and efficiency while addressing the specific challenges faced by developing countries. Through a qualitative approach, the study highlights key opportunities, including improved risk detection, optimized regulatory policies, and greater financial inclusivity in less developed regions. However, it also emphasizes challenges such as cybersecurity risks, the need for regulatory adaptation, and the inequalities that AI may exacerbate. The findings underline AI's pivotal role in modernizing financial regulatory practices and fostering international cooperation, offering critical insights into how AI is shaping the future of financial governance and regulation.

The twelfth chapter "Sustainable Finance Effect On The Green Economy By The Mediation Of Corporate Governance In The Horn Of Africa", examines the interdependencies among financial sustainability, governance by community-based corporates, and the economics of green ecosystem. Through the use of a quantitative investigation approach, the results show that good governance by community-based corporates has a major positive impact on sustainable financing activities, which in turn helps to advance the development of a strong economics of green ecosystem. Regression analysis reveals that financial sustainability plays a key role in promoting environmental sustainability and governance by community-based corporates. It also delivers convincing experiential indications in support of including ecological, communal, and authority deliberations in commercial decision-making. This chapter highlights the need for companies to create comprehensive governance structures that link their financial plans to their sustainability goals. It also offers executives and policymakers practical guidance on collaborative initiatives that can foster and support sustainable practices.

The thirteenth chapter "A Systematic Analysis Approach of AI's Role in Enhancing Financial Decision-Making", aims to analyze the intellectual structure and research directions about the impacts of AI on financial decision-making. A systematic bibliometric review was conducted, in which datasets were retrieved from both Scopus and Web of Science databases. After merging and applying all inclusion criteria, a final set of 235 datasets was analyzed in October 2024 using software tools provided by RStudio-Biblioshiny and IRaMuTeQ. This mirrors the intellectual structuring around the clusters in predictive modeling, risk management, and responsible finance. This research enhances a better understanding of the applications of AI and their impact on financial decision-making. These include looking at the effect of AI on ethics and transparency in the governance of financial systems. This paper contributes to new knowledge of advanced technologies integrated into finance and suggests ways to pursue further research.

The fourteen chapter "A Study on Understanding the Transformative Role of Artificial Intelligence in Fostering Financial Literacy in the Manufacturing Sector" explores AI-driven tools like machine learning, natural language processing, and predictive analytics to enhance financial decision-making. By bridging knowledge gaps and simplifying complexities, AI fosters better understanding and sustainable growth. It provides insights for leaders and policymakers, emphasizing AI's role in shaping financial literacy and driving innovation.

The final chapter, "Algorithmic Governance in ESG Ratings - Addressing Bias & Enhancing Transparency in AI Driven Sustainable Finance" explores the impact of firm size, industry sector, and regional regulatory environments on ESG scores. Findings reveal that energy-intensive sectors receive lower ratings due to sustainability concerns, while larger corporations tend to score higher because of superior disclosure practices. Additionally, companies operating in regions with stricter regulations generally achieve better ESG performance. These inconsistencies are further illustrated through case studies of BlackRock and Tesla, highlighting the shortcomings in current rating methodologies.

This book makes a significant contribution to the evolving intersection of Artificial Intelligence, Behavioral Finance, and Sustainability, offering both theoretical depth and practical applications. By exploring how AI can analyze and mitigate financial biases, it enhances understanding of irrational investor behaviors and their impact on market dynamics. The book also provides actionable insights for integrating AI into sustainable investment strategies, ESG compliance, and risk management.

Its impact extends beyond academia, serving as a valuable resource for finance professionals, policymakers, and technology experts, helping them harness AI to drive responsible financial decision-making. By bridging the gap between behavioral finance theory and AI-driven applications, this book lays the foundation for a more data-driven, ethical, and sustainable financial ecosystem, shaping future research and industry practices.

Chapter 1
Technological Options for Implementing Central Bank Digital Currency and Its Potential Impacts on Financial Economy:
A Prospective Analysis

Hicham Sadok
https://orcid.org/0000-0003-4402-0954
Mohammed V University in Rabat, Morocco

ABSTRACT

This chapter reviews the main technical and regulatory issues that would need to be faced in the event of a Central Bank's decision to operate a public digital currency scheme, also called a 'central bank digital currency' (CBDC). It reviews in particular the conditions and motivations that might warrant such monetary innovation; its modalities of implementation; the effects of the CBDC issue on the financial stability and its consequences for monetary policy. In so doing, it addresses a gap in digital currency literature, thus far overly focused on private schemes, whilst neglecting the opportunities and challenges involved in a central bank-issued scheme.

INTRODUCTION

> 'Because we are a successful and large enough company, we are now able to build systems without precedent ... more sophisticated than many governments have done'
> (Maquet, 2020).

These were the words of Meta (Facebook) CEO, Mark Zuckerberg, on the eve of launching the Libra virtual currency project in 2019. These words capture the potential that virtual currencies have opened, for different societal actors (and particularly large corporations) to transcend central bank monopoly over currency issue, Governments have been slow to register the idea—which Zuckerberg's words appear to

DOI: 10.4018/979-8-3693-9684-1.ch001

imply—that a private company could exert a comparable degree of control over monetary flows, and thereby take on some aspects of the role traditionally ascribed to central banks.

Over the course of history, Means of payment have continued to evolve and technical developments continue to change their form, and with it the uses of money. After the appearance of the check in the 19th century, credit cards and the first ATMs in the mid-20th century, it is the turn of digital and contactless payment to emerge at the beginning of this millennium.

While central banks have so far played a secondary role in these developments, many of them are now exploring the possibility of creating a Central Bank Digital Currency (CBDC). This would mean making central bank money accessible to the general public, whereas today it is only usable by commercial banks during "wholesale" transactions, particularly on the interbank market (Sadok & El Maknouzi, 2020). With the issuance of a CBDC, the central bank could also play a role as a "retail" currency, which would considerably transform the role of the Central Bank in this area: from a simple settlement institution for financial intermediaries, it would become the operator of a payment system accessible to all (Mahboub & Sadok, 2024; Hossain, 2021).

According to the latest survey conducted by the Bank for International Settlements, 44 central banks have started exploratory work on CBDCs, nine of which are exploring the subject at varying stages and half of these nine are already in the development, experimentation or deployment phase[1].Their motivations vary depending on the context: financial stability, implementation of monetary policy, financial inclusion, improving the efficiency and security of payment systems (Barontini & Holden, 2019). There are now five officially launched CBDCs: the Sand dollar in the Bahamas, DCash in the Eastern Caribbean Currency Union, eNaira in Nigeria and jam-Dex in Jamaica and the Chinese e-CNY (digital yuan).

While there is much interest in how such a CBDC monetary system might work in practice, there is less interest in how this public digital currency might be used by the actors it is supposed to bypass in their quest to reduce reliance on the traditional banking system, and in particular private banks, following the financial crisis of 2008. However, such public digital currencies also have the potential to resurrect public monetary power, and thus begin to address some of the reasons underlying distrust in traditional banking institutions.

To this end, it will be interesting to examine in more detail what CBDCs—as hybrids between crypto-currency and sovereign currency—might look and work like. This horizon of inquiry yields such questions as: what could their effects on monetary policy and financial stability be? How could they be practically implemented, and how might their uptake be incentivised?

Questions such as these provide the focus for a growing group of researchers, and of financial and monetary actors and institutions. This chapter is an attempt to begin mapping and unpacking those questions in an organic way, and thereby contribute to an understanding of the effects of CBDC issue. In particular, this study addresses the issues arising along the following four dimensions: (i) the motivations and modalities of implementation that might warrant such monetary innovation; (ii) the effects of CBDC issue on financial stability; (iv) and its consequences for monetary policy. The following sections address each of these issues in turn, and are followed by a conclusion.

1. MOTIVATIONS AND OPTIONS FOR CBDC SETUP

A CBDC can be thought of as a virtual representation of *fiat* money, albeit with some differences—first and foremost regarding anonymity. A CBDC would be a coin 'minted'—not on a material substrate but—as a code encrypted through an algorithm. Like the physical coin, this 'coded coin' would originate from the central bank, which would determine its face value. Issue by a central bank means that the ledger needed to record and validate transactions might as well be maintained by the central bank (centralised ledger), as opposed to using distributed ledger technology (DLT), i.e. the blockchain, as used for instance by Bitcoin.

For a central bank, several trends would justify introducing a digital public currency: money, as a "monetary anchor," could be threatened if a means of payment independent of the national currency, such as a foreign CBDC or a stablecoin issued by a large technology company as Meta (Libra Association, 2019), were to be used as an independent means of payment. And if the use of cash were to decline, the entire payments market, which would now be completely electronic, would be dominated by foreign intermediaries. Visa and Mastercard currently manage 87.4% of electronic transactions worldwide, which poses a real problem of sovereignty, often very little explored (J.P. Morgan, 2021). Another major reason for adopting a CBDC is that, amidst trends towards the increasing digitisation of payments, these digital currency schemes would help preserve the seigniorage of the State over money issue in the long term, through an increase (and diversification) of the monetary base, and a reduction in costs (Niepelt, 2019).

Given the state of thinking on digital currencies, the question of the interest of this monetary project is entirely legitimate since free competition applied to the management and provision of means of payment does not result in the optimal situation that central banks should be monitoring. Money is a network good, which leads to the creation of oligopolies on the payment markets. At the same time, a significant part of the world's population is in a situation of financial exclusion due to the fact that it does not have access to all the necessary banking services, starting with those of electronic payment. This exclusion is due, on the one hand, to the commercial nature of the provision of these services, which responds to profitability constraints and leaves aside those who do not represent a sufficiently lucrative clientele; and on the other hand, to a lack of incentives, infrastructure and payment equipment in working-class neighbourhoods and remote areas (Sadok & Assadi, 2022).

In designing the CBDC, it should first be a more inclusive means of payment than existing solutions. Central banks should consider how it can be implemented and used by everyone, including those who are currently excluded from the financial system and territories with the necessary infrastructure.

For the central bank, the CBDC would therefore be a new means of electronic payment mobilizing a form of risk-free public currency, operating through national systems, usable throughout the territory and accessible to all. Issue by a central bank means that the ledger needed to record and validate transactions might as well be maintained by the central bank (centralised ledger), as opposed to using distributed ledger technology (DLT), i.e. the blockchain, as used by Bitcoin.

Several possible models are available for its implementation and they can be approached through two main criteria: the monetary architecture and the currency transfer mechanism.

The architecture of the CBDC corresponds to its operational and institutional organization with the different types of actors that can intervene in its circulation. Regardless of the specific technical form, a first question concerning CBDC development would be around who it should contemplate as its users, whether individuals and families, companies, or only banking institutions. In this respect, it seems a general trend is emerging in the pioneering work of 'early adopter' central banks, suggesting there might really be two kinds of CBDCs in the works: retail (CBDC-R) and wholesale (CBDC-W) CBDCs (European central Bank – ECB, 2020). Wholesale virtual currencies would be reserved to financial intermediaries (banks), while retail virtual currencies would be intended for general use by businesses and households (Berentsen & Schär, 2018; Pfister, 2017, 2019). States could therefore choose to develop either, both, or neither of these two digital currency variants. Since 2016 the Swedish central bank has been exploring the issue of a CBDC-R, under the name e-krona (Skingsley, 2016; Sveriges Riksbank, 2017, 2018; Ingves, 2018).

Indeed, the idea that the central bank ensures the provision of all CBDC services is not necessarily realistic. All central banks consider that they must collaborate with the market. The question then arises of the distribution of roles between these two poles. The primary characteristic of the CBDC is that these units represent claims of the central bank, in the same way as for cash; consequently, the prerogative to create and issue CBDC units naturally falls to the latter.

But after this first step, several questions remain open: who keeps track of the transactions and account balances of each user? Who manages the execution of transactions? Who interacts with users to offer them CBDC services?

Depending on the entity that performs these different tasks, a CBDC, from the point of view of its architecture, can be described as either "direct", in the case where the central bank takes charge of all the tasks related to its circulation, or "intermediated", in the case where private actors, more particularly commercial banks, perform the majority of the tasks.

The second main feature of the CBDC is its transfer mechanism that determines the terms of circulation of these units between users. These terms can be compared with those of current currencies. In electronic form, these are necessarily linked to an account: the transfer of a unit results in the debit of one account and the credit of another. These accounts are managed by an institution with which it is necessary to communicate to make a transfer, and each account is necessarily linked to a natural or legal person. In contrast, in their physical form, in coins or notes, currencies are bearer; to use them, their simple possession is enough. No third-party institution is involved in the exchanges and the parties to the exchange do not need to be identified. However, this possibility that a means of payment is bearer is not necessarily reserved for physical cash. Currencies stored in an electronic wallet (a card or a Smartphone) can also be bearer and circulate peer-to-peer like cash, but in this case, via NFC (Near Field Communication) or Bluetooth technology (Sadok, 2023). Depending on the transfer mechanism available, the CBDC could thus be linked to an account and/or to the bearer like cash.

These two characteristics, architecture and transfer mechanisms, make it possible to differentiate at least four possible modalities for the implementation of the CBDC: (i) CBDC account domiciled with the central bank, (ii) CBDC similar to cash and provided by the central bank, (iii) CBDC account whose management is delegated to commercial banks and (iiii) CBDC similar to cash and provided by a private intermediary.

If central banks are already well engaged in the implementation of CBDCs (at least the ECB in view of the 2024 report), what do we know then about the direction they want to take and the solutions that are attracting attention?

2. CONSEQUENCES OF CBDE ISSUE ON FINANCIAL STABILITY

In developing digital public currencies, central banks seem particularly concerned about not crowding out private players from the payments market; however, this is the potential of the CBDC, particularly in its direct form. If it is possible to hold an account with the central bank, it is no longer necessary to have one with a commercial bank: if the citizen can make payments in central currency via a solution offered by the central bank (an application for example), payment service providers therefore become largely superfluous.

The main modality currently being considered in the central banks' reflection projects for the implementation of CBDCs is that of a digital currency with a private intermediary, mainly a commercial bank. The central bank would only be in charge of issuing the digital currency and settling transactions. Concretely, in addition to the current account, the commercial bank would also provide access to a digital currency account that could be topped up from the current account and chosen to use when paying for a purchase.

This solution would indeed bring very little added value. It would be largely redundant with existing card payment solutions, and the consumer would have little direct interest in using it. Consequently, one can doubt the success of a public digital currency offered only in this form. It may seem odd to want to innovate while fearing that the innovation introduced will be successful. But here it reveals the suspicion of central banks towards this monetary innovation, even if it would be distributed by a commercial bank.

In their perception of CBDCs, central banks believe that the latter would pose a problem of disintermediation of the banking sector, which, lacking deposits, would be less able to carry out its functions, particularly that of financing the economy (Sadok et al., 2023). Central banks could therefore plan to limit the latitude with which customers use digital currency by setting up a ceiling, exorbitant management fees or a disincentive remuneration structure.

However, CBDC architectures are not mutually exclusive. Thus, while the concept of this public digital currency would be primarily intermediated, there is nothing to prevent a complementary direct modality: the central bank, via a smartphone application, from directly providing CBDC accounts to those who want them. At present, the possibility of a central bank being able to maintain such direct relationships with citizens appears to be a red line. This would not, however, require the central bank to recruit as many employees and open as many counters as commercial banks, as some often claim in a caricatured manner to rule out this possibility. But above all, it presents an ideological stance that empties this financial innovation of its great interest, namely the democratization of means of payment and giving substance to the public character of money (Sadok & El Maknouzi, 2020).

In this context, what should a CBDC developed to serve the collective interest, rather than to safeguard the position of existing actors, look like?

A first step would be to broaden the range of intermediaries that can offer CBDCc services. While the central bank is only considering involving private intermediaries, there is no obligation to limit itself to this type of actor. For its e-Krona, the Bank of Sweden plans to involve both private and public intermediaries, recognising that the market cannot meet all needs and that it must be supplemented by non-market channels.

The underlying issue is this: knowing whether money and the payment services linked to it should constitute private goods falling within the commercial domain or whether, on the contrary, they should constitute public goods.

The issuance of the CBDC is not simply a change in the nature of the contractual link underlying the central bank. It is a monetary innovation that should be accessible and free for users. To this end, only a public implementation option (CBDC-R) would guarantee this; not only by diversifying the modalities of access to the public digital currency, but also by generating a competitive effect on the entire banking sector. Issuing a CBDC-R could also help reduce the social costs connected with retail payment infrastructure (e.g. the costs of production, issue, distribution, storage, management, security, and destruction of cash). These have been estimated at almost 1% of GDP in the euro area, and half of that amount is specifically attributable to performance of cash payments (Schmiedel et al., 2012). With specific reference to Sweden, Juks (2018) estimates that the arrival of CBDCs on the market could lower banks' financing costs by 0.22%. A reduction of those costs would particularly benefit those sections of society that, due to their vulnerability, face the greatest costs in accessing bank-managed payment services (Banque de France, 2018). Moreover, a CBDC-R could promote financial inclusion, especially in developing countries where sections of the population are excluded from the banking system

This option does not need to be exclusive, but it is a necessary complement to what can reasonably be expected of the central bank in its contribution to the digital transformation. The challenges of resilience of the payment system, which lie in the existence of several systems that are autonomous from each other, and of strategic independence from foreign suppliers or proprietary technological systems, also justify the in-depth exploration of the design of the CBDC based on the public option.

All these options relating to the design and implementation of the CBDC are ultimately political choices, which should, in truth, not be left to the sole choice of central bank governors, but should be the subject of an informed and democratic citizen debate.

3. CONSEQUENCES OF CBDC ISSUE ON MONETARY POLICY

In the medium to long term, the appearance of CBDCs would lead to important shifts in the functioning of the monetary and financial system. For one, a CBDC would catalyse greater competition and productivity gains in the payment services sector, with spillover on all trading activity (Sadok & El Maknouzi, 2020). Unlike scriptural money—i.e. account balances held with private banks and spent through wire transfers, cheques, or payment cards—the circulation of a CBDC would not be tied to a countervailing requirement of holding fractional reserves: this would reduce the loss to the economy that comes from tying up resources to guarantee the liquidity of private banks.

A CBDC would additionally stimulate excess demand by enabling transactions that fail to happen on grounds of security, confidentiality, non-monetary barriers(e.g. time allocation, physical distance from a bank or ATM), or transaction costs tied to online or point-of-sale purchases (Fung & Halaburda, 2016, Mouline & Sadok, 2021).Enlarging the horizon to an international level, CBDCs denominated in highly sought-after currencies would—if made available also to non-residents—have a disciplining effect on countries with more expansive monetary policies. Furthermore, if international investors were to consider CBDCs as an option for portfolio diversification, this might increase the volatility of exchange rates (Armelius et al., 2018).

CBDCs would also impact interbank and money markets by enabling instant tracking of intraday transactions, in a way that would allow the central bank to better track the evolution of monetary payments in real time (Federal Reserve System – FED, 2019; Pfister, 2018). In turn, this would significantly remove disturbances in the transmission of monetary policy decisions via central bank interest rates.

Another area of concern is how a CBDC could impact liquidity risk in the event of a bank failure (Carney, 2016; Bank for International Settlements – BIS, 2018). The increasing recurrence of financial crises makes this issue a crucial one, which overrides all the other possible benefits of a CBDC system on the economy and financial markets (Armelius et al., 2018). In response, it should be considered that the liquidity risk associated with the failure of a private bank would be mitigated in the presence of a CBDC system, since the main holder of CBDC deposits would remain the central bank. In such a case, CBDC users are unlikely to suffer losses on their CBDC holdings, as would be the case with bank accounts held with a commercial bank in the event of a liquidity crisis (Pfister & Valla, 2017). Similarly, CBDCs would also mitigate the risk of financial instability following a bank run, for example following the dissemination of misleading information. Another factor suggesting a positive assessment of CBDCs in the event of a financial crisis is that, thanks to their direct link to the central bank, any unusual movements (e.g. a sudden influx of bank transfers or requests to exchange with another currency) would be reported more quickly to the central bank, allowing for faster preventive measures to be taken to stop contagion and address financial instability (Kumhof & Noone, 2018; Nobanee et al., 2023).

Besides making available a secure, liquid, and dematerialised means of payment to preserve the continuity of transactions, another goal of CBDC adoption would be to put in place a flexible tool for of conducting monetary policy. It is well known that the ultimate goal of monetary policy is price stability. In this respect, Japan is a textbook example of the difficulties that arise, once inflation has dropped below target, to raise it again. For a CBDC to serve central bank efforts to remedy one such predicament, its adoption must be capable of stimulating enough demand to counterbalance the decline in prices. Hence, the introduction of a CBDC requires some thought to go into the design of this scheme, to establish appropriate transmission mechanisms that will place it in service of more effective monetary policy.

In this respect, a CBDC needs to be implemented in such a way as to counteract the risk of increased volatility in the supply of central bank-issued money, due to the fluctuations stemming from demand by non-residents and during financial crises. However, issuing CBDCs can also create an opportunity for other financial intermediaries, beyond banks, to operate on the money market and to access a central bank-issued asset. According to Pfister (2018), this widening of access could usher an instant payment system in which monetary policy could be conducted in real time, by establishing an intraday market for CBDCs. Such arrangement would make it possible to adjust the base interest rate instantly, in response to feedback from the intraday market. Finally, this adjustment could take into account, and influence, the demand for other financial assets whose remuneration is correlated to the bank base rate—like banknotes, bank deposits, reserves, and the main refinancing instruments (Drumetz et al., 2015).

Ultimately, the impact of CBDC issue on the transmission mechanism for monetary policy would depend on the choice as to whether to remunerate the new digital currency. Awarding a remuneration to CBDC holdings—however symbolic—would create a remunerated asset backed by the central bank, something that would reverberate on the interest rates offered on all other assets existing in the economy (Armelius et al., 2018). Andolfatto (2018) explores a few possible scenarios. For instance, he estimates that the competition generated by the restructuring of interest rates following the issue of a CBDC would incentivise banks to raise deposit rates, potentially increasing the volume of bank deposits. However, this scenario might not be the most likely, in the absence of vigorous competition in the banking sector. In such a case, the resulting increase in banks' costs of securing financial resources could be passed on to loans. Finally, in connection with the control of inflation, issuing a remunerated CBDC would actually reduce the opportunity cost of holding fiat currency in an inflationary environment, and therefore remove a source of potential disturbance to the integrity of interest rate setting as a tool for monetary policy

(Pfister & Valla, 2017). In the opposite case of an unremunerated CBDC, this would make negative (real) interest rates on central bank-issued assets a reality to be reckoned with, in the conduct of monetary policy (Nessen et al., 2018). However, a nominal interest of zero would only be viable for assets with the shortest maturities, whereas assets with longer maturities would be expected to carry a positive interest rate—save for the long-term permanence of exceptional circumstances like those brought about by the 2008 or 2020 financial crises. In view of this, the remuneration structure of a CBDC could react on compensation expected on government securities (Armelieus et al., 2018). Moreover, a move away from government securities might drive up demand for other more remunerative assets, like commodities, which would however drive up inflation. In view of these complications, from the standpoint of inflation control, it seems that remuneration of the CBDC would introduce a better balance in the interest rate structure, allowing adequate remuneration for holders of government securities, and simultaneously easing the pursuit of monetary policy objectives.

To summarize what has been said so far: for inflation control purposes, the interest rate on central bank deposits held as required reserves should be equal to or higher than the possible interest rate on a CBDC. Finally, all of these rates should be higher than or equal to the minimum rate that could be retained as a floor in the interest rate structure.

CONCLUSION

In this chapter, we have charted some of the principal questions concerning the prospect of digital currency issue on the part of central banks. Despite the obvious benefit of having a dematerialised and highly liquid asset to ease payments in the economy, this would still demand attention with respect to repercussions for financial stability and for the conduct of monetary policy. Concerning financial stability, widening access to the digital currency would introduce unpredictable fluctuations in the demand for central bank-issued money. The repercussions of remunerating a digital asset of this kind would also have to be considered carefully, for the arbitrage opportunities they might introduce in the economy, between different central bank-issued assets and between different assets classes across the economy. Secondly, the new digital assets could—under certain conditions—prompt a rethinking of the mechanism for monetary policy transmission, and would have to be so implemented as to expand the tools for the conduct of monetary policy at the disposal of central banking authorities—rather than undermining them through interferences at cross-purposes with central bank interventions.

With respect to different models of CBDCs, CBDC-W would pose the least disruption to the functioning of the financial system, by being offered solely to financial institutions. On the other hand, for countries where financial exclusion were a severe issue, a CBDC-R might be able to take advantage of the rapid spread of mobile phones to make available fast and reliable digital payment methods to wider chunks of the population.

Finally, the issue of a new digital currency also creates broader policy questions—beyond the realm of financial stability and monetary policy—which would need to be addressed in the appropriate *for a* and with the participation of citizens.

DECLARATION

The author declares that the manuscript follows ethical standards and there are no potential conflicts of interest with respect to the research, authorship and/or publication of this chapter.

DISCLAIMER

The contents and views of this chapter are expressed by the author in his personal capacity. It is not necessary for the Editor and the Publisher to agree with these viewpoints, and they are not responsible for any duty of care in this regard.

ACKNOWLEDGMENT

The author extends sincere gratitude to

• The Editor and the International Editorial Advisory Board (IEAB) of this book who initially desk reviewed, arranged a rigorous double/triple blind review process, and conducted a thorough, minute, and critical final review before accepting the chapter for publication.

• All anonymous reviewers who will provide very constructive feedbacks for thorough revision, improvement, extension, and fine tuning of the chapter.

• All colleagues, assistants and well-wishers who assisted to complete this task.

REFERENCES

Andolfatto, D. (2018). Assessing the Impact of Central Bank Digital Currency on Private Banks. Federal Reserve Bank of St. Louis, Working Paper2018-026C. Retrieved from:https://s3.amazonaws.com/realstlouisfed.org/wp/2018/2018-026.pdf(accessed 11 September 2020)

Armelius, H., Boel, P., Claussen, C. A., & Nessen, M. (2018).The E-Krona and the Macroeconomy. *SverigesRiksbank Economic Review*, 2018(3), 43–65. Retrieved from:https://www.riksbank.se/globalassets/media/rapporter/pov/engelska/2018/economic-review-3-2018.pdf (accessed 06April 2021)

Bank for International Settlements (BIS). (2018).*Rapport du Committee on Payments and Market Infrastructure et du Markets Committee*. Basel: Bank for International Settlements. Retrieved from: https://www.bis.org/cpmi/publ/d174.htm (accessed 13 September 2020)

Banque de France. (2018). *Rapport annuel de l'Observatoire de l'inclusion bancaire*. Paris: Banque de France. Retrieved from: https://publications.banque-france.fr/sites/default/files/medias/documents/oib2018_web_signets.pdf (accessed 06April 2021)

Barontini, C., & Holden, H. (2019). Proceeding with Caution – a Survey on Central Bank Digital Currency.Bank for International Settlements, BIS Papers 101. Retrieved from: https://www.bis.org/publ/bppdf/bispap101.pdf (accessed 3 October 2020)

Berentsen, A., & Schar, F. (2018). The Case for Central Bank Electronic Money and the Non-Case for Central Bank Cryptocurrencies. *Review - Federal Reserve Bank of St. Louis*, *100*(2), 97–106. Retrieved September 15, 2020, from https://research.stlouisfed.org/publications/review/2018/02/13/the-case-for-central-bank-electronic-m

Candus, E., Pfister, C., & Sedillot, F. (2017). Où s'investit l'épargne des Français? *Bulletin de la Banque de France*, *214*, 5–21. https://publications.banque-france.fr/sites/default/files/medias/documents/bulletin-bf-214_web.pdf(accessed 21 October 2020)

Carney, M. (2016).*Enabling the FinTech Transformation: Revolution, Restoration, or Reformation?* London: Bank of England. Retrieved from:https://www.bankofengland.co.uk/-/media/boe/files/speech/2016/enabling-the-fintech-transformation-revolution-restoration-or-reformation.pdf (accessed 6April 2021)

Drumetz, F., Pfister, S., & Sahuc, J.-G. (2015). *Politique monétaire* (2 ed.).Louvain-la-Neuve: de Boeck.

Engert, W., & Fung, S. C. (2019). Motivations and Implications of a Central Bank Digital Currency. In E. Gnan & D. Masciandaro (Eds.), Do We Need Central Bank Digital Currency? Economics, Technology and Institutions (pp. 56–71). SUERF., Retrieved from https://www.suerf.org/studies/7025/do-we-need-centralbank-digital-currency-economics-technology-and-institutions, Retrieved September 18, 2020, from.

European Central Bank (ECB). (2020). *Report on a digital euro*. Frankfurt: European Central Bank. Retrieved from:www.ecb.europa.eu/pub/pdf/other/Report_on_a_digital_euro~4d7268b458.en.pdf (accessed 24 September 2020)

Federal Reserve System (FED). (2019).*Federal Reserve Actions to Support Interbank Settlement of Faster Payments*. Washington, D.C.: Board of Governors of the Federal Reserve System. Retrieved from:https://www.federalreserve.gov/newsevents/pressreleases/files/other20190805a1.pdf(accessed 14 September 2020)

Fung, B. S. C., & Halaburda, H. (2016). Central Bank Digital Currencies: a Framework for Assessing Why and How. Bank of Canada, Discussion Paper 2016-22. Retrieved from: https://www.researchgate.net/publication/318555671_Central_Bank_Digital_Currencies_A_Framework_for_Assessing_Why_and_How (accessed 15 November 2020)

Hossain, M. S. (2021). What do we know about cryptocurrency? Past, present, future. *China Finance Review International*. Advance online publication. DOI: 10.1108/CFRI-03-2020-0026

Ingves, S. (2018). *The E-Krona and the Payments of the Future*. Stockholm: Sveriges Riksbank. retrieved from:https://www.riksbank.se/globalassets/media/tal/engelska/ingves/2018/the-e-krona-and-the-payments-of-the-future.pdf (accessed 27 September 2020)

Juks, R. (2018). When a Central Bank Digital Currency Meets Private Money. *Sveriges Riksbank Economic Review*, 2018(3), 79–99. Retrieved from:http://prod-upp-image-read.ft.com/c080e86a-966c-11e9-8cfb-30c211dcd229 (accessed 21 October 2020)

Kumhof, M., & Noone, C. (2018). Central Bank Digital Currencies – Design Principles and Balance Sheet Implications. Bank of England, Staff Discussion Paper 725. Retrieved from: https://www.bankofengland.co.uk/working-paper/2018/central-bank-digital-currencies---design-principles-and-balance-sheet-implications (accessed 27 September 2020)

Libra Association. (2019).*White Paper*. Geneva: Libra Association. Retrieved from: https://libra.org/en-US/wp-content/uploads/sites/23/2019/06/LibraWhitePaper_en_US.pdf (accessed 03 October 2020)

Mahboub, H. M., & Sadok, H. (2024). Barriers to digital transformation: The case of Moroccan companies. *Journal of Telecommunications and the Digital Economy*, *12*(1), 261–276. https://search.informit.org/doi/10.3316/informit.T2024040300010000142251162

Maquet, C. (2020). MNBC: tout comprendre de la monnaie numérique de demain. Retrieved from:https://siecledigital.fr/2020/11/02/mnbc-tout-savoir-monnaie-numerique/ (accessed 6 April 2021)

Morgan, J. P. (2021).J.P. Morgan Creates Digital Coin for Payments. Retrieved from:https://www.jpmorgan.com/solutions/cib/news/digital-coin-payments (accessed 6 April 2021)

Mouline, B., & Sadok, H. (2021). Determinants of corporate cash holdings: Evidence from the Moroccan market. *Accounting*, *7*(6), 1231–1240.

Nakamoto, S. (2009).Bitcoin: A Peer-to-Peer Electronic Cash System. Retrieved from: https://bitcoin.org/bitcoin.pdf (accessed 18 August 2020)

Nessen, M., Sellin, P., & Sommar, P. Å. (2018).The Implications of an E-Krona for the Riksbank's Operational Framework for Implementing Monetary Policy. *Sveriges Riksbank Economic Review*, 2018(3), 29–42. retrieved from:https://www.riksbank.se/globalassets/media/rapporter/pov/artiklar/engelska/2018/181105/20183-the-implications-of-an-e-krona-for-the-riksbanks-operational-framework-for-implementing-monetary-policy.pdf (accessed 11 November 2020)

Niepelt, D. (2019). Reserves for All? Central Bank Digital Currency, Deposits, and their (Non)-Equivalence. *International Journal of Central Banking*, *16*(3), 211–238.

Nobanee, H., El Hadi El Maknouzi, M., Sadok, H., & Alodat, A. Y. (2024). Analysis of insurance entrepreneurship as a hedge in times of crisis: A literature review. *Sustainable Technology and Entrepreneurship*, *3*(2), 100065. Advance online publication. DOI: 10.1016/j.stae.2023.100065

Pfister, C. (2017). Politique monétaire et monnaies digitales: beaucoup de bruit pour rien? *Revue française d'économie*, 32(2), 37–63

Pfister,C. (2018). Le temps (réel), c'est de l'argent. *Revue française d'économie*, 32(4), 195–212.

Pfister, C. (2019). Les monnaies digitales, un nouvel univers? *Regards croisés sur l'économie*, 24(1), 40–52

Pfister, C., & Valla, N. (2017). Nouvelle Normale ou Nouvelle Orthodoxie? Éléments d'un nouveau cadre d'action pour les banques centrales. *Revue économique*, *68*, 41–62.

Riksbank, S. (2017). The Riksbank's E-Krona Project Report. Sveriges Riksbank., Retrieved from https://www.riksbank.se/globalassets/media/rapporter/e-krona/2017/rapport_ekrona_uppdaterad_170920_eng.pdf, Retrieved October 6, 2020, from.

Riksbank, S. (2018). The Riksbank's E-krona Project Report 2. Sveriges Riksbank., Retrieved from https://www.riksbank.se/globalassets/media/rapporter/e-krona/2018/the-riksbanks-e-krona-project-report-2.pdf, Retrieved October 16, 2020, from.

Ryan-Collin, J., Greenham, T., Werner, R., & Jackson, A. (2012). *Where Does Money Come From? A Guide to the UK Monetary and Banking System*. New Economics Foundation.

Sadok, H. (2023). The Initial Coin Offering: Is It a Profitable Tool for Investment? In Jallouli, R., Bach Tobji, M. A., Belkhir, M., Soares, A. M., & Casais, B. (Eds.), *Digital Economy. Emerging Technologies and Business Innovation. ICDEc 2023. Lecture Notes in Business Information Processing* (Vol. 485). Springer., DOI: 10.1007/978-3-031-42788-6_12

Sadok, H., & Assadi, D. (2023). The Contribution of AI-Based Analysis and Rating Models to Financial Inclusion. In *Artificial Intelligence, Fintech, and Financial Inclusion* (pp. 11–25). CRC Press., DOI: 10.1201/9781003125204-2

Sadok, H., Chaibi, H., & Saadane, R. (2023). An exploratory study on the contribution of Artificial Intelligence in improving the bank credit analysis process. In: Proceedings of the 6th International Conference on Networking, Intelligent Systems & Security. pp. 1–4. ACM, Larache Morocco. https://doi.org/DOI: 10.1145/3607720.3607784

Sadok, H &El Maknouzi,M.H, (2020). The Regulation of Virtual Currencies in Comparative Perspective: New Private Money or Niche Technological Innovation? *Journal of Money Laundering Control*. https://doi.org/DOI: 10.1108/JMLC-09-2020-0101

Schmiedel, H., Gergana, K., & Ruttenberg, W. (2012). The Social and Private Costs of Retail Payment Instruments – A European Perspective. European Central Bank, Occasional Paper 137. Retrieved from: https://www.ecb.europa.eu/pub/pdf/scpops/ecbocp137.pdf? 33f4f6bcb83613df99dd634b89e2c8a0 (accessed 19 November 2020)

Segendorf, B. (2018). How Many E-Krona Are Needed for Payments? *Sveriges Riksbank Economic Review*, 2018(3), 66–78. retrieved from:https://www.riksbank.se/globalassets/media/rapporter/pov/artiklar/engelska/2018/181105/20183-how-many-e-krona-are-needed-for-payments.pdf (accessed 14 September 2020)

Skingsley, C. (2016). Should the Riksbank Issue E-Krona? Sveriges Riksbank., Retrieved from https://www.riksbank.se/globalassets/media/tal/svenska/skingsley/2016/tal_skingsley_161116_eng.pdf, Retrieved November 19, 2020, from.

ENDNOTE

1 Anneke Kosse et Ilaroa Mattei « Gaining Momentum-Results of the 2021 BIS Survey on Central Bank Digital Currencies" BIS Papers n° 125, mai 2022.

Chapter 2
Deep Learning Approaches to Market Sentiment and Stock Returns:
A Cross-Country Analysis in Africa in the Time of the COVID-19 Pandemic

Imane Boudri
https://orcid.org/0009-0007-5163-108X
Groupe Institut Supérieur de Commerce et d'Administration des Entreprises, Morocco

Abdelhamid El Bouhadi
Sidi Mohamed Ben Abdellah University, Morocco

Mimoun Benali
Sidi Mohamed Ben Abdellah University, Morocco

ABSTRACT

This chapter explores the intersection of behavioral finance and artificial intelligence through an analysis of market sentiment and stock returns in three African financial markets: the Casablanca Stock Exchange (MASI), the Tunisian Stock Exchange (TUNINDEX), and the Regional African Stock Exchange (BRVM Composite). Using advanced natural language processing techniques, particularly BERT, the study analyzes sentiment from news articles to evaluate its influence on stock performance during the COVID-19 pandemic. The findings reveal diverse dynamics: the BRVM Composite exhibited a significant causal relationship between sentiment and returns, while the MASI and TUNINDEX showed weaker correlations, highlighting the complexity of sentiment-driven behavior. Structural factors, policy interventions, and market-specific dynamics emerged as key influences. This research contributes to behavioral finance by deepening our understanding of sentiment's impact in emerging markets and offering actionable insights for investors and policymakers during crises.

DOI: 10.4018/979-8-3693-9684-1.ch002

1 INTRODUCTION

In a world where words matter and where markets pulse with the collective emotions of billions, understanding the interplay between market sentiment and financial performance is no longer just a curiosity-it's a necessity!

This need has been underscored for the last two decades by researchers in behavioral finance, challenging the accepted traditional Efficient Market Hypothesis (EMH). While EMH considers markets completely rational and the prices reflect all the available information, behavioral finance presents a contrasting perspective; psychological biases and emotions play a major role in investors' behavior and, as such, in market outcomes.

At the heart of every human behaviors and interactions, psychology emerges as a key actor and a driving force that influences and guides decisions. Whether, it's the sophisticated trading floors of Wall Street or Nasdaq, or the lively streets of Casablanca, Tunis or Abidjan, it is the collective emotions, perceptions, and biases of individuals that guide societies. After all, markets aren't just cold, rational systems; they breathe with the emotions of investors; panic in times of crisis, excitement in moments of growth, and hesitation when uncertainty prevails. Understanding this deep connection between psychology and financial behavior isn't just interesting, it's a game-changer for analyzing and predicting future market trends.

This raises a fundamental question: Is the investor truly a rational agent, as traditional financial theories assume? Historical events like the 2008 global financial crisis or the dot-com bubble of the early 2000s reveal a stark contrast between theoretical assumptions of rationality and the emotional, often erratic, decisions of market participants. Fear, panic, greed, euphoria and overconfidence can easily override careful analysis, leading to market anomalies and deviations from expected performance. These episodes highlight the need to delve deeper into the psychological foundations of investor behavior to better comprehend and predict market trends and dynamics.

The COVID-19 pandemic has further illuminated this divergence between rationality and reality in financial markets. The unprecedented economic disruptions it caused led to extreme volatility, with global markets experiencing sharp declines and subsequent recoveries, all in a very short time. Bansal (2020) observes that this crisis exposed the limitations of traditional finance models, as they failed to account for the cognitive biases and emotional reactions that drove investor behavior during this period. Overconfidence, herding behavior, and heightened risk aversion emerged as dominant forces, shaping market movements in ways that were inconsistent with purely rational decision-making. Investors, overwhelmed by uncertainty and fear, often relied on heuristics and analogies to previous crises, such as the 2008 financial meltdown, further amplifying volatility.

Such behavior underscores the importance of incorporating psychological insights into financial theories, especially during crises, when emotions often overshadow logic. This brings into focus the dual nature of human decision-making.

In his seminal work *Thinking, Fast and Slow*, Daniel Kahneman (2011) highlights the dual processes of human thought: the fast, intuitive 'System 1' and the slow, deliberate 'System 2.' In financial markets, time-sensitive decisions often amplify reliance on System 1, driven by emotions and heuristics. While adaptive in crises, this reliance frequently leads to biases such as overreaction, herd behavior, or excessive risk aversion. Kahneman's insights challenge the notion of rational markets, emphasizing the need to account for emotional and cognitive factors in financial models.

Understanding the psychological foundations of market behavior highlights the importance of sentiment analysis, especially during crises like the COVID-19 pandemic. Market sentiment or market mood, derived from textual data such as news, social media and forums, captures the collective emotions of investors, often serving as a driver to market movements.

Leveraging advances in Deep Learning, particularly transformer-based models like BERT, this study investigates the relationship between market sentiment and stock returns in three African markets: MASI (Morocco), TUNINDEX (Tunisia), and BRVM Composite (West Africa). By applying these advanced techniques, we aim to explore whether sentiment influence returns and to provide a cross-country analysis, shedding light on the dynamics of emerging and frontier (pre-emerging) markets during a global crisis.

The findings seek to contribute to behavioral finance literature and its interaction with artificial intelligence by demonstrating the value of Deep Learning in understanding financial markets dynamics.

2 LITERATURE REVIEW

The early acknowledgment of psychology's role in economics in general and investment decision-making in particular can be traced back to Charles Mackay's classic work, *Memoirs of Extraordinary Popular Delusions and the Madness of Crowds* (1841). Mackay's study of historical financial manias such as the Mississippi Scheme (1719-1720), the South Sea Bubble (1720), and earlier the Tulip Mania (1630s), illustrates how collective emotions like fear and greed can lead to widespread economic irrationality. His story puts in a nutshell that even people who seemed so rational could become victims of the power of crowd dynamics - to forsake logic in the tide of popular trends. By underlining the psychological principles of economic decisions, Mackay's work laid the ground for a broader understanding of how human behavior, driven by emotions and social influence, drives economic phenomena. These lessons, rooted in historical episodes, still echo today, underlining the timeless interplay between psychology and economic systems.

Despite these early insights of the psychological dimensions of economic behavior, the mid-20th century marked a definitive turntoward a more stochastic, mathematically based view of market dynamics. The Efficient Market Hypothesis, formally tated by Eugene Fama in the 1970s but with precursors in Bachelier (1900) and Samuelson (1965), held that markets are 'informationally efficient.' In such a setup, all information is immediately and correctly reflected in asset prices, with no systematic possibilities for arbitrage. In this paradigm, market participants were presumed to act rationally, with their expectations revised constantly in response to new data. The EMH was set out in weak, semi-strong, and strong forms, an elegant theoretical underpinning of the price movement, emphasizing randomness of market fluctuations and the futility of trying to outperform the market without taking additional risk (Fama, 1970).

However, the emphasis on rationality and stochastic processes within the EMH strongly deviated from earlier observations regarding crowd psychology and emotional biases underlined by Mackay (1841). Even though the hypothesis played the leading role in academic debate for decades, it started to show its shortcomings in front of recurring market anomalies, such as overreaction to news, momentum effects, and speculative bubbles (De Bondt & Thaler, 1985; Jegadeesh & Titman, 1993). These various inconsistencies thus provided a fertile ground for reviews which would contest the universality of market efficiency by insisting that economic models needed more psychological and behavioral underpinning. The shift from the more anecdotal Mackay through to the formalism of the EMH well mirrors the wider pendulum-like swing of economics between the rational and emotional poles of choice.

While the EMH had an appealing narrative of rationality and informational efficiency, there started to appear a number of cracks in its foundation, with an ever-increasing awareness of systematic market anomalies and a role of psychological biases. Such inconsistencies showed that the real investors' behavior is far from the model of a rational agent, especially under the conditions of uncertainty and risk (De Bondt et al., 2013). That intellectual turning point crystallized with the development, by Kahneman & Tversky back in 1979, of the so-called Prospect Theory that really reconstituted how decision-making was understood. Their seminal work underlined the fact that individuals assess possible outcomes not in absolute terms but rather relative to a reference point while valuing losses more intensely than symmetric gains. The principle of loss aversion, for the first time bundled with systematic distortions in probability judgment, unraveled the cognitive processes underlying violations of optimum decisions.

The turning point-Prospect Theory-cemented the realization and conceptual, systematic space where the then-emerging domain now known as behavioral finance belonged. It replaced the mathematical determinism of the underlying theory in the EMHs with deepened psychological and emotional characteristics present within human behavior. This evolution was further supported by empirical evidence, for instance, when in 1985 Shefrin & Statman singled out what is known as the disposition effect: how investors' aversion to realizing losses and premature realization of gains could distort market efficiency. In this respect, Odean (1998) has extended this idea by large-scale empirical verification and has shown, based on actual trading data, how cognitive biases manifest in real-world financial decisions. These contributions not only questioned the axiom of rationality but also enriched the view of financial markets as a playground of human psychology and bounded rationality. For example, the "weekend effect" documented by French (1980) demonstrated systematic patterns in stock returns that could not be explained by traditional efficient market theory. Further, Barberis et al. (1998) integrated these insights to propose a behavioral model of investor sentiment, overreaction to news, and the formation of bubbles. Their model also provided an integrated explanation for various market anomalies, which violated assumptions of rationality implicit in the Efficient Market Hypothesis by Fama (1970). Prospect Theory remains a landmark in behavioral finance literature, where research is ongoing into the interplay between human psychology and economic decisions. According to Barberis (2013), it is an integral building block of market anomalies such as the equity premium puzzle and disposition effect; how such concepts as loss aversion and probability weighting bridge rational models with real-world investor behavior.

Building on the roots of Prospect Theory, De Bondt & Driehaus (2005) continued the behavioral finance debate with their seminal work, *The Psychology of World Equity Markets*. This research examines the psychological dynamics of worldwide equity markets, highlighting how cognitive biases-systematic errors in judgment-drive various phenomena such as fluctuations in stock prices, financial bubbles, and predictable reversals. These findings also support Barberis's (2013) observations and further demonstrate how psychological elements, such as loss aversion and probability weighting, become embedded in market behavior. Further development of this view has come in work such as Shiller's (2003) analysis of speculative bubbles and irrational exuberance, and the work of Grinblatt & Keloharju's (2000) examination into cultural and emotional influences on trading. Together, these articles represent a paradigm shift in the direction of finance theory from the rational stochastic model to a much more subtle conception of markets as complex systems interwoven through human psychology and bounded rationality.

However, Andrew Lo's Adaptive Market Hypothesis (AMH) is a strong synthesis of Efficient Market Hypothesis (EMH) and behavioral finance, closing the gap between the rationality of traditional finance and the psychological biases emphasized by behavioral economists. While EMH assumes markets to be efficient and asset prices to accurately reflect available information, AMH does not agree with market efficiency as a given but rather as something dynamic with evolving market conditions and adaptive behavior on the part of the market players. Lo's model employs concepts from evolutionary biology to propose that investors learn from experience and modify the strategy accordingly over time, thus resulting in a balance between rational choice and biases like loss aversion and overconfidence. In Lo's model, there is space for market anomalies - for example, overreactions to news or sentiment-driven mispricings - within a broader framework of adaptive efficiency. Accordingly, the AMH offers a more sophisticated and fuller image of market behavior, recognizing that financial markets are complex systems in which rational and behavioral forces exist together, influenced by adaptive and evolving cycles (Lo, 2004; 2005; 2012).

In this adaptive and dynamic environment, the position of investor sentiment is a key driver in influencing market behavior. Sentiment, as motivated by emotional response and cognitive bias, not only indicates the interaction of rationality with behavioral determinants but also provides a measurable aspect through which such subtleties may be identified. The incorporation of sentiment analysis within behavioral finance has therefore emerged as an effective means of analyzing the role of emotion and perception in financial decision-making (Ángeles López-Cabarcos et al., 2020).

Adaptive Market Hypothesis (AMH) has been utilized to investigate emerging and pre-emerging markets in-depth, offering insight into the unique characteristics of such markets. For instance, Lahboub et al. (2022) empirically tested Moroccan stock market efficiency based on the AMH and demonstrated the occurrence of alternating efficiency and inefficiency as influenced by market volatility and economic fundamentals. Their findings align with the AMH's underlying principles that propose market efficiency evolves dynamically with changing conditions and adaptive behavior of participants. Similarly, Lekhal & El Oubani (2020) pointed out that the AMH offers a more nuanced explanation of market behavior than the static assumptions of the Efficient Market Hypothesis (EMH).

The incorporation of sentiment analysis in behavioral finance has revolutionized investor behavior research through the provision of empirical tools to measure emotions and perceptions that drive market movements. Sentiment analysis uses natural language processing (NLP) techniques to glean information from text-based data such as news reports, financial announcements, and now social media posts. This strategy is in accordance with the teachings of behavioral finance, which accentuate the part played by emotional and cognitive biases in financial choices. Early research, like that of Baker & Wurgler (2006; 2007), showed how investor sentiment is to blame for market anomalies, as asset prices balloon with excessive optimism and pessimism leads to massive sell-offs.

Social media sentiment predictability has become a foundation of behavioral finance studies, with Nguyen et al. (2015) illustrating the manner in which collective emotional trends extrapolated from sources such as Twitter are able to successfully forecast market directions, augmenting conventional financial models through the addition of real-time data-driven input. Likewise, research by Makrehchi et al. (2013) and Oh & Sheng (2011) has shown the potential of social media sentiment metrics in predicting direction of stock prices and detecting emerging market trends. The advent of microblogging sites, as noted by Piñeiro-Chousa et al. (2016), has also made it easier to gather real-time sentiment information, allowing researchers to analyze its relationship with conventional financial indicators. These advances not only enrich theoretical models in behavioral finance but also offer empirical instruments to investors who struggle to make sense of the unpredictabilities of modern financial markets.

More recently, as part of the artificial intelligence revolution, the application of deep learning instruments in sentiment analysis has revolutionized the study of investor behavior and market dynamics. As unstructured text data increases exponentially from sources like social media, news, and financial reports, deep learning methods such as Recurrent Neural Networks (RNNs), Convolutional Neural Networks (CNNs) and Transformers have been found to be very effective at extracting and understanding sentiment. For example, Aattouchi et al. (2022) illustrated the use of CNNs together with Latent Dirichlet Allocation (LDA) in analyzing financial tweets at a performance rate of 99% on a dataset of one million entries. This high performance rate reflects the potential of deep learning models in detecting complex sentiments that would be otherwise overlooked using conventional methodologies. In addition, natural language processing (NLP) methods allow for feature extraction of sentiment from various sources of text to provide a holistic view of investor sentiment. Du et al. (2024) further highlight how such models can forecast market directions using sentiment change analysis, providing actionable intelligence for investment and facilitating real-time decision-making. The advent of machine learning and deep learning methods has created new opportunities for behavioral finance research, transforming the landscape of investor sentiment analysis and usage.

Pioneering research, including Das & Chen's (2007) early exploration into message board analysis, showed the potential for automated sentiment detection. Following this, Ding et al. (2015) established neural network architectures for event-based stock prediction, demonstrating the potential of deep learning in incorporating multiple sources of data for more accurate market prediction. Another advancement involves the creation of financial language models specific to the financial domain, such as BERT (Devlin et al., 2019) and FinBERT (Araci, 2019), which has allowed for the more accurate evaluation of market sentiment and behavioral dynamics.

In addition, recent research has investigated investor sentiment's impact on stock returns using sophisticated sentiment analysis methods for extracting information from textual data. For example, Baker & Wurgler (2006) showed that high investor sentiment is associated with greater stock returns, especially in small-cap stocks, implying that positive sentiment can push prices above their intrinsic values. Li et al. (2014) also examine the connection between news sentiment and stock returns, illustrating how the sentiment of news articles affects investors' behavior and market direction. Their article demonstrates that positive news sentiment drives stock price rises, and negative sentiment leads to falls, illustrating the predictive power of sentiment analysis. The authors point out the promise of incorporating sentiment information in investment decision-making to enhance decision-making and develop more accurate stock price predictive models, emphasizing the powerful role of news sentiment on market reaction.

Other research using machine learning algorithms in sentiment analysis has also reported encouraging outcomes in forecasting stock market directions. For instance, Kolasani & Assaf (2020) employed neural networks models in a study of Twitter sentiment analysis and discovered that positive sentiment is a robust predictor of future stock price improvement. This kind of incorporation of sentiment analysis into financial prediction models demonstrates the potential of sentiment analysis to improve conventional techniques through the addition of real-time emotional information, thus enabling investors to gain improved insights into market dynamics (Du et al., 2024). In general, the relationship involving stock market returns and sentiment analysis highlights the significance of psychological aspects in the determination of financial decision-making and market performance.

Building on these developments, Zhu & Yen (2024) applied BERTopic, a cutting-edge NLP method, to mine sentiment information from stock market analysis. Their study illustrated that the incorporation of topic-level sentiment into predictive models greatly enhanced the precision of stock price forecasting, highlighting the importance of fine-grained sentiment analysis in predicting market trends.

In total, the use of deep learning techniques on sentiment analysis offers a highly effective prism through which to view the interaction between stock market returns and market sentiment. Although the existing literature has largely concentrated on developed markets, applying the techniques to emerging and pre-emerging markets - particularly during a time of increased uncertainty such as the COVID-19 pandemic - offers distinctive insights. This kind of study not only addresses important gaps in the literature but also generates a richer understanding of the relationship between stock returns and market sentiment, providing revealing insights into the intricacies of financial system development.

3 MATERIAL AND METHODS

In this section, we present the method used in examining the connection between market sentiment and stock returns of the chosen African financial markets within the period of the COVID-19 pandemic and zooming in on March 2020, when the markets were highly volatile. Three markets are examined in the study: Morocco (MASI), Tunisia (TUNINDEX), and the West African Economic and Monetary Union[1] (BRVM Composite). These markets were chosen not merely due to their local relevance but also for the potential to gain insight into the dynamics of investor sentiment within emerging and pre-emerging settings. The crux of this research is the application of Deep Learning models, in this instance BERT, that employs dynamic word embeddings and a transformer-based model to read news articles with contextual precision and determine its correlation with numerical market data. By fine-tuning BERT on financial information, the model worked better at detecting subtle variations in sentiment, making way for incorporating unstructured text data into analysis.

3.1 Data Collection

The data was collected for news published between March 1, 2020, and March 31, 2020, in local online newspapers. News sources related to both general news and those with a specific interest in financial news platforms targeted at sophisticated investors were included. In this period, for each day of it, we collected the news on three categories: updates about the situation of the pandemic, economic developments in the respective country, and performance of the national and international stock market-the latter included to control for contagion that often arises in financial markets when the period is volatile and amidst a crisis period (Paskaleva & Stoykova, 2021; Longstaff, 2010). This categorization is designed to capture the comprehensive view of the information ecosystem influencing investor sentiment during this volatile period.

The table 1 presents the various sources utilized in this study:

Table 1. Sources of data collection by region

Morocco	Tunisia	West Africa
- Financialafrik.com **- ilBoursa.com** **- Le 360** **- Fr.Hespress.com** **- Le Matin** **- L'Economiste** **- Al Alam** **- Al Massae** **- Libération** **- Aujourd'hui le Maroc** **- L'Opinion**	- Fr.Hespress.com - Businessnews.com.tn - ilBoursa.com - Lapresse.tn	- Financialafrik.com - Lemonde.fr - Brvm.org - France24.com - Unocha.org - Mfwa.org - Francetvinfo.fr - Afrique.latribune.fr - World Bank Group (Banquemondiale.org) - West African Health Organization (Wahooas.org) - Radio France international (Rfi.fr) - Africa Centre for Strategic Studies (africacentre.org) - African Development Bank Group (afdb.org)

Simultaneously, daily returns for the MASI (Morocco), TUNINDEX (Tunisia), and BRVM Composite (West Africa) indices were calculated using the logarithmic return formula:

$$R_t = \ln\left(\frac{P_t - P_{t-1}}{P_{t-1}}\right)$$

Where R_t represents the return on day t, P_t is the closing price of the index on day t, and P_{t-1} is the closing price on the previous day.

The daily price data for these three indices were collected from the platform: *Investing.com*, which provides complete and reliable dataset. This dual dataset combining qualitative news sentiment and quantitative market returns, provides a robust foundation for analyzing the interplay between market sentiment and stock performance during the COVID-19 crisis.

3.2 Data Pre-Processing

After data collection, rigorous pre-processing was performed to ensure the quality and usability of the datasets, as shown in Figure 1. Textual data from news articles were cleaned to remove irrelevant information such as advertisements, metadata, and non-textual elements. Standard NLP techniques such as tokenization, stop-word removal, and stemming were applied to prepare the text for sentiment analysis. This was a quintessential step, which allowed ensuring that noise and inconsistency in the textual data were not affecting sentiment extraction.

Figure 1. Textual data pre-processing for sentiment analysis

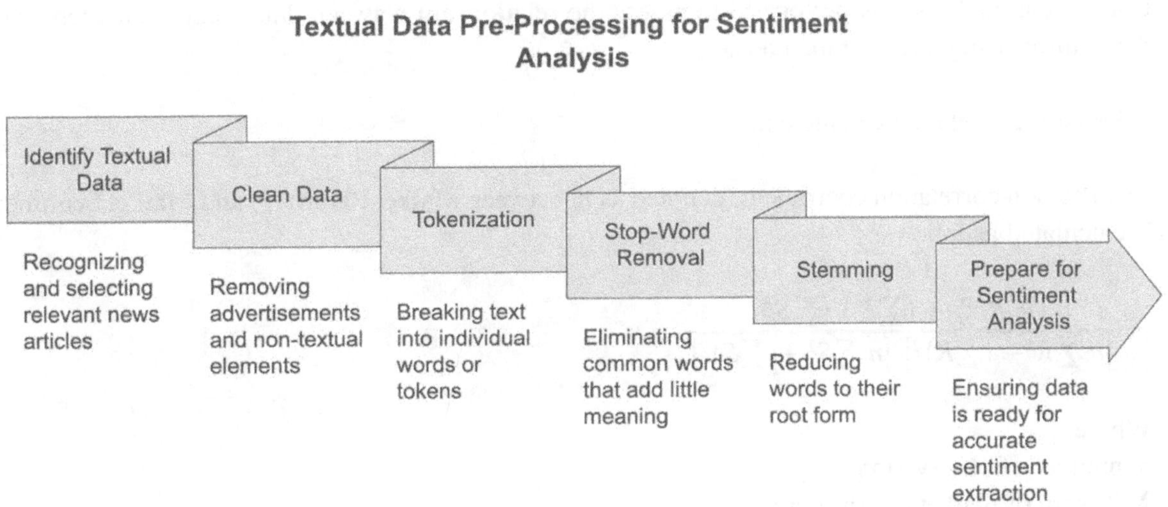

3.3 Sentiment Score Calculation

The present study used the pre-trained BERT (Bidirectional Encoder Representations from Transformers) model to quantify the investor sentiments in news data. This approach makes it possible to analyze the exact sentiment expressed within the texts and to perform more robust analyses than before. A BERT model was used which assigned a score S_i from the continuous scale, ranging from -1 (very negative) to +1 (very positive), for each text that is a news article or a comment. The model's critical ability to understand the context and nuances of financial language in context was essential in capturing the emotional tone embedded in news content.

For each day, sentiment scores were then aggregated across three categories: pandemic situation, economic developments, and stock market performance in both national and international contexts. A daily sentiment index for each market is computed as the average of the many texts collected and their individual sentiment scores. This index, denoted $\overline{S}_d$, was calculated using the formula:

$$\overline{S}_d = \frac{1}{n} \sum_{i=1}^{n} S_i$$

Where n represents the total number of texts analyzed for a given day, and S_i is the sentiment score of the *i-th* text.

The computed daily average sentiment indexes were further classified into three categories to improve interpretability. Days with a positive index ($\overline{S}_d > 0$) were classified as having an overall positive sentiment, those with a negative index ($\overline{S}_d < 0$) were labeled as negative, and days where the average index was zero ($\overline{S}_d = 0$) were categorized as neutral. This classification enabled a more nuanced understanding of the daily sentiment dynamics across different markets during a period marked by extreme stress.

3.4 Correlation and Lagged Correlation Analysis

Correlation analysis was performed to assess the relationship between daily sentiment scores and market returns using different methods:

- Pearson Correlation Coefficient:

The Pearson correlation coefficient (denoted as *r*) between Market Return (*r*) and Market Sentiment (*s*) is calculated as follows:

$$r = \frac{n\,(\sum R_i S_i) - (\sum R_i)\,(\sum S_i)}{\sqrt{[n \sum R^2 - (\sum R)^2]\,[n \sum S^2 - (\sum S)^2]}}$$

Where:
n: number of observations.
$\sum R_i$: sum of market return scores.
$\sum S_i$: sum of market sentiment scores.

- Spearman Rank Correlation Coefficient:

The Spearman rank correlation coefficient (denoted as ρ_s) between Market Return (*r*) and Market Sentiment (*s*) is calculated as follows:

$$\rho_s = 1 - \frac{6 \sum d_i^2}{n\,(n^2 - 1)}$$

Where:
d_i: difference between ranks for each pair of observations (Market Return and Market Sentiment).

- Kendall's Tau Correlation Coefficient:

$$\tau = \frac{(n_c - n_d)}{\frac{1}{2}\,n\,(n - 1)}$$

Where:
n_c: number of concordant pairs (where the ranks for both variables agree).
n_d: number of discordant pairs (where the ranks for both variables disagree).

These various tests were designed to ascertain whether positive or negative sentiment had an influence on market movements during the COVID-19 period for both linear and monotonic relationships. The linear relationship between sentiment and market returns was checked using Pearson's correlation coefficient. The null hypothesis (H_0) was considered to state that there is no linear relationship between the two variables, and any observed correlation is only a coincidence. On the other hand, monotonic relationships were explored using Spearman's rank correlation, indicating whether one variable consistently increases or decreases when the other variable increases independent of linearity. Here, the null hypothesis (H_0) is that ranks of the two variables are independent, and this would mean there is no monotonic relationship. Besides, Kendall's tau introduced another insight into the monotone relationships by testing concordance and discordance in paired observation while setting their null hypothesis (H_0) to suggesting no association thus subjects variables result in equal measures concordant to discord pairs. Put altogether, these two tests provided one comprehensive way through which one gets a proper glimpse as to what exactly sentimenting had on it within this area in that respective timeframe.

To check the possibility of potential delayed effects from sentiment on market returns, the correlation analysis has been done using lagged regressions by applying various lags, ranging between one and five days. With this method, the relation was studied between today's market returns and the score of sentiment calculated for the days preceding it to allow the time course of short to medium horizons in capturing sentiment-driven behaviors. Through systematic investigation of these lags, we investigated whether investor sentiment contemporaneously or with delay affects the performance of stock markets. Several periods of lag estimation would present a nuanced view of persistence and decay features of the effects of sentiment, thereby underlining dynamics in the reactions by market participants over time due to changes in collective sentiment.

3.5 Causality Analysis

To deepen our understanding of the relationship between market sentiment and stock market returns, we employed the Granger Causality Test. The analysis is conducted using an unrestricted model, which allows us to assess whether past values of market sentiment can predict future values of market return. The null hypothesis H_0 for this test states that market sentiment does not Granger-cause market return.

The unrestricted model is specified as follows:

$$r_t = \alpha_0 + \sum_{i=1}^{p} \beta_i R_{t-i} + \sum_{j=1}^{q} \gamma_j S_{t-j} + \epsilon_t$$

Where:

R_t: market return at time t.

S_{t-j}: market sentiment at lagged time periods.

α_0, β_i and γ_j: coefficients that will be estimated through regression analysis.

ϵ_t: error term.

In summary, our methodological approach is outlined in Figure 2 below:

Figure 2. Analytical workflow of the proposed study

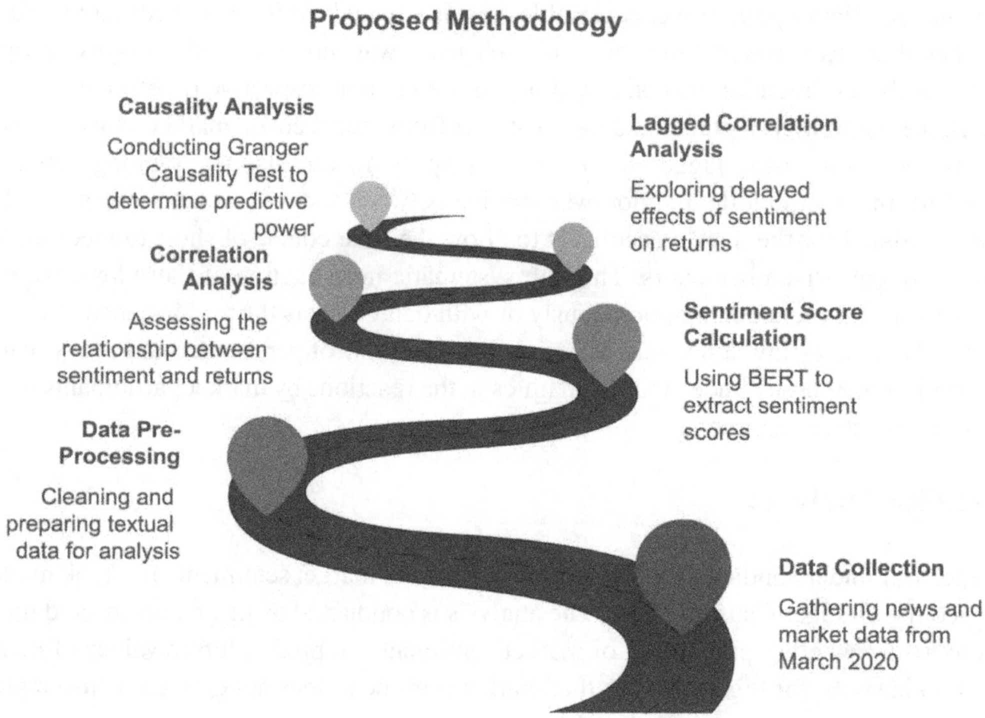

4 RESULTS AND FINDINGS

4.1 Sentiment Analysis

To provide a preliminary analysis, we deemed it appropriate to conduct a sentiment distribution analysis to better understand market perceptions during the study period. The results are shown in figure 3 below:

Figure 3. Positive, negative and neutral sentiment distribution

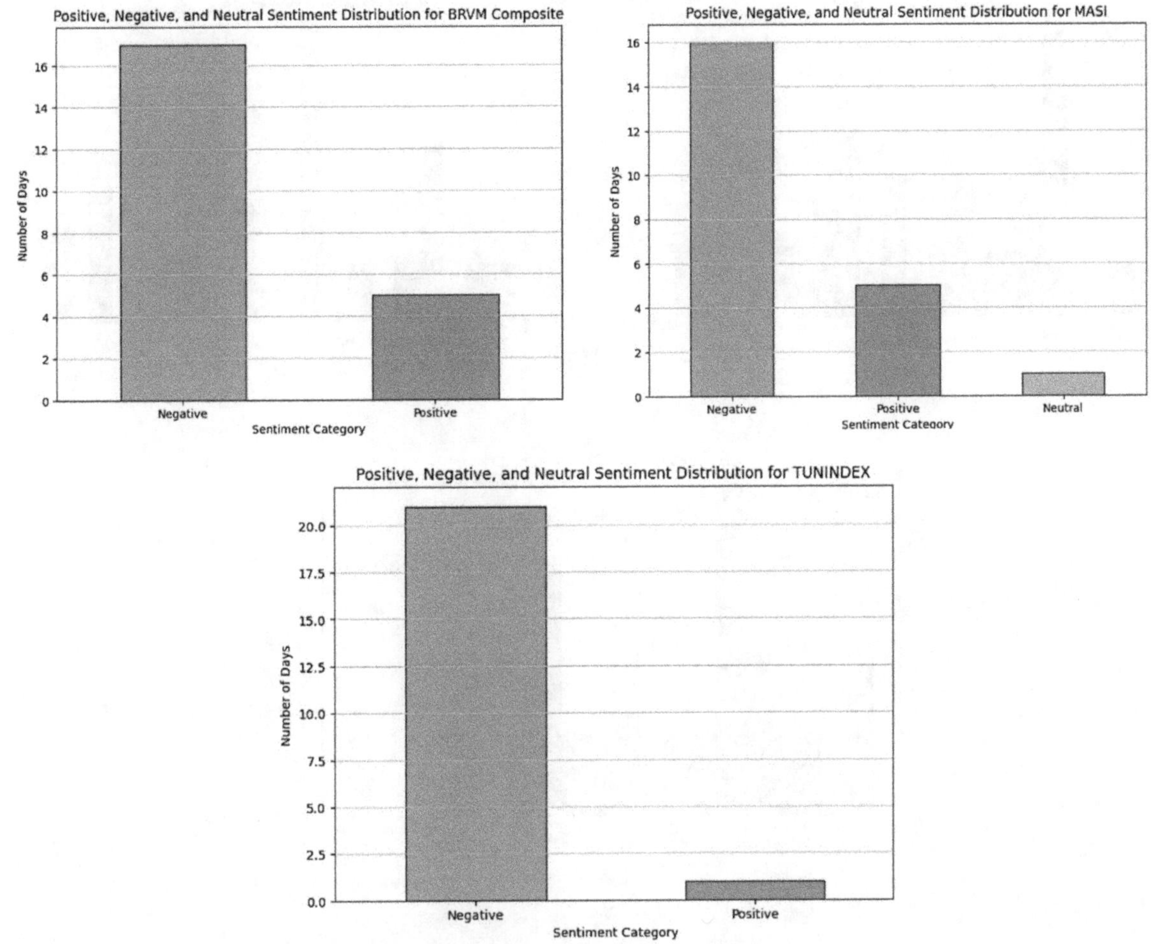

The sentiment distribution across MASI, TUNINDEX, and BRVM Composite highlights a predominance of negative sentiment, reflecting widespread pessimism likely caused by COVID-19 uncertainties. TUNINDEX exhibited the highest negativity, while MASI and BRVM showed slightly more positive sentiment. The scarcity of neutral sentiment underscores a polarized market environment, providing essential context for analyzing the relationship between sentiment and market movements.

To further deepen these insights, we now turn to a sentiment volatility analysis, which aims to examine the fluctuations in market sentiment and their potential implications for market behavior during the study period.

Figure 4. Sentiment volatility analysis

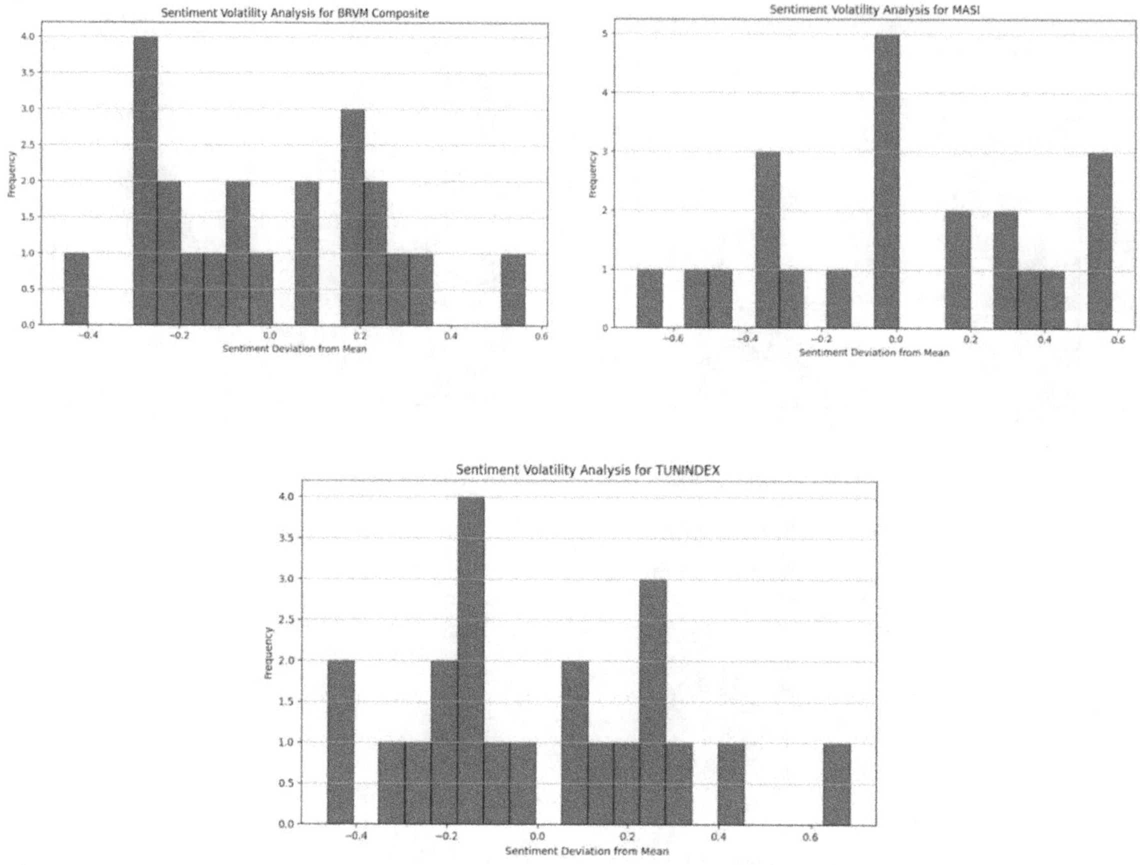

The sentiment volatility analysis for the MASI, TUNINDEX, and BRVM Composite markets presented in figure 4, reveals that most sentiment values are concentrated around the mean, indicating overall stability in sentiment during the study period. However, notable deviations, both positive and negative, reflect occasional significant shifts likely influenced by major events, such as the announcement of the first confirmed COVID-19 cases and lockdown measures. These deviations underscore the markets' sensitivity to external shocks, amplifying uncertainty during this critical period.

Among the three markets, the TUNINDEX exhibits more frequent and pronounced negative deviations, consistent with its predominantly negative sentiment. This suggests heightened market stress and a greater impact of negative news. Conversely, the MASI and BRVM Composite markets show more balanced sentiment distributions, with fluctuations on both sides of the mean, though negative deviations are slightly more frequent.

4.2 Correlation Analysis

Building on our preliminary analysis, we now move to examine the relationship between market sentiment and market returns for the three studied markets. To this end, Figure 5 illustrates the evolution of market sentiment and market returns during the study period.

Figure 5. Market sentiment and market returns over time

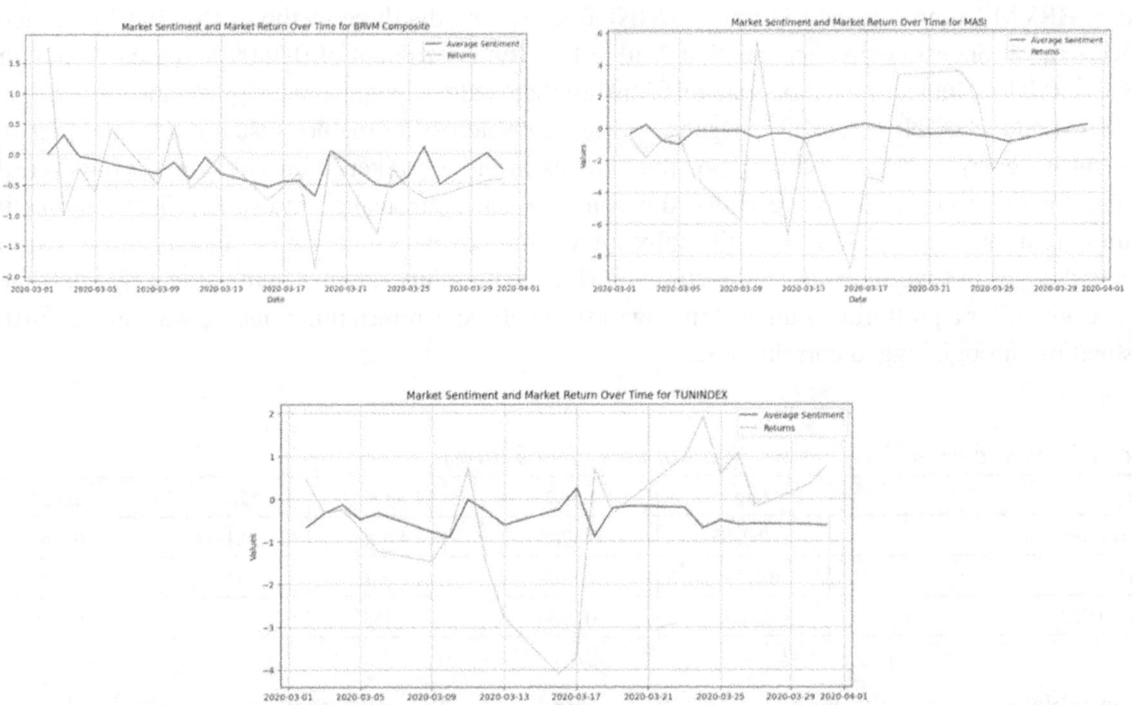

The curves in figure 5 illustrate the temporal variations in market sentiment and returns for the BRVM Composite, MASI, and TUNINDEX markets during the study period. These visualizations provide a comparative view of how market sentiment aligns with or diverges from market returns over time. Notably, sentiment trends appear smoother and more stable, while market returns demonstrate greater fluctuations, reflecting the inherent volatility of financial markets. The overlay of these trends facilitates an initial exploration of potential relationships and lagged effects between sentiment and returns, serving as a foundation for subsequent analyses, including correlation (Table 2) and lagged correlation (Table 3) assessments.

Table 2. Correlation and P-value analysis results

Index	Pearson	P-value	Spearman	P-value	Kendall	P-value
BRVM Composite	0.3809	0.0803	0.3360	0.1263	0.2814	0.0708
MASI	-0.2901	0.1903	-0.2551	0.2519	-0.1663	0.2828
TUNINDEX	-0.3388	0.1229	-0.1963	0.3812	-0.1609	0.2964

The table 2 summarizes the correlation coefficients (Pearson, Spearman, and Kendall) and their corresponding p-values, assessing the relationship between market sentiment and returns for the three markets: BRVM Composite, MASI, and TUNINDEX. Among the three methods, the BRVM Composite shows the strongest positive correlation, with a Pearson coefficient of 0.3809 and a corresponding p-value of 0.0803, indicating a moderate relationship that is close to statistical significance. In contrast, both MASI and TUNINDEX exhibit negative correlations across all methods, suggesting that negative sentiment is generally associated with positive returns in these markets, and vice versa. However, the *p-values* for these correlations are above the conventional significance threshold (0.05), indicating that these relationships may not be statistically robust, thereby necessitating a causality test to explore whether changes in sentiment have a directional influence on returns, rather than being only correlated. These results offer a preliminary understanding of the sentiment-return relationship, warranting further investigation through lagged correlations.

Table 3. Lagged correlations across different lags (1 to 5 days)

Index	Lag 1	Lag 2	Lag 3	Lag 4	Lag 5
BRVM Composite	-0.0585	0.3088	0.4408	0.1884	0.2091
MASI	0.1711	0.4711	0.1266	-0.0375	0.3846
TUNINDEX	-0.0277	-0.0636	-0.0468	0.1734	0.5942

The table 3 presents the lagged correlations between market sentiment and returns for the three markets calculated over time lags ranging from 1 to 5 days, recognizing that investors typically respond to announcements or news starting the following day. These results provide insights into the potential delayed effects of sentiment on market performance.

For the BRVM Composite, the correlations become increasingly positive with longer time lags, reaching a peak at lag 3 ($r = 0.4408$) before decreasing slightly. This suggests that the impact of sentiment on returns in this market materializes most strongly after approximately three days.

In the case of the MASI, a similar trend is observed, with the highest correlation at lag 2 ($r = 0.4711$), followed by a decline at longer lags. This pattern indicates a shorter lagged influence of sentiment on market returns compared to the BRVM Composite.

The TUNINDEX market, however, shows weaker correlations across all lags, with the highest value at lag 5 ($r = 0.5942$). This result suggests that sentiment's influence on returns in TUNINDEX may take longer to manifest, or that the relationship is less direct and more dependent on external factors.

These results become more apparent when observing figure 6, which clearly illustrate the trends in rolling averages of sentiment and returns for the three markets. The visualizations offer valuable insights into the temporal alignment and divergence between sentiment and market performance.

Figure 6. Rolling averages of sentiment and returns

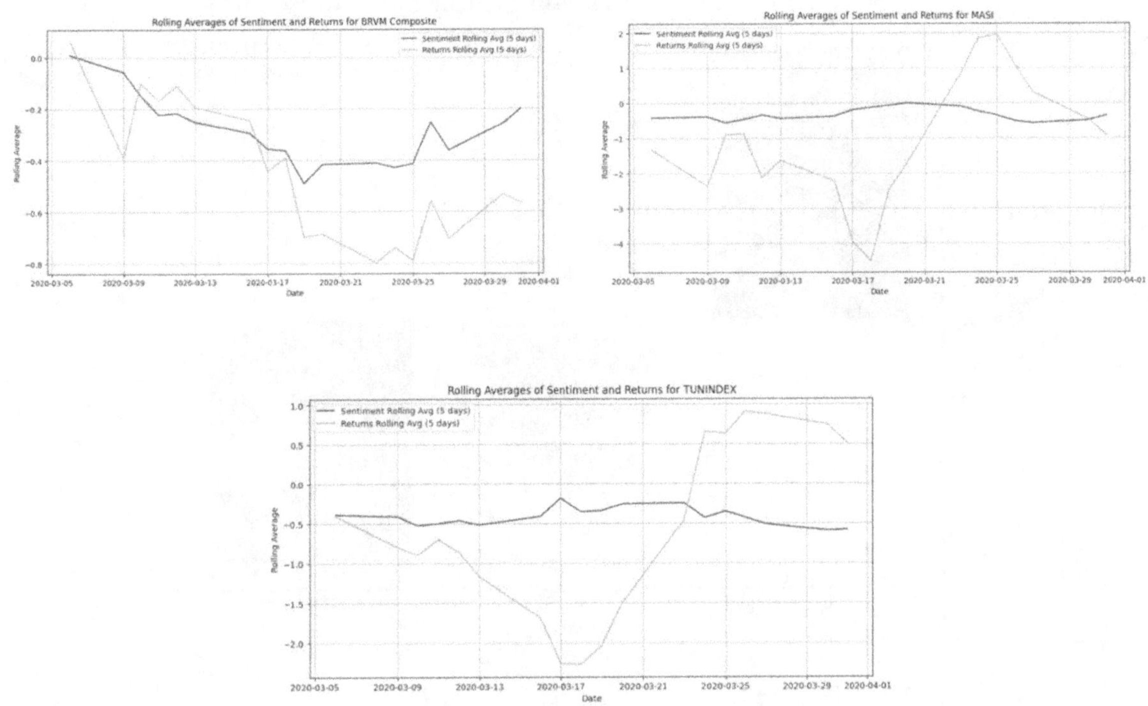

For the BRVM Composite, rolling averages show a persistent fall in sentiment, closely accompanied by a similar fall in market returns. There is a divergence, however, towards the later part of the period, with an improvement in sentiment and sustained volatility in returns. This development shows that shifts in sentiment can follow in the direction of market moves, with predictive value in sentiment.

For both the MASI and TUNINDEX, a strong divergence between sentiment and returns can be seen. For both markets, for most of the period, sentiment is relatively calm, but for both, high volatility in market returns can be seen. For the MASI, a sharp rise in returns can be seen following a long period of negativity, and for the TUNINDEX, a sharp fall in returns in mid-March, following an improvement thereafter. These trends show that in both the MASI and TUNINDEX, market returns can follow factors not derived through sentiment, such as external shocks, structural factors in a market, or liquidity.

In general, figure 7 shows a comparative overview of global correlations between sentiment and returns in the three respective markets. According to it, BRVM Composite has a high positive correlation, indicating a strong relation between sentiment and market returns. For both the MASI and TUNINDEX, a reverse correlation can be seen, indicating a reverse relation in which a fall in sentiment can follow an improvement in positive market returns, and vice versa.

Figure 7. Global correlations between market sentiment and market returns

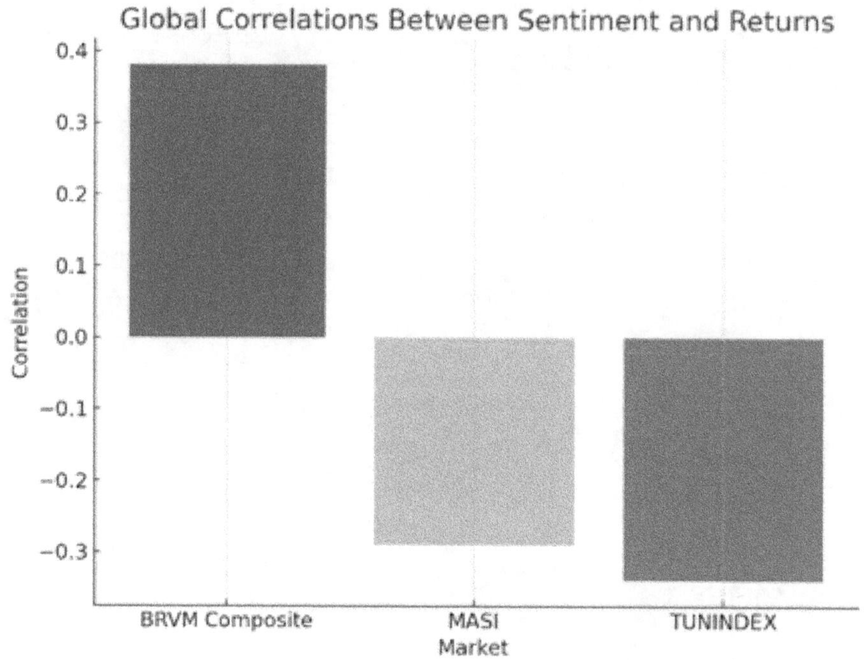

This comparative study points out the varying dynamics of sentiment-return relationships in the respective markets, and re-emphasizes the necessity of considering market-specific factors in explaining such interactions.

4.3 Causality Analysis

To deeper examine, directionality of relationship between market sentiment and stock returns, Granger causality testing at several lags was conducted, in an attempt to validate whether changes in sentiment occur in anticipation and with an influence over returns.

Table 4. Causality test results

Index	Lag	P-value	Interpretation
BRVM Composite	1	0.598	No significant causality
	2	0.700	No significant causality
	3	0.069	Tendency towards causality
	4	0.034	Significant causality
	5	0.097	Tendency towards causality

continued on following page

Table 4. Continued

Index	Lag	P-value	Interpretation
MASI	1	0.336	No significant causality
	2	0.093	Tendency towards causality
	3	0.259	No significant causality
	4	0.434	No significant causality
	5	0.074	Tendency towards causality
TUNINDEX	1	0.363	No significant causality
	2	0.609	No significant causality
	3	0.850	No significant causality
	4	0.875	No significant causality
	5	0.133	No significant causality

The Granger causality test results in table 4, offers additional details regarding causality between market sentiment and stock returns in the three markets under examination. For BRVM Composite, causality is significant at lag 4 (p= 0.034) and trending towards causality at lag 3 (p= 0.069) and lag 5 (p= 0.097). All these conform to positive and significant relationships found for BRVM, and points towards a significant role played by sentiment in determining returns, but with a lag in terms of days. This reinforces the idea that sentiment changes take time to propagate through investor behavior and market performance in this regional context.

In contrast, neither TUNINDEX nor MASI have causality at most lags, with a general causality at lag 2 ($p = 0.093$) and lag 5 ($p = 0.074$) for the MASI, but no causality in any case for the TUNINDEX. As with less strong and negative relations in these two markets, such estimates validate difficulty in distinguishing causality between return and sentiment. For the MASI, a general causality can represent delayed reaction of the market towards a change in sentiment but with no apparent effect. Similarly, a failure in causality in the TUNINDEX could represent that external factors, even structural variance, dominate over sentiment in producing returns.

5 DISCUSSION AND CONCLUSION

The analysis of the relationship between market sentiment and returns of stocks showed mixed dynamics between the three markets under investigation: BRVM Composite, MASI, and TUNINDEX. The BRVM Composite exhibited a moderate positive correlation, indicating that positive sentiment was generally associated with higher market returns. This relationship was further confirmed by the Granger causality test, which identified significant causality at a four-day lag and a tendency towards causality at three- and five-day lags. These results suggest that sentiment changes play a directional and a strong force in determining market behavior in the BRVM, particularly over short to medium term horizons. In contrast, the MASI and TUNINDEX showed negative correlations, where negative sentiment often aligned with positive market returns, and vice versa. However, the Granger causality test revealed limited or no significant causality for these markets, with only tendencies observed at certain lags, indicating that sentiment may not directly drive returns and that external factors could play a larger role.

Further, the analysis of lagged correlations and rolling averages also highlighted these time dynamics. For the BRVM Composite, the strong correlation at three-day lag and correlated rolling averages reinforced the finding that sentiment change happens before and drives market stabilization. That there is strong causality provides further emphasis on the thesis that sentiment is an important predictor of market changes in this region. In contrast, although the MASI and TUNINDEX had their highest correlations at two-day and five-day lags, respectively, their rolling averages picked up stable sentiment patterns together with volatile returns. Together with the absence of strong causality, these results imply that the impact of sentiment is weaker in these markets and could be overshadowed by structural differences or external shocks that drive investor behavior.

In the same context, Bai et al. (2023) implemented a large-scale cross-country study of the interconnectedness between financial market sentiment and stock returns under the COVID-19 pandemic circumstances, having applied LIWC (Linguistic Inquiry and Word Count) for analyzing more than 1.2 million pieces of textual content from news media across 47 countries. Their results showed that good financial market sentiment greatly amplified stock returns, even at the peak of the pandemic, and bad sentiment augmented the negative impact of the crisis on stock performance. Importantly, negative sentiment affected market returns more than positive sentiment, highlighting its amplification effect in times of increased uncertainty. These findings are consistent with and augment previous research by Smales (2017), which demonstrated that sentiment is more closely linked to market returns during periods of recession, again showing the pivotal role played by investor sentiment during economically turbulent times.

While the BRVM Composite confirms the positive correlation between sentiment and returns established by Bai et al. (2023), the MASI and TUNINDEX demonstrate the intricacy of this relation in individual regional and less developed markets, where negative sentiment is commonly associated with volatile or positive returns.

It is relevant at this stage of discussion to ask the question: was the event anticipated, and have investors learned from previous crises, such as the 2008 financial crisis? The divergence that we observe between returns and sentiment in certain markets, such as Morocco and Tunisia, comes with the possibility that investors may have drawn on experience from previous crises to ride out the uncertainty of the COVID-19 pandemic. Despite predominantly negative sentiment, returns in these markets did not all move in the same direction, implying a more cautious or strategic investor reaction.

This double-sided question about anticipation and learning from past crises opens a pathway to examine the broader dynamics at play in the COVID-19 pandemic. The findings of Takyi and Bentum-Ennin (2020) indicate that, despite increased awareness of systemic risks following the 2008 financial crisis, many investors were still caught off guard by the rapid increase of the pandemic. Their observation of sharp market declines, ranging from -2.7% to -21% for African countries, resonates with the volatile returns that we observe in the MASI and TUNINDEX. That the disconnect between sentiment and returns exists in these markets suggests that perhaps some investors were more rational in their approach, potentially informed by their experiences during prior crises.

In addition, Iyke and Ho (2021) cite lagged market response to early warnings of COVID-19 economic effect, illustrating the reactive inclination of most investors. This confirms our results of weak or non-significant causality in the MASI and TUNINDEX, in which sentiment alone could not decisively determine the direction of the market. Instead, the moving averages of these markets displayed steady sentiment patterns with extreme return volatility, indicating the presence of external shocks, structural differences, or regional economic forces that dominated the immediate effect of sentiment.

In contrast, the BRVM Composite presents an exception. The significant causality observed at the four-day lag and the positive correlation between returns and sentiment suggest a tighter relation, in which not only did changes in sentiment precede but also influenced market stabilization. This may be a sign of stronger reliance on sentiment as a proxy for market adjustments in the BRVM region, where investors appeared to integrate news, moods and sentiment signals more systematically into their decision-making process. This is supported by the empirical evidence of Zaremba et al. (2020), which demonstrated that stock markets react strongly to real-time indicators, i.e., confirmed cases of COVID-19, relative to lagged indicators such as deaths. Under the BRVM context, the sensitivity of such change in sentiments underscores the usefulness of timely change in sentiment to influence market performance.

Furthermore, such findings form part of the more general argument over how and in what manner government responses and public health measures have the potential to affect market behavior and sentiment. Zaremba et al. (2020) emphasized that policy responses to the pandemic effectively moderated market volatility. Along the same lines, Kartobi et al. (2024) investigated the asymmetric impact of COVID-19 on the Casablanca Stock Exchange (CSE) and concluded that stock prices reacted more strongly to bad pandemic news than to good news. This asymmetric reaction aligns with our findings of negative sentiment being inversely related to returns in the MASI and underscores the defensive investor behavior amidst heightened uncertainty. At the same time, Alaoui Mdaghri et al. (2021) investigated the influence of the pandemic on MENA countries' stock market liquidity and recorded substantial reductions in liquidity depth and tightness. These liquidity constraints offer additional insights into the volatility experienced on the MASI and TUNINDEX, where structural market conditions can have intensified sensitivity to exogenous shocks and sentiment fluctuations.

Another important aspect is the methodological contribution of this study. By applying BERT to sentiment analysis, we introduced a more nuanced and contextual approach to capturing investor sentiment compared to traditional tools. Unlike static methods such as LIWC, BERT's ability to interpret linguistic subtleties provided a richer understanding of how sentiment evolves over time and interacts with market dynamics.

These findings collectively suggest that sentiment, during times of crises, plays a dual role in both reinforcing a barometer of investor confidence, one that directly impinges on market returns, including the BRVM Composite, while, on the other hand, this divergence in evidence obtained through the MASI and TUNINDEX underlines the fact that sentiment as a determinant and predictor, *prima facie* and at best, can only relate broad trends, making it essential to incorporate macroeconomic, structural, and liquidity factors.

While this study presents a significant contribution to understanding the dynamics between market sentiment and stock returns for African financial markets during the COVID-19 pandemic, it also has some limitations. First, the analysis concentrates on three markets: BRVM Composite, MASI, and TUNINDEX. While providing regional diversity, these markets may not capture the larger dynamics of the sentiment-return relationships across the continent or other emerging and pre-emerging markets. Second, basing sentiment data on news articles alone rules out other possible drivers, such as social media or macroeconomic announcements, which would be potentially larger and more complete sources. Third, the time frame of this study, which focuses on March 2020, is essentially short-term, representing the highest volatility of the market; it might not reflect long-term dynamics of sentiment and returns[2].

Future research could address these limitations by expanding the dataset to include additional markets, alternative sentiment sources, and a longer time frame to assess the persistence of sentiment's impact. Moreover, incorporating control variables, such as policy measures, macroeconomic indicators, and global market trends, could enrich the analysis and provide a more holistic understanding of sentiment-driven market behavior. Additionally, future studies could include a placebo effect analysis to test whether the observed relationships are robust and not driven by spurious correlations, further strengthening the validity of the findings. Methodologically, exploring advanced machine learning models or integrating nonlinear approaches to sentiment analysis could further enhance the accuracy and depth of findings. By building on these foundations, future studies can better inform policymakers and investors navigating the complexities of market behavior in times of crisis.

REFERENCES

Aattouchi, I., Ait Kerroum, M., el Mendili, S., & Elmendili, F. (2022). Financial sentiment analysis of tweets based on deep learning approach. *Indonesian Journal of Electrical Engineering and Computer Science, 25*(3), 1759–1770. DOI: 10.11591/ijeecs.v25.i3.pp1759-1770

Ángeles López-Cabarcos, M., & Pérez-Pico, M., A., Vázquez Rodríguez, P., & López Perez, M. L. (2020). Investor sentiment in the theoretical field of behavioural finance. *Economic Research -. Ekonomska Istrazivanja, 33*(1), 2101–2228. DOI: 10.1080/1331677X.2018.1559748

Araci, D. (2019). *FinBERT: Financial Sentiment Analysis with Pre-trained Language Models* (arXiv:1908.10063). arXiv. https://doi.org//arXiv.1908.10063DOI: 10.48550

Bachelier, L. (1900). Theory of speculation. *Translation of the 1900 french edition. In P. Cootner, editor, The Random Character of Stock Market Prices*, 17–78. MIT Press, Cambridge, MA, 1964.

Bai, C., Duan, Y., Fan, X., & Tang, S. (2023). Financial market sentiment and stock return during the COVID-19 pandemic. *Finance Research Letters, 54*, 103709. DOI: 10.1016/j.frl.2023.103709 PMID: 36811022

Baker, M., & Wurgler, J. (2006). Investor Sentiment and the Cross-Section of Stock Returns. *The Journal of Finance, 61*(4), 1645–1680. DOI: 10.1111/j.1540-6261.2006.00885.x

Bansal, T. (2020). *Behavioral Finance and COVID-19: Cognitive Errors that Determine the Financial Future* (SSRN Scholarly Paper 3595749). https://doi.org/DOI: 10.2139/ssrn.3595749

Barberis, N. C. (2013). Thirty Years of Prospect Theory in Economics: A Review and Assessment. *The Journal of Economic Perspectives, 27*(1), 173–196. DOI: 10.1257/jep.27.1.173

Bondt, W. D., Mayoral, R. M., & Vallelado, E. (2013). Behavioral decision-making in finance: An overview and assessment of selected research. *Spanish Journal of Finance and Accounting / Revista Española de Financiación y Contabilidad*. https://www.tandfonline.com/doi/abs/10.1080/02102412.2013.10779742

Bourezk, H., Raji, A., Acha, N., & Barka, H. (2020). Analyzing Moroccan Stock Market using Machine Learning and Sentiment Analysis. *2020 1st International Conference on Innovative Research in Applied Science, Engineering and Technology (IRASET)*, 1–5. https://doi.org/DOI: 10.1109/IRASET48871.2020.9092304

Cevik, E., Kirci Altinkeski, B., Cevik, E. I., & Dibooglu, S. (2022). Investor sentiments and stock markets during the COVID-19 pandemic. *Financial Innovation, 8*(1), 69. DOI: 10.1186/s40854-022-00375-0 PMID: 35814528

Das, S. R., & Chen, M. Y. (2007). Yahoo! for Amazon: Sentiment Extraction from Small Talk on the Web. *Management Science, 53*(9), 1375–1388. DOI: 10.1287/mnsc.1070.0704

De Bondt, W., & Driehaus, R. H. (2005). *The Psychology of World Equity Markets*. Edward Elgar Publishing. https://econpapers.repec.org/bookchap/elgeebook/2773.htm

De Bondt, W., & Thaler, R. (1985). Does the Stock Market Overreact? *The Journal of Finance, 40*(3), 793–805. DOI: 10.1111/j.1540-6261.1985.tb05004.x

Devlin, J., Chang, M. W., Lee, K., & Toutanova, K. (2019). BERT: Pre-training of deep bidirectional transformers for language understanding. In *Proceedings of NAACL-HLT*. 4171–4186.

Ding, X., Zhang, Y., Liu, T., & Duan, J. (2015). Deep Learning for Event-Driven Stock Prediction. *Proceedings of the Twenty-Fourth International Joint Conference on Artificial Intelligence (IJCAI 2015).*

Du, K., Xing, F., Mao, R., & Cambria, E. (2024). Financial Sentiment Analysis: Techniques and Applications. *ACM Comput. Surv., 56*(9), 220:1-220:42. https://doi.org/DOI: 10.1145/3649451

Fama, E. F. (1965). The Behavior of Stock-Market Prices. *The Journal of Business, 38*(1), 34–105.

Fama, E. F. (1970). Efficient Capital Markets: A Review of Theory and Empirical Work. *The Journal of Finance, 25*(2), 383–417. DOI: 10.2307/2325486

French, K. R. (1980). Stock returns and the weekend effect. *Journal of Financial Economics, 8*(1), 55–69. DOI: 10.1016/0304-405X(80)90021-5

Grinblatt, M., & Keloharju, M. (2000). The investment behavior and performance of various investor types: A study of Finland's unique data set. *Journal of Financial Economics, 55*(1), 43–67. DOI: 10.1016/S0304-405X(99)00044-6

Iyke, B. N., & Ho, S.-Y. (2021). Investor attention on COVID-19 and African stock returns. *MethodsX, 8*, 101195. DOI: 10.1016/j.mex.2020.101195 PMID: 34434722

Jegadeesh, N., & Titman, S. (1993). Returns to Buying Winners and Selling Losers: Implications for Stock Market Efficiency. *The Journal of Finance, 48*(1), 65–91. DOI: 10.1111/j.1540-6261.1993.tb04702.x

Kahneman, D. (2011). *Thinking, Fast and Slow* (1st ed.). Farrar, Straus and Giroux.

Kahneman, D., & Tversky, A. (1979). Prospect Theory: An Analysis of Decision under Risk. *Econometrica, 47*(2), 263–292.

Kartobi, S. E., Oubida, M. A. A., & Elhachimi, Z. (2024). Asymmetric impact of the COVID-19 on the Moroccan stock exchange. *Review of Behavioral Finance, ahead-of-print*(ahead-of-print). https://doi.org/DOI: 10.1108/RBF-03-2024-0078

Kolasani, S. V., & Assaf, R. (2020). Predicting Stock Movement Using Sentiment Analysis of Twitter Feed with Neural Networks. *Journal of Data Analysis and Information Processing, 8*(4), 4. Advance online publication. DOI: 10.4236/jdaip.2020.84018

Lahboub, K., Benali, M., & Moufdi, G. (2022). Evaluation of the adaptive market hypothesis as an evolutionary perspective on market efficiency: Evidence from the Moroccan Stock Market. *Cuadernos de Economía (Santiago, Chile), 45*(129), 48–59.

Lekhal, M., & Oubani, A. E. (2020). Réexamen de l'efficience du marché financier marocain à la lumière de l'Hypothèse des Marchés adaptatifs. Revue du contrôle, de la comptabilité et de l'audit, 4(1), Article 1. https://www.revuecca.com/index.php/home/article/view/500

Li, X., Xie, H., Chen, L., Wang, J., & Deng, X. (2014). News impact on stock price return via sentiment analysis. *Knowledge-Based Systems, 69*, 14–23. DOI: 10.1016/j.knosys.2014.04.022

Lo, A. W. (2004). The Adaptive Markets Hypothesis: Market Efficiency from an Evolutionary Perspective. *Journal of Portfolio Management, 30*(5), 15–29.

Lo, A. W. (2005). Reconciling Efficient Markets with Behavioral Finance: The Adaptive Markets Hypothesis. *The Journal of Investment Consulting*, *7*(2), 21–44.

Lo, A. W. (2012). Adaptive Markets and the New World Order. *Financial Analysts Journal*, *68*(2). Advance online publication. DOI: 10.2469/faj.v68.n2.6

Lo, M. (2022). Market Efficiency Hypothesis. In Lee, C.-F., & Lee, A. C. (Eds.), *Encyclopedia of Finance* (pp. 937–943). Springer International Publishing., DOI: 10.1007/978-3-030-91231-4_30

Longstaff, F. A. (2010). The subprime credit crisis and contagion in financial markets. *Journal of Financial Economics*, *97*(3), 436–450. DOI: 10.1016/j.jfineco.2010.01.002

Mackay, C. (1869). *Memoirs of Extraordinary Popular Dilusions.*

Makrehchi, M., Shah, S., & Liao, W. (2013). Stock Prediction Using Event-Based Sentiment Analysis. *2013 IEEE/WIC/ACM International Joint Conferences on Web Intelligence (WI) and Intelligent Agent Technologies (IAT), 1*, 337–342. https://doi.org/DOI: 10.1109/WI-IAT.2013.48

Mdaghri, A. A., Raghibi, A., Thanh, C. N., & Oubdi, L. (2020). Stock market liquidity, the great lockdown and the COVID-19 global pandemic nexus in MENA countries. *Review of Behavioral Finance*, *13*(1), 51–68. DOI: 10.1108/RBF-06-2020-0132

Nguyen, T. H., Shirai, K., & Velcin, J. (2015). Sentiment analysis on social media for stock movement prediction. *Expert Systems with Applications*, *42*(24), 9603–9611. DOI: 10.1016/j.eswa.2015.07.052

Odean, T. (1998). Are Investors Reluctant to Realize Their Losses? *The Journal of Finance*, *53*(5), 1775–1798. DOI: 10.1111/0022-1082.00072

Oh, C., & Sheng, O. (2011). Investigating Predictive Power of Stock Micro Blog Sentiment in Forecasting Future Stock Price Directional Movement. *ICIS 2011 Proceedings*. https://aisel.aisnet.org/icis2011/proceedings/knowledge/17

Paskaleva, M., & Stoykova, A. (2021). GLOBALIZATION EFFECTS ON CONTAGION RISKS IN FINANCIAL MARKETS. *Ekonomicko-Manazerske Spektrum*, *15*(1), 38–54.

Piñeiro-Chousa, J. R., López-Cabarcos, M. Á., & Pérez-Pico, A. M. (2016). Examining the influence of stock market variables on microblogging sentiment. *Journal of Business Research*, *69*(6), 2087–2092. DOI: 10.1016/j.jbusres.2015.12.013

Samuelson, P. A. (1965). Proof That Properly Anticipated Prices Fluctuate Randomly. *Industrial Management Review*, *6*(2), 41.

Samuelson, P. A. (2015). Rational Theory of Warrant Pricing. In Grünbaum, F. A., van Moerbeke, P., & Moll, V. H. (Eds.), *Henry P. McKean Jr. Selecta* (pp. 195–232). Springer International Publishing., DOI: 10.1007/978-3-319-22237-0_11

Shefrin, H., & Statman, M. (1985). The Disposition to Sell Winners Too Early and Ride Losers Too Long: Theory and Evidence. *The Journal of Finance*, *40*(3), 777–790. DOI: 10.1111/j.1540-6261.1985.tb05002.x

Shiller, R. J. (2003). From Efficient Markets Theory to Behavioral Finance. *The Journal of Economic Perspectives*, *17*(1), 83–104. DOI: 10.1257/089533003321164967

Smales, L. A. (2017). The importance of fear: Investor sentiment and stock market returns. *Applied Economics*, *49*(34), 3395–3421.

Takyi, P. O., & Bentum-Ennin, I. (2021). The impact of COVID-19 on stock market performance in Africa: A Bayesian structural time series approach. *Journal of Economics and Business*, *115*, 105968. DOI: 10.1016/j.jeconbus.2020.105968 PMID: 33318718

Zaremba, A., Kizys, R., Aharon, D. Y., & Demir, E. (2020). Infected Markets: Novel Coronavirus, Government Interventions, and Stock Return Volatility around the Globe. *Finance Research Letters*, *35*, 101597. DOI: 10.1016/j.frl.2020.101597 PMID: 32550842

Zhu, E., & Yen, J. (2024). *BERTopic-Driven Stock Market Predictions: Unraveling Sentiment Insights* (arXiv:2404.02053). arXiv. https://doi.org//arXiv.2404.02053DOI: 10.48550

ENDNOTES

1 The West African Economic and Monetary Union, or WAEMU, is an organization of eight-member states which include Benin, Burkina Faso, Côte d'Ivoire, Guinea-Bissau, Mali, Niger, Senegal, and Togo. They share a common currency (the CFA franc) and centralized their stock market activities through the Bourse Régionale des Valeurs Mobilières (BRVM), located in Abidjan, Côte d'Ivoire. The BRVM constitutes a unified financial market, providing a platform for listing and trading of firms from the WAEMU area. This domestic stock market is also a barometer of the financial health of West African nations in general, mirroring economic trends and investors' sentiments within the region.

2 We remind that the main objective of our study in to examine the relationship between sentiment and market return during a period of crises and uncertainty marked by high volatility.

Chapter 3
Behavioral and Financial Barriers to the Integration of Artificial Intelligence in the Tourism and Hospitality Industry:
A Systematic Approach

Mouhcine Rhouiri
https://orcid.org/0009-0007-7115-871X
Sidi Mohamed Ben Abdellah University, Morocco

Mohamed Habiboullah Meyabe
https://orcid.org/0009-0005-0935-7211
Nouakchott Business School, Mauritania

Mehdi Bensouda
https://orcid.org/0000-0002-7320-3795
Sidi Mohamed Ben Abdellah University, Morocco

Fouad Daidai
https://orcid.org/0000-0003-2165-5551
National School of Business and Management, Morocco

ABSTRACT

As artificial intelligence (AI) transforms tourism and hospitality practices, this chapter examines the behavioral and financial barriers to its adoption. The study highlights major challenges such as resistance to change, high implementation costs and lack of resources. A systematic analysis of key themes from 29 recent articles, carried out with IRaMuTeQ, reveals that these barriers are holding back technology adoption. The results underline the need for inclusive strategies, including incentive policies and training programs, to ensure an equitable and sustainable digital transition.

DOI: 10.4018/979-8-3693-9684-1.ch003

INTRODUCTION

With artificial intelligence gaining prominence, major technology revolutions have remapped traditional practices and strategies in various sectors. From recommendation systems by e-commerce sites to supply chain optimization algorithms within manufacturing, the new face of operations is being refashioned using various automated solutions for an integrative solution (Kaplan and Haenlein, 2019; Dwivedi et al., 2021). In a global context marked by increasing digitalization and heightened competitiveness, the tourism and hospitality sector is no exception to this transformation. Faced with rapidly changing customer expectations, companies in the sector are forced to adapt by integrating technologies capable of meeting increased demands for personalization, responsiveness and operational efficiency (Gretzel et al., 2015).

One role for AI involves personalized customer experience: personalization of service, ordering or booking in itself, with resource management all set for even smoother and easier procedures. That is where 24/7 service through chatbots powered by AI and, again, revenue-maximizing price adjustments from machine-learning-based dynamic pricing come into play for customer service (Tussyadiah, 2020). Internally, AI improves operations management, with intelligent tools for inventory management and forecasts based on data analysis (Ivanov and Webster, 2017).

Despite these promising benefits, AI adoption in the tourism and hospitality sector remains low compared to other industries, such as logistics or finance, where this technology has already been tried and tested (Mariani and Baggio, 2022). The peculiarities of the sector, like heavy reliance on human interaction, sometimes rigid organizational structures, and cultural resistance to technological change, are acting as barriers to this transition (Bilgihan et al., 2016).

Artificial intelligence (AI) has been a tremendous technological revolution that has brought multi-faceted changes in business practices and strategies in several industries (Kaplan & Haenlein, 2019). Particularly from recommendation systems in e-commerce to supply chain optimization algorithms in manufacturing, AI is redefining traditional operating models through innovative and automated solutions (Dwivedi et al., 2021). Therefore, in the world of increased digitalization and fierce competition, the tourism and hospitality industry is not an exception to this evolution. Subjected to the increasingly changing customers' expectations, the companies within this sector must develop ways of fitting technologies that could help satisfy the growing needs for personalization, responsiveness, and operational efficiency (Gretzel et al., 2015).

Artificial intelligence is at the very core of facilitating individualized experiences for customers; it personalizes customer service, optimizes bookings, and pro-actively allocates resources. Specifically, online chatbots with artificial intelligence have enabled 24-hour customer support. Dynamic pricing systems supported by machine-learning algorithms adjust real-time rates for greater revenue (Tussyadiah, 2020). From an internal perspective, artificial intelligence supports operations with intelligent inventory management and forecasting with the aid of data analysis (Ivanov & Webster, 2017).

However, however, the rate at which AI is adopted in the hospitality industry is relatively slow when compared with other industries such as finance and transportation, to which this useful technology has gained economic validation (Mariani & Baggio, 2022). Extreme dependence on human interaction along with sluggish organizational structure and culture inherent in the tourism and hospitality industries impede this transition (Bilgihan et al., 2016).

Tourism and the hospitality industry represent some of the huge pillars of the world economy. Before the COVID-19 pandemic began to have its impact, tourism contributed 10.3% of the world GDP and supported approximately 330 million jobs (Slaoui, 2021). Additionally, it serves as a source for foreign currency, investment, and an economic opportunity that many countries, especially whose economies rely a lot on revenues from tourism, need so much.

In this context, it is actually proving to be a strategic lever as it enables companies to offer customized, smooth travel experiences in today's market where increasing expectations are set by the modern consumer (Buhalis et al., 2019). In fact, the satisfaction of the customer can be raised and their loyalty can be increased through tailor-made travel proposals created by AI systems that analyze every customer's preferences. Second, AI serves in operational resilience by automating operations that are repetitive in nature while optimizing operation costs, which are increasingly required under a highly competitive environment where pressures on profit margins are high (Ivanov et al., 2019).

However, despite its potential, AI remains little used in this sector, not least because of behavioral and financial barriers. Identifying and understanding these obstacles is thus crucial to fully exploiting such technology's benefits and changing the sector into a competitive and sustainable model capable of facing current challenges on all fronts, from tourism flows to environmental sustainability and the enhancement of consumer experience.

Despite the obvious potential of AI in tourism and hospitality, its adoption remains fragmented, largely due to behavioral and financial breaks, hindering the sector's ability to take full advantage of the opportunities offered by this technology. Thus, the central issue of this study can be formulated as follows: *What are the main behavioral and financial obstacles to the integration of artificial intelligence in the tourism and hospitality sector?*

This is a very important issue in a sector where the expectations of consumers are changing very fast. Indeed, finding an effective answer to this question could improve the performance and resilience against market challenges of tourism and hospitality businesses.

Few works, however, have demonstrated the benefits of AI in tourism and hospitality, and fewer still examine the barriers from both behavioral and financial perspectives. Most existing studies either focus on successful use cases or technological analyses but do not go in-depth to explore the reasons why some companies remain reluctant to adopt AI.

The key purpose of this article would be to spot, analyze, and propose solutions for a few of the critical behavioral and financial barriers that hamper AI adoption in the tourism and hospitality sector.

This chapter is concerned with the integration of AI into the tourism and hospitality industries, with a focus on its adoption based on important behavioral and financial factors. The aim is to find the barriers to the adoption of this technology, both in behavioral and financial terms, with a structured approach supported by IRaMuTeQ software. It starts with the presentation of evidence on huge behavioral barriers created through resistance to change, fear of automation, and lack of digital skills. The paper goes ahead to outline some important financial hurdles relating to AI integration. Key themes within the discussion were identified by utilizing a robust literature review. This is then followed by an in-depth results discussion to handle the objectives of implications and the limitation of the approach developed here in this chapter.

BACKGROUND

Artificial intelligence (AI) is redefining many sectors, including tourism and hospitality, by transforming customer experiences, optimizing operations and boosting revenues. Indeed, tourism, a key sector of the global economy, accounted for over 10% of global GDP before the COVID-19 pandemic

(CESE, 2020). Consequently, the integration of AI makes it possible to meet modern consumers' expectations for personalized, seamless and efficient services. Notably, among its flagship applications are intelligent chatbots, dynamic pricing algorithms and proactive resource management tools (Tussyadiah, 2020; Ivanov & Webster, 2017).

In particular, the use of AI-based chatbots enables 24/7 customer interaction, reducing response times while improving customer satisfaction (Davenport & Ronanki, 2018). In addition, dynamic pricing algorithms powered by AI and Machine Learning analyze data in real time to adjust prices according to demand and market conditions, thereby increasing companies' revenues (Nguyen, H. T., Tran, T. T., Nham, P. T., Nguyen, N. U. B., & Le, A. D., 2023; Gao, J., 2024). In addition, proactive resource management tools help optimize inventory and human resource management, improving overall operational efficiency (Ivanov et al., 2019).

However, despite its promise, the adoption of artificial intelligence (AI) in the tourism sector remains slower than in other industries such as finance or logistics. Indeed, several obstacles are holding back this transition. Firstly, dependence on human interaction is a major challenge. Being an inherently human-centric industry, many customers prefer interactions with physical staff, which limits the acceptance of automated technologies (Bilgihan et al., 2016). Secondly, the rigid organizational structures of companies in the sector, often made up of small and medium-sized enterprises (SMEs), lack the flexibility to adopt new technologies (Garzella et al., 2021). In addition, cultural resistance plays a significant role. The perception of AI as a threat to employment or as a dehumanizing factor hinders its integration (Wannemo, F., 2024).

In addition, the implications of geopolitical factors, such as local and international regulations and political tensions, can slow AI adoption by creating uncertainties and legal barriers (Dwivedi et al., 2021). Furthermore, regional disparities, particularly in terms of technological infrastructure and levels of economic development, exacerbate inequalities in access to and implementation of AI in the tourism sector (Mhlanga, D., 2021). Consequently, these combined obstacles explain why the tourism sector is slow to fully exploit the potential of AI.

This chapter looks specifically at behavioral and financial barriers to the integration of AI in the tourism sector, based on a systematic analysis of qualitative data using IRaMuTeQ software. This methodology categorizes and visualizes key themes through lexical and co-occurrence analyses (Ramos, M. G., do Rosário Lima, V. M., & Rosa, M. P. A., 2018). The aim is to identify concrete and strategic solutions to overcome these challenges and leverage the transformative potential of AI in this strategic sector.

1. LITERATURE REVIEW

The integration of artificial intelligence (AI) into the tourism and hospitality industry represents a major transformation, enabling improved operational efficiency, personalized services and a richer customer experience. This section of the literature review examines two key aspects: (1) the integration of AI in these sectors and (2) the behavioral, financial and geopolitical factors influencing this adoption. In addition, it also explores government initiatives, socio-economic factors and ethical concerns related to data confidentiality.

1.1. The integration of artificial intelligence (AI) in the tourism and hospitality industry

AI is increasingly being used in the tourism and hospitality sector to automate processes, improve the customer experience and optimize operations. The integration of AI in these sectors revolves around several axes, including reservations management, improving service personalization, and optimizing internal processes (Avula and Sithole 2024).

Automatisation et gestion des réservations

AI plays a key role in automating booking processes and optimizing prices. Indeed, accommodation management systems can use AI algorithms to predict demand, adjust prices in real time and thus maximize revenue (Kim, H., So, K. K. F., Shin, S., & Li, J., 2024). In addition, chatbots and virtual assistants, often powered by AI, enable customers to book rooms, ask questions and solve problems without human intervention. As such, these tools improve not only operational efficiency, but also customer satisfaction by offering 24/7 availability (Tussyadiah & Park, 2018). Along these lines, Praharaj et al. 2023 explore the impact of automated reservation services (AS) on value creation (VC) and guest experience (GE) in the hotel industry. Based on a survey of 290 Indian customers and structural modeling analysis (SEM), the results show that SA and VC positively influence customer experience, with VC playing a mediating role. These findings underline the importance of automation in enhancing the customer experience by optimizing value creation (Praharaj et al., 2023).

Personalizing the customer experience

One of the major contributions of AI in the hotel sector is the personalization of services. AI systems can analyze customer data (booking history, food preferences, online behaviors) to offer tailored recommendations, special offers or personalized services (Park, S., 2021; Mishra et al., 2025). These solutions contribute to a smoother, more personalized experience, boosting customer loyalty. Indeed, hotels can adapt room temperatures or suggest tourist activities based on customer interests, thanks to intelligent systems (Lv et al., 2024).

Another concrete case of control is the Hotel by Marriott, which uses a combination of technologies to personalize services while improving the customer experience. One is one of the highlights of their innovations; Alexa for Hospitality-an altered version of Amazon Alexa that seeks to improve upon it for the hotel industry's needs. This technology allows guests to set room temperature, light adjustments, room service requests, and virtual check-outs among a myriad of other things through voice commands. This system was installed in two hotels in Los Angeles by the Marriott, improving its efficiency in operations and guest comfort (Huang et al., 2021; Amazon Alexa, 2023).

Additionally, Marriott introduced facial recognition check-in kiosks at two of its hotels in China-Hangzhou and Sanya -in 2018. Guests can scan in their ID, sign the digital form, and receive room keys in under three minutes, reducing the check-in time by two-thirds (Huang et al., 2021). Marriott also uses bots, including Alexa voice assistants and concierge bots- such as Mario-used in its Belgium properties-to ensure service is both fast and efficient. On the other hand, the Botlr chatbot from Marriott is used in lieu of automated phone calls and emails, improving the responsiveness of customer service (Rawal et al., 2022; Uniyal & Sharma, 2020).

Optimizing internal processes

AI optimizes human resources and inventory management in the hotel industry. The tools replace manual labor with robots and intelligent assistants that handle tasks like cleaning and deliver room service. These help in enhancing operation efficiency while reducing expenses (Ivanov et al., 2020). Ivanova et al. showed in their work that robot use and, consequently, automation of services within agencies and tourist information facilities have increased efficiency, reducing repetitive work for humans (Ivanova, 2019). Moreover, Ivanov and Webster (2019) prove that the adoption of robots and service automation in industries such as travel, tourism, and hospitality has also contributed to internal processes, inventory management, and human resources.

Impact on marketing strategy

AI also makes it possible to analyze the massive data generated by consumer behavior to develop more targeted marketing strategies. Indeed, recommendation systems, which are forms of AI, analyze customer preferences to propose personalized offers, thereby increasing cross-selling and conversion. These tools also enable companies to better understand consumer trends, and adjust their offers accordingly (Buhalis and Sinarta, 2019). The study by Florido-Benítez and del Alcázar Martínez shows that artificial intelligence has a notable impact on tourism marketing, optimizing resources and improving the attractiveness of tourist sites (Florido-Benítez and del Alcázar Martínez, 2024).

1.2. Behavioral and financial factors critical to AI integration in the tourism and hospitality industry

The adoption of AI in the tourism and hospitality sector depends not only on the technological advances available, but also on behavioral and financial factors that influence how these technologies are integrated into business practices.

Behavioral factors

There are various major challenges that come in the way of integration of artificial intelligence in the hospitality and tourism sector, mainly in the fields of organizational change management and acceptance of this technology by employees and customers (Rane et al., 2024). On the employee's part, receptivity to AI can be influenced by concern about their work being replaced by machines or robots. Lee et al. (2019) suggested that hotel companies must support such a transition through training that enables the staff to competently understand and apply these new technologies for their operations. Besides, the inclusion of employees in the process of change may improve the acceptance of AI. Furthermore, explaining the benefits related to reducing repetitive tasks and improving their performances is another added value.

On the consumer side, their perception of AI technologies is another key issue. As Zhong et al (2021) point out, some customers remain reluctant to interact with robots or automated systems, preferring human contact. However, this perception may change thanks to improved customer experience, greater transparency in processes and a commitment to service quality on the part of companies. Indeed, the work of Kong et al (2023), shows that customer perception of artificial intelligence technologies is an important topic, and that this perception varies according to cultural and generational factors.

Finally, AI in this sector raises a very important ethical and privacy issue: the collection and usage of personal data. Many customers are concerned about the security of their information, and that requires strong data protection policies, with strict adherence to regulations such as the GDPR. As Belk (2021) said, companies need to be transparent about data usage and use ethical practices if they are to engender trust in consumers for the beneficial adoption of AI technologies. Xu et al. (2021) investigated hotel guests' adoption of such services regarding aspects of security, privacy, and trust. A study carried out by Xu et al. (2021) investigated adopting facial recognition service for check-in by the hotel guests: "security-privacy-trust perspective of facial recognition check-in service adoption in hotels". Indeed, a hotel with transparent and ethical policy on the processing of biometric data, Xu et al. (2021) found, uses facial Recognition to establish that 81.3% Guests were satisfied in this technology adoption.

Financial factors

The significant financial outlay needed to integrate artificial intelligence (AI) into the travel and hospitality industry can be a significant barrier, especially for small and medium-sized businesses (SMEs). For many businesses, the expenses of personnel training, infrastructure, and technology are a major deterrent (García-Madurga and Grilló-Méndez, 2023).

A key aspect in overcoming this obstacle lies in the analysis of return on investment (ROI). As Buhalis and Sinarta (2019) point out, a thorough ROI assessment is essential to convince decision-makers to commit to AI adoption. Although these technologies involve high initial costs, they can generate substantial gains in the long term, notably through reduced operational costs, improved process efficiency and increased revenues thanks to more personalized services. Indeed, Challoumis (2024) shows that AI technologies implemented in companies have had significant ROI.

In addition, financial constraints can be alleviated through access to public subsidies or the establishment of strategic partnerships with technology companies. Vinodan et al. (2023) highlight the role of government initiatives and public-private collaborations in supporting companies in this transition, reducing the financial burden associated with AI adoption. In this sense, Vinodan et al. (2023) show that public incentives for smart tourism services play a major role in strengthening tourism infrastructures and improving visitor experience.

2. METHODOLOGICAL APPROACH AND TOOLS USED

The methodology adopted in this study combines a rigorous systematic review of the literature with a textual factorial analysis, using IRaMuTeQ software. This approach has been chosen for its potential to provide an overview of the subject under study while allowing the detailed exploration of emerging themes from scientific publications. The overarching methodological aim would then be to outline and systematically organize the information that is available in regard to behavioral and financial barriers, related to the implementation of AI within the tourism and hospitality industry.

The methodology is structured around three interdependent stages: (1) selection of relevant articles, (2) textual factorial analysis to identify recurring themes, and (3) interpretation of the results obtained to draw relevant conclusions.

2.1. Article selection

Articles relevant to the study were selected. A systematic search in the SCOPUS academic database was independently performed by two researchers. For this paper, we have preferred SCOPUS because of its wealth of high-quality scientific content with international coverage, ensuring a variety of positions on the subject. PRISMA has then been used as our methodology to guarantee rigor and transparency in this selection process.

Inclusion and exclusion criteria

In order to ensure relevance and quality, strict inclusion and exclusion criteria were defined for the selection of articles that would form the basis of this study. These criteria ensure that the analyzed articles respond directly to the problematic of the present study, which is the identification of behavioral and financial barriers to the adoption of AI in the tourism and hospitality sector.

Inclusion criteria

In addition, for subject matters, the publication should specifically address the integration of AI in the tourism or hospitality sector, focusing on behavioral barriers to implementation or diffusion-such as resistance to change and fear of automation-and/or financial barriers, including costs and uncertain return on investment. Lastly, with respect to the language, only those published in the English language were considered for this review. From the period of publication, only articles that were published between 2013 and 2024 were chosen to reflect the recent advances in AI and its implications on the studied sector. The SCOPUS academic database was selected due to the quality of scientific publications. After selection, a total of 29 articles was selected to create the corpus of analysis.

Exclusion criteria

Articles that did not meet the following criteria were excluded from the analysis. First, with regard to sector relevance, only those publications dealing exclusively with AI in sectors other than tourism or hospitality, such as health or finance, were excluded. Second, with regard to languages, only those in English or French were taken into consideration, thus excluding the ones in other languages. Finally, conference reviews and reports were also excluded from the analysis. Indeed, these kinds of publications do not always undergo the same severe peer-reviewing process as regular articles published in academic journals, which may question the reliability of the scientific rigor of the information they contain.

Selection results

As shown in Figure 1, this study elucidated 29 relevant articles for the period, 2019-2024. In total, 374 articles were excluded as they met the selection criteria set. The main language of the articles, reviews, book chapters, and books is English. The presented works have been carried out within a wide range of divergent fields, including: Business, Management and Accounting; Economics, Econometrics and Finance; Engineering; Social Sciences, and Computer Science.

The keywords with the highest occurrence among the selected articles are: green finance, investments, finance, decision-making and carbon emissions. All these terms were mentioned frequently in the corpus and reflect their importance in the context of the study.

All of the selected publications date back 5 years now-from 2019 to 2024-this shows just how novel the theme addressed is.

Figure 1. Adapted PRISMA flow diagram.

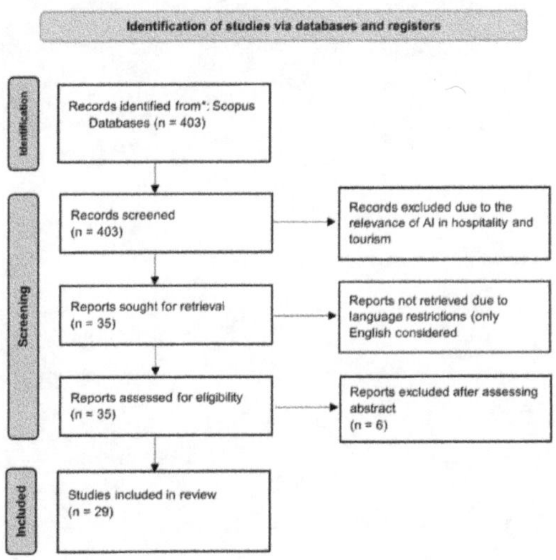

2.2. Textual Factorial Analysis with IRaMuTeQ

Once the articles had been selected, the textual corpus comprising the abstracts of the publications was analyzed using IRaMuTeQ software. This software, based on advanced textual statistics, is particularly well suited to extracting recurring themes and conceptual relationships from a voluminous corpus.

Corpus construction

The abstracts of the 29 articles were grouped together to form a unified corpus. This corpus was then imported into IRaMuTeQ to perform a hierarchical top-down classification (DHC), grouping text segments into distinct thematic classes.

Descending hierarchical classification (DHC)

DHC is a statistical method that divides the corpus into homogeneous text segments, grouped into classes according to their lexical content. Each class represents a recurring theme or sub-theme in the articles analyzed. This approach is particularly useful for identifying hidden patterns and complex conceptual structures.

Figure 2. Distribution of descending hierarchical classes (DHC) in our study

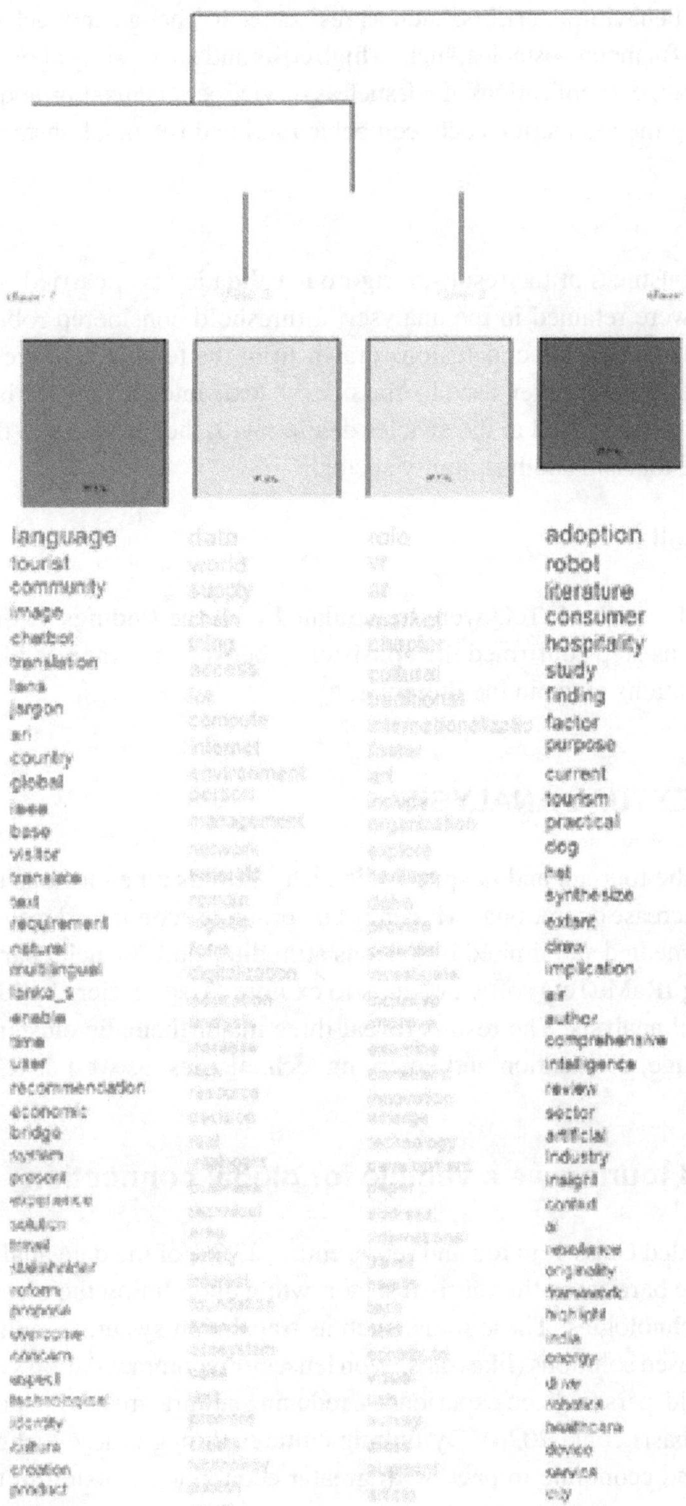

In this study, DHC was used to identify four main classes:

1. A class focused on behavioral barriers, such as resistance to change and lack of technical skills.
2. A class dedicated to financial obstacles, such as high costs and uncertainty about return on investment.
3. A class exploring practical applications of AI, such as service personalization and process optimization.
4. A class synthesizing the interactions between behavioral and financial obstacles.

Validation of results

To guarantee the robustness of the results, a rigorous validation was carried out. In this study, over 70% of text segments were retained in the analyses, a threshold considered robust in similar studies. This high retention ensures that the conclusions drawn from the textual data are representative of the overall corpus. These results were then used to classify the texts into clusters (or broad classes) in order to identify the key themes addressed in the articles dealing with the obstacles to the integration of artificial intelligence in the tourism and hospitality sector.

Triangulation of results

The results obtained via IRaMuTeQ were triangulated with the findings of the original studies included in the corpus. This step confirmed the consistency between the themes identified in the textual analysis and the observations made in the literature.

3. RESULTS OF TEXTUAL ANALYSIS

AI integration into the tourism and hospitality industry affords an enormous opportunity to extend customer experience, increase operational efficiency and promote economic development. Nevertheless, its adoption is still fragmented and limited by various attitudinal and financial barriers. This systematic study, carried out using IRaMuTeQ software, aims to explore these barriers by identifying key themes through rigorous textual analysis. The results reveal three major thematic clusters that highlight challenges related to language, digitization and emerging technologies, as well as the adoption of AI and robots in services.

3.1. Language and tourism as a vehicle for global connection

The first group, entitled Class 1, in red and representing 27.3% of the data analyzed, highlights ways of overcoming language barriers in the tourism sector, while underlining the essential role of language and communication technologies. These tools, such as translation systems, multilingual chatbots and artificial intelligence-based solutions (like translation lenses or recommendation systems), meet tourists' growing demand for fluid, personalized experiences, reducing cultural misunderstandings and improving visitor satisfaction (Rubasri et al., 2024). By linking cultures through these technologies, there is also a significant cultural and economic impact, with greater economic inclusion in tourist regions. Local products benefit from greater visibility, while local players are able to offer more tailored experiences to international visitors (Ma, 2024).

However, despite their many advantages, these technologies face major challenges. Attitudinally, tourism operators are sometimes reluctant to adopt them, either because of a lack of familiarity with digital tools, or for fear that they will replace traditional human interaction. Travelers, especially the elderly, can also be reluctant, fearing mistakes or a loss of spontaneity in their experiences (Reddy and Sailesh, 2024). In addition, financial barriers are a major obstacle: the high cost of developing, maintaining and updating these solutions limits their adoption, particularly for small local businesses, which often prefer traditional methods for lack of sufficient resources, to the detriment of the expectations of modern tourists (Reddy and Sailesh, 2024).

This group therefore illustrates a balance between the opportunities offered by language technologies to enrich tourism experiences and the challenges to be overcome for sustainable adoption in the sector.

3.2. Digitalization, IoT and immersive realities as drivers of economic and cultural transformation

The second cluster is made up of class 2 (green, 25.8%) and class 3 (cyan, 25.8%), focusing on two axes: the integration of digitalization and IoT technologies in resource and supply chain management, and the adoption of immersive technologies, such as augmented reality (AR) and virtual reality (VR), for promoting cultural innovation and international collaborations. These two axes therefore underline how emerging technologies are transforming economic and cultural practices.

In Class 2, analysis reveals that the Internet of Things (IoT) is revolutionizing supply chains by offering advanced logistics flow tracking and predictive inventory management capabilities (Car et al., 2019). Access to massive data enables companies to make informed decisions, reducing waste while promoting sustainable ecosystems (Khan et al., 2024). However, challenges remain. Behaviorally, resistance to change is a major obstacle. Companies with an organizational culture centered on traditional practices, as well as employees, often perceive automation as a threat, fearing loss of control or jobs (Bihari Singh et al., 2024). In financial terms, IoT adoption requires significant investment in infrastructure, smart sensors and analysis tools. This financial constraint particularly limits small and medium-sized enterprises (SMEs), accentuating the economic divide within supply chains (McKinsey, 2022).

Class 3 highlights the potential of immersive technologies to foster cultural innovation. Augmented reality and virtual reality make it possible to recreate historical and cultural experiences, making knowledge more accessible and engaging (Semwal et al., 2024). These technologies also contribute to internationalization by fostering cross-cultural collaborations and creating new opportunities in the tourism, education and arts sectors (Zhang et al., 2024). However, attitudinal barriers hinder their adoption. Cultural and educational organizations, often attached to traditional approaches, perceive these tools as complex or unreliable. Similarly, end-users may feel intimidated by these innovations, not least due to a lack of digital skills (Benckendorff et al., 2019). Financial barriers are also significant: the high costs of hardware, software and maintenance limit their use, particularly in economically disadvantaged regions. Smaller organizations, such as local museums or tourism businesses, struggle to access these technologies for lack of sufficient budgetary resources (Rane et al., 2023).

The group's global analysis highlights that digitalization, IoT and immersive technologies play a central role in economic and cultural transformation. These technologies enable greater inclusion and contribute to sustainable development in an interconnected world. However, to maximize their impact, it is necessary to overcome technological and economic gaps, particularly between developed and developing countries. Further research and targeted support policies are essential to democratize access to these innovations.

3.3. Adoption of artificial intelligence and robots in the service sector

Class 4, in purple and representing 21.1% of the data analyzed, explores the adoption of artificial intelligence (AI) and robots in service sectors such as tourism, healthcare and hospitality. These technologies are increasingly being used to optimize operations, reduce costs and personalize services. In the hospitality sector, robots play a crucial role in greeting customers and managing simple requests, offering standardized and efficient responses (Ivanov and Webster, 2017). In addition, research frameworks are emerging to ensure ethical and effective integration of these innovations, minimizing negative impacts on employees and consumers. The aim is to combine technological benefits with attention to human well-being.

However, widespread adoption of AI and robotics remains held back by several behavioral and financial obstacles. On the one hand, consumers often lack confidence in these tools, fearing technical errors or the dehumanization of services. Ethical concerns about replacing human jobs also reinforce reluctance, particularly among employees and companies. On the other hand, financial barriers, such as high initial costs, maintenance expenses and the need for costly training programs, limit access to these technologies, particularly for SMEs. In addition, inadequate digital infrastructures in some regions represent a further obstacle, requiring considerable investment to upgrade them. These challenges underline the need for appropriate strategies to promote the gradual, sustainable adoption of these technologies in services.

4. DISCUSSION OF RESULTS

4.1. Discussion of the results of the cluster analysis

Based on the results obtained from this systematic study, analyzed using IRaMuTeQ software, we have identified several significant clusters, each grouping specific themes related to technology adoption in the tourism sector. These clusters reflect distinct dynamics in terms of technological barriers and opportunities. A discussion of the results by cluster is presented below:

Cluster 1: Language and tourism as a vehicle for global connectivity

Language technologies appear to be promising tools for reducing language barriers in tourism. These findings confirm the work of Wang, X., and Leou, C. H. (2015). which highlight their ability to facilitate interactions between tourists and service providers. However, these technologies raise challenges regarding the authenticity of cultural interactions, potentially compromised by excessive standardization of experiences. In addition, their adoption remains hampered by behavioral and financial barriers, particularly in economically disadvantaged regions where resources for deploying these solutions are limited. These observations underline the need to strike a balance between technological progress and the preservation of local cultural wealth. Furthermore, investment in infrastructure and adequate financial resources remain essential to ensure wider, equitable adoption.

Cluster 2: Digitalization, IoT and immersive realities as drivers of economic and cultural transformation

The results highlight the complementary roles of Internet of Things (IoT) technologies and immersive technologies such as augmented reality (AR) and virtual reality (VR). These findings are in line with the work of Lukita et al, (2018) on AR/VR, which demonstrates the potential of these tools to transform tourism experiences. However, technological and financial barriers hinder their adoption, particularly in developing countries. High installation costs and a lack of suitable infrastructure widen disparities between rich and poor regions, exacerbating the digital divide. This unequal access to digital technologies and skills limits the ability of disadvantaged regions to take full advantage of innovations, reinforcing economic and social imbalances on a global scale. As such, the results reinforce the idea that investment in technology infrastructure development and skills training is crucial to overcoming these barriers. Such an approach could also reduce technological inequalities on an international scale.

Cluster 3: Adoption of artificial intelligence and robots in services

Applications of artificial intelligence (AI) and robotics in the service sector confirm the findings of Ivanov and Webster (2017), who highlight their benefits in improving the efficiency and quality of services. However, they raise ethical concerns linked, among other things, to confidentiality, social equity and the substitution of human jobs. Consumers are also showing behavioral resistance to AI, often perceived as a threat to the authenticity of human relationships. Furthermore, the high cost of implementing these technologies is a major brake, particularly for small and medium-sized enterprises (SMEs). The ethical adoption of AI, based on appropriate regulatory frameworks, therefore appears to be a promising way of minimizing negative impacts while taking economic constraints into account.

4.2. Discussion of objectives versus results

The results of this systematic study address the main objectives set. Through the analysis carried out via IRaMuTeQ, behavioral and financial barriers, as well as strategic avenues for overcoming them, were identified and discussed.

Identification of behavioral barriers

The objective of this research is the behavioral impediments inhibiting the use of artificial intelligence (AI) in the tourism and hospitality sector. Two major obstacles come into focus.

The first is that resistance to change poses a major problem. It is this kind of resistance that stems from the distrust of new technologies, like AI and robotics, which are viewed as interfering with the quality of human contact and endangering job availability. Such findings correspond with the work by Duan, Edwards and Dwivedi (2019) who claimed that negative perceptions tend to adversely affect the adoption of technology.

Lack of digital skills is another major barrier that SMEs face. These firms frequently do not have adequate training, which leads to employees not using these technologies effectively. This observation corresponds to the work done by Carlisle S Ivanov S Dijkmans C. (2023) emphasizing on the needed digital skills in innovation within tourism industries.

Promoting the adoption of AI technology will require increased educational and awareness programs to lessen the impact of these barriers.

Identifying financial barriers

Identifying financial constraints to AI adoption was also a central objective of this research. The analyses reveal two major financial barriers.

On the one hand, the high initial costs of installation, maintenance and technological upgrades represent a major challenge, particularly for SMEs with limited resources. These findings concur with those of Kamble, Gunasekaran, and Gawankar (2020), who indicate that budgetary constraints hinder the integration of technological innovations in the tourism sector.

On the other hand, uncertainty about return on investment is a major barrier. Companies are reluctant to invest in expensive technologies because of the long-term benefits that are difficult to assess, especially in an uncertain economic climate. These findings are consistent with observations by McKinsey and Company (2022), who point out that the lack of convincing economic data often holds back technology investments.

This underscores the crucial importance of implementing robust financial and policy mechanisms to overcome the identified barriers to the adoption of artificial intelligence (AI) in the tourism industry. Public policies, such as subsidies, tax incentives and public-private partnerships, play a key role in reducing the initial costs associated with integrating emerging technologies. These approaches are corroborated by Kamble, Gunasekaran and Gawankar (2020), who demonstrate that companies facing budget constraints benefit significantly from external finance. In addition, tax incentives can act as gas pedals to stimulate technological investment (McKinsey and Company, 2022).

In addition, the establishment of clear regulatory frameworks and awareness programs is essential to allay fears related to privacy, employment and the ethical impacts of AI technologies. Such frameworks not only build stakeholder trust, but also promote responsible and socially acceptable adoption, as suggested by the work of Duan, Edwards and Dwivedi (2019). Such initiatives promote a smooth transition by mitigating behavioral resistance often exacerbated by distrust of technological innovations.

In sum, this study validates the initial objectives by identifying and analyzing the behavioral and financial barriers holding back AI adoption. The results also highlight the urgent need for an integrated approach, combining financial, political and educational measures, to remove these barriers. Such an approach is essential to ensure the equitable and sustainable adoption of AI technologies in the tourism industry, in line with the recommendations of Skubis, Wolniak, and Grebski (2024), who emphasize the role of multi-sector strategies in promoting technological innovation.

ISSUES, CONTROVERSIES AND PROBLEMS

In order to mitigate the behavioral and financial costs of incorporating artificial intelligence (AI) within the tourism and hospitality industry, it is important to create targeted strategies that best suit the businesses, particularly SMEs. First, strengthening the involvement of the employees in digital skills training is extremely important in order to combat change aversion. Employees are more likely to accept new technologies (Lee et al., 2019) when there is targeted training that builds their digital skills, for example workshops on how to use AI tools such as chatbots or automated reservation systems. Companies can reduce resistance to technology integration by showing employees how AI can eliminate tedious work.

Furthermore, consumer education and consumer trust are important because the customer's view strongly influences the acceptance of AI technologies. To gain their trust, it is important to demonstrate the value these technologies can bring such as responses to services becoming more personalized and efficient. In this regard, hotels can demonstrate to the customers how the information obtained through the services will be put to use in enhancing the customer's experience while upholding regulations such as GDPR.

Adopting face recognition technologies has proven to be helpful to the hospitality business, as guests tend to have 81.3 percent positive reviews when hotels are open to surveillance, according to Xu et al (2021).

Moreover, promoting public-private collaboration and providing support through subsidies is an important answer for the steep costs of adopting AI associated with SMEs. Supporting public-private collaboration and motivating the government to subsidize technology investments for business is vital. In the Indian context, over 500 hotel SMEs have enhanced their infrastructure as well as integrated AI technologies into their systems due to government subsidization, and they are now more competitive globally (AL-Romeedy & El-Sisi, 2024).

Cooperative approaches of funding also solve financial challenges. Taking a cue from other industries, hotel SMEs can adopt collaborative cost-sharing models for AI technologies through collaborative management systems. For instance, several hotels could collectively invest in an automated reservation system; it would cut down costs and allow all users to gain the advantage of the technology (Ivanov, S., & Webster, C., 2019).

These other essential things regarding data security and ethical issues should be strengthened in relation to the future use of personal data-how companies should have data protection policies in place and comply with regulations. Yes, proper ethical frameworks developed along with the use of AI technologies will help boost trust from customers and employees.

On the other hand, advanced technological tools like AR and predictive analytics bring in more gratitude towards AI. A virtual tour of rooms or facilities in hotels through AR improves the experience of customers even before they come. Predictive analytics can anticipate customer wishes and streamline operations, such as optimizing inventory management and workforce planning.

Lastly, KPIs need a system set up to ascertain whether AI technology works properly. These can be measures of customer satisfaction, operational efficiency, and return on investment (ROI). Hotels could assess whether customer satisfaction evolved after introducing the chatbot, or what savings were achieved through the automation of administrative tasks.

By taking these recommendations into account, the tourism-hospitality sector shall overcome the barriers in ushering AI and embrace the benefits that accrue from the deployment of these technologies whilst retaining its unique character in terms of humanism and culture.

SOLUTIONS AND RECOMMENDATIONS

To overcome the behavioral, financial and ethical obstacles associated with AI integration in tourism and hospitality, a multi-faceted approach is essential. Firstly, implementing training programs to strengthen digital skills and reduce fears related to job loss, while involving employees in technology integration processes, can encourage their buy-in (Lee et al., 2019). At the same time, raising consumer awareness of the benefits of AI, such as personalized services and improved responsiveness, is essential to building trust and acceptance.

From a practical point of view, the results offer concrete avenues for encouraging inclusion and reducing technological inequalities. They highlight the need to invest in suitable infrastructures and develop targeted strategies to overcome behavioral resistance and financial constraints. In addition, the study confirms that financial incentives and awareness-raising campaigns, as suggested by Kamble, Gunasekaran and Gawankar (2020), can play a key role in fostering stakeholder acceptance of technologies.

In terms of solutions to overcome financial barriers, it is recommended that public-private partnerships be encouraged, prompting governments to support SMEs through subsidies for technology investments (Oyegbade, I. K., Igwe, A. N., Chrisanctus, O., & Ofodile, C. A., 2022). Furthermore, pooling resources can prove effective by setting up collaborative models that enable SMEs to share the costs associated with AI adoption.

In addition, strengthening data protection and ensuring compliance with regulations such as the GDPR are crucial to addressing ethical concerns. Similarly, developing transparent ethical frameworks to frame the use of AI technologies is essential to preserve stakeholder trust (Belk, 2021).

Finally, to develop technologies and performance indicators, it is pertinent to exploit tools such as augmented reality (AR) and predictive analytics to offer immersive experiences and optimize processes. According to Kamble and others, they are recommending the key performance indicators (KPIs) to assess the impact of AI on customer satisfaction, operational efficiency, and financial performance.

By taking a cue from these recommendations, the tourism and hospitality sector will guarantee that it will not only accelerate the adoption of AI technology but will also do so responsibly while safeguarding its human and cultural essence.

CONCLUSION

This study set out to analyze the behavioral and financial barriers limiting the adoption of artificial intelligence (AI) in the tourism and hospitality industry while exploring solutions to overcome these obstacles. The analysis showed three major themes. Firstly, AI-enabled language-based technologies, such as multilingual chatbots and instant translation systems, play an important role in reducing language barriers and improving customer experience in a globalized industry. However, these aids adversely affect intercultural exchanges because they risk standardizing interactions and thereby homogenizing tourism experiences.

Therefore, to overcome this limitation, the introduction of these technologies has to be backed by initiatives that preserve cultural authenticity. Secondly, IoT technologies and immersive tools such as VR and AR are becoming critical drivers of economic and cultural shifts in tourism. IoT optimizes logistical and operational processes, while the use of immersive technologies contributes to cultural innovation by offering more engaging experiences. Nevertheless, their adoption is limited by financial and structural constraints, particularly in economically disadvantaged regions.

Moreover, it is crucial to put in place funding mechanisms to support their adoption in these regions. Finally, the use of AI and robots in services, particularly in the hotel industry, is helping to personalize services and improve operational efficiency. However, these technologies face behavioral resistance, including ethical concerns about their impact on employment and data privacy.

Thus, to mitigate such resistance, it is essential to develop sound ethical frameworks and confidentiality policies. The results of the study help to answer the research questions by highlighting the main behavioral and financial obstacles. Resistance to change, lack of digital skills and fear of dehumanizing services are major brakes on AI adoption. High initial costs, uncertainties regarding ROI, and lack of infrastructure represent other significant barriers, especially for SMEs.

These results add to the body of knowledge that puts a face on the specific challenges at the very core of the tourism and hospitality sectors wherein human interaction and cultural diversity play an integral role. On a theoretical level, this study fills a gap in the literature by focusing on the specific impediments to AI adoption in the tourism sector, an aspect that is often overlooked. In contrast to existing work that focuses primarily on the benefits of technologies, this research proposes a systematic framework for understanding behavioral and financial barriers. By incorporating innovative methodological perspectives, such as the use of IRaMuTeQ for textual analysis, it enriches models on technological adoption and opens the way to cross-sectoral and contextual reflections.

In addition, the integration of artificial intelligence (AI) in the tourism and hospitality sector faces several limitations that influence the analysis of barriers to its adoption. Firstly, the exclusive use of the Scopus database, although of high quality, restricts the coverage of certain scientific contributions available in other databases such as Web of Science. In addition, the absence of publications prior to 2019 underlines the emerging nature of this theme, limiting our understanding of behavioral barriers, such as resistance to change and mistrust of automation, but also financial barriers, notably high implementation costs and uncertainties over return on investment.

On the other hand, these methodological limitations, notably the absence of empirical approaches such as surveys or interviews, could restrict the depth of the results. It is also important to note that the impact of differences between large companies and SMEs has not been explored in depth. This could offer complementary insights into the specific challenges faced by each type of company. To overcome these limitations, database expansion and the inclusion of future empirical research are needed to provide a more comprehensive and nuanced view of the challenges and opportunities associated with AI adoption in this strategic sector.

FUTURE RESEARCH DIRECTIONS

To round out the limitations identified and help appreciate the challenges accompanying the integration of artificial intelligence (AI) in the tourism and hospitality sector, some research directions could be offered. First, extending the database to add several more sources, including Web of Science, would broaden the coverage of publications and give wrestled into these challenges met by AI adoption.

Longitudinal research could also track the changing nexus of barriers like these over several years, giving a clearer perspective on how these barriers change dynamically over time.

Additionally, a qualitative-quantitative survey must be incorporated in future studies to attain the perception of divergent industry players such as hotel managers, employees and customers. This will open a way to validate the findings secured and appreciate the practical realities of practitioners.

Comparative analyses between various tourism subsectors (hotels, catering, travel agencies) on and across various geographical units could afford good insight into regional and sectoral irregularities. Additionally, this can extend to being able to tell the specific features that characterize each context-whether in behavioral, financial, or technological barriers.

Importantly, future research should also pay keen attention to small and medium-sized enterprises (SMEs), which account for a large part of the tourism sector. Their specific needs should be studied taking into consideration budget and organizational constraints, giving rise to suitable solutions for the respective SMEs. Exploring collaborative models, such as resource pooling for technology, could be a way that would help reduce the cost of adopting AI.

Meanwhile, examination of emerging technologies could yield more insight into enabling AI adoption, such as augmented reality, virtual reality, or the internet of things. Their interaction with artificial intelligence can enhance tourism experience (as for virtual tours of historic sites) while at the same time improving operational efficiency (like automated inventory management).

Ultimately, it is worthwhile to look into how cultural differences affect acceptance of AI, particularly developed versus developing regions; and to analyze, in-depth, the ethical issues regarding AI: data privacy, cultural diversity, and the impact on employment. Such research directed toward this class of problems could also lend itself to an agenda for institutional mechanisms to promote inclusive and responsible policies that ensure equality and ethicality in the adoption of AI in the sector.

These research lines will inform not only on the opportunities and impediments of AI in tourism and its hospitality but will also provide solutions to problems that pertain to a very dynamic sector. Empirical approaches by inclusion of a focus on the SMEs and exploration of emerging technologies would add value to future research aimed at making this complex domain develop a more effective and balanced AI integration.

This is one of the main conclusions of this research: how AI serves as a transformative lever in the tourism and hospitality industry while identifying the most important barriers to its uptake. The research provides a strong case for the adoption of inclusive technology: a quest for innovation, social inclusion and respect for cultural preservation. They also provide a proper guide for the tourism and hospitality industries and policymakers interested in making the transition to a sustainable and equitable digital future. First, the research proves the AI hotspot details with what they can effectively improve and enhance in saving operational cycles, personalizing services and optimizing the customer experience. Nevertheless, it is discovered that other challenges must be overcome if widespread adoption is to be realized. Such challenges include resistance to change, financial constraints and ethical considerations.

Second, the study's findings are reminders of a balanced approach in which changes in technological innovation are coupled with attention to human and cultural dimensions. Therefore, near the heart of strategies for integrating AI should go into preserving human interaction, cultural diversity, and the sector where these values are paramount. Finally, this research invites a further reflection on how emerging technologies-R, AR, virtual reality, and IoT-can contribute to coherent economic and social development. Of particular interest will be future research that examines how to feed these technologies into the specificities and specific needs of small and medium-sized enterprises and regions that are financially disadvantaged, within the scope of contemporary ethical principles and regulations. In other words, this study opens the way to more reflective and responsible AI adoption in tourism and hospitality, giving actionable strategies to transform barriers into opportunities for maximum benefit. In doing so, it represents an essential contribution to the thought on the future of a key sector in the global economy, in which innovation and human values should go hand in hand.

REFERENCES

AL-Romeedy. B. S., & El-Sisi, S. A. W. (2024). Does AI Have an Effective Role in Applying Sustainable Entrepreneurship in the Tourism Industry? In Sustainable Tourism, Part A (pp. 3-22). Emerald Publishing Limited.

Amazon Alexa. (2024), "Alexa Smart Properties for Hospitality", Retrieved: https://www.amazon.com/alexahospitalityhttps://developer.amazon.com/en-US/alexa/alexasmartproperties/hospitality (consulted on January 26, 2025)

Avula, M., & Sithole, T. (2024). Artificial Intelligence's Potential to Improve Operational Efficiency and Customer Experience in the Hospitality and Tourism Sectors. In Impact of AI and Tech-Driven Solutions in Hospitality and Tourism (pp. 351-382). IGI Global.

Belk, R. (2021). Ethical issues in service robotics and artificial intelligence. *Service Industries Journal, 41*(13-14), 860–876.

Benckendorff, P. J., Xiang, Z., & Sheldon, P. J. (2019). *Tourism information technology*. Cabi.

Bihari Singh, A., Gaurav, G., Sarkar, P., Sharan Dangayach, G., & Lal Meena, M. (2024). Current understanding, motivations, and barriers towards implementing sustainable initiatives in the hospitality industry in the age of automation and artificial intelligence. *Recent Patents on Engineering, 18*(7), 2–25.

Bilgihan, A., Kandampully, J., & Zhang, T. (2016). Towards a unified customer experience in online shopping environments: Antecedents and outcomes. *International Journal of Quality and Service Sciences, 8*(1), 102–119.

Bilgihan, A., Nejad, M., & Cobanoglu, C. (2016). The impact of information technology innovations on hotels. In *Advances in Hospitality and Leisure* (Vol. 12, pp. 109–127). Emerald Group Publishing Limited., DOI: 10.1108/S1745-354220160000012005

Buhalis, D., & Sinarta, Y. (2019). Real-time co-creation and nowness service: Lessons from tourism and hospitality. *Journal of Travel & Tourism Marketing, 36*(5), 563–582.

Car, T., Stifanich, L. P., & Šimunić, M. (2019). Internet of things (iot) in tourism and hospitality: Opportunities and challenges. *Tourism in South East Europe, 5*(3), 163–175.

Carlisle, S., Ivanov, S., & Dijkmans, C. (2023). The digital skills divide: evidence from the European tourism industry. *Journal of tourism futures, 9*(2), 240-266.

CESE. Conseil Economique, Social et Environnemental. (2020). Le tourisme, levier de développement durable et d'intégration. In *Avis Du Conseil Economique, Social Et Environnemental*. https://www.cese.ma/media/2023/09/Avis-tourisme-VF.pdf

Challoumis, C. (2024). THE FUTURE OF BUSINESS-INTEGRATING AI INTO THE FINANCIAL CYCLE. In *XIV International Scientific Conference* (pp. 44-78).

Colliers International. (2018). *Ukraine hotel market research & forecast report*. Colliers International. Retrieved: https://www.colliers.com/-/media/Files/EMEA/Ukraine/Reports-Eng/Hotels_Eng.ashx (consulted on January 26, 2025)

Davenport, T. H., & Ronanki, R. (2018). Artificial intelligence for the real world. *Harvard Business Review, 96*(1), 108–116.

Duan, Y., Edwards, J. S., & Dwivedi, Y. K. (2019). Artificial intelligence for decision making in the era of Big Data–evolution, challenges and research agenda. *International Journal of Information Management, 48*, 63–71.

Dwivedi, Y. K., Hughes, D. L., & Ismagilova, E.. (2021). Artificial Intelligence (AI): Multidisciplinary perspectives on emerging challenges, opportunities, and agenda for research, practice, and policy. *International Journal of Information Management, 57*, 101994. DOI: 10.1016/j.ijinfomgt.2019.08.002

Dwivedi, Y. K., Hughes, L., Ismagilova, E., Aarts, G., Coombs, C., Crick, T., & Williams, M. D. (2021). Artificial Intelligence (AI): Multidisciplinary perspectives on emerging challenges, opportunities, and agenda for research, practice and policy. *International Journal of Information Management, 57*, 101994.

Florido-Benítez, L., & del Alcázar Martínez, B. (2024). How artificial intelligence (ai) is powering new tourism marketing and the future agenda for smart tourist destinations. *Electronics (Basel), 13*(21), 4151.

Gao, J. (2024). Optimizing hotel revenue management through dynamic pricing algorithms and data analysis. *Journal of Computational Methods in Science and Engineering*, 14727978241298467.

García-Madurga, M. Á., & Grilló-Méndez, A. J. (2023). Artificial Intelligence in the tourism industry: An overview of reviews. *Administrative Sciences, 13*(8), 172.

Garzella, S., Fiorentino, R., Caputo, A., & Lardo, A. (2021). Business model innovation in SMEs: The role of boundaries in the digital era. *Technology Analysis and Strategic Management, 33*(1), 31–43.

Gretzel, U., Sigala, M., Xiang, Z., & Koo, C. (2015). Smart tourism: Foundations and developments. *Electronic Markets, 25*, 179–188.

Huang, A., Chao, Y., de la Mora Velasco, E., Bilgihan, A., & Wei, W. (2022). When artificial intelligence meets the hospitality and tourism industry: An assessment framework to inform theory and management. *Journal of Hospitality and Tourism Insights, 5*(5), 1080–1100.

Ivanov, S., & Webster, C. (2017). Adoption of robots, artificial intelligence, and service automation by travel, tourism, and hospitality companies – A cost-benefit analysis. *International Journal of Contemporary Hospitality Management, 29*(6), 1577–1598.

Ivanov, S., & Webster, C. (2017). Adoption of robots, artificial intelligence, and service automation by travel, tourism, and hospitality companies – A cost-benefit analysis. *International Conference on Tourism (ICOT) Proceedings*, 190–204.

Ivanov, S., & Webster, C. (2019). Conceptual framework of the use of robots, artificial intelligence and service automation in travel, tourism, and hospitality companies. *Robots, artificial intelligence, and service automation in travel, tourism and hospitality*, 7-37.

Ivanov, S., & Webster, C. (2019). Economic fundamentals of the use of robots, artificial intelligence, and service automation in travel, tourism, and hospitality. In *Robots, artificial intelligence, and service automation in travel, tourism and hospitality* (pp. 39-55). Emerald Publishing limited.

Ivanov, S., & Webster, C. (2020). Robots in tourism: A research agenda for tourism economics. *Tourism Economics*, *26*(7), 1065–1085.

Ivanov, S., Webster, C., & Berezina, K. (2019). Adoption of robots and service automation by tourism and hospitality companies. In *Robots, Artificial Intelligence, and Service Automation in Travel, Tourism and Hospitality* (pp. 10–32). Emerald Publishing.

Ivanova, M. (2019). Robots, artificial intelligence, and service automation in travel agencies and tourist information centers. In *Robots, artificial intelligence, and service automation in travel, tourism and hospitality* (pp. 221–237). Emerald Publishing Limited.

Kamble, S. S., Gunasekaran, A., & Gawankar, S. A. (2020). Achieving sustainable performance in a data-driven agriculture supply chain: A review for research and applications. *International Journal of Production Economics*, *219*, 179–194.

Kaplan, A., & Haenlein, M. (2019). Siri, Siri, in my hand: Who's the fairest in the land? On the interpretations, illustrations, and implications of artificial intelligence. *Business Horizons*, *62*(1), 15–25. DOI: 10.1016/j.bushor.2018.08.004

Khan, N., Khan, W., Humayun, M., & Naz, A. (2024). Unlocking the Potential: Artificial Intelligence Applications in Sustainable Tourism. *The Role of Artificial Intelligence in Regenerative Tourism and Green Destinations*, 303-316.

Kong, H., Wang, K., Qiu, X., Cheung, C., & Bu, N. (2023). 30 years of artificial intelligence (AI) research relating to the hospitality and tourism industry. *International Journal of Contemporary Hospitality Management*, *35*(6), 2157–2177.

Lee, C., Hallak, R., & Sardeshmukh, S. R. (2019). Creativity and innovation in the restaurant sector: Supply-side processes and barriers to implementation. *Tourism Management Perspectives*, *31*, 54–62.

Lukita, C., Pangilinan, G. A., Chakim, M. H. R., & Saputra, D. B. (2023). Examining the impact of artificial intelligence and internet of things on smart tourism destinations: A comprehensive study. [ATT]. *Aptisi Transactions on Technopreneurship*, *5*(2sp), 135–145.

Lv, L., Chen, S., Liu, G. G., & Benckendorff, P. (2024). Enhancing customers' life satisfaction through AI-powered personalized luxury recommendations in luxury tourism marketing. *International Journal of Hospitality Management*, *123*, 103914.

Ma, S. (2024). Enhancing Tourists' Satisfaction: Leveraging Artificial Intelligence in the Tourism Sector. *Pacific International Journal*, *7*(3), 89–98.

Mariani, M., & Baggio, R. (2022). Big data and analytics in tourism and hospitality: A perspective article. *Tourism Review*, *77*(1), 6–10. DOI: 10.1108/TR-09-2019-0383

McKinsey & Company. (2022). The state of AI in 2022–and a half-decade in review. Retrieved from https://www.mckinsey.com (consulted on January 26, 2025)

Mhlanga, D. (2021). Artificial intelligence in the industry 4.0, and its impact on poverty, innovation, infrastructure development, and the sustainable development goals: Lessons from emerging economies? *Sustainability*, *13*(11), 5788.

Mishra, S., Anifa, M., & Naidu, J. (2025). AI-Driven Personalization in Tourism Services: Enhancing Tourist Experiences and Business Performance. In *Integrating Architecture and Design Into Sustainable Tourism Development* (pp. 1-20). IGI Global Scientific Publishing

Nguyen, H. T., Tran, T. T., Nham, P. T., Nguyen, N. U. B., & Le, A. D. (2023). AI Chatbot for Tourist Recommendations: A Case Study in Vietnam. *Applied Computer Systems*, *28*(2), 232–244.

Park, S. (2021). Big data in smart tourism: A perspective article. *Journal of Smart Tourism*, *1*(3), 3–5.

Praharaj, S., Mishra, B. B., Mishra, U. S., Panigrahi, R. R., & Mishra, P. C. (2023). Role of service automation on guest experience of hotel industry. *Tourism and Hospitality Management*, *29*(2), 265–278.

Ramos, M. G., do Rosário Lima, V. M., & Rosa, M. P. A. (2018). Contribuições do software IRAMUTEQ para a Análise Textual Discursiva. *Atas CIAIQ2018-Investigação Qualitativa em Educação, 2018, Brasil.*

Rane, N., Choudhary, S., & Rane, J. (2023). Sustainable tourism development using leading-edge Artificial Intelligence (AI), Blockchain, Internet of Things (IoT), Augmented Reality (AR) and Virtual Reality (VR) technologies. *Blockchain, Internet of Things (IoT), Augmented Reality (AR) and Virtual Reality (VR) technologies (October 31, 2023).*

Rane, N., Choudhary, S. P., & Rane, J. (2024). Acceptance of artificial intelligence: Key factors, challenges, and implementation strategies. *Journal of Applied Artificial Intelligence*, *5*(2), 50–70.

Rawal, Y. S., Soni, H., Dani, R., & Bagchi, P. (2022, July). A review on service delivery in tourism and hospitality industry through artificial intelligence. In *Proceedings of Third International Conference on Computing, Communications, and Cyber-Security: IC4S 2021* (pp. 427-436). Singapore: Springer Nature Singapore.

Reddy, K., & Sailesh, B. (2024). Technology Adoption in Tourism and Its Effects on Tourist Behaviour. *Journal of Tourism Quarterly*, *6*(3-4), 53–73.

Rubasri, S., NF, S. R., Prasath, R., & Krishna, B. V. (2024, April). *AI-Enhanced Image Translation for Seamless Communication in Global Tourism.In2024 International Conference on Advances in Data Engineering and Intelligent Computing Systems (ADICS)(pp.1-5).IEEE.*

Semwal, R., Tripathi, N., Singh, A., & Saxena, S. R. (2024). Reviving Narratives: Virtual Reality and Historical Reconstruction in Tourism. In *Dimensions of Regenerative Practices in Tourism and Hospitality* (pp. 269-284). IGI Global.

Skubis, I., Wolniak, R., & Grebski, W. W. (2024). AI and Human-Centric Approach in Smart Cities Management: Case Studies from Silesian and Lesser Poland Voivodships. *Sustainability*, *16*(18), 8279.

Slaoui, H. (2021). *The Impact of Covid-19 on the Hospitality Industry and How to Recover from Such Global Pandemic* (Doctoral dissertation, HEC Montréal).

Tussyadiah, I. (2020). A review of research into automation in tourism: Launching the robotics and AI in tourism and hospitality research agenda. *Journal of Hospitality & Tourism Research (Washington, D.C.)*, *44*(7), 1085–1111.

Tussyadiah, I. P. (2020). A review of research into automation in tourism: Launching the Annals of Tourism Research Curated Collection on AI and Robotics in Tourism. *Annals of Tourism Research, 81*, 102883. DOI: 10.1016/j.annals.2020.102883

Uniyal, R. S. D. M., & Sharma, N. (2020). Emerging Use of Artificial Intelligence, Robots & Service Automation in Hotel Industry. *International Journal of Future Generation Communication and Networking, 13*(3), 2785–2790.

Vinodan, A., Meera, S., & Shreeansh, M. (2023). Incentivized adoption of smart tourism services: Host community perspective. *Smart Tourism, 4*(2), 2454.

Wang, X., & Leou, C. H. (2015). A study of tourism motivation, perceived value and destination loyalty for Macao cultural and heritage tourists. *International journal of marketing studies, 7*(6), 83-91.

Wannemo, F. (2024). Post-human Hospitality? Opportunities and risks with AI: An exploratative case study of AI in the hospitality industry of Värmland.

Zhang, L., Zou, L., & Shi, M. (2024, July). Immersing and Perceiving in Tourism Scenarios: The Interaction Mechanism between Digital Technologies and Tourists. In *2024 IEEE 24th International Conference on Software Quality, Reliability, and Security Companion (QRS-C)* (pp. 1292-1301). IEEE.

Zhong, L., Sun, S., Law, R., & Zhang, X. (2021). Impact of artificial intelligence on service employee engagement and organizational performance: A conceptual framework. *International Journal of Hospitality Management, 93*, 102768.

Zhong, L., Zhang, X., Rong, J., Chan, H. K., Xiao, J., & Kong, H. (2021). Construction and empirical research on acceptance model of service robots applied in hotel industry. *Industrial Management & Data Systems, 121*(6), 1325–1352.

KEY TERMS AND DEFINITIONS

Artificial Intelligence: The computer science field dedicated to the development of systems with functionalities that enable them to behave like human intelligence. AI applications in tourism and hospitality range from chatbots and dynamic pricing algorithms through to personalized recommendations, thus allowing substantial improvement in operational efficiency and customer experience. Such technologies are powered by machine learning, natural language processing, and robotics.

Behavioral barriers: These are the psychological and cultural factors that slow down the adoption of new technologies. In tourism, these range from employees' resistance to the acceptance of automation due to perceived threats to their jobs to customers' reluctance to deal with automated systems as not being personal enough. Awareness, training, and demonstrations of how technology will complement human efforts are what it takes to overcome these obstacles.

Financial barriers: these are cost-related challenges, essentially building and adopting these technologies such as AI. It may involve infrastructure investment, investment in training and maintenance costs, or even uncertainty about returns on investment. SMEs in the tourism sector face specific resource constraints. The necessary subsidies, partnerships, and pooling models become required to overcome these challenges.

Smart Tourism: This merges AI, IoT, and other superior technologies in managing destinations and adding to the visitor experience. Intelligence in tourism depends on data collected and analyzed in real time to enable personalized services, sustainable management, and optimization of resources utilization.

Dynamic Pricing: Flexible pricing using an AI-driven strategy that centers on real-time adjustment of prices for a given service relative to demand, supply, and other market factors. Dynamic pricing is already adopted widely in the tourism industry to maximize revenues for competitive rates in periods of low demand and premium prices during high seasons.

Augmented Reality: This technology indicates that the actual world is combined with information of the digital realm to aid the user experience tremendously. This might open up, for example, the possibility of proposing interactive visitors or historical or cultural fullness in a destination.

Digital divide: The gap between those individuals or regions with access to advanced technologies, like AI, and others without. This is another inequality that makes it difficult to adopt AI equitably in tourism, especially in developing countries where infrastructure and investment are mostly inadequate. Overcoming this divide is critical for inclusive digital transformation.

Resistance to Change: A behavioral obstacle where individuals or organizations resist technological or structural innovation due to fear, uncertainty, or lack of confidence. In tourism, this resistance usually manifests itself in the form of job security concerns or skepticism that AI can replicate human-centered services.

Data Privacy: It involves the protection of personal information collected through the use of AI systems, like booking data and customer preferences. Compliance with legislation, such as the GDPR, is key in consumer confidence and in ensuring ethics within the tourism and hospitality industries when using that data.

Chapter 4
Investor Sentiment Contagion: An Industry Perspective of Investors' Heterogeneity Presented by "Informational Cycle Cascade" With AI's Algorithm

Feng Sun
https://orcid.org/0000-0001-8737-3034
South China Normal University, China

ABSTRACT

This chapter uses the FEM algorithm of artificial intelligence (AI) to analyze the rule of investor sentiment contagion under "informational cycle cascade". There are five big up or down phases of investor sentiment contagion for the industry average at the whole period. Bad information contagion under the influence of the global finance crisis and good information contagion under the influence of an economic stimulating plan of on big scale indicate that investor sentiment contagion differentiates between the up phase and down phase. The FEM coupling model of investor sentiment is created to compute and analyze investor sentiment contagion among the industries. Cloud picture presents the average space distribution of investor sentiment contagion. In the real capital market, some investors often adjust their investment decisions, and the informational cycle cascade can well explain this phenomenon.

INTRODUCTION

Investors' personal knowledge, investment experience, risk preference and psychology are different when they make the decision. Some investors have cognitive biases and heterogeneous beliefs for asset pricing. This irrational phenomenon for the investor is called investor sentiment in behavioral finance. There are many kinds of individual investor sentiment, and the common kinds are over optimistic sentiment, over pessimistic sentiment, overconfidence, overreaction, etc. When the investors make the decision under sequence choice, the subsequent investors observe the choice made by the preceding investors and the public information in the market. The subsequent investors make the same choice with

DOI: 10.4018/979-8-3693-9684-1.ch004

the preceding investors under public information, while not considering their own private information. This phenomenon is called informational cascade.

There are specific running rules for investor sentiment contagion among the industries. The management of investor sentiment can better supervise the normal running of capital market and create the sustainable capital market. The research problem of this chapter is that it uses finite element method (FEM) of the algorithm of artificial intelligence (AI) to compute and analyze flowing velocity, flowing direction and space distribution of "informational cycle cascade" among the industries. The research objective is that this chapter can be used to describe and express the running theory of investor sentiment intuitively. To the best of our knowledge, this chapter is the first to analyze the contagious process of investor sentiment with FEM algorithm among the industries.

The research plan of this chapter is that it first uses factor analysis method to extract investor sentiment factor from industry stock turnover and industry stock volume share. It computes and analyzes empirical data with second GICS industries of listed companies. Generally, investor sentiment contagion among all the industries is either in up phase or in down phase. There are five big up or down phases for industry average at whole period. This chapter creates FEM coupling model of investor sentiment, which can be used to compute and analyze investor sentiment contagion among the industries.

Second, according to the contagious process of investor sentiment at the whole period, two typical phases of industry average are chosen. After information transmits from the first investor to the last investor for the first round, the first investor observes subsequent new information and adjusts the decision, and information contagion starts another new round. So this creates the phenomenon of "informational cycle cascade". For example, in the real capital market, some investors often adjust their investment decisions, and informational cycle cascade can well explain this phenomenon. Good information contagion is basically anticlockwise, while bad information contagion is basically clockwise. Information contagion among noise investors isn't fixed in single direction, while information contagion is multi directions at the same time. Cloud picture presents the average space distribution of investor sentiment contagion.

Because of cognitive biases and heterogeneous beliefs, individual investor can have sentiment in the investment decision (García, 2013; Mclean & Zhao, 2014; Stambaugh et al., 2012). Baker and Wurgler (2006) examine how the cross-section of subsequent stock returns varies with proxies for beginning-of-period investor sentiment. When sentiment is low, subsequent returns are relatively high on smaller stocks, high volatility stocks, unprofitable stocks, non-dividend-paying stocks, extreme-growth stocks, and distressed stocks. Brown and Cliff (2004) investigate investor sentiment and its relation to near-term stock market returns, and point out that individual sentiment is strongly positive to its past levels and positively related to recent large stock returns.

Individual investor sentiment often gather to produce group investor sentiment. Group investor sentiment is mainly caused by herd effect. Herd effect is that noise investors don't pay attention to private information about market and corporation operation, while simulate investment decision made by other investors (Cipriani & Guarino, 2005; Froot et al., 1992; Hirshleifer & Teoh, 2003; Welch, 2000). Shiller (1995) shows that people interacting with each other regularly will tend to think and behave similarly, and this is the reason of herd effect.

In this case "informational cascade" will occur. When the investors make the decision under sequence choice, the subsequent investors observe the choice made by the preceding investors and the public information in the market. The subsequent investors make the same choice with the preceding investors under public information, while not considering their own private information. This phenomenon is called informational cascade. Bikhchandani et al. (1992) indicate that in sequential choices of BHW model, an informational cascade occurs when it is optimal for an individual who has observed the actions of those ahead of him to follow the behaviour of the preceding individual without regard to his own information.

Based on BHW model, many papers analyze sequence decision process of informational cascade. Kuran and Sunstein (1999) point out that through the rising availability in public disclosure, an availability cascade occurs when subsequent decision makers with incomplete personal information on a particular matter base their own beliefs on the apparent beliefs of the preceding decision makers. Hirshleifer and Teoh (2003) indicate that investors 'cascade' in deciding whether to participate in the market and whether or not buy or sell and what securities to trade, and in sequence decision process they ignore their private information signals. Duan et al. (2009) examine informational cascade in the context of online software adoption, and Seog (2008) investigates the cascade effect in insurance market purchase. Wu et al. (2013) point out potential lenders may influence contract terms via informational cascade in the syndicated loan market.[1]

Gossner and Melissas (2006) explain how an informational cascade makes truth-telling incentive compatible in a dynamic investment model, and Wang et al. (2014) indicate that people with different strength of ties to friends and relatives make huge differences on decision-making on the basis of an informational cascade.[2]Spiwoks et al. (2008) present experimental evidence that only a small number of the subjects (<6%) make rational decisions systematically and consistently to test informational cascade.

Morone et al. (2009), Huck and Oechssler (2000), Anderson and Holt (1997), Kübler and Weizsäcker (2004) analyze the cascade of subjects' decision-making in the laboratory setting. Alevy et al. (2007) compare the cascade behaviour of market professionals with that of college students in an experimental setting.

These subsequent investors are noise investors who have investor sentiment, and investor sentiment contagion will arrive at more and more noise investors. The subsequent decision makers take the same choice as that of preceding decision makers. When good/bad information occurs in the market, some preceding noise investors misjudge the prospect and have over optimistic/pessimistic sentiment, and subsequent noise investors observe the public information of preceding noise investors. They also have over optimistic/pessimistic sentiment. Accompanying with the information flowing among more and more noise investors, informational cascade will occur in the market.

When informational cascade transmits to more investors, it is not that all the investors will be affected by public information and have investor sentiment. Some investors have abundant personal knowledge and investment experience, and they make the decision more on private information while not public information. These investors will not have investor sentiment, while only noise investors can be affected by informational cascade. Kuran and Sunstein (1999) point out that not every member of a society experiencing an informational cascade need be influenced and those with considerable private information may not be influenced.

EMPIRICAL DATA ANALYSIS FOR FEM COUPLING MODEL

Investor Sentiment Factor among the Industries

To analyze space distribution for investor sentiment contagion in different industries, this chapter uses GICS (Global Industries Classification Standard) second industries category of listed companies from January, 2007 to December, 2017 in China. The industries number for GICS second industries category can be used to give a good comparison and analysis. There are 25 industries including industry average. Industry average is computed in order to compare with other industries. The result of this chapter indicates that the stock market of China's industry is suitable to analyze the running theory of investor sentiment. There are 26,976 observations, and data source is from Wind information database.

Investor sentiment belongs to psychological variable which is unable to be directly observed, and it can only be extracted from some observed indicators (Chhaochharia et al., 2019; Jiang et al., 2019; Tai, 2014). Baker and Stein (2004) indicate that both stock turnover and the equity share have considerable forecasting power for the market liquidity and investor sentiment. Baker and Wurgler (2006) use the sample of common stocks to consider six proxies for investor sentiment, including NYSE share turnover, equity share in new issues, average first-day returns on IPOs, average closed-end fund discount, dividend premium and the number on IPOs. Baker et al. (2012) construct investor sentiment indices for six major stock markets, using log turnover, log number of IPO, average first-day returns of IPO and log-ratio of the equal-weighted average market-to-book ratio for investor sentiment proxies. Baker and Wurgler (2007) propose 12 potential proxies to measure investor sentiment, including trading volume, equity issues over total new issues, investor mood, insider trading, option implied volatility, etc.

Stock turnover and stock volume share are suitable to measure the abnormal volatility of stock market, and the latent reason is the existence of investor sentiment. Too many variables probably produce several factors, which are difficult to be explained and analyzed according to the aim of this chapter. Considering this point, this chapter uses factor analysis method with dimensions decreasing technology to extract investor sentiment factor from industry stock turnover and industry stock volume share. The advantage of factor analysis method is that one factor or several factors can be extracted from some variables in multi dimensions space. The coordinate axis is made rigid rotation to extract the factors at biggest extent to give better further explanation for the factors.

Assume industry stock volume share is N_i and industry stock turnover is T_i for $i(i = 1, 2, \cdots M)$ industry. Investor sentiment factor $\psi_i(\ln N_i, \ln T_i)$ is extracted from log industry volume share and log industry turnover, then:

$$\ln N_i = \omega_i^N + \beta_i^N \psi_i(\ln N_i, \ln T_i) + \varepsilon_i^N \quad (1)$$

$$\ln T_i = \omega_i^T + \beta_i^T \psi_i(\ln N_i, \ln T_i) + \varepsilon_i^T \quad . \quad (2)$$

The expectation and variance of the investor sentiment are satisfied with $E\psi_i(\ln N_i, \ln T_i) = 0$ and $Var\ \psi_i(\ln N_i, \ln T_i) = 1$.[3]

For the covariance between investor sentiment and error item, the following relations are satisfied:

$$Cov(\psi_i(\ln N_i, \ln T_i), \varepsilon_i^N) = 0 \quad , \quad (3)$$

$$Cov(\psi_i(\ln N_i, \ln T_i), \varepsilon_i^T) = 0 \quad . \quad (4)$$

To acquire investor sentiment, this chapter uses factor analysis to extract sentiment factor from industry turnover and industry stock volume. Industry turnover is listed in Table 1. Different industries have different turnover means and volatility numbers. Software & Services industry has the biggest mean 40.56‰, which indicates that the stock turnover in this industry has the highest average value. Insurance industry has the smallest mean 11.87‰, which indicates that the stock turnover in this industry has the lowest average value. Insurance industry has the biggest variation coefficient 1.21, which indicates that the volatility of turnover in this industry is the highest. Technology Hardware & Equipment industry has the smallest variation coefficient 0.4, which indicates that the volatility of turnover in this industry is the lowest. For all industries, the scope of industry turnover is in the interval [1.26‰, 232.64‰]. Banks industry has the minimum turnover and Insurance industry has the maximum turnover.

Industry stock volume is listed in Table 2. Table 2 indicates that the means and volatility numbers of industry stock volume change in different industries. Materials industry has the biggest mean 4791.81 million shares, which indicates that the investors sell or buy the stocks in this industry with the highest frequency on average. Household & Personal Products industry has the smallest mean 58.21 million shares, which indicates that the investors sell or buy the stocks in this industry with the lowest frequency on average. Banks industry has the biggest variation coefficient 1.29, which indicates that the volatility of volume in this industry is the highest.[4] For all the industries, the scope of industry volume is in the interval [3.29, 23955.19] million shares. Telecommunication Services industry has the minimum volume and Materials industry has the maximum volume. This indicates that there is huge difference for trading volume among the industries.

Bartlett's Test of Sphericity indicates that log turnover and log stock volume are suitable for dimensions decreasing. One common factor is extracted from standardized data for log stock volume and log turnover. Its correlation numbers to log stock volume and log turnover are both 0.799. It explains 63.91% variance information. So it well explains the information of two indicators. This common factor can be explained as expectation confidence factor $\psi_i(\ln N_i, \ln T_i)$.

Accompanying with the change of market and economic condition, investor sentiment is also changing all the time. Figure 1 lists the time series tendency of investor sentiment factor for all the industries from January, 2007 to December, 2017. Figure 1 indicates that all 25 industries have obvious phase reversion of investor sentiment. Generally, investor sentiment contagion among these industries is either in up phase or in down phase. Among these industries, the time series tendency of Industry Average (IA) is listed in Figure 2. It clearly indicates that investor sentiment contagion of industry average is obvious phase reversion, which is the same character for all 25 industries. Considering the length of this chapter, we choose industry average to analyze the running theory of investor sentiment contagion. For the robustness, we also make the computation of flowing velocity and direction for other industries, and the results present the same running rule like industry average.

Table 1. Industry turnover for the GICS second industries category of listed companies from January, 2007 to December, 2017

Industry	Abbreviation	Mean	Std. Dev.	VC	Min	Max
Energy	EN	28.86	14.11	0.49	8.05	92.98
Materials	MA	31.79	14.04	0.44	11.17	81.47
Capital Goods	CG	32.89	13.88	0.42	12.07	90.43
Commercial and Special Services	CS	40.43	19.56	0.48	9.66	199.30
Transportation	TR	20.63	12.51	0.61	3.66	73.38
Automobiles & Components	AC	29.39	14.16	0.48	8.46	84.24
Consumer Durables & Apparel	CD	29.94	13.59	0.45	8.59	92.59
Consumer Services	CO	25.04	14.96	0.60	4.07	83.23
Media	ME	33.49	15.79	0.47	6.77	104.92
Retailing	RT	24.18	13.29	0.55	6.49	77.71
Food & Staples Retailing	FS	23.99	13.77	0.57	5.74	82.42
Food, Beverage & Tobacco	FB	29.30	14.25	0.49	9.20	95.99
Household & Personal Products	HP	24.20	15.59	0.64	4.92	119.03
Health Care Equipment & Services	HC	29.80	15.38	0.52	7.63	147.74
Pharmaceuticals,Biotechnology&Life Sciences	PB	26.77	13.36	0.50	8.54	86.25
Banks	BA	12.74	14.10	1.11	1.26	122.47
Diversified Financials	DF	30.53	19.87	0.65	6.76	109.15
Insurance	IN	11.87	14.31	1.21	1.32	232.64
Software & Services	SS	40.56	18.12	0.45	8.56	139.82
Technology Hardware & Equipment	TH	35.98	14.25	0.40	9.57	84.93
Semiconductors & Semiconductor Equipment	SE	38.02	17.61	0.46	8.77	132.46
Telecommunication Services	TE	30.71	21.23	0.69	4.58	197.73
Utilities	UT	21.53	13.48	0.63	5.39	74.47
Real Estate	RE	23.73	13.80	0.58	5.90	75.06
Industry Average	IA	28.18	11.73	0.42	9.93	70.12

Notes: Industry turnover(‰) from 01/2007 to 12/2017 is listed in this table. Factor analysis method and dimensions decreasing technology are used to extract investor sentiment factor. Assume industry stock volume is N_i and industry turnover is T_i for $i(i = 1,2,\cdots M)$ industry. Investor sentiment factor $\psi_i(\ln N_i, \ln T_i)$ is extracted from log industry stock volume and log industry turnover. So $\ln N_i = \omega_i^N + \beta_i^N \psi_i(\ln N_i, \ln T_i) + \varepsilon_i^N$ and $\ln T_i = \omega_i^T + \beta_i^T \psi_i(\ln N_i, \ln T_i) + \varepsilon_i^T$ are set up. VC is variation coefficient, which is used to measure the volatility of investor sentiment among the industries. Variation coefficient is equal to standard deviation divided by mean for the investor sentiment factor.

Table 2. Industry stock volume for the GICS second industries category of listed companies from January, 2007 to December, 2017

Industry	Mean	Std. Dev.	VC	Min	Max
Energy	973.51	888.33	0.91	153.49	6648.53
Materials	4791.81	3474.52	0.73	777.60	23955.19
Capital Goods	4538.41	3631.87	0.80	588.59	21852.41
Commercial and Special Services	169.87	184.11	1.08	7.51	974.69
Transportation	1275.32	1122.42	0.88	203.08	8056.94
Automobiles & Components	740.98	473.70	0.64	124.17	2869.05
Consumer Durables & Apparel	1191.33	763.07	0.64	194.31	4937.71
Consumer Services	193.77	130.42	0.67	41.71	817.24
Media	354.43	322.20	0.91	9.53	1421.95
Retailing	615.27	404.11	0.66	138.06	2750.03
Food & Staples Retailing	121.22	101.93	0.84	16.17	580.04
Food, Beverage & Tobacco	1003.48	611.56	0.61	198.55	4082.37
Household & Personal Products	58.21	39.25	0.67	11.75	324.11
Health Care Equipment & Services	164.79	109.42	0.66	20.55	659.62
Pharmaceuticals, Biotechnology & Life Sciences	803.37	500.83	0.62	149.27	3205.08
Banks	1494.32	1930.20	1.29	226.97	17739.09
Diversified Financials	905.57	1070.23	1.18	39.18	7499.13
Insurance	110.12	118.78	1.08	6.11	782.21
Software & Services	669.65	714.43	1.07	32.16	3271.14
Technology Hardware & Equipment	1471.56	1221.26	0.83	156.27	7390.40
Semiconductors & Semiconductor Equipment	357.41	349.88	0.98	20.73	1836.49
Telecommunication Services	212.17	186.13	0.88	3.29	1802.75
Utilities	1110.56	1087.21	0.98	150.29	7398.22
Real Estate	1759.13	1219.69	0.69	282.02	8600.42
Industry Average	1045.26	778.56	0.74	182.77	5068.51

Notes: Industry stock volume(Million shares) from 01/2007 to 12/2017 is listed in this table. Factor analysis method and dimensions decreasing technology are used to extract investor sentiment factor. Assume industry stock volume is N_i and industry turnover is T_i for i($i = 1, 2, \cdots M$) industry. Investor sentiment factor $\psi_i(\ln N_i, \ln T_i)$is extracted from log industry stock volume and log industry turnover. So $\ln N_i = \omega_i^N + \beta_i^N \psi_i(\ln N_i, \ln T_i) + \varepsilon_i^N$ and $\ln T_i = \omega_i^T + \beta_i^T \psi_i(\ln N_i, \ln T_i) + \varepsilon_i^T$ are set up. VC is variation coefficient, which is used to measure the volatility of investor sentiment among the industries. Variation coefficient is equal to standard deviation divided by mean for the investor sentiment factor.

Figure 1. Time series tendency of investor sentiment for all the industries from January,2007 to December 2017

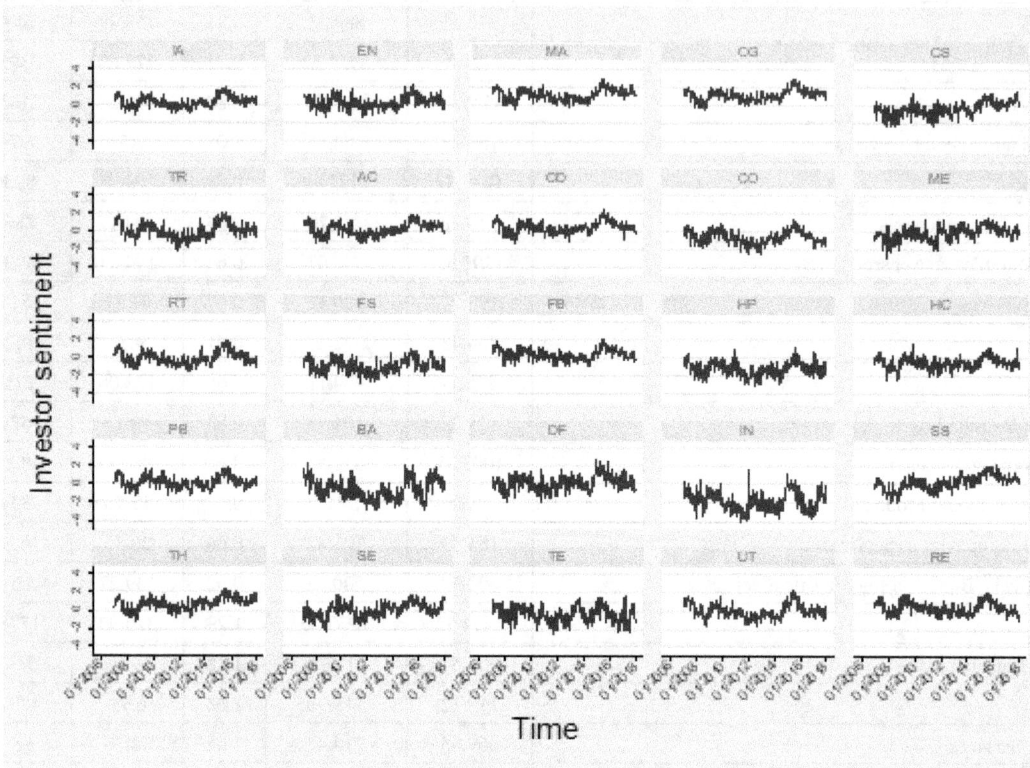

Figure 1. Time series tendency of investor sentiment for all the industries from January, 2007 to December, 2017 is listed. This figure reports the tendency of investor sentiment factor for all 25 industries. The abbreviation codes for 25 industries are listed in Table 1. IA represents industry average, which is computed from other industries. X axis is the time from January, 2007 to December, 2017. Y axis is investor sentiment factor $\psi_i(\ln N_i, \ln T_i)$ extracted from log industry turnover and log industry stock volume.

Generally, Figure 2 indicates that there are five big up or down phases for industry average between May 25, 2007 and February 3, 2017. For each of these five big phases, there are many small reversion phases. But the total tendency for each of these five big phases is up or down phase. It is down phase from May 25, 2007 to September 12, 2008, which indicates that noise investors have over pessimistic sentiment under the gradual influence of a series of bad events of global finance crisis, and investor sentiment drastically decreases in this phase. It is up phase from September 12, 2008 to December 4, 2009, which indicates that noise investors have over optimistic sentiment under the influence of economic stimulating plan of big scale made by the government, and investor sentiment rapidly increases in this phase. These two phases are chosen to analyze and other three phases have similar characters for investor sentiment contagion.

Figure 2. Time series tendency of investor sentiment for industry average from January 2007 to December 2017

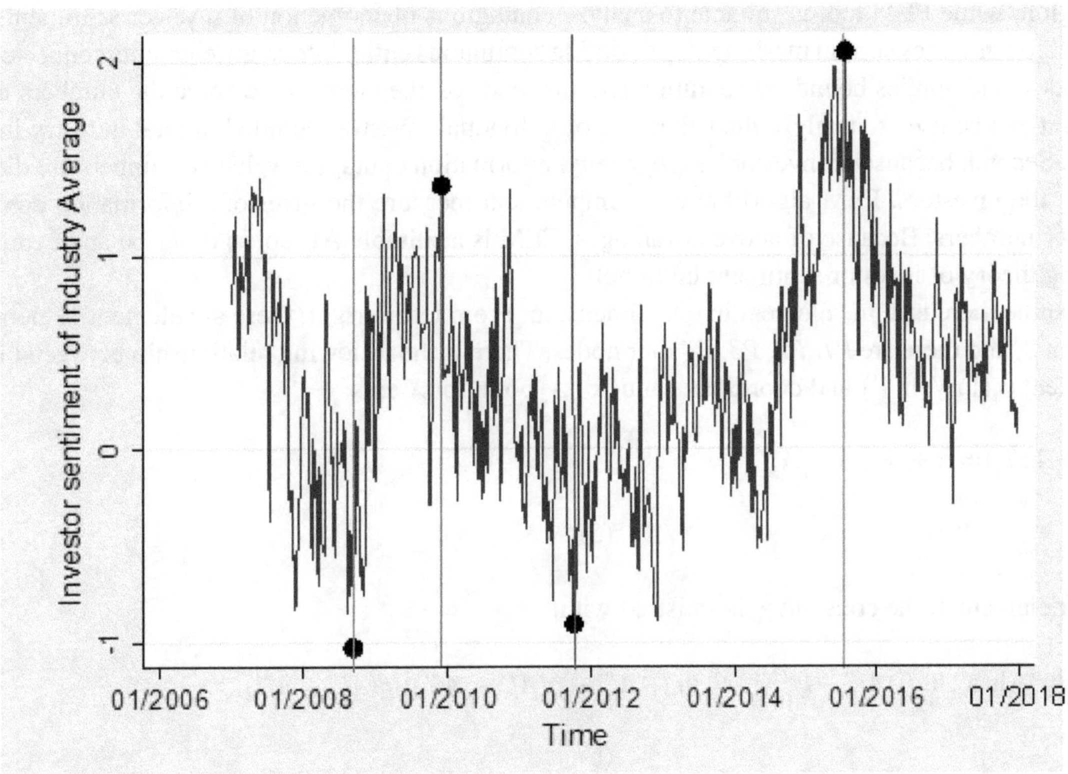

Figure 2. Time series tendency of investor sentiment for Industry Average from January, 2007 to December, 2017 is listed. This figure reports the tendency of investor sentiment for industry average. Y axis is investor sentiment factor $\psi_i(\ln N_i, \ln T_i)$ extracted from log industry turnover and log industry stock volume. There are five big reversion phases. The down phases include the phase from 25/05/2007 to 12/09/2008, the phase from 04/12/2009 to 30/09/2011 and the phase from 24/07/2015 to 03/02/2017. The up phases include the phase from 12/09/2008 to 04/12/2009 and the phase from 30/09/2011 to 24/07/2015.

FEM Coupling Model of Investor Sentiment among the Industries

FEM is a number analysis tool with AI's algorithm, and it is mainly used for computer visualization. FEM has been used to analyze some financial phenomena and theories. A front-fixing FEM is used to analyze American call and put options pricing under regime-switching model, and especially a conjecture about the asymptotic behaviour of the early exercise prices near expiration is proposed (Holmes et al., 2012). The effectiveness of the DWR (dual weighted residual) method is investigated for FEM to solve partial differential equations associated with European option pricing using local volatility Black-Scholes model (Ern et al., 2004).

Most visualization software can't solve the velocity and direction numbers for investor sentiment contagion, while FEM tool is suitable to analyze contagious phenomenon of investor sentiment. First, FEM algorithm uses certain meshing step to divide continuous entity into many elements connected with the nodes, and applies boundary condition and the loads on the elements to solve the numbers in total entity. It can be used to analyze the behaviour of individual investor included in total industry investor group. Second, because of investor heterogeneity, information contagion velocity numbers are different among the investors. FEM algorithm can compute and measure the investors' information contagion velocity numbers. Because of above advantages, FEM is a suitable AI tool to describe and express the running theory of investor sentiment intuitively.

Assume there is a line element in one dimension. From left to right, there are element 1, element 2, element 3, and there are *P1, P2, P3, P4* four nodes. There is the following relationship between investor sentiment $\psi_i(\ln N_i, \ln T_i)$ and coordinate value of A_x point for X axis:

$$\psi_i(\ln N_i, \ln T_i) = \alpha + \beta(\gamma_0 + \gamma_1 A_x) \tag{5}$$

.

For element 1, the constant γ_0 is satisfied with:

$$\gamma_0 = \left[\psi_i^{P1}(\ln N_i, \ln T_i) A_x^{P2} - \psi_i^{P2}(\ln N_i, \ln T_i) A_x^{P1} - \alpha(A_x^{P2} - A_x^{P1})\right] / \beta(A_x^{P2} - A_x^{P1}) \tag{6}$$

.

The coordinate coefficient γ_1 is:

$$\gamma_1 = \psi_i^{P2}(\ln N_i, \ln T_i) - \psi_i^{P1}(\ln N_i, \ln T_i) / \beta(A_x^{P2} - A_x^{P1}) . \tag{7}$$

The investor sentiment value inside element 1 is:

$$\psi_i(\ln N_i, \ln T_i) = \frac{A_x^{P2} - A_x}{A_x^{P2} - A_x^{P1}} \psi_i^{P1}(\ln N_i, \ln T_i) + \frac{A_x - A_x^{P1}}{A_x^{P2} - A_x^{P1}} \psi_i^{P2}(\ln N_i, \ln T_i) \tag{8}$$

.

For *P1* and *P2* nodes, there is the following relationship:

$$\int_{A_x^{P1}}^{A_x^{P2}} \frac{A_x^{P2} - A_x}{A_x^{P2} - A_x^{P1}} \left\{ \varphi_i^{\psi} \frac{\partial^2 [\psi_i(\ln N_i, \ln T_i) - \alpha] / \beta}{\partial (A_x)^2} - \omega_i^{\psi} \frac{\psi_i^{O}(\ln N_i, \ln T_i) - \psi_i^{I}(\ln N_i, \ln T_i)}{\beta} \right\}^1 dA_x = 0 \tag{9}$$

.

For *P1, P2,* and *P3* nodes, there is the following relationship:

$$\int_{A_x^{P2}}^{A_x^{P3}} \frac{A_x^{P3}-A_x}{A_x^{P3}-A_x^{P2}} \left\{ \varphi_i^{\psi} \frac{\partial^2[\psi_i(\ln N_i,\ln T_i)-\alpha]/\beta}{\partial(A_x)^2} - \omega_i^{\psi} \frac{\psi_i^O(\ln N_i,\ln T_i)-\psi_i^I(\ln N_i,\ln T_i)}{\beta} \right\}^2 dA_x$$

$$+\int_{A_x^{P1}}^{A_x^{P2}} \frac{A_x-A_x^{P1}}{A_x^{P2}-A_x^{P1}} \left\{ \varphi_i^{\psi} \frac{\partial^2[\psi_i(\ln N_i,\ln T_i)-\alpha]/\beta}{\partial(A_x)^2} - \omega_i^{\psi} \frac{\psi_i^O(\ln N_i,\ln T_i)-\psi_i^I(\ln N_i,\ln T_i)}{\beta} \right\}^1 dA_x = 0 \quad (10)$$

For *P2, P3,* and *P4* nodes, there is the following relationship:

$$\int_{A_x^{P3}}^{A_x^{P4}} \frac{A_x^{P4}-A_x}{A_x^{P4}-A_x^{P3}} \left\{ \varphi_i^{\psi} \frac{\partial^2[\psi_i(\ln N_i,\ln T_i)-\alpha]/\beta}{\partial(A_x)^2} - \omega_i^{\psi} \frac{\psi_i^O(\ln N_i,\ln T_i)-\psi_i^I(\ln N_i,\ln T_i)}{\beta} \right\}^3 dA_x$$

$$+\int_{A_x^{P2}}^{A_x^{P3}} \frac{A_x-A_x^{P2}}{A_x^{P3}-A_x^{P2}} \left\{ \varphi_i^{\psi} \frac{\partial^2[\psi_i(\ln N_i,\ln T_i)-\alpha]/\beta}{\partial(A_x)^2} - \omega_i^{\psi} \frac{\psi_i^O(\ln N_i,\ln T_i)-\psi_i^I(\ln N_i,\ln T_i)}{\beta} \right\}^2 dA_x = 0 \quad (11)$$

For *P3* and *P4* nodes, there is the following relationship:

$$\int_{A_x^{P3}}^{A_x^{P4}} \frac{A_x-A_x^{P3}}{A_x^{P4}-A_x^{P3}} \left\{ \varphi_i^{\psi} \frac{\partial^2[\psi_i(\ln N_i,\ln T_i)-\alpha]/\beta}{\partial(A_x)^2} - \omega_i^{\psi} \frac{\psi_i^O(\ln N_i,\ln T_i)-\psi_i^I(\ln N_i,\ln T_i)}{\beta} \right\}^3 dA_x = 0$$

$$(12)$$

$\psi_i^O(\ln N_i, \ln T_i)$ is investor sentiment output value, and $\psi_i^I(\ln N_i, \ln T_i)$ is investor sentiment input value. ψ_t^{ψ} is conductive coefficient of investor sentiment, and ω_t^{ψ} is transfer coefficient of investor sentiment.

To analyze space distribution for investor sentiment contagion, FEM coupling model of investor sentiment is created (Figure 3). Assume that the blue square district represents one industry such as industry average, and the countless points in the square district represent many individual noise investors with investor sentiment. Investor sentiment loads are applied on left boundary line and right boundary line of this model. To compute space distribution of investor sentiment contagion among the industries, this model is divided into FEM grids using meshing technology. If fineness of element grids is high, it will increase the precision of computing result, but more computing time will be used.[5] This model adopts element grids with middle fineness. Every boundary line is divided into 25 parts, and total model includes 625 FEM elements.

Table 3. The change of investor sentiment for industry average between May 25, 2007 and February 3, 2017

Time Phase		Phase Character	Investor Sentiment	
Starting Time	Ending Time		Starting Value	Ending Value
May 25, 2007	September 12, 2008	Down phase	1.39978	-1.04144
September 12, 2008	December 4, 2009	Up phase	-1.04144	1.36678
December 4, 2009	September 30, 2011	Down phase	1.36678	-0.91868

continued on following page

Table 3. Continued

Time Phase		Phase Character	Investor Sentiment	
Starting Time	Ending Time		Starting Value	Ending Value
September 30, 2011	July 24, 2015	Up phase	-0.91868	2.05622
July 24, 2015	February 3, 2017	Down phase	2.05622	-0.28421

Notes: This table reports the starting value and ending value of investor sentiment among the five big up or down phases. Assume there is element 1 in one dimension with *P1* and *P2* nodes. The investor sentiment value $\psi_i(\ln N_i, \ln T_i)$ is satisfied with coordinate value of A_x point for x axis, that is, $\psi_i(\ln N_i, \ln T_i) = \alpha + \beta(\gamma_0 + \gamma_1 A_x)$. The investor sentiment value inside element 1 is satisfied with $\psi_i(\ln N_i, \ln T_i) = \psi_i^{P1}(\ln N_i, \ln T_i)(A_x^{P2} - A_x)/(A_x^{P2} - A_x^{P1}) + \psi_i^{P2}(\ln N_i, \ln T_i)(A_x - A_x^{P1})/(A_x^{P2} - A_x^{P1})$. From the change of positive value and negative value for starting investor sentiment and ending investor sentiment, it can be found that investor sentiment experiences obvious phase reversion.

Figure 3. FEM coupling model of investor sentiment representing many individual noise investors among the industries

Figure 3. FEM coupling model of investor sentiment representing many individual noise investors among the industries is listed. This figure creates a model with FEM to compute and solve the flowing velocity, flowing direction and space distribution of investor sentiment contagion. Assume that the blue square district represents one industry such as industry average, and the countless points (similar with countless points in a plane in Mathematics) in the square district represent many individual noise investors with investor sentiment. Investor sentiment loads are applied on left boundary line and right boundary line. The top and bottom boundaries are set as insulated boundaries with FEM. The square

coupling model is suitable to analyze investor sentiment contagion in this chapter and can simplify the analysis. Every boundary line of the square district is divided into 25 parts, and there are total 625 FEM elements in this model.

From May 25, 2007 to September 12, 2008, investor sentiment of industry average decreases from 1.39978 to -1.04144. From September 12, 2008 to December 4, 2009, investor sentiment of industry average increases from -1.04144 to 1.36678. Table 3 lists the change of investor sentiment among the five big up or down phases between May 25, 2007 and February 3, 2017. For the FEM analysis, the computation value for parameter a is -3.213445 and the computation value for parameter β is 0.066349.

When good/bad information occurs in the market, a noise investor misjudges the information because of cognitive bias and begins to have investor sentiment. Accompanying with information contagion among noise investors, more and more noise investors observe the choice of preceding noise investors and public information, and they make the same choice under herd effect (Bicchieri & Fukui, 1999; Cai et al., 2019). This phenomenon of information contagion produces informational cascade. When public information transmits to more noise investors, herd effect becomes wider and wider, and investor sentiment contagion with large scale occurs (Feng et al., 2017; Goeree et al., 2007; Grebe et al., 2008; Doherty, 2018).

Different with sequential decision BHW model of "informational cascade" from the first investor to the last investor in one round analyzed by Bikhchandani et al. (1992), this chapter thinks information flowing as "informational cycle cascade". The 1992 BHW model creates an excellent framework of sequence decision of information contagion in one round, while this chapter analyzes the novel phenomenon of flowing velocity, flowing direction and space distribution of informational cycle cascade in many rounds extended from this model. After information transmits from the first investor to the last investor for the first round, the first investor observes subsequent new information and adjusts the decision, and information contagion starts another new round. So this creates the phenomenon of informational cycle cascade. For example, in the real capital market, some investors often adjust their investment decision, and informational cycle cascade can well explain this phenomenon.

Analysis of Investor Sentiment Contagion under "Informational Cycle Cascade" Among the Industries

Information Flowing Velocity of Informational Cycle Cascade

From May 25, 2007 to September 12, 2008, investor sentiment load 1.39978 is applied on left boundary line of FEM coupling model of investor sentiment for industry average. Investor sentiment load -1.04144 is applied on right boundary line. This is down phase of investor sentiment contagion, and investor sentiment drastically decreases under the influence of global finance crisis. The preceding noise investors are affected by bad information of global finance crisis, and misjudge the influence of bad information and have over pessimistic investor sentiment. More and more subsequent noise investors also have over pessimistic sentiment under herd effect for the first round. The preceding noise investors observe the action of subsequent noise investors, and misjudge the bad information again and adjust the investment decision. The subsequent noise investors are affected by the bad public information again under herd effect. So investor sentiment contagion starts the second round. Accompanying with more rounds, informational cycle cascade of bad information occurs.

Investor sentiment decreases from 1.39978 at the beginning of this period to -1.04144 at the end of this period. This process is shown out in steady coupling field in Figure 4. Bad information contagion is basically clockwise, which presents the main down tendency of sentiment contagion for this period in Figure 2. The bad information contagion isn't uniform distribution. The colour of the arrows represents different bad information contagion velocity among noise investors. Red arrows represent the highest range of information flowing velocities in [0.22077, 0.248366], and blue arrows represent the lowest range of information flowing velocities in [0, 0.027596].

Figure 4. Information Flowing velocity of informational cycle cascade from May 25, 2007 to September 12, 2008

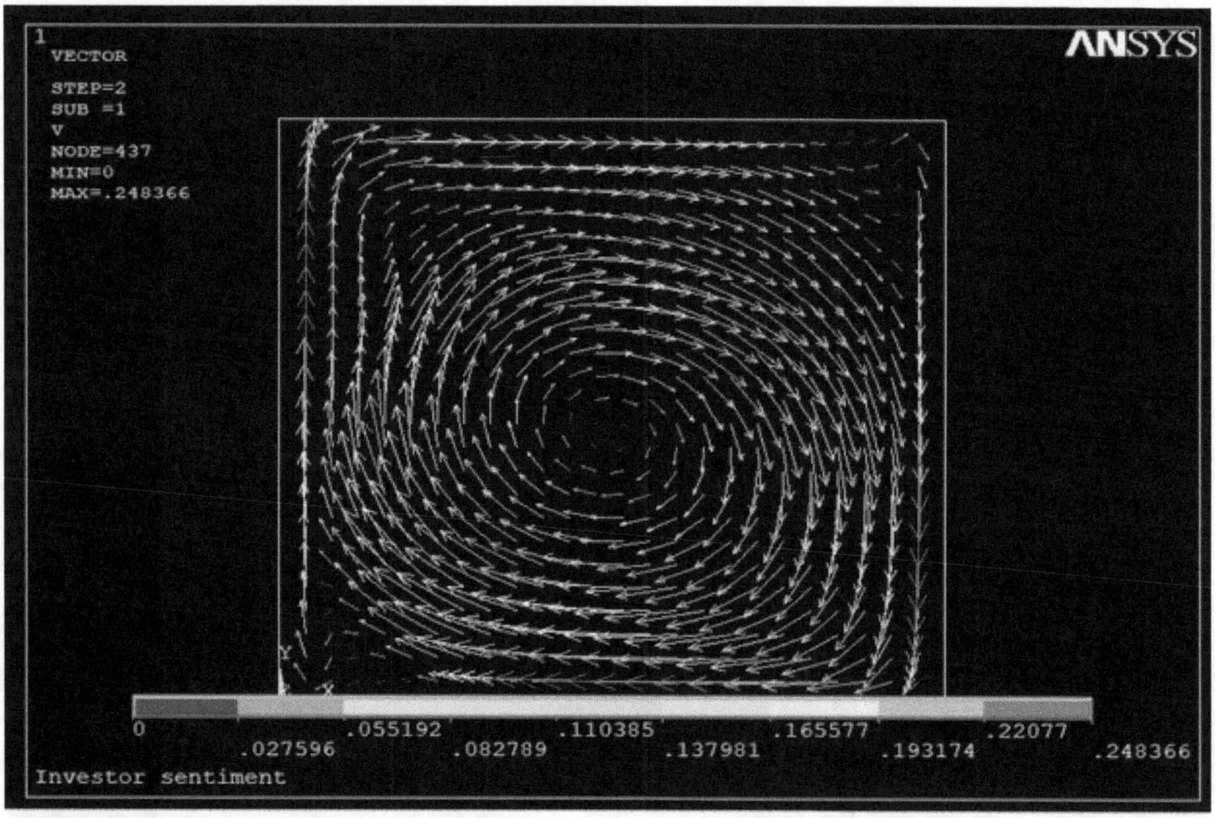

Figure 4. Information flowing velocity of informational cycle cascade from May 25, 2007 to September 12, 2008 is listed. This figure reports the information flowing velocity of bad information contagion. Investor sentiment decreases from 1.39978 to -1.04144 in this phase under the influence of global finance crisis. The colour of the arrows represents different bad information contagion velocity among noise investors. Red arrows represent the highest range of information flowing velocity number in [0.22077, 0.248366], and blue arrows represent the lowest range of information flowing velocity number in [0, 0.027596].

When information arrives at a noise investor, he will make a decision from this information. He misjudges the information because of cognitive bias and has investor sentiment (Celen & Kariv, 2004; Fiore & Morone, 2008). Then this information continues to arrive at next noise investor. Noise investor need some time to make the decision from the information. This is expressed on information flowing velocity. For some noise investors, the velocity of information flowing is high. For other noise investors, the velocity of information flowing is low. The difference of information flowing velocity numbers among noise investors is caused by the heterogeneity of noise investors. If noise investors haven't enough knowledge and investment experience, they are easily affected by herd effect to have cognitive bias. They will quickly have investor sentiment, and information flowing velocity numbers for them are high. If noise investors have enough knowledge and investment experience, they are uneasily affected by herd effect.[6]

From September 12, 2008 to December 4, 2009, investor sentiment load -1.04144 is applied on left boundary line of FEM coupling model for industry average. Investor sentiment load 1.36678 is applied on right boundary line. This period is up phase of investor sentiment contagion, and investor sentiment rapidly increases under the influence of economic stimulating plan of big scale made by the government. The preceding noise investors are affected by good information of economic stimulating plan, and misjudge the influence of good information and have over optimistic sentiment. More and more subsequent noise investors also have over optimistic sentiment under herd effect for the first round. The preceding noise investors observe the action of subsequent noise investors, and misjudge the good information again and adjust the investment decision. The subsequent noise investors are affected by the good public information again under herd effect. So investor sentiment contagion starts the second round. Accompanying with more rounds, informational cycle cascade of good information occurs.

Investor sentiment increases from -1.04144 at the beginning of this period to 1.36678 at the end of this period. This process is shown out in Figure 5. Good information contagion is basically anticlockwise, which presents the main up tendency of sentiment contagion for this period in Figure 2.[7] The colour of arrows represents different good information contagion velocity among noise investors. Red arrows represent the highest range of information flowing velocity numbers, while blue arrows represent the lowest range of information flowing velocity numbers. The anticlockwise direction in this period is contrary to the clockwise direction from May 25, 2007 to September 12, 2008, which presents the up or down contagion for investor sentiment. Figure 4 and Figure 5 present the different investor sentiment contagion for the down phase and up phase.

Figure 5. Information flowing velocity of informational cycle cascade from September 12, 2008 to December 4, 2009

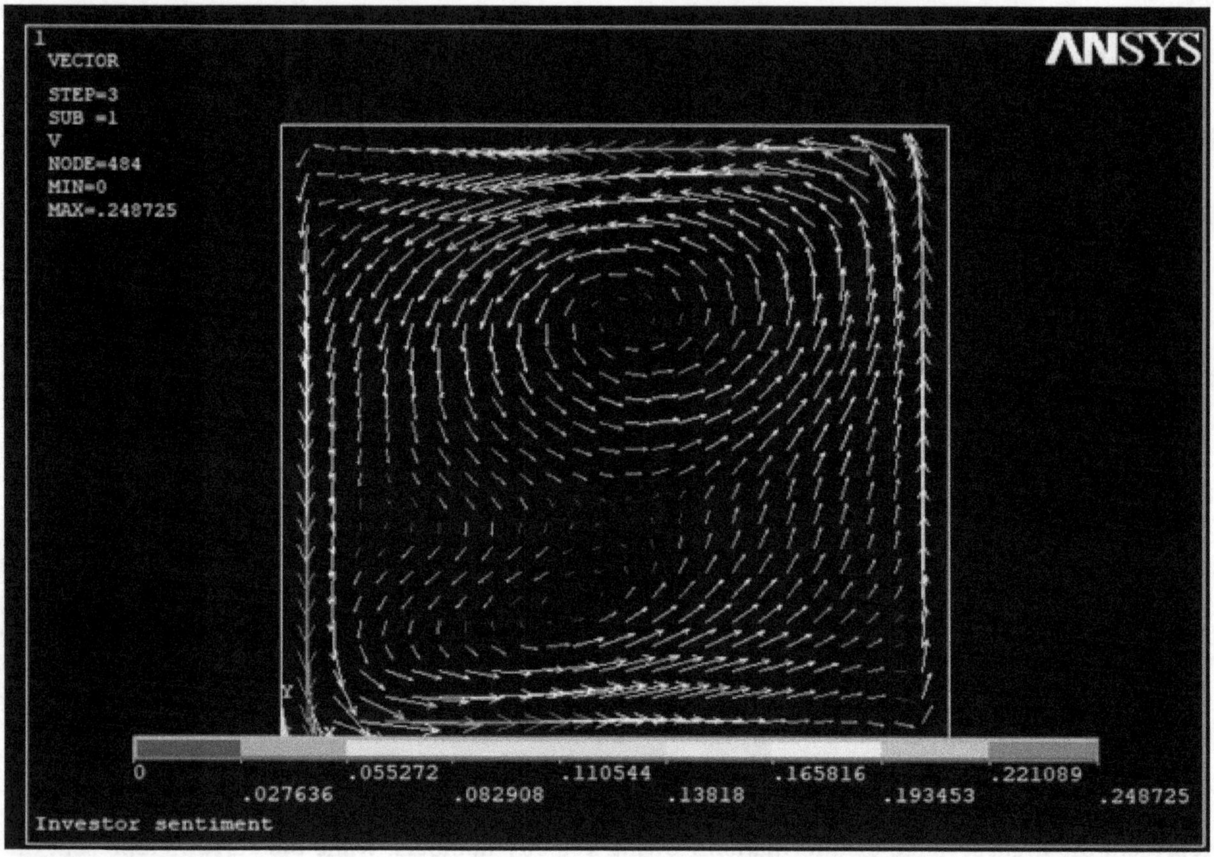

Figure 5. Information flowing velocity of informational cycle cascade from September 12, 2008 to December 4, 2009 is listed. This figure reports the information flowing velocity of good information contagion. Investor sentiment increases from -1.04144 to 1.36678 in this phase under the influence of economic stimulating plan of big scale made by the government. The colour of arrows represents different good information contagion velocity among noise investors. Red arrows represent the highest range of information flowing velocity numbers in [0.221089, 0.248725], and blue arrows represent the lowest range of information flowing velocity numbers in [0, 0.027636].

From December 4, 2009 to September 30, 2011, investor sentiment load 1.36678 is applied on left boundary line of FEM coupling model of investor sentiment for industry average. Investor sentiment load -0.91868 is applied on right boundary line. This is down phase of investor sentiment contagion. From September 30, 2011 to July 24, 2015, investor sentiment load -0.91868 is applied on left boundary line. Investor sentiment load 2.05622 is applied on right boundary line. This period is up phase of investor sentiment contagion. From July 24, 2015 to February 3, 2017, investor sentiment load 2.05622 is applied on left boundary line. Investor sentiment load -0.28421 is applied on right boundary line. This is down phase of investor sentiment contagion. These three up or down phases have the similar characters like the above two up/down phases.

Flowing Direction and Space Distribution of Informational Cycle Cascade

Information contagion among noise investors isn't fixed in single direction, while information contagion is multi directions at the same time. The contagion is in X direction and Y direction at the same time, which indicates the multi directions for the contagion. Cloud picture of average flowing velocity for informational cycle cascade in X direction from May 25, 2007 to September 12, 2008 is listed in Figure 6. The colour of areas represents different bad information contagion velocity in X direction among noise investors. The positive values and negative values represent the flowing velocity numbers in different directions. Red areas represent the highest range of information flowing velocity numbers in [0.149744, 0.199508], and blue areas represent the lowest range of information flowing velocity numbers in [-0.248366, -0.198602].

Figure 6. Average flowing velocity of informational cycle cascade in X direction from May 25, 2007 to September 12, 2008

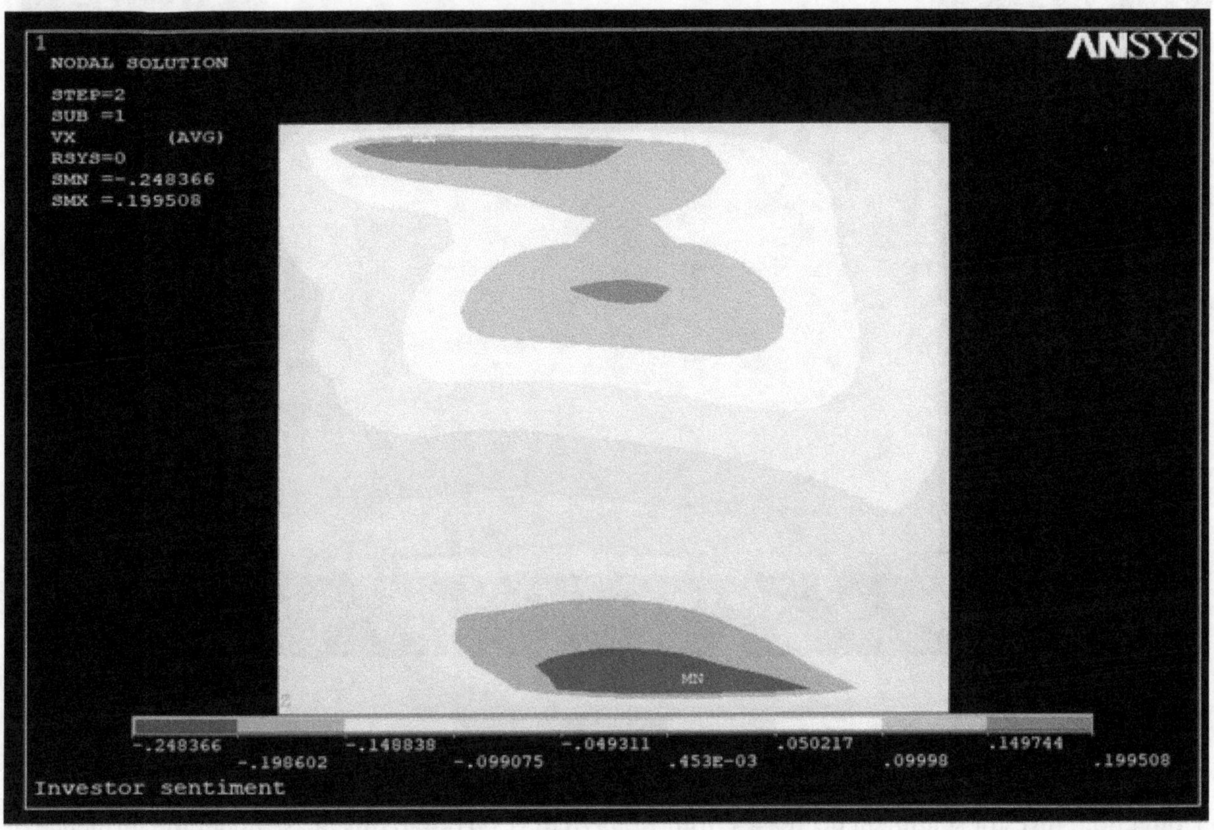

Figure 6. Average flowing velocity of informational cycle cascade in X direction from May 25, 2007 to September 12, 2008 is listed. This figure reports the flowing velocity of bad information contagion in X direction. Investor sentiment decreases from 1.39978 to -1.04144 in this phase under the influence of global finance crisis. The colour of areas represents different bad information contagion velocity in X direction among noise investors. The positive values and negative values represent the flowing velocity

numbers in different directions. Red areas represent the highest range of information flowing velocity numbers in [0.149744, 0.199508], and blue areas represent the lowest range of information flowing velocity numbers in [-0.248366, -0.198602].

Cloud picture of average flowing velocity in Y direction from May 25, 2007 to September 12, 2008 is listed in Figure 7. The colour of areas represents different bad information contagion velocity in Y direction among noise investors.[8] Red areas represent the highest range of information flowing velocity numbers, while blue areas represent the lowest range of information flowing velocity numbers.

Figure 7. Average flowing velocity of informational cycle cascade in Y direction from May 25, 2007 to September 12, 2008

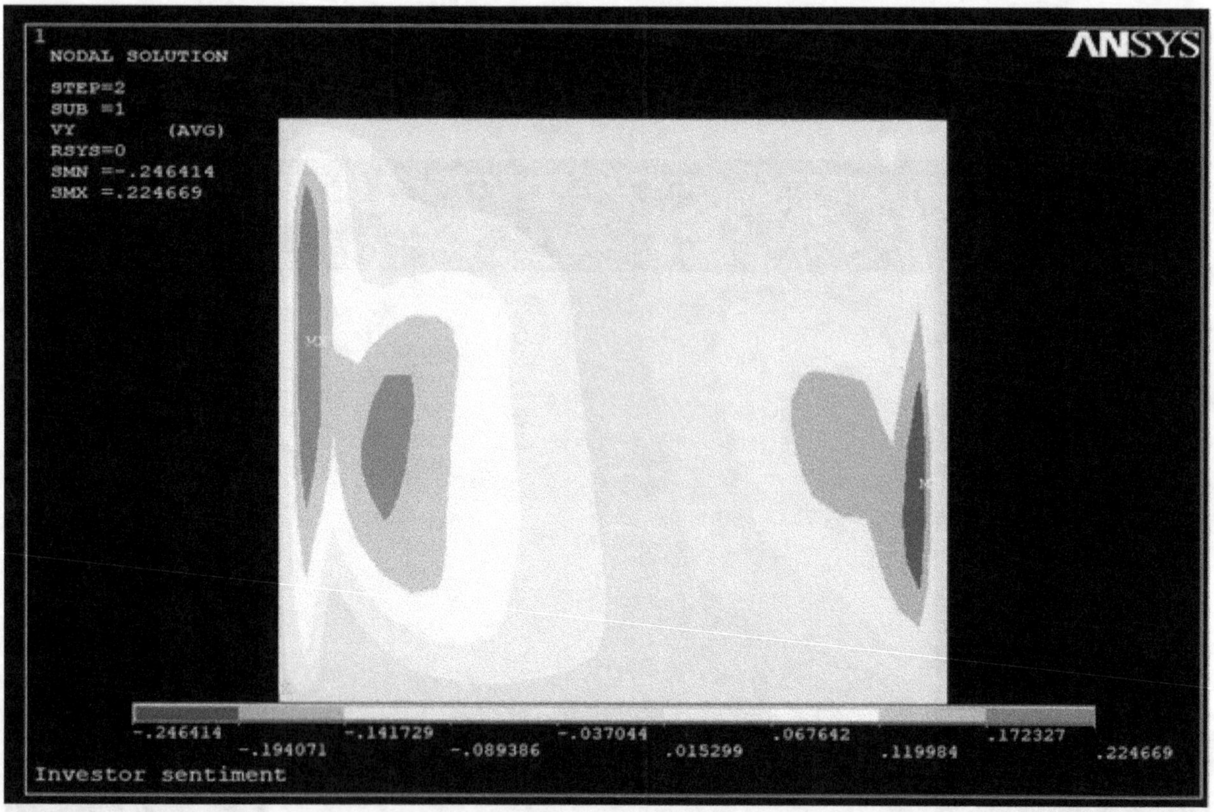

Figure 7. Average flowing velocity of informational cycle cascade in Y direction from May 25, 2007 to September 12, 2008 is listed. This figure reports the flowing velocity of bad information contagion in Y direction. Investor sentiment decreases from 1.39978 to -1.04144 in this phase under the influence of global finance crisis. The colour of areas represents different bad information contagion velocity in Y direction among noise investors. The positive values and negative values represent the flowing velocity numbers in different directions. Red areas represent the highest range of information flowing velocity numbers in [0.172327, 0.224669], and blue areas represent the lowest range of information flowing velocity numbers in [-0.246414, -0.194071].

When bad information under the influence of global finance crisis arrives at noise investor A, A misjudges the influence of bad information and has over pessimistic sentiment. Then the information arrives at noise investor B, and B also has over pessimistic sentiment under herd effect. Then the information continues to arrive at other noise investors. Furthermore, the decision information of noise investor A also arrives at noise investor C, noise investor D, etc. Then the information continues to arrive at subsequent noise investors from noise investor C, noise investor D, etc. So over pessimistic sentiment makes forward contagion in multi directions at the same time. For plane rectangular coordinate system in Mathematics, a contagious velocity can be divided into X axis direction and Y axis direction, and the information contagion of informational cycle cascade is also analyzed with this method.

From September 12, 2008 to December 4, 2009, cloud picture of average flowing velocity in X direction is listed in Figure 8. The colour of areas represents different good information contagion velocity in X direction among noise investors. The positive values and negative values represent the flowing velocity numbers in different directions. Red areas represent the highest range of information flowing velocity numbers in [0.18331, 0.237315], and blue areas represent the lowest range of information flowing velocity numbers in [-0.248722, -0.194718].

Figure 8. Average flowing velocity of informational cycle cascade in X direction from September 12, 2008 to December 4, 2009

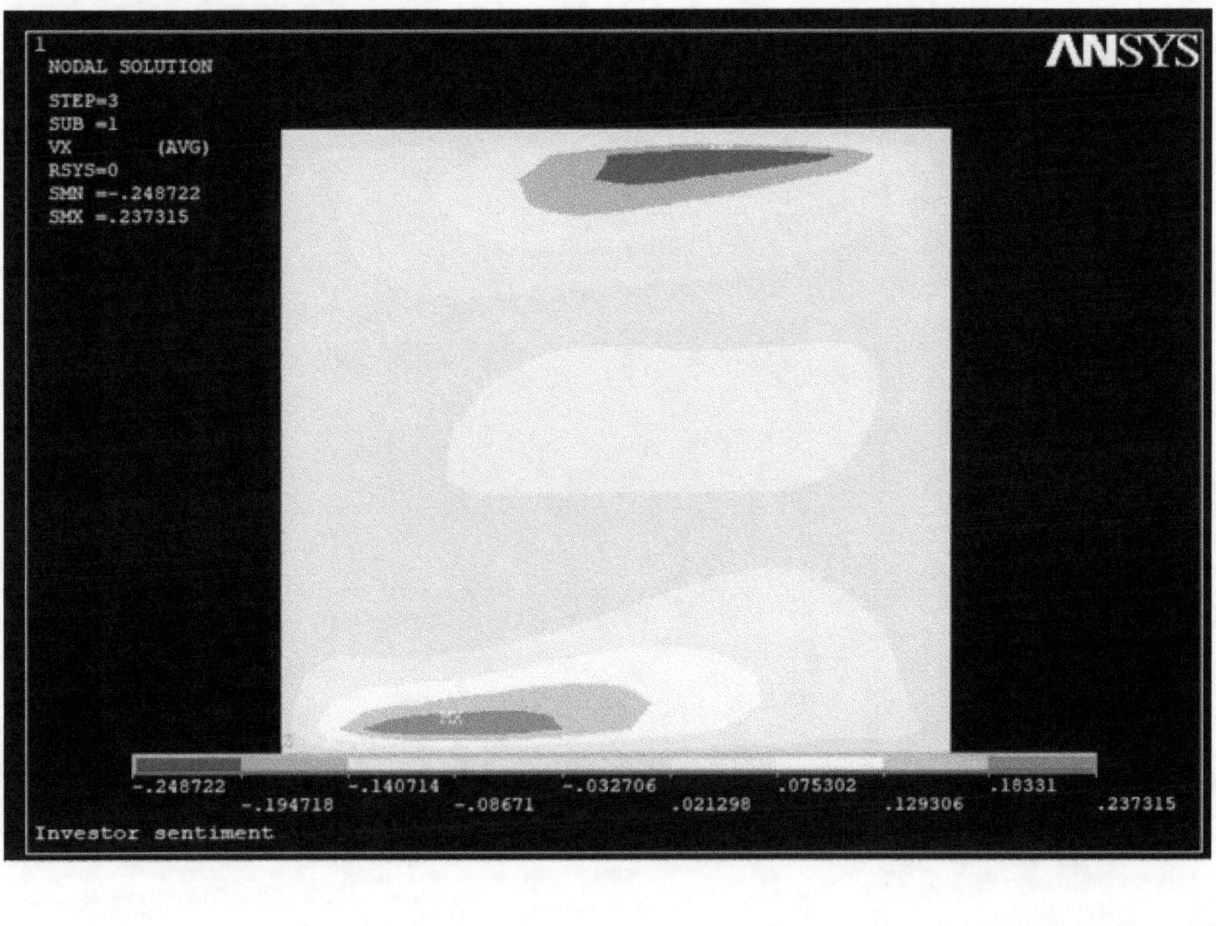

Figure 8. Average flowing velocity of informational cycle cascade in X direction from September 12, 2008 to December 4, 2009 is listed. This figure reports the flowing velocity of good information contagion in X direction. Investor sentiment increases from -1.04144 to 1.36678 in this phase under the influence of economic stimulating plan of big scale made by the government. The colour of areas represents different good information contagion velocity in X direction among noise investors. The positive values and negative values represent the flowing velocity numbers in different directions. Red areas represent the highest range of information flowing velocity numbers in [0.18331, 0.237315], and blue areas represent the lowest range of information flowing velocity numbers in [-0.248722, -0.194718].

Cloud picture of average flowing velocity in Y direction from September 12, 2008 to December 4, 2009 is listed in Figure 9. The colour of areas represents different good information contagion velocity in Y direction among noise investors. The positive values and negative values also represent the flowing velocity numbers in different directions.[9]

This phase is up phase of investor sentiment contagion. When good information under the influence of economic stimulating plan of big scale made by the government arrives at one noise investor, this noise investor misjudges the influence of good information and has over optimistic sentiment. Just as above, over optimistic sentiment will also make forward contagion in multi directions at the same time. Figure 6-9 present that investor sentiment contagion has different information contagion velocity numbers in up or down phase.

Figure 9. Average flowing velocity of informational cycle cascade in Y direction from September 12, 2008 to December 4, 2009

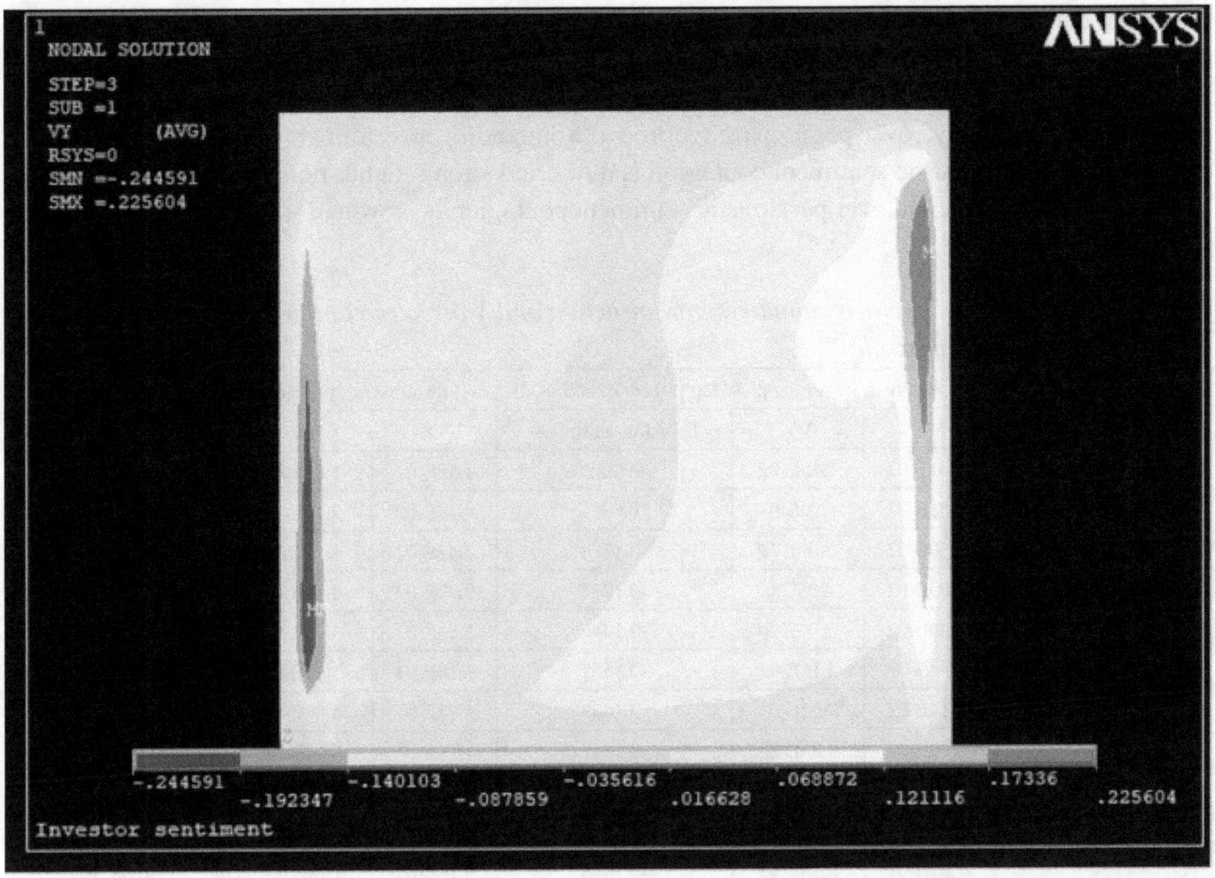

Figure 9. Average flowing velocity of informational cycle cascade in Y direction from September 12, 2008 to December 4, 2009 is listed. This figure reports the flowing velocity of good information contagion in Y direction. Investor sentiment increases from -1.04144 to 1.36678 in this phase under the influence of economic stimulating plan of big scale made by the government. The colour of areas represents different good information contagion velocity in Y direction among noise investors. The positive values and negative values represent the flowing velocity numbers in different directions. Red areas represent the highest range of information flowing velocity numbers in [0.17336, 0.225604], and blue areas represent the lowest range of information flowing velocity numbers in [-0.244591, -0.192347].

Cloud picture of average flowing velocity can be used to indicate average flowing velocity of the information. Besides this, divided FEM grids can be used to precisely compute average flowing velocity in X direction and Y direction. Table 4 shows average flowing velocity values of informational cycle cascade for industry average in X direction and Y direction from May 25, 2007 to September 12, 2008 and from September 12, 2008 to December 4, 2009. Computing values of first 20 elements are selected to list. The precise average flowing velocity numbers in X direction and Y direction for first 20 elements can be found in Table 4.

Figure 10 is average space distribution of investor sentiment of informational cycle cascade for industry average from May 25, 2007 to September 12, 2008. Investor sentiment decreases from 1.39978 to -1.04144 in this phase under the influence of global finance crisis. Space distribution values of investor sentiment can be found from the colour of the areas. Red areas represent the highest range of investor sentiment values in [1.12853, 1.39978], and blue areas represent the lowest range of investor sentiment values in [-1.04144, -0.77019]. When bad information under the influence of global finance crisis occurs, noise investors will have over pessimistic sentiment. Some noise investors are easily affected by herd effect, and over pessimistic sentiment contagion is quick and strong. Other noise investors are uneasily affected by herd effect, and over pessimistic sentiment contagion is slow and weak.

Table 4. Average flowing velocity numbers in X direction and Y direction and investor sentiment values of informational cycle cascade

	Industry average 25/05/2007-12/09/2008			Industry average 12/09/2008-04/12/2009		
Element Number	**VX**	**VY**	**Investor sentiment**	**VX**	**VY**	**Investor sentiment**
1	-6.41E-03	1.13E-02	0.5235	1.35E-02	-1.03E-02	-0.8709
2	-1.55E-02	6.00E-03	0.031	4.33E-02	-2.15E-02	-0.5715
3	-1.50E-02	-8.48E-03	-0.1318	7.47E-02	-1.72E-02	-0.3499
4	-1.03E-02	-4.26E-03	-0.1274	9.92E-02	-8.48E-03	-0.2421
5	-1.03E-02	-2.01E-04	-0.1446	1.13E-01	-3.40E-03	-0.1904
6	-1.74E-02	4.11E-03	-0.1587	1.18E-01	-1.48E-03	-0.1589
7	-3.14E-02	7.94E-03	-0.1607	1.18E-01	-6.58E-04	-0.1352
8	-5.00E-02	9.83E-03	-0.1542	1.15E-01	2.26E-04	-0.1164
9	-6.97E-02	9.57E-03	-0.1472	1.09E-01	1.37E-03	-0.1019
10	-8.74E-02	7.96E-03	-0.1426	1.01E-01	2.50E-03	-0.0911
11	-1.01E-01	5.95E-03	-0.1415	9.13E-02	3.28E-03	-0.0827
12	-1.12E-01	4.08E-03	-0.1438	8.06E-02	3.55E-03	-0.0752
13	-1.18E-01	2.56E-03	-0.1493	7.00E-02	3.36E-03	-0.0673
14	-1.22E-01	1.34E-03	-0.1576	6.02E-02	2.91E-03	-0.0584
15	-1.24E-01	3.11E-04	-0.1685	5.16E-02	2.41E-03	-0.0483
16	-1.24E-01	-5.95E-04	-0.182	4.41E-02	1.99E-03	-0.0377
17	-1.21E-01	-1.41E-03	-0.1984	3.76E-02	1.69E-03	-0.0271
18	-1.17E-01	-2.14E-03	-0.2181	3.19E-02	1.46E-03	-0.0171
19	-1.11E-01	-2.78E-03	-0.2416	2.68E-02	1.22E-03	-0.0081
20	-1.03E-01	-3.46E-03	-0.2697	2.25E-02	8.34E-04	0.0002

Notes: This table reports the investor sentiment values of first 20 FEM elements and precise average flowing velocity numbers in X direction and Y direction from May 25, 2007 to September 12, 2008 and from September 12, 2008 to December 4, 2009. VX is average flowing velocity in X direction, and VY is average flowing velocity in Y direction.

Figure 10. Average space distribution of investor sentiment for informational cycle cascade from May 25, 2007 to September 12, 2008

Figure 10 reports space distribution of investor sentiment for bad information contagion from May 25, 2007 to September 12, 2008. Investor sentiment decreases from 1.39978 to -1.04144 in this phase under the influence of global finance crisis. Space distribution values of investor sentiment can be found from the colour of areas. Red areas represent the highest range of investor sentiment values in [1.12853, 1.39978], and blue areas represent the lowest range of investor sentiment values in [-1.04144, -0.77019].

Figure 11. Average space distribution of investor sentiment for informational cycle cascade from September 12, 2008 to December 4, 2009

Figure 11 reports space distribution of investor sentiment for good information contagion from September 12, 2008 to December 4, 2009. Investor sentiment increases from -1.04144 to 1.36678 in this phase under the influence of economic stimulating plan of big scale made by the government. Red areas represent the highest range of investor sentiment values in [1.09920, 1.36678], and blue areas represent the lowest range of investor sentiment values in [-1.04144, -0.77386].

Figure 11 is average space distribution of investor sentiment of informational cycle cascade for industry average from September 12, 2008 to December 4, 2009. Investor sentiment increases from -1.04144 to 1.36678 in this phase under the influence of economic stimulating plan of big scale made by the government. Red areas represent the highest range of investor sentiment values in [1.09920, 1.36678], and blue areas represent the lowest range of investor sentiment values in [-1.04144, -0.77386]. When good information under the influence of economic stimulating plan of big scale made by the government occurs, noise investors will have over optimistic sentiment. Some noise investors are easily affected by herd effect, and over optimistic sentiment contagion is quick and strong.[10]

After informational cycle cascade starts in the market, more and more noise investors make investment decision based on public information while not private information, and investor sentiment transmits to other noise investors. But the contagion of informational cycle cascade isn't for ever, it can be broken up by new information occurring in the market. New information can change investment decision of the investors, which will change flowing velocity, flowing direction and space distribution. In some cases informational cycle cascade even can reverse the flowing direction.

FUTURE RESEARCH DIRECTIONS

Because of the heterogeneity of noise investors, the information flowing velocity numbers among noise investors are different. Some noise investors will quickly have investor sentiment, while other noise investors will slowly have investor sentiment. The management of investor sentiment is important, which can better supervise and manage the normal running of capital market and create the sustainable capital market (Chinco et al., 2022; Jiang & Verardo, 2018; Welch, 2022). For example, the investor sentiment can be presented by the information flowing velocity. If the information flowing velocity for one investor is high, he will be easy to be contagious and the investor sentiment is high. If most investors will quickly have investor sentiment, the capital market is more possible to get high volatility and the stock price goes forward in a bigger range. To avoid huge risks probably produced by capital market, the authority can supervise the changing tendency of investor sentiment, and can adopt suitable management policy to prevent or decrease the probable risks. They can explain the dynamic status of the economy and the market to the investors, give the hint of the probable huge risks to the investors, and make stricter punishment to some abnormal accidents in the capital market, etc. The future research can give the measurement and analysis on flowing velocity for individual's investor sentiment, on the flowing direction and space distribution of investor sentiment for a certain group, and on their possible influences to the capital market. Through the measurement and analysis, the investor sentiment can be well managed to better supervise the normal running of capital market and create the sustainable capital market.

CONCLUSION

This chapter uses FEM algorithm of artificial intelligence to compute and analyze flowing velocity, flowing direction and space distribution of "informational cycle cascade" among the industries, which can be used to describe and express the running theory of investor sentiment intuitively. It uses factor analysis method to extract investor sentiment factor from log industry turnover and log industry stock volume with GICS second industries category of listed companies. Generally, all 25 industries have obvious phase reversion for investor sentiment contagion. There are five big up or down phases for industry average. For each of these five big phases, there are many small reversion phases. Two typical phases of industry average are chosen to compute and analyze the flowing velocity, flowing direction and space distribution. For bad information contagion under the influence of global finance crisis and good information contagion under the influence of economic stimulating plan of big scale made by the government, both indicate that the contagious process of investor sentiment accompanies with different phases.

After information transmits from the first investor to the last investor for the first round, the first investor observes subsequent new information and adjusts the decision, and information contagion starts another new round. So this creates the phenomenon of informational cycle cascade. In the real capital market, some investors often adjust their investment decision, and informational cycle cascade can well explain this phenomenon. Bad/good information contagion is basically clockwise/anticlockwise and information

contagion is multi directions at the same time. Cloud picture computes and shows average space distribution among the industries. New information can change investment decision of the investors, which will change flowing velocity, flowing direction and space distribution of informational cycle cascade.

REFERENCES

Alevy, J. E., Haigh, M. S., & List, J. A. (2007). Information cascades: Evidence from a field experiment with financial market professionals. *The Journal of Finance*, *LXII*(1), 151–180. DOI: 10.1111/j.1540-6261.2007.01204.x

Anderson, L. R., & Holt, C. A. (1997). Information cascades in the laboratory. *The American Economic Review*, *87*, 847–862. https://www.jstor.org/stable/2951328

Baker, M., & Stein, J. C. (2004). Market liquidity as a sentiment indicator. *Journal of Financial Markets*, *7*, 271–299. DOI: 10.1016/j.finmar.2003.11.005

Baker, M., & Wurgler, J. (2006). Investor sentiment and the cross-section of stock returns. *The Journal of Finance*, *61*, 1645–1680. DOI: 10.1111/j.1540-6261.2006.00885.x

Baker, M., Wurgler, J., & Yuan, Y. (2012). Global, local, and contagious investor sentiment. *Journal of Financial Economics*, *104*, 272–287. DOI: 10.1016/j.jfineco.2011.11.002

Bicchieri, C., & Fukui, Y. (1999). The great illusion: Ignorance, informational cascades, and the persistence of unpopular norms. *Business Ethics Quarterly*, *9*, 127–155. DOI: 10.2307/3857639

Bikhchandani, S., Hirshleifer, D., & Welch, I. (1992). A theory of fads, fashion, custom, and cultural change as informational cascades. *Journal of Political Economy*, *100*, 992–1026. DOI: 10.1086/261849

Brown, G. W., & Cliff, M. T. (2004). Investor sentiment and the near-term stock market. *Journal of Empirical Finance*, *11*, 1–27. DOI: 10.2139/ssrn.282915

Cai, F., Han, S., Li, D., & Li, Y. (2019). Institutional herding and its price impact: Evidence from the corporate bond market. *Journal of Financial Economics*, *131*, 139–167. DOI: 10.1016/j.jfineco.2018.07.012

Celen, B., & Kariv, S. (2004). Distinguishing informational cascades from herd behaviour in the laboratory. *The American Economic Review*, *94*, 484–498. DOI: 10.1257/0002828041464461

Chhaochharia, V., Kim, D., Korniotis, G. M., & Kumar, A. (2019). Mood, firm behaviour, and aggregate economic outcomes. *Journal of Financial Economics*, *132*, 427–450. DOI: 10.1016/j.jfineco.2018.10.010

Chinco, A., Hartzmark, S. M., & Sussman, A. B. (2022). A new test of risk factor relevance. *The Journal of Finance*, *77*, 2183–2238. DOI: 10.1111/jofi.13135

Cipriani, M., & Guarino, A. (2005). Herd behaviour in a laboratory financial market. *The American Economic Review*, *95*, 1427–1443. DOI: 10.1257/000282805775014443

Décamps, J. P., & Lovo, S. (2006). Informational cascades with endogenous prices: The role of risk aversion. *Journal of Mathematical Economics*, *42*, 109–120. DOI: 10.1016/j.jmateco.2005.03.002

Doherty, O. (2018). Infomational cascades in financial markets: Review and synthesis. *Review of Behavioral Finance*, *10*, 53–69. DOI: 10.1108/RBF-05-2016-0030

Duan, W. J., Gu, B., & Whinston, A. B. (2009). Informational cascades and software adoption on the Internet: An empirical investigation. *Management Information Systems Quarterly*, *33*, 23–48. DOI: 10.2307/20650277

Ern, A., Villeneuve, S., & Zanette, A. (2004). Adaptive finite element methods for local volatility European option pricing. *International Journal of Theoretical and Applied Finance*, *7*, 659–684. DOI: 10.1142/S0219024904002669

Feng, S., Cheng, L., & Guang, Z. X. (2017). Analysis of industry risk premium with MVS three dimensions vector factor model. *Cogent Economics & Finance*, *5*(1), 1374814. DOI: 10.1080/23322039.2017.1374814

Fiore, A., & Morone, A. (2008). A simple note on informational cascades. *Economics*, *1*, 1–21. DOI: 10.5018/economics-ejournal.ja.2008-1

Froot, K. A., Scharfstein, D. S., & Stein, J. C. (1992). Herd on the street: Informational inefficiencies in a market with short-term speculation. *The Journal of Finance*, *47*, 1461–1484. DOI: 10.3386/w3250

García, D. (2013). Sentiment during recessions. *The Journal of Finance*, *68*, 1267–1300. DOI: 10.1111/jofi.12027

Goeree, J. K., Palfrey, T. R., Rogers, B. W., & Mckelvey, R. D. (2007). Self-correcting information cascades. *The Review of Economic Studies*, *74*, 733–762. DOI: 10.1111/j.1467-937X.2007.00438.x

Gossner, O., & Melissas, N. (2006). Informational cascades elicit private information. *International Economic Review*, *47*, 297–325. DOI: 10.1111/j.1468-2354.2006.00380.x

Grebe, T., Schmid, J., & Stiehler, A. (2008). Do individuals recognize cascade behaviour of others?- An experimental study. *Journal of Economic Psychology*, *29*, 197–209. DOI: 10.1016/j.joep.2007.05.003

Hirshleifer, D., & Teoh, S. H. (2003). Herd behaviour and cascading in capital markets: A review and synthesis. *European Financial Management*, *9*, 25–66. DOI: 10.1111/1468-036X.00207

Holmes, A. D., Yang, H. T., & Zhang, S. H. (2012). A front-fixing finite element method for the valuation of American options with regime switching. *International Journal of Computer Mathematics*, *89*, 1094–1111. DOI: 10.1080/00207160.2012.663911

Huck, S., & Oechssler, J. (2000). Informational cascades in the laboratory: Do they occur for the right reasons? *Journal of Economic Psychology*, *21*, 661–671. DOI: 10.1016/S0167-4870(00)00025-8

Jiang, F. W., Lee, J., Martin, X. M., & Zhou, G. F. (2019). Manager sentiment and stock returns. *Journal of Financial Economics*, *132*, 126–149. DOI: 10.1016/j.jfineco.2018.10.001

Jiang, H., & Verardo, M. (2018). Does herding behaviour reveal skill? An analysis of mutual fund performance. *The Journal of Finance*, *LXXIII*, 2229–2269. DOI: 10.1111/jofi.12699

Kübler, D., & Weizsäcker, G. (2004). Limited depth of reasoning and failure of cascade formation in the laboratory. *The Review of Economic Studies*, *71*, 425–441. http://hdl.handle.net/10.1111/0034-6527.00290

Kuran, T., & Sunstein, C. R. (1999). Availability cascades and risk regulation. *Stanford Law Review*, *51*, 683–768. DOI: 10.2307/1229439

Mclean, R. D., & Zhao, M. X. (2014). The business cycle, investor sentiment, and costly external finance. *The Journal of Finance*, *69*, 1377–1409. DOI: 10.1111/jofi.12047

Morone, A., Sandri, S., & Fiore, A. (2009). On the absorbability of informational cascades in the laboratory. *Journal of Socio-Economics*, *38*, 728–738. DOI: 10.1016/j.socec.2009.06.014

Seog, S. H. (2008). Informational cascade in the insurance market. *The Journal of Risk and Insurance*, *75*, 145–165. https://www.jstor.org/stable/25145267

Shiller, R. J. (1995). Conversation, information, and herd behaviour. *The American Economic Review*, *85*, 181–185. https://www.jstor.org/stable/2117915

Spiwoks, M., Bizer, K., & Hein, O. (2008). Informational cascades: A mirage? *Journal of Economic Behavior & Organization*, *67*, 193–199. DOI: 10.1016/j.jebo.2007.06.005

Stambaugh, R. F., Yu, J. F., & Yuan, Y. (2012). The short of it: Investor sentiment and anomalies. *Journal of Financial Economics*, *104*, 288–302. DOI: 10.1016/j.jfineco.2011.12.001

Tai, C. S. (2014). Can investor sentiment be a channel of contagion during the 1997 Asian crisis? Evidence from closed-end country funds. *Journal of Accounting and Finance*, *14*, 142–170. DOI: 10.2139/ssrn.1464130

Wang, F., Wei, J. C., & Zhao, D. T. (2014). A quantifiable risky decision model in corporating individual memory into informational cascade. *Systems Research and Behavioral Science*, *31*, 537–553. DOI: 10.1002/sres.2294

Welch, I. (2000). Herding among security analysts. *Journal of Financial Economics*, *58*, 369–396. DOI: 10.1016/S0304-405X(00)00076-3

Welch, I. (2022). The wisdom of the robinhood crowd. *The Journal of Finance*, *LXXVII*, 1489–1527. DOI: 10.3386/W27866

Wu, J. M. (2015). Helpful laymen in informational cascades. *Journal of Economic Behavior & Organization*, *116*, 407–415. DOI: 10.1016/j.jebo.2015.05.002

Wu, W. S., Chang, H. H., Suardi, S., & Chang, Y. C. (2013). The cascade effect on lending conditions: Evidence from the syndicated loan market. *Journal of Business Finance & Accounting*, *40*, 1247–1275. DOI: 10.1111/jbfa.12050

ADDITIONAL READING

Cai, F., Han, S., Li, D., & Li, Y. (2019). Institutional herding and its price impact: Evidence from the corporate bond market. *Journal of Financial Economics*, *131*, 139–167. DOI: 10.1016/j.jfineco.2018.07.012

Décamps, J. P., & Lovo, S. (2006). Informational cascades with endogenous prices: The role of risk aversion. *Journal of Mathematical Economics*, *42*, 109–120.

Grebe, T., Schmid, J., & Stiehler, A. (2008). Do individuals recognize cascade behaviour of others?- An experimental study. *Journal of Economic Psychology*, *29*, 197–209. DOI: 10.1016/j.joep.2007.05.003

Mclean, R. D., & Zhao, M. X. (2014). The business cycle, investor sentiment, and costly external finance. *The Journal of Finance*, *69*, 1377–1409.

Stambaugh, R. F., Yu, J. F., & Yuan, Y. (2012). The short of it: Investor sentiment and anomalies. *Journal of Financial Economics*, *104*, 288–302.

Wang, F., Wei, J. C., & Zhao, D. T. (2014). A quantifiable risky decision model in corporating individual memory into informational cascade. *Systems Research and Behavioral Science*, *31*, 537–553. DOI: 10.1002/sres.2294

KEY TERMS AND DEFINITIONS

Factor Analysis: This chapter uses factor analysis method with dimensions decreasing technology to extract investor sentiment factor from industry stock turnover and industry stock volume share. The advantage of factor analysis method is that one factor or several factors can be extracted from some variables in multi dimensions space. The coordinate axis is made rigid rotation to extract the factors at biggest extent to give better further explanation for the factors.

Finite Element Method: FEM is a number analysis tool with AI's algorithm, and it is mainly used for computer visualization. FEM has been used to analyze some financial phenomena and theories. FEM algorithm uses certain meshing step to divide continuous entity into many elements connected with the nodes, and applies boundary condition and the loads on the elements to solve the numbers in total entity. It can be used to analyze the behaviour of individual investor included in total industry investor group. Because of investor heterogeneity, information contagion velocity is different among the investors. FEM algorithm can compute and measure investors' information contagion velocity numbers.

Flowing Direction of Information Contagion: Information contagion among noise investors isn't fixed in single direction, while information contagion is multi directions at the same time. The contagion is in X direction and Y direction at the same time, which indicates the multi directions for the contagion. For example, when bad information under the influence of global finance crisis arrives at noise investor A, A misjudges the influence of bad information and has over pessimistic sentiment. Then information arrives at noise investor B, and B also has over pessimistic sentiment under herd effect. Then information continues to arrive at other noise investors. Furthermore, decision information of noise investor A also arrives at noise investor C, noise investor D, etc. Then information continues to arrive at subsequent noise investors from noise investor C, noise investor D, etc. So over pessimistic sentiment makes forward contagion in multi directions at the same time.

Herd Effect: Herd effect is that noise investors don't pay attention to private information about market and corporation operation, while simulate investment decision made by other investors.

"Informational Cycle Cascade": After information transmits from the first investor to the last investor for the first round, the first investor observes subsequent new information and adjusts the decision, and information contagion starts another new round. So this creates the phenomenon of informational cycle cascade. For example, in the real capital market, some investors often adjust their investment decision, and informational cycle cascade can well explain this phenomenon.

Informational Cycle Cascade of Bad Information: This is down phase of investor sentiment contagion, and investor sentiment drastically decreases under the influence of global finance crisis. The preceding noise investors are affected by bad information of global finance crisis, and misjudge the influence of bad information and have over pessimistic investor sentiment. More and more subsequent noise investors also have over pessimistic sentiment under herd effect for the first round. The preceding noise investors observe the action of subsequent noise investors, and misjudge the bad information again and adjust the investment decision. The subsequent noise investors are affected by the bad public information again under herd effect. So investor sentiment contagion starts the second round. Accompanying with more rounds, informational cycle cascade of bad information occurs.

Informational Cycle Cascade of Good Information: This period is up phase of investor sentiment contagion, and investor sentiment rapidly increases under the influence of economic stimulating plan of big scale made by the government. The preceding noise investors are affected by good information of economic stimulating plan, and misjudge the influence of good information and have over optimistic sentiment. More and more subsequent noise investors also have over optimistic sentiment under herd effect for the first round. The preceding noise investors observe the action of subsequent noise investors, and misjudge the good information again and adjust the investment decision. The subsequent noise investors are affected by the good public information again under herd effect. So investor sentiment contagion starts the second round. Accompanying with more rounds, informational cycle cascade of good information occurs.

Investor Sentiment: Investors' personal knowledge, investment experience, risk preference and psychology are different when they make the decision. Some investors have cognitive biases and heterogeneous beliefs for asset pricing. This irrational phenomenon for the investors is called investor sentiment.

Velocity of Information Flowing: Noise investors need some time to make the decision from the information. This is expressed on velocity of information flowing. For some noise investors, velocity of information flowing is high. For other noise investors, velocity of information flowing is low. The difference of information flowing velocity numbers among noise investors is caused by the heterogeneity of noise investors. If noise investors haven't enough knowledge and investment experience, they are easily affected by herd effect to have cognitive bias. They will quickly have investor sentiment, and information flowing velocity numbers for them are high.

ENDNOTES

1 The cascade effect of two types of players including expert with high signal accuracy and layman with low signal accuracy is introduced in Wu (2015).

2 Décamps and Lovo (2006) consider a sequential trade model of informational cascade and find that endogenous prices cannot fully incorporate private information.

3 For stochastic error item, there are $E\varepsilon_i^N = 0$ and $E\varepsilon_i^T = 0$.

4 Food, Beverage & Tobacco industry has the smallest variation coefficient 0.61, which indicates that the volatility of volume in this industry is the lowest.

5 If fineness of element grids is low, less computing time will be used, but the precision of computing result will be decreased.

6 They will slowly have investor sentiment, and information flowing velocity numbers for them are low.

7 The good information contagion isn't uniform distribution.

8 The positive values and negative values represent the flowing velocity numbers in different directions.

9 Red areas represent the highest range of information flowing velocity numbers, while blue areas represent the lowest range of information flowing velocity numbers.

10 Other noise investors are uneasily affected by herd effect, and over optimistic sentiment contagion is slow and weak.

Chapter 5
Enhancing Portfolio Optimization With Deep Learning:
Evidence From African Stock Markets

Gharmili Meryem
https://orcid.org/0009-0003-1323-6039
Université Moulay Ismail Meknès, Morocco

Alj Abdelkamel
Université Moulay Ismail Meknès, Morocco

ABSTRACT

Emerging markets, particularly in Africa, present unique challenges for portfolio optimization due to increased volatility and limited historical data. This study explores the potential of deep learning models, specifically Long Short-Term Memory (LSTM), Deep Multilayer Perceptron (DMLP), and Convolutional Neural Networks (CNN), to predict the movements of three key African stock indices: MASI (Morocco), BRVM Composite (West Africa) and TUNINDEX (Tunisia). By comparing the performance of these architectures, this research aims to identify the models most suitable for prediction in a the context of limited data and high volatility. The results of this study will provide crucial insights for investors, portfolio managers, and researchers, thereby contributing to the development of more robust and effective portfolio optimization strategies for African markets, often overlooked by traditional methods.

1. INTRODUCTION

The field of portfolio optimization has long been a crucial aspect of financial management, as investors and financial professionals strive to construct portfolios that maximize returns while minimizing risks. Traditional approaches, such as the mean-variance optimization model developed by Harry Markowitz (1952), have provided valuable insights and tools for portfolio selection. However, the mean-variance (MV) model, while foundational in portfolio optimization, rests on several restrictive assumptions. One key assumption is the normal distribution of stock returns, which rarely holds true in real-world financial

DOI: 10.4018/979-8-3693-9684-1.ch005

markets. Recognizing this limitation, researchers have explored alternative approaches to improve model accuracy. The Mean Absolute Deviation model, (Konno, H., & Yamazaki, H.1991) aims to replace the MV model. This model utilizes absolute deviation as a risk measure, thus providing ease of calculation for large-scale portfolio optimization problems. Furthermore, they demonstrate that this absolute deviation measure is equivalent to the variance measure when stock returns follow a normal distribution. The ARIMA (Autoregressive Integrated Moving Average) model (Saboia, 1977; Tsay, 2000), is another traditional statistical method used in portfolio optimization, it allows to predict time series based on linear relationships between past and present values. It is effective for stationary time series and has the advantage of being interpretable, allowing to understand the components of the series (trend, seasonality, etc.). On the other hand, ARIMA has its limitations, its primary weakness lies in its assumption of linearity, unable to capture complex and non-linear relationships present in many real data, which can lead to inaccurate forecasts. In addition, the ARIMA model primarily focuses on short-term temporal dependence, neglecting longer-term trends and structural changes in volatility, its sensitivity to outliers and the need for a precise model specification add additional complexity, increasing the risk of biased estimates and erroneous results. Although more sophisticated approaches such as the bilinear model (Poskitt & Tremayne, 1986), the threshold autoregressive model (Stark, 1992), and the autoregressive conditional heteroskedasticity (ARCH) model (Engle, 1982), are capable of extracting nonlinear signals in time series, they still require the series to be stationary. Proposed by Tim Bollerslev (1986), GARCH generalizes the ARCH model by including terms related to the past conditional variance. The GARCH model makes it possible to capture the effects of persistent volatility more efficiently with fewer parameters, which simplifies the estimation, as well as thanks to its components q (past variance) and p (past residuals), it captures long-term dynamics better.

The GARCH model offers a major advance to analyze time series with volatility fluctuations, an area where ARIMA and ARCH show their limits. Its effectiveness in financial data has made it an essential tool for researchers such as Engle and Bollerslev, who have revolutionized the modeling of conditional volatility.

Faced with the increased instability of financial markets, traditional portfolio optimization models struggle to effectively manage risks and maximize returns. The rise in volatility questions the validity of the linearity and stability assumptions on which this models are based. The emergence of deep learning, a branch of machine learning, offers new perspectives to improve financial forecasting and portfolio optimization (Heaton et al., 2017). Many studies have demonstrated the benefits of deep learning in portfolio optimization. For example, Gu, Kelly, and Xiu (2020) demonstrated that deep learning models can outperform traditional statistical models in terms of risk-adjusted performance. Similarly, the study of Jiang, Xu, Liang, (2017), indicate that deep learning can help better capture non-linear relationships and interactions between assets, leading to more efficient portfolios.

Recently, the use of various types of machine learning (ML) models deep neural networks especially, has become widespread for predicting financial markets, thereby contributing to improving portfolio optimization. Deep neural networks (DNNs) have shown better performance in predicting the financial market, so it is of great worth to explore the application of DNNs in formulating portfolio optimization models based on prediction.

This study explores the use of deep neural networks (DNN) to improve stock return predictions and optimize portfolio construction on three African stock markets: the MASI in Morocco, the BVRM in West Africa, and the TUNINDEX in Tunisia. The main objective is to evaluate and compare out-of-sample three types of DNN - the deep multilayer perceptron (DMLP), the long short-term memory neural network (LSTM), and the convolutional neural network (CNN) - in predicting stock returns. The stock market data of the MASI, BRVM and TUNINDEX indices will be collected for the period from March 19, 2019 to March 19, 2024 from reliable sources such as Investing. After their retrieval, these data will be cleaned to eliminate errors and missing values, then transformed into 10-, 20- and 30-day time sequences in order to predict future returns of the indices. The study will be carried out using Python, evaluating the models with three metrics (MAE, RMSE, MASE). Several configurations will be tested, including three batch sizes (32, 64, 128) and four optimizers (Nadam, Adam, RMSProp, SGD). Using these predictions, the study calculates the expected portfolio returns and assesses the risk associated with each stock based on the semi-absolute deviation of prediction errors. This analysis focuses on African markets, often underestimated in quantitative research, and aims to fill this gap by providing valuable insights for investors interested in this region. Driving this study on African stock markets is of significant importance in several respects and is essential for visionary investors who wish to diversify their portfolios and take advantage of the continent's economic growth potential, by discovering promising sectors and companies that are often overlooked, thus minimizing risks and maximizing potential gains while contributing to the economic and social development of Africa.

This article therefore raises an essential question to explore and analyze: **What Deep Learning model (LSTM, DMLP, or CNN) provides the highest accuracy and reliability in predicting trends in African stock markets? And to what extent can Deep Learning models, taking into account the specific challenges of African stock markets such as volatility, limited data availability, and unique economic context?**

The results of this study will help to identify the most effective DNN models for each specific market, thus providing investors with crucial data to refine their investment strategies and navigate efficiently in these evolving markets.

The document is organized as follows: In section 2, a literature review is conducted to explore previous research on portfolio optimization models. Section 3 then outlines the materials and methods, including the prediction-based portfolio optimization models, such as LSTM, DMLP, and CNN. The optimizers used in the experiments are discussed in section 4. Section 5 defines the evaluation metrics to assess the performance of the models. The results and discussion of the experiments conducted on prediction-based portfolio models are presented in section 6. Finally, a conclusion is drawn in section 7.

2. LITERATURE REVIEW

Financial analysts rely on various models of Artificial Neural Networks (ANNs) to predict stock market values. Financial time series models, based on economic concepts and theories, are essential for predicting data series in the 21st century. However, these concepts cannot always predict market fluctuations influenced by external factors. The concept of a multilayer network improves the performance of ANNs, making them more effective than other prediction methods. Deep neural networks, a paradigm of machine learning, model the complex and nonlinear relationships between inputs and outputs. Internal parameters are iteratively updated to adjust inputs to target outputs. The multilayer perceptron (MLP) model is an important and widely used prediction technique. MLP is believed to be able to approximate arbitrary functions. Regression analysis is a diagnostic and analytical process that analyzes the interdependence of features and variables. Nonlinear models include techniques such as ARCH, GARCH, TAR, and deep learning algorithms like MLP, LSTM (Long Short-Term Memory), RNNs (Recurrent Neural Networks), and CNNs (Convolutional Neural Networks). LSTM is an exceptional variant of RNNs, introduced by Hochreiter and Schmidhuber (2000). Time-dependent data analysis is enhanced through LSTM networks, which can retain previous information. Sadon, A. N., Ismail, S. et al (2021) compares the performance of the recurrent neural network, the gated recurrent unit, and the LSTM neural network for stock return prediction. The experimental results demonstrated that the LSTM neural network outperformed the other models. They also proposed portfolios based on predictive thresholds using the predictive results of the LSTM neural network and achieved satisfactory performance. Fischer and Krauss (2018) also used an LSTM neural network, a random forest, a multilayer perceptron (MLP), and logistic regression to predict future stock returns. Their main finding was that the LSTM neural network outperformed the other memoryless models in terms of performance. Using the predictions from the LSTM neural network, they constructed a portfolio following the same approach. Experimental results showed that this portfolio outperformed the overall market from 1992 to 2009, but experienced a deterioration in 2010.

A study conducted by Selvin, Menon, Soman, (2017) and their colleagues compared the effectiveness of three deep learning models - CNN, RNN, and LSTM - for predicting stock prices using a sliding window approach. The results showed that the CNN outperformed the other two models in terms of accuracy. This superiority of the CNN is attributed to its ability to focus solely on the information in the current window to predict stock prices. This approach allows the CNN to capture dynamic changes and patterns occurring in the present, without being influenced by historical data from previous periods.

In contrast, the RNN and LSTM models incorporate information from previous time steps in their predictions. This reliance on historical data may hinder their ability to identify rapid changes and emerging trends in the current window.

These results suggest that the CNN could be a valuable tool for short-term prediction of stock prices, especially in volatile markets where rapid changes are frequent.

Additionally, Mahanta and his colleagues (Mahanta, R., et al. 2016). explored the use of different neural networks to predict the closing prices of the Sensex and Nifty indices. They tested the Radial Basis Function Network (RBFN), the Multilayer Perceptron (MLP) model, and an optimized RBFN using technical indicators. Their results demonstrated that the optimized RBF model outperformed both the MLP and the standard RBFN. These studies illustrate the growing interest in neural networks for predicting financial markets, which are characterized by their chaotic and volatile nature. However, results vary depending on the models used and the available data. Further research is needed to identify the most effective models in different contexts.

The "gate recurrent unit" (GRU), introduced by Dey & Salem in 2017, presents also an attractive alternative to traditional recurrent neural networks (RNNs). It operates using two types of gates: a reset gate and an update gate. These gates allow the GRU to manage the flow of information within the network, enabling it to learn complex temporal dependencies. Compared to LSTM, the GRU is characterized by its simplified structure and reduced number of parameters, which can make it more efficient and performant in certain learning contexts.

From the review of the literature, it is understood that each deep learning model has specific characteristics and strengths for predicting time series. CNNs excel in extracting spatial features, DMLPs offer flexibility in modeling non-linear relationships, and LSTMs are particularly suited for handling temporal dependencies. This article focuses on exploring these three promising models - CNN, DMLP, and LSTM - for predicting the three stock indices: MASI, BRVM, and TUNINDEX. The objective is to compare their performances and identify the model most suitable for predicting these specific stock indices, thus contributing to a better understanding of the capabilities of deep learning in the financial domain.

3. MATERIALS AND METHODS

The aim of this research is to predict future returns on the MASI, BRVM and TUNINDEX stock market indices. The methodology involves several key steps, from data collection to analysis and prediction (Figure1).

Firstly, stock market data for the MASI, BRVM and TUNINDEX indices will be retrieved for the period March 19, 2019 to March 19, 2024 from reliable sources of financial data. This data will then be cleaned and pre-processed to eliminate errors and missing values. Once cleaned, the data will be transformed into 10-, 20- and 30-day time sequences, which will be used to predict target values, i.e. future index returns.

Next, the prepared data will be divided into two sets: a training set (80% of the data) and a test set (20%) using a hold-out validation technique. These sets will be used to train and evaluate the deep learning models.

Three deep learning models will be trained on the training set: LSTM, CNN and DMLP. To improve model performance, optimization techniques such as SGD, Adam and RMSprop will be applied. In addition, different parameter configurations, such as batch size (32, 64, 128) and epochs (100, 200, 400), will be tested to find the best possible configuration.

Once the models have been trained, they will be evaluated on the test set using the MAE, RMSE and MAPE metrics. The model with the best performance, i.e. with the lowest values of MAE, RMSE and MASE, will be selected. This model will then be used to predict future returns for the MASI, BRVM and TUNINDEX indices.

Figure 1. Research methodology

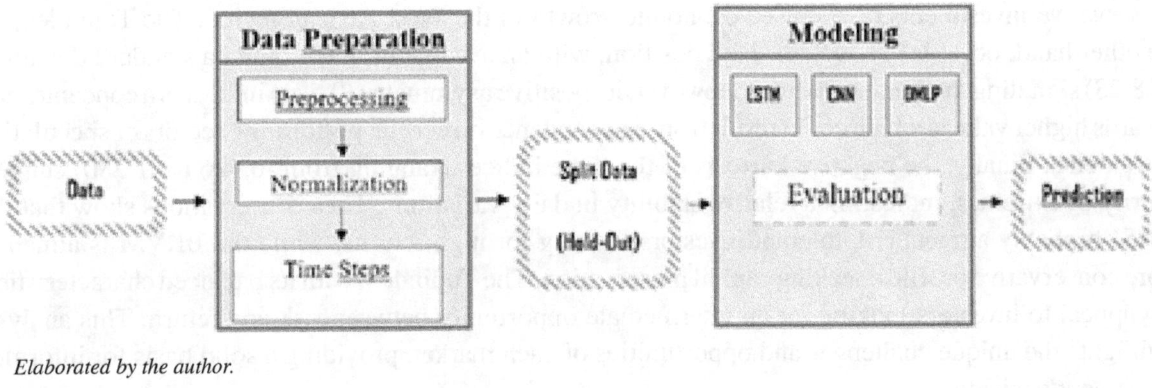

Elaborated by the author.

3.1. Descriptive Data Exploration

Data collection was carried out via the investing.com website, using Python as the software for this study. This research focuses on stock market data from three pre-emerging African stock markets: the Moroccan stock market (MASI), the Tunisian stock market (TUNINDEX) and the Regional Stock Exchange (BRVM), which includes eight West African countries (Benin, Burkina Faso, Guinea-Bissau, Ivory Coast, Mali, Niger, Senegal and Togo). The data covers a five-year period, from March 19, 2019 to March 19, 2024.

3.1.1. Visualization of Time Trends:

Table 1. Descriptive Statics for MASI, BRVM, and TUNINDEX

Market	Mean	Median	Std Dev	Kurtosis	Skewness
MASI	11637.72	11661.97	1035.05	-0.42	-0.13
BRVM	148.15	151.290	18.79	-1.28	-0.27
Tunindex	7456.12	7193.85	728.27	-0.88	0.57

The analysis of the MASI, BRVM and Tunindex (Table 1) indices highlights distinct market dynamics that reflect their respective economic and financial contexts. The MASI, with a high average (11,637.72) and a notable standard deviation (1,035.05), shows a market with a large capitalization, but marked by significant volatility. This volatility can be interpreted as an indicator of sensitivity to economic fluctuations, sectoral variations or global macroeconomic pressures. A median close to the average (11,661.97) and a slight negative asymmetry (-0.127) reflect a balanced distribution of values around their central trend, which is typical of relatively mature markets with a diversified investor base. On the other hand, the BRVM presents a fundamentally different profile. Its low average (148.15) combined with a very low standard deviation (18.80) reflects a regional market characterized by high stability, but also by a reduced capitalization and limited trading volumes. The more pronounced negative asymmetry (-0.274) reveals a concentration of values towards the bottom, which could reflect a predominance of conservative investments or a slowed economic growth in the West African region. The Tunindex, on the other hand, occupies an intermediate position, with an average (7,456.12) and a standard deviation (728.28) signaling moderate volatility. However, its positive asymmetry (0.571) indicates a concentration towards higher values, which could result from a dependence on certain performing sectors or speculative movements. Finally, the negative kurtosis of the three indices (ranging from -0.426 to -1.280) suggest a rarity of extremes, indicating a relative stability in daily variations. These observations show that the MASI probably attracts risk-tolerant investors looking for high returns, while the BRVM is aimed at more conservative profiles, seeking capital preservation. The Tunindex, with its balanced characteristics, can appeal to investors looking for an intermediate opportunity between risk and return. This analysis highlights the unique challenges and opportunities of each market, providing a solid basis for informed investment decisions.

3.1.2. Analysis of Volatility Regimes

Figure 2. The volatility regimes of the MASI, BRVM, and TUNINDEX indices

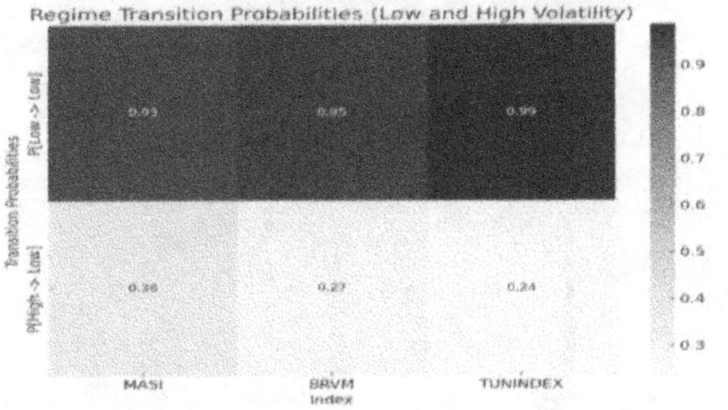

The analysis of the volatility regimes (the Markov Switching Model) of the MASI, BRVM, and TUNINDEX indices (figure 2) reveals distinct dynamics in their behavior in the face of volatility. The transition probabilities and the smoothed probabilities of high volatility make it possible to identify the dominant regimes and the relative stability of each market.

The TUNINDEX stands out for its high stability, with a probability o(f 98.71% of remaining in a low volatility regime and a relatively low probability of 23.65% of returning to a stable regime after a period of high volatility. These results reflect a low exposure to extreme fluctuations and a well-established market structure, making it the most predictable and least risky market of the three.

The MASI, with a probability of 93.09% of maintaining a low volatility regime, shows a frequent alternation between stable periods and phases of moderate volatility. The probability of transition from high volatility to stability (35.77%) indicates a moderate resilience to shocks, characteristic of a market in balance between risk and stability. Periods of moderate volatility probably reflect the impact of Moroccan economic policies and variations in the dirham.

On the other hand, the BRVM is clearly the most volatile and risky market, with a probability of 94.73% of remaining in a stable regime, but a probability of only 27.22% of returning to a stable regime after a period of high volatility. This highlights an increased exposure to regional shocks and political, economic and structural risks. The smoothed probabilities reveal prolonged periods of high volatility, confirming the relative instability of the West African market.

In summary, this analysis confirms that the TUNINDEX offers favorable market conditions for investors seeking stability and low volatility. The MASI, with its balance between stability and moderation of risks, is suitable for investors looking for a compromise. Finally, the BRVM, although the most speculative, can offer high-risk opportunities for investors tolerant of extreme fluctuations. These results highlight the structural and economic particularities of each market, thus guiding potential investment strategies.

The Descriptive Data Exploration section highlights the distinct characteristics of the MASI, BRVM and TUNINDEX indices. The MASI has moderate volatility and a slightly symmetrical distribution, offering a balance between stability and risk. The BRVM is the most volatile, with more frequent extreme declines and prolonged periods of high volatility, reflecting a risky and speculative market. On the other hand, the TUNINDEX stands out for its high stability, with low volatility and returns concentrated around the average. The analyses of volatility regimes confirm the predominance of stable regimes for the TUNINDEX, while the BRVM is more prone to extreme fluctuations.

3.1.3. Analysis of Yield Distributions

Figure 3. Histograms of the returns of the MASI, BRVM, and TUNINDEX

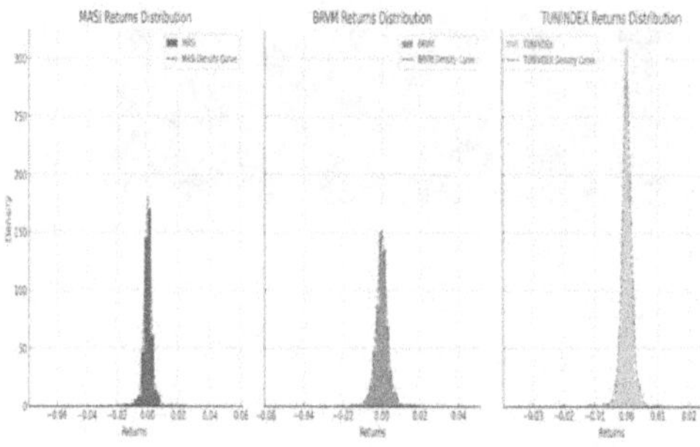

The histograms of the returns of the MASI, BRVM, and TUNINDEX (figure 3) indices highlight distinct characteristics of their distributions, supported by precise values. The MASI has a slightly symmetrical distribution with thick tails, characterized by a kurtosis of 5.92, indicating an increased probability of extreme events. Its moderate volatility, measured by a standard deviation of 0.00296 (0.296%), reflects a relatively stable market. The BRVM, on the other hand, shows a negative asymmetric distribution (skewness of -0.45) with a high kurtosis of 8.34, reflecting increased instability and a high exposure to extreme declines. Its standard deviation of 0.00775 (0.775%) makes it the most risky and volatile market. Finally, the TUNINDEX reveals a distribution concentrated around the average with a kurtosis of 4.02 and a skewness close to zero (-0.08), highlighting a great stability. Its standard deviation of 0.00142 (0.142%) shows that it is the least volatile and most predictable market. These observations confirm that the BRVM is the most speculative market, while the TUNINDEX stands out for its low volatility, the MASI offering a balance between risk and stability.

3.2. Prediction Models:

3.2.1. Portfolio Optimization Model Based on LSTM Neural Network

The LSTM Recurrent Neural Network (RNN), introduced by Hochreiter and Schmidhuber (1997) was specifically designed to counter the problem of « vanishing gradients », a major obstacle in the processing of sequential data.

Traditional RNNs, which use internal loops to process sequential information, have difficulty storing information over the long term. The LSTM, on the other hand, solves this problem thanks to its unique structure, which comprises several elements:

- Forgetting gate: Determines which information from the previous state is to be forgotten.
- Input gate: Decides what information is to be added to the unit's memory.
- Update cell: Updates the unit's memory according to the information retained.
- Output gate: Produces a new long-term memory based on the unit's information.

These elements enable the LSTM to store information over long sequences, making it particularly suitable for time series prediction. Indeed, time series prediction poses considerable challenges due to long-term trends, seasonal and cyclical fluctuations, and random noise.

Here are the mathematical equations that describe how the LSTM algorithm works:

$$
\begin{aligned}
i_t &= \sigma\left(W_i X_t + U_i h_{t-1} + b_i\right) \\
f_t &= \sigma\left(W_f X_t + U_f h_{t-1} + b_f\right) \\
\tilde{c}_t &= \tanh\left(W_c X_t + U_c h_{t-1} + b_c\right) \\
c_t &= i_t \cdot \tilde{c}_t + f_t \cdot c_{t-1} \\
h_t &= o_t \cdot \tanh\left(c_t\right)
\end{aligned}
$$

This formula represents the basic equations of an LSTM (Long Short-Term Memory) cell, which is a type of recurrent neural network (RNN) designed to model long-term dependencies in data sequences. Here is an explanation of the different elements of these equations:

- Entrance door (i_t): It determines the amount of information coming from the financial data current values (X_t) that must be added to the memory model. This helps the model to assess whether a variation in current prices, transaction volumes or other financial indicators is relevant for future forecasts.
- Door of Oblivion (f_t): It decides the amount of the information passed (for example, the trends observed in the previous days or months) to keep or forget. This allows to reduce the impact of outdated trends, focusing only on information recent data that may influence future forecasts.
- New candidate cell state ($\tilde{c}_t$): This value represents the new information that the cell considered to be added to long-term memory. It integrates the changes potential changes in financial data, such as a new peak in volatility or a decline significant price fluctuation, which could influence future forecasts.
- Cellular State (c_t): This is the long-term memory of the model, which combines the new relevant information with those that have been kept from the history. In a context financial, this may mean the preservation of previously observed market trends, but also the addition of important new dynamics.
- Hidden state / Output (h_t): This value represents the output of the cell at time t, indicating the forecasts or the current understanding of the model in relation to financial data. She integrates current and past information to produce a prediction, for example, the future trend in the price of a share. All the considered hyperparameters are presented in Table 1.

Table 2. Parameters of LSTM neural network.

Parameters	Value
Hidden nodes	5, 10, 15, 20, 25, 30
Hidden layers	1, 2, 3,…,10
Learning rate	0.0001, 0.001, 0.01, 0.1
Batch size	32, 64, 128
Epochs	100, 200, 400

3.2.2. Portfolio Optimization Model Based On CNN:

Convolutional neural networks (CNNs), a class of deep neural networks widely used in computer vision, have also found promising applications in financial prediction.

Unlike traditional neural networks, which rely on matrix multiplication, CNNs use a mathematical operation called convolution. This technique, which involves combining two functions to create a third function, enables CNNs to extract specific features from input data, such as trends and patterns in financial data. In convolutional neural networks, the convolution operation is applied to multidimensional data, such as (2D) images or (1D) time series (Figure 4), to produce a feature map (Goodfellow et al, 2016).

Figure 4. CNN for time series forecasting

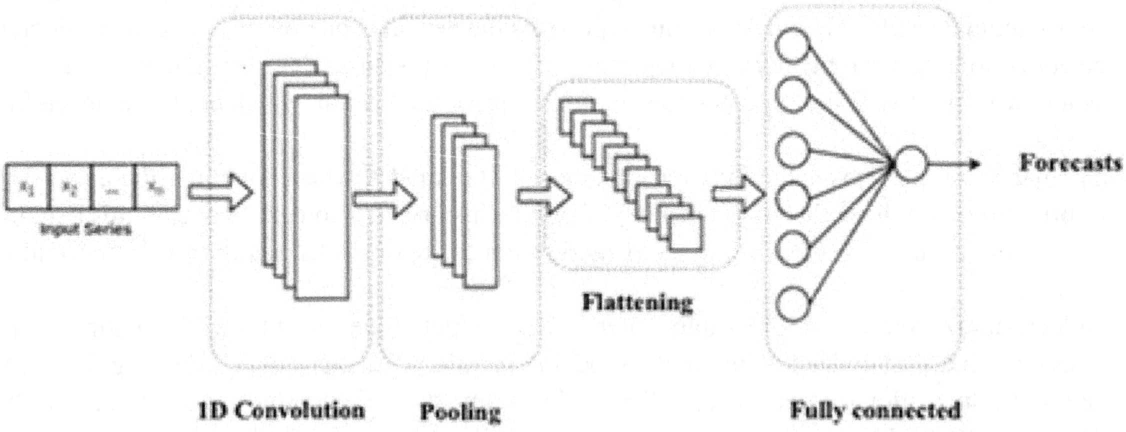

For a 1D convolutional layer with an input of size (N, C_{in}, L) and a size output (N, C_{out}, L_{out}), the formula is:

$$\text{Out}\left(\mathbf{N}_i, \mathbf{C}_{out\,j}\right) = \text{bias}\left(\mathbf{C}_{out\,j}\right) + \sum_{k=0}^{C_{in}-1} \boldsymbol{weight}\left(\mathbf{C}_{out\,j}, k\right) * \text{input}\left(\mathbf{N}_i, \boldsymbol{k}\right)$$

In this formula, each component plays a specific role in modeling the relationship between inputs and outputs in time-series prediction.

Out $(N_i, C_{out\,j})$: This term represents the output for the output channel $(C_{out\,j})$ and the time point (N_i). This output is calculated by combining the input values with learned weights and bias. In the context of CNNs, it corresponds to the final activation, which is passed on to the next layer or used to make predictions.

bias $(C_{out\,j})$: The bias associated with the output channel $(\mathbf{C}_{out\,j})$, is a constant added to each output. It makes it possible to capture general trends and offsets in the data, regardless of the input values. By adding a bias, the model is able to better adjust to the data, capturing the components of the time series that do not vary according to past values, such as averages or background trends.

$\sum_{k=0}^{C_{in}-1} weight\ (C_{out\,j}, k) * input\ (N_i, k)$: This sum represents a weighted combination of the input values. Each input value input (N_i, k) is multiplied by a corresponding weight $(C_{out\,j}, k)$, which is a parameter adjusted during the training of the model. These weights allow the model to capture the temporal dependencies in the input data, giving more or less importance to the values depending on their impact on the prediction. In the context of time series, this weighted sum is essential, because it allows the CNN to identify specific patterns in the time sequences.

it is important to mention that k represents the index of the input channels, ranging from 0 to $C_{in} - 1$. In other words, k traverses the different input channels or characteristics which feed the calculation of the output. Each input channel contributes to the output of the layer, with an associated weight $(C_{out\,j}, k)$ which indicates the importance of this channel for the output channel $C_{out\,j}$ *and* N_i represents the time index of the entry or the position of the sample in the time series. Thus, N_i indicates the moment or point in time for which we calculate the output of the layer. For example, if the time series represents daily data, N_i could designate a specific day in the sequence. The consider hypeparameters of CNN are presented in Table 2.

Table 3. Parameters of CNN.

Parameters	**Value**
Filer numbers	2, 4, 8, 16, 32, 64
convolutional layers	1, 2, 3,…,10
Maxpooling layers	1, 2, 3,…,10
Batch size	32, 64, 128
Epochs	100, 200, 400

3.2.3. Portfolio Optimization Model Based On Deep Multilayer Perceptron (DMLP):

The DMLP (Deep Multilayer Perceptron) is a classic type of ANN, distinguished from the MLP (Multilayer Perceptron) by its hidden multi-layer structure. Although MLP is theoretically capable of approximating any function (Principe et al., 1999), DMLP generally performs better in practice, especially when using a limited number of hidden layers (Hornik, K., Stinchcombe, M., et al 1989). As recommended by Orimoloye et al. (2020), the Relu function is used as the activation function.

Here is an explanation of its mathematical components:

- Activation of Neurons in the Layer l:

For each layer l, each neuron j receives inputs $x_i^{(l-1)}$ of the neurons in the previous layer. The weighted sum $Z_j^{(l)}$ for each neuron is calculated as follows:

$$\mathbf{Z}_j^{(l)} = \sum_{i=1}^{n_{(l-1)}} \boldsymbol{w}_{ij}^{(l)} \boldsymbol{x}_i^{(l-1)} + \boldsymbol{b}_j^{(l)}$$

in which:
$\boldsymbol{w}_{ij}^{(l)}$: is the weight linking the neuron i of the layer $(l-1)$ to the neuron j layer l
$\boldsymbol{b}_j^{(l)}$: is the bias term for the neuron j in layer l

- Activation function:

The activation function (f) plays a crucial role by introducing non-linearity into the calculation of the weighted sum.

$$\mathbf{Z}_j^{(l)} = f\left(\mathbf{Z}_j^{(l)}\right)$$

Activation functions such as the sigmoid, the hyperbolic tangent (tanh) and the Relu are often employed.

- Front Spread:

The architecture of a DMLP involves forward propagation, where the output of one layer is the input of the next, resulting in the final prediction of the output layer.

$$\hat{y} = f^{(L)}\left(\boldsymbol{W}^{(L)} \cdot f^{(L-1)}\left(\ldots f^{(1)}(\boldsymbol{W}^{(1)} \cdot \boldsymbol{X} + \boldsymbol{b}^{(1)}) + \cdots \; + \boldsymbol{b}^{(L-1)}\right) + \boldsymbol{b}^{(L)}\right)$$

The network has L layers. It is important to note that the activation function can vary from one layer to another, $f^{(L)}$ designating the function of the layer l.

- Loss function:

The loss function L is used to evaluate the error of the model by comparing the prediction ($\hat{y}$) to the real value (y).

$$\mathcal{L} = \frac{1}{N}\sum_{i=1}^{N} \ell(y^{(i)}, \hat{y}^{(i)})$$

The loss function ℓ can be chosen from different functions, such as the mean squared error (MSE) for the regression and the cross entropy for the classification.

- Backpropagation and Optimization:

The backpropagation allows the calculation of the gradients of the loss function relative to the weights and biases. These gradients are then exploited by an optimization algorithm (gradient descent, Adam, RMSProp, etc.) in order to update the parameters of the model.

$$W^{(l)} = W^{(l)} - \eta \cdot \frac{\partial \mathcal{L}}{\partial W^{(l)}}$$

The learning rate η controls the size of the step taken during the descent into the parameter space. This value, in conjunction with the backpropagation and the optimizer, allows deep DMLP networks to learn complex representations and make accurate predictions.

DMLP neural network contains similar hyperparameters with LSTM, all the discussed hyperparameters are presented in Table 4.

Table 4. Parameters of DMLP.

Parameters	Value
Hidden nodes	5, 10, 15, 20, 25, 30
Hidden layers	1, 2, 3,...,10
Learning rate	0.0001, 0.001, 0.01, 0.1
Batch size	32, 64, 128
Epochs	100, 200, 400

4. OPTIMIZER

To improve the performance of the time series prediction algorithm, several optimizations are available. Among the most commonly used are stochastic gradient descent (SGD), the moment adaptation algorithm (Adam), root mean square propagation (RMSprop) and the Nesterov Accelerated Adaptive Moment Estimation (Nadam).

The SGD, is an optimization algorithm widely used to train machine learning models, in particular deep neural networks. Its objective is to minimize a loss function, which represents the error of the model, by gradually adjusting the parameters of this model to reduce this error. The operation of SGD is based on several stages. First of all, the algorithm begins by calculating the gradient of the loss function relative to the current parameters of the model. This gradient provides the direction in which the parameters should be adjusted to reduce the error. Then, unlike the classic gradient descent, where the gradient is calculated on all the training data (which can be costly in terms of time and resources), SGD updates the parameters according to individual samples or small subsets called mini-batches. This introduces a stochastic (random) aspect into the algorithm, because each update is based on a different subset of the data. The parameters of the model are adjusted after each sample or mini-batch according to the following formula: $\theta = \theta - \eta \cdot \nabla L(\theta)$, where θ represents the parameters of the model, η is the learning rate which determines the size of the steps for each update, and ∇L(θ) is the gradient of the loss function with respect to the current parameters. SGD has advantages and limitations. Among its advantages, it is fast and efficient for large data sets, and frequent parameter updates allow the model to converge more quickly to an optimal solution. However, due to updates based on individual samples, the convergence trajectory of SGD can be unstable and erratic, which can make the convergence less reliable compared to that of the classic gradient descent. In practice, techniques such as momentum or variants of DMS such as Adam and RMSProp are often used to stabilize the trajectory and accelerate the convergence of the model, thus making DMS even more efficient for large data sets R. Hinton, et al. (2012).

Adam is a sophisticated optimization method combining the advantages of Momentum and RMSprop for fast, stable gradient descent. It individually adapts the learning rate to each parameter, taking into account not only the direction (Momentum) but also the amplitude (RMSprop) of the gradients, making it particularly effective for deep neural networks. This adaptation mechanism is based on the calculation and use of the first and second moments of the gradients (Kingma, et al, 2015).

At each iteration, Adam calculates the first moment, m_t an exponentially decreasing weighted average of the previous gradients. m_t thus represents the average direction of the recent gradients, integrating the history of the gradients for a better estimation of the optimal direction.

This first moment is calculated $m_t = \beta_1 \cdot m_{t-1} + (1 - \beta_1) \cdot g_t$, where g_t represents the current gradient and β_1 is the weighting rate, often set to 0.9 to give more weight to recent gradients. In parallel, Adam calculates a second moment, denoted v_t, which is an estimate of the variance of the gradients, which helps to avoid too large or too small updates when the gradients vary in amplitude. This step is carried out by par $v_t = \beta_2 \cdot v_{t-1} + (1 - \beta_2) \cdot g_t^2$, with a weighting parameter β_2, typically set at 0.999. Since m_t et and v_t are initialized to zero, the first values may be biased. To correct this, Adam introduces correction biases by calculating $\hat{m}_t = \frac{m_t}{1 - \beta_1^t}$ and $\hat{v}_t = \frac{v_t}{1 - \beta_2^t}$, in order to obtain more accurate estimates of the moments. Finally, the parameters are updated according to the corrected moments, by applying the formula $\theta = \theta - \eta \cdot \frac{\hat{m}_t}{\sqrt{\hat{v}_t} + \epsilon}$, where η is the learning rate, and ϵ is a small constant (in general, $= 10^{-8}$) to avoid division by zero. The advantage of Adam is his ability to dynamically adapt to variations in gradients, which allows a faster and more stable gradient descent, without having to manually adjust the learning rate during training. In summary, Adam uses the properties of moments to stabilize and accelerate convergence, making him a first-rate choice for training 0deep learning models.

RMSProp is an optimization algorithm that improves the convergence of the gradient descent, especially for deep neural networks. It alleviates the problems related to the variability of the gradients by dynamically adapting the learning rate for each parameter. This is done by using an exponentially decreasing moving average of the squares of the gradients, thus normalizing the updates and avoiding significant oscillations due to large amplitude gradients (Sebastian Ruder, et al, 1992).

RMSProp calculates the gradient of the loss function with respect to the parameters g_t. Then, it maintains an exponential estimate of the mean of the squares of the gradients, denoted v_t, which is updated at each iteration by the following formula:

$$v_t = \beta v_{t-1} + (1 - \beta) g_t^2$$

β (generally fixed at 0.9) controls the influence of the past gradients on the moving average of the squares of the gradients v_t. The model parameters are then updated using this average.

$$\theta = \theta - \frac{\eta}{\sqrt{v_t} + \epsilon} g_t$$

where θ represents the parameters of the model, η is the learning rate, g_t is the gradient of the loss function at iteration and epsilon is a small constant (in general, $\epsilon = 10^{-8}$) to avoid division by zero. The effectiveness of RMSProp lies in its adaptation of the learning rate to each parameter, depending on the variance of its gradients. This effectively prevents divergence and oscillations, which are frequent when the gradients have significant differences between parameters. This dynamic adaptation is particularly advantageous for deep neural networks, where the complexity of the data and models makes optimization more difficult.

Now we come to a more robust and modified version of the Adam optimizer, called Nadam, which stands for "Nesterov Accelerated Adaptive Moment"."Nadam integrates Adam's techniques, based on the moving averages of the gradients, while adding a component of anticipation thanks to Nesterov's momentum.

Nadam uses, like Adam, the moments of order one m_t (mean of the gradients) and two v_t (mean of the squares of the gradients) to update the parameters. The addition of the Nesterov momentum anticipates the direction of the gradient, thus stabilizing the descent and accelerating the convergence.

The Nadam optimization mechanism is enriched by the inclusion of the Nesterov momentum, which allows an anticipatory correction of the descent trajectory. The algorithm does not just follow the calculated gradient, but extrapolates its future direction. This predictive calculation makes it possible to dampen the oscillations inherent in the gradient descent and, consequently, to improve the stability and to accelerate the convergence towards the minimum (Reddi, Sashank J., et al. 2018)

Therefore, the Nadam update formula, taking into account this directional anticipation, is written:

$$\theta_{t+1} = \theta_t - \alpha \cdot \left(\frac{\beta_1 \cdot \hat{m}_{t-1} + (1-\beta_1) \cdot g_t}{\sqrt{\hat{v}_t} + \epsilon} \right)$$

By combining the current gradient, g_t, and an anticipated estimation of the gradient, $\beta_1 \cdot \hat{m}_{t-1}$ this correction ensures a more stable and rapid descent towards the minimum of the cost function.

5. EVALUATION

Mean Squared Error (MSE) is a common measure used to evaluate the performance of a predictive model. It quantifies the mean difference between the values predicted by the model and the actual values.

In simple terms, MSE calculates the average squared error between predictions and actual values. MSE value can be calculated using Eq:

$$\text{MSE} = \frac{1}{n} \sum_{i=1}^{n} (y_i - \hat{y}_i)^2$$

where:

y_i : is the actual value for the data point;
$\hat{y}_i$: is the predicted value;
n : is the total number of observations.

The logic behind choosing the square of the errors rather than their absolute value (as in the MAE) is that it imposes a greater penalty on significant errors, which may encourage the models to adapt better to all values.

The MSE gives a measure of the magnitude of the mean squared error between the predictions and the actual values:

- The lower the MSE, the better the quality of the predictions, because it means that the predicted values are close to the real values.
- Since the MSE is a quadratic measurement, it amplifies large errors (squared), which means that it is particularly sensitive to outliers

The MSE is particularly useful in the following areas:

- Regression: In supervised learning, it is commonly used as a loss function to evaluate linear regression models, logistic regression, or other regression models.
- Model optimization: In machine learning, many regression algorithms try to minimize the MSE to fit the model to the data.
- Model Comparison: The MSE can be used to compare the performance of several different models: the one that gets the lowest MSE is usually considered the best model for the data.

The MSE, although very useful and widely used in the evaluation of regression models, has several limitations that can affect the quality of the analysis of the models.

First of all, one of the main limitations of the MSE is its sensitivity to outliers. Since the MSE calculates the square of the errors, any significant difference between the predicted value and the observed value will be amplified significantly. This means that a single observation that is far from the general trend can significantly increase the MSE, thereby distorting the overall assessment of the model. In contexts where the data contain extreme values or anomalies, the MSE can make the performance of the model apparently poor, even if, for the majority of the data, the predictions are reasonably accurate. This sensitivity can lead analysts to adjust the model disproportionately to reduce the impact of these extreme errors, often to the detriment of overall performance. (Armstrong and Collopy, 1992)

Then, the MSE can pose a problem of direct interpretability. Since this is the mean of the high squared errors, the MSE unit does not correspond to that of the observed values, but rather to this squared unit. For example, for a price prediction in euros, the MSE would be in square euros, which has no intuitive meaning. This makes it more difficult to concretely interpret the average error of the model in the context of the target variable. To overcome this difficulty, it is common to take the square root of the MSE, thus obtaining the RMSE (Root Mean Squared Error), which brings the unit of measurement back to that of the prediction variable and makes the error more easily interpretable. However, this transformation adds an additional step that is not always necessary in other metrics such as the MAE (Mean Absolute Error).

In addition, the MSE is only relevant for regression tasks and is not usable for classification problems. In classification, models are usually evaluated in terms of error rates or by using measures such as cross entropy, which are better suited to handle categorical class outputs. Since the MSE is based on the differences between continuous values, it cannot account for errors on discrete values, which limits its application to regression models and makes it useless for a wide variety of models in machine learning.

In some cases of model optimization, minimizing the MSE can lead to an excessive adjustment of the data. By focusing excessively on reducing the mean squared error, the model can adjust to specific variations in the training data, including noise and anomalies. This situation, called overfitting, can degrade the performance of the model on new data, because the model becomes too specialized on the training set and loses its generalization ability. In this context, it is sometimes preferable to use metrics that are less sensitive to large errors, such as the MAE, to balance the adjustment to the real data without focusing excessively on the particularities of the training sample.

Root mean square error (RMSE) is a measure of prediction error used in statistics and machine learning. It is the square root of the mean square error (MSE), which is the average of squared errors between predicted and actual values. In simple terms, RMSE measures the average dispersion of prediction errors.

RMSE is expressed in the same unit as the target variable. It is always a positive number, and the lower the RMSE value, the better the prediction model.

$$RMSE = \sqrt{\frac{1}{n}\sum_{i=1}^{n}(y_i - \hat{y}_i)^2}$$

The RMSE therefore takes the average of the squares of the errors like the MSE, but by applying the square root at the end, it makes it possible to bring the metric back to the unit of the response variable, which facilitates the interpretation of the average error.

The RMSE represents the mean of the squared deviations, therefore an estimate of the average prediction error in the units of the target variable. This means that the RMSE tells us, on average, by how much the predictions of a model deviate from the observed values. For example, if the RMSE for a temperature prediction model is 3°C, this indicates that, on average, the model is wrong by about 3°C in its predictions, a more understandable information than the MSE which would be in square degrees Celsius (°C2).

A lower RMSE is desirable, as it means that the model predictions are broadly close to the real values. On the other hand, a high RMSE suggests that the model does not adjust well to the data, which may be an indicator of under-learning or of a poorly adapted model.

The RMSE and the MSE share important limitations, mainly due to their sensitivity to large errors and the difficulty of interpreting the MSE relative to the original unit of the target variable. The choice between MSE and RMSE depends on the need for interpretation and the level of tolerance for outliers in the data, but they both remain relevant in contexts where large errors need to be correcte (Makridakis, S, & al. 1998).

Mean Absolute Scaled Error (MASE) is an error measure commonly used to assess the accuracy of time series forecasts. Introduced by Rob J. Hyndman and Anne B. Koehler in 2006, MASE offers several advantages over traditional error measures such as MAE or RMSE.

The MASE is defined in such a way as to make the average prediction error staggered or normalized according to the difficulty of the prediction. It is based on the comparison between the mean absolute error of the model and the mean absolute error of a simple reference model, often a naive model. This means that the MASE compares the model in evaluation with a basic method to determine if the model really brings an improvement (Armstrong, J. S., & Collopy, F., 1992).

Its main features are:

- Scale independence: MASE is independent of the scale of the time series data. This means it can be used to compare forecast accuracy between different time series, even if they have different scales.
- Interpretability: MASE is easy to interpret. An MASE value of less than 1 indicates that the model's forecasts are, on average, more accurate than a naive forecasting method, which uses the last observed value to predict the next value.
- Robustness to outliers: MASE is less sensitive to outliers than RMSE, as it uses the median instead of the mean in its formula.

The mathematical formula of the MASE is as follows:

$$\textbf{MASE} = \frac{\textbf{MAE}}{Q} = \frac{\frac{1}{T}\sum_{t=1}^{T}\left|y_t - \hat{y}_t\right|}{\frac{1}{T_0 1}\sum_{t=2}^{T}\left|y_t - y_{t-1}\right|}$$

The upper part of the formula corresponds to the MAE of the forecasts. the denominator represents the average absolute error of a naive model (typically a persistence model that predicts that the next observation will be equal to the previous observation), taking into account the seasonality of the series. Thus, the MASE becomes a relative performance report. In other words, the MASE is the ratio between the error of your model and the error of a base model.

The MASE is a staggered metric that can be interpreted as follows:

MASE < 1: The forecast model is more accurate than the naive reference model.
MASE = 1: The forecast model is as accurate as the naive reference model.
MASE > 1: The forecast model is less accurate than the naive reference model.

This scale makes the MASE independent of the scale of the data. This means that it is possible to compare model errors over time series of different nature using the same performance scale.

The MASE has several advantages that make it a metric of choice for evaluating forecasting models, especially in the context of time series. One of its main advantages is its independence of the scale of the data: unlike metrics such as the MSE or the RMSE, the MASE normalizes errors with respect to a reference error, making the results comparable between series of different natures, whether for example sales volumes, temperatures, or economic indices. In addition, the MASE takes into account the seasonality and the difficulty of forecasting in the time series, which makes it possible to obtain a more realistic measurement of the performance of a model in contexts where the data show seasonal variations or regular trends. Finally, the MASE facilitates comparison with simple models: by comparing the studied model to a naive reference model (often a persistence forecast), it makes it possible to verify if we really gain in accuracy by using a complex model, instead of a basic forecast. Another major advantage is the robustness of the MASE against extreme values, because it is based on absolute errors and not on squared errors, like the MSE or the RMSE. This means that it is less influenced by outliers, which makes it a particularly useful tool in real, often noisy data.

However, the MASE also has certain limitations, that may restrict its usefulness in certain contexts. It is first important to note that its performance strongly depends on the reference model chosen for the evaluation. If this reference model is inadequate or poorly adapted, as in the case of time series with very complex trends or characteristics, the MASE may not accurately reflect the performance of the evaluated model. In addition, although the MASE is standardized, its interpretation is not as intuitive as that of the MAE or the RMSE, which give a direct estimate of the average error in concrete units. Since the MASE is a relative measurement, it expresses the error in the form of a report, which requires contextualizing it in relation to the reference model. In addition, the calculation of the MASE can be more complex and less immediate than that of simple metrics such as the MAE or the RMSE, especially if seasonal effects or special variations in time series are taken into account. This can complicate the analysis for users who need quick or less sophisticated evaluations.

In short, the MASE is a powerful metric for evaluating time series forecasting models by offering a fair comparison and a standardized scale. However, it is essential to interpret it correctly and make sure that the chosen reference model is well adapted, since its meaning depends on this relative comparison (Hyndman, R. J., & Koehler, A. B. 2006).

6. RESULTS AND DISCUSSION

The LSTM, CNN and DMLP algorithms were modeled to predict the stock prices of the 3 stock market indices (MASI -TUNIDEX-BRVM10) with several experiments to generate an optimal model. Experiments included optimization metrics (SGD, Adam and RMSprop, NADAM), lot sizes (32, 64, 128) and epochs (100, 200, 400).

6.1 Performance of Algorithms:

a. MASI Performance:

Figure 5. Performance of prediction models on the MASI test set

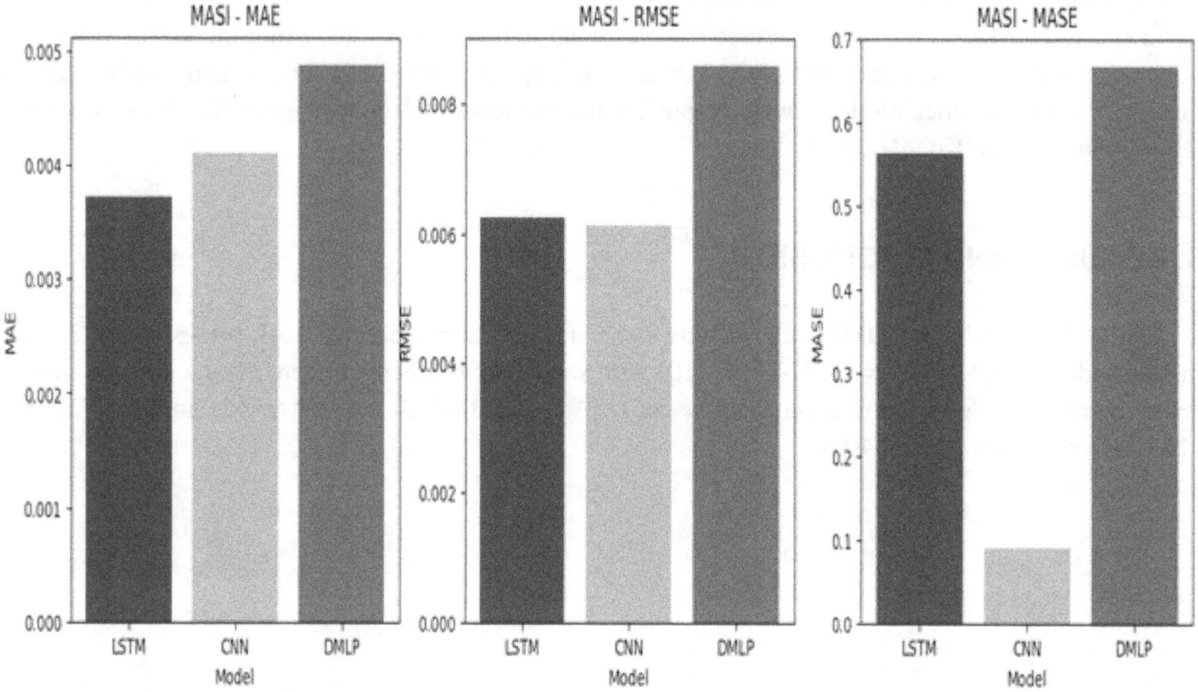

This study compares the performance of three prediction model architectures – Recurrent long-term memory neural networks (LSTM), Convolutional neural networks (CNN) and Multilayer Perceptrons (DMLP) - applied to a MASI dataset. The objective is to identify the most efficient model for the prediction of the MASI time series and to analyze the strengths and weaknesses of each approach.

The LSTM model obtains the lowest MAE (between 0.001 and 0.005), followed by the CNN and finally the DMLP, which has the highest EAW. This indicates that the LSTM is able to capture the trends of the MASI dataset with greater average accuracy (figure 5).

The low MAE of the LSTM shows that it effectively minimizes global errors, which could be explained by its ability to model temporal sequences and take into account sequential data dependencies. The CNN, although efficient, is less accurate than the LSTM in terms of MAE, perhaps because of its structure which captures spatial patterns better than temporal. The DMLP, being a classic neural network model (non-recurrent nor convolutional), has difficulty grasping temporal relationships, thus explaining its inferior performance in MAE.

The CNN obtains the lowest RMSE (0,00612), followed by the LSTM (0,00624) . The DMLP again presents the highest RMSE here (0,00859). Since the RMSE is more sensitive to large errors than the MAE, these results suggest that the CNN is slightly more effective in limiting large errors.

The better performance of the CNN in RMSE indicates that it is relatively more robust to extreme errors, which could be due to its ability to extract stable structural patterns in the data, thus limiting major deviations. The LSTM follows closely, suggesting that it is also effective in avoiding big mistakes, but less than the CNN for this specific task. The poor performance of the DMLP in RMSE highlights an inability to control large deviations, suggesting a possible sensitivity to outliers.

The CNN shows the weakest MASE, showing its superiority in terms of generalization compared to a naive prediction. On the other hand, the DMLP has the highest MASE, followed by the LSTM. Interpretation: A low MASE for the CNN implies that it adapts well to the characteristics of the time series of the MASI dataset, surpassing a naive reference model. The LSTM is less efficient in terms of relative generalization, and the DMLP is largely behind, which could be due to an inability to adapt to variations in seasonality or trend of the dataset.

For the MASI dataset, CNN and LSTM stand out, with a preference for CNN due to its performance in RMSE and MASE. The DMLP, on the other hand, seems unsuitable, probably because of its simpler structure which does not allow it to capture the temporal and structural relationships in the data.

b. TUNINDEX Performance:

Figure 6. Performance of prediction models on the TUNINDEX test set

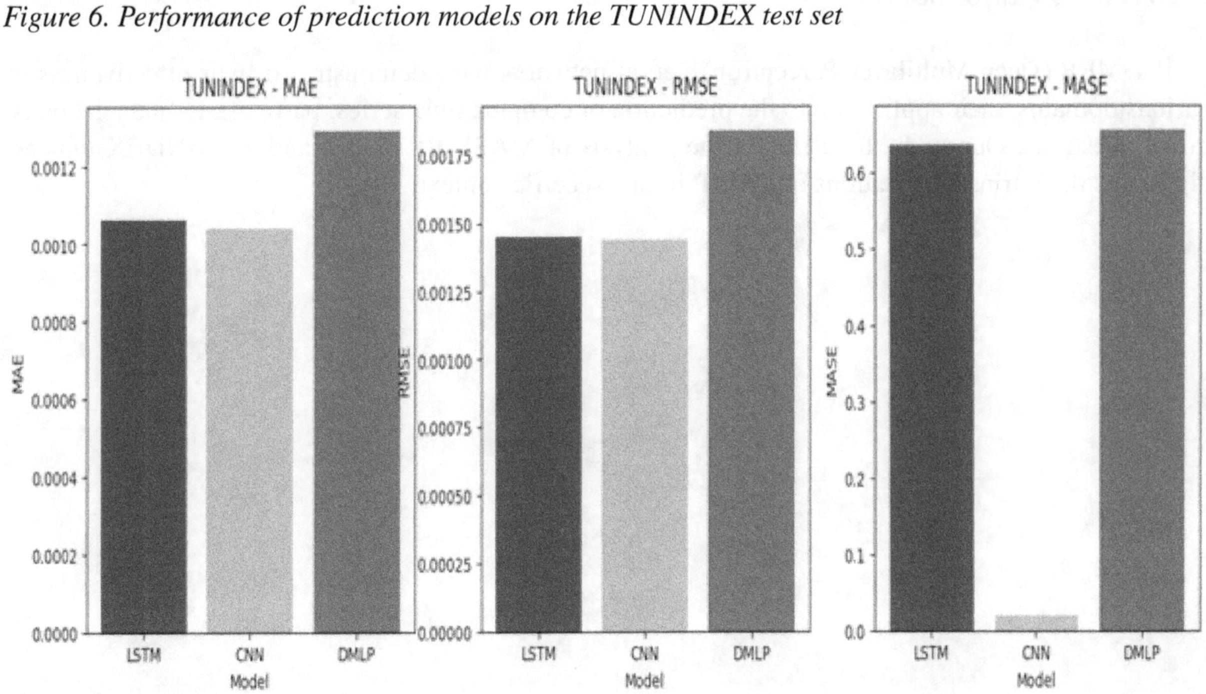

As we can see from figure 6, the lowest MAE is given by the CNN, with the LSTM closely following, while the highest MAE is trailed by the DMLP.

The performance of CNNs in MAE also demonstrates their capabilities in minimizing the overall error. Given its spatial structure, the CNN would be more handy given the periodical fluctuation types of motifs in the TUNINDEX dataset. The LSTM follows it closely, with this model capturing the temporal dependencies nicely but failing to outperform the CNN on this occasion. Still, DMLP, with its highest MAE, confirms that it struggles to catch the trends of this particular dataset.

CNN also has the lowest RMSE, while DMLP remains with the highest RMSE. The CNN succeeds in limiting significant errors in the TUNINDEX dataset, which could indicate that it adapts well to large amplitude variations or sudden changes. The LSTM is slightly less efficient in RMSE, but remains a robust option to reduce average errors. The DMLP, once again, is not performing well, suggesting that it lacks flexibility to manage the complex variations of this dataset. The MASE of CNN is by far the lowest, indicating a strong generalization capacity, while DMLP has a very high MASE.

A weak MASE for the CNN suggests that it is particularly adapted to the characteristics of the TUNINDEX, surpassing the naive prediction. This shows an increased ability to adjust to the specificities of time series data, which is less the case for LSTM and even less for DMLP. Summary: In the context of the TUNINDEX, the CNN is the most efficient model on all criteria, confirming its superiority for this type of data. LSTM remains an acceptable alternative, while DMLP is clearly ineffective for capturing TUNINDEX patterns.

c. BRVM10 Performance:

If DMLP (Deep Multilayer Perceptron) neural networks have demonstrated their effectiveness in various domains, their application to the prediction of complex time series, particularly financial ones, raises questions. Our study, focusing on the analysis of MASI, BRVM10, and TUNINDEX indices, highlights the intrinsic limitations of DMLP in this specific context.

Figure 7. Performance of prediction models on the BRVM10 test set

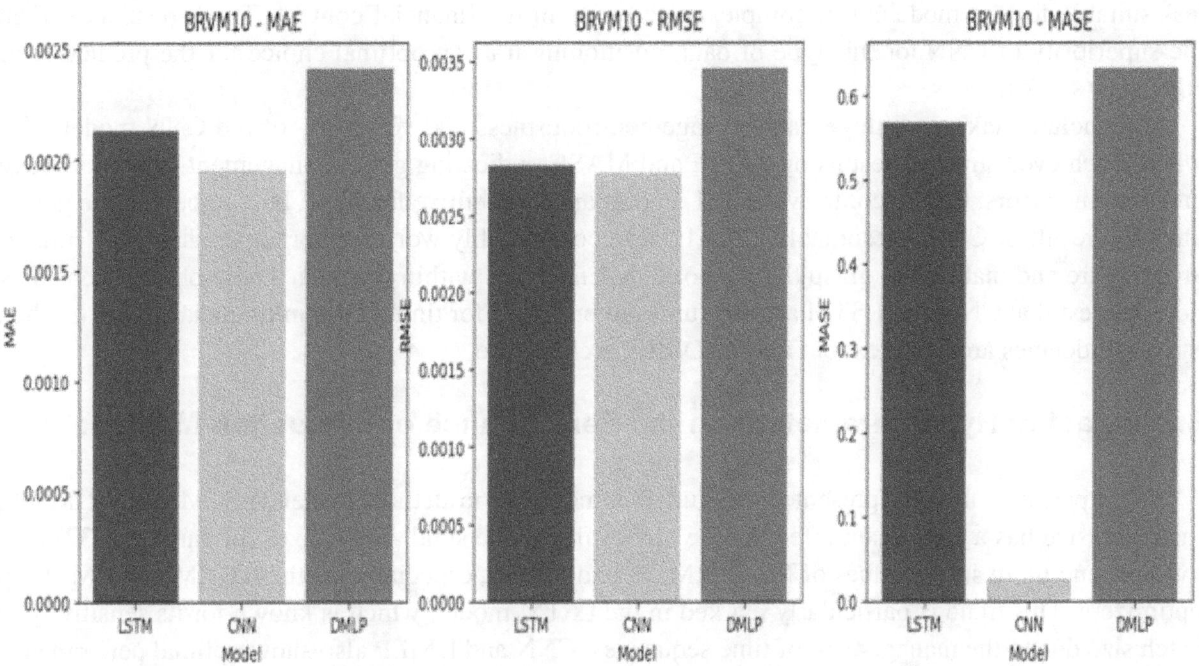

The analysis of the results of the BRVM10 dataset (figure 7) reveals contrasting performances between the LSTM, CNN and DMLP models in the prediction of financial time series. In terms of mean absolute error (MAE), the CNN shows the best accuracy with an MAE of 0.002, closely followed by the LSTM with an MAE of 0.0021, while the DMLP, with an MAE of 0.0025, shows a more limited ability to minimize global errors. This low MA of the CNN indicates that it better captures the global trends of the BRVM10 dataset, reducing the average deviation between the predicted and actual values compared to other models.

By analyzing the mean squared error (RMSE), a similar trend is observed: the CNN obtains an RMSE of 0.0025, which confirms its ability to limit large errors, an essential factor in the prediction of financial indices where extreme variations can induce significant losses. The LSTM, with a slightly higher RMSE of 0.003, shows a certain robustness but remains less efficient than the CNN in the management of significant deviations. The DMLP, on the other hand, records the highest RMSE of 0.0035, illustrating its difficulty in containing important errors and in following the complexity of the variations in the dataset.

The analysis of the normalized mean absolute error (MASE) highlights the generalization capacity of the models compared to a naive prediction. The CNN still stands out with a MASE of 0.1, indicating that it is not only accurate, but also able to generalize effectively beyond a simple naive approach. The LSTM, with a MASE of 0.65, and the DMLP, with a MASE of 0.7, are significantly underperforming on this indicator, which suggests that they fail to satisfactorily exceed a basic prediction for this dataset.

In summary, the CNN proves to be the most efficient model for the prediction of financial data from the BRVM10 dataset, by obtaining the best values in all the metrics, which underlines its accuracy, its robustness and its generalization capacity. The LSTM, although effective, remains slightly behind due to its inability to reduce extreme errors as effectively as the CNN. Finally, the DMLP shows significant limitations, particularly for the minimization of large errors and generalization, suggesting that it is less suitable for the modeling of complex time series in the financial context. These results confirm the superiority of CNN for this type of data, positioning it as an optimal choice for the prediction of BRVM10 stock indices.

To conclude, taking all three datasets together, robustness and versatility of the CNN model arise when it achieved superior results on RMSE and MASE, indicating good management of both average and extreme errors. On the contrary, LSTM models are competitive for MAE but lag behind the generalization result of CNN. Presumably, DMLP has a considerably worse performance due to its simpler architecture and inability to grasp the temporal dependencies within the data. These observations may now suggest that CNN and LSTM architectures are preferred for time series in financial contexts when the dependencies are complex, but not the DMLP architecture.

6.2 Impact of Hyperparameters on the Performance of Evaluation Metrics:

The experimental results presented in Figure 8, demonstrate in all three models (LSTM, CNN, DMLP), the batch size has a significant effect on the error values. The small batch sizes (in particular 32) lead to lower and more stable values of MAE, RMSE, and MASE, especially for the ADAM and RMSProp optimizers. This trend is particularly marked in the LSTM model, which is known for its sensitivity to batch size due to the management of time sequences. CNN and DMLP also show optimal performance with small batch sizes, but the effect is less pronounced compared to LSTM. Among the three architectures, an increased batch size of 128 generally amplifies the errors and reduces the stability of the model across runs, hence pointing toward poorer convergence with larger batches.

Figure 8. Influence of Batch Size and Epochs on LSTM Evaluation Metrics

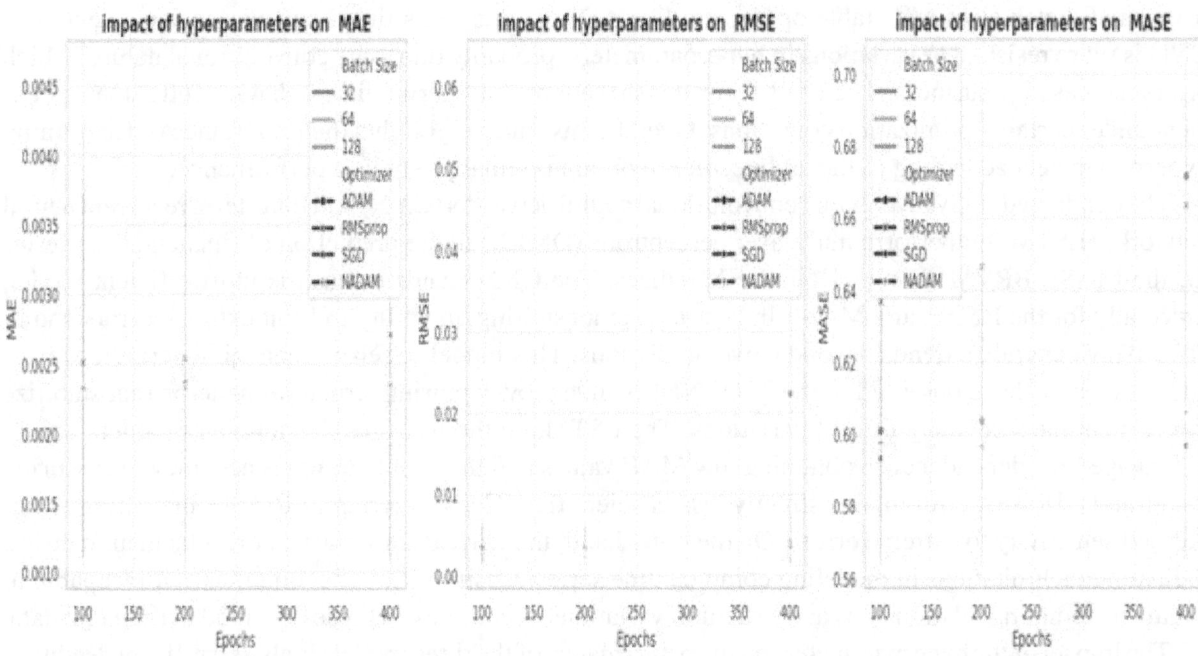

In this respect, the most effective optimizers coming out of the three models are those of ADAM and RMSprop. They give more stable results for the low error values of the three metrics irrespective of the used model. On the other hand, the highly volatile nature of the SGD optimizer shows its worst for the LSTM and DMLP, indicating less effective convergence inside the architectures that demand more accurate handling of back-propagation. NADAM, although a little more efficient than SGD, remains less stable than ADAM and RMSProp in most cases, with more variable performance depending on the batch size and the number of epochs.

In all three architectures, increasing the number of epochs generally reduces the error, although it also depends on the batch size and the optimizer. However, for very high epochs (in particular at 400), a slight increase in the variability of the errors in the LSTM model is observed, particularly with a large batch size. This may indicate overfitting or saturation of convergence for LSTM, while CNN and DMLP seem to maintain acceptable stability, even with a high number of epochs.

In terms of similarity, the three architectures show optimal performance with smaller batch sizes (32 and 64) and optimizers like ADAM and RMSProp. These configurations favor a better stability and a reduction of errors for MAE, RMSE, and MASE in all cases. The large batch size (128) usually leads to an increase in errors and a reduction in stability, a trend shared between the three architectures.

However, distinct differences appear between the models. The LSTM shows a greater sensitivity to variations in the batch size and the optimizer, probably due to its complex management of time sequences. The CNN, being designed for image processing, seems to be less affected by hyperparameter changes, showing better overall robustness. Finally, the DMLP, with its fully connected structure, presents intermediate performances: it is sensitive to hyperparameters but less markedly than the LSTM.

These analyses show that the choice of hyperparameters is crucial to optimize the performance of neural network models, and that each architecture has its specificities. The LSTM particularly benefits from small batch sizes and stable optimizers like ADAM, due to its time sequence management. The CNN is more resistant to variations in hyperparameters, probably due to its convolutional nature, which offers increased robustness. The DMLP, for its part, adopts an intermediate behavior and remains efficient under certain optimization conditions. Overall, this study highlights the importance of fine-tuning hyperparameters according to the architecture to obtain optimal prediction performance.

The conducted study reveals that convolutional neural networks (CNN) and long-term recurrent neural networks (LSTM) outperform multilayer perceptrons (DMLP) in the prediction of financial time series for the MASI, BRVM10 and TUNINDEX indices. The CNN stands out as the most efficient model, especially for the RMSE and MASE indicators, demonstrating an ability to limit extreme errors and to effectively generalize trends beyond naive predictions. This model excels in managing periodic fluctuations, such as those observed in the TUNINDEX index, by capturing structural patterns that stabilize forecasts in the face of significant variations. The LSTM, on the other hand, shows an excellent ability to manage time dependencies, obtaining low MAE values and thus confirming its accuracy in capturing data trends. However, it remains slightly less efficient than CNN in terms of RMSE, indicating an increased sensitivity to extreme errors. On the other hand, the DMLP shows weaker results in all metrics, indicating its limitations in modeling complex time series; its simple architecture makes it incapable of capturing temporal relationships and structural variations as complex as those observed in financial data.

The impact of the hyperparameters on the performance of the three models is also significant. Reduced batch sizes (32 or 64) associated with the ADAM and RMSProp optimizers produce more stable results for the MAE, RMSE and MASE, especially for the LSTM model which is sensitive to these parameters due to the management of time sequences. Larger batch sizes (128), on the other hand, increase errors and reduce stability, a trend common to all three architectures. Regarding the number of epochs, a moderate increase generally reduces the errors, but a very high number of epochs, especially for the LSTM, tends to cause an overfitting, reducing the generalization of the model.

To improve performance, several avenues can be explored. The stability of the LSTM and DMLP models could benefit from an advanced search for hyperparameters via techniques such as Bayesian networks, to optimize the configuration in a more robust way. To overcome the limitations of DMLP, in particular its difficulty in capturing temporal relationships, the integration of temporal transformation layers (such as Transformers) could offer significant improvements. Moreover, a hybrid architecture combining CNN layers for the detection of periodic patterns and LSTM layers for temporal dependencies could take advantage of the strengths of each approach, offering increased accuracy on all performance indicators. Finally, to limit the effects of over-adjustment observed in the LSTM with a high number of epochs, regularization techniques such as dropout or early shutdown would be advantageous.

In sum, the study confirms the superiority of the CNN for the prediction of financial indices, positioning it as the most effective option to manage extreme variations and generalize complex trends, with the LSTM as a robust alternative for the management of temporal dependencies. The DMLP, for its part, is limited in this context, and its use for complex time series would require significant adaptations of its architecture and its hyperparameters to compete with other models.

7. CONCLUSION

This in-depth study of African stock markets (MASI, BRVM10, TUNINDEX), marked by their own challenges and specificities, reveals crucial insights into the performance of three deep learning models (LSTM, DMLP, CNN) using four optimizers (Adam, Nadam, SGD, RMSprop) and various training parameters (epochs: 100, 200, 400 and batch size: 32, 64, 128).

The results show that each African stock market requires a specific approach to optimize model performance. Overall, the LSTM and CNN models demonstrated superiority over the DMLP. This improved performance of LSTM and CNN can be attributed to their ability to capture complex temporal and spatial relationships, respectively, which are essential in the analysis of time series data and market structures.

For the MASI, the LSTM showed great variability in performance depending on the parameters used. An increase in epochs and batch size did not systematically improve the results, suggesting that the volatile nature of the Moroccan market requires a more nuanced approach. The CNN, however, benefited from increasing epochs and batch size, demonstrating a better ability to generalize with more training data.

On the BRVM10 market, the CNN also performed better, with specific optimizations (notably with Nadam and Adam) showing promising results. LSTM once again performed inconsistently, requiring specific fine-tuning for each set of parameters.

In Tunisia, LSTM showed better adaptation to market variations, with superior performance when coupled with optimizers such as Nadam and Adam. The CNN also showed robust results, particularly with an increase in epochs and batch size, while the DMLP lagged behind.

The optimizers played a crucial role in the performance of the models. The Nadam and Adam optimizers showed favorable signs in all markets, underlining their ability to adapt to the different dynamics of the African market. The SGD also showed promising performance, although its effectiveness is highly dependent on specific tuning parameters.

This analysis not only revealed the relative performance of deep learning models on African stock markets, but also highlighted the importance of customizing parameters and optimizers for each market context. African stock markets, with their unique challenges and volatility, require a sophisticated and bespoke modelling approach. LSTM and CNN, while effective, need to be carefully adjusted for each specific market, while Nadam and Adam optimizers are proving to be robust and reliable choices.

Our conclusions open up promising prospects for future investigations. The exploration of hybrid architectures combining LSTM and CNN, as well as the automation of hyperparameter optimization via techniques such as Bayesian optimization (Snoek et al., 2012) or reinforcement search (Zoph & Le, 2016), are particularly stimulating avenues of research. In short, this study contributes to a better understanding of the challenges and opportunities associated with the application of Deep Learning for stock market prediction.

REFERENCES

Armstrong, J. S., & Collopy, F. (1992). Error measures for generalizing about forecasting methods: Empirical comparisons. *International Journal of Forecasting*, *8*(1), 69–80.

. Armstrong, J. S., & Collopy, F. (1992). Evaluating the forecasting performance of ex ante predictors.

Bollerslev, T. (1986). Generalized autoregressive conditional heteroskedasticity. *Journal of Econometrics*, *31*(3), 307–327.

Dey, R., & Salem, F. M. (2017). Gate-variants of Gated Recurrent Unit (GRU) neural networks. 2017 IEEE 60th International Midwest Symposium on Circuits and Systems (MWSCAS), 1597–1600.

Engle, R. F. (1982). Autoregressive conditional heteroscedasticity with estimates of the variance of United Kingdom inflation. *Econometrica*, *50*(4), 987–1007.

Fischer, T., & Krauss, C. (2018). Deep learning with long short-term memory networks for financial market predictions. *European Journal of Operational Research*, *270*(2), 654–669.

Goodfellow, I., Bengio, Y., & Courville, A. (2016). *Deep learning*. MIT Press.

Gu, S., Kelly, B., & Xiu, D. (2020). Empirical asset pricing via machine learning. *Review of Financial Studies*, *33*(5), 2223–2273.

Heaton, J. B., Polson, N. G., & Witte, J. H. (2017). Deep learning in finance. *Applied Stochastic Models in Business and Industry*, *33*(1), 3–12.

Hochreiter, S., & Schmidhuber, J. (1997). Long short-term memory. *Neural Computation*, *9*(8), 1735–1780. PMID: 9377276

Hornik, K., Stinchcombe, M., & White, H. (1989). Multilayer feedforward networks are universal approximators. *Neural Networks*, *2*(5), 359–366.

Hyndman, R. J., & Koehler, A. B. (2006). Another look at measures of forecast accuracy. *International Journal of Forecasting*, *22*(4), 679–688.

Jiang, Z., Xu, D., & Liang, J. (2017). A deep reinforcement learning framework for the financial portfolio management problem. arXiv preprint arXiv:1706.10059.

Kingma, D. P., & Ba, J. (2015). Adam: A method for stochastic optimization. arXiv preprint arXiv:1412.6980.

Konno, H., & Yamazaki, H. (1991). Mean-absolute deviation portfolio optimization model and its applications to Tokyo stock market. *Management Science*, *37*(5), 519–531.

Mahanta, R., Pandey, T. N., Jagadev, A. K., & Dehuri, S. (2016). Optimized Radial Basis Functional Neural Network for Stock Index Prediction. Dans *Proceedings of the International Conference on Electrical, Electronics, and Optimization Techniques (ICEEOT)* (pp. 775–780).

Makridakis, S., Wheelwright, S. C., & Hyndman, R. J. (1998). Forecasting: Methods and applications (3rd ed.).

Orimoloye, L. O., Sung, M. C., Ma, T., & Johnson, J. E. (2020). Comparing the effectiveness of deep feedforward neural networks and shallow architectures for predicting stock price indices. *Expert Systems with Applications*, *139*, 112828.

Ortu, M., Casu, M., & Lazzari, R. (2022). On technical trading and social media indicators for cryptocurrency price classification through deep learning. *Expert Systems with Applications*, •••, 198.

Poskitt, D. S., & Tremayne, A. R. (1986). The selection and use of linear and bilinear time series models. *International Journal of Forecasting*, *2*(1), 101–114.

Principe, J. C., Euliano, N. R., & Lefebvre, W. C. (1999). *Neural and adaptive systems: Fundamentals through simulations*. Wiley.

Reddi, S. J., Kale, S., & Kumar, S. (2018). On the convergence of Adam and beyond.

Ruder, S. (2017). An overview of gradient descent optimization algorithms.

Saboia, J. L. M. (1977). Autoregressive integrated moving average (ARIMA) models for birth forecasting. *Journal of the American Statistical Association*, *72*(358), 264–270.

Sadon, A. N., Ismail, S., Jafri, N. S. B., & Shaharudin, S. M. (2021). Long short-term vs gated recurrent unit recurrent neural network for Google stock price prediction. In *2021 2nd International Conference on Artificial Intelligence and Data Sciences (AiDAS)* (pp. 1-6). IEEE.

Sebastian, R., & Collopy, F. (1992). Evaluating the forecasting performance of ex ante predictors.

Selvin, S., Vinayakumar, R., Gopalakrishnan, E. A., Menon, V. K., & Soman, K. P. (2017). Stock price prediction using LSTM, RNN, and CNN-sliding window model. *2017 International Conference on Advances in Computing, Communications and Informatics (ICACCI)*, 1643–1647.

Snoek, J., Larochelle, H., & Adams, R. P. (2012). Practical Bayesian optimization of machine learning algorithms. *Advances in Neural Information Processing Systems*, *25*, 2951–2959.

Stark, C. R. (1992). *Non-linear series: A dynamical system approach*. Howell Tong.

Tsay, R. S. (2000). *Analysis of financial time series*. Wiley.

Zoph, B., & Le, Q. V. (2016). Neural architecture search with reinforcement learning. arXiv preprint arXiv:1611.01578.

Chapter 6
Ethics in AI-Driven Sustainable Finance:
Balancing Innovation With Integrity

Quazi Tafsirul Islam
https://orcid.org/0000-0003-3451-1346
North South University, Bangladesh

Munshura Hossain Faria
https://orcid.org/0009-0002-7540-7166
North South University, Bangladesh

ABSTRACT

Artificial intelligence (AI) has made its way through sustainable finance to make it more efficient in data-driven decision-making with machine learning (ML) and data analytics while evaluating sustainability risks, optimize resource allocation, and ensuring ensure informed investment decisions. All these are crucial for long-term economic growth, staying within the boundaries of the Environmental, Social, and Governance (ESG) framework that opens a future scope for technology-driven financial practices along with global sustainability goals. However, along with the profound blessings, AI has brought many systematic risks like bias, lack of ethical governance, data privacy, regulatory issues, exploitation of developing countries, etc. AI is still developing and should be observed and regulated correctly. These unregulated AI systems in finance pose significant risks to Sustainable Development Goals (SDGs). Hence, this chapter stresses the significance of ethical governance with competent regulation, which promotes sustainability without impeding growth.

1. INTRODUCTION

AI is an advanced technology which has improved various sectors including sustainable finance by providing a new effective dimension to decision making through data. With the help of data analysis and machine learning, sustainability matters in business are addressed properly so that the decisions made are firm and resources are well managed. These new technologies will pave the way for advanced

DOI: 10.4018/979-8-3693-9684-1.ch006

technologies in financial applications that respect the ESG principles ensuring economic growth while also targeting global sustainability goals and advocating for other forms of financing.

The ability of AI to analyze huge amounts of data accurately and within a short period of time makes it easier to understand and mitigate sustainability risks which is quite an important factor given the fact that many investors are beginning to look for investments that have ESG scores. It helps to better define green investments, to improve resource use, and to minimize carbon emissions during financial transactions. This technology makes the use of AI much more effective in tackling the challenges of sustainable finance and contributes to the general aim of creating a more sustainable model of the world economy. Say for instance, AI-powered techniques such as the Financial Maximally Filtered Graph (FMFG) have been effective in determining the best green finance approach and have a reasonable success rate in locating environmental enhancement opportunities. This is facilitated by real-time data processing and decision-making frameworks that emphasize digitalization and sustainable growth (Guo & Polák, 2021). AI has shifted green finance via automation, identification, and evaluation of sustainable projects, thereby increasing scalability and accuracy (Behrooz et al., 2023).

However, although AI holds great promise for sustainable finance, one must also admit the challenges and risks it presents. AI systems, being quite complex, may produce biased results or come to decisions that lack transparency. In addition, legislation may not have the pace and capabilities to keep up with the rapid changes that artificial intelligence technologies undergo, and this can result in ethical problems and governance issues. All of these should be addressed in order to prove that indeed AI is moving in the right direction with regard to promoting sustainability goals and economic growth through the advances it makes in finance. Adeyelu et al. (2024) addressed the dual aspect of AI in various areas, but within finance, the AI accelerates the ability to make correct decisions yet also adds other fierced data privacy and algorithmic race issues, and hence demands clear ethical frameworks for managing such issues. Even though AI holds amazing possibilities for integrating sustainable finance, considerable ethical questions accompany this matter. Unsupervised AI poses a significant threat to SDGs, as manifested today. Among those concerns is the existing disparity AI may amplify in addition to the current biases. Up to 134 SDG targets may enable AI while about 59 of them may inhibit AI. Such conditions reveal regulatory oversight, given the risk of imbalance between benefits and threats posed (Vinuesa et al., 2019). Careful development and proper commissioning of such algorithms also foster continued practice of biased norms and behaviors into norms available for accessing finance resources and services (Truby, 2020).

Ethical governance in AI applications does not mean that it favours privacy. Data is everything for a financial institution to conduct business; indeed, many sensitive personal data comprise the enormous amount of data possessed, or processed, by AI systems. There are no ways that can prevent that data from misuse; thus, this leads to violations of privacy and loss of consumers' trust.

Further, regulation will take strides in the new-age technology of AI towards sustainable finance. Speed is in the growing pace of its technology development, and unfortunately, it is still futile in framing significant legal measures and laws that create uncertainties. There can be a situation where a financial practice is solely under the conduct of an AI application and appears illegal without being within the bounds of legal sanction, which may either benefit or harm the consumers or cast doubt on the very source of such financing. The other major ethical dilemma is that of transnational exploitation. History shows that powerful financial institutions have used AI technologies to create inequalities among markets in the world. Countries with fewer financial resources or poorer infrastructure are put at a disadvantage, forcing them to face heavy odds to compete with other countries at their own game. Such situations further increase economic disparities and delay achievement of global sustainability goals (Svetlova, 2022).

Therefore, strengthening solid moral-governance frameworks is necessary for assuring AI applications in sustainable finance to be transparent, fair and accountable. Ethical governance would induce the use of reliable AI technologies to contribute to sustainability without impeding development. Implementing very strong regulatory measures over AI-oriented financial practices is part of the initiative, and thesethresh-old will always enjoy an environment where they can flourish within ethical boundaries. Sustainable AI frameworks postulate the lifecycle management of AI.

2. ETHICAL CONSIDERATIONS IN AI DEPLOYMENT

2.1 Algorithmic Bias

Artificial intelligence in finance unleashes serious ethical quandaries around algorithmic bias, which results from the unintentional aggravation of bias by AI systems. Typically, decision-model training relies on the same data when developing this sort of process, leading to these sorts of bias. Historical data that teach artificial-intelligence systems have already pointed out that they highlight systematic inequalities in the social fabric and personal biases. When biases are embedded into data, AI eternalizes and amplifies them into unfair and discriminatory outcomes.

Reflect on algorithmic bias first by understanding that those involved in AI systems do not come with neutrality. AI systems, after all, imitate biases present in their training data. For instance, financial algorithms which are used in credit scoring or hiring processes tend to devalue underrepresented groups. This happens because the data operated to train these algorithms often comprises implicit biases based on race, gender, socioeconomic status, and other facets (Fazelpour & Danks, 2021). Such being the case, if a dataset reflects historical discrimination against a particular group, the AI system would replicate those patterns producing biased results.

Commonly referenced examples of algorithmic bias in finance include allocating consumer credits on the basis of gender. Of particular note, in 2022, the algorithms used by Apple were widely condemned when it was discovered that women were assigned much lower credit limits than men with commensurate credit profiles. According to analysts, this was not an intentional outcome but rather a byproduct of the data and algorithms that the system utilized (Pérez, 2022). Such examples illuminate the persistent call for rigorous testing and assurance of AI systems before field deployment to detect and mitigate biases.

One of the clear manifestations of algorithmic bias in finance is gender discrimination with respect to credit allocations. It was discovered that, in 2022, under the fire of critical attacks, Apple's AI has allocated women lower credit limits against men envisaging similar financial history. The bias under discussion was not deliberate; it resulted from the data and the algorithms used in the system (Pérez, 2022). Such incidents necessitate the rigorous testing and assurance of AI systems before putting them into real-world applications in order to find and address the biases.

AI structure bias is not limited to gender discrimination; the race bias can also be included. A classic case in the health sector, which obviously has its analogy in financial services, is the analysis of Obermeyer et al. (2019). The authors show that a mechanism that supposedly forecasts people's future healthcare needs is highly biased concerning race. This algorithm was relatively less likely to capture the medical needs of black patients than those of white ones. The sparse use of black people in healthcare services makes them have lower costs; thus, the algorithm's substitution of healthcare expenditure to healthcare needs brought about this bias (Obermeyer et al., 2019). There could be a similar manifestation reporting financial algorithms, which suffer bias from historical inequalities in access to financial services that may lead to discriminatory outcomes.

These ethical implications of algorithmic bias are so profound because biased decisions made by AI systems tend to reinforce pre-existing inequalities and create new forms of discrimination. This is worrying in sustainable finance, which aims to promote equitable and just economic welfare. Given the extent to which AI systems are likely to be biased, their objectives will then be defeated by upholding inequalities in access to financial resources and opportunities.

A comprehensive strategy is essential in dealing with algorithmic biases. Artificial intelligence training is centered around using representative datasets with various characteristics. This will ensure that the statistics will cover the entire cross-section of people and not favor any group over another. Financial organizations must conduct exhaust testing in conjunction with all the rigorous validation techniques to help solve bias issues in AI. Recent tools like bias audits and fairness assessment might be necessary to ascertain that AI systems yield unbiased results.

Transparency remains very prominent as this enables financial firms to demonstrate transparency regarding the data and techniques with which AI systems operate. Stakeholders can thus increase their confidence, and external inquiries can also be done over the artificial intelligence systems. Last but not least, continuous evaluation and monitoring are needed for the AI systems to maintain neutrality and fairness over time meaning often looking for biases in AI systems and changing them to help minimize them.Wang (2024) argues that AI systems in the financial sector must be reviewed by the regulatory framework and that any hidden fairness and bias features that must be removed should be voiced out to society.

Algorithmic bias represents a most grave ethical issue concerning the application of AI in the finance industry. These institutions might ensure that their AI systems embody justice and fairness and not merely cast a shadow before existing disparities if they comprehend and address such biases.

2.2 Fairness and Accountability

AI-forced mechanics responsible for creating the necessary scales of accountability were supposedly erected to avert risks caused by decision-making having been automated or placed into AI systems. Although integrating AI into all public financial systems may significantly enhance efficiency and decision-making, it raises significant ethical questions about fairness and accountability without foreclosing some involvement by the emergent interpretation techniques. It is by far one of the best insights into aiding fairness by having well-specified design principles, for instance, algorithmic fairness as constraints, and XAI or explainable AI. (Hajian et al., 2016).

Framework for accountability: Accountability and fairness are provided in the mode governing the development of AI systems, while the other principle to ensure the desired; such kind of aspectuality with AI can guarantee biased algorithms and biased outcomes. Therefore, more ethical and fair systems can be provided for development with preclusion of bias from data and algorithms. Yet another crucial construct contributing to operational accountability would be Explainable AI, comprising AI models and an explanation-like capability of providing reasoning about results, making them interpretable to stakeholders so they can trust the findings. Transparency and explanation in AI decision-making processes remain indispensable to foster trust and ensure that systems are used responsibly (Hajian et al., 2016).

The construction of strategies that entail fairness-aware data mining is crucial to recognize and eliminate date-mindedly the discriminatory patterns in algorithms examining finance. Data mining is all about examining huge data sources to extract patterns or associations and as far as fairness is concerned, it seeks the recognition of biases or inequalities that may have crept into data before they affect decisions made by the AI systems that govern them. Fairness-aware data mining seeks the result that the outputs produced by the AI system are not in any way making excessive disadvantages to a particular group, thereby engendering and propagating fairness and equity in financial decision-making.

Methods to achieve fairness: Chakraborty and Gummadi (2020) stress fairness in recommendation systems and present techniques that will harmonize stakeholder preferences while guaranteeing non-discriminatory consequences while emphasizing fairness in recommendation systems from both patron and producer viewpoints, as they center on understanding equity for both parties through simplifying the fair recommendation problem into a more condensed form of indivisible indeed distribution problem. Hence, it will help decrease instances of bias and, therefore, promote fairness in sharing the benefits of AI systems.

Fairness of AI systems requires different methods. One approach is embedding fairness constraints within the algorithms from the development. This means defining the certain properties that algorithms need to be able to satisfy while producing fair and non-discriminative outputs. By inserting such constraints, it is possible to design the entire AI system that cannot give any biased results. Explicit AI being focused on transparency and interpretability is essential for fairness. The most feasible way for AI systems to make right judgments will be having the decision-making processes as transparent as possible to the stakeholders so they can have understanding on it.

Continuous monitoring requires evaluation for fairness in AI systems. That means continuously checking an algorithm's performance to detect and mitigate new biases. However, continuously auditing and assessing an AI system for fairness and accountability is what it takes to keep it compliant. All that guarantees fairness and accountability in Al is on the concerted efforts of developers, authorities, and users. Collaboration in developing the best practices and guidelines for the ethical and responsible use of AI technologies can yield open access to the use of those technologies.

2.3 Ethical Frameworks for AI in Finance

Moral norms are necessary in making sure that AI technologies adhere to social and legal standards. Continuing this integration of Ai within the financial sector includes developing good frameworks of ethical practice that mitigate risks and provide opportunities for responsible use. It directs the designs of AI systems as implemented in practice and oversight to guarantee that they are made equitable, transparent, and accountable.

Evaluation of Ethical Guidelines: The ethical AI guidelines at the moment articulate some of the most important principles such as transparency, fairness, and dependability. Unfortunately, these principles are often not put into practical use. Translucent makes an understanding of AI decision-making processes possible for stakeholders to see how decisions are made and why. Fairness ensures that there is no discrimination against any group by AI systems and that their output is equally just. According to Kordzadeh and Ghasemaghaei, individuals and organizations need to be liable for results that follow AI system decisions and actions (2021).

For this purpose, they (2021) put digital put into a model with algorithmic biases and fair manner and decision-making behaviors. After approval, they stressed that it is crucial to identify and fix biases at the data collection step and in algorithm development. For instance, nowadays, people appear to use partial shades in answering such questions. How do demographic elements that relate to bias factor into fairness perceptions, and how do these two elements increase biases in fairness perceptions? Only by understanding how biases contribute to fairness perceptions can organizations design mechanisms by which they can counterbalance them to be certain in their AI-based systems; otherwise, fairness regarding any possible outcomes shall remain dubious. At the end of the day, it involves continuous monitoring and evaluating to counteract bias that may be created over time. (Kordzadeh & Ghasemaghaei, 2021).

Democratic fairness of algorithms calls for the political establishment to offer additional input on matters of fairness which can hinder the monopolization of definitions of fairness. This is why regulation is important for codes or guidelines on ethical AI. Contrastingly, governments could enact legislative and policy instruments that would help promote fairness, transparency and accountability in running and designing AI technologies and ensuring that they would follow societal pursuants and legal standards (Wong, 2019).

It can also subvert the power imbalances that exists in the AI ecosystem by democratizing the definitions and standards of fairness, which in this context goes a long way to ensure that the vast arrays of perspectives in fairness are well represented to mirror the broader society. This should be translated into inclusive policymaking processes that invite stakeholders from different sectors like the tech, finance domain, academia and civil society (Wong, 2019).

Regulation itself can give a structure toward accountability as it lays down duties and consequences for non-respect of such duties. Such measures may include transparency reporting, routine auditing, and punitive measures related to nonconformity to ethical norms for organizations. Introduction of such measures in the AI development and application process may motivate firms to prioritize ethics in their operations.

3. GOVERNANCE STRUCTURES FOR AI IN SUSTAINABLE FINANCE

3.1 Overview of AI Governance in Financial Services

AI governance is all about ensuring that AI technology is used fairly and safely, with due account to the principles of fairness, accountability and stakeholder engagement. Thereby, financial service firms are required to continuously build strongly governed structures that harmonize AI's ethical and responsible use. Governance frameworks are very germane in containing the threats posed by AI systems, especially since they find applications in the most critical decision-making processes.

Necessity of Governance Frameworks: Institutional governance goes a long way to contain risk of the rise of Ai systems within financial services and particularly tapping into significant decision-making processes. Compliance, fairness, and operational transparency become top priorities amidst the governance frameworks. Therefore, to ensure sound AI Governance, a clear set of guiding principles and standards should be adopted for the designing, deployment, and operation of AI technology, which particularly ensures the adherence to ethical principles as well as legal conditions, such as personal data protection laws and anti-discrimination regulations, by these AI systems (Kurshan et al., 2020).

In addition, the governance institutes also assure the AI system's transparency and accountability. Transparency in AI is making the procedures understandable to the stakeholders, including how decisions are taken using the data to inform those decisions. Accountability involves acknowledging of individuals and institutions for the outcomes derived from AI systems. This may include enforcing tools for auditing and tracking AI systems to guarantee that it operates as intended and avoid producing biased or discriminatory outcomes. By prioritizing compliance, fairness, and transparency, governance frameworks help build trust over AI procedures and ethical use in financial services (Kurshan et al., 2020).

Integrating in Risk Management the Governance of AI: Various frameworks push for AI governance considerations in the context of risk management to ensure an organization innovates with a clear conscience when dealing with fairness and operational risk issues. The purpose of including AI governance in a risk management system is to systematically identify, assess, and mitigate the risks of introducing AI technologies. In the process of accomplishing this, implications include addressing algorithmic biases or fairness, maintaining data privacy, and establishing cyber protection mechanisms (Lee et al., 2020).

One way to embed AI governance in risk management includes regular examination of the AIs' operations to identify potential risks and areas for improvement and in compliance with ethical and legal standards. With the provision of clear guidelines, institutions can now combine these with risk management policies that adequately address the unique challenges entailed in the implementation of AI in their systems, so as to provide guidance with respect to ethical use of data, protocols for addressing algorithmic biases, and systems to assure transparency and accountability in AI decision processes (Lee et al., 2020).

Such use of AI governance could render the institutions quite sufficiently prepared to address multiple levels of AI applications with regard to ethical considerations applicable to the envisaged practice; thus, by maintaining effective AI governance and ethics, institutions can ensure responsible use of AI technology and derive the benefits without jeopardizing fairness and transparency. Furthermore, organizations would be capable of embedding AI governance into their risk management initiatives and could act as a driving factor in anticipating and addressing emerging risks and challenges to facilitate continual improvement and venturous innovation.

3.2 Regulatory Approaches to AI

Features of regulation must be such that they facilitate healthy practice of ethical AI while balancing innovation and risk. In this respect, the financial services sector relies on the increasing connection of AI and regulatory feature development with roles in making rules and ensuring enforcement. These directions further provide regulators with flexibility in creativity and innovation. Good regulation should help in risk mitigation due to AI; algorithm misuse, systemic failures, and consumer-centered innovations should not cover loss of consumer safety.

The role of regulatory bodies: commercial and financial application of AI should be regulated as it is in other industrial sectors. Important regulatory requirements would include effective regulations that provide safety and protection to the consumer. These would include some of the necessary conditions for avoiding the risks presented by algorithm misuse. It provides a moral compass for AI use, associated standards of practice that must meet by financial institutions to make it difficult to cause systemic market failure and direct protection of consumer interests. As described by Lee (2019), the framework of regulations has to some extent mitigated the following classified risks on AI, in terms of privacy in data, decisions, and market manipulation possibilities. In defining explicit criteria and monitoring compliance, it can help ensure appropriate and moral use of AI systems (Lee, 2019).

In addition, regulations can hold companies responsible for the consequences arising from their AI systems and introduce regulations that encourage transparency about AI implication measures, such as requiring financial institutions to clarify the way in which AI algorithms operate and what data they leverage. Regulatory authorities can also set rules for fairness, thereby assuring that AI does not discriminate against any groups or make uneven decisions among them. Importantly, the regulatory authorities define and enforce this measurement system, thereby favoring moral application in financial services among AI.

International frameworks for compliance: Global AI governance frameworks really give a master-program in the transparency, fairness, and accountability of AI systems. Of course, a practical demonstration is the European Union General Data Protection Regulation (GDPR), which put its tentacles worldwide. Very tough under the GDPR are the privacy and data protection rules, not guaranteeing that people will control their private data, but even requiring companies to be transparent and forward in their use of such information. Such principles are the bedrock of public faith in AI systems operating ethically.

International guidelines under proper AI management have equity as well as accountability. Many guidelines were to be formulated regarding the responsible, open, inclusive, and transparent use and engineering of AI systems. The OECD's AI Principles, which the G20 has adopted, outline values-based policies on AI that encompass fairness, translucency, and responsibility, just one example. Such regulation intends toward making, creating, and implementing AI as welfare for humanity.

Proactive regulation, as promoted by Truby et al. (2020), emphasizes preemptive measures to control detriments before surfacing. In such a case, it means that regulatory stipulations would be enacted for awareness of risks early on developing while deploying an AI system. By being proactive, risk regulators can identify those risks that would occur in order to provide a framework for squashing that before it would start harming the intended promise. Actions that would fall under pre-emptive regulation include impact assessments, ethics review boards, and periodic auditing of AI systems. Proactive regulation helps confirm that AI technologies are developed and deployed within an appropriately managed environment that prevents harm and nurtures public trust in AI systems (Truby et al., 2020).

3.3 Algorithmic Transparency and Accountability

Such openness has to play a central role in winning the trust of stakeholders and ethical usage of financial AI systems. Transparency and accountability are important in imparting confidence and promote ethical use of AI systems especially considering their increasing application in financial services. To attain algorithmic transparency, stakeholders must be able to comprehend the decision making process in artificial intelligence systems as well as observe their reasoning. Accountability will ensure that an individual and organization have artificial intelligence systems adhere to moral standards and societal norms and answer for the results they generate. Algorithmic transparency is increasingly being recognized as a basic right. Much work is being done on enforcing provisions on transparency measures in the EU and the US, through acts like the AI Act itself and along industry-specific lines. The proposed AI Act of the European Commission aims to exert control over AI systems in order to advance accountability, transparency, and fairness. It contains provisions with respect to the transparency obligations, in turn requiring AI developers to release translucent information about how their systems work and the data they process. So that trust is built up in processes, and legitimate usage is ensured (Engelmann, 2023).

Honest and forthright communication about such predicaments is the best way to discover them and consequently confront the justice systems. The decision-making process by which the AI systems penetrate is open to the shareholders, ensuring that the algorithms and the data do not give rise to skewed or discriminatory outputs. The systems are also maintained by promoting ethical standards. This motivates equity and accountability. In view of the right to transparency, Engelmann (2023) argues that developers should be made to answer such kind of a question, while at the same time emphasizing letting ethical issues run throughout the development processes and implementation of their systems.

Efforts across regions: Numerous strategies have been implemented; the various regions have attempted to ensure algorithmic transparency and accountability in different ways. There is a need for strong governance structures, including transparency audits and compliance protocols as stated by the European Union. Such criteria provide transparency on the systems and thus make them accountable, often creating faith and responsible use. In such cases, transparency audits involve an independent assessment of that system and determination of its transparency and fairness to ensure operation according to ethical and legal standards.(Gasser & Almeida 2017).

Being exactly of opposite kind, the United States emphasis is more like self-regulations and adaptive governance codes to promote the innovations alongside the control. Self-regulation is where the industry actors outline their own guidelines and standards that allow for a further level of flexibility and innovation since they can adjust to the evolving technologies and market demands. A category of adaptive governance is thus regulatory frameworks that would evolve towards the given emerging risk and challenge dynamics associated with the technologies for them to ensure the openness (Gasser & Almeida, 2017).

They are approaches for which the outcome to be achieved is thus the balancing of transparency and accountability on the one hand and innovation and flexibility on the other. These are AI tickers for financial services. It's amazing; however, it has its obviously unique benefits and perils. Each of the geographical regions has different strategies with which to cope with it. Transparency and accountability have to be algorithmically into the systems so that they may be trusted and used wisely and ethically in the terms and lay values of the society.

4. ADDRESSING ALGORITHMIC BIAS AND ENSURING TRANSPARENCY IN AI

4.1 Sources of Bias in AI Models

Two main reasons for algorithmic bias related to data selection and the algorithm design. Understanding and addressing these reasons can make AI's consistency and transparency concepts true because the AI prejudice can lead to discrimination, which destroys the user's trust and effectiveness of AIdriven financial services.

Data selection bias: The training datasets often simply ingest historical prejudice or misunderstand certain minority data; this gives rise to biased AI predictions. All too often while training upon it actually understands this and tries to copy or imitate the biases, resulting unfairness. For example, it has been shown that the biases in algorithms for credit approval are mostly due to the scanty data into which this credit decision-making analysis is made. If the most affluent citizens predominantly define the data set, a model of AI will not be able in general to perform useful measurements for other groups, and unfair practices will occur. This is particularly important because biased and unrepresentative credit approval algorithms can deny people loans or credit who historically do not subscribe to the foundation but are not considered worthwhile in their eyes because of their race (Daneshjou et al., 2021).

Bias from data selection: Diversified and figurative datasets are vital to the empowerment of models in building an environment of training by gathering diverse demographic groups and ensuring that the dataset represents the accurate population for which it is going to be served. Data augmentation and synthetic data generation can yield balanced data sets. Regular audits and evaluations of training data will also identify and address biases. According to Daneshjou et al. (2021), AI creators can render forecasts less biased and facilitate the right in AI systems through this.

Algorithmic design flaws: Badly designed models propagate the bias in the data or even introduce biases unknowingly. This happens even when neutral training data are included; biased outcomes are ensured by the algorithmic design. An example is where an AI model has been designed without consideration for fairness constraints and is thus optimizing for accuracy alone: it produces discriminatory results. Schmidt and Biessmann (2020) indicate that measurement of transparency, when not done carefully, can also propagate bias. For instance, AI biased decision explanations can add fuel to a fire of bias and further distance the actual workings of your algorithm behavior (Schmidt and Biessmann, 2020).

There must be multifaceted solutions to algorithmic design flaws. One best way tends to be an incorporation of fairness constraints directly into the algorithm while developing it. This involves imposing criteria on the algorithm so as to ensure that its computation outputs match the definitions of unbiasedness and nondiscrimination. Regularisation and fairness-aware machine learning included in the algorithmic learning will also tend to minimize data prejudice effects. Moreover, explainable AI (XAI) bring transparency and understandable reasoning into AI judgments; thus, in this way, it will allow stakeholders to examine and trust the system outputs (Schmidt & Biessmann, 2020).

Periodic testing and validating of the AI models are also very important to detect and rectify defects in the algorithms. It involves the assessment of the algorithms using diverse datasets to ensure that a fair and equal end product is produced. Keeping constant check and improvement of AI models ensures that models in future will hover around their thresholds of fairness and transparency. Algorithmic design flaws can be attended to in developing AI systems that operate with ethics and promote user trust.

4.2 Strategies for Bias Mitigation

Active methods, such as the use of diversified datasets, continuous auditing, and explainable AI mechanisms, are required to mitigate bias in AI. Algorithmic Prejudice is a way to ensure right and fairness in the AI-Powered Financial Services. Approaches identified to take care of the issues are several.

Diverse datasets: Data from different populations has been used to make up for any bias involved and to achieve more generalization of models. Such AI trained models on diverse datasets and encompassing wide demographic ranges would give fairer and objective results. Research shows that public datasets import a wider variety regarding their demographic in contributing to better fairness benchmarks (Giunchiglia et al. 2021).

Many datasets ensure that an AI model learns from a variety of sources so that no one group can be made to gain or lose disproportionately. Such strategy could promote wider acceptance of AI-based financial services while enhancing precision and reliability of AI in forecasting-the builders of a system could hence minimize bias and raise equality within their models by relying on training data representative of the target population.

Constant auditing: Algorithmic audits are crucial for identifying and correcting AI biases. The continuous auditing of AI models aims towards finding and fixing loopholes in these models by analytics at regular intervals. Raji and Buolamwini's "Gender Shades" study, which was published in 2019, is an excellent example of an algorithmic audit. This paper uncovered gender-and-skin-type biases in commercial artificial intelligence face recognition systems. After the biased results from the study were made available to the public, these systems underwent massive changes. Regular auditing reports an assurance of fairness by verifying and updating AI models and facilitating accountability and transparency. Thus, developers are very much suited to spot and fix bias-causing factors, such as unevenly represented datasets or flawed computations. Continuous audits ensure trust in AI systems and ethical and responsible behavior-Raji & Buolamwini, 2019.

Explains the fact that explainable AI (XAI): Interpretability-prone models allow stakeholders to understand and argue with the idea of biases. With the role in de-mystifying those decision-making systems, explainable AI frameworks count upon their utility in the areas of eliminating ambiguity in such systems. The third portion of explainability is to make all the AI models' used decision-making processes intelligible and clear to the stakeholders. This should enable a scrutiny of the AI system's outputs, so that decisions are fair and just. XAI makes it possible for both internal and external auditors and stakeholders to be aware of the nature of the systems and algorithms involved and hence enables identification and treatment of such biases. For instance, according to Lu et al. (2020), the significance of explainability in AI systems can improve accountability and transparency in processes of decision-making and risk management. Such frameworks allow explainable AI to develop an in-depth understanding of AI models, allowing developers to make sure their systems are performing ethically and not producing biased consequences. Bringing the black box of AI to light promotes fairness and trust in AI monetary sectors by making clear the AI decision-making process. (Lu et al., 2020)

4.3 Enhancing Transparency Through Explainable AI (XAI)

XAI, or explainable artificial intelligence, augments a decision made by AI alongside its reliability and comprehensibility, which brings along accurate and easily available justification of the AI models' decision-making process and thus facilitates communication between end users and technology engineers.

Role of XAI in stakeholder trust: XAI helps develop confidence among stakeholders. It describes how the process of arriving at a decision occurs, thereby filling a gap between the technical developer and the end user. Increasing understandability by making AI models more trustworthy among stakeholders such as consumers, regulators, and business leaders would improve trust in AI systems. Transparency mechanisms such as interpretability checkpoints would allow stakeholders to look within the decision to some of the factors and data points driving particular decisions. This will develop trust because users can understand and evaluate the fairness as well as accuracy with which AI has driven its decisions. For instance, how interpretability checkpoints might improve transparency and ensure that all parties in the decision-making are sufficiently and straightforwardly grasped by it.

The promotion of fairness and accountability among stakeholders, empowering them to ensure that AI models are ethical and not biased, is achieved by providing clear explanations, which are also essential in addressing algorithmic bias and discrimination concerns. When stakeholders can see how decisions are made, they are better equipped to identify and manage the present biases in the system. Further, XAI may provide much-needed transparency to demonstrate compliance with eligibility criteria by organizations in their AI systems, proving regulatory sufficiency on their part.

Regulatory implications: It enshrines the "right to explanation" covering an important aspect of the top enables: individual access to understanding the effects of algorithms in decision-making processes affecting them. The GDPR orders companies to explain adequately and explicably the decisions taken by AI algorithms, especially where data-related events have direct consequences on individuals. That is, as stated under an important principle of the law of data protection and privacy, it assumes to be the sole indication that subjects are informed as to how their data is being processed and how decisions are taking place.

The insistence that XAI should form a part of any regulatory framework hanging out pretty much the value of its exponent-from clarity to accountability. To such regulations as the GDPR, organizations are bound to promote faith and conviction of the living in AI procedures by requiring clear explanations for algorithmic conclusions. It brings in place those regulatory measures for organizations to build solid systems through which XAI could uphold the transparency of output from the model used. These laws push for transparency in the same line with the ultimate goal of protecting subjective rights through fostering ethical AI practices.

Implementation challenges: Besides creating an answer, the task is to provide transparency without overwhelming the users with excessive details. Almost all of the Effective XAI frameworks need detail without sacrificing clearness or compressible understanding with technical jargon or complexities. It is not the least possible knowledge that confuses users but actually differentiates the focus of the same, not-all-clear guidelines for persons while being over-detailed. Several sources show that some higher matters must be taken into account when deciding how to do this. With that definition, it is firm that strong XAI should be understood as an access-providing frame for meaningful explanations fitted for easy understanding and hence usable by the common masses.

It can be well accomplished using techniques like visualization, simplification of technical terminology, and contextualized explanations-all of which will stack organizational purposes into the benefits of XAI for users, making AI-natural learning processes. Further, constant user feedback will enable organizations to continuously evolve their XAI frameworks for different kinds of stakeholders while sustaining the necessary transparency.

5. REGULATORY FRAMEWORKS FOR ETHICAL AI GOVERNANCE

Using AI in finance has many benefits. Major benefits include efficient decision making, risk management and efficient operation. At the same time, using AI might also introduce some risks associated with bias, lack of transparenct, and ethical concerns. Hence, it is very important to establish a reliable AI use guideline in order to protect AI usage. Ethical implementation of AI is as important as new innovation in AI application. According to Krijger (2023) extensive work was done by Volksbank on the framework for its ethical AI shows organizational conceptualization, ethical governance structure, and even triggers concerning ethical inquiry. The EU guidelines on ethical issues in AI and financial industries are described, with the inclusion of case studies related to mortgage automation, trade reconciliations, and algo trading (Huang et al., 2021).

5.1. Global AI Ethics Guidelines

There are many well-established AI ethics guidelines available. Many countries, universities, research labs, and large companies have developed their handbook to use AI efficiently and easily protect their future from AI-related threats. These guidelines are introduced to protect the core principles such as transparency, fairness, accountability and privacy. However, different policies vary on how to address such concerns and how the core principles are interpreted (Jobin et al., 2019).

The European Union (EU), for example, has been a pioneer in establishing guidelines through its "Ethics Guidelines for Trustworthy AI." These guidelines emphasize seven key principles. The seven principles proposed by EU in their AI ethics manual are human agency and oversight, technical robustness and safety, privacy and data governance, transparency, diversity and fairness, societal well-being, and accountability (Floridi, 2019). While they set a solid ethical foundation, they primarily serve as recommendations rather than enforceable rules. EU attempts to consistently implement AI ethics across their member states (Hickman & Petrin, 2020).

Guidelines have been more decentralized in the United States. The policy has seen efforts from individual states, federal agencies, and private organizations. For example, the National Institute of Standards and Technology (NIST) released a voluntary framework for AI risk management, focusing on AI's ethical design and implementation (Daly et al., 2020). But, the lack of a cohesive national policy has created gaps in enforcement and ethical compliance (Fukuda-Parr & Gibbons, 2021).

Globally, several organizations, such as the OECD and UNESCO, have developed guidelines aiming to standardize AI ethics. Although there have been several attempts, the OECD AI Principles, which 38 countries have adopted, emphasize inclusivity, accountability, and transparency. It promotes for AI systems that benefit society while minimizing risks (Hagendorff, 2019). UNESCO's "Recommendation on the Ethics of Artificial Intelligence," adopted in 2021, extends beyond technical guidelines to emphasize ethical considerations in AI research, design, and development, promoting human rights and sustainable development (Khan et al., 2021).

5.2. Implementation of Ethical AI in Financial Regulations

Integrating AI ethics into financial regulations is essential for aligning AI deployment with sustainable development goals (SDGs) and protecting consumer interests. The EU has significantly improved this area by embedding AI ethics principles within financial regulations. The European framework aims to ensure that AI systems used in finance adhere to fairness, transparency, and accountability. They have given special attention to credit scoring, trading algorithms, and anti-money laundering measures (Rodriguez, 2022). This integration aligns AI with ethical principles and supports financial inclusion and consumer protection.

The EU's regulatory approach includes mandatory compliance measures such as impact assessments, algorithmic transparency, and data protection audits. For instance, AI systems deployed in financial decision-making must undergo ex-ante risk assessments to identify potential ethical and legal issues before deployment (Huang et al., 2021). This proactive approach aims to minimize risks while supporting innovation.

In contrast, the United States has adopted a more laissez-faire approach, focusing on innovation-driven policies rather than stringent regulations. However, this has raised concerns about consumer protection and market integrity, prompting calls for more robust regulatory measures to govern AI use in financial services (Lee, 2019). Experts argue that without clear legal frameworks, AI systems can exacerbate inequalities and increase risks, making ethical governance a pressing need (Maple et al., 2023).

International organizations like the Financial Stability Board (FSB) and the International Monetary Fund (IMF) have also advocated for ethical AI governance in finance. They recommend incorporating ethical considerations into global financial regulations, emphasizing the importance of transparency, accountability, and fairness in AI-powered financial services (Héder, 2020).

5.3. Practical Governance Tools

Practical tools for implementing ethical AI governance in finance include algorithmic audits, certification processes, and compliance checks. Algorithmic audits involve reviewing AI models to ensure they operate within ethical and legal boundaries. These audits assess fairness, transparency, and potential biases, providing a mechanism to detect and mitigate risks before AI systems are deployed in financial markets (Truby et al., 2020).

Certification processes are another practical tool, offering a standardized approach to verifying AI systems' compliance with ethical guidelines. For example, the "Trustworthy AI Certification" in the EU ensures that AI systems meet specified ethical standards, including non-discrimination and data protection (Agbese et al., 2023). Certification encourages adherence to moral principles, incentivizing developers to prioritize ethical AI design.

Compliance checks are critical to maintaining ethical standards in AI deployment. These checks involve monitoring AI systems to ensure they comply with established ethical and regulatory requirements. In finance, compliance checks are essential to maintaining trust and integrity. They help prevent issues like discriminatory lending, fraud, and privacy breaches (Vakkuri et al., 2020).

Combining these tools ensures that ethical AI is not only a theoretical ideal but a practical reality in financial services. By implementing algorithmic audits, certification processes, and compliance checks, financial institutions can develop AI systems that are fair, transparent, and accountable.

6. CHALLENGES IN ETHICAL AI IMPLEMENTATION

6.1. Barriers to Transparency and Accountability

The complexity of AI systems presents substantial barriers to transparency and accountability. Given high-stakes sectors like finance, monitoring and implementing policies is difficult. Transparency in AI refers to stakeholders' ability to understand how AI algorithms process information, make decisions, and produce outcomes. However, maintaining transparency in complex AI models is challenging due to several factors:

AI models, especially those based on deep learning, often operate as "black boxes," making their decision-making processes opaque. This lack of clarity can prevent users from understanding why a particular decision was made, complicating efforts to establish accountability (Kempton & Vassilakopoulou, 2021). For example, in financial applications like credit scoring, AI models can generate risk assessments that are difficult to explain to regulators or end-users. Thus potentially undermining trust in AI-driven financial systems.

While AI ethics guidelines emphasize the importance of transparency, current legal frameworks often fail to enforce these principles effectively. Existing regulations like the European Union's AI Act attempt to promote transparency but face implementation challenges. Defining adequate transparency is difficult (Kiseleva et al., 2022). There is also a lack of standardized requirements across jurisdictions, creating inconsistent applications of transparency principles.

The technical challenges in achieving transparency in AI include limited interpretability of complex models and insufficient tools for explainable AI (XAI). Current XAI tools focus on making AI more understandable but often fail to offer meaningful insights for non-technical users. For example, while AI developers may find some interpretability techniques helpful, financial regulators or consumers may not understand the technical jargon or statistical outputs used to explain AI decisions (Kempton & Vassilakopoulou, 2021).

Transparency must be embedded across different layers of AI systems, ranging from the development phase to the end-user interactions. However, current AI governance often narrows on algorithmic transparency, neglecting broader systemic factors such as organizational accountability and data governance. Without clear roles and responsibilities among stakeholders (e.g., AI developers, users, and regulators) further complicates accountability (Kiseleva et al., 2022).

Ensuring transparency may sometimes conflict with other ethical requirements, such as privacy or data protection. For example, disclosing certain information to enhance transparency could expose sensitive data, thus violating data protection laws (Kempton & Vassilakopoulou, 2021). In financial applications, this tension between openness and privacy is particularly evident, as financial institutions are legally obligated to protect customer information while also being required to explain AI-driven decisions.

AI systems must incorporate comprehensive transparency measures throughout their development and deployment processes. Multi-disciplinary collaboration involving computer scientists, ethicists, legal experts, and financial regulators is crucial to creating transparent AI models that can be effectively explained to diverse stakeholders. Besides, implementing user-centered design principles can enhance the interpretability of AI models, making them more accessible and understandable to non-technical users (Kiseleva et al., 2022).

6.2. Risks of Unregulated AI Use

Using AI in finance without proper regulation poses significant risks to financial stability, consumer protection, and the broader economy. Several case examples highlight the potential consequences of unregulated AI:

AI models trained on biased data can produce discriminatory outcomes in financial services, such as credit scoring or loan approvals. For instance, AI systems that have learned from historical lending data may inadvertently favor certain demographic groups over others, perpetuating existing social inequalities (Truby et al., 2020). This lack of regulation can result in discriminatory lending practices, harming marginalized communities and reducing trust in financial institutions.

The use of AI in high-frequency trading and other automated financial systems has introduced new systemic risks. AI algorithms can make rapid trading decisions based on minimal data, sometimes leading to unintended market fluctuations and economic crises. For example, the 2010 Flash Crash in the US stock market was partly attributed to high-frequency trading algorithms acting on limited information, causing a sudden and significant drop in stock prices (Truby et al., 2020).

In financial services, AI models are increasingly used to provide personalized advice through robo-advisors. However, without adequate regulation, these systems may offer misleading or incomplete advice, exposing consumers to financial losses (Truby et al., 2020). Moreover, consumers may not fully understand the recommendations made by AI systems, leading to over-reliance or misuse of AI-driven advice.

Unregulated AI systems are vulnerable to exploitation by malicious actors. For instance, AI can be used to develop sophisticated fraud techniques, such as deepfakes for identity theft or AI-powered attacks on financial systems. These threats pose significant risks to economic security, consumer data, and overall market stability (Truby et al., 2020).

AI's rapid evolution has outpaced existing legal and ethical frameworks, leading to a regulatory gap that exacerbates the risks associated with unregulated AI use. The absence of clear guidelines for ethical AI deployment allows companies to prioritize efficiency over fairness, transparency, and accountability, leading to unethical outcomes in financial decisions (Truby et al., 2020).

To mitigate these risks, it is essential to develop robust regulatory frameworks that align AI applications with ethical principles, particularly in finance. Proactive regulation, including real-time audits, compliance checks, and ethical guidelines, can ensure AI systems operate responsibly and equitably. Additionally, regulatory bodies need to adopt a risk-based approach, focusing on areas where AI poses the most significant risks to financial stability and consumer protection (Truby et al., 2020).

7. CONCLUSION

7.1. Summary of Ethical and Governance Needs

Applying AI in sustainable finance introduces opportunities for enhanced decision-making, improved resource allocation, and long-term growth aligned with environmental, social, and governance (ESG) principles. However, ethical considerations such as transparency, accountability, and robust governance are critical to ensuring that AI promotes fairness, supports sustainable development goals (SDGs), and protects stakeholders.

Transparency is essential for building trust in AI systems and making them interpretable for stakeholders. It ensures that decision-making processes are clear and understandable, enabling financial institutions to provide explanations for AI-driven decisions. This is particularly important in finance, where transparency helps address concerns about algorithmic biases and opaque decision-making, which can perpetuate inequalities in credit scoring, loan approvals, and investment management. Despite its importance, transparency is often limited by the "black-box" nature of complex AI models, making it challenging to understand and regulate AI's impact on financial outcomes (Ofori-Sasu et al., 2023).

Establishing accountability in AI systems is crucial to ensuring that decisions are ethical and comply with regulatory standards. Effective accountability measures involve clarifying roles and responsibilities among AI developers, users, and regulatory bodies. These measures enable organizations to trace AI decisions back to their sources, allowing stakeholders to assess the fairness and accuracy of AI systems. However, achieving accountability in AI governance remains a complex task due to the rapid evolution of AI technologies and the challenges of implementing uniform regulations across jurisdictions (Elamin, 2023).

The integration of robust governance structures is essential for regulating AI in sustainable finance. These structures should be designed to uphold ethical principles, mitigate risks, and ensure compliance with sustainability criteria. Effective governance frameworks must incorporate regular audits, impact assessments, and feedback mechanisms to address potential biases and unintended consequences. Additionally, governance structures should include guidelines that align with global standards for sustainable finance, such as the EU's Sustainable Finance Disclosure Regulation (SFDR) and the proposed AI Act, which emphasize transparency, accountability, and ethical AI deployment in financial sectors (Ofori-Sasu et al., 2023).

Implementing ethical frameworks that align AI technologies with sustainability goals is critical for promoting responsible finance. These frameworks should be developed in consultation with diverse stakeholders, including regulatory authorities, financial institutions, and civil society organizations, to ensure that AI systems are inclusive, fair, and adaptable to changing societal needs. Ethical frameworks should address both technical and social dimensions of AI, considering not only model design and data inputs but also the broader socio-economic impacts of AI on financial inclusion, fairness, and access to resources (Elamin, 2023).

To achieve ethical AI in sustainable finance, it is vital to integrate transparency, accountability, and robust governance structures at every stage of AI development and deployment. These measures will enhance trust in AI systems and ensure that they contribute positively to financial stability, sustainable growth, and social equity.

7.2. Future Directions for Research and Practice

As AI continues to evolve and play a central role in sustainable finance, there is an urgent need for ongoing research and policy development to address emerging ethical challenges. The following directions are proposed for advancing ethical AI governance and aligning AI applications with sustainability goals:

Future research should focus on creating more comprehensive regulatory standards that govern AI use in sustainable finance. These standards should address the risks posed by AI systems, such as biases in credit scoring, investment recommendations, and financial decision-making. Regulatory bodies must collaborate with AI developers, financial institutions, and other stakeholders to create adaptable regulations that can respond to rapid technological changes while maintaining consistency with global sustainability goals (Ofori-Sasu et al., 2023).

There is a continuous need to improve ethical guidelines for AI applications in finance. Ethical guidelines should emphasize fairness, transparency, and accountability while also considering the unique challenges of sustainable finance, such as environmental and social impacts. Research should focus on developing sector-specific ethical guidelines that align AI applications with broader sustainability frameworks like the UN SDGs and ESG standards. This approach can help ensure that AI systems optimize financial outcomes and contribute to social equity and environmental sustainability (Elamin, 2023).

Explainable AI (XAI) is crucial for making AI models more interpretable and understandable to both technical and non-technical users. Future research should explore advanced XAI techniques that can enhance transparency and accountability in financial decision-making processes. These techniques should be designed to provide meaningful explanations that can be understood by diverse stakeholders, including financial regulators, investors, and consumers. Additionally, XAI tools should be integrated into governance frameworks to ensure that AI systems remain compliant with ethical standards throughout their lifecycle (Ofori-Sasu et al., 2023).

To promote fairness and inclusion, future AI research should prioritize the development of models that can address systemic biases in financial services. This involves improving algorithmic fairness and considering socio-economic factors that may affect AI outcomes, such as disparities in access to financial services or biased historical data. Research should also focus on creating tools that can detect and correct biases in real time, ensuring that AI systems provide equitable financial services to all stakeholders (Elamin, 2023).

Advancing ethical AI in sustainable finance requires collaboration between regulators, financial institutions, AI developers, and civil society. Future research should explore ways to facilitate cross-sector partnerships that can support ethical AI development and deployment. These collaborations can lead to the creation of best practices, training programs, and public awareness campaigns that promote ethical AI use in finance. Additionally, collaborative efforts can help bridge gaps in understanding and implementation, ensuring that AI technologies are developed and deployed responsibly (Ofori-Sasu et al., 2023).

For ethical AI to have a meaningful impact, it must be integrated into the core operations of financial institutions. Research should investigate practical ways to embed ethical AI principles into financial workflows, risk assessments, and investment strategies. This includes developing tools for continuous monitoring, auditing, and improvement of AI systems and training financial professionals to understand and implement ethical AI guidelines. By making ethical AI a standard practice in finance, institutions can enhance their contributions to sustainability while reducing risks associated with AI deployment (Elamin, 2023).

Continued development of regulatory standards, ethical guidelines, and practical tools is necessary to ensure that AI in sustainable finance supports long-term growth, fairness, and compliance with global sustainability goals. By addressing transparency, accountability, and inclusion, AI can be a powerful tool for driving positive social and environmental outcomes in finance.

8. KEY TAKEAWAYS FOR PRACTITIONERS

The implementation of ethical AI governance in sustainable finance is crucial for ensuring responsible AI deployment. Practitioners can adopt the following practical guidelines and steps to enhance governance structures, mitigate biases, and promote transparency in AI systems.

1. Implementing Ethical Governance Structures for AI

To ensure ethical governance in AI, practitioners should integrate governance frameworks that address ethical principles throughout the AI lifecycle, from development to deployment. Here are key strategies:

AI governance should involve frameworks that are holistic and adaptable. For example, the "Hourglass Model" of AI governance, as described by Mäntymäki et al. (2022), emphasizes a multi-level approach that incorporates organizational and AI system-level governance, ensuring alignment with ethical standards across AI processes (Mäntymäki et al., 2022). This model includes mechanisms such as ethical risk assessments, impact evaluations, and regular audits, which can help organizations comply with evolving ethical requirements and align AI with sustainable finance goals.

Practitioners should conduct regular audits to identify ethical risks and biases in AI systems. Compliance checks can verify adherence to ethical guidelines, helping prevent unintended ethical lapses during AI deployment. Regular audits allow organizations to assess AI models' fairness, transparency, and accountability, fostering trust among stakeholders (Agbese et al., 2023).

AI governance must be inclusive, incorporating feedback from diverse stakeholders, including financial regulators, AI developers, and end-users. Engaging stakeholders ensures that governance measures are practical, context-sensitive, and aligned with real-world financial needs. Such engagement fosters a culture of ethical responsibility across organizations, enhancing both governance and AI performance in sustainable finance contexts (Arcilla et al., 2023).

2. Steps for Mitigating Bias and Ensuring Transparency

Mitigating bias and enhancing transparency in AI models is crucial for promoting fairness in sustainable finance. Practitioners can take the following steps:

AI models should be trained on datasets representing diverse populations and financial contexts to reduce biases. Diverse datasets help prevent biases that can result from over-representation of specific demographic groups. Practitioners should implement processes to update datasets to maintain their relevance and inclusivity regularly (Agbese et al., 2023).

XAI techniques can enhance transparency by making AI models' decision-making processes more understandable to non-technical users. This helps financial institutions explain AI-driven decisions, such as loan approvals or investment recommendations, to clients and regulators. XAI tools should be integrated into AI governance frameworks to ensure that decision-making processes are both transparent and interpretable (Mäntymäki et al., 2022).

Continuous monitoring and adjustment of AI models are essential for detecting biases that may emerge over time. Practitioners should use bias detection tools and conduct periodic evaluations to identify potential biases, ensuring that AI models remain fair and accurate throughout their use in sustainable finance. These evaluations can include algorithmic impact assessments and user feedback mechanisms (Arcilla et al., 2023).

By implementing ethical governance structures, mitigating biases, and enhancing transparency, practitioners can ensure that AI systems in sustainable finance contribute to fairer, more ethical financial outcomes while supporting global sustainability goals.

REFERENCES

Adeyelu, O. O., Ugochukwu, C. E., & Shonibare, M. A. (2024). Ethical implications of ai in financial decision – making: A review with real world applications. *International Journal of Applied Research in Social Sciences*, *6*(4), 608–630. DOI: 10.51594/ijarss.v6i4.1033

Agbese, M., Mohanani, R., Khan, A., & Abrahamsson, P. (2023). Implementing AI Ethics: Making Sense of the Ethical Requirements. *Proceedings of the 27th International Conference on Evaluation and Assessment in Software Engineering*.

Arcilla, A. O., Espallardo, A. K. V., Gomez, C. A. J., Viado, E. M. P., Ladion, V. J. T., Naanep, R. A. T., Pascual, A. R. L., & Artificio, E. B. (2023). Ethics in AI Governance: Comparative Analysis, Implication, and Policy Recommendations for the Philippines. 2023 27th International Computer Science and Engineering Conference (ICSEC), 319-326.

Chakraborty, A., & Gummadi, K. (2020). Fairness in Algorithmic Decision Making. *Proceedings of the 7th ACM IKDD CoDS and 25th COMAD*.https://doi.org/DOI: 10.1145/3371158.3371234

Choung, H., David, P., & Seberger, J. (2023). A multilevel framework for AI governance. *ArXiv*,abs/2307.03198. https://doi.org//arXiv.2307.03198.DOI: 10.48550

Daly, A., Hagendorff, T., Li, H., Mann, M., Marda, V., & Wagner, B. (2020). AI, Governance and Ethics: Global Perspectives. SSRN *Electronic Journal*.

Daneshjou, R., Smith, M., Sun, M., Rotemberg, V., & Zou, J. (2021). Lack of Transparency and Potential Bias in Artificial Intelligence Data Sets and Algorithms: A Scoping Review. *JAMA Dermatology*. Advance online publication. DOI: 10.1001/jamadermatol.2021.3129 PMID: 34550305

Elamin, M. O. I. (2023). Advancing Ethical and Sustainable Economy: Islamic Finance Solutions for Environmental, Social, & Economic Challenges in the Digital Age. *International Journal of Membrane Science and Technology*.

Fazelpour, S., & Danks, D. (2021). Algorithmic bias: Senses, sources, solutions. *Philosophy Compass*. Advance online publication. DOI: 10.1111/PHC3.12760

Floridi, L. (2019). Establishing the rules for building trustworthy AI. *Nature Machine Intelligence*, *1*(5), 261–262.

Fukuda-Parr, S., & Gibbons, E. (2021). Emerging Consensus on 'Ethical AI'. *Global Policy*, *12*(2), 272–284. https://consensus.app/papers/emerging-consensus-ethical-human-rights-critique-fukuda-parr/c1df02a41d7e540fa6de040534b096df

Gasser, U., & Almeida, V. (2017). A Layered Model for AI Governance. *IEEE Internet Computing*, *21*, 58–62. DOI: 10.1109/MIC.2017.4180835

Giunchiglia, F., Otterbacher, J., Kleanthous, S., Batsuren, K., Bogina, V., Kuflik, T., & Tal, A. (2021). Towards Algorithmic Transparency: A Diversity Perspective. *ArXiv*, abs/2104.05658.

Guo, H., & Polák, P. (2021). Artificial Intelligence and Financial Technology FinTech: How AI Is Being Used Under the Pandemic in 2020. *Studies in computational intelligence*, 935, 169-186. https://doi.org/.DOI: 10.1007/978-3-030-62796-6_9

Hagendorff, T. (2019). The Ethics of AI Ethics: An Evaluation of Guidelines. *Minds and Machines, 30*(1), 99–120.

Hajian, S., Bonchi, F., & Castillo, C. (2016). Algorithmic Bias: From Discrimination Discovery to Fairness-aware Data Mining. *Proceedings of the 22nd ACM SIGKDD International Conference on Knowledge Discovery and Data Mining*.https://doi.org/DOI: 10.1145/2939672.2945386

Hemanand, D., Mishra, N., Premalatha, G., Mavaluru, D., Vajpayee, A., Kushwaha, S., & Sahile, K. (2022). Applications of Intelligent Model to Analyze the Green Finance for Environmental Development in the Context of Artificial Intelligence. *Computational Intelligence and Neuroscience*. Advance online publication. DOI: 10.1155/2022/2977824 PMID: 35845917

Hickman, E., & Petrin, M. (2020). Trustworthy AI and Corporate Governance. *European Business Organization Law Review*, *22*, 593–625.

Huang, J., Gupta, A., & Youn, M. (2021). Survey of EU ethical guidelines for commercial AI: Case studies in financial services. *AI and Ethics*, *1*, 569–577. DOI: 10.1007/s43681-021-00048-1

Jobin, A., Ienca, M., & Vayena, E. (2019). The global landscape of AI ethics guidelines. *Nature Machine Intelligence*, *1*, 1–11.

Kempton, A., & Vassilakopoulou, P. (2021). Accountability, Transparency and Explainability in AI for Healthcare. *Frontiers in Artificial Intelligence*.

Kiseleva, A., Kotzinos, D., & Hert, P. (2022). Transparency of AI in Healthcare as a Multilayered System of Accountabilities. *Frontiers in Artificial Intelligence*, 5.

Kordzadeh, N., & Ghasemaghaei, M. (2021). Algorithmic bias: Review, synthesis, and future research directions. *European Journal of Information Systems*, *31*, 388–409. DOI: 10.1080/0960085X.2021.1927212

Krijger, J. (2023). Operationalising ethics for AI in the financial industry: Insights from the Volksbank case study. *Journal of Digital Banking*. https://doi.org/.DOI: 10.69554/yqzc2796

Kurshan, E., Shen, H., & Chen, J. (2020). Towards self-regulating AI: challenges and opportunities of AI model governance in financial services. *Proceedings of the First ACM International Conference on AI in Finance*. https://doi.org/DOI: 10.1145/3383455.3422564

Lee, J. (2019). Access to Finance for Artificial Intelligence Regulation in the Financial Services Industry. *European Business Organization Law Review*, *21*, 731–757. DOI: 10.1007/s40804-020-00200-0

Lee, M., Floridi, L., & Denev, A. (2020). Innovating with Confidence - Embedding AI Governance and Fairness in a Financial Services Risk Management Framework. *Social Science Research Network*. https://doi.org/DOI: 10.2139/SSRN.3830579

Lu, J., Lee, D., Kim, T., & Danks, D. (2020). Good Explanation for Algorithmic Transparency. *Proceedings of the AAAI/ACM Conference on AI, Ethics, and Society*.https://doi.org/DOI: 10.1145/3375627.3375821

Mäntymäki, M., Minkkinen, M., Birkstedt, T., & Viljanen, M. (2022). *Putting AI Ethics into Practice: The Hourglass Model of Organizational AI Governance*. ArXiv.

Maple, C., Szpruch, L., Epiphaniou, G., Staykova, K. S., Singh, S., Penwarden, W., Wen, Y., Wang, Z., Hariharan, J., & Avramović, P. (2023). The AI Revolution. *ArXiv*, *2308*, 16538.

Obermeyer, Z., Powers, B., Vogeli, C., & Mullainathan, S. (2019). Dissecting racial bias in an algorithm used to manage the health of populations. *Science*, *366*, 447–453. DOI: 10.1126/science.aax2342 PMID: 31649194

Ofori-Sasu, D., Donkor, G. N. A., & Abor, J. (2023). Do sustainability ethics explain the impact of country-level corporate governance on financial stability in developing economies? *Journal of Sustainable Finance & Investment*, *13*, 1415–1450.

Raji, I., & Buolamwini, J. (2019). Actionable Auditing: Investigating the Impact of Publicly Naming Biased Performance Results of Commercial AI Products. *Proceedings of the 2019 AAAI/ACM Conference on AI, Ethics, and Society*. https://doi.org/DOI: 10.1145/3306618.3314244

Schmidt, P., & Biessmann, F. (2020). Calibrating Human-AI Collaboration: Impact of Risk, Ambiguity and Transparency on Algorithmic Bias., 431-449. https://doi.org/.DOI: 10.1007/978-3-030-57321-8_24

Truby, J. (2020). Governing Artificial Intelligence to benefit the UN Sustainable Development Goals. *ERN: Regulation (IO) (Topic)*. https://doi.org/.DOI: 10.1002/sd.2048

Truby, J., Brown, R., & Dahdal, A. (2020). Banking on AI. *Law and Financial Markets Review*, *14*(2), 110–120.

Truby, J., Brown, R., & Dahdal, A. (2020). Banking on AI: Mandating a Proactive Approach to AI Regulation in the Financial Sector. *Law and Financial Markets Review*, *14*(2), 110–120.

Vakkuri, V., Kemell, K.-K., Kultanen, J., & Abrahamsson, P. (2020). The Current State of Industrial Practice in AI Ethics. *IEEE Software*, *37*(5), 50–57.

Van Wynsberghe, A. (2021). Sustainable AI: AI for sustainability and the sustainability of AI. *AI and Ethics*, *1*, 213–218. DOI: 10.1007/s43681-021-00043-6

Vinuesa, R., Azizpour, H., Leite, I., Balaam, M., Dignum, V., Domisch, S., Felländer, A., Langhans, S., Tegmark, M., & Nerini, F. (2019). The role of artificial intelligence in achieving the Sustainable Development Goals. *Nature Communications*, *11*. Advance online publication. DOI: 10.1038/s41467-019-14108-y PMID: 31932590

Wang, Y. (2024). Ethical considerations of AI in financial decision. *Computers and Artificial Intelligence*. Advance online publication. DOI: 10.59400/cai.v2i1.1290

Wong, P. (2019). Democratizing Algorithmic Fairness. *Philosophy & Technology*, *33*, 225–244. DOI: 10.1007/s13347-019-00355-w

Chapter 7
AI Chatbots and Market Dynamics:
Analyzing the Impact of AI on the Indian Stock Market

Swagatam Saha
https://orcid.org/0009-0000-1825-2693
Christ University, Bangalore, India

Babita Chaudhary
https://orcid.org/0009-0000-9765-5705
Christ University, Bangalore, India

ABSTRACT

This study examines the potential of ChatGPT v4.0 for stock market analysis, particularly within the Indian stock market. The research uses prompt engineering to assess ChatGPT's ability to recommend stocks, construct portfolios, provide fundamental analysis, and understand price movements. The study combines sentiment analysis of news data with historical price data to forecast future price movements. Results demonstrate ChatGPT's effectiveness in identifying investment opportunities and providing insights for decision-making. The study also evaluates the accuracy of ChatGPT's predictions, finding an 88.89% accuracy rate based on news sentiment analysis and a 94% accuracy rate when integrating sentiment analysis with historical price data. Despite limitations, including constraints in handling large datasets, ChatGPT exhibits promise for supporting investors in the Indian stock market. Future research should focus on refining models and addressing ethical considerations to ensure responsible AI integration in finance.

1. INTRODUCTION

The rapid evolution of financial markets has been closely connected with technological advancements, and one of the most transformative technologies in recent years has been Artificial Intelligence (AI). The emergence of AI chatbots, particularly those driven by Large Language Models (LLMs) such as ChatGPT, is one of its most disruptive uses, redefining the way investors engage with markets and make

DOI: 10.4018/979-8-3693-9684-1.ch007

choices. Thanks to these conversational AI solutions, financial information is now accessible to everyone and is no longer limited to experts or institutional investors. AI chatbots have the potential to usher in a new age in the Indian stock market, where retail involvement is increasing and financial knowledge is becoming increasingly important. These bots are more than simply tools; they are catalysts that help democratize access to financial data, improve market efficiency, and help investors navigate the intricate and stormy waters of the stock market.

AI's introduction into the financial industry has established conventions and brought about relevant changes to trading tactics, portfolio management, and investment decision-making. At the forefront of this change are conversational models like ChatGPT, Gemini, and Co-Pilot, which have drawn notice for their ability to enhance financial decision-making procedures. These AI-driven assistants are crucial in India, a nation where stock market involvement is increasing. An AI interested in financial markets specifically academicians and beginners who are new to the market would be highly beneficial by optimizing both the traditional ways and modern technologies for a better understanding of the market. AI Chatbots have the ability not only to improve investment results but also to greatly increase financial literacy for all types of investors (Das *et al.*, 2024).

1.1 The Role of AI Chatbots in Financial Decision-Making

AI chatbots are more than simply a cutting-edge development in the financial industry; it is radically changing the way that financial decisions are made. Chatbots like ChatGPT can process enormous volumes of data in real-time and provide investors insights that would normally need years of training and in-depth knowledge by utilizing the enormous processing capacity of LLMs. Because these chatbots simplify down sophisticated stock evaluations and market movements into simple English, consumers no longer need to be financial experts to understand them. For instance, an investor may ask for a complete study of a company, and the chatbot would provide it without the need for technical language by pulling information from news, historical data, and current market patterns (Khan & Umer, 2024).

1.2 Enhancing Financial Literacy and Democratizing Access to Financial Markets

Artificial Intelligence has already had a significant impact on the banking industry with its use in fraud detection and algorithmic trading. However, the focus of this research is specifically on the role of the conversational AI in the Indian stock market. India still has a poor level of financial literacy, especially amongst the retail investors. This includes understanding personal money, budgeting, and investing. AI chatbots can be introduced as a tool which possess the exceptional capability of converting intricate financial ideas into comprehensible English. For many, this is the first step towards making well-informed choices and avoiding typical pitfalls like mindlessly adhering to market rumours or giving in to peer pressure.

AI chatbots also provide a fair playing field, which has typically been controlled by financial specialists or institutional investors. Personalized insights that were previously exclusive to the limited ones are now available to retail investors according to their preferences, financial goals, and risk tolerance. The widespread accessibility of excellent financial knowledge marks a revolutionary change in a market like India, where only selected & few well-informed individuals have traditionally held control. Investors are already finding it easier to negotiate the complexities of market volatility and risk due to the integration of these AI-driven technologies; chatbots, that can provide detailed analysis and takes into account both structured financial data and unstructured sources like news (Zheng, 2024).

1.3. The Impact of AI on Market Dynamics

The impact of artificial intelligence (AI) on the Indian stock market is being felt much beyond the reach of regular investors. Artificial intelligence (AI) chatbots are increasing the market participation, enhancing liquidity, and reducing the knowledge gap between institutional and ordinary investors by offering real-time data and tailored recommendations. Thanks to AI's ability to sort through enormous databases and deliver actionable information at previously unheard-of speeds, markets—long chastised for their inefficiencies—may finally be ready for more responsive, agile behaviour (Agarwal *et al.*, 2023).

However, there are certain difficulties with AI's development in the financial markets. When trading choices are influenced by transient changes, an over-reliance on algorithmic models may expose markets to new types of vulnerability and perhaps increase market volatility. These technologies have the potential to worsen price volatility rather than to stabilize them during periods of market stress. While AI can improve portfolio management, (Agarwal *et al.*, 2023) warn that it is important to closely monitor its interaction with larger market circumstances, especially in times of market turbulence. Even with their great capability, AI tools can sometimes go wrong.

1.4. Ethical and Operational Challenges of AI in Finance

Notwithstanding the advantages, there are a number of moral and practical concerns with AI chatbots being widely used in the banking industry. Given that these models frequently inherit the biases present in the datasets they are trained on, bias in AI-generated recommendations is a serious cause for worry. These prejudices, which may be based on socioeconomic class, gender, or race, may quietly seep into financial advice and unfairly cause disadvantage to some investment groups (Khan & Umer, 2024). The uncertainty of AI decision-making, which distinguishes AI chatbots from human advisers in that they never offer clear justifications for their suggestions, exacerbates this problem.

Data privacy is still another important concern. AI chatbots frequently need access to sensitive financial data in order to provide tailored advice. There is a persistent risk of data breaches or improper use of this information, which begs the question of how to protect user trust while guaranteeing the security of personal financial data. The advent of artificial intelligence (AI) involves social as well as technological hazards. The automation of financial processes has the potential to displace employment in customer assistance and advisory services, among other industries, with far-reaching economic ramifications.

Important challenges also count the reliability of AI-generated financial predictions. While AI tools like Gemini or ChatGPT can process vast amounts of data and provide insights that are difficult for humans to generate manually, they are not infallible. Inaccuracies in data or misinterpretations of markets sentiment can lead to flawed predictions, which in turn could result in financial losses for investors (Zheng, 2024). Hence AI tools should not be relied upon as the sole source of investment advice. (Alnefaie, A., 2021).

1.5. The Future of AI Chatbots in the Indian Stock Market

AI chatbots are poised to become vital resources for Indian investors in the future. Market involvement will probably increase as more individuals use these tools, which will help create a more effective and equitable financial environment. However, resolving the moral, practical, and legal issues raised by its use will be necessary for AI-driven finance to continue to advance. The development of frameworks that support equity, transparency, and data security would be greatly aided by SEBI and other regulatory agencies. To guarantee that these instruments continue to be dependable, financial institutions must also exercise caution, upgrading their AI models often and resolving any biases in the system (Agarwal *et al.*, 2023).

2. LITERATURE REVIEW

2.1. AI Chatbots in Financial Services

The integration of Artificial intelligence (AI) in the financial sector has profoundly altered the investment decision-making landscape, since the advent of AI chatbots such as ChatGPT. These AI-driven conversational agents use Natural Language Processing (NLP) that are capable of processing large-scale financial data and delivering an intuitive, data-rich investment-related insight. Eisfeldt and Schubert (2024) stress that AI technologies are redefining the financial industry both by increasing market efficiency, enabling automated decision-making, and by improving data analytics, but they also call for adequate regulatory frameworks to address systemic risk (Eisfeldt & Schubert, 2024).

AI chatbots offer personalized financial services that were once only accessible to institutional investors. Cao (2022) explains how the convergence of AI, big data, and ML makes it possible for chatbots to deliver truly accurate and real-time financial analysis which opens the doors of the financial insights to retail investors (Cao, 2022). This change is especially important for the Indian stock market, where retail participation is increasing, but financial literacy is still inadequate. Chatbots can break down complex financial jargon and market data, allowing investors to make informed decisions without requiring specialized knowledge.

2.2. Impact on Investor Behavior

AI chatbots have a deep impact on investor psychology and investor decision processes. Dowling and Lucey (2023) claim that AI agents such as ChatGPT shape public confidence in the market by delivering stable, data-rich, and actionable insights into the market. However, they caution that the overreliance on AI tools can lead to cognitive biases if the outputs are not critically evaluated (Dowling & Lucey, 2023).

In the Indian context, Agarwal *et al.* (2023) have shown how AI chatbots can overcome behavioural biases such as herding and overreaction by delivering rational, current information. This is of particular relevance in emotionally-oriented markets such as India, where speculative trading seems to dominate over rationality (Agarwal *et al.*, 2023).

Example ChatGPT's Role in Managing Market Rumors

During the COVID-19 market crash in 2020, many retail investors in India faced panic-driven selling due to misinformation. Hypothetically, if ChatGPT had been integrated into brokerage platforms during this time, it could have countered panic by providing verified news and data-driven risk assessments, encouraging rational decision-making over fear-driven actions.

Dong *et al.* (2024) further supports this by examining the how ChatGPT reduces the psychological wall of entry for retail investors by providing tailored information to push market participation to a wider level. Their research suggests that AI chatbots can enhance investor confidence by simplifying complex financial data into actionable advice (Dong *et al.*, 2024).

2.3. Enhancing Market Efficiency and Dynamics

AI chatbots greatly enhance market efficiency by lowering information asymmetry between institutional and retail investors. Zaremba and Demir (2023) claim that market analysis is simplified by AI based chatbots that run with NLP capabilities as they provide real-time, context-aware information which facilitates quicker and more efficient decision making (Zaremba & Demir, 2023).

Case Study Upstox and Behavioral Nudges

Upstox, a popular stock trading platform in India, integrates AI tools to analyze user behavior and market trends. During periods of market volatility, Upstox's AI system sends automated alerts and recommendations to help users avoid impulsive trading.

In the volatile Indian stock market, this capability is particularly crucial. Zheng (2024) discusses the dynamic, real-time capabilities that a chatbot with financial data APIs such as Yahoo Finance and Screener.in affords - which (as relevant in this discussion) enable immediate profit from market changes (Zheng, 2024). This leads to the inherent informational gap, which drives more efficient markets and thus liquidity.

Also, Cao (2022) argues that the building capacity of AI tools empowers them to handle the huge amounts of data that would be impossible for human analysts, thus providing an advantage for AI tool users (Cao, 2022).

2.4. Financial Inclusion and Digital Literacy

AI chatbots are pivotal in advancing financial inclusion and literacy in emerging economies like India. Mhlanga (2020) highlights an important function of AI related to filling the financial services gap of the unbanked and underbanked segments by providing individual financial advisor services to a general public (Mhlanga, 2020).

Das *et al.* (2024) argue that chatbots like ChatGPT are instrumental in improving financial literacy by simplifying technical investment concepts and guiding novice investors in constructing balanced portfolios (Das *et al.*, 2024). This is significant in India, where retail investor participation has increased, but has not been matched by improvement in financial literacy.

Case Study Groww's Simplified Investment Guidance

Groww, a leading Indian investment platform, employs AI algorithms to assist new investors in selecting mutual funds and stocks. The chatbot guides users through the entire investment process, simplifying jargon-heavy information and encouraging participation in equity markets.

Moreover, Zarifhonarvar (2024) also proposes that the general availability of AI technologies may require workforce upskilling, potentially improving overall financial literacy and market participation (Zarifhonarvar, 2024).

2.5. Challenges and Risks of AI Chatbots in Finance

Nevertheless, AI chatbots are associated with ethical, operational, and security issues. Eisfeldt and Schubert (2024) caution that embedding of AI into financial platforms could lead to systemic risks, particularly if AI algorithms falter or are exploited to boost market volatility (Eisfeldt & Schubert, 2024).

Additionally, Thach *et al.* (2021) highlight the cybersecurity risks associated with AI chatbots, emphasizing the need for robust data protection measures due to the sensitive nature of financial data handled by these systems (Thach *et al.*, 2021).

Khan & Umer (2024) further argues that there are potential pitfalls of algorithmic bias in AI models, that could result in unfair financial advice if the models are not properly observed and, thus, reconfigured. (Dong *et al.*, 2024) echo these worries, highlighting the importance of transparency in AI decisioning so as to gain user trust.

2.6. Future Research Directions

Although AI chatbots such as ChatGPT promise to improve investment decision-making, more research is required about the long-term effects of such technologies on market dynamics and investor behavior, in the specific Indian context. Eisfeldt & Schubert (2024) also advocate for the construction of regulatory structures that will guarantee the responsible use of AI in financial markets (Eisfeldt & Schubert, 2024).

Future studies should, in addition, be directed to upgrading AI models to improve transparency and decrease algorithmic bias. Dowling Lucey (2023) propose use of hybrid models of AI-based insight cross-checked by human supervision to reconcile automation with reflection (Dowling Lucey, 2023).

Additionally, the emerging field of explainable AI (XAI) has the potential to improve the interpretability of chatbot advice, thereby encouraging trust among retail investors. Increasing models for sentiment analysis to include real-time data may further enhance predictive performance, in turn increasingly yielding better investment results.

3. DATA

The research will delve into the historical data and real time data related to Indian stocks, majorly the prediction accuracy of share price and news articles with the help of running tests and experiments. The data will be sourced from sites like NSE official, Screener and Yahoo Finance. For understanding the market conditions financial news sites like Money control, Live mint, Economic Times, etc. These sources will be used to improve the accuracy of the information provided by ChatGPT.

3.1. Adjusted Closing Price

We have used the adjusted stock close price to calculate the stock return. While analysing stock returns in academic papers, the use of adjusted close prices, using adjusted close pricing becomes essential for a thorough and precise analysis. This method takes into account a number of variables that impact stock prices after closing, giving a more accurate picture of a stock's worth and returns in time. We have outlined and discussed the importance of utilizing adjusted close prices to compute stock returns in academic settings below. The utilization of adjusted close prices is essential for a thorough and precise assessment. This methodology accounts for several elements influencing stock prices after market closure, yielding a more accurate representation of a stock's worth and its returns. In the following, We present and elucidate the importance of utilizing adjusted close prices for the calculation of stock returns in academic settings.

3.1.1. Introduction to Adjusted Close Price

The adjusted close price is basically the stock's closing price that is modified to include any circumstances that occurs at any time after the market close. This adjustment includes dividends, stock splits also any rights offered in the market. The main purpose of adjusting the closing price is ensuring that the stock's performance accurately represents its value, free from distortions brought on by corporate actions.

3.1.2. Adjustment of Dividend

While paying dividend, it distributes a portion of its earnings to shareholders. This results in a decrease in the stock price, equivalent to the dividend amount, on the ex-dividend date. Hence the adjustment of dividend and closing price offers a clarity of the stock's performance by incorporating the total return of shareholders, which contains both price appreciation and dividend received.

3.1.3. Stock Splits and Reverse Splits

Stock splits and reverse splits modify the quantity of shares outstanding without affecting the company's market capitalisation. A stock split decreases the price per share and increases the total number of shares, but a reverse split has the contrary effect. Modifying the closing price for these events guarantees that the analysis accurately represents the stock's value and performance, free from distortions due to fluctuations in share quantity.

3.2 Data Collection

3.2.1 Stock Price Data

In the data collection process, we will utilize the Yahoo Finance to acquire stock price data for the selected corporations. Yahoo finance is a popular open-source website that provides a convenient method to access historical and real-time financial data.

Key features of the Yahoo finance:

Historical Data Retrieval

The website enables users to download historical stock price data, including open, high, low, close prices, and trading volume, for specified time periods. This feature is crucial for our research, as we will analyse the efficacy of the ChatGPT structure in predicting stock price movements based on historical data.

Real-time Data Access

Yahoo finance and Google finance provides access to real-time stock price data, allowing users to obtain the most recent transaction information. Although our study primarily concentrates on historical data, the ability to integrate real-time data can be valuable for future extensions or applications of our proposed structure.

Dividend and Stock Split Adjustments

ChatGPT automatically adjusts historical price data for dividends and stock splits, ensuring that the retrieved data accurately reflects the stock's performance over time. This feature saves substantial data preprocessing efforts and ensures the integrity of our analysis.

3.2.2. Stock News Data

The new ChatGPT 4.o now can access to web search and has the access to real time and historical market data, including stock prices, company's fundamentals and related news.

4. METHODOLOGY

4.1. Research Design and Approach

This research adopts a qualitative and quantitative mixed-methods approach to examine how ChatGPT, through prompt engineering, can serve as an advisory tool in stock selection, portfolio construction, and fundamental analysis in the Indian stock market. Using carefully engineered prompts, the study probes the limits of ChatGPT's capabilities to grasp financial information and build and recommend stable portfolios under the setting of the Indian market conditions and selecting stock with sound performance. In order to get better stock analysis, we used ChatGPT's Stock-Market Analyst GPT developed by *Ivan Petrov*. This is a built in ML model in ChatGPT which helps specifically for stock market analysis and data interpretation to the users.

The research focuses on the following key areas:

- **Stock Picking:** Computation of investment decisions based on the stock proposed by the conversational agent, the ChatGPT, based on the input of the underlying fundamental indicators.
- **Portfolio Building:** Natural language representation of and coverage by guidelines used for portfolio diversification in support of multiple investment objectives.
- **Fundamental Analysis Explanation:** Analysis of the utility of ChatGPT for delivering concise explanations of the key parameters shaping stock recommendations.

- **Understanding of price movements:** With the help of data interpretation and data visualization model of ChatGPT, how we can have a good understanding of stock market movements for effective decision making.
- **Sentiment analysis and its impact on stock market forecasting:** With the help of news headlines and news data and integration of historical prices, we developed a prediction model to test the forecasting capabilities of ChatGPT 4.0.

4.2. Prompt Engineering Process for ChatGPT

This study employs prompt engineering, which involves designing specific queries and commands to guide ChatGPT in producing responses that meet investment analysis requirements. The process involves an iterative enhancement of prompts in order to achieve the most accuracy and relevance of ChatGPT's responses to financial questions.

- **Prompt Structuring**: Prompts are designed to get certain interpretations, both of the underlying entities (intrinsic indicators, e.g., P/E ratio, EPS, debt-to-equity ratio) and of the stock selection criteria (e.g., good earnings growth, low debt, high return on equity).
- **Iterative Prompt Refinement**: Under the given inputs, each prompt is tuned up by considering the response of ChatGPT, so as to make the answers of the prompt in a way that it can meet the given condition of stock analysis in the Indian market.

User Prompts Samples:
"Can you give an idea if I start invest for RS 10,000/Month in the form of SIP and I want to continue this for 5 years and hold this for 5 years hence give me the best strategy to maximize return out of it. How many companies shall I keep in my portfolio and how much should be the allocation large cap, mid cap and small cap?"
"Can you give me the latest fundamental analysis of the stocks you have recommended and interpret this to me in an easier manner"

4.3. Data Analysis

Data analysis involves two primary processes: Rating ChatGPT's advice in terms of past performance and discussing the clarity and utility of ChatGPT's justifications for key indicators.

4.3.1. Quantitative Analysis

- **Prediction Accuracy:** Comprehensively measure how well ChatGPT's stock recommendations perform in comparison to macroeconomic factors and news sentiments. Predict returns for suggested stocks and compare with established performance measures and predict the movement of stocks.
- **Performance Analysis:** Compare the performance of the ChatGPT-proposed portfolio construction strategies by adopting the techniques like Percentage Error and Mean Absolute Error to the proposed portfolios. This will allow it to establish the relevance of ChatGPT's recommendation in generating returns with respect to risk in the Indian stock market.

4.3.2. Qualitative Analysis

- **Clarity and Depth of Explanations:** Evaluate the ability of ChatGPT to define the fundamental performance metrics used in the stock recommendations. This includes the examination of the ability of ChatGPT's output to convey nuanced financial ideas to aid investor comprehension.
- **Thematic Analysis:** Cluster and categorize ChatGPT's response on themes such as Value Investments", and `Defensive Stocks" according to its recommendations and commentary. Code the patterns in ChatGPT's way of making stock and portfolio recommendations.
- **Comparative Analysis:** As part of an effort to assess the quality of the explanations that ChatGPT provides of the topic, the subject of this paper, in comparison with the explanations provided on financial education web sites, this paper compares ChatGPT's explanation of the topic to what can be found on financial education web sites.

4.4. Tools and Instruments

- **ChatGPT:** Prompt engineering using the main instrument of stock recommendations, portfolios advice, data analysis, data visualization and explanations.
- **MS Excel**: In the domain of stock data management, the calculation of return and the comparison of performance metrics.

5. RESULTS

In order to test ChatGPT's capability in stock market analysis and how it helps retail investors to gain financial knowledge about the market, we have instructed ChatGPT about the current requirements and knowledge I need to start investing,

5.1. Strategies in Stock Picking

Prompt1: "I am starting to invest in Indian stock market can you assist me in picking best stocks and make me understand the steps you are taking in to consider it."

Result: So, at first ChatGPT has asked to Define our Investment Goals, clarify the investment horizon and risk tolerance

- Long-term growth (5 years+) which are generally growth stocks, and high growth sectors with great potential.
- Short-term gains (i.e., >3 years) could be handled through value stocks or growth stocks, etc., which are perceived as having short-term growth.

It also has asked us what level of risk we can take for this invest since risk tolerance is crucial. In the case of a high-risk tolerance person, small-cap stocks might be watched; in the case of a low-risk portfolio, large-cap or blue-chip stocks appear more secure.

Secondly it has asked us to, Analyze Key Sectors in the Indian Market. Since India's economy is diverse, with sectors like IT, banking, pharmaceuticals, consumer products, and renewables, however renewable industry is now the trending in the market. Understanding the comprehension of pattern in the domain may then be used to guide towards possible market winners.

Here ChatGPT not only explained the sector and sector's growth but also gave the result with some real time examples.

- **IT and Software Services**: Strong global demand for tech services makes this a high growth sector.
- **Banking and Financial Services:** Stable sector, important for economy's growth, leading by companies like HDFC Bank and ICICI Bank.
- **Pharma and Healthcare:** Important to the home and foreign markets, as there is expanding demand for health care.
- **Renewable Energy:** An emerging sector and India's adoption of sustainability (Such as Adani Green Energy entering the action).

Next thing ChatGPT suggested is to Screen for Quality Stocks. Here's a simple framework suggested by ChatGPT for high-quality stocks:

a) **Market Leaders:** Large-cap or blue-chip stocks are also typically a more stable, e.g., Reliance Industries, TCS, etc.
b) **Strong Financials:**
   - **Consistent Revenue and Profit Growth:** Growing companies (CAGR of 10%+) often indicate stability.
   - **Low Debt-to-Equity Ratio:** Generally, under 1 is safer.
   - **High Return on Equity (ROE):** Moreover, the turnover of more than 15% on equity (ROE) would indicate management effectiveness.
c) **Valuation Metrics:**
   - **Price-to-Earnings Ratio (P/E):** Lower P/E relative to the sector indicates value.
   - **Price-to-Book Ratio (P/B):** Particularly important for sectors like banking and finance.
   - **Dividend Yield:** Useful for stable returns, especially in large-cap companies.
d) **Growth Potential and Market Share:**

Firms looking to expand their market, innovate, and do business in fast-growing markets are going to pose the highest proposition.

ChatGPT then recommends to Review Economic and Industry Trends. Look for macroeconomic trends like GDP growth, inflation, and actions of the RBI as this is likely to affect share performance:

- **RBI Interest Rates:** Lowering interest rates could, for instance, encourage real estate, or consumer goods industries, etc.
- **GDP Growth and Infrastructure Investment:** Plays a major role in the trend analysis of the construction, affiliated construction, utilities and capital goods technologies.

Last but not the least it also has suggested the Diversification of Portfolio. It has further explained the benefits of diversification below:

To allocate across sectors and stock types (large-cap, mid-cap, small-cap). Restrict exposure to investments into the number of stocks/sectors exposed to an attempt to minimize the exposure to risk of potential loss.

Now in order to understand the intelligence of ChatGPT and to understand whether it really can help us picking stocks we further instructed it with prompt engineering and this time we gave some command and real-life scenario to test its capabilities for stock analysis.

5.2. Portfolio Building and Capital Allocation

Prompt2:" Can you give an idea if I start invest for RS 10,000/Month in the form of SIP and I want to continue this for 5 years and hold this for 5 years hence give me the best strategy to maximize return out of it. How many companies shall I keep in my portfolio and how much should be the allocation large cap, mid cap and small cap?"

Result: Here again ChatGPT has suggested a strategic plan to start the investment;

Starting a monthly investment of 10,000 in the form of a Systematic Investment Plan (SIP) for a 5-year investment phase with a 5-year holding period afterward is a great way to benefit from rupee-cost averaging and potentially maximize returns over the long term. Here's a strategic breakdown of how to structure your investments for the best balance of risk and growth.

1. **Portfolio Allocation Strategy**
    - Due to our investment horizon is quite long (10 years in total), GPT suggested a balanced portfolio from large-cap, mid-cap, and small-cap stock can provide the stability and growth trade-off. Here's an optimal allocation to balance risk and returns:
    - Large-Cap Stocks (40%) – Reason is they are the stable and less volatile stocks, and they have consistent growth and dividend capability.
    - Mid-Cap Stocks (35%) – Due to their growth potential is very high, but there is a slightly higher risk than large-cap companies.
    - Small-Cap Stocks (25%) -Having greater risk but hold the potential for big bang returns if chosen wisely.

This split provides us exposure to rapidly growing areas whilst maintaining a large, stable, large-cap portfolio.

2. **Suggested Number of Companies in Portfolio:** It has suggested for a monthly SIP of 10,000, a focused portfolio of 8–12 companies will help maintain diversification without diluting returns. Large-Cap: 3–4 companies (well-established blue-chip stocks), Mid-Cap: 3-4 companies (market-leading high-growth companies in specialized sectors), Small-Cap: 2–4 companies (emerging companies with significant growth potential).
3. **Suggested Monthly Allocation (SIP) by Market Cap:** Here's how we could allocate our 10,000 monthly investment as per the recommendation: For Large-Cap: 4,000 (40%) - Distributed over 3–4 mega-caps, at (1,000–1,300) respectively, Mid-Cap: 3,500 (35%) - Distributed in 3–4 mid-cap stocks at (900–1,200) each, Small-Cap: Spread out over 2-4 small cap stocks at (600- 1,250),

respectively. By using this setting each of the stock categories is able to expand, large-cap stocks provide stability in order to offset the increased variability of mid-cap and small-cap stocks.

4. **Choosing Stocks in Each Segment:** Now ChatGPT identifies the companies that would be suitable within each segment. Following are examples of criteria for stock selection. Specific stock choices should be considered based on recent financials, market conditions, and sector analysis.

Large-Cap Stocks (Stable, foundational investments)

- **HDFC Bank (Banking)** A stable performer in the banking sector.
- **Reliance Industries (Energy, Telecom, Retail)** revenue diversity with growth potential.
- **Infosys (IT)** Global IT company with high earnings stability.

Mid-Cap Stocks (Growth potential with moderate risk)

- **Bharat Electronics (Défense, Electronics)** Residing in the tailwind of the government's defence manufacturing drive.
- **Crompton Greaves Consumer Electricals (Household items)** expanding consumption of consumer durables.
- **Adani Green Energy (Renewable Energy)** operating in the high-growth renewable energy market.

Small-Cap Stocks (High growth but high risk)

- **Vaibhav Global (E-commerce Retail)** Growth in international markets with an attractive e-commerce business model.
- **IDFC First Bank (Banking)** Growing digital banking services and expanding reach.
- **APL Apollo Tubes (Construction Materials)** Large market share in steel pipes and construction materials.

5. **Monitoring and Rebalancing Strategy:** It has provided some strategies to maximize returns, review and rebalance your portfolio annually like:

- Track stock performance: Reassess underperforming stocks and consider replacing them if they consistently underperform their sector.
- Adjust allocation: If a specific sector is performing well, consider reallocating gains toward more stable large-cap stocks.
- Dividend Reinvestment: If any large-cap stocks pay Dividend, reinvest them Back into your SIP can generate growth on growth.

6. **Estimated Growth Potential:** ChatGPT has also given an average annual return estimation of 12 -15% which can be reasonable for a balanced portfolio in the Indian stock market, for the investment growth. 5-Year SIP Contribution: 6,00,000 (10,000/month); 12-14 Lakhs. This projection is based on the amount of growth during the SIP period as well as an additional 5 years of compounding on the holdings period.

This method provides an optimum mixture of growth opportunity and risk mitigation while securing high and rerating as the cost of money grows over time.

In order to support this result, we referred to Google Finance to understand the accuracy of the result. We have noticed that actually that the results and stock recommendations given by ChatGPT is pretty decent, since all the recommended stock performed well in 5 years.

Figure 1. Reliance Industries Ltd has given a return of 72.05% in 5 years

Source: https://www.google.com/finance/

Figure 2. HDFC Bank has given a return of 46.49% in 5 years

Source: https://www.google.com/finance/

Figure 3. Infosys Ltd has given a return of 164.30% in 5 years

Source: https://www.google.com/finance/

Figure 4. Bharat Electronics Ltd has given a return of 811.75% in 5 years

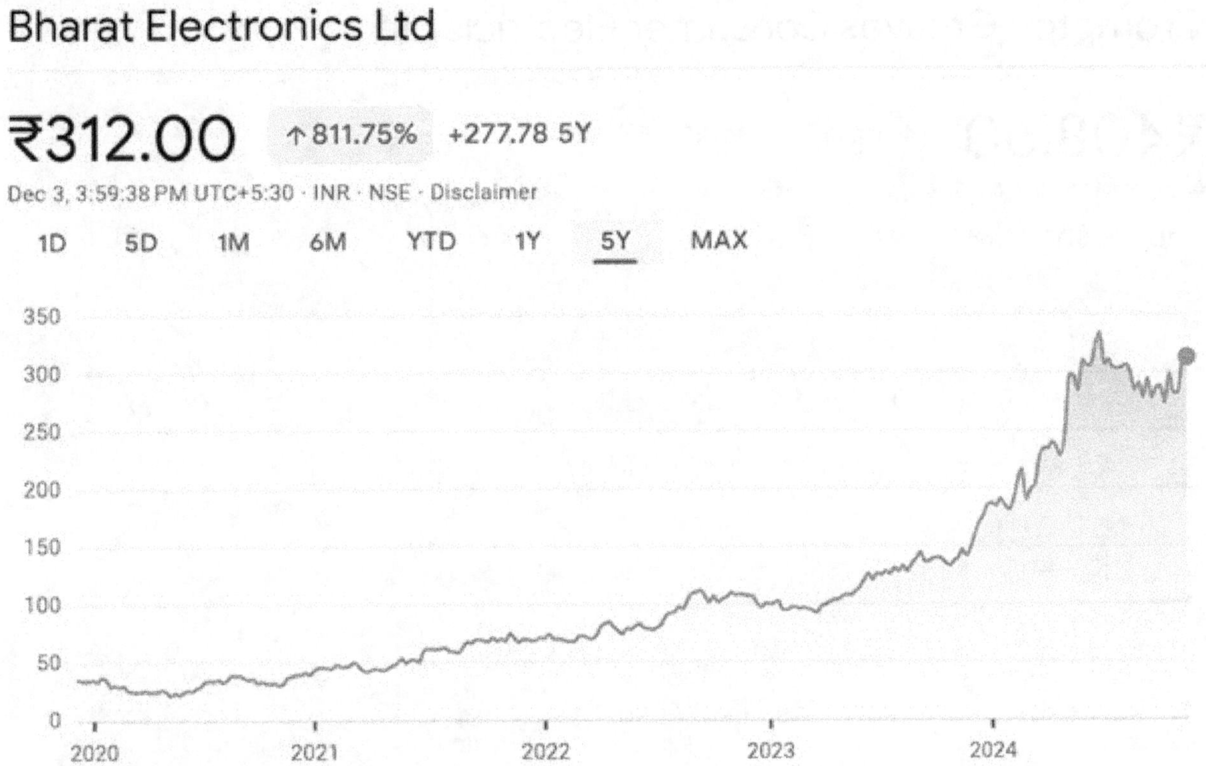

Source: https://www.google.com/finance/

Figure 5. Crompton Greaves Consumer Electricals Ltd has given a return of 64.99% in 5 years

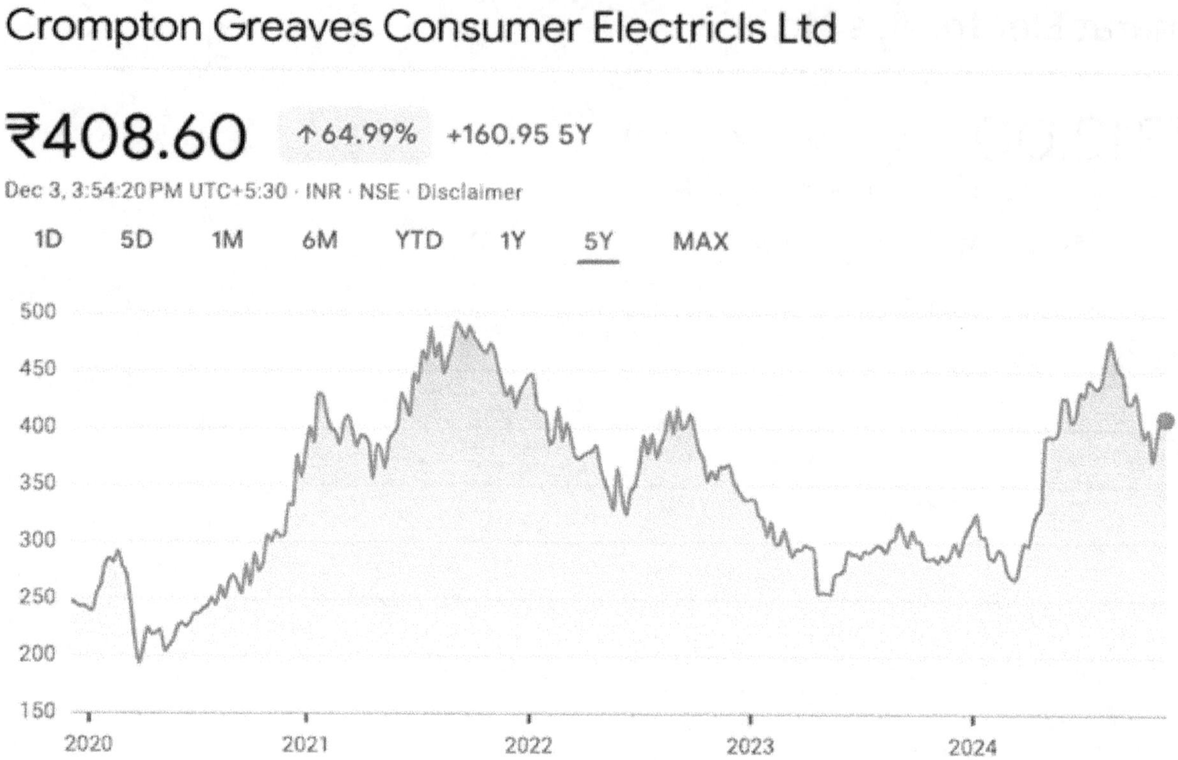

Source: https://www.google.com/finance/

Figure 6. Adani Green Energy Ltd has given a return of 937.97% in 5 years

Source: https://www.google.com/finance/

Figure 7. Vaibhav Global Ltd has given a return of 75.15% in 5 years

Source: https://www.google.com/finance/

Figure 8. IDFC First Bank Ltd has given a return of 50.46% in 5 years

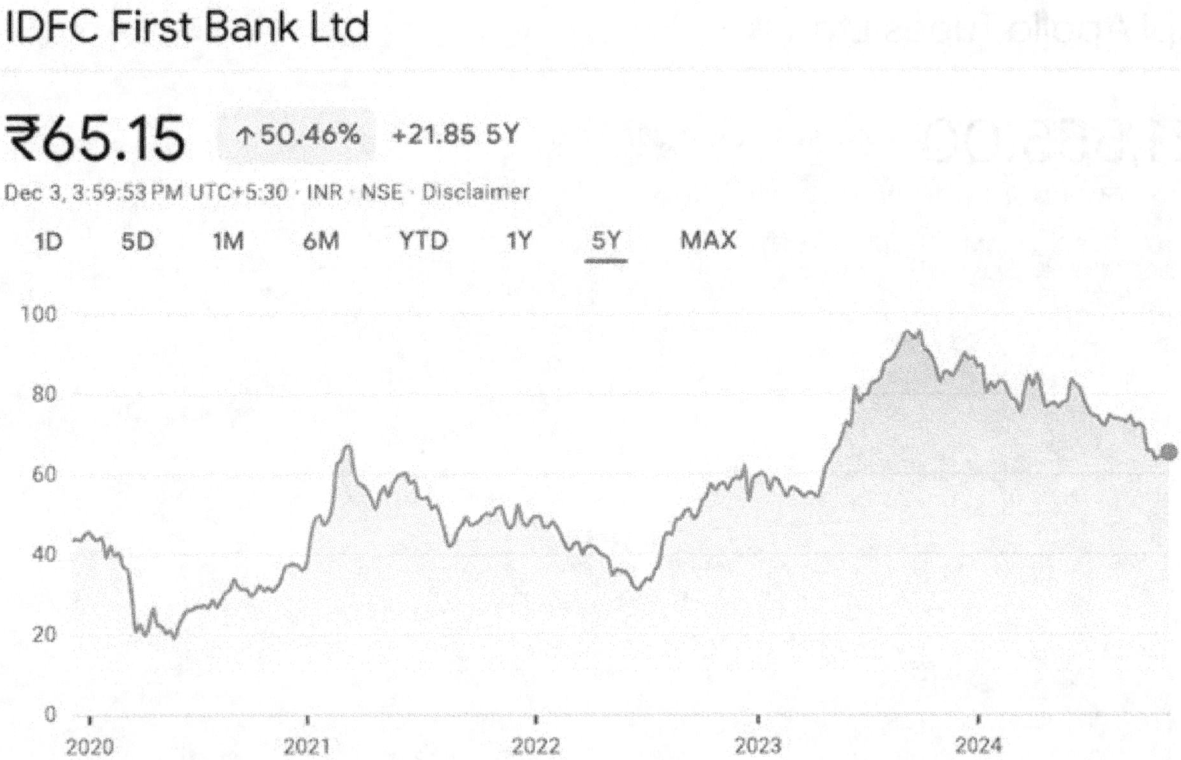

Source: https://www.google.com/finance/

Figure 9. Apl Apollo Tubes Ltd has given a return of 893.36% in 5 years

Source: https://www.google.com/finance/

For further testing we asked ChatGPT to give us the fundamental analysis of the company what are the considerations it took for the decision making, why it recommended these stocks to me? and how it is helping novice retail investors who are new in the market.

5.3. Fundamental Analysis

Prompt 3: "Give me this in tabular form with all the fundamentals mentioned of each company like P/E ratio, ROE, P/B ratio, EPS, etc according to you and then interpret me each and every aspect you have considered for the decisions"

Result: ChatGPT has given us the result, so here it has interpreted all the things that are considered in a fundamental analysis of a company such as Market Capital, P/E Ratio, EPS, etc. On what basis it has chosen the stocks what are the positive indicators it has noticed everything has been mentioned properly. ChatGPT also has created a tabular sheet to organise the data, but it couldn't process the dividend yield of Adani Greens since it has not announced any dividend since 2018. Now the latest ChatGPT 4.o has the capability of web search facility which can search results through websites so get latest results.

The AI Chatbot explained Metric Interpretation and Investment Rationale which are important for fundamental analysis, that includes importance of Market Cap which represents the company's valuation. Large-caps (e.g., HDFC Bank, Reliance), P/E Ratio (Price-to-Earnings): Measures how much investors are willing to pay per rupee of earnings. Higher P/E (e.g., Adani Green, Crompton) often indicates growth expectations but may also reflect overvaluation. Large-cap stocks like Reliance and HDFC Bank have reasonable P/Es around 25, indicating stability with modest growth, P/B Ratio (Price-to-Book): A high P/B ratio, like Adani Green's 10.5, can signal expectations of high growth or overvaluation. Mid-range P/B ratios (2-4) in large-caps like Reliance suggest a balance between growth and value, ROE (Return on Equity): A measure of profitability relative to shareholders' equity. Higher ROE (above 15%) in Infosys, Bharat Electronics, and APL Apollo Tubes suggests efficient use of capital. Infosys is particularly strong at 21%, making it attractive for consistent returns, EPS (Earnings Per Share): Reflects profitability on a per-share basis, important for understanding earning potential. Higher EPS in Reliance and HDFC Bank signals strong profit generation, while lower EPS in Adani Green shows reliance on future growth, Debt/ Equity Ratio: Indicates financial leverage. A higher ratio, as seen in Adani Green (3.2), means more debt financing, which may increase risk, especially in uncertain markets. Lower ratios in Infosys and Bharat Electronics reflect conservative financial management, Dividend Yield: Provides insights into income generation. Higher dividend yield in Infosys (2.5%) makes it attractive for steady income, whereas no yield in Adani Green reflects its reinvestment-focused growth approach.

Table 1. Fundamentals of company

Company	Market Cap	P/E Ratio	P/B Ratio	ROE	EPS	Debt/Equity	Dividend Yield
HDFC Bank	11.6 lakh cr	25.4	3.8	17%	75	0.9	0.9%
Reliance Industries	16 lakh cr	24.5	2.2	13%	104	0.3	0.4%
Infosys	6 lakh cr	28.0	6.2	21%	57	0.1	2.5%
Bharat Electronics	98,000 cr	20.2	4.1	19%	8.2	0.1	1.2%
Crompton Greaves	25,661 cr	54.2	8.3	16%	7.25	0.2	0.7%
Adani Green Energy	2.3 lakh cr	110	10.5	7%	5.4	3.2	N/A
Vaibhav Global	9,000 cr	36.0	5.8	12%	11.8	0.2	0.6%
IDFC First Bank	55,000 cr	16.0	1.8	10%	5.6	1.1	0.4%
APL Apollo Tubes	34,500 cr	35.5	6.5	15%	18	0.5	0.8%

Source: Author's Calculation

5.4. Data Visualization

Moving ahead we asked ChatGPT for data analysis and data visualization here we have provided the historical data of all the stocks and feed them into the system for better understanding of price movement, moving average, EMA, MACD and so on.

Prompt4: "Analyse the historical price data and price movement of these stocks in the file"

Result: We got the analysis of all the stocks so here it plotted line chart for price movements of all the stocks with the help of coding, we didn't need to run a single code which signifies how it is useful for traders who lacks in programming language. They can easily instruct ChatGPT to plot the line chart and get their work done. These data visualization will help traders in technical analysis and understanding of price movements in stock market.

Figure 10. Line Chart Adani Green

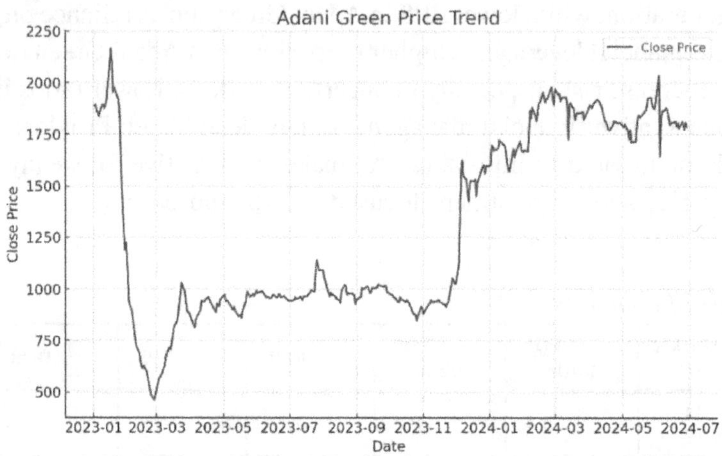

- **Average Close Price:** 1295.10
- **High Volatility:** Standard deviation of close prices at 452.97.
- **Price Range:** Min: 462.20, Max: 2166.15.

Figure 11. Line Chart Apollo Tubes

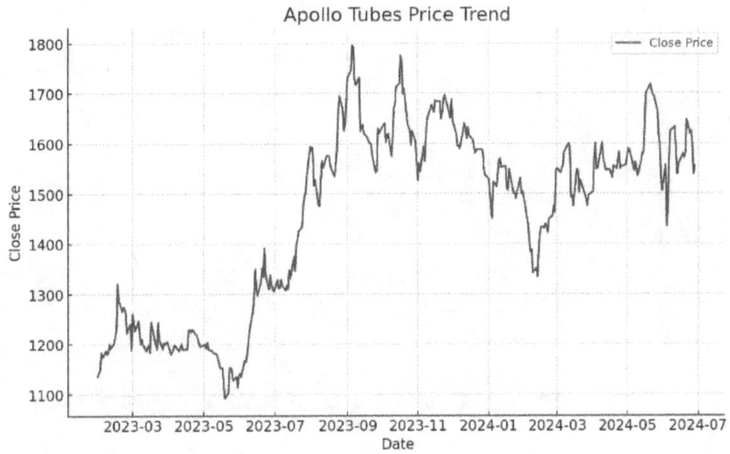

- **Average Close Price:** 1456.40
- **Standard Deviation:** 182.04 (moderate volatility).
- **Price Range:** Min: 1092.70, Max: 1795.30.

Figure 12. Line Chart Bharat Electronics

- **Average Close Price:** 155.76
- **Standard Deviation:** 57.79.
- **Price Range:** Min: 88.95, Max: 318.65.

Figure 13. Line Chart Crompton Greaves

- **Average Close Price:** 305.01
- **Standard Deviation:** 35.29 (low volatility).
- **Price Range:** Min: 252.55, Max: 431.05.

Figure 14. Line Chart Crompton Greaves

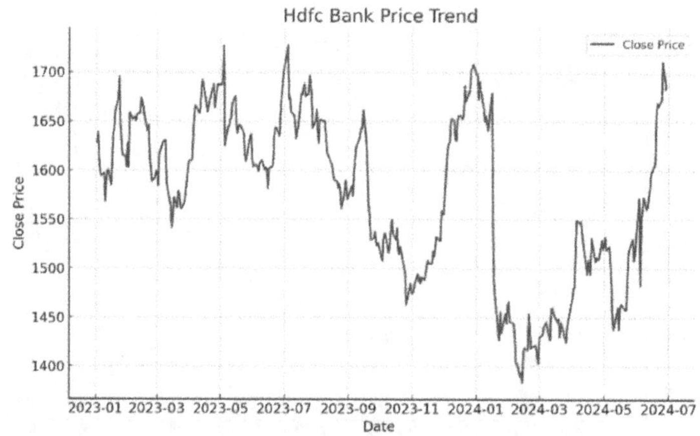

- **Average Close Price:** 1577.26
- **Standard Deviation:** 84.17 (stable performance).
- **Price Range:** Min: 1384.05, Max: 1728.20.

Figure 15. Line Chart IDFC First Bank

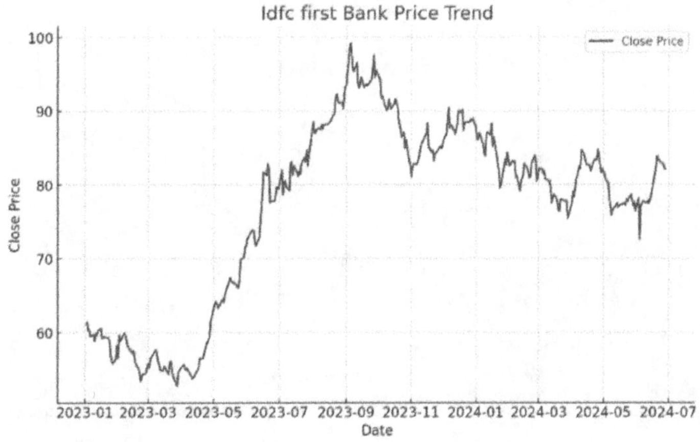

- **Average Close Price:** 77.05
- **Standard Deviation:** 12.37.
- **Price Range:** Min: 52.75, Max: 99.20.

Figure 16. Line Chart Infosys

- **Average Close Price:** 1458.06
- **Standard Deviation:** 114.11 (moderate volatility).
- **Price Range:** Min: 1223.40, Max: 1729.45.

Figure 17. Line Chart RIL (Reliance Industries)

- **Average Close Price:** 1255.37
- **Standard Deviation:** 144.25 (moderate volatility).
- **Price Range:** Min: 1015.88, Max: 1565.40.

Figure 18. Line Chart Vaibhav Global

- **Average Close Price:** 367.94
- **Standard Deviation:** 59.23 (moderate volatility).
- **Price Range:** Min: 271.25, Max: 528.55.

For better understanding we asked ChatGPT to provide the EMA10 and EMA20 in colour green and red, plot RSI14 value with red colour. Alongside we asked for the volume data for all stocks.

Prompt5: "Plot the line chart Plot the EMA10 and EMA20 in colour green and red Plot RSI14 value with red colour Plot Volume data 200 days Display for all the 9 stocks"

Adani Greens Ltd.

Figure 19. Adani Greens EMA &, RSI14

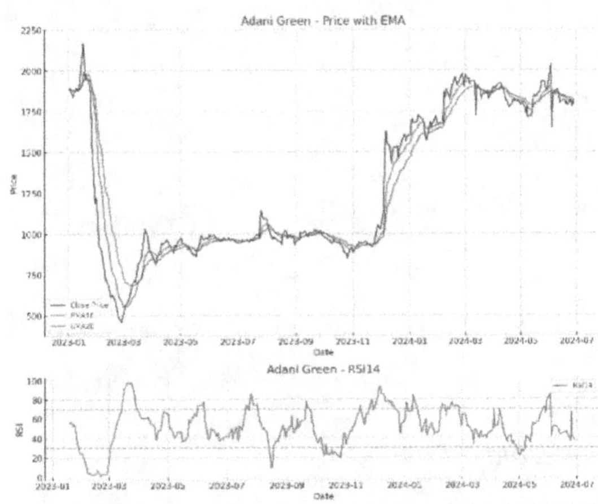

Figure 20. Adani Greens Volume Data

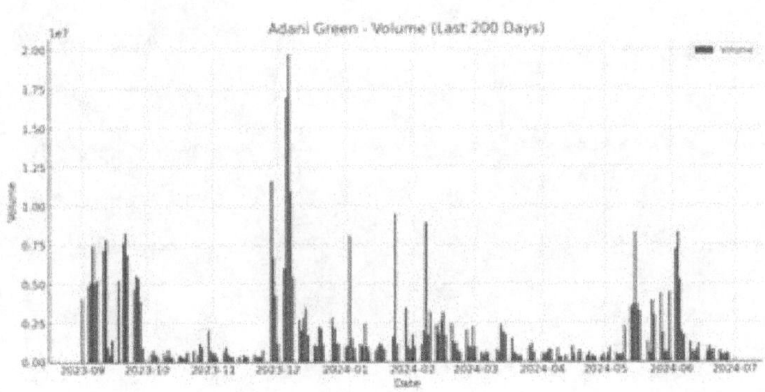

APL Apollo Tubes Ltd.

Figure 21: Apollo Tubes EMA &, RSI14

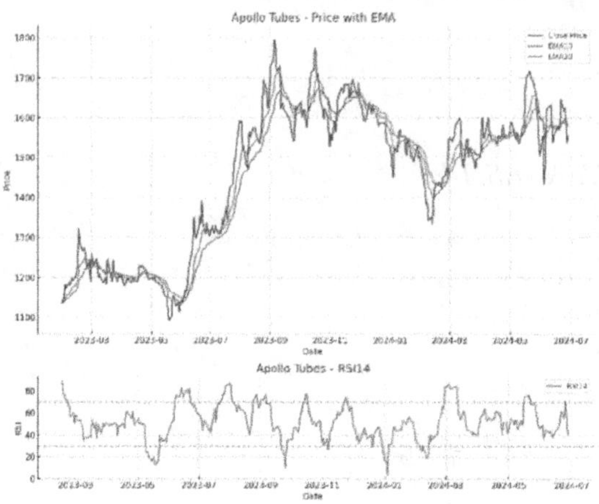

Figure 22. Apollo Tubes Volume Data

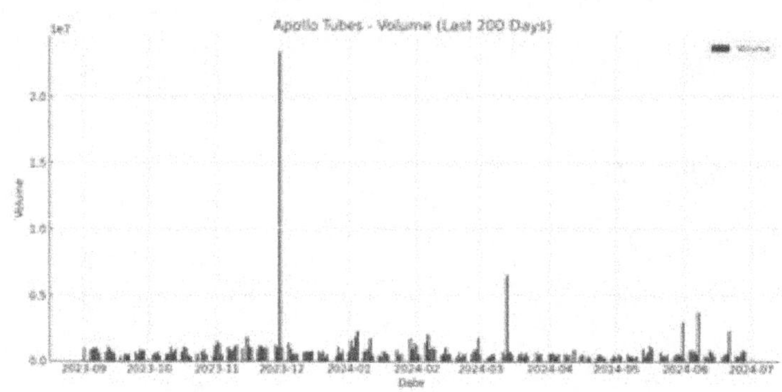

Bharat Electronics Ltd.

Figure 23. Bharat Electronics EMA & RSI

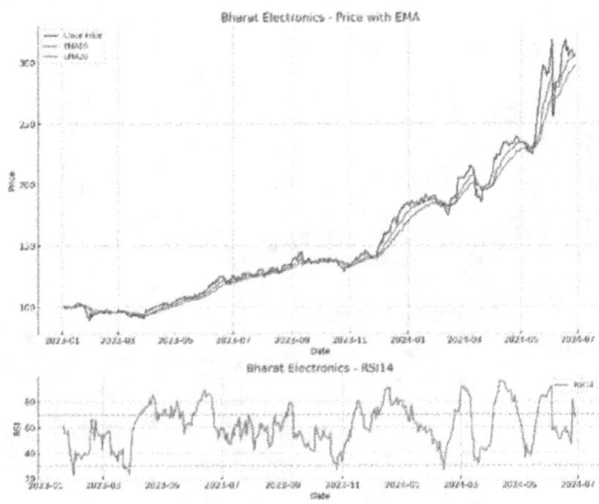

Figure 24. Bharat Electronics Volume Data

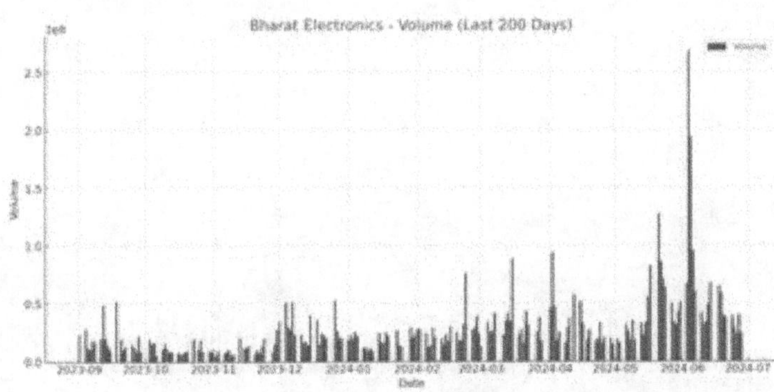

Crompton Greaves Ltd.

Figure 25. Crompton Greaves EMA & RSI

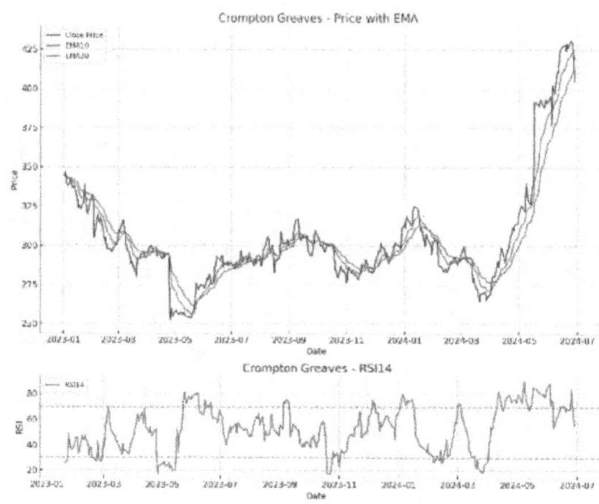

Figure 26. Crompton Greaves Volume Data

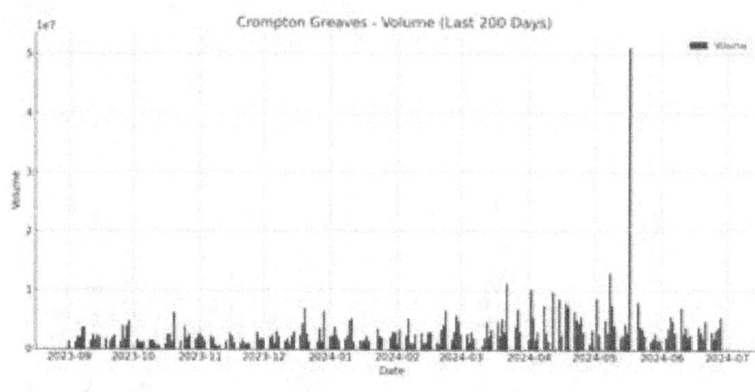

HDFC Bank Ltd.

Figure 27. HDFC Bank EMA & RSI

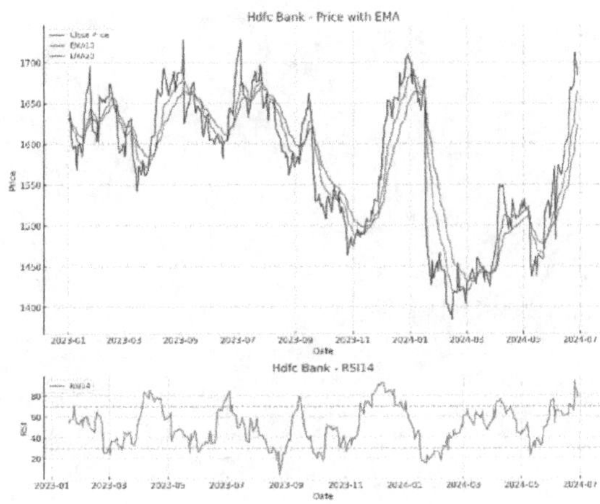

Figure 28. HDFC Bank Volume Data

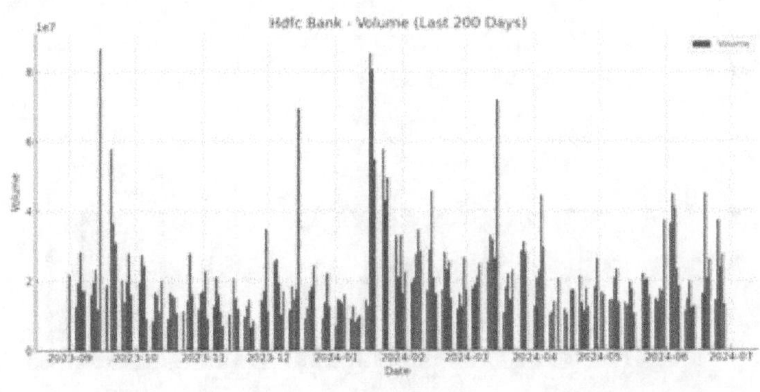

IDFC First Bank Ltd.

Figure 29. IDFC First Bank EMA & RSI

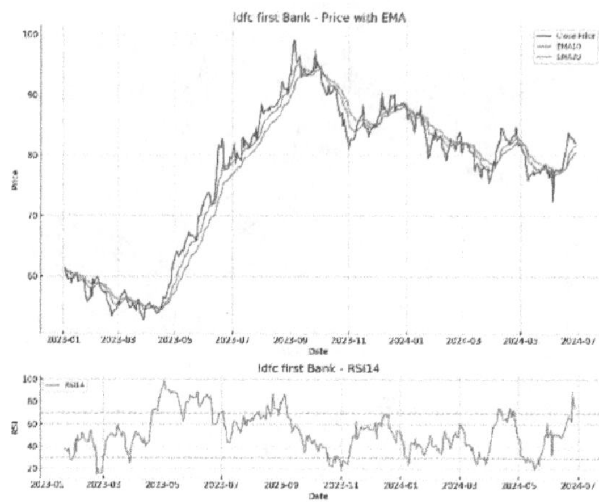

Figure 30. IDFC First Volume Data

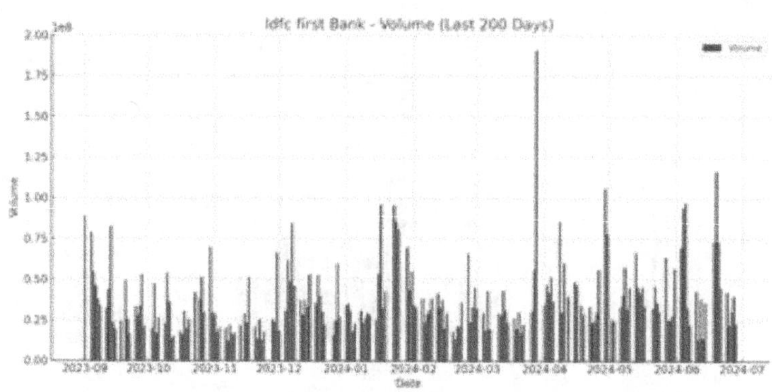

Infosys Ltd.

Figure 31. Infosys EMA & RSI

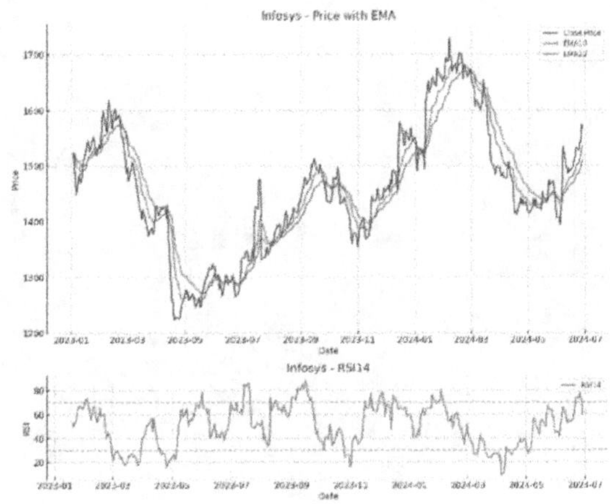

Figure 32. Infosys Volume Data

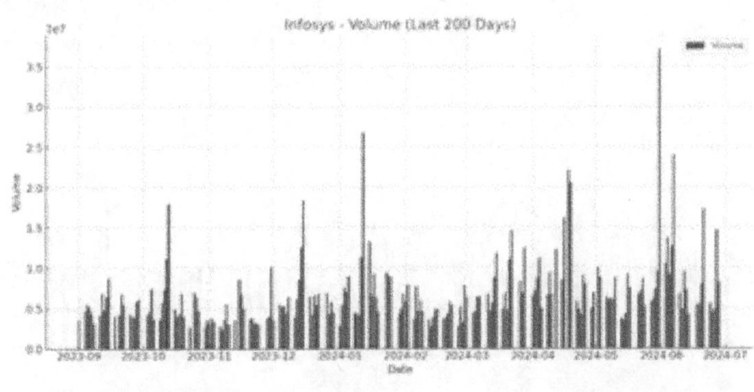

Reliance Industries Ltd.

Figure 33. RIL EMA & RSI

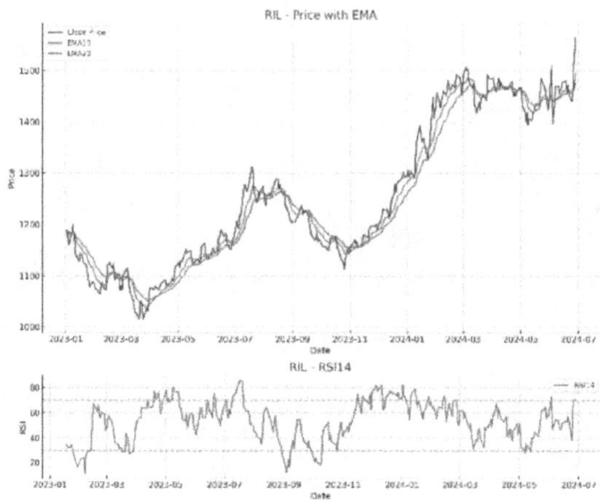

Figure 34. RIL Volume Data

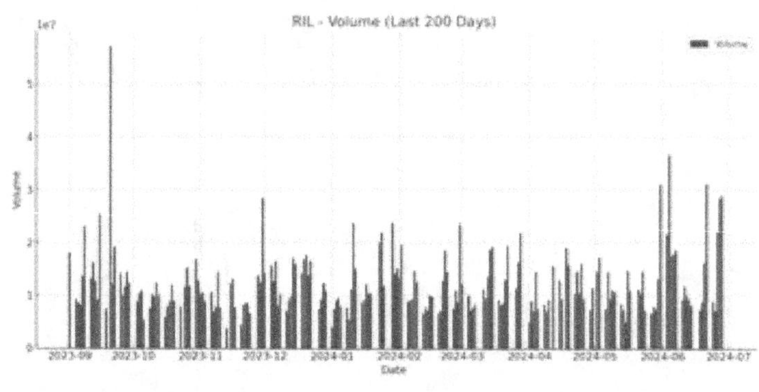

Vaibhav Global Ltd.

Figure 35. Vaibhav Global EMA & RSI

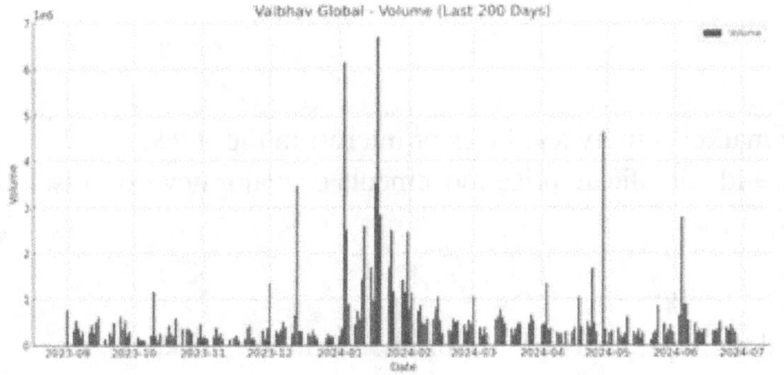

Figure 36. Vaibhav Global Volume Data

EMA10 (Green Line) and EMA20 (Red Line): Exponential Moving Averages are weighted moving averages that give more importance to recent prices. EMA10 focuses on short-term trends (last 10 days). EMA20 represents medium-term trends (last 20 days). The Significance of this metrics are helping in identifying trends and momentum of the stocks. Also, when EMA10 crosses above EMA20, it signals bullish momentum. When EMA10 crosses below EMA20, it signals bearish momentum. Here stocks like Infosys or HDFC Bank, frequent crossovers suggest sideways movement or consolidation and for more directional stocks like Adani Green, EMA10 generally stays above EMA20 during bullish phases.

RSI14 (Red Line): The Relative Strength Index measures the speed and change of price movements over a 14-day period. Values above 70, indicates the stock is overbought (potentially overvalued). Values below 30 indicates the stock is oversold (potentially undervalued). RSI generally signifies insight into potential reversals or continuation of trends. As we can observe stocks like IDFC First Bank show RSI moving in and out of overbought conditions, reflecting strong price momentum. Crompton Greaves had periods where RSI dropped below 30, suggesting potential entry points for buyers.

Volume refers to the total number of shares traded during a given period (e.g., daily). It is a critical indicator of market activity and provides insights into investor interest and stock liquidity.

High Volume

- Indicates strong market activity and investor interest in the stock.
- Often correlates with significant price movements or major news/events.

Low Volume

- Suggests reduced market activity or lack of interest in the stock.
- May indicate consolidation periods, where the stock is neither significantly rising nor falling.

Volume Spikes

- Sudden and extreme increases in volume often signify major events like earnings releases, new contracts, or macroeconomic news.

Adani Green indicates Consistent trading volumes reflect sustained investor interest, especially in renewable energy. Occasional spikes align with announcements of large-scale projects or renewable energy policies globally. High volume during uptrends confirms strong bullish momentum and institutional participation. Technical Interaction like EMA Trends, EMA10 is significantly dominant over EMA20 indicates strong uptrend phases. RSI value briefs the periods in the overbought zone signify exuberant buying but return to neutral levels indicate controlled optimism. Market Dynamics suggests growth in the renewable energy sector globally and Adani Green's expansion strategies maintain steady interest, visible in sustained high trading volumes.

Apollo Tubes indicates moderate volumes with occasional surges likely tied to the cyclical demand for steel and infrastructure-related products. Surges often coincide with sectoral news like government infrastructure spending or industry expansions. Technical Interaction where EMA Crossovers signify moderate volatility with crossovers suggesting consolidation phases. Investors may accumulate the stock during these periods. Balanced RSI indicates minimal overbought or oversold conditions, suggesting a steady market sentiment. Market Dynamics suggest being a mid-cap industrial stock, volume rises with industrial or macroeconomic growth trends.

Bharat Electronics indicates stable, high trading volumes due to its status as a defence sector leader. Volume spikes occur around announcements of defence contracts/policy shifts, indicating trader confidence in BEL's dominance in the sector. EMA Alignment is consistent EMA trends signify a strong baseline for institutional trading interest. RSI indicates rare situation of extreme zones, reflecting consistent, long-term investor confidence. Market Dynamics is favourite among investors seeking defence exposure. Stable volumes make it less risky for short-term trading and highly reliable for long-term investment.

Crompton Greaves indicates moderate trading volumes with sharp spikes during result announcements or product launches in the home appliances sector. Limited participation from large investors, as seen by relatively low average volumes. EMA Crossovers indicate short-term volatility, useful for swing traders. RSI value is indicating periodic dips below 30 suggest undervaluation and potential entry points for value investors. Market Dynamics, investors monitor Crompton for product innovation or earnings surprises; lower liquidity during off-peak periods highlights niche appeal.

HDFC Bank indicating exceptionally high trading volumes, given its blue-chip status and representation in major indices. Volume surges align with quarterly results and major banking sector developments. EMA Trends showing consistent upward trajectory in EMA aligns with its long-term bullish sentiment. RSI value signifies limited excursions into extreme zones signify a balanced market perception. According to Market Dynamics high liquidity, market-wide importance, and institutional ownership drive consistent volume activity.

IDFC First Bank is having high trading activity, reflecting strong interest from both retail and institutional investors. Spikes correspond with announcements of loan growth, expansion strategies, or broader banking sector rallies. EMA Trends reflects periods of short-term bullish and bearish phases, suitable for traders. RSI value is signifying frequent movements into the overbought zone signal strong price momentum, attracting short-term traders. Market Dynamics effects, positioned as a growth-oriented bank, IDFC First attracts high volumes due to retail investor participation.

Infosys has consistent volume indicates strong investor interest due to Infosys's global IT dominance. Occasional volume spikes align with earnings announcements or significant global tech news. EMA Crossovers, indicate consolidation and alignment with broader tech sector movements. RSI value signifies occasional overbought conditions show increased activity during earnings-driven growth phases. Market Dynamics effect is being a technology leader, Infosys remains highly liquid, making it attractive for both long-term and short-term investors.

Reliance Industries (RIL) is also reflecting exceptional high and stable trading volumes, shows its dominance in multiple sectors like telecom, energy, and retail. Spikes correspond with significant announcements (e.g., Jio launches, retail expansions, or new energy ventures). **RIL** significantly showing EMA Crossovers, indicating moderate trends with occasional reversals, highlighting trading opportunities. RSI movement shows the stock is overbought/oversold regions often predicts price action shifts. Market Dynamic effect of RIL's massive market cap and diversified operations ensure continuous trading activity.

Vaibhav Global significantly having lower average volume reflecting niche market appeal and limited large-scale investor participation. Spikes correlate with earnings announcements or dividend declarations. **EMA Crossover** Suggests volatility and short-term trading opportunities. RSI value signifies occasional dips into oversold zones indicate potential undervaluation for contrarian investors. Market Dynamics effect of Vaibhav Global since a mid-cap stock, it's trading patterns are sensitive to sector-specific news and retail investor sentiment.

5.5. Forecasting of Price Movement & Expected Price

To Determine the capabilities of ChatGPT in price forecasting, we have developed a model where we fed news data and instructed to run a sentimental analysis based on news headlines. The prediction forecast period we considered is for the next quarter Q2 (July-September). If the news is positive, it is indicated as "Good", if the news seems negative it is indicated as "Bad" otherwise indicate as "Neutral". Therefore "Good" indicates "UP" otherwise "Negative" indicates "DOWN". Here out of 9 predictions 8 predictions were correct and 1 was incorrect. Correct values are "TRUE", incorrect were indicated as "False".

Table 2. Price forecasting using sentiment analysis

Companies	CMP (Jun-2024)	CMP (Sep-2024)	FPM(UP/DOWN/NEUTRAL)	True/False
Adani Greens	1788.8	2070.55	UP	TRUE
APL Apollo Tubes	1549.35	1584.15	UP	TRUE
Bharat Electronic	305.07	285.1	UP	FALSE
Crompton Greaves	402.5	469.6	UP	TRUE
HDFC Bank	1683.8	1768.05	UP	TRUE
IDFC First Bank	82.16	74.35	DOWN	TRUE
Infosys	1549.11	1854	UP	TRUE
RIL	1554.55	1476.57	DOWN	TRUE
Vaibhav Global	305.38	309.51	NEUTRAL	TRUE
Accuracy Ratio				**88.89%**

Source: Author's Calculation

Indicators*

CMP= Current Market Price

FPM= Forecasted Price Movement

The Accuracy Ratio suggests that the model's prediction of stocks is 88.89% correct. This indicates a relatively high level of accuracy in predicting the direction of stock price movement for this particular dataset.

Specific Observations: Adani Greens, APL Apollo Tubes, Crompton Greaves, HDFC Bank, Infosys: The model correctly predicted that these stocks would move UP in price. Bharat Electronic: The model incorrectly predicted that this stock would move UP, while it actually went DOWN. RIL: The model correctly predicted that these stocks would move DOWN in price. Whereas Vaibhav Global was between the resistance and support level remaining as NEUTRAL

Nevertheless, it is important to remember that past performance is not indicative of future results. Stock prices are influenced by various factors, and no model can perfectly predict future movements.

Followed by this, we have asked ChatGPT to integrate the news sentiments along with the historical price movements for getting better results. Here we fed the price data from January 2023-June 2024 to finely tune our model and asked the expected price and return % for next quarterly results.

Table 3. Price forecasting integrating sentiment analysis & historical price

Companies	CMP (Jun-2024)	Predicted Price (PP)	Actual Price (AP)	Accuracy Ratio
Adani Greens	1,788.80	1,878.24	2,070.55	91%
Infosys	1,549.11	1,610.50	1,854.00	87%
HDFC Bank	1,683.80	1,869.02	1,783.00	95%
BEL	305.90	330.00	293.30	87%
Crompton Greaves	405.90	450.00	441.55	98%
IDFC First Bank	82.16	77.50	74.35	96%
APL Apollo Tubes	1,549.35	1,679.70	1,584.15	94%

continued on following page

Table 3. Continued

Companies	CMP (Jun-2024)	Predicted Price (PP)	Actual Price (AP)	Accuracy Ratio
RIL	1,554.55	1,510.50	1,476.57	98%
Vaibhav Global	305.38	305.00	309.51	99%
Avg. Accuracy Ratio				**94%**

Source: Author's Calculation
Accuracy Ratio *f(x):1-ABS(PP/AP-1)*

Interpretation

The model achieved an average accuracy ratio of 94%. This suggests that the model was generally quite accurate in predicting the direction of stock price movement for the given period.

Individual Stock Performance

- **Adani Greens:** The model predicted a price increase, which was accurate, but the actual price was significantly higher than predicted.
- **Infosys:** The model predicted a price increase, which was accurate, but the actual price observed significantly higher than predicted.
- **HDFC Bank:** The model predicted a price increase, which was accurate, and the actual price increase was significantly close to the predicted one.
- **BEL:** The model predicted a price increase, which was inaccurate as the price actually decreased.
- **Crompton Greaves:** The model predicted a price increase, which was accurate, and the actual price increase was significantly close to the predicted one.
- **IDFC First Bank:** The model predicted a price decrease, which was accurate, and the actual price decrease was significantly close to the predicted one.
- **APL Apollo Tubes:** The model predicted a price increase, which was accurate, but the actual price increase was significantly lower than predicted.
- **RIL:** The model predicted a price decrease, which was accurate, and the actual price decrease was significantly close to the predicted one.
- **Vaibhav Global:** The model predicted to stay moderately flat to downward movement with a price band of 300-310, which was accurate as the price actually was between the price band.

Mean Absolute Error is a metric that calculates the average magnitude of the absolute errors between the predicted and actual values, The table provided shows the predicted stock prices for various companies as of June 2024, along with their actual prices in September 2024, and two error metrics: Absolute Bias (ABS) and Mean Absolute Error (MAE).

Table 4. Price Forecasting integrating Sentiment Analysis & Historical Price (ABS & MAE)

Companies	CMP (Jun-2024)	Expected Price (E)	Observed Price (O)	ABS	MAE
Adani Greens	1,788.80	1,878.24	2,070.55	192.31	
Infosys	1,549.11	1,610.50	1,854.00	243.5	
HDFC Bank	1,683.80	1,869.02	1,783.00	86.02	
BEL	305.90	330.00	293.30	36.7	
Crompton Greaves	405.90	450.00	441.55	8.45	
IDFC First Bank	82.16	77.50	74.35	3.15	
APL Apollo Tubes	1,549.35	1,679.70	1,584.15	95.55	
RIL	1,554.55	1,510.50	1,476.57	33.93	
Vaibhav Global	305.38	305.00	309.51	4.51	
Total ABS				**704.12**	**78.23556**

Source: Author's Calculation

Interpretation

The model achieved an average MAE of 78.23556. This suggests that, on average, the model's predictions were off by approximately 78.24 points from the actual prices.

Individual Stock Performance

- **Adani Greens:** The model predicted a price increase, which was accurate, but the actual price was significantly higher than predicted (ABS = 192.31).
- **Infosys:** The model predicted a price increase, which was accurate, but the actual price was significantly higher than predicted (ABS = 243.5).
- **HDFC Bank:** The model predicted a price increase, which was accurate, and the actual price increase was significantly close to the predicted one (ABS = 86.02).
- **BEL:** The model predicted a price increase, which was inaccurate as the price actually decreased (ABS = 36.7).
- **Crompton Greaves:** The model predicted a price increase, which was accurate, and the actual price was significantly close to the predicted one (ABS = 8.45).
- **IDFC First Bank:** The model predicted a price decrease, which was accurate, and the actual price was significantly close to the predicted one (ABS = 3.15).
- **APL Apollo Tubes:** The model predicted a price increase, which was accurate, but the actual price increase was lower than predicted (ABS = 95.55).
- **RIL:** The model predicted a price decrease, which was accurate, and the actual price was significantly close to the predicted one (ABS = 33.93).
- **Vaibhav Global:** The model predicted a flat movement to downward in price with a resistance and support band between 300-310, which was significantly accurate as the price actually stayed between the price band (ABS = 4.51).

Percentage error is a measure of how close a measured or estimated value is to the actual or known value. It's expressed as a percentage. The table provided shows the predicted stock prices for various companies as of June 2024, along with their actual prices in September 2024, and the percentage error between the predicted and observed prices.

Table 5. Price Forecasting integrating Sentiment Analysis & Historical Price (Percent Error)

Companies	CMP (Jun-2024)	Expected Price	Observed Price	Percentage Error
Adani Greens	1,788.80	1,878.24	2,070.55	-9.29%
Infosys	1,549.11	1,610.50	1,854.00	-13.13%
HDFC Bank	1,683.80	1,869.02	1,783.00	4.82%
BEL	305.90	330.00	293.30	12.51%
Crompton Greaves	405.90	450.00	441.55	1.91%
IDFC First Bank	82.16	77.50	74.35	4.24%
APL Apollo Tubes	1,549.35	1,679.70	1,584.15	6.03%
RIL	1,554.55	1,510.50	1,476.57	2.30%
Vaibhav Global	305.38	305.00	309.51	-1.46%
Avg. Percentage Error				1%

Source: Author's Calculation
Percentage Error $f(x)$= (|Expected Price - Actual Price| / Actual Price) * 100

Interpretation

The model achieved an average percentage error of 1%. This suggests that, on average, the model's predictions were off by approximately 1% from the actual prices.

Individual Stock Performance

- **Adani Greens:** The model predicted a price increase, which was accurate, but the actual price increase was higher than predicted (-9.29% error).
- **Infosys:** The model predicted a price increase, which was accurate, but the actual price increase was higher than predicted (-13.13% error).
- **HDFC Bank:** The model predicted a price increase, which was accurate, and the actual price increase was close to the predicted one (4.82% error).
- **BEL:** The model predicted a price increase, which was inaccurate as the price actually decreased (12.51% error).
- **Crompton Greaves:** The model predicted a price increase, which was accurate, and the actual price increase was close to the predicted one (1.91% error).
- **IDFC First Bank:** The model predicted a price decrease, which was accurate, and the actual price decrease was close to the predicted one (4.24% error).
- **APL Apollo Tubes:** The model predicted a price increase, which was accurate, but the actual price increase was lower than predicted (6.03% error).

- **RIL:** The model predicted a price decrease, which was accurate, and the actual price decrease was close to the predicted one (2.30% error).
- **Vaibhav Global:** The model predicted a price increase, which was inaccurate as the price actually decreased (-1.46% error).

6. FINDINGS

Based on the comprehensive evaluation of the AI-Chatbot i.e., ChatGPT structure's performance in stock market analysis, several key findings emerge:

- **Improved Version 4.0:** As compared to ChatGPT 3.5, ChatGPT 4.0 is now capable of understanding Indian stock market with the help of pre-built models like Stock Market Analyst-GPT, which is specifically built for better interpretation of stock market information. It also has file upload feature which enables user to provide data directly to GPT for interpretation of the provided data.
- **Strategic Portfolio Building:** AI-Chatbots are now capable of generating portfolio based on user's financial need and purpose. It would suggest the number of stocks, capital allocation, companies recommended according to the risk appetite and duration of holding period.
- **Web Searching Access:** The new version of ChatGPT is capable to access real time data through web search function. We found that this might help in getting latest stock news, fundamentals or any related information required.
- **Limited Access to GPT 4.0:** ChatGPT 4.0 has limited access for free users to use its advanced features. To get access for the complete version we need to subscribe to ChatGPT Plus which costs around $20/per month which is around Rs.1950/per month INR. This relevantly seems to be a costly option for Indian users to afford.
- **Coder for Non-Coders:** Ai-Chatbots are now capable of generating complex python codes which is a life-saver to non-Coders. Since in data analytics languages like python is essential but now ChatGPT generates those codes within seconds for functions like sentiment analysis, stock price forecast even for data interpretation and data visualization.
- **Data visualization:** Now AI-Chatbots like ChatGPT can generate data and visualize them through images and charts, we observed that with simple prompt instructions we were able to generate complex charts within seconds.
- **Limited capabilities in running Big Data:** ChatGPT has limited capabilities in running large files, since it was observed that ChatGPT wasn't able to interpret EMA 50, EMA 200 since it lacks in interpreting files with large dataset for which we required to feed only historical data of 1 year period using EMA10 and EMA20. Using EMA50 and EMA200 would have given a better interpretation of data, resulting a better analysis.
- **Limitations of the dataset and evaluation period:** The findings are based on a specific dataset and evaluation period, which was not fully captured by the model's performance across different market conditions and over longer time horizons. Since ChatGPT also has limitation in document analysing. This limitation highlights the importance of conducting more extensive evaluations with larger and more diverse datasets to assess the model's robustness and generalizability.

- **Potential for further improvement:** While ChatGPT 4.0 structure demonstrates promising results in predicting stock price movements, there is room for improvement. Further optimization is required since some functions have bugs and glitches and are not well-optimized. New improved AI-Chatbots can be developed to reduce the errors we found in Open Ai's ChatGPT. Better predictive and sentimental analysis models can be developed and the integration of these models can lead to more accurate results.
- **Implications for stock market analysis and investment strategies:** The findings underscore the potential of ChatGPT's prediction structure to provide valuable insights and support decision-making in the field of stock market analysis and investment strategies. It needs more improvements to understand the market dynamics of India, since in some scenarios we have observed unsatisfactory results due to lack of market understanding of the model. However, the practical implementation of the model requires careful consideration of the trade-offs between performance, cost, and the specific requirements of the use case.

7. LIMITATIONS & CHALLENGES

Although prompt engineering provides a versatile and practical way to direct ChatGPT, there are intrinsic limitations:

- **Model Constraints:** Because of ChatGPT's knowledge cutoff and training constraints, it is not possible to obtain real-time information. Accordingly, for prompts design is paramount for mitigation through exploring historical/generic examples, without any specific examples.
- **Lack of Predictive Validity:** As a result, the responses generated by ChatGPT are historical outputs rather than real-time market behaviour, should be treated as indicative only and not as invocations to invest directly.
- **Lack of Large Document Breakdown:** Though we can use ChatGPT for analysing files, images and documents yet it fails to interpret documents which are larger in size. It surely fails to scan the file and sometimes gives unsatisfactory results.
- **Financial Planning and Analysis**: Financial Planning and Analysis (FP&A) involves forecasting and making strategic financial decisions. Generative AI models enhance this process by predicting future financial trends using historical data. However, challenges emerge during unexpected events like economic crises, where market behavior deviates sharply from past patterns. Adapting AI algorithms to navigate such unpredictable scenarios remains a significant challenge in financial planning and analysis.
- **Risk Management:** Risk management involves identifying and mitigating various risks. Generative AI models analyze historical data but may overlook emerging risks or interconnectedness between different risk factors. Additionally, ensuring ethical AI use, avoiding biases, remains a critical challenge in risk management.
- **Ethical Challenges in Using AI Chatbots like ChatGPT for Stock Market Analysis:** In the context of using AI chatbots like ChatGPT for investment decision-making in the Indian stock market, several ethical challenges arise. These challenges can impact investor trust, market integrity, and the broader financial ecosystem. Below are key ethical concerns.

1. Data Privacy and Security

- **Challenge:** AI chatbots require access to sensitive financial and personal data to provide personalized investment advice. Mishandling or unauthorized access to this data can lead to privacy breaches.
- **Implications**: Investors' confidential information (e.g., financial goals, transaction history) could be exposed or misused, violating data protection laws.
- **Example**: If ChatGPT integrates with brokerage accounts without strict data protection measures, it could become a target for cyberattacks.
- **Mitigation:** Compliance with India's *Digital Personal Data Protection Act, 2023* and implementation of advanced encryption protocols are necessary.

2. Algorithmic Bias and Discrimination

- **Challenge:** AI models like ChatGPT can inherit biases from the data they are trained on, leading to biased or discriminatory investment advice.
- **Implications:** Certain investor groups (e.g., rural investors, women, or minority communities) may receive skewed or less favorable recommendations, limiting fair access to financial opportunities.
- **Example:** A biased algorithm might prioritize high-risk financial products for certain demographics while recommending safer options to others.
- **Mitigation:** Regular bias audits, diverse training datasets, and fairness metrics in model evaluation.

3. Accountability and Liability Issues

- **Challenge:** Determining responsibility for financial losses caused by AI-generated advice is unclear.
- **Implications:** If investors suffer losses due to inaccurate or misleading recommendations, it is difficult to hold the AI model or the financial institution accountable.
- **Example:** If ChatGPT misinterprets market trends and suggests a failing stock, the investor bears the loss, raising questions about legal responsibility.
- **Mitigation:** Establishing clear accountability frameworks for AI-generated financial advice and regulatory oversight.

4. Market Manipulation and Ethical Misuse

- **Challenge:** AI chatbots could be exploited to spread misleading financial information or manipulate market trends.
- **Implications:** Malicious use of AI for pumping false market data could influence stock prices, leading to market volatility and unfair trading advantages.
- **Example:** Chatbots could be programmed to generate positive sentiment around weak stocks, artificially inflating prices (*pump-and-dump schemes*).
- **Mitigation:** Implementing strict monitoring systems and regulatory controls to detect and prevent market manipulation.

5. Overdependence on AI for Financial Decisions

- **Challenge:** Investors may become overly reliant on AI recommendations, reducing their own critical thinking and due diligence.
- **Implications:** Blind trust in AI could lead to poor financial decisions, especially during market disruptions where AI models may fail to adapt.
- **Example:** An investor following ChatGPT's advice during an economic crisis without cross-verifying market signals could incur significant losses.
- **Mitigation:** Educating users to treat AI recommendations as supplementary, not definitive, and encouraging human oversight.

8. CONCLUSION

This study aimed to determine the potential of ChatGPT v4.0's capabilities in stock market analysis by developing an analysis model that integrates stock price and news data. The main findings indicate the incorporation of external data sources and prompt engineering techniques can significantly improve ChatGPT's capabilities in picking stocks, capital allocation, predicting stock price movements and valuable information for investment decision-making.

From this study we got to know how AI chatbots and LLMs are efficient and effective to analyse the Indian stock market and give results as the investment needs of the investors through prompt engineering techniques. Findings suggests ChatGPT is capable for suggesting stocks, capital allocation and building a balanced portfolio taking the risk in factor. This highlights the potential of AI chatbots like ChatGPT to support more informed and efficient decision-making in equity market investments.

Although, it is essential to acknowledge the limitations and drawbacks of this research. This study relies on specific dataset and evaluation timeframe, which may not represent the true capabilities of the model's performance across different market conditions. In future research it is recommended to find out better models of AI Chatbots that can analyse the stocks more precisely which would help investors to participate fairly in the stock market.

The evaluation results showed how ChatGPT suggested stocks for investments, capital allocation in different sectors and based on its recommendations we referred to Google Finance to get the actual idea how much returns the stocks have made for the past 5 years. The model also has achieved 88.89% accuracy in predicting the price movements based on stocks news. With historical data it had further predicted the estimated price and return% for next quarter where it has achieved 94% accuracy. Mean Absolute Error signified the prediction was off by 78.24 points, suggesting a good score.

In conclusion, the integration of AI chatbots like ChatGPT in financial decision-making presents a promising future for investors in the Indian stock market. By continuously refining these models and addressing existing limitations, AI-powered financial tools can significantly enhance market participation and investment outcome.

REFERENCES

Agarwal, S., Chakravarti, S., Ghosh, O., & Chakrabarti, G. (2023). Dynamic market risk and portfolio choice: Evidence from Indian stock market. *IIMB Management Review*, *35*(3), 240–257.

Alnefaie, A., Singh, S., Kocaballi, B., & Prasad, M. (2021, January). An overview of conversational agent: applications, challenges and future directions. In *17th International Conference on Web Information Systems and Technologies*. SCITEPRESS-Science and Technology Publications.

Bahoo, S., Cucculelli, M., Goga, X., & Mondolo, J. (2024). Artificial intelligence in Finance: A comprehensive review through bibliometric and content analysis. *SN Business & Economics*, *4*(2), 23.

Cao, L. (2022). Ai in finance: Challenges, techniques, and opportunities. *ACM Computing Surveys*, *55*(3), 1–38.

Dakalbab, F., Talib, M. A., Nassir, Q., & Ishak, T. (2024). Artificial intelligence techniques in financial trading: A systematic literature review. *Journal of King Saud University. Computer and Information Sciences*, •••, 102015.

Das, S. K., Anwar, S., Tulsyan, U., Gupta, Y., Vudatha, R., Hassan, S., & Gardezi, I. (2024). The Role of AI in Financial Markets: Impacts on Trading, Portfolio Management, and Price Prediction. *Journal of Electrical Systems*, *20*(6s), 1000–1006.

Dong, M. M., Stratopoulos, T. C., & Wang, V. X. (2024). A scoping review of ChatGPT research in accounting and finance. *International Journal of Accounting Information Systems*, *55*, 100715.

Dowling, M., & Lucey, B. (2023). ChatGPT for (finance) research: The Bananarama conjecture. *Finance Research Letters*, *53*, 103662.

Eisfeldt, A. L., & Schubert, G. (2024). *AI and Finance* (No. w33076). National Bureau of Economic Research.

Fotheringham, D., & Wiles, M. A. (2023). The effect of implementing chatbot customer service on stock returns: An event study analysis. *Journal of the Academy of Marketing Science*, *51*(4), 802–822.

. Goel, J., Nihalani, S. V., Bhagwat, S., & Agarwal, V. Artificial Intelligence in Stock Market: Concepts, Applications and Limitations.

Gurdgiev, C., & O'Loughlin, D. (2020). Herding and anchoring in cryptocurrency markets: Investor reaction to fear and uncertainty. *Journal of Behavioral and Experimental Finance*, *25*, 100271.

Jain, R., & Vanzara, R. (2023). Emerging Trends in AI-Based Stock Market Prediction: A Comprehensive and Systematic Review. *Engineering Proceedings*, *56*(1), 254.

Khan, M. S., & Umer, H. (2024). ChatGPT in finance: Applications, challenges, and solutions. *Heliyon*, *10*(2). PMID: 38304767

Lin, C. Y., & Marques, J. A. L. (2024). Stock market prediction using Artificial Intelligence: A systematic review of Systematic Reviews. *Social Sciences & Humanities Open*, *9*, 100864.

Lopez-Lira, A., & Tang, Y. (2023). Can chatgpt forecast stock price movements? return predictability and large language models. *arXiv preprint arXiv:2304.07619*.

Mhlanga, D. (2020). Industry 4.0 in finance: The impact of artificial intelligence (ai) on digital financial inclusion. *International Journal of Financial Studies*, *8*(3), 45.

Mumtaz, U., & Mumtaz, S. (2023). Potential of ChatGPT in predicting stock market trends based on Twitter Sentiment Analysis. *arXiv preprint arXiv:2311.06273*.

Pelster, M., & Val, J. (2024). Can ChatGPT assist in picking stocks? *Finance Research Letters*, *59*, 104786.

Possati, L. M. (2023). Psychoanalyzing artificial intelligence: The case of Replika. *AI & Society*, *38*(4), 1725–1738.

Thach, N. N., Hanh, H. T., Huy, D. T. N., & Vu, Q. N. (2021). technology quality management of the industry 4.0 and cybersecurity risk management on current banking activities in emerging markets-the case in Vietnam. *International Journal of Qualitative Research*, *15*(3), 845.

Zaremba, A., & Demir, E. (2023). ChatGPT: Unlocking the future of NLP in finance. *Modern Finance*, *1*(1), 93–98.

Zarifhonarvar, A. (2024). Economics of chatgpt: A labor market view on the occupational impact of artificial intelligence. *Journal of Electronic Business & Digital Economics*, *3*(2), 100–116.

. Zheng, Q. (2024). How can we use ChatGPT better: A research of API-Enhanced ChatGPT in stock prediction.

Chapter 8
Navigating Towards Sustainability:
The Role of Corporate Governance and AI-Driven Behavioral Interventions

Mohammad Irfan
https://orcid.org/0000-0002-4956-1170
Christ University, Bengaluru, India

Rui Teixeira Dias
https://orcid.org/0000-0002-6138-3098
ESCAD, IPLUSO, Intrepid Lab, Lisboa, Portugal

Manas Khemka
https://orcid.org/0009-0001-6748-4076
Christ University, Bengaluru, India

Pragya Mondal
https://orcid.org/0009-0004-3508-6454
Christ University, Bengaluru, India

N. Mohan
https://orcid.org/0000-0002-2729-960X
CMR Institute of Technology, Bengaluru, India

ABSTRACT

The paper explores how corporate governance practices influence non-financial performance, particularly sustainability. Strong governance ensures that ESG principles are integrated into business operations, promoting long-term sustainability. The study examines the effectiveness of AI-assisted behavioral interventions in advancing sustainable practices. AI can mitigate cognitive biases and irrational decisions, pushing individuals and organizations toward sustainability. AI-driven governance frameworks can enhance non-financial performance, including environmental stewardship, social responsibility, and ethical governance. Through case studies and analysis, the paper provides insights into how AI and corporate governance can optimize sustainability strategies beyond traditional financial metrics.

DOI: 10.4018/979-8-3693-9684-1.ch008

INTRODUCTION

Sustainability has emerged as a prominent narrative of the corporate world with intensifying challenges from climate change, dwindling natural resources, and rising social inequalities. This would have once been considered ancillary in the corporation's strategy and its way of doing business but, rather than that, has now formed one of the very central pillars to corporate strategy. This way of transformation is growing where companies begin to understand that success should not just be about finance and that a company can judge and measure how well it will fare in an ever-changing environment by some non-financial metrics—environmental, social responsibility, and governance (ESG), (Raman et al., 2024). This paradigm shift calls for organizations to align their corporate governance frameworks in such a way that sustainability becomes integrated into the core of their activities.

Corporate governance is defined as the system of principles, processes, and practices that give direction to organizational decision-making. This system not only tells how companies are directed and controlled but also influences their strategic priorities and responses to emerging issues. Strong governance frameworks ensure that businesses are adequately prepared to navigate the complexities of sustainability, aligning objectives with ESG principles and ensuring accountability, transparency, and ethical behavior. Corporate governance plays a very important role in the pursuit of sustainability. Well-governed organizations are more likely to adopt proactive approaches to sustainability, leveraging their governance structures to embed ESG considerations into their strategies (Isalm, 2024).

By doing so, they enhance their reputation, mitigate risks, and create long-term value for stakeholders. Integration of ESG principles into corporate governance frameworks also helps organizations to forecast and respond to the growing expectations of investors, customers, and regulators as leaders in sustainability (Aagaard, 2024). Non-financial performance, which encompasses a wide range of metrics such as energy efficiency, waste management, employee well-being, and community engagement, has emerged as a key focus for organizations striving to meet sustainability goals. In response to growing stakeholder demands for transparency and accountability, companies are increasingly prioritizing non-financial performance as a measure of their commitment to ESG principles. The organizations build trust and loyalty among their stakeholders by setting aligning sustainability objectives with stakeholder interests, thus further strengthening corporate credibility (Zhao & Fariñas, 2022).

The rapid advancements in artificial intelligence (AI) have opened new doors for corporate governance to better non-financial performance. AI technologies, with their capacity to process great volumes of data and generating actionable insights, provide transformative power for organizations seeking better sustainability practice. (Aagaard, 2024) By leveraging AI, companies can develop innovative solutions for complex sustainability challenges, including optimizing resource allocation and minimizing carbon footprints. One of the most promising fields of AI application in sustainability is in behavioural interventions. AI-driven behavioral interventions alter stakeholder behavior by urging them to undertake actions relevant to sustainability objectives. Such interventions focus on insights from behavioral science and AI analytics to create pointed nudges that push people in the direction of sustainable practice, such as recommending to specific employees how to reduce consumption of energy or implement better environmental practices. Behavioral interventions are valuable for attacking the cognitive biases and irrational patterns of decision making that characteristically impede progress toward sustainability. Cognitive biases - such as overconfidence, loss aversion, and status quo bias - can cause people and organizations to focus on immediate payoffs rather than sustainability goals. An example could be a company that prioritizes cost-cutting measures with short-term benefits over long-term operational cost savings through investments in renewable sources of energy (Aagaard, 2024).

AI-driven behavioral interventions can address these biases by providing data-informed insights that make decision-making processes consistent with sustainability goals. Through a culture of evidence-based decision-making, AI empowers organizations to overcome psychological barriers that stand in the way of their journey toward sustainability. This not only increases their chances of achieving their sustainability targets but also improves their resilience against environmental and social challenges.

This is the unique opportunity that corporations have to catalyze transformation through corporate governance and AI. A sound governance framework sets the stage for ESG integration into organizational strategies, while AI technologies give birth to innovative solutions for addressing complex sustainability challenges. Herein lies a powerful synergy enhancing non-financial performance and enabling long-term value creation (Raman et al., 2024). This paper expands on the dynamic relationship between corporate governance and non-financial performance, with a specific focus on the role of AI in advancing sustainability. It looks into whether better-governed organizations are positioned to score higher on superior sustainability performance, utilizing their governance structures to more effectively embed ESG principles into their strategies. Finally, it also explores how AI-powered behavioral interventions could go about shaping stakeholder behavior towards more sustainable practices. To provide a comprehensive understanding of these issues, the paper incorporates case studies of successful organizations that have harnessed the power of AI to enhance their sustainability performance. The examples illustrate how innovative governance practices and cutting-edge technology can drive meaningful progress toward sustainability goals (Ajmera et al., 2024). They also highlight the importance of stakeholder engagement in fostering a culture of sustainability, emphasizing the role of transparency and inclusivity in decision-making processes. Stakeholder engagement is a critical component of sustainability initiatives because it fosters buy-in and support for non-financial performance objectives. Through stakeholder engagement, organizations build trust and create a sense of shared ownership over sustainability goals. This not only enhances their credibility as responsible corporate citizens but also strengthens their ability to navigate the complexities of sustainability challenges.

Sustainability is a vital ingredient in corporate governance frameworks that integrate it into the organization of today's world. Organizations placing sustainability at the heart of their strategies are better placed to capitalize on opportunities, mitigate risks, and create long-term value. By using AI technologies and behavioral insights, companies can revolutionize their approach to sustainability, making them leaders in ethical and responsible business practices (Adisa et al., 2024).

This paper aims to contribute to the emerging body of literature on corporate governance and sustainability by examining the intersections between governance practices, non-financial performance, and AI-assisted behavioral interventions. It aims to provide insights and recommendations that would equip organizations with the tools and strategies needed to achieve their sustainability objectives while fostering innovation and inclusivity. In conclusion, convergence between corporate governance and AI-driven behavioral interventions can be a transformational way to advance sustainability (Isalm, 2024). Through these tools, organizations are able to not only strengthen their non-financial performance but also take the lead in finding solutions to the social and environmental challenges of our time. This paper attempts to shine light on the pathways that corporate governance and AI may use to drive meaningful progress toward a sustainable future (Raman et al., 2024).

LITERATURE REVIEW

The depth of the influence of AI on different aspects of human life is engraved in its development. Recently, it has become a pivotal force in overcoming developmental challenges, especially those related to SD. Despite the growing relevance, there is a distinct lack of systematic studies on the role of AI research in the contribution to SD. The bibliometric approach presented here attempts to fill this gap by unearthing some of the essential trends and traces of evolution in concepts in the domain of AI applications for sustainable development goals. The aim of the paper is to discuss Industry 5.0, where sustainability merges with technology in transforming organizational culture and workforce management. It gives insight into the shift from traditional HRM to the use of ICT and e-HRM to improve effectiveness and inculcate sustainability into business operations. (N. Rane et al., 2024) This chapter examines various strategies to enhance innovation, the integration of HR strategies in the attainment of sustainability, and human capabilities integrated into technology. The frameworks that secure organizational resilience and underlines HRM's role in driving digital transformations. This chapter looks at building up a sustainable culture-featured by adaptability, collaboration, and sustainability principles. It outlines strategies to enhance employee engagement in sustainability initiatives, addresses challenges in integrating sustainable HRM practices, and highlights opportunities for innovation in Industry 5.0 (Aagaard, 2024).

Climate change and environmental degradation are pressing issues that call for a reevaluation of how we approach economic activities. Both leaders and corporations now shift their focus toward adopting practices and embracing the concept of the circular economy. The food and beverage industry is highly promising for potential transformations, given the fact that it plays a crucial role in terms of greenhouse gas emissions. This paper deals with understanding the role AI can play in enabling Circular Economy principles within the food and beverages industry (Rathod et al., 2024). This paper discusses the role of AI in shaping functionalities and enhancing user engagement in the Metaverse-an immersive digital world powered by virtual reality-in response to the increasing interest in it. Our research, focused on recent advancements, prevailing challenges, and potential future developments, draws from a comprehensive analysis grounded in meticulous methodology. The research study, informed by credible sources, is supported by the sources that include SD, Scopus, IEEE, and WoS, and encompasses 846 retrieved studies. After careful filtration, 54 research papers had been identified for relevance to form a basis in the specific taxonomy of AI in Metaverse applications. (Ajmera et al., 2024) the study has spanned a wide gamut of dimensions of Metaverse: augmented reality, virtual reality, mixed reality, Blockchain, Agent Systems, Intelligent NPCs, Societal and Educational Impact, HCI and Systems Design, and Technical Aspects. Our findings bring forward the importance of trustworthy AI adoption in the Metaverse that may enable improvement in user experience, protection of privacy, and responsibility of technology use. The present paper does not only elucidate scholarly interest in the Metaverse but also elaborates on the influence of the Metaverse on human behavior, education, societal norms, and community dynamics. (Aagaard, 2024) It provides the basis for further development and responsible implementation of the concept of the Metaverse, pointing out and discussing seven open issues which will provide invaluable insights for subsequent studies on integrating AI in the Metaverse.

The growth of artificial intelligence evidently denotes the impact that AI has brought into human life. Of late, it has tended to become a critical player in addressing developmental challenges in subsets, particularly in the realm of SD. Despite its ever-increasing relevance, striking rarity characterizes systematic studies relative to assessing the various contributions of AI research to the field of SD. The following chapter tries to bridge this gap by unmasking important bibliometric trends and conceptual evolution within the area of AI applications to sustainable development goals (Balcıoğlu et al., 2024).

Artificial Intelligence basically stands for a set of technologies with gigantic applications, ranging from autonomous automobiles to chatbots, including even fraud detection and diagnosis in medicine. While the domain of AI research has over a 50-year history, recent technological advances have facilitated their utilization and deployment in real-world applications. Despite the growing rates of AI deployment in organizations, many struggle to fully realize the business value from such technologies. Furthermore, AI is no exception to adverse or unintended effects, either. Growing concerns about AI adoption and cases of failed AI deployments-some resulting in deaths, the loss of jobs, and/or racial discrimination-have underlined the dire need for responsible AI governance. Thus, a gap exists between design, deployment, and usage and its business value for AI. (Aagaard, 2024) This thesis is based on a sequential multiple methods design. It started with an exploratory approach of identifying important aspects of RAIG and responsible principles (Adisa et al., 2024).

An exploratory literature review on the use of AI and its business value was first conducted. This was followed by a second literature review on RAIG to achieve the purposes of understanding principles and methods that guide responsible use of AI. Following the two literature reviews, a set of empirical studies is performed. We begin with a multi-case study involving three organizations to explore how responsible AI governance is implemented in practice and promotes the development of robust AI applications that introduce no negative effects. Subsequently, a case study was done with 14 expert interviews in order to investigate in-depth the importance of RAIG and dark side effects occurring if RAIG is missing. (Balcıoğlu et al., 2024) Research extended the idea to construct a conceptual framework showing the basic processes that involve AI resource orchestration. This framework represents an attempt to explain activities using strategic orchestration of resources by creating business value. Finally, an empirical questionnaire survey of 300 responses was conducted within Europe and the USA to determine whether RAIG generates value and, if so, by which mechanisms and processes this value is created. (Isalm, 2024) The results contribute to our understanding of how RAIG is implemented in organizations and what its resulting business value is by: first, developing a conceptual model that explores the basic dimensions of relevance for RAIG within organizations and discloses the supporting practices behind them; second, by determining the negative or unintended outcomes of AI when RAIG is lacking, grouped into three clusters regarding the nature of work, conflicts and effects, and responsibility; lastly, through a conceptual model presenting and explaining how firms manage their RAIG practices in order to enhance competitiveness. (Sklavos et al., 2024) Finally, the study discusses implications for research, practice, and policy, and also presents avenues for future investigation.

This presents an ever-changing tapestry of financial planning wherein integration using artificial intelligence is a pivotal force that will redefine the top contours of strategic decision-making, right to their operational efficiency. The historical growth and development, contemporary applications, and multifaceted impact of AI in financial planning are discussed in this paper with the intention of presenting the complexities and transformation possibilities from using the emergent AI technologies.

It does this through the critical analysis of existing peer-reviewed literature and empirical studies that trace the route of AI integration into finance-from foundational levels to the current positioning as a cornerstone of financial innovation. The methodology, in this respect, is based on a qualitative analysis that has systematically looked into the enhancement of AI in financial decision-making, challenges thrown up by it in terms of ethical and regulatory compliance issues, and qualitative changes in financial strategies brought about by the adoption of AI. (Aagaard, 2024) The findings highlight that AI is acting both as a catalyst for unprecedented efficiency and a harbinger of new challenges; hence, its integration should be balanced. Finally, the paper concludes by calling for a judicious blend of innovation and ethical stewardship, recommending that financial institutions welcome AI's potential while assiduously meeting its challenges through continuous learning, adaptability, and ethical vigilance. These recommendations, therefore, try to lead the different stakeholders through the maze of AI integration in a way that financial planning becomes more efficient and strategic, yet fair and transparent. The study below has been a lighthouse for any future exploration of how to maneuverer such intricacies as AI-driven financial planning. (Balcıoğlu et al., 2024) Artificial Intelligence is changing the ESG criteria and considerably strengthening business practices that are more sustainable. The paper throws light on those AI-driven methodologies that have bettered ESG performance across different sectors.

With the rise in regulatory demands and stakeholder expectations to be more transparent, companies are now embracing AI technologies for monitoring and reporting ESG metrics with unprecedented accuracy. AI enables the collection and analysis of data in real time, which could help companies track environmental impacts, optimize resource use, and decrease carbon emissions. Socially, AI fosters workforce diversity and inclusion through unbiased recruitment algorithms, improving workplace safety with predictive analytics in occupational health and safety. (Mayuranathan et al., 2024) In governance, AI-driven risk management tools and blockchain technologies enhance corporate governance by ensuring compliance and transparency in supply chains and financial reporting. It enables the use of NLP and machine learning algorithms in ESG data analytics to give sustainability reporting more robustness and insightfulness, hence helping business strategies align with global sustainability goals. Besides that, AI-powered predictive models pinpoint future ESG risks and opportunities, too, thus helping a business make informed decisions in the best interest of its long-term objectives related to sustainability. This review, therefore, looks at recent development evidencing AI's effectiveness in the implementation of ESG and zooms in on the role that AI plays in encouraging a culture of sustainability in organizations. (Pashang & Weber, 2023) As AI technologies continue to evolve, their transformative potential for ESG practices will make great strides toward contributing to resilient and sustainable businesses for the future. This research paper aims to discuss the transformative potentialities of AI in corporate finance and how this facilitation of efficiency would improve decision-making processes. Using machine learning, NLP, and RPA, AI introduces innovative ways to improve corporate governance and sustainability practices.

Today, every corporation faces an increasing challenge to operate efficiently and, at the same time, be conscious of environmental, social, and governance issues. Traditional ways of finance cannot handle big data efficiently and extract actionable insight in no time. AI introduced a paradigm shift that allowed automatic data analysis, pattern recognition, and predictive modeling. These allowed finance professionals to make fast and accurate decisions based on data. (Lehtimäki, 2024) The machine learning algorithms provided insights into patterns and correlation within financial data, which allowed proactive risk management and strategic planning. NLP technologies are also gaining valuable insights from unstructured data sources such as regulatory filings, news articles, and social media to support corporate governance and informed decision-making in sustainability. (Fadhel et al., 2024) Furthermore, RPA smooths out repetitive tasks and workflows that, in turn, reduces operation costs while freeing up human resources to pursue higher value activities. Through automation of routine processes like data entry, reconciliation, and reporting, RPA improves operational efficiencies and compliances. (Mayuranathan et al., 2024) With AI technologies, companies can unlock new opportunities for innovation, resource optimization, and sustainable growth in today's dynamic business environment. The future of companies and society in our fast-growing world is going to be shaped by AI integrated with ESG factors. This combination has huge potential for solving critical issues like mitigating the effects of climate change, social integration, and corporate governance. (Fadhel et al., 2024).

However, AI adoption also raises complex issues and concerns, as it introduces a unique set of risks and ethical considerations for ESG performance. (Isalm, 2024) This is why the present study tries to fill this gap by gathering and providing a current analysis of the impact of emerging technologies on the role of strategic leadership in pursuit of the business objective in the context of ESG issues. Materials, Methods, and Procedure: We performed the bibliometric analysis on the subject of this study through R Studio version 4.2.0; we used the bibliometric applications VOSviewer version 1.6.20 and Biblioshiny version 4.2.0. The data were collected from the Scopus database. Using the PRISMA method, 205 research publications were appropriately selected. According to the results, it can be shown that AI and ESG are two important requirements for the digitization of the boardroom. Meanwhile, it also has to be secured through an advanced detection system. Later, CEOs have to address issues regarding transparency and cybersecurity to avoid those specific risks and successfully earn the trust in business processes. Artificial intelligence is a two-edged sword in dealing with corporate sustainability challenges. (Mayuranathan et al., 2024) Artificial intelligence can make great leaps toward solving some of the most complicated environmental and social problems that mankind faces.

Efficiencies and innovations generated by AI may also bring new risks-for example, automated bias and conflict with human ethics. We argue that companies and governments should make a collective effort to address sustainability challenges and risks brought by AI. (Lehtimäki, 2024) Accountable and sustainable AI can be realized through a proactive regulatory framework supported by rigorous corporate policies and reports. With a view to this area of technological development, which is moving particularly fast, we recommend a harmonized regulatory approach considering the risks and allowing the coming on-stream of many different AI solutions for the common good. Ensuring a sufficient degree of technological neutrality and proportionality of the regulation will mitigate many of the varied risks that may be inherent in the use of AI. (Isalm, 2024) Instead of augmenting sustainability, unregulated AI would pose a threat since its effects on economy, society, and the environment would not be effectively put under surveillance. Such a suitable regulatory framework would create not only a consensus concerning the risks to avoid and how to do so, but also include enforcement mechanisms which would make sure that trustworthy and ethical use of AI in the boardroom is ensured. (Lehtimäki, 2024) It can then be referred to as a common good in itself and constitute an important asset to human development. The paper consequently goes on to discuss the dynamic interaction involving AI, digital transformation, and sustainable business development. It begins by setting the scene through the exploration of the ever-growing integration of AI and digital transformation within business practices today. It gives a backdrop wherein technological innovation reshapes the very configuration of organizations and gives birth to cross-sector innovation (Fadhel et al., 2024).

It underscores the criticality of sustainability for the global business landscape, from compliance to strategic imperative for long-term success. It dissects the role of AI in operational efficiency, environmental impact, and promotion of circular economy practices within sustainable business development. (Kalai et al., 2024) Real-life examples provide a tangible illustration of how businesses strategically transform models toward sustainability through digital means and are able to evidence the power of technology in fostering innovation and environmental consciousness in the practice of business. The research also illustrates how digital transformation increases stakeholder engagement, especially in customer relationships and community involvement. It follows through with strategic recommendations for businesses in this evolving landscape on integrating AI for sustainability, investing in ethical AI governance, continuous stakeholder engagement, and innovative business model strategies. (Zhao & Fariñas, 2022) It goes on to reiterate that responsible deployment of AI and digital transformation is about committing to a future that is ethical, resilient, and socially conscious.

Success Rates of Sustainability Initiatives

Figure 1. Success rates of sustainability initiatives

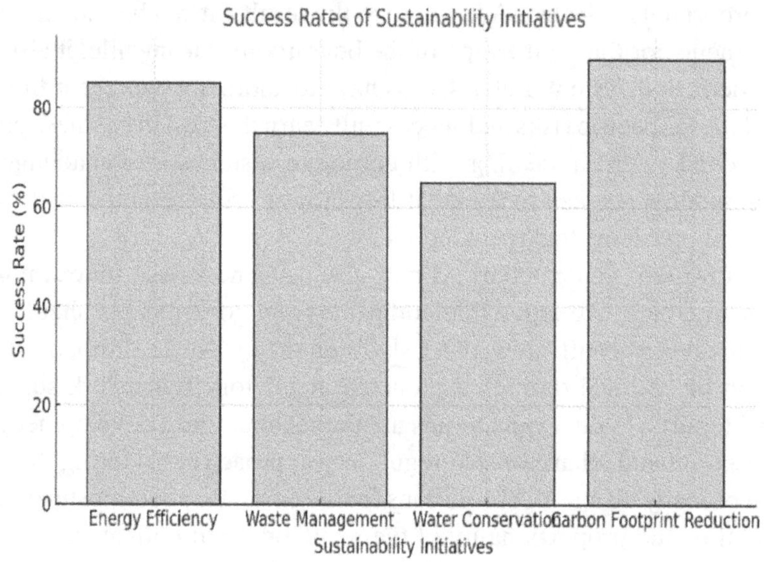

The bar graph provides a comparative analysis of the success rates of four key sustainability initiatives in corporate governance: Energy Efficiency, Waste Management, Water Conservation, and Carbon Footprint Reduction. Energy Efficiency (85%): Organizations have shown substantial progress in implementing energy-efficient technologies such as LED lighting, smart grids, and optimized industrial processes. High success in this area is attributed to cost-saving benefits, government incentives, and the availability of mature technologies. Waste Management (75%): Waste management initiatives have achieved a respectable success rate, driven by the increasing focus on reducing landfill waste and promoting recycling. However, challenges such as inadequate infrastructure in developing regions and a lack of consumer awareness affect further improvement (Aguilera, Aragon-Correa, Marano, & Tashman, 2022). Water Conservation (65%): Despite significant efforts, water conservation lags behind other initiatives. Success is constrained by challenges like aging water systems, limited public-private collaboration, and insufficient data analytics for efficient water use. Carbon Footprint Reduction (90%): This category exhibits the highest success rate, reflecting effective policies, widespread adoption of renewable energy sources, and carbon offset programs. Companies have increasingly prioritized reducing greenhouse gas emissions due to stakeholder pressure and global climate commitments. The bar graph emphasizes the diverse levels of success across these initiatives and identifies areas requiring additional focus, such as water conservation (Aguilera, Aragon-Correa, Marano, & Tashman, 2022).

Adoption of AI in Corporate Governance Over Time

Figure 2. Sources: McKinsey, Adoption of AI in Corporate Governance Over Time

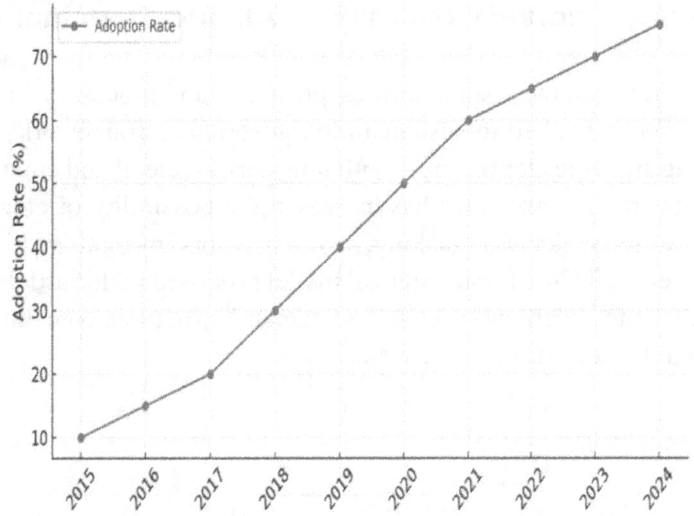

This line graph captures the year-on-year progression in the adoption of AI technologies within corporate governance frameworks, highlighting significant trends from 2015 to 2024.

Initial Slow Growth (2015-2018): During this period, the adoption rate grew slowly as organizations were in the exploratory phase of AI integration. Limited awareness and skepticism about AI's potential benefits in governance were major barriers. Rapid Acceleration (2019-2022): This period marked a steep increase in AI adoption. Technological advancements such as natural language processing (NLP), machine learning (ML), and predictive analytics allowed companies to use AI for compliance monitoring, fraud detection, and decision-making. Simultaneously, regulatory pressures and a competitive business environment pushed organizations to leverage AI for enhanced governance (Fadhel et al., 2024).. Plateauing Adoption (2023-2024): The adoption curve flattens in recent years, suggesting that a majority of early adopters have already implemented AI solutions. The plateau could be due to barriers such as high implementation costs, lack of skilled personnel, and the need for cultural adaptation within organizations. The line graph not only reflects the growing importance of AI in corporate governance but also indicates that future growth may require overcoming structural and financial challenges.

CONCEPTUAL FRAMEWORK

Corporate governance and sustainability have emerged as interdependent constructs in the current corporate landscape, reflecting the increasing recognition of the importance of non-financial performance metrics. Governance, traditionally focused on accountability and value creation, now encompasses environmental, social, and governance (ESG) considerations as a core dimension. Simultaneously, artificial intelligence (AI) has emerged as a transformative tool, offering capabilities that extend beyond operational efficiencies to support strategic decision-making in sustainability. (Isalm, 2024) This chapter presents a conceptual framework showing the interplay between corporate governance, AI, and sustainability. At the same time, it underscores the criticality of ESG principles in governance structures and explains how AI improves their implementation.

Interconnectedness: Corporate Governance, AI, and Sustainability

Corporate governance refers to the system of rules, practices, and processes through which firms are directed and controlled. When applied to sustainability, governance frameworks come to play a very prominent role in aligning strategies for business with long-term societal and environmental objectives. Implementing AI into governance structures has increased the possibility of creating sustainable outcomes by providing for definitive decision-making, avoiding errors in cognitive biases, and introducing a culture of data (Ajmera et al., 2024). The theoretical model proposed in this article depicts the dynamic relationship between corporate governance, AI, and sustainability in three core dimensions: governance foundations, AI as an enabler, and sustainability outcomes.

Figure 3. Sources: Author's Estimated

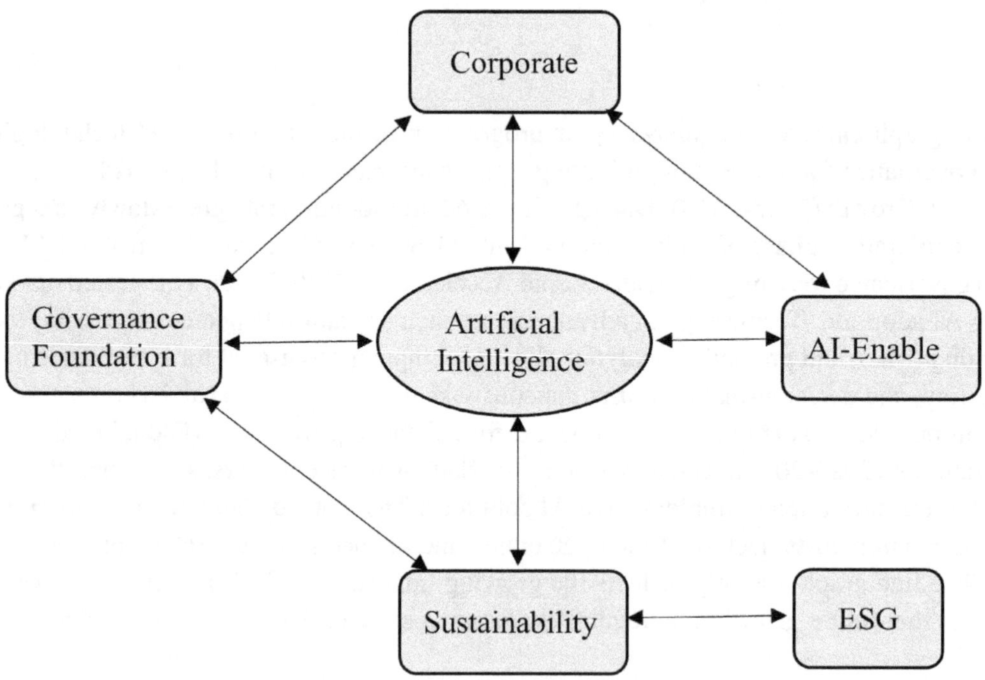

Governance foundations provide the structural and procedural base from which sustainability initiatives draw legitimacy and efficacy.

Role of Governance in Sustainability: Corporate governance helps organizations align their operations with ESG principles. This alignment means that sustainability is integrated into decision-making processes, ensuring that financial performance does not overshadow environmental and social considerations. Governance practices that prioritize ethical accountability, transparency, and stakeholder inclusivity are better positioned to achieve sustainability targets. Stakeholder Engagement: An essential part of governance is stakeholder engagement that will ensure diverse groups' viewpoints and interests are reflected in the sustainability strategy. (Isalm, 2024) This way, involving stakeholders in active ways with investors, employees, customers, and local communities, ESG initiatives are not only more legitimate but also more feasible. Risk Management: Governance frameworks that integrate sustainability considerations into risk assessment and mitigation enhance organizational resilience. Climate risks, regulatory shifts, and changing societal expectations call for governance mechanisms that proactively anticipate and address these challenges.

AI as an Enabler

Artificial intelligence serves as an enabler of governance and sustainability by improving decision-making processes, automating routine tasks, and generating actionable insights from complex datasets. Data-Driven Insights: AI technologies, such as machine learning and predictive analytics, help organizations process extensive datasets and derive meaningful insights. The insights thus generated support governance by identifying inefficiencies, predicting trends, and optimizing resource allocation. For example, AI-powered tools can analyze carbon footprints across the supply chain, allowing for targeted interventions to reduce emissions. (Isalm, 2024) Mitigating Cognitive Bias: Cognitive biases, including overconfidence, loss aversion, and status quo bias, often interfere with sustainable decision-making. AI-driven behavioral interventions can overcome such biases by providing data-informed alternatives that align short-term actions with long-term sustainability goals. AI-facilitated nudging strategies can influence employees and stakeholders to engage in behaviors that are environmentally and socially responsible. Real-Time Monitoring and Feedback: AI systems allow for sustainability metrics to be monitored in real-time, giving immediate feedback to decision-makers. This facility allows organizations to change strategies as needed to keep in alignment with ESG goals. AI-driven dashboards and visualizations make information accessible for stakeholders, increasing transparency and accountability. (Ajmera et al., 2024)

Sustainability Outcomes:The harmony between corporate governance and AI results in measurable sustainability outcomes including environmental stewardship, social responsibility, and ethical governance. Environmental Stewardship: AI-enhanced governance frameworks drive environmental sustainability by optimizing resource utilization, minimizing waste, and reducing greenhouse gas emissions. Predictive modeling and scenario analysis empower organizations to anticipate environmental impacts and implement proactive measures. Social Responsibility: Governance practices augmented by AI foster social equity by addressing issues such as diversity, inclusion, and community engagement. AI tools can assess demographic data to identify underrepresented groups and design initiatives that promote inclusivity and social well-being (Mikalef & Krogstie, 2024). Ethical Governance: The detection and mitigation of unethical practices through AI strengthen governance systems. ESG compliance monitoring through automated compliance systems and audits using AI helps improve the transparency in reporting and accountability.

ESG Integration as a Governance Imperative: ESG principles have developed from voluntary guidelines to being integral parts of corporate governance. The incorporation of ESG factors into governance structures not only helps in the improvement of non-financial performance but also places organizations in harmony with the sustainability objectives of the world, such as the United Nations' Sustainable Development Goals (SDGs). AI technologies make this integration possible by making ESG metrics operational and incorporating them into the core business processes. (Pashang & Weber, 2023). Role of ESG in Governance Structures: Environmental Considerations Governance systems that value environmental sustainability develop policies on energy efficiency, waste reduction, and climate change adaptation. AI technologies can measure accurately the environmental impact of their activities and give information for use in policy and operations. Social Pillar: The social pillar of ESG is all about human rights, labor practices, and community development. (Isalm, 2024) Governance systems that have AI can design just policies, monitor workplace conditions, and determine the societal implications of corporate initiatives.

Governance Principles: Governance, as the foundation of ESG, ensures accountability and ethical conduct. AI-driven systems improve governance through checks on compliance, detection of anomalies, and better clarity in reporting. Role of AI in ESG Implementation ESG principles are augmented with AI technologies in the following aspects:

Enhanced Reporting and Transparency AI simplifies ESG reporting by automating data gathering, analysis, and visualization. This makes sustainability disclosures more precise and accessible, fulfilling regulatory and other stakeholder expectations. (Mikalef & Krogstie, 2024)

Predictive Capabilities: AI's predictive capabilities allow organizations to anticipate ESG risks and opportunities, enabling preemptive action. For example, predictive models can forecast climate-related disruptions, informing risk mitigation strategies. Personalized Interventions: AI-driven behavioral interventions target specific organizational needs, promoting sustainable practices among employees and stakeholders. Personalized nudges, informed by behavioral analytics, align individual actions with organizational ESG objectives. (Aagaard, 2024)

The conceptual framework presented here underscores the transformative potential of combining corporate governance and AI to achieve sustainability goals. By aligning governance practices with ESG principles and leveraging AI's capabilities, organizations can drive meaningful non-financial performance outcomes. This interplay not only enhances environmental stewardship, social responsibility, and ethical governance but also positions organizations as leaders in the global transition toward sustainability. As the business landscape changes, the integration of AI in governance frameworks will become a necessity. (Oyeniyi et al., 2024) Future research and practice should focus on refining these frameworks and exploring innovative applications of AI to further embed sustainability into organizational strategies. (Zavrazhnyi, 2024).

The Role of AI-Assisted Behavioural Interventions in Governance

Frameworks guiding governance always are an existence to the extent that this corresponds to ensure that the corporate operations align towards the broader visions that also encompass matters of ecological integrity, social balance, and even issues of accountability. However, the decision-making processes behind implementing them face shortcomings that include those aspects brought forward from individual thought biasness plus also complexity that characterize a modern business context. AI is a new transformative tool for governance. It takes enormous data sets, identifies patterns that help provide actionable insights into enhancing decision-making. According to (Oyeniyi et al., 2024), This section explores the possible role of AI-driven behavioral interventions in aiding governance through cognitive biases, optimization of decisions and sustainability.

AI-Driven Decision Support

With modern governance frameworks in place, AI technologies incorporate the three most important elements: machine learning, natural language processing, and advanced data analytics. These tools help organizations streamline their decision-making process and improve their operational levels while aligning their strategy with sustainable goals.

Machine Learning and Data Analytics for Decision Support: Machine learning algorithms can analyze historical and real-time data to extract trends, predict future outcomes, and recommend optimal courses of action. In governance, this translates into an improvement in ESG performance. For example, it can determine the carbon footprint of different configurations of supply chains and advise on greener practices. (Isalm, 2024)

Data analytics aggregates and synthesizes information from various sources to improve decision making. Data visualization tools enable governance bodies to present sustainability metrics on which stakeholders can base their decisions. For instance, analytics platforms can track the pattern of energy usage, offer suggestions of potential measures for saving energy, and do so according to organizational needs.

AI for Scenario Planning and Risk Assessment: AI-driven scenario planning helps governance teams model the possible outcomes of different strategies. It helps organizations to plan and analyze long-term effects of decisions made, especially if the issue is related to sustainability. For example, an AI model can simulate the financial and environmental impacts of renewable energy sources with financial aspects balanced against short-term costs versus long-term gains.

Another area to which AI technologies are really applying themselves is risk assessment. (Oyeniyi et al., 2024) While taking environmental, social, and geopolitical considerations into account, AI determines the risks that emerge and provides suggestions on how to counteract them. For example, AI may predict disruptions in raw material supply chains with regard to climate change, and hence, allows organizations to diversify their sourcing strategies.

Mitigating Cognitive Biases with AI: The most common barriers to the attainment of sustainability goals are cognitive biases, systematic deviations from rational decision-making. These systematically influence both individual and organizational behavior by leading to suboptimal decisions in favor of short-term gains rather than long-term objectives. AI-assisted interventions deal with these cognitive biases through data-driven recommendations and nudges guiding decision-makers toward sustainable choices. (Zavrazhnyi, 2024)

Present Bias: Present bias is the tendency to give up future benefits for immediate rewards. This is a huge challenge in sustainability governance because an organization may prefer short-term cost-cutting measures rather than investment in energy-efficient technologies that may bring long-term benefits. (Pashang & Weber, 2023) AI can overcome present bias by quantifying future benefits of sustainable actions and representing them in easily digestible formats. For instance, a dash-figure representation in an AI-driven dashboard of long-term savings in cost and environmental effects from installing solar panels may bring the future benefits into tangible view for decision-makers.

Loss Aversion: The loss aversion bias, whereby the majority of people fear to lose something they value as much as they value gaining equivalent gain, deters many firms from embracing new sustainability solutions. Sustainability solutions framed using AI would be seen not in terms of losses but gains by the organization: For instance, an AI would argue that the ESG practices will yield greater reputational and financial benefits, making resistance to change less likely.

Status Quo Bias: The status quo bias will make an organization resist change even if the alternative strategy is a lot better. AI-driven insights can help beat this inertia by bringing evidence that the new approach would work out much better. For instance, AI might analyze how well peer organizations have succeeded in sustainability initiatives and present the findings as evidence for the need to do the same thing. (Isalm, 2024) Confirmation Bias: Confirmation bias makes the decision-makers seek supportive information whereas ignoring contradictory information. Thus, AI systems, that can process diverse data sources, bring a balance perspective on issues of sustainability to be used by governance in taking decisions.

Example AI Interventions

AI-driven behavioral interventions are subtle, yet powerful means to influence a wide range of decisions. They function on the triad of data analytics, personalization, and behavioral science in achieving sustainable behavioral change in employees, stakeholders, and organizations.

Targeted alerts: AI-based systems can provide decision-makers with targeted alerts filled with messages about opportunities to adopt green practices. For instance, an in-house governance team may automatically receive alert dates about the deadlines of ESG reporting, matched with tips on how to boost the sustainability metrics. It is also possible that personalized alerts go toward workers to change their behavior and become "greener", such as saving less energy or participating in neighborhood service projects.

Targeted nudges are also known as micro-persuasion- gentle nudges in a proper direction, free of imposing certain choices. With the help of data insights, AI-facilitated nudges show the most promising effect; for example, by leveraging employee traffic patterns to optimize carpooling options and routes that make them prefer more environmentally friendly alternatives such as public transportation. Another way for targeted nudges would be to stimulate stakeholders into investing in more green technologies and show such investments through various incentives that look attractive both to finances and their environment.

Data-Driven Prompts: AI can provide data-driven prompts that will make decisions at the governance meetings and strategic planning sustainable. The new product development governance team will receive live prompts focused on identifying the differing materials and the production methods that would influence environmental impacts in the environment. This would make sustainability be considered with every level of decision-making.

Gamification of Sustainable Practices: AI-facilitated gamification strategies make initiatives at sustainability very engaging and rewarding. Organizations use AI to design interactive platforms where employees and other stakeholders earn points or rewards for adopting sustainable behaviors. A good example is the development of a sustainability leaderboard where individual contributions in waste reduction or energy savings are tracked. In this respect, AI will ensure that the gamification strategy dovetails with the goals of the organization and the motivation of the individuals. (Zhao & Fariñas, 2022)

Case Studies on AI Interventions

Case 1: Using AI to Enhance Supply Chain Sustainability

A multinational company applied AI-based optimization towards sustainability to its supply chain. It utilized supplier data, transport routes, and production processes at the identification of opportunities for improvement with the help of AI recommendations. It achieved a carbon footprint of 20% while bringing about big cost savings. Supplier nudging in a sustainability culture towards greener practice was an excellent target for nudges in chains.

Case Study 2: AI for Employee Engagement

An organization installed the use of AI behavioral analytics that urged the employees to adopt sustainable practices. The system monitored the consumption of energy by office buildings after which it dispatched targeted notifications advising that the employees switch off light and equipment once they leave the offices. Through the interventions, energy consumption declined by 15% after some time with a higher sensitization of employees to issues related to sustainability.

Case Study 3: AI in Stakeholder Communications

A bank utilized AI to advance ESG reporting and communicate better with its stakeholders. Through a set of multiple data collection points, the AI provided stakeholders with up-to-date reports on metrics regarding sustainability. Stakeholders were thus empowered through individual dashboards, tracking performance on various specific ESG targets and facilitating accountability and transparency. Investor nudges for investing in green activities encouraged higher investments into renewable energy initiatives.

Behavioral interventions are the key which adds value to governance and brings about more sustainability. An AI system allows an organization to have long-term ESG goals in sight as it is the platform through which there is reduction of cognitive biases and provision of data-driven insights, while offering personalized nudges allows making an informed decision. AI-based interventions like custom notification and targeted nudge or data-driven prompt really bring change in the influence of various industries.

Introduction of AI in the governance frameworks brings into question whether the same technology sustains enough moral value. To make stakeholders place their trust, it is quintessential to keep the AI system transparent, accountable, and inclusive. Determining scalability for AI intervention in the future would require understanding how it might be impactful on the organizational culture. Then, some facts could be unfolded as to how technology will make future sustainable. Then, governing frameworks are all freed up from traditional bonds because these AI powers will now be utilized for a just and sustainable world.

CASE STUDIES AND REAL-WORLD APPLICATIONS

AI in corporate governance has evolved to become an adaptive mechanism for sustainability challenges. ESG-compliant decision-making via AI technologies helps organizations achieve actual changes in those things that cannot be financially quantified-from the point of view of energy efficiency, waste, and employee engagement. The following chapter now describes real-life examples of companies that have embraced AI-driven governance models for sustainability. It also elaborates on the quantifiable impacts of such interventions and draws key lessons for other organizations interested in pursuing similar approaches.

Companies Using AI in Governance for Sustainability

Case Study 1: Unilever – AI-Driven Sustainable Supply Chains

The company Unilever is one of the leading companies using AI to improve sustainability in supply chain governance. It developed AI analytics platforms that track the practice of suppliers, assess the environmental effects, and predict the occurrence of disruptions in supply chains due to climate change. The use of real-time data combined with predictive analytics helped Unilever to optimize its procurement process in order to minimize waste and achieve sustainability standards.

Key AI Interventions:

AI-based algorithms were tracking suppliers on ESG compliance. Algorithms through machine learning were being used for forecasting the scarcity of raw material from climate risk. Data analytics revealed the opportunities to reduce packaging waste.

Unilever was able to reduce the carbon footprint through their supply chain by 15%. Simultaneously, it could save a lot of money by optimizing resource utilization. Emphasis on sustainability would also improve the brand reputation and help develop closer relationships with concerned consumers who may care about the environment.

Case Study 2: Microsoft – AI for Carbon Reduction

In this context, Microsoft has even hardwired AI into its governance structures to reach the extremely ambitious target of becoming carbon negative by 2030. The company utilizes AI-based technologies in measuring, tracking, and minimizing carbon footprint across all its operations. AI-based models study energy consumption trends, maximize the use of renewable energy sources, and point out which data centers need improvement.

AI systems monitored carbon emissions at facilities. Advanced analytics indicated energy-efficient changes in operations. Predictive tools evaluated the effect of renewable energy adoption on overall sustainability goals.

Through these interventions, Microsoft reduced its operational carbon footprint by 30% in key facilities. The company also developed scalable AI solutions for other organizations, reinforcing its leadership in sustainability-focused innovation.

Case Study 3: IKEA – AI in Waste Management

IKEA has also developed AI technologies that promote the growth of waste management through circular economy principles. The company uses AI-based systems to track the amount of waste generated in its stores and warehouses. These systems have allowed the company to come up with actionable insights on how to reduce waste and recycle materials.

Critical AI Interferences:

AI tools identified on-time patterns of waste generation. Predictive models helped to identify strategies of reuse and recycling. Data analytics helped the firm in designing sustainable products.

IKEA managed to reduce the waste that was sent to landfills by 25% and also increased its recycling rate by 40%. The company increased its product lines using recycled materials following its vision of sustainability.

Measurable Impact of AI Interventions

AI-based governance frameworks bring tangible improvements across several dimensions of sustainability, as shown in the following examples of measurable outcomes that organizations might achieve while applying AI for sustainability-focused governance.

Energy Efficiency

AI interventions strongly increase energy efficiency through optimized patterns of consumption and integration with renewable energy sources.

For example, Google applied AI technologies to systems for controlling the cooling process of data centers; they achieved 40% energy saving on cooling processes. These effects were both reduced operation cost and reduced environmental degradation. Thus, Google took a front position regarding the operation of sustainable technologies. Employee Involvement in Sustainable Activities

AI technologies are stimulants in inspiring employees to engage in sustainability practices.

Illustration: A multinational company applied AI-based platforms to gamify energy consumption reduction and participation in recycling programs.

Outcome: Engagement of employees in sustainability activities increased by 30% and made the workplace more environmentally responsible.

Waste Minimization: AI initiatives have successfully reduced waste across sectors.

Example: AI-based predictive analytics helps a manufacturing company reduce inventory and eliminate unnecessary production or wastage.

Benefits: The waste produced declined by 20% and ensured the operations to be in compliance with circular economy.

ESG Reporting

Quality of ESG reporting increases as well as the transparency that AI-based tools provide to an organization to comply with the regulation and meet the requirements of the stakeholder.

Example: Bankers used AI-based system for collecting data from different sources and presented detailed reports about how much progress had been done toward sustainability goals.

Impact: Stakeholder confidence was enhanced while attracting the "green" investors.

Conclusion and Best Practice Lesson Learnt

There are several lessons and best practices as culled from the above case studies as an outcome of integrating AI into governance framework for sustainability. Some of the lessons include,

1. Adopt Data-Based Decision Making

AI systems feed on data and hence, organizations have to invest in good data collection and management practices for optimal reaping of AI interventions.

Best Practice: Design central data hubs that bring together data from all sources so that AI solutions can extract useful insights from it.

2. Alignment of AI Strategy with Business Strategy

The best implementations are those where AI technologies support and align to wider organizational goals, where sustainability initiatives contribute to business objectives.

Best Practice: Clearly define the goals of sustainability and leverage AI for means identification to achieve the goal with an interplay of short-term financial performance and long-term environmental impact.

3. Cross Functional Collaboration

AI governance frameworks need cross-functional collaboration from departments involved at the levels of IT, Sustainability, and Operations.

Best Practice: Organize interdisciplinary teams for implementing AI based on organizational capabilities that need to match the needs of governance.

4. Ethical AI Development

Governance using AI should apply all principles that make it ethical, such as transparency, accountability, and fairness.

Best Practice: Have an audit system on AI for identifying and addressing bias by interventions that are for equity and inclusion.

5. Scalability and Adaptability

AI systems must be designed to scale up with the needs of organizations and changing challenges in sustainability.

Best Practice: Invest in modular AI solutions that can be scaled up or customized with changing opportunities and challenges.

6. Leverage Stakeholder Engagement

Engaging stakeholders, including employees, investors, and customers, is critical for the success of AI-driven sustainability initiatives.

Best Practice: Implement AI-based communication tools for sustainability performance information to facilitate stakeholder feedback for building a transparent and accountable organization.

AI as a force in corporate governance has transformed this area into a tool to help enhance performance in terms of sustainability. Some examples include the benefits for the most influential companies: Unilever, Microsoft, and IKEA regarding their utilization of AI governance frameworks in carbon emissions, waste elimination, employee engagement, and improving ESG reports. The impact of these AI interventions, therefore is measurable and speaks to potential actual applications in cooperative ways tackling highly important environmental and social issues. Organizations would achieve maximum effectiveness from AI through governance by adopting good practices in data-driven decision-making, including ethical development of AI, and cross-functional collaboration.

With increasing global demands for sustainability, the effects of AI on governance frameworks will be more evident. Future research should then focus on how AI is innovatively utilized in governance and assess its long-term effects on organizational performance, societal well-being, and environmental health. More innovation and collaboration will propel AI-driven governance toward an equitable and sustainable future.

NON-FINANCIAL PERFORMANCE MEASUREMENT METRICS AND FRAMEWORKS

Non-financial performance has become a very important indicator of the sustainability and long-term value of an organization. Hence, ESG metrics are very necessary to measure ESG performance. This would imply that organizations need well-defined metrics and frameworks that provide structure, add consistency, and provide transparency in reporting. Artificial Intelligence (AI) is gradually becoming the transformative tool to help better make the measurement and track such metrics in an increasingly efficient manner by advancing capacity in data aggregation, analysis, and predictive modeling. The main discussion of the chapter looks at key performance indicators relevant to sustainability, the established frameworks on ESG measurements, and the role of AI in optimizing such processes. (Aagaard, 2024)

Important Performance Indicators for Sustainability

KPIs are defined as specific, measurable metrics that organizations monitor and measure against their sustainability goals. They provide actionable insights into the various dimensions of ESG performance.

1. Environmental KPI: The environmental KPIs look to measure the impact of any organization on natural resources and ecosystems. These indicators help organizations know how much to reduce and minimize their environmental footprint.

Carbon Footprint: It measures the aggregate of GHG emissions associated with all of an organization's operations, directly or indirectly. This includes scope 1, scope 2, and scope 3.

Energy Efficiency: It compares energy consumption to the output it has generated, which helps organizations in finding areas where they could save energy. Waste Minimization: Tracks the volume of waste generation and calculates the percentage of waste taken out from landfills by recycling, reusing, etc. (Adisa et al., 2024) Water Footprint: Measures the amount of water consumption and activities on decreasing water use or increasing reuse of water. Biodiversity: Tracks the effect that an organization has on the local ecosystem, like deforestation, loss of habitats, and preservation of biodiversity.

2. Social KPIs: KPIs related to social involve the benefits of the company to society, its ties with employees, customers and communities.

Employee Engagement: Measures the level of engagement of the employees and whether they care for the sustainability initiatives, by surveys or participation rate. Diversity and Inclusion: The composition of the demographic groups within the organization and then the activities of such inclusiveness. Community Engagement: Evaluation of the engagement by the organization in the development of the community through charitable contributions, volunteer hours, and social impact initiatives.

Health and Safety Metrics: Tracking workplace incidents, injury rate, and safety deployment that can improve employee welfare. Consumer Satisfaction of Sustainability Initiatives: Measurement of consumer attitude and engagement with the firm's green and social responsibility offerings. (Adisa et al., 2024)

3. Governance KPIs: Governance KPIs will examine the ethical practice, compliance, and accountability of a leader within an organization. Board Diversity: This will assess the diversity in the structure of the board of directors in the organization.

ESG Integration into Corporate Strategy: How much has the corporation integrated ESG principles into its decision-making and strategies. Anti-Corruption Measures: Implementation and effectives of anti-corruption policies and practices.

Transparency in ESG Reporting: It determines the availability and quality of disclosures on ESG-related information provided to stakeholders. Stakeholder Engagement: It tracks the effort in engaging stakeholders for sustainability activities and decision-making. Frameworks and Standards for Measuring Non-Financial Performance

There are some internationally recognized frameworks and standards that organizations use in their measurement and reporting of ESG performance. This assists in ensuring that there would be consistency, comparability, and reliability in reporting sustainability.

1. Global Reporting Initiative (GRI)

The GRI Standards remain the most widely used reporting framework for sustainability. It delivers highly detailed guidelines for organizations for disclosing environmental, social, and governance impacts.

Focus Areas: The GRI deals with a broad range of issues including emissions, labor practices, human rights, and governance.

Structure: The framework consists of general application standards that are applicable to all, and industry or sector-specific standards about specific issues.

AI Applications: Analyzing large datasets to detect trends through AI, automating data collecting processes, and preparing GRI-compliant reports in a more streamlined manner.

2. Sustainability Accounting Standards Board (SASB)

The SASB offers industry-specific standards for disclosure of sustainability matters, in terms of financially material ESG issues.

Focus Areas: SASB focuses on ESG factors that impact financial performance, such as supply chain risks, regulatory compliance, resource efficiency. Structure: Standards are industry-specific to 77 industries, ensuring highly specific and relevant reporting. AI Applications: AI enhances ESG data integration with financial performance metrics, hence enhancing decision-making to determine risks and opportunities

3. Task Force on Climate-Related Financial Disclosures (TCFD)

The TCFD framework sees risks and opportunities on climate matters as a way of goading organizations to disclose what strategies they have adopted regarding their approach towards dealing with climate change. Governance and strategy; Risk management, metrics and targets on climate Structure: The framework puts emphasis upon forward-looking disclosures, like scenario analysis, in order to evaluate what resilience organizational strategies have through various climate scenarios.

AI Applications: AI-based climate models enable the enterprise to perform scenario analysis and assess the potential impact of climate on operations and financial performance. (Adisa et al., 2024)

4. Integrated Reporting (IR)

The IR framework for an organization provides an all-rounded view of value creation by integrating financial and non-financial performance into one report. Focus Areas: types of capital, which are: financial manufactured intellectual human social and natural. Structure: The framework therefore invites organizations to show how their activities, outputs, and outcomes are building value over time. AI Applications: AI automates data integration across multiple capital types to improve the quality and efficiency of integrated reporting.

5. UN SDGs

The UN SDGs are a universal blueprint for achieving sustainability, with 17 goals and 169 targets to tackle the most significant societal and environmental challenges. Focus Areas: Poverty, health, education, gender equality, clean energy, climate action, and more. Structure: Organizations target specific SDGs that their efforts align with and report on progress toward achieving them.

AI Applications: AI technologies determine business activities and link them with appropriate SDGs and provide a measure of contribution towards global sustainability goals.

The Role of AI in Measurement and Framework Tracking

The use of AI technology has transformed the practice of measurement, tracking, and reporting on non-financial performance. This is mainly due to it solving problems of volume, complexity, and accuracy in data.

1. Data Acquisition and Consolidation

AI makes it simple to collect and integrate ESG data from internal systems, external databases, and IoT devices.

Example: Real-time monitoring of energy consumption through AI-powered sensors provides precise data for the energy efficiency metrics.

Impact: The increased accuracy and specificity of data allow for a more precise measurement of KPIs.

2. Monitoring and Measurement in Real Time

AI measures sustainability metrics in real time, so anomalies can be traced and dealt with immediately by an organization.

Example: Anomaly detection of waste management procedures that may include unexpected increases in the generation of waste.

Impact: This enhances response to sustainability-related challenges through continuous improvement.

3. Predictive Analysis

AI uses predictive analytics to foretell future trends in performance from historical information.

Example: AI models forecast carbon emissions based on various operational scenarios, and organizations can prepare mitigation strategies.

Impact: Proactive decision-making reduces risks and enhances long-term sustainability.

4. Automating Compliance

AI automates compliance with reporting frameworks by mapping data to specific requirements and generating standardized reports.

Example: AI tools automatically populate GRI-compliant templates with relevant ESG data.

Impact: Reduced manual effort and increased reporting accuracy improve compliance and stakeholder trust.

5. Enhancing Stakeholder Engagement

AI technologies enable stakeholder engagement through interactive and accessible ESG data.

Example: AI-powered dashboards enable stakeholders to dynamically explore ESG performance metrics.

Impact: Improved transparency and communication establish stronger relationships with stakeholders.

Challenges and Opportunities in AI-Driven Measurement

Challenges

Data Gaps: In some regions or industries, the availability of ESG data is limited, and the effectiveness of AI is accordingly limited.

Bias and Fairness: AI systems can incidentally mirror biases present in the underlying data, hence giving biased insights.

Resource Intensity: AI-based measurement tools require significant investments in technology and expertise-intensive investment.

Opportunities

Scalability: AI-based solutions support the scalability of growing volumes of data and changing reporting requirements.

Customization: Advanced AI models can be customized to specific industries or organizations' unique requirements.

Collaboration: Organisational, government and technology vendor collaboration would accelerate the adoption of AI in measurement of sustainability. Adisa et al., 2024

To the concerned organizations embracing sustainability and the ESG approach, that means implementing KPIs and traditional frameworks used for measuring nonfinancial performance. AI technologies would allow organisations to overcome some of the constraints of ESG tracking related to data complexity and resource limitation. AI offers real-time monitoring, predictive analytics, and automation of compliance-a transformative ability to improve the quality, transparency, and impact of sustainability reporting. More and more organizations will adopt AI-driven solutions, which will require more research on fine-tuning these technologies to overcome the problems that include data gaps, bias, and resource intensity. By facilitating collaboration and innovation, AI-driven metrics and frameworks are well positioned to bring meaningful progress toward global sustainability goals.

REFERENCES

Aagaard, A. (Ed.). (2024). *Business model innovation: game changers and contemporary issues* (By Aarhus University). https://library.oapen.org/bitstream/handle/20.500.12657/92666/978-3-031-57511-2.pdf?sequence=1#page=167

Adisa, O., Ajadi, T. H., & Keshtiban, A. (2024). Navigating Human-Technology Nexus for Environmental and Organizational Sustainability in Industry 5.0. In *Practice, progress, and proficiency in sustainability* (pp. 222–246). https://doi.org/DOI: 10.4018/979-8-3693-7322-4.ch011

Aguilera, R. V., Aragón-Correa, J. A., Marano, V., & Tashman, P. A. (2021). The Corporate Governance of Environmental Sustainability: A Review and Proposal for More Integrated Research. *Journal of Management*, *47*(6), 1468–1497. DOI: 10.1177/0149206321991212

Ajmera, D., Kharub, M., Krishna, A., & Gupta, H. (2024). Navigating the challenges of AI-enabled circular economy in the food and beverage sector: Strategies for sustainable transformation. *International Journal of Logistics Management*. Advance online publication. DOI: 10.1108/ijlm-09-2023-0408

Balcıoğlu, Y. S., Çelik, A. A., & Altındağ, E. (2024). Artificial intelligence integration in Sustainable Business Practices: A text mining analysis of USA firms. *Sustainability*, *16*(15), 6334. DOI: 10.3390/su16156334

Fadhel, M. A., Duhaim, A. M., Albahri, A. S., Al-Qaysi, Z. T., Aktham, M. A., Chyad, M. A., Abd-Alaziz, W., Albahri, O. S., Alamoodi, A., Alzubaidi, L., Gupta, A., & Gu, Y. (2024). Navigating the metaverse: Unraveling the impact of artificial intelligence—a comprehensive review and gap analysis. *Artificial Intelligence Review*, *57*(10). Advance online publication. DOI: 10.1007/s10462-024-10881-5

Isalm, M. (2024). AI for Sustainable Development: Addressing Environmental and Social Challenges. *Deleted Journal*, *3*(1), 97–105. DOI: 10.60087/jaigs.v3i1.70

Islam, R. (2024). *Sustainable entrepreneurship in the Digital Age : The role of AI in Green Business Practices*. Theseus. https://www.theseus.fi/handle/10024/862779

Kalai, L., Jmaii, A., & Tanwar, S. (2024). Exploring the intersection of sustainability challenges and artificial intelligence. In *Advances in finance, accounting, and economics book series* (pp. 33–58). https://doi.org/DOI: 10.4018/979-8-3693-3282-5.ch003

Lehtimäki, M. (2024). *Navigating ethical and practical challenges in AI-Driven visual content creation*. Theseus. https://www.theseus.fi/handle/10024/865896

Mayuranathan, M., Nahar, G., Vijayakumar, A., Naveen, N., Mamodiya, U., & Babu, D. M. (2024). Sustainable business models for smart city using artificial intelligence techniques. In *Practice, progress, and proficiency in sustainability* (pp. 263–294). https://doi.org/DOI: 10.4018/979-8-3693-2827-9.ch009

Mikalef, P., & Krogstie, J. (2024). *Responsible AI governance in practice: The strategic impact of responsible AI governance on business value and competitiveness*. https://ntnuopen.ntnu.no/ntnu-xmlui/handle/11250/3129623

Oyeniyi, N. L. D., Ugochukwu, N. C. E., & Mhlongo, N. N. Z. (2024). TRANSFORMING FINANCIAL PLANNING WITH AI-DRIVEN ANALYSIS: A REVIEW AND APPLICATION INSIGHTS. *Finance & Accounting Research Journal*, *6*(4), 626–647. DOI: 10.51594/farj.v6i4.1037

Pashang, S., & Weber, O. (2023). AI for Sustainable Finance: Governance Mechanisms for Institutional and Societal Approaches. In *Philosophical studies series* (pp. 203–229). https://doi.org/DOI: 10.1007/978-3-031-21147-8_12

Raman, R., Pattnaik, D., Lathabai, H. H., Kumar, C., Govindan, K., & Nedungadi, P. (2024). Green and sustainable AI research: An integrated thematic and topic modeling analysis. *Journal of Big Data*, *11*(1). Advance online publication. DOI: 10.1186/s40537-024-00920-x

Rane, N., Choudhary, S., & Rane, J. (2024). Artificial intelligence driven approaches to strengthening Environmental, Social, and Governance (ESG) criteria in sustainable business practices: a review. SSRN *Electronic Journal*. https://doi.org/DOI: 10.2139/ssrn.4843215

Rane, N. L., Choudhary, S. P., & Rane, J. (2024). Artificial Intelligence-driven corporate finance: Enhancing efficiency and decision-making through machine learning, natural language processing, and robotic process automation in corporate governance and sustainability. *Studies in Economics and Business Relations*, *5*(2), 1–22. DOI: 10.48185/sebr.v5i2.1050

Rathod, S. B., Ponnusamy, S., Mahajan, R. A., & Khan, R. H. (2024). Echoes of tomorrow. In *Advances in business information systems and analytics book series* (pp. 158–174). https://doi.org/DOI: 10.4018/979-8-3693-3234-4.ch012

Sklavos, G., Theodossiou, G., Papanikolaou, Z., Karelakis, C., & Ragazou, K. (2024). Environmental, Social, and Governance-Based Artificial Intelligence Governance: Digitalizing firms' leadership and human resources management. *Sustainability*, *16*(16), 7154. DOI: 10.3390/su16167154

The role of artificial intelligence in promoting sustainable business operations and autonomy. (2023, December 1). IEEE Conference Publication | IEEE Xplore. https://ieeexplore.ieee.org/abstract/document/10434654/

Zavrazhnyi, K. Y. (2024). *The impact of the use of artificial intelligence and digital transformation on sustainable business development*. https://essuir.sumdu.edu.ua/handle/123456789/95082

Zhao, J., & Fariñas, B. G. (2022). Artificial intelligence and sustainable decisions. *European Business Organization Law Review*, *24*(1), 1–39. DOI: 10.1007/s40804-022-00262-2

Chapter 9
Impact of ESG Factors on the Financial Performance of Corporates in India

Anand Patil
https://orcid.org/0000-0003-4736-6571
Christ University, Bangalore, India

Neha Sanwal
https://orcid.org/0009-0002-4928-9346
Christ University, Bangalore, India

ABSTRACT

This study investigates the connection between Indian companies' financial results and Environmental, Social, and Governance (ESG) performance, with a focus on socially and environmentally sensitive industries. There is little data on the financial effects of ESG integration in developing nations like India, even though it is becoming more and more crucial for long-term value development. Using a quantitative approach involving ESG ratings and financial indicators (Return on Equity [ROE], Return on Assets [ROA], and Return on Capital Employed [ROCE]) we analyze the performance of firms from 2021 to 2023 in five different sectors. Among the pillars, environmental issues had the most significant effect on material financial success, showing a positive but weak correlation with ESG scores. However, the study also investigates into sectoral distinctions, pointing to differential financial outcomes associated with ESG across industries.

1. INTRODUCTION

The modern-day global economy has come to recognize ESG (Environmental, Social, Governance), which now influencing company strategy and investment selections. Corporations are anticipated to incorporate sustainability into their business strategies as a means to fulfil investors growing demand for ethics and responsibility (Smith & Jones, 2020). ESG – Environmental, Social and Governance (Focus on these areas has become an imperative in the creation of lasting value.) The increasing environmental

DOI: 10.4018/979-8-3693-9684-1.ch009

crises, social inequalities, and governance failings are forcing stakeholders to demand that firms be held more accountable for its costs (Lee et al., 2019).

We are seeing an increased trend towards ESG integration particularly in the Indian economy, which is a rapidly growing one. National Voluntary Guidelines on Social, Environmental, and Economic Responsibilities and ESG reporting requirement drive Indian corporations towards social and environmental accountability; Government from within the List of Abbreviations encourages companies to become conscious about their social and environmental effects (Kumar et al., 2021). Although recent times have shown a rise in ESG performance scores of Indian enterprises, their power to drive financial results across organizations is still shrouded in relative obscurity. The research is also providing no definitive answer in terms of the relationship between ESG practices and financial performance (Gupta & Das, 2022). This gap highlights the need for further research on the association between ESG practices and financial performance in a developing economy such as India.

The term ESG integration refers to the process of embedding environmental, social and governance considerations into a company's operations that are crucial in assessing its long-term performance Sustainability Criteria Initiative, 2020)ll. Social aspects include community involvement, labor relations and diversity, while environmental factors cover execution around carbon footprint and resource efficiency. Implementation of governance is key focused on board composition, CEO compensation, and openness. A conglomerate ESG score formed by these factors effects financial productivity of a firm (Brown & Clark, 2021). On one hand, whereas the research on ESG and financial performance in Indian corporate sector is increasing, however most of the studies on this topic are from developed economies; hence, it left a significant research gap.

The purpose of this study is to fill that gap by studying the impact of ESG practices on major financial ratios such as Return on Equity (ROE), Return on Assets (ROA) and Return on Capital Employed (ROCE) in Indian companies (Patel, 2021). The basic issue arises due to lack of comprehensive study and understanding which has been done on the impact of these ESG factors on financial performance of our diverse companies in India as particularly those which have externalities attached with them socially or environmentally (Sharma, 2020).

The very purpose of present study is to assess the impact of ESG factors on the financial performance Indian Companies with a major focus on the manufacturing and energy segment.(Agarwal,2022). To look at the relation between Environmental, Social and Governance (ESG) performance and Financial Performance is one of the primary purposes of this study along with assesses those factors influence financial opportunities separately, explores sectors which are relevant to the Indian economy from Environment, Social as well Governance perspective on their impact on financial results. Some limitations of this study, the extent of coverage and quality ESG data for different industries and companies available at that time which may complicate the identification of long-term effects of ESG practices on financial performance, no consideration was given to non-public companies, small businesses or risk considerations; a relatively short period studied (Singh & Verma & 2021).

2. LITERATURE REVIEW

The authors of this paper (Ray and Goel 2023) investigate the complex link between a company's ESG score and its financial success in light of India's recent ESG reporting legislation. They use static and dynamic panel regression models to examine the impact of ESG scores on various financial variables such as ROA, ROE, firm size, market capitalization, profitability, and share price, using a representative sample of 48 Indian companies from the BSE-100 index from 2011 to 2019. Their findings show that ESG has a dynamic influence on these variables, with time delays in the expression of the effects. Notably, the analysis finds a significant and favourable long-term relationship between robust ESG disclosure and average yearly share price. This ground-breaking work emphasises the potential of ESG scores as a critical indicator for predicting future financial performance and developing effective risk mitigation measures, implying their significant relevance from both business and policy perspectives in the Indian context.

As organisations negotiate the changing global context, sustainability is increasingly seen as a critical driver of long-term value development. "The Business Value of ESG Performance: The Indian Context." (Chelawat and Trivedi 2016) addresses this critical topic. While research has found a correlation between strong environmental, social, and governance (ESG) practices and greater financial performance in a variety of nations, this relationship has received less attention in rising economies such as India. To close this gap, the authors used panel regression models to investigate the influence of ESG performance on the financial results of Indian enterprises. Their findings provide hopeful evidence: improved ESG performance significantly improves financial outcomes. This significant work adds to the current knowledge base by illustrating the importance of ESG integration in the Indian context, providing valuable insights for investors, business management, and politicians alike. By recognising the financial benefits of ethical business practices, stakeholders can work together to create a more sustainable and prosperous future for India.

Understanding the influence of environmental, social, and governance (ESG) standards on healthcare firms' financial performance remains a difficult issue. The author addresses this issue in their study, "Examining the impact of ESG score on the financial performance of healthcare companies," (Kalia and Aggarwal 2022) which analyses data from 468 healthcare firms in 2020. Their findings reveal an important nuance: the link between ESG and financial success is not ubiquitous. While good ESG practices benefit healthcare organisations in rich economies, the same may not hold true in underdeveloped markets, where the link may be negative or inconsequential. This revolutionary discovery, the first to look at the ESG-financial performance nexus via the development lens, reveals that a one-size-fits-all strategy is insufficient. Policymakers looking to promote ESG adoption in healthcare must evaluate country-specific situations and modify their approach appropriately. This significant contribution emphasises the need for more study to understand better the underlying mechanisms driving these distinct interactions, as well as how healthcare organisations in various markets may use ESG principles to achieve long-term development.

In his research, "ESG factors and corporate financial performance," (Mardini 2022), the author investigates the link between environmental, social, and governance (ESG) practices and corporate financial performance (CFP). Mardini examines a large dataset of over 7,000 non-financial firms from 2012 to 2020 and discovers that strong ESG performance, particularly strong environmental and governance practices, has a positive impact on both market-based (Tobin's Q) and accounting-based (return on assets and return on equity) CFP measures. This shows that firms that prioritise environmental and governance considerations not only improve their financial health but also attract investors by raising their market worth. Interestingly, the study found a negative and substantial relationship between social variables and market-based CFP. While this conclusion has no substantial impact on accounting-based measurements, it does show that while expenditures in social efforts are important, they may temporarily drain resources and alter reputation, potentially resulting in a competitive disadvantage. This thorough analysis emphasises the necessity of treating each ESG aspect independently while noting their overall influence on CFP, adding vital worldwide evidence to the current discussion over sustainable corporate practices and their financial repercussions.

The complex link between Environmental, Social, and Governance (ESG) disclosure and company sustainable growth has spawned several disputes in the academic community. Chai et al. (2023), in their paper "Exploring the Nexus between ESG Disclosure and Corporate Sustainable Growth: Moderating Role of Media Attention," look at this relationship in the case of Chinese corporations from 2012 to 2022. Using a quantile regression technique, they discover a positive and substantial impact of ESG disclosure on the sustainable growth rate (SGR). Notably, the effectiveness of ESG disclosure in encouraging SGR increases with increased degrees of transparency, demonstrating its potential as a strong instrument for sustainable development. Furthermore, the study emphasises the moderating influence of media attention, finding that firms with more media coverage had a stronger positive association between ESG disclosure and SGR. However, the authors note digitalization's possible moderating effect, recommending additional investigation into its effects on the varied impact of ESG across different SGR levels. Chai et al.'s contribution, therefore, advocates for a sophisticated view of the ESG-SGR nexus, taking into account disclosure levels, media involvement, and digitalization variables, in order to realise its full potential for fostering sustainable corporate development.

This study called, "Understanding the Impact of ESG Practices in Corporate Finance" (Kim and Li 2021) conducts a thorough examination of the link between Environmental, Social, and Governance (ESG) aspects and business financial performance. Drawing on a large body of literature, the study emphasises the growing relevance of ESG factors in investing decision-making and portfolio development. Previous research has repeatedly found a favourable relationship between ESG characteristics and financial performance, with the majority having a good influence on business profitability. Notably, the study emphasises the importance of corporate governance as a critical ESG factor impacting business value, profitability, and other financial indicators. The findings show that ESG aspects improve corporate profitability, particularly for bigger enterprises, with corporate governance appearing as the most significant category, especially for companies with weaker governance systems. Surprisingly, whereas social elements influence credit ratings positively, environmental scores have a detrimental impact. Overall, the study presents solid evidence for incorporating ESG concerns into investment strategies to increase value generation and reduce risks in the corporate finance sector.

Unravelling the complex relationship between Environmental, Social, and Governance (ESG) performance and financial results remains a top research priority. Bruna et al. (2022) explore this complicated link in their paper, "Investigating the marginal impact of ESG results on corporate financial performance." They overcome past research' methodological weaknesses by using a time-lagged panel regression model and a complete indicator for both ESG and financial performance to 350 European listed businesses from 2014 to 2019. Their findings reveal a nonlinear, complicated connection in which the influence of ESG on financial performance varies with firm size and amount of ESG commitment. Notably, mandated ESG disclosure rules are linked to higher ESG ratings and better financial performance, implying a favourable impact on both dimensions. This significant addition emphasises the need of taking into account non-linearity and company-specific aspects when studying the ESG-financial performance nexus, as well as the potential benefits of obligatory disclosure in fostering sustainable and financially sound business practices.

The complex link between business ESG performance and financial results has sparked extensive scholarly attention. Velte's (2017) study on German corporations, titled "Does ESG performance have an impact on financial performance?" investigates this dynamic in the context of Germany. His complete methodology, which examines both accounting-based (ROA) and market-based (Tobin's Q) financial performance indicators as well as individual evaluations of each ESG component (environmental, social, and governance), provides valuable insights. Velte's major discovery demonstrated a favourable impact of ESG performance on ROA, notably through good governance standards, implying that German firms gain financially from thorough ESG integration. However, the lack of a link between ESG and Tobin's Q raises additional concerns regarding its impact on market pricing. This valuable contribution to the field, which breaks down ESG performance and incorporates a variety of financial measures, emphasises the need for additional research into the mechanisms underlying these relationships, their generalizability, and practical implementation strategies for businesses to fully realise the financial potential of strong ESG practices.

The study (Dalal and Thaker 2019) examines the influence of ESG parameters on the financial performance of Indian firms listed on the NSE 100 ESG Index between 2015 and 2017. It uses panel data regression models to investigate the link between ESG ratings, business size, leverage, and financial performance metrics such as ROA and Tobin's Q. The study builds on previous work by Naik (2014) and Atan et al. (2017) to evaluate how ESG practices affect profitability and corporate value. The findings imply that organisations with superior ESG policies are more likely to attract investors and achieve long-term financial performance. The study also emphasises the relevance of sustainability reporting and the necessity for regulators to broaden obligatory disclosures to include ESG factors in order to improve sustainable business practices and shareholder wealth in India.

Research on the relationship between environmental, social, and governance (ESG) concerns and business financial performance has produced a variety of outcomes. Examining the work of Landi and Sciarelli (2018), who evaluated the influence of ESG ratings on anomalous returns in Italian firms, provides interesting insights into this continuing discussion. Their study, which focused on the FTSE MIB index from 2007 to 2015, used panel data analysis and the Fama-French technique to assess returns. While they discovered a rise in Italian firms adopting ESG and increased rating quality, their study revealed no statistically significant positive impact of ethical investments on market returns. This article provides important insights into the Italian market while also raising issues regarding generalizability and possible causes for the observed lack of market premium for ethical investments. By combining more studies and connecting them to your own research, you can build on this foundation to produce a full and educated discussion of the ESG-financial performance link.

Egorova et al. (2022) investigate the essential junction between ESG elements and the performance of information technology (IT) enterprises. The authors emphasise the rising relevance of sustainable development in the global business landscape, emphasising the necessity for corporations to achieve the environmental, social, and governance goals embodied in the ESG framework. Examining IT businesses' ESG scores in comparison to other industries indicates that they currently trail behind in ESG performance, notably in the environmental (E) and social (S) components. Despite this, the study highlights the potential for IT firms to increase market value and attract investors by improving their ESG processes. The literature study highlights the financial impact of ESG commitments, with research demonstrating that firms that adhere to sustainable principles have higher market capitalization and value measures. While some studies have found a detrimental impact of ESG on financial performance, the overwhelming consensus indicates a favourable association between ESG performance and financial results. This study adds to the literature by providing insight into the ESG environment in the IT industry and developing hypotheses to investigate the impact of ESG ratings on market value. The findings imply that improving ESG standards might be a potential way for IT firms to improve their market position and attract long-term investments.

As the global narrative shifts towards incorporating environmental, social, and governance (ESG) factors into corporate behaviour, Dayanandan, Donker, and Kuntlurus look into the potential impact of International Financial Reporting Standards (IFRS) on ESG disclosure practices in India (Dayanandan et al. 2023). Their study, driven by the Securities and Exchange Board of India's (SEBI) demand for integrated reporting by listed enterprises, looks at 104 non-financial organisations from 2013 to 2021. The findings indicate a favourable association between IFRS adoption and the degree of ESG disclosures provided by Indian enterprises. Interestingly, the analysis finds that business performance (measured by return on assets) and leverage have a negative influence on ESG disclosure, implying that financial variables may play a complicated role in determining corporate transparency about ESG practices. This significant addition to the area throws light on the possible impact of accounting standards on ESG reporting, spurring more investigation into the processes at work and their implications for stakeholders in the Indian business sector.

Digar (2023) investigates the relationship between environmental, social, and governance (ESG) standards and financial success in India, examining 37 firms listed on the S&P ESG 100 from 2018 to 2022. Using static and dynamic panel regression models, the study explores how ESG ratings affect important financial measures such as ROA, ROE, and ROCE. Their findings show a positive and substantial association between good ESG performance and capital efficiency, implying that Indian enterprises gain financially from adopting sustainable practices. This work, which investigates the influence of ESG not only on profitability but also on sustainable development, provides useful information for stakeholders such as legislators, business executives, and investors. However, limitations such as sample size and data availability highlight the need for additional research with larger datasets and cross-country comparisons to confirm the findings' generalizability and advance our understanding of the nuanced relationship between ESG and financial performance in India.

In “Exploring the relationship of ESG score and firm value using cross-lagged panel analyses: case of the Indian energy sector,” Behl et al. (2021) look at the dynamic interaction between environmental, social, and governance (ESG) performance and firm value in the Indian energy sector. Recognising the changing relevance of ESG integration and its variable influence across settings, they use a four-wave cross-lagged panel structural equation model to go beyond static analysis. Their findings call into question the premise that there is a simple, bidirectional link between ESG disclosure and business value, indicating a more complex dynamic. While they find no general bidirectional causation, certain ESG aspects have lagged impacts on company value, with negative connections in the near term and favourable ones in the long run. This insightful investigation reveals the intricacies of the ESG-firm value link in the Indian energy industry, with implications for investors, fund managers, politicians, and energy business management. Notably, it offers recommendations on ESG investment methods and the timescales required to fully realise their influence on business value.

Growing investor interest in the financial benefits of Environmental, Social, and Governance (ESG) initiatives has prompted researchers to investigate their influence on stock performance. Suresha et al. (2022) examined Indian companies in their study, 'The impact of ESG inclusion on price, liquidity, and financial performance of Indian stocks: Evidence from stocks listed in BSE and NSE ESG indices', which investigated the influence of inclusion in the BSE100 ESG and Nifty 100 ESG indices on stock price, liquidity, and financial performance. They used event research methods to evaluate changes before and after inclusion in 150 firms from both indexes. Interestingly, while firms in the BSE100 ESG saw a large short-term price drop on the announcement day, both indexes produced positive long-term returns (CAAR). Additionally, liquidity for BSE100 ESG equities has greatly improved, indicating increasing investor interest. Notably, the study shows that inclusion in ESG indexes significantly improves firms' financial success, as assessed by EPS and market capitalization. These findings show the potential benefits of excellent ESG policies for Indian firms, including recruiting investors and improving long-term financial health.

Identifying the real impact of Environmental, Social, and Governance (ESG) performance on financial results remains difficult. Madison and Schiehll (2021) address this intricacy in their paper, "The Effect of Financial Materiality on ESG Performance Assessment." They look at how "financial materiality," or the possible financial implications of certain ESG concerns, affects ESG scores and rankings. Using data from Morgan Stanley Capital International (MSCI) ESG Ratings and the Sustainability Accounting Standards Board (SASB) Materiality Map®, their study demonstrates substantial changes in both scores and ranks when financial materiality is taken into account. The report identifies environmental challenges, particularly those concerning natural resource utilisation, as driving these changes. This illustrates that including financial materiality has a major impact on the value of ESG scores and rankings, possibly revealing previously unnoticed investment possibilities in firms that perform well on financially essential ESG aspects. The authors contend that such consideration can lead to more informed investment decisions based on ESG performance, hence leading to a better comprehension and assessment of the entire information content.

Junius et al. (2020) examined the possible relationship between ESG performance and financial results in four Southeast Asian nations (Indonesia, Malaysia, Singapore, and Thailand) between 2013 and 2017. Their study, which included 271 publicly traded businesses and 1355 firm-year data, utilised multiple regression analysis and focused on a larger variety of dependent variables such as returns on assets, equity, Tobin's Q, and price-earnings ratio. Notably, they found no meaningful association between ESG rankings and business performance or market value. According to the authors, this might be attributable to the ongoing incorporation of ESG criteria into standard performance measurements. While noting difficulties in analysing lag effects and the sample size of enterprises with available ESG ratings, Junius et al.'s contribution expands the study area by focusing on emerging economies and including less commonly utilised market value indicators. This study emphasises the need for more research on the increasing relationship between ESG and financial success, particularly in emerging markets, given the limitations noted by the authors.

Kang and Jung (2020) investigated the complex link between Environmental, Social, and Governance (ESG) activities and business value, focusing on how a company's financial features influence the effectiveness of ESG initiatives. Recognising the limits of relying exclusively on quantitative ESG ratings, they investigated the qualitative differences in how ESG activities influence business value based on certain financial factors. Using data from numerous ESG rating institutes over a four-year period, their study demonstrated a positive relationship between excellent ESG performance and company value, with differences across key ESG dimensions. Interestingly, the study found a stronger favourable effect on enterprises with more profitability or foreign ownership. This shows that robust financial health or active participation of foreign investors, as well as transparency and discipline, might increase the value generation potential of ESG initiatives. Notably, their findings were consistent even after accounting for potential reverse causation between ESG performance and financial factors. This useful research emphasises the significance of boosting market confidence through solid financial practices in order to maximise the value generated by ESG initiatives, urging businesses to explore strategic financial levers as they pursue long-term success.

In their study, "The Influence of Environmental, Social, and Governance (ESG) Disclosure on Firm Financial Performance," Almeyda and Darmansya (2019) look at how ESG disclosure affects corporate financial results in the real estate industry across seven major nations (G7). They address previous study discrepancies on the ESG-financial performance link by concentrating on long-term real estate investments and taking into consideration both accounting and stock market metrics (ROA, ROC, stock price, P/E). Their findings show a statistically significant positive relationship between high ESG disclosure transparency and ROA and ROC, implying that organisations with excellent ESG standards would perform well financially. Surprisingly, no substantial impact was detected on stock price or P/E ratio, although the environmental element alone had a beneficial effect on ROC and stock price. However, neither social nor governance elements were shown to be statistically significant predictors of financial performance. This study emphasises the potential for greater ESG disclosure to improve a company's financial health, emphasising its importance to investors, executives, legislators, and industry regulators in promoting openness and sustainable business practices.

Rodríguez-Fernández et al. (2019) in their study, 'Influence of ESGC Indicators on Financial Performance of Listed Travel and Leisure Companies' examined how environmental, social, governance, and controversies (ESGC) aspects affect financial performance in the travel and leisure business. Using data from multinational corporations listed on stock exchanges, their study, which included both parametric and nonparametric tests, found that governance procedures had a considerable influence on financial performance. This study not only adds to the existing body of information on ESGC and financial success, but it also takes an innovative method by creating particular ESGC indicators and analysing their link with financial outcomes using a binary regression logistic model. Importantly, their findings are applicable to the international tourist environment, giving useful insights for players in this industry.

Research Gap

In developing economies, the relationship between ESG activities and economic achievement is yet vague, particularly in cases of sectoral initiatives. Although research results actually draw long-term economic advantages from proper ESG reporting, sectoral disparities call for more nuanced studies; for example, the weaker or adverse effects in sectors such as health care demonstrate the necessity for further research. In addition, although governance and transparency are important contrarians of ESG performance, their impact in emerging countries is not highly regarded.

There are still holes in the temporal dimensions—such as the distinction between short- and long-term effects—and the market-specific difficulties—such as changing regulatory frameworks and uneven disclosure requirements. To fully grasp how ESG might contribute to these regions' sustainable financial performance, more research is required.

3. OBJECTIVES OF THE STUDY

- Evaluate the overall relationship between ESG performance and financial performance of Indian corporates.

- Examine the individual impact of each ESG pillar (Environmental, Social, and Governance) on the financial performance of Indian corporates.
- Analyse the relationship between ESG and financial performance in companies operating in environmentally and socially critical sectors.

4. HYPOTHESES STATEMENTS

Statement 1: There is a positive relationship between the financial performance and the combined ESG score of the companies

- H0: There is no significant relationship between the financial performance and the combined ESG score of the companies.
- H1: There is a significant positive relationship between the financial performance and the combined ESG score of the companies.

Statement 2: Environmental factors positively impacts financial performance.

- H0: There is no positive impact of environment score on financial performance.
- H1: There is a positive relationship between environment score and financial performance.

Statement 3: Social responsibility practices positively impacts financial performance.

- H0: There is no positive impact of strong social scores on financial performance.
- H1: There is a positive relationship between social scores and financial performance.

Statement 4: Corporate governance practices positively impacts financial performance.

- H0: There is no positive impact of strong corporate governance practices on financial performance.
- H1: There is a positive relationship between governance score and financial performance.

Statement 5: the relationship between ESG scores and financial performance varies across different sectors

- H0: The relationship between ESG factors and financial performance does not vary significantly across different sectors in the Indian market.
- H1: There are significant sector-specific differences in the relationship between ESG factors and financial performance, with certain sectors exhibiting stronger correlations than others.

5. THEORETICAL FRAMEWORK

Figure 1. Theoretical framework

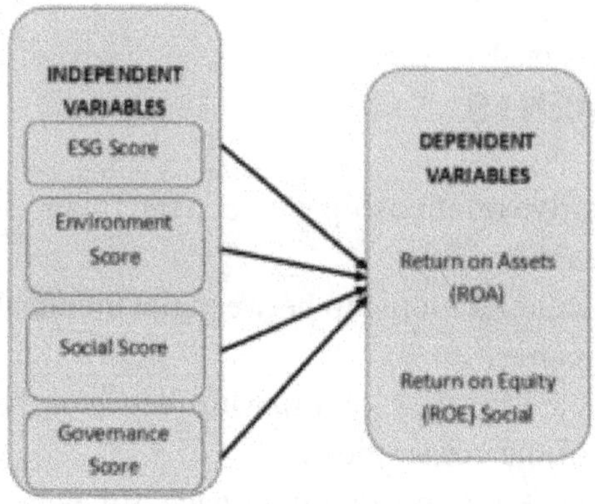

Variables of The Study

ESG Score

The ESG (Environmental, Social, and Governance) score is a composite statistic that assesses a company's environmental sustainability, social responsibility, and corporate governance policies. It gives investors and stakeholders an overall assessment of a company's ESG performance, which is frequently based on data from many sources, such as ESG rating agencies and sustainability reports.

Environment Score

The environmental score reflects a company's ability to manage environmental risks and opportunities. It considers carbon emissions, energy efficiency, waste management, and resource conservation. A higher environmental score implies better environmental management and adherence to environmental rules.

Social Score

The social score assesses a company's efforts to address social concerns and promote social well-being. It encompasses labour practices, employee diversity and inclusion, community participation, human rights, and product safety. A higher social score indicates improved social responsibility activities and a good social effect.

Governance Score

The governance score measures the effectiveness of a company's corporate governance structures and procedures. It includes topics including board composition, CEO remuneration, shareholder rights, transparency, and risk management. A higher governance score suggests better corporate governance norms and oversight procedures.

Return on Assets (ROA)

Return on Assets (ROA) is a financial ratio that assesses a company's profitability by dividing net income by total assets. It measures how well a corporation produces income from its assets. Higher ROA indicates better asset utilisation and operational efficiency.

Return on Equity (ROE)

Return on Equity (ROE) is a financial ratio that assesses a company's profitability by dividing net income by shareholders' equity. It analyses the return on shareholders' investments. A higher ROE suggests increased profitability and better management of shareholder money.

Return on Capital Employed (ROCE)

ROCE is a financial ratio that determines a company's profitability by dividing operating income by capital employed (total assets less current liabilities). It analyses how well a corporation uses its money to produce profit. A greater ROCE indicates efficient capital allocation and operational success.

6. RESEARCH METHODOLOGY

The most effective technique for this kind of research is the quantitative analytical approach. The research utilizes secondary data, specifically financial performance metrics and ESG (Environmental, Social, and Governance) scores, to ascertain the impact of ESG practices on business success. Between 2021 and 2023, data from reputable sources like S&P Global and CRISIL was gathered for Indian enterprises across five industries. The study examined the research themes and evaluated the relationship between ESG scores and financial performance measurements, such as ROA, ROE, and ROCE. Panel data regression was employed in conjunction with correlation matrices and descriptive statistics. Fifty-five companies from each of the following sectors—healthcare, banking, IT, power, and FMCG—were selected through the use of probability-stratified random sampling. The results were confirmed to be robust using appropriate statistical analyses, and the data dependability was ensured through the use of the Augmented Dickey-Fuller stationarity test. This methodology provides informative information regarding the impact of ESG policies on corporate profitability while ensuring accurate assessment of variables.

7. ANALYSIS AND INTERPRETATION

7.1 Descriptive Statistics:

The E-score (56.707) lags behind the S-score (57.427) and G-score (66.360), suggesting higher performance in the social and governance domains. The descriptive statistics show that the typical company has a relatively favourable ESG score of 60.747. Higher levels of variability in social and environmental performance are suggested by the standard deviations. Financially, the enterprises have positive returns on equity (ROE), capital employed (ROCE), and assets (ROA), with notable variability (averages of 8.419, 20.072, and 12.837, respectively). A plausible correlation between ESG ratings and financial success is indicated by the statistical significance of the means, which is supported by the probability values of 0.000 for all metrics. These numbers do not, however, make clear the linkages or causative elements at work.

Table 1. Descriptive statistics

Statistics	ESG Score	E-Score	S-Score	G-Score	ROA	ROE	ROCE
Mean	60.747	56.707	57.427	66.360	8.419	20.072	12.837
Median	63.000	57.000	59.000	71.000	4.500	21.000	9.000
Maximum	86.000	89.000	86.000	87.000	33.900	77.400	54.500
Minimum	20.000	14.000	17.000	20.000	-4.000	-7.700	-10.200
Std. Dev.	14.234	18.448	13.978	15.352	8.529	14.540	12.240
Skewness	-1.056	-0.270	-0.569	-1.475	1.046	1.812	1.241
Kurtosis	3.719	2.203	3.269	4.624	3.482	8.849	5.229
Probability	0.000	0.000	0.000	0.000	0.000	0.000	0.000
Observations	75	75	75	75	75	75	75

7.2 Stationarity Tests

Table 2. Stationarity yest (ADF Unit Root Test)

Variables	Level	First Diff.
ESG Score	0.0000	0.0000
E-Score	0.0000	0.0000
S-Score	0.0000	0.0000
G-Score	0.0000	0.0000
ROA	0.0893	0.0000
ROE	0.0744	0.0000
ROCE	0.3333	0.0002

The panel data is examined for stationarity—that is, whether its statistical characteristics hold true across time—using the Augmented Dickey-Fuller (ADF) unit root test. Table 7.2's findings show that, with p-values of 0.0000, the ESG score and each of its constituent parts (the E-, S-, and G-scores) are stationary at both the level and first difference. On the other hand, p-values of 0.0000 for ROA and ROE and 0.0002 for ROCE indicate that the financial measures ROA, ROE, and ROCE are non-stationary at the level but become stationary after initial differencing. At the 1% significance level, all variables are essentially stationary following the first difference.

7.3 Correlation Matrix

Table 3. Correlation matrix

Variables	ESG Score	E-Score	S-Score	G-Score	ROA	ROE	ROCE
ESG Score	1	-	-	-	-	-	-
E-score	0.89089	1	-	-	-	-	-
S-score	0.89928	0.77727	1	-	-	-	-
G-score	0.88753	0.64163	0.70651	1	-	-	-
ROA	0.28853	0.31313	0.25071	0.21936	1	-	-
ROE	0.22156	0.23019	0.14103	0.19329	0.84376	1	-
ROCE	0.25948	0.2728	0.20503	0.21172	0.96879	0.92733	1

The correlations between financial performance measures and ESG ratings are shown in Table 7.3's correlation matrix. The financial measures, Return on Capital Employed (ROCE) (0.259), Return on Equity (ROE) (0.222), and Return on Assets (ROA) (0.289), show a significant positive correlation that is moderate to strong. The environmental score, which ranges from 0.230 to 0.313, has somewhat positive associations with ROA, ROE, and ROCE. With values ranging from 0.141 to 0.251, the social score likewise shows weakly positive relationships with these financial measures. As opposed to environmental and social aspects, the governance score has lesser correlations, ranging from 0.193 to 0.219, indicating that it has less of an impact on financial performance. Overall, while the correlations are statistically significant, they are not strong, indicating that other unmeasured factors may influence these relationships.

7.4 Ordinary Least Squares (OLS) Regression Analysis

Table 4. Regression Analysis (ROA)

Variables	Co-efficient	Std. Error	Probability
ESG Score	0.1728	0.0671	0.0121
E-Score	0.1447	0.0513	0.0062
S-Score	0.1529	0.0691	0.03

continued on following page

Table 4. Continued

Variables	Co-efficient	Std. Error	Probability
G-Score	0.1218	0.0634	0.0486
Dependent Variable	ROA		
R-squared	0.4737		

The correlation between Return on Assets (ROA) and ESG components (ESG Score, E-Score, S-Score, and G-Score) is strongly favourable, as Table 7.4 demonstrates. The E-Score, S-Score, and G-Score each contribute 0.1447, 0.1529, and 0.1218 units, therefore ROA rises by 0.1728 units for every unit increase in the ESG Score. At the 0.05 level, these data are statistically significant, suggesting a low likelihood of coincidence. With a 47.37% explanation of ROA variance, the model demonstrates the substantial influence of ESG on financial success.

7.5 Ordinary Least Squares - Regression Analysis (ROE)

Table 5. Regression Analysis (ROE)

Variables	Co-efficient	Std. Error	Probability
ESG Score	0.2263	0.1165	0.0461
E-Score	0.1814	0.0897	0.0469
S-Score	0.1467	0.1205	0.0506
G-Score	0.1830	0.1087	0.0509
Dependent Variable	**ROE**		
R-squared	0.1989		

The OLS model in Table 7.5 demonstrates a weaker but positive correlation between Return on Equity (ROE) and ESG components. With certain coefficients not being statistically significant at the 0.05 level, the model appears to explain 19.89% of the variation in ROE, according to the R-squared value of 0.1989. This suggests that the model's limited prediction ability for ROE based on ESG ratings is accurate.

7.6 Ordinary Least Squares – Regression Analysis(ROCE)

Table 6. Regression Analysis (ROCE)

Variables	Co-efficient	Std. Error	Probability
ESG Score	0.2231	0.0972	0.0246
E-Score	0.1810	0.0747	0.0179
S-Score	0.1795	0.1003	0.0576

continued on following page

Table 6. Continued

Variables	Co-efficient	Std. Error	Probability
G-Score	0.1688	0.0912	0.0482
Dependent Variable	ROCE		
R-squared	0.3446		

Table 7.6 shows that Return on Capital Employed (ROCE) and ESG factors (ESG Score, E-Score, S-Score, and G-Score) are positively correlated. The E-Score contributes 0.1810 units to the 0.2231 unit increase in ROCE that occurs with a one unit increase in ESG Score. To be statistically significant at the 0.05 level are the ESG Score and the E-Score. Nonetheless, there is less statistical significance indicated by the S-Score and G-Score coefficients, which have p-values of 0.0576 and 0.0482, respectively. With an R-squared value of 0.3446, the model has moderate predictive power, meaning that ESG factors account for 34.46% of the variation in ROCE.

The null hypothesis (H1) is rejected based on the findings of the hypothesis testing, which show a positive correlation between the financial success of businesses and their total ESG scores, as demonstrated by a moderately to substantially positive correlation with ROA, ROE, and ROCE. There is a weak to moderately positive correlation between environmental factors and financial performance (H2), and a weak but positive correlation between social responsibility practices and financial indicators (H3). Scores on governance have a smaller correlation with financial performance than with environmental and social issues, notwithstanding their positive correlation (H4). The alternative hypothesis that the relationship between ESG scores and financial performance is sector-dependent (H5) is supported by the fact that the relationship between ESG scores and financial success varies significantly across sectors, with correlation coefficients indicating differences in strength and direction depending on the industry.

Correlation (Sector Specific)

In the Power sector, the correlation coefficients between ESG scores and financial performance indicators (ROA, ROE, and ROCE) are all negative, showing an unfavourable relationship. This implies that organisations with better ESG scores in the Power sector tend to have lower financial performance measures. The correlations are modest, with coefficients ranging from -0.4676 to -0.4779, implying a somewhat negative relationship between ESG ratings and financial success in this industry.

7.7 Correlation Matrix for the Power Sector

Table 7. Correlation matrix for the power sector

Correlation Matrix - Power				
Variables	**ESG Score**	**ROA**	**ROE**	**ROCE**
ESG Score	1	-	-	-
ROA	-0.4766	1	-	-
ROE	-0.4676	0.9891	1	-
ROCE	-0.4779	0.9939	0.9923	1

The correlations between ESG ratings and financial performance measures in the IT industry are unfavourable, although not as strong as those in the Power sector. This points to a less strong adverse association between ESG rankings and financial success in the IT industry. However, the negative associations suggest that organisations with greater ESG scores in the IT sector may face worse financial performance indicators, but to a smaller extent than in the Power sector.

7.8 Correlation Matrix for the IT Sector

Table 8. Correlation matrix for the IT sector

Correlation Matrix - IT				
Variables	**ESG Score**	**ROA**	**ROE**	**ROCE**
ESG Score	1	-	-	-
ROA	-0.2252	1	-	-
ROE	-0.5572	0.8696	1	-
ROCE	-0.2972	0.9917	0.9139	1

The relationships between ESG scores and financial performance measurements are often weak and inconsistent in the FMCG sector. The correlation coefficients vary greatly, with both positive and negative correlations. This implies that the association between ESG scores and financial success in the FMCG industry is less constant and may differ amongst firms within the sector.

7.9 Correlation Matrix for the FMCG Sector

Table 9. Correlation matrix for the FMCG sector

Correlation Matrix - FMCG				
Variables	**ESG Score**	**ROA**	**ROE**	**ROCE**
ESG Score	1	-	-	-
ROA	-0.016	1	-	-
ROE	0.4231	0.903	1	-
ROCE	-0.0522	0.956	0.9734	1

In the banking industry, correlations between ESG scores and financial performance indicators are often positive, implying a favourable association between ESG scores and financial success. However, the relationships are minor, suggesting that the impact of ESG scores on financial performance in the banking sector may be limited.

7.10 Correlation Matrix for the Banking Sector

Table 10. Correlation matrix for the banking sector

Correlation Matrix - Banking				
Variables	**ESG Score**	**ROA**	**ROE**	**ROCE**
ESG Score	1	-	-	-
ROA	0.1663	1	-	-
ROE	0.1980	0.9621	1	-
ROCE	0.2971	0.8194	0.8862	1

In contrast, in the healthcare industry, the correlations between ESG scores and financial success indicators are continuously favourable and rather significant. This demonstrates a strong positive association between ESG scores and financial performance in the healthcare industry, with firms with higher ESG scores reporting better financial performance measures.

7.11 Correlation Matrix for the Healthcare Sector

Table 11. Correlation matrix for the healthcare sector

Correlation Matrix - Healthcare				
Variables	**ESG Score**	**ROA**	**ROE**	**ROCE**
ESG Score	1	-	-	-
ROA	0.7390	1	-	-
ROE	0.6487	0.926	1	-
ROCE	0.7204	0.9878	0.9707	1

8. HYPOTHESIS TESTING

1. H1 - There is a positive relationship between the financial performance and the combined ESG score of the companies.

The correlation matrix and OLS regression analysis show that ESG score correlate positively with financial performance indicators (ROA, ROE, and ROCE). The correlation coefficients indicate a moderately to strongly favourable association between ESG ratings and financial success metrics. It is identified that there is a positive relationship between the financial performance and the combined ESG score of the companies, hence rejecting the null hypothesis.

2. H2 - Environment factors positively impacts financial performance.

The correlation matrix and OLS regression analysis reveal a favourable relationship between environment scores and financial performance indicators (ROA, ROE, and ROCE). The correlation coefficients show a weak to moderately favourable association between environmental performance and financial results. It is identified that there is a positive relationship between Environment scores and financial performance of the Indian corporates in the chosen sample.

3. H3 - Social responsibility practices positively impacts financial performance.

The correlation matrix and OLS regression analysis show that social scores have positive but less significant relationships with financial performance indicators (ROA, ROE, and ROCE). The correlation coefficients point to a weak positive association between social responsibility activities and financial outcomes. It is identified that there is a weak positive relationship between social score and financial performance of the companies in this sample.

4. H4 - Corporate governance practices positively impacts financial performance.

The correlation matrix and OLS regression analysis show that governance scores are positively correlated with financial performance indicators (ROA, ROE, and ROCE). However, the relationship is weaker than the environmental and social scores. It is identified that there is a weak positive relationship between governance score and financial performance of the companies in this sample.

5. H5 - The relationship between ESG scores and financial performance varies across different sectors

Based on the analysis and interpretation of correlation matrices for firms in certain sectors, there is evidence to support the alternative hypothesis (H1) that the link between ESG variables and financial success varies significantly by sector. The correlation coefficients between ESG ratings and financial performance measurements change between sectors, demonstrating that the relationship's strength and direction vary by sector. As a result, the results do not support the null hypothesis, which states that there are no significant differences between sectors. Instead, the study reveals that the association between ESG scores and financial performance in India varies significantly by sector.

9. RESULTS AND DISCUSSIONS

The association between ESG scores and financial success for a selection of organizations was thoroughly examined in this study. The results indicate a favorable, if slight, link between ESG scores and financial performance metrics including ROA, ROE, and ROCE using descriptive statistics, correlation matrices, and Ordinary Least Squares (OLS) regression. With a governance score of 60.747, the average ESG score indicates that corporations do quite well in the environmental, social, and governance domains. Significant variations in the ESG performance of different companies are indicated by the variability and standard deviations.

The ESG scores and financial performance measures become stable after first differencing, according to the stationarity tests, particularly the Augmented Dickey-Fuller (ADF) unit root test, indicating the constancy of the data across time. ESG scores and financial indicators have moderately favourable relationships, according to the correlation matrix, with environmental scores exhibiting the strongest relationship. This supports the theory that businesses that do better environmentally also typically have greater financial success.

ESG components have a strong positive impact on ROA, ROE, and ROCE, according to OLS regression analysis, which lends more credence to the idea. The financial performance variance can be moderately explained by ESG aspects, according to the R-squared values. Although environmental performance has a bigger impact than social and governance scores, the study shows that ESG elements still have a favourable impact on financial outcomes. An additional indication that other factors entirely may influence financial performance arises from the fact that the relationship of ESG with financial success is different for various industries. The results help develop the body of work on sustainability and corporate success by providing better clarification of how ESG relates to financial performance.

10. SCOPE FOR FURTHER STUDY

The study's scope might have been limited because the sample consisted of businesses from only one industry. Future studies should widen the sample size to include companies from a wider variety of industries and geographical locations in order to more precisely generalize the findings.

A more comprehensive understanding of Economic Value Added (EVA) would arise from a focused analysis of how particular financial adjustments, such as those regarding research and development, affect the creation of value. Additionally, studying managerial actions would shed light on the effects on EVA results. Future evaluations might similarly scrutinize ambiguities about financial statement revisions and their implications vis-a-vis the EVA framework. As far as EVA is concerned, the road ahead would be to further develop the metric to accommodate an added dimension to value creation, thereby underscoring the complexity of modern financial management.

11. LIMITATIONS OF THE STUDY

One of the most significant limitations is the availability and quality of data on ESG performance and financial measures. Furthermore, the accuracy and consistency of ESG data across different sources and reporting formats may differ, influencing the analysis's robustness. The study's conclusions may be impacted by sample selection bias, since the research may be limited to publicly traded businesses or those with easily available ESG disclosures. This may ignore the ESG performance of smaller enterprises, non-listed entities, or those operating in specific industries, reducing the findings' generalizability. The influence of ESG issues may differ dramatically amongst industries with varying environmental footprints or social repercussions. Similarly, major organisations may have greater resources and visibility to prioritise ESG, which might affect their financial performance differently than smaller firms. Because of the study's short timeline, the long-term impacts of ESG integration on financial performance may be missed.

12. CONCLUSION

The descriptive data analysis showed that there is a positive relationship between Environmental, Social, and Governance (ESG) scores and key environmental factors such as consumption and efficiency. The results from the Descriptive statistics highlighted that corporations generally perform well in social aspects, such as social relations and decision-making, and in governance-related ESG elements. On the other hand the environmental indicators like carbon dioxide emissions reflected relatively strong corporate performance, each ESG component contributed to explaining variations in the financial performance of organisations.

The results from the Correlation analysis exhibited a significant relation between financial metric such as returns on equity (ROE),, returns on assets (ROA) and returns on capital employed (ROCE) and ESG scores. The findings from the Regression analyses further validated these results, with significance levels approaching zero, reinforcing the robustness of the correlation. Remarkably, while ROA, ROE, and ROCE looked most influenced by environmental factors, it is crucial to admit the deviation between traditional financial performance measures and how ESG performance is scored.

However, supplementary data analysis using ADF unit root tests established the stationarity of the data. Ordinary Least Squares (OLS) regression analysis discovered that variations in financial performance were mainly determined by ESG factors, with environmental aspects having the most considerable positive effect on financial results.

Industry-specific results emphasized that the strength of the correlation between ESG factors and financial performance differs significantly across sectors. This underlines the status of sector-specific research to address unique ESG challenges and opportunities. Thus, further studies are suggested, focusing on larger and more varied geographical regions. Expanding our understanding of ESG performance, its impact on financial success, and improving literacy on environmental issues could foster enhanced overall or dual bottom-line outcomes for corporations.

REFERENCES

Almeyda, R., & Darmansya, A. (2019). The Influence of Environmental, Social, and Governance (ESG) Disclosure on Firm Financial Performance. *IPTEK Journal of Proceedings Series*, *0*(5), 278–290.

Behl, A., Kumari, P. S. R., Makhija, H., & Sharma, D. (2021). Exploring the relationship of ESG score and firm value using cross-lagged panel analyses: Case of the Indian energy sector. *Annals of Operations Research*, *313*(1), 231–256.

Bruna, M. G., Loprevite, S., Raucci, D., Ricca, B., & Rupo, D. (2022). Investigating the marginal impact of ESG results on corporate financial performance. *Finance Research Letters*, *47*, 102828.

Chai, S., Cao, M., Li, Q., Ji, Q., & Liu, Z. (2023). Exploring the nexus between ESG disclosure and corporate sustainable growth: Moderating role of media attention. *Finance Research Letters*, *58*(104519), 104519.

Chelawat, H., & Trivedi, I. V. (2016). The business value of ESG performance: The Indian context. *Asian Journal of Business Ethics*, *5*(1), 195–210.

Chong, T., Chong, T., Loh, L., & Loh, L. (2023). Innovating ESG Integration as Sustainable Strategy: ESG Transparency and Firm Valuation in the Palm Oil Sector. *Sustainability*, *15*(22), 15943.

Dayanandan, A., Donker, H., & Kuntluru, S. (2023). IFRS and ESG Disclosure in Indian Corporate Sector. Journal of Emerging Market Finance. https://doi.org/DOI: 10.1177/09726527231197328

Deb, S., Sajit, S. K., & Digar, B. (2023). *Does ESG Improve Firm Performance?* Evidence from Indian Companies.

Dodman, D., Diep, L., & Colenbrander, S. (2017). Making the case for the nexus between resilience and resource efficiency at the city scale. *International Journal of Urban Sustainable Development*. Advance online publication. DOI: 10.1080/19463138.2017.1345740

Egorova, A. A., Grishunin, S. V., & Karminsky, A. M. (2022). The Impact of ESG factors on the performance of Information Technology Companies. *Procedia Computer Science*, *199*, 339–345.

Gupta, J., & Das, N. (2022). Multidimensional corporate social responsibility disclosure and financial performance: A meta-analytical review. *Corporate Social Responsibility and Environmental Management*, *29*(4), 731–748.

Junius, D., Adisurjo, A., Arief Rijanto, Y., & Adelina, Y. E. (2020). THE IMPACT OF ESG PERFORMANCE TO FIRM PERFORMANCE AND MARKET VALUE. *JAAPA: Official Journal of the American Academy of Physician Assistants*, *5*(1), 21–41.

Kalia, D., & Aggarwal, D. (2022). Examining impact of ESG score on financial performance of healthcare companies. *Journal of Global Responsibility*, *14*(1), 155–176.

Kang, W., & Jung, M. (2020). Effect of ESG Activities and Firm's Financial Characteristics. *Korean Journal of Financial Studies*, *49*(5), 681–707.

Kim, J., Son, S., Son, S., & Jin, I. (2022). The Effects of Shareholding of the National Pension Fund on Environmental, Social, Governance, and Financial Performance: Evidence from the Korean Manufacturing Industry. *Sustainability, 14*(18), 11788.

Kim, S., & Li, Z. (frank). (2021). Understanding the Impact of ESG Practices in Corporate Finance. Sustainability. *Science Practice and Policy, 13*(7), 3746.

Landi, G., & Sciarelli, M. (2018). Towards a more ethical market: The impact of ESG rating on corporate financial performance. *Social Responsibility, Journalism, Law, Medicine, 15*(1), 11–27.

Lee, S. H., Williams, P. D., & Frame, T. H. (2019). Increased shear in the North Atlantic upper-level jet stream over the past four decades. *Nature, 572*(7771), 639–642. PMID: 31391588

Madison, N., & Schiehll, E. (2021). The Effect of Financial Materiality on ESG Performance Assessment. Sustainability. *Science Practice and Policy, 13*(7), 3652.

Mardini, G. H. (2022). ESG factors and corporate financial performance. *International Journal of Managerial and Financial Accounting, 1*(1), 1.

Masud, M. M., Al-Amin, A. Q., Ha, J., Ahmed, F., Yahaya, S. R. B., Akhtar, R., & Banna, H. (2016). Climate change issue and theory of planned behaviour: Relationship by empirical evidence. *Journal of Cleaner Production*. Advance online publication. DOI: 10.1016/j.jclepro.2015.11.080

Ray, R. S., & Goel, S. (2023). Impact of ESG score on financial performance of Indian firms: Static and dynamic panel regression analyses. *Applied Economics*. Advance online publication. DOI: 10.1080/00036846.2022.2101611

Rodríguez-Fernández, M., Sánchez-Teba, E. M., López-Toro, A. A., & Borrego-Domínguez, S. (2019). Influence of ESGC Indicators on Financial Performance of Listed Travel and Leisure Companies. Sustainability. *Science Practice and Policy, 11*(19), 5529.

Suresha, B., Srinidhi, V. R., Verma, D., Manu, K. S., & Krishna, T. A. (2022). The impact of ESG inclusion on price, liquidity and financial performance of Indian stocks: Evidence from stocks listed in BSE and NSE ESG indices. *Investment Management and Financial Innovations, 19*(4), 40–50.

Terdpaopong, K., Terdpaopong, K., & Rickards, R. (2021). Thai Non-Life Insurance Companies' Resilience and the Historic 2011 Floods: Some Recommendations for Greater Sustainability. *Sustainability, 13*(16), 8890.

Velte, P. (2017). Does ESG Performance Have an Impact on Financial Performance? Evidence from Germany. https://papers.ssrn.com/abstract=2916741

Yahya, M. R. (2023). *Exploring the Relationship Between Corporate Governance Mechanism and Financial Performance: Evidence From Listed Companies*. West Science Accounting and Finance., DOI: 10.58812/wsaf.v1i02.133

Chapter 10
Artificial Intelligence, Open Innovation, and Financial Sustainability:
Trends, Perspectives, and Future Research Directions

Hicham Saidi
https://orcid.org/0009-0008-0764-8201
Industrial Technologies and Services Laboratory, Superior School of Technology of Fez, Morocco

Yousra Chnigri
https://orcid.org/0000-0001-5121-6600
Laboratory of Studies and Research in Management of Organisations and Territories, FSJES Fes, Morocco

Fatima Zahra Madhat
Industrial Technologies and Services Laboratory, Superior School of Technology of Fez, Morocco

ABSTRACT

This study examines the intersection of finance, AI and open innovation, emphasizing decision-making, operational efficiency and financial inclusion. Using bibliometric methods on 420 Wos publications and co-author network analysis with VOSviewer, we identified key contributors and thematic clusters. It is found that research grew exponentially from 2016, peaking in 2023, with strong AI and OI synergies in finance's digital transformation. Co-authorship analysis highlighted core themes: AI applications, innovation management and financial sustainability. The co-author network shows three principal collaborative clusters knew centers of these networks included the National University of Singapore. There is, however, very little cross cluster collaboration and the regions of Africa and MENA are largely absent. Achieving a greater degree of multi-regional collaboration will make it possible to support the development of more sustainable financial practices. This study contributes to understanding the impact of AIs and OI on the creation of inclusive financial ecosystems.

DOI: 10.4018/979-8-3693-9684-1.ch010

1. INTRODUCTION

The evolution of technology is something that has completely changed industries around the world. These include changes in Open Innovation and AI where perhaps the most profound impact has been seen in the financial industry. Companies are modernizing the way they conduct business using artificial intelligent such as chatbots among other tools, which helps them make better decisions and increases productivity. In addition to that, sharing ideas and insights that transcend organizational and geographic boundaries is now possible due to Open Innovation. As discussed by Sætra (2023), Bouteraa et al. (2024), and Ali and Aysan (2023), Artificial Intelligence can actually be analyzed as a type of Open Innovation that has changed the way financial institutions operate. The early implementers of these technologies are clearly enjoying a head start in competition, managing to adapt to changes in the market, improve business processes, and serve customers better.

In particular, AI-powered solutions are revolutionizing areas such as customer service, virtual assistants, support, information retrieval, trade reconciliation, and decision-making within the financial markets (Ali and Aysan, 2023; Bouteraa et al., 2024). The integration of Open Innovation practices, exemplified by models like Open Banking, facilitates collaboration between financial institutions (banks), enterprises, and consumers, driving new business models and fostering a more inclusive, transparent financial ecosystem, and (Yun, 2021; Bloomberg, 2023; Reuters, 2023). As AI and Open Innovation continue to evolve, their combined impact is expected to reshape the competitive landscape in the financial sector, creating new opportunities and challenges for both established institutions and emerging enterprises to growth and to be more sustainable (Hernandez et al., 2024).

The current research explores the intersection relationship between transformative technologies and subsequent changes within the realm of finance, selecting particular attention to the roles of AI and Open Innovation in fostering innovation, competitiveness, and performance. With the use of bibliometric analysis, this study assesses the gaps, existing trends, and themes that literature covers, and consequently, it helps to build a foundation for what should be done in the future. In particular, we analyze the structure and evolution of this field, its prominent authors and journals, as well as the spatial distribution of the research activities.

2. LITERATURE REVIEW

2.1 Open Innovation in the Financial Sector

Open Innovation, as defined by Chesbrough (2003), involves the purposeful inflow and outflow of knowledge to accelerate internal innovation processes and expand market opportunities. (De Groote & Backmann, 2020) defined open innovation as the ability of companies to use their knowledge on both side internal and external way to enhance innovation design and development in product, process or service form. This concept has gained a lot of traction in the financial sector as institutions are trying to cope with the extremely fluctuating market conditions as well as expectations of consumers. The shift towards Open Banking, a model that allows consumers and SMEs to access a wider range of financial services, exemplifies the potential of Open Innovation in creating more dynamic and transparent ecosystems through: viewing accounts in one place, managing debt and sharing information securely (Yun, 2021; Openbanking, 2020). This model basing on using digital platform facilitates the exchange of information between financial companies, external partners and stakeholders, encouraging collaboration and knowledge-sharing that drives innovation in products and services (Pollari, 2018).

The focus on Open Innovation is however, congruent to the definition of Finance 4.0, whereby financial services are becoming more personalized and digitally transformed to the preferences of customers (Yun, 2021). The integration of AI, blockchain, Internet of Things (IoT) and other digital technologies into financial services is facilitating this transformation, creating opportunities for both incumbents and companies to develop new business models and enhance their service offerings (Yun, 2021). Furthermore, the collaborative nature of Open Innovation has been shown to support SMEs and startups by providing them with access to cutting-edge technologies and to attain financial resources from various stakeholders, because were previously out of reach and some of them have started to offer artificial intelligence and internet of things (Iot) products and services (Capinzaiki & Pomim, 2021; Hernandez et al., 2024).

As noted by Rothwell et al. (1985), Open Innovation is rooted in the innovation networks model, where knowledge flows in and out of organizations, driving the creation of new solutions and enhancing competitiveness. This collaborative approach is especially appropriate in the finance industry, since technological changes along with the demands of customers are compelling business to innovate and work together. By establishing external partnerships and incorporating a variety of technologies including AI, financial institutions can adapt to changes in the marketplace in a timely manner to stay ahead of market trends and even surpass competition (Sætra, 2023).

2.2 Artificial Intelligence in Financial Services

Artificial Intelligence (AI) is an engineering technology that deals with cognitive activities (Shinde et al., 2021). This latest has had a profound impact on the financial sector, enabling institutions to streamline operations, improve decision-making, and enhance customer interactions. (Hernandez et al., 2024, Gama & Magistretti, 2023) in their explain that artificial intelligence (AI) can effectively impact innovation and firms' performance specially in finance. AI-powered tools, such as chatbots, are being deployed across various areas within the financial industry, including customer service, sales, marketing, and even complex processes like trade reconciliation and risk management (Ali and Aysan, 2023; Bouteraa et al., 2024). AI has allowed financial institutions to automate routine tasks, reducing operational costs and improving service efficiency. For instance, AI-driven chatbots have revolutionized customer service by providing immediate assistance, processing transactions, and answering customer queries, all while reducing the need for human intervention (Bouteraa et al., 2024).

AI also plays a critical role in enhancing the decision-making processes within financial firms and their ability to respond effectively to market (Bag et al., 2021; Ramadan et al., 2020). By analyzing vast amounts of data, AI algorithms can provide more accurate and timely insights, enabling banks and other financial entities to make better-informed decisions, especially in areas such as investment, lending, brainstorming, human-AI product design and development and finally risk assessment (Feuerriegel et al., 2022; Bouteraa et al., 2024). This data-driven decision-making process, coupled with the automation of tasks, not only boosts productivity but also enables financial companies to better respond to market changes and customer needs.

As AI technologies continue to advance, they are expected to further revolutionize the financial services industry by enhancing personalization, improving operational efficiency, and reducing costs. According to (Wamba, 2022 ; Olan et al., 2022; Feuerriegel et al. 2022), the integration of AI into financial decision-making processes can significantly improve a firm's operational performance, especially in dynamic and competitive environments like financial markets.

2.3 Synergy Between Open Innovation and AI

The convergence of Open Innovation and AI offers a unique opportunity for financial institutions to foster innovation and enhance operational performance. For instance, according to Bouteraa et al. (2024) the use of AI spearheaded ChatGPT as Open Innovation platform, has made considerable impact. These tools offer for financial institutions the capacity to work on diverse financial goals and improving decision making with data analysis (Bouteraa et al., 2024). This synergy can lead the firms, to enhance their capability to deploy AI and to develop new products, services, and business models that address emerging market needs and challenges (Shinde et al., 2021). The collaboration between enterprises, financial institutions, and technology providers, fueled by AI and Open Innovation, can create a more agile, efficient, and customer-centric financial ecosystem.

Enterprises specially (SMEs and startups), in emerging economies, stand to benefit from the integration of AI and Open Innovation by gaining access to the latest technological advancements and external expertise, which can help them scale rapidly and compete with larger institutions. By participating in open innovation platforms, these companies can collaborate with established firms and technology suppliers to create cutting-edge solutions, develop their business plan, share knowledge and seek investment, solve problems and address business challenges that meet the needs of modern consumers (Capinzaiki & Pomim, 2021; Hernandez et al., 2024). Moreover, by strengthening their position within the market, AI allows them to optimize business processes, eliminate routine tasks, and enhance the service delivery quality to clients (Hernandez et al, 2024). Studies realized by (Mikalef & Gupta, 2021 ; Wu et al., 2023) confirm that AI can lead to better outcomes on innovation management and performance.

Despite the significant potential of AI and Open Innovation, several challenges remain in their widespread adoption and implementation. As Kuckertz et al. (2019) point out, effective management of innovation processes, particularly when integrating advanced technologies like AI, requires strong leadership, adequate financial support, and robust technological infrastructure. Furthermore, based on (Yun, 2021) the successful deployment of open innovation in financial services is presented in the real world as AI, machine learning, customised service (individual/ corporate), cyber currencies, Smart system, cloud computing, digitalisation, Big data, FinTech, InsurTech, distributed ledger technology (DLT). As a result all of which can impede as an open innovation sources in financial sector (Kuckertz et al., 2019).

As Feng et al. (2021) and Hernandez et al. (2024) highlight, there is a need for further investigation and exploration into the role of emerging enterprises and developing economies in adopting AI and Open Innovation, because the developed countries might have reached maturity in the innovation cycle while the emerging economies are not embracing it. Numerous studies confirm the significant impact of AI on innovation processes across various sectors, including (Gama & Magistretti, 2023), retail and marketing (Mariani et al., 2023). A few studies, such as Shinde et al. (2021), have ventured into bibliometric analyses in this domain, like the role of blockchain in securing AI applications (Saidi & Madhat, 2024) or the intersection of open innovation and digital transformation, though they often focus on more specific aspects. Future research should therefore aim to explore the financial sector, institutions, and enterprises to better navigate the challenges and leverage the combined potential of Open Innovation and AI for sustainable growth.

3. METHODOLOGY AND DATA COLLECTION

The aim of the study is to develop a quantitative research method known as bibliometric analysis. This approach enables us to analyze the current trends in the literature related to a specific area of research and provides a comprehensive overview and structure of the field (Amin et al., 2019; Donthu et al., 2021; Ramos-Rodríguez & Ruíz-Navarro, 2004). In this analysis, we analyzed 420 publications using the Web of Science (WoS) database retrieved on 25 November. The data gathering period excludes the ongoing calendar year of 2024 as it is not yet complete. This was done in order to prevent any possible bias of the thematic trends of our bibliometric analysis. The choice of these databases was made as they seem to have the widest coverage of references, abstracts, and summaries, in accordance with standard procedures (Fink, 2019; Song et al., 2019).

For this purpose, the following keywords were utilized during the search: ("open innv*" AND " financ* " AND " iA* " OR " artific* " AND techno*). Focus was placed on document types of articles and only those published in English were retrieved so as to preserve the language, in compliance with Bonilla, Merigó and Torres-Abad (2015) (see Table 1).

Table 1. Protocol for data collection.

Topic	Definition
Keywords	AK=("open innv*" AND " financ* " AND " iA* " OR " artific* " AND techno*)
Query Link	https://www.webofscience.com/wos/woscc/summary/31dc0c5c-9505-4632-9fe1-cf7284f20b83-012b4434e7/relevance/1
Database	Web of science
Search type	Author keywords
Language	English
Document type filter	articles
Research Area	Business Economics
Period	From 1994 -until 2024

We followed the three main steps proposed by (Da Silva & Martha De Souza, 2021): data collection, data processing, and results extraction (see Fig.1).

Figure 1. Bibliometric literature mapping method

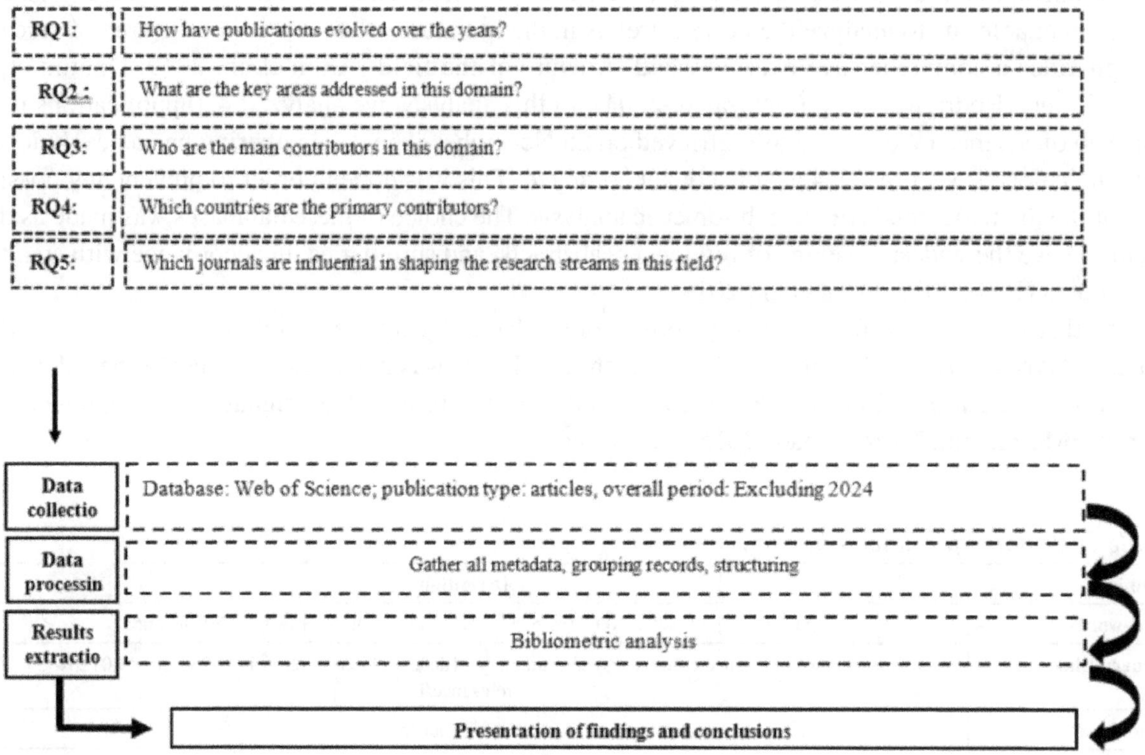

source: (CHNIGRI et al., 2024)

VOSviewer software (version 1.6.20) was utilized to conduct the bibliometric analysis. This works well as an open source for building and visualizing bibliometric networks to find patterns and clusters in literature. (Van Eck & Waltman, 20120). It has been very useful when designing and showcasing the information as well as conducting network analysis.

We have also used data from Clarivate analytics, which offers rich bibliographic databases like the Web of Sciences (WoS). This contributed to the selection of other peer-reviewed studies relevant to the research topic. For data set preparation and data set cleaning, we employed Microsoft Office Excel whereby the data should be made ready to fit with the tools of the bibliometric analysis.

With the assistance of the above tools, it was possible to conduct the analysis trend investigations in a more systematic manner, offering the analysis influencer and thematic cluster in the Artificial Intelligence, Open Innovation and financial practices circles. Their subsequent application improved the overall quality and detail of our results.

4. RESULTS AND DISCUSSION

4.1 Search Growth Basing On Publications And Citations

An analysis of the evolution of academic writing on open innovation, artificial intelligence (AI), and sustainable finance shows a steady increase in complexity since the advent of these topics in 1994. The earliest publications, although sparse and exploratory, laid the conceptual foundations necessary for understanding these fields. The first researches were mainly theoretical, focusing on fundamental definitions, as is seen in the work of Chesbrough's (2003) in the field of open innovation, and the early developments in AI with limited applicability to financial issues.

Figure 2. Search growth TP and TC

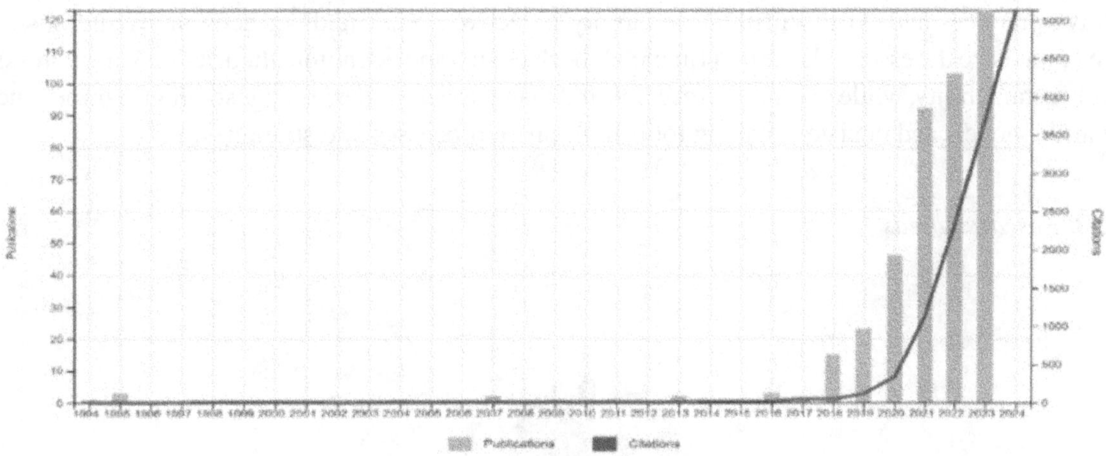

Source: *Author's elaboration based on WOS data base*

From 1994 to 2014, research in this area was marked by a narrow focus and low volume, reflecting an initial interest at the intersection of these domains. A critical turning point occurred in 2015, which was marked by a significant increase in academic output. This period saw the emergence of applied studies that introduced topics such as the use of AI for automating financial tasks and Open Banking (Behera et al., 2016).

The period from 2018 to 2020 marked a turning point, characterized by a substantial acceleration in research output and a diversification of topics addressing the transformative role of emerging technologies across various sectors, including financial reporting (Türegün, 2019). Since 2021, research activity has surged significantly, reaching a peak in 2024 with nearly 5,000 publications and citations. This period has been marked by increasingly complex and strategic themes, such as the adoption and impact of new technologies in financial sectors, customer perceptions of digital transformation, and the role of innovations like artificial intelligence (AI) and FinTech (Aloulou et al., 2024). Studies have emphasized the transformative potential of cloud computing, AI, and machine learning (ML) in banking and insurance (Iwanicz-Drozdowska et al., 2023), while also underscoring the critical importance of regulatory compliance and strategic implementation to enhance the performance and inclusivity of digital financial services, particularly in emerging economies (Bharti et al., 2024).

However, the chronological sequence of all these concepts reveals a strong correlation with the level of progress in technological development and sustainability efforts globally. It also points to the fact that these gaps need to be bridged in geographical and thematic counterparts to understand the impact of AI and open innovation in the economic spheres. This progress grounds the ways forward in promoting inclusive and sustainable financial practices globally.

4.2 Most Frequent Areas Of Research

The examination of the research domains reveals the significantly interdisciplinary characteristics at the convergence of open innovation, artificial intelligence (AI), and sustainable behavioral finance. The dominance of disciplines such as management and business emphasizes the strategic and organizational emphasis of this research area, illustrating the methods by which firms and industries incorporate innovative practices and AI to fulfill sustainability objectives. The fields of economics and business finance emphasize the essential role that financial mechanisms and economic theories play in addressing issues of sustainability, while operations research and management science suggest reliance on advanced quantitative models and decision-making tools to improve processes and strategies.

Figure 3. Research areas

Source: *Author's elaboration based on WOS data base*

Disciplines like industrial relations, regional urban planning, and industrial engineering show the practical implications of this research, which span from workforce dynamics and sustainable urban development to the improvement of industrial systems through innovations powered by artificial intelligence. The existence of fields like information science and library science points out a growing interest in data-centric methodologies and the importance of knowledge management in furthering sustainable financial practices. Conversely, applied psychology emphasizes the importance of understanding human behavior in order to promote responsible decision-making and to integrate sustainability into both individual and organizational practices. These diverse areas of research fields indicate the broad nature of the discipline, combining theoretical constructs, empirical applications, and emerging technologies.

It embodies a holistic approach in which established academic disciplines intersect with emerging fields to explore the leading solutions for fostering sustainable financial systems. Such interdisciplinary emphasis not only broadens the breadth of research inquiry but also cements the critical role that cross-disciplinary research plays in addressing the most complex global issues. The diverse framework instituted places the discipline at the cutting edge of both scholarly and practical developments, hence facilitating influential research and praxis in real-world conditions.

4.3 Most Productive And Highly Cited Authors

The following table shows the top 10 author metrics from WOS, which provide an overview of the most contributing authors in the field of open innovation, AI, and sustainable behavioral finance. The ranking of the authors is done based on TP and TC, showing how influential each is in terms of their research productivity. Fang Z leads in terms of total citations with 673, even though he has only three publications, which reflects the high impact and quality of his work. Similarly, Dwivedi YK, with the highest number of publications (4) and a substantial citation count of 372, shows a balance between research volume and influence, making him a pivotal figure in the field.

Other authors, such as Gupta S and Kim J, show significant citation counts of 165 and 129, respectively, highlighting the importance of their contributions despite fewer publications. Meanwhile, authors like Kumar A, with six publications but relatively lower citations (41), suggest a focus on quantity over immediate impact, potentially addressing niche or emerging areas. The presence of Al-Emran M and Al-Sharafi MA (both with 110 citations) underscores growing contributions from regions traditionally underrepresented in global research, such as the MENA region.

Table 2. Top 10 author metrics in (WOS).

R	WOS		
	Auteurs	**TP**	**TC**
1	Fang Z	3	673
2	Dwivedi YK	4	372
3	Gupta S	3	165
4	Kim J	3	129
5	Al-emran M	3	110
6	Al-sharafi MA	3	110
7	Islam N	3	67
8	Gherhes C	3	46
9	Kumar A	6	41
10	Ferreira FAF	3	25

Total Authors =1187

While this table reflects the prominence of the top 10 contributors, it also points to a vast pool of authors (1,187 in total), suggesting a highly collaborative and diverse research field. However, it has to be noted that there are no authors from Africa in this collection, which definitely brings into light the need for more investment in research infrastructure and collaboration in the African environment. The representation of MENA authors, albeit limited, is a promising sign of the region's growing engagement in the field, yet further efforts are needed to integrate their perspectives into the global discourse.

This data shows the strong influence wielded by a few top authors, while at the same time opening up a wide collaborative potential within the field. It underlines the need to encourage inclusiveness and expand opportunities for contributions from underrepresented regions to take part in and shape this vibrant research area. This would enrich the academic discourse and drive innovations that are tailored to different socio-economic contexts, thus helping to create a more equitable and global academic landscape.

4.4 Country-Wise Analysis

The geographical distribution of research contributions suggests a significant of research efforts within a few most active countries, with the United States at the top of the list with 119 publications, followed by England with 52 and China with 50. The said countries boast advanced research facilities, ample funding schemes, and strong international cooperation, hence becoming leading contributors to the advancement of research on open innovation, artificial intelligence, and sustainable behavioral finance. Other emerging economies, such as India with 41 and Germany at 32, are also showing significant activity, evidence of growing focus on research and innovation in these countries. Countries such as France at 29 and Italy at 25 in Europe remain actively engaged, reaping the fruits of collaborative frameworks developed in the European Union to promote interdisciplinary and cross-border research.

Figure 4. Country-wise analysis

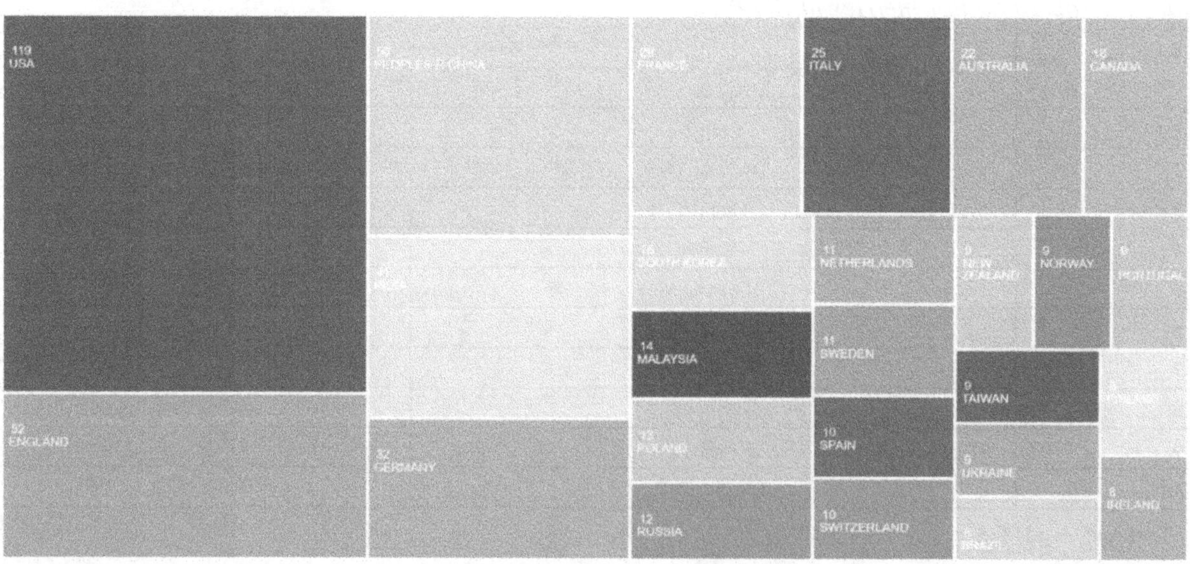

out of 76 countries
Source: *Author's elaboration based on WOS data base*

To exemplify, countries such as Australia (22), Canada (18), and South Korea (15) make a moderate contribution, reflecting open engagement in applied research and international cooperation. On the other hand, smaller but diverse contributors, such as Malaysia, Brazil, and Norway, depict the growing globalization of the field, a slow but assured development of knowledge creation spreading beyond the traditional centers. This may signal new avenues toward greater diversity in research methodologies and more inclusive ways of cooperation across different economic and academic contexts.

However, the map highlights a glaring absence of contributions from the MENA region and Africa, underscoring a significant gap in research output from these areas. This lack of representation may be attributed to several challenges, including limited research funding, insufficient access to advanced technological infrastructures, and weaker integration into global research networks. The disparity is particularly concerning given the growing importance of these regions in addressing global sustainability and innovation challenges. MENA countries, for instance, are uniquely positioned to explore the intersection of sustainability and finance given their resource-driven economies and the increasing demand for diversification. Similarly, African nations, with their rapidly growing populations and unique socio-economic challenges, have the potential to contribute valuable perspectives on behavioral finance and sustainable innovation.

Addressing these gaps requires targeted strategies to foster research capacity in underrepresented regions, including increasing funding opportunities, encouraging international collaboration, and enhancing access to technological and academic resources. Bridging this divide is essential not only for advancing global knowledge but also for ensuring that the benefits of innovation and sustainability practices are equitably distributed. These findings bring urgency to the inclusion of MENA and African voices in the global academic landscape, as it would bring new dimensions to the discourse and provide contextually-relevant solutions for some of the most compelling problems facing the world today.

4.5 Co-Authorship Based On Organizations

Figure 5. Co-authorship based on organizations

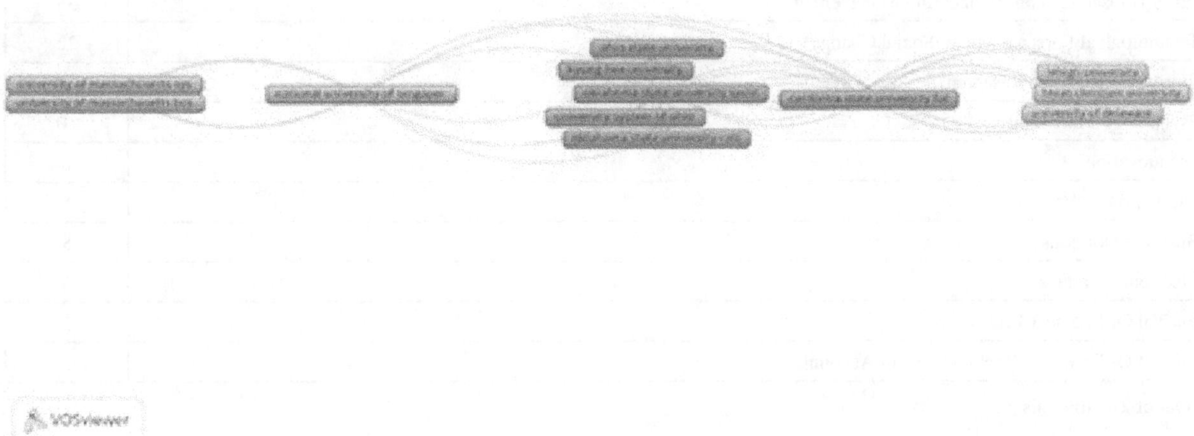

The co-authorship network visualization represents the collaborative relations among universities based on their shared academic outputs. There are three clusters in this network, which are marked in different colors. The blue cluster consists of such institutions as the University of Massachusetts System, the University of Massachusetts Boston, and the National University of Singapore; this strongly implies that there is good international collaboration between the United States and Asia. The red cluster, dominated by U.S. based universities such as Ohio State University, Oklahoma State University, and California State University Fullerton, reflects regional collaborations concentrated within the United States. Universities such as Lehigh University, Texas Christian University, and the University of Delaware are part of the green cluster which indicates an increased area of collaboration within US institutions.

This clusters have been bridged by some key nodes within the network. For instance, the California State University representatives, Fullerton are major links between the red and green clusters. Additionally, National University of Singapore connects the blue and red clusters which exemplifies their importance in tying international partnerships together. Collaboration strength is represented through the connection medium, where ties within clusters are thicker than those outside.

The visualization illustrates the strengths and gaps within the co-authorship patterns. Although there are strong intra-cluster collaborations, cross cluster partnerships seem to be less frequent which shows there is great potential towards building both interdisciplinary and international research networks. For instance, the institutions within the green cluster can strengthen their connection with the blue and red clusters which increases their reach out globally. The network highlights the interconnected structure of academic research and the importance of fostering collaboration over regions and disciplines to simplify the complexity of global issues.

4.6 Main Journals Of Publication

Table 3. Main journals of publication in (WOS).

WOS	
Revues	**TP**
IEEE Transactions on Engineering Management	35
Technological Forecasting and Social Change	22
Journal Of Business Research	11
Psychology Marketing	10
Technovation	8
Futures	6
Business Horizons	5
Electronic Markets	5
Journal Of Business Ethics	5
Journal Of Emerging Technologies in Accounting	5

Out of 211 Journals

The table shows the leading journals which contain research papers on open innovation, AI, and sustainable behavioral finance. IEEE Transactions on Engineering Management is the first with 35 publications, which reflects the technology and management-related aspects of this field. Forecasting Technological and Social Trends Change Practices "22" publications include a deeper explanation on why these practices are so important for the development of sustainable finance. Other major players include the Journal of Business Research (11 publications) and Psychology & Marketing (10 publications) that depict the blend of business practices and behavior.

The focus on technological innovation and digital transformation is also found in specialized journals such as Technovation and Electronic Markets with 8 publications each. The presence of Journal of Business Ethics and Journal of Emerging Technologies in Accounting (5 publications each) reflects the wide interest in ethical issues and the new reporting requirements arising from the technological and sustainability revolution in finance.

Even though there are a lot of journals, there is a significant absence of coverage from sources that center around Africa and MENA regions. This fact reveals a more general deficiency in terms of dealing with regional issues and possibilities that emerge in the field of sustainability and innovation. Promoting research in these areas and integrating them into the international academic community would add great value as well as the needed variance to the debate.

4.7 Co-Occurrence Analysis Based On The Authors' Keyword "WoS":

In this section, we have used the VOSviewer, which is the most widely used information visualization software to select the topmost keywords used by the authors in their papers. (CHNIGRI et al., 2024; Muhuri et al., 2019).

Due to the abundance of keywords, the construction of the co-occurrence network was carried out by considering only terms that appeared at least twice across the collected documents.

In WOS, a total of 153 author-keywords met the mentioned threshold and are organized into 6 clusters interconnected by 198 links. The significance of each keyword is depicted by the size of the circles in the visualization. The most common keywords within each cluster are as follows: cluster 1 (80 items); cluster 2 (21 items); cluster 3 (16 items); cluster 4 (14 items); cluster 5 (11 items); cluster 6 (11 items).

Figure 6. Most popular author keywords in WOS.

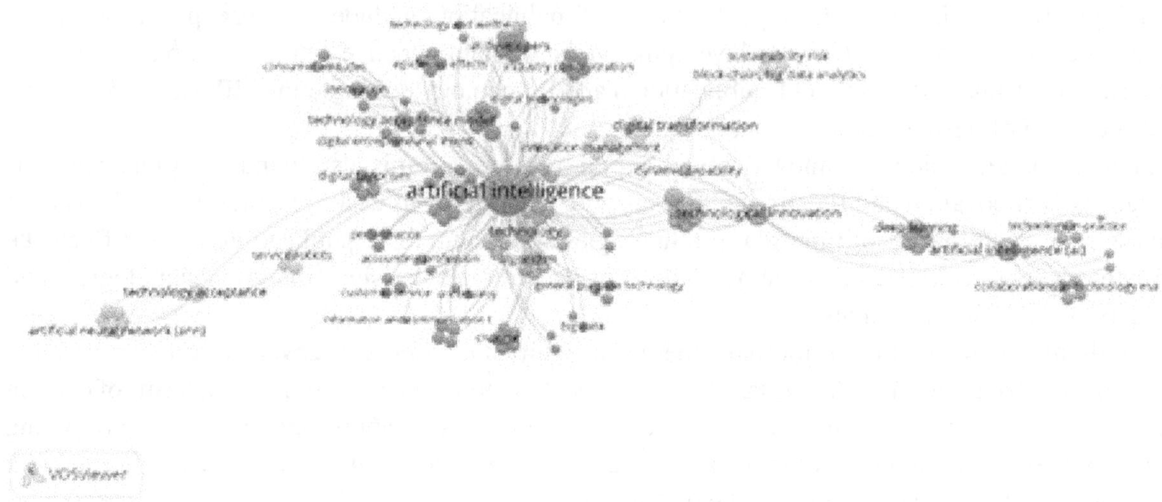

Source: *Author's elaboration based on the WOS analytics with VOSviewer software.*

Cluster 1 "In Red": Emerging Technologies and Digital Transformation in the Financial Sector: Innovation, Ethics, and the Future of Work: This cluster in red covers a wide range of items related to emerging technologies, artificial intelligence (AI), digital transformation, and their impact on industries, particularly in the financial sector. These items are interconnected as part of the technological revolutions that are redefining business practices, innovation and performance in different areas, especially in financial way, we have chosen to divide these elements into parts and program them as follows:

- **Emerging technologies and AI**: AI (artificial intelligence) technology, including artificial neural networks and automation, has a central role in the banking and financial sector, as highlighted by the literature on the impact of AI on business innovation and performance. AI enables better decision-making by analyzing large amounts of data, which improves the efficiency of financial services, reduces operational costs and creates new opportunities to personalize services (Bouteraa et al., 2024; Hernandez et al., 2024). These technologies also include the use of service robots and automation tools to manage repetitive tasks and improve customer interaction. The associated items are: *Artificial Intelligence, AI Technology, Artificial Neural Network, Automation, Big Data, Generative AI, FinTech, Service Technology, Technology Adoption, Technology Acceptance, Technology and Service, Human-Machine Interactions.*
- **Digital banking and digital currencies**: Digital currencies and CBDCs (central bank digital currencies) are changing the payments and transactions landscape. They are enabling greater digital financial inclusion and accelerating the digitalisation of financial services (Yun, 2021). Digital payments and the rise of fintechs are facilitating access to new financial services for consumers and SMEs, particularly in emerging markets. Related items are: *Central Bank Digital Currencies, Digital Currency, Digital Payments, Digital Financial Inclusion, Digital Literacy, FinTech, Digital Era, E-commerce, Digital Technologies, Digital Responsibility, Digital Wellbeing.*

- **Social responsibility and ethics**: Companies must now take into account their corporate social responsibility (CSR) in an increasingly digital context. AI ethics is becoming a major topic, as the use of AI in financial services raises issues of transparency, fairness and privacy (Feuerriegel et al., 2022). Companies are encouraged to integrate digital responsibility practices and ensure that technological innovations comply with ethical standards. The items are: *Corporate Social Responsibility, Ethics, AI Ethics, Corporate Responsibility, Digital Responsibility, Technology Policy, Sociology of Technological Expectations.*
- **Digital transformation and new customer expectations**: Digital transformation is in the heart of customer experience and customer relationship management. As the emergence of new technologies enables making services more personalized for users and expectations shift among consumers (Sætra, 2023). Tools such as ChatGPT can enable businesses to efficiently provide automated support and minimize consumer expectations through customization of services. Related items: *Customer Relationship Management, Customer Service, Customer Experience, Service Robots, ChatGPT, Service Delivery, Technology and Wellbeing, User Experience, Digital Technologies, Technology Receptivity.*
- **Technologies and digital inclusion:** The adoption of digital technologies contributes to financial inclusion and the reduction of economic inequalities. Digital literacy and digital financial inclusion enable more people, including those in remote areas, to access financial services via digital platforms (Yun, 2021). These changes are also supported by the rise of the Internet of Things (IoT) and blockchain-based technologies. Items: *Digital Financial Inclusion, Digital Literacy, Digital Payments, Emerging Technologies, FinTech, Economic Growth, Digital Era, Information and Communication Technologies.*
- **Product innovation and sustainability:** Product innovation and sustainable competitiveness are enhanced by the integration of green technologies and green intellectual capital into innovation processes (Shinde et al., 2021). Companies in the financial sector are increasingly integrating innovations linked to sustainability and ecology, not only to meet new societal expectations, but also to differentiate themselves in an increasingly competitive market. Items: *Green Technology Innovation, Green Intellectual Capital, Green Knowledge Management, Sustainable Competitiveness, Sustainable Performance, Corporate Social Responsibility, Product Innovation.*
- **The future of work and skills:** The future of work in an increasingly automated and technologized environment involves employee training and a reassessment of the skills required. The automation of routine tasks and the management of technology must be accompanied by an evolution in the skills of employees, who must be trained to use these technologies effectively while remaining competitive in the marketplace (Bag et al., 2021). Items: *Employee Motivation, Engagement and Training, Task Routineness, Task-Technology Fit, Technology Receptivity, Technology Acceptance, Future of Work, Human Labor.*
- **Impact of the technologies convergence:** This is where different technologies, from AI to large technical systems and even to open innovation, converge to drastically alter how companies innovate and position themselves within the market. This convergence gives rise to a dynamic environment that requires companies to constantly evolve in order to remain competitive and meet societal and technological expectations (Capinzaiki & Pomim, 2021; Yun, 2021). Items: *Innovation, Inter-Firm Diffusion, Blockchain, General Purpose Technology, Product Matching, Large Technical System, Technology Indicator, Technology Adoption, Fintech, User Experience.*

Indeed, this cluster demonstrates the connection between the adoption of technology and the ethics and sustainability issues surrounding it in the sphere of finance, in this case, regard the impact of AI, automation and digitalization of financial services. The effects of these changes on competitiveness, performance and customer relationship management indicate a shift toward more open innovations in the defined space, which can be evidenced, for instance, by the growing importance of overseas collaborations and new technologies in the industry.

80 items of cluster 1: Accounting profession, adopting technology, ai developers, ai technology, artificial intelligence, artificial neural network, automation, banking industry sector, big data, central bank digital currencies, ChatGPT, corporate responsibility, corporate social responsibility, corporate website, customer experience, customer relationship management, customer service, data security, digital currency, digital era, digital financial inclusion, digital literacy, digital payments, digital responsibility, digital Taylorism, digital technologies, digital wellbeing, digitalization, e-commerce, economic growth, emerging technologies, employee motivation, engagement and training, epidemic effects, ethics, ethics of IA, expectations, fintech, future of technology, future of work, general purpose technology, generative AI, Green intellectual capital, green knowledge management, green technology innovation, human labor, human-machine interactions, industry concentration, information and communication, information technology, infrastructure, intangible capital, inter-firm diffusion, large technical system, performance, product innovation, product matching, service delivery, service robots, service technology, sociology of technological expectations, superstar firms, sustainable competitiveness, sustainable performance, task routineness, task-technology fit, techno-functional framework, technological change, technological readiness, technology acceptance, technology adoption, technology and service, technology and wellbering, technology indicator, technology policy, technology receptivity, uncertainty, user experience, web data.

Cluster 2 "In green": Digital Transformation: From AI to Human Resource Management for Training and facilitating the Work: Digital technologies such as AI, robots and self-service are redefining human resources and working conditions. They are automating tasks, improving efficiency and creating new training needs, notably through virtual reality for skills development. These changes also affect global value chains and require adjustments in talent management. However, the impact of automation raises ethical questions, notably about digital inclusion and the role of the human being in an increasingly technological world.

Cluster 2 Items: AI, bot, data analytics, digital technology, education needs, global value chains, human enhancement, human resource management, organization, organizational affects, post human, robot, self- service technology, society, technology, training needs, virtual human resource development, virtual reality, working conditions.

Cluster 3 "In purple": Technological Advancements and Organizational Resilience in the Modern Economy: Artificial neural networks and deep learning are transforming businesses by enhancing their dynamic capacity to innovate, especially in the context of Industry 4.0. These technologies, coupled with social robots, are influencing corporate governance and business continuity, essential for navigating through crises such as pandemics. Behavioral sciences and psychology help to understand human interaction with these technologies, while innovation policies support long-term sustainability in global economic systems.

cluster 3 (16 items): Artificial neural network, behavioral sciences, business continuity, corporate governance, deep learning, dynamic capability, economic systems, economics, industry 4.0, innovation policy, pandemic, psychology, social robots, sustainability, systems of innovation, technological innovation.

Cluster 4 "In yellow": riving Digitalization in Finance: The Role of Open Innovation: Open innovation serves to accelerate the process of digitalization of the financial industry by integrating external partners into the development of modern technologies such as blockchain, AI, or cloud computing. This encourages more marriage of the physical and virtual worlds, resulting in the Finance 4.0 phenomenon where consumers have more specific expectations of financial services. Open innovation enables financial firms to adopt more agile business strategies, enhance their fiscal health, undertake risk management in an anticipatory manner, and accelerate digital transformation all while improving their standing within the industry.

Cluster 4 (14 items); "block-chain, big data analytics, the internet of thing, cloud computing, artificial intelligence", change management, digital transformation, educational sustainability, financial performance, financial risk, future of education, industry 4.0 technologies, innovation focused strategies, innovation management, smart university, strategic management, sustainability risk, technology implementation.

Cluster 5 "In sky-blue": AI, Open Banking, and Consumer Acceptance: Driving the Future of Finance: AI, robotics, and other emerging technologies have greatly transformed the improvement of banking automation services such as transaction reconciliation and virtual assistance. These new technologies are also boosting the efficiency and improving the transparency in the industry. Through open innovation using models like Open Banking, there is collaboration between consumers, banks, and businesses which creates new business opportunities that are much more inclusive and accessible. This acceptability of technology by consumers and its impact on digital entrepreneurship is very crucial to the success of this transformation as it fosters sustainable business growth in a more digital world.

Cluster 5 (11 items); banking industry, cloud computing, consumer attitudes, customer acceptance, digital entrepreneurial intentions, digital entrepreneurship, innovation, mobile banking, new technologies, robotics, artificial intelligence and service automatization, technology acceptance.

Cluster 6 "In bleu": Transforming Finance: AI, Innovation Efficiency, and Open Systems in Technology Management: The adoption of AI in the financial sector is revolutionizing decision-making processes by enabling more accurate data analysis, improving the efficiency of investment, lending and risk assessment (Feuerriegel et al., 2022). Artificial intelligence (AI) and techniques such as data envelopment analysis (DEA) are helping to measure the effectiveness of innovation in financial institutions, optimizing their performance. Technology management collaborations are crucial to the successful integration of AI, fostering an open innovation environment. Open systems theory shows that institutions need to remain flexible in the face of rapidly evolving technologies, and technological developments and trends point to a growing adoption of AI to improve financial services. Concepts such as smart homes also illustrate the practical application of AI in other sectors, highlighting its role in digital transformation. Finally, technology in practice enables businesses to maximize the impact of AI on a day-to-day basis, improving operational efficiency and personalizing services.

Cluster 6 (11 items): Ai adoption, artificial intelligence, collaborations in technology management, data envelopment analysis, innovation efficiency, open systems theory, smart homes, technology development trend, technology evolution, technology roadmap, technology in practice.

4.8 Leading Studies in the Field of AI and Open Innovation

Open innovation, artificial intelligence (AI), and sustainable behavioral finance has a range of themes which are connected to each other and interdisciplinary. Open innovation, artificial intelligence (AI), and sustainable behavioral finance has a range of themes which are connected to each other and interdisciplinary. These include the work of Luo et al. (2019) "*The Impact of Artificial Intelligence Chatbot Disclosure on Customer Purchases*" where they noted how AI chatbots influence customer selling conversations with the customers and purchase decision respectively. Similarly, Puntoni et al. (2021), in their article "*Consumers and Artificial Intelligence: An Experiential Perspective,*" demonstrate how consumer experience is technologically influenced providing an interaction approach to AI systems which underlines the reliance on trust and usability. In the same context, Cheerchan (2021) analyzes the ethics of AI application in performance within finance sectors and the need for responsible, transparent and equitable automated decision making.

Table 4. Top 10 highly cited papers in WOS

R	Authors & Year	Title	TC
1	(Luo et al., 2019)	Frontiers: Machines vs. Humans: The Impact of Artificial Intelligence Chatbot Disclosure on Customer Purchases	470
2	(Puntoni et al., 2021)	Consumers and Artificial Intelligence: An Experiential Perspective	354
3	(Fernandes & Oliveira, 2021)	Understanding consumers' acceptance of automated technologies in service encounters: Drivers of digital voice assistants adoption	282
4	(Longoni & Cian, 2022)	Artificial Intelligence in Utilitarian vs. Hedonic Contexts: The "Word-of-Machine" Effect	268
5	(Sheehan et al., 2020)	Customer service chatbots: Anthropomorphism and adoption	257
6	(Liu et al., 2020)	Influence of artificial intelligence on technological innovation: Evidence from the panel data of China's manufacturing sectors	247
7	(Kumar et al., 2019)	Understanding the Role of Artificial Intelligence in Personalized Engagement Marketing	227
8	(Martin, 2019)	Ethical Implications and Accountability of Algorithms	221
9	(Pitardi & Marriott, 2021)	Alexa, she's not human but horizontal ellipsis Unveiling the drivers of consumers' trust in voice-based artificial intelligence	190
10	(Thiebes et al., 2021)	Trustworthy artificial intelligence	187

Longoni and Cian (2020), in their in their work 'Artificial Intelligence in Utilitarian vs. Hedonic Contexts' reveal the variation of AI applications across different customers and organizations, arguing the possible capabilities of AI in both productivity and creativity. In addition, Sheehan et al. (2021) in their study "Customer Service Chatbots: Anthropomorphism and AI," focus on the anthropomorphism of AI technologies and human-like traits. They highlight that these traits are important in building trust and satisfaction towards AI technologies.. Kumar et al. (2021) focus on the strategies of engagement marketing through their publication "The Role of Artificial Intelligence in Personalizing Engagement Marketing," where he underscores the innovative ways businesses can enhance customer engagement and loyalty through automation.

In the ethical and trust dimensions of AI are further addressed by Marriott (2021) in his article "Alexa, She's Not Human But Horizontal," elaborates on the trust and ethical dimensions of AI while emphasizing where behavioral finance is concerned. Additionally, the emphasis by Thiebes et al. (2021) on "Trustworthy Artificial Intelligence," describes frameworks for ethical AI deployment, particularly in critical areas such as finance and innovation. Collectively, these documents, taken together, point to an intersection of AI, open innovation and behavioral finance, and the need for ethical, sustainable human-centered approaches that provide the desired leverage for AI to contribute to the global sustainability strategy.

5. CONCLUSION

This study examined the intersection of AI, Open Innovation, and sustainable behavioral finance of sustainability and empowerment in the financial sector. Using bibliometric analysis on 420 publications from the Web of Science database, we examined trends, prominent actors and recent topics of interest in the literature. Notwithstanding these insights, our results also uncover boundaries, suggesting ways in which future research can enrich understanding in this interdisciplinary domain.

First, our descriptive analysis of research trends shows the dynamic rise of interest in AI and Open Innovation in the financial industry. In 2016, the number of publications more than doubled and has continuously grown since, demonstrating the increasing acknowledgment of collaborative efforts to tackle complex problems in finance. Perhaps most notably, for example that of Bouteraa et al. (2024) and Ali and Aysan (2023) highlight the transformative impact of AI on decision making, operational efficiency, and customer engagement. The research activity based on the number of publications peaked in 2023, highlighting the increasing relevance of these topics. Geographically, The USA is the leader in terms of contributions with 119 works made, followed by England and China, whereas some regions, such as Africa and MENA, have considerably fewer works developed while demonstrating the increased urgency of technological integration and innovation.

Our results highlight the powerful synergy among AI and Open Innovation. AI facilitates data-centric decision-making at its best and streamlines operational efficiencies whereas Open Innovation fosters collaboration and knowledge-sharing between stakeholders. Collectively, such technologies spur innovation, enable financial inclusion, and sustain competitiveness in an environmentally responsible manner. In turn, supporting this perspective, findings by Capinzaiki and Pomim (2021) and Hernandez et al. (2024) reveal that SMEs and startups in emerging economies can reap huge rewards from these innovations, avoiding technologies and know-how previously thought available only to global businesses.

Further, our bibliometric and co-authorship analyses, provide additional insights into collaborative networks forming within this subject of research. The co-authorship network highlighted three separate clusters of university collaboration (see fig 5), in which California State University Fullerton, for example, played a hallmark node in connecting different silos of research groups, as did the National University of Singapore. The small pale blue and red clusters are indicative of strong regional and international collaboratives while the green cluster reflects localized partnerships. Yet, cross-cluster collaborations are still relatively few, indicating the room to support wider interdisciplinary and global science. The visualization also highlights how crucial institutions such as the National University of Singapore also serve to connect international research clusters at their intersection, while smaller clusters (to the left in the green group) may be better served by fuller engagement with larger networks.

Additionally, our bibliometric analyses revealed heterogeneous research directions, with clusters converging on digital transformation, innovation management, and sustainable financial practices. At the same time, the prominent keywords that emerged from the co-occurrence analysis such as "AI," "digital inclusion," and "sustainability," suggest that the field overemphasizes concerns about whether technological integration can adequately tackle global challenges. Nonetheless, due to the lack of African and MENA context in these analyses, there is an apparent research gap. The divergence in local interest highlights the need for intentional investments to engage local actors and address region -specific problems- particularly in less-tapped sectors such as agriculture and manufacturing.

Our study, however, has limitations despite these contributions. Limiting the scope of the present study to only resources that can be found in the Web of Science database, however, may have omitted relevant studies published elsewhere, possibly reducing the breadth of outcomes identified. Moreover, bibliometric data is notoriously aggregated, which prevents us from making detailed examinations of case-specific findings or the localized implication on the policy-setting of AI and Open Innovation. Given that the authorship pool is minuscule, proper examining of Africana and MENA authors will reveal a pressing issue of dearth of regional representation for a shared understanding of the region.

However, this study lays the foundation for further research on the relationships between AI, Open Innovation, and finance, as well as perspectives on the trends and opportunities present in the literature. These limitations should be addressed in future research to rectify this imbalance by studying the contextual dynamics of these technologies in emerging economies as well as bringing varied experiences to the broader conversation. One way to do this is to build even stronger cross-cluster collaborations and to introduce greater regional representation. These will help the financial sector make the most out of AI and Open Innovation, while also advancing sustainable development, inclusivity and integration in a globalized world.

REFERENCES

Ali, H., & Aysan, A. F. (2023). What will ChatGPT revolutionise in financial industry? SSRN *Electron. J.*https://doi.org/DOI: 10.2139/ssrn.4403372

Aloulou, M., Grati, R., Al-Qudah, A. A., & Al-Okaily, M. (2024). Does FinTech adoption increase the diffusion rate of digital financial inclusion? A study of the banking industry sector. *Journal of Financial Reporting and Accounting*, *22*(2), 289–307. DOI: 10.1108/JFRA-05-2023-0224

Amin, M. T., Khan, F., & Amyotte, P. (2019). A bibliometric review of process safety and risk analysis. *Process Safety and Environmental Protection*, *126*, 366–381.

Bag, S., Yadav, G., Dhamija, P., & Kataria, K. K. (2021). Key resources for industry 4.0 adoption and its effect on sustainable production and circular economy: An empirical study. *Journal of Cleaner Production*, *281*, 125233. DOI: 10.1016/j.jclepro.2020.125233

Behera, A. K., Nayak, N. C., & Das, H. C. (2016). Performance of Indian Service Industries Due to IT Adoption. *Global Business Review*, *17*(5), 1073–1093. DOI: 10.1177/0972150916656657

Bharti, S. S., Prasad, K., Sudha, S., & Kumari, V. (2024). Correction to : Customer acceptability towards AI-enabled digital banking: a PLS-SEM approach. *Journal of Financial Services Marketing*, *29*(4), 1653–1653. DOI: 10.1057/s41264-023-00250-8

Bloomberg. (2023). *Wall Street Banks Are Cracking Down on AI-Powered ChatGPT. Technology*. Singap World Sci.

Bouteraa, M., Chekima, B., Thurasamy, R., Bin-Nashwan, S. A., Al-Daihani, M., Baddou, A., & Ansar, R. (2024). Open Innovation in the Financial Sector: A Mixed-Methods Approach to Assess Bankers' Willingness to Embrace Open-AI ChatGPT. *Journal of Open Innovation*, *10*(1), 100216. DOI: 10.1016/j.joitmc.2024.100216

Capinzaiki Ottonicar, S. L., & Pomim Valentim, M. L. (2021). Industry 4.0 and open innovation in startups accelerators. DOI: .DOI: 10.5380/atoz.v10i3.81882

Chesbrough, H. (2003). Open innovation: The new imperative for creating and profiting from technology.

Chnigri, Y., Sadik, M., & Slimani, H. (2024). Mapping the Literature on Intelligent Systems and Decision Support in Higher Education: A Bibliometric Analysis. https://doi.org/DOI: 10.5281/ZENODO.13700094

Da Silva, R. F., & Martha De Souza, G. F. (2021). Mapping the Literature on Asset Management: A Bibliometric Analysis. *Journal of Scientometric Research*, *10*(1), 27–36. DOI: 10.5530/jscires.10.1.4

Donthu, N., Kumar, S., Mukherjee, D., Pandey, N., & Lim, W. M. (2021). How to conduct a bibliometric analysis: An overview and guidelines. *Journal of Business Research*, *133*, 285–296. DOI: 10.1016/j.jbusres.2021.04.070

Feng, C., Ma, R., & Jiang, L. (2021). The impact of service innovation on firm performance: A meta-analysis. *Journal of Service Management*, *32*(3), 289–314. DOI: 10.1108/JOSM-03-2019-0089

Fernandes, T., & Oliveira, E. (2021). Understanding consumers' acceptance of automated technologies in service encounters: Drivers of digital voice assistants adoption. *Journal of Business Research, 122*, 180–191. DOI: 10.1016/j.jbusres.2020.08.058

Feuerriegel, S., Shrestha, Y. R., von Krogh, G., & Zhang, C. (2022). Bringing artificial intelligence to business management. *Nature Machine Intelligence*, *4*(7), 611–613. DOI: 10.1038/s42256-022-00512-5

Fink, A. (2019). *Conducting research literature reviews: From the internet to paper*. Sage publications.

Gama, F., & Magistretti, S. (2023). Artificial intelligence in innovation management: A review of innovation capabilities and a taxonomy of AI applications. *Journal of Product Innovation Management*. Advance online publication. DOI: 10.1111/jpim.12698

Hernandez, A. A., Sacdalan, R. V., Sopoco, C. T., Villapando, J. E., & Garcia, P. M. (2024, February). Predicting the Innovation Capability for Firm Performance: the role of Artificial Intelligence in the Philippines Startups Perspective. In 2024 16th International Conference on Knowledge and Smart Technology (KST) (pp. 195-200). IEEE. DOI: DOI: 10.1109/KST61284.2024.10499661

Iwanicz-Drozdowska, M., Cichowicz, E., Cicirko, M., Kawiński, M., & Nowak, A. K. (2023). New technologies in the financial industry : Case of Poland. *Economics and Business Review*, *9*(3). Advance online publication. DOI: 10.18559/ebr.2023.3.926

Kuckertz, A., Berger, E. S., & Gaudig, A. (2019). Responding to the greatest challenges? Value creation in ecological startups. *Journal of Cleaner Production*, *230*, 1138–1147. DOI: 10.1016/j.jclepro.2019.05.149

Kumar, V., Rajan, B., Venkatesan, R., & Lecinski, J. (2019). Understanding the Role of Artificial Intelligence in Personalized Engagement Marketing. *California Management Review*, *61*(4), 135–155. DOI: 10.1177/0008125619859317

Liu, J., Chang, H., Forrest, J. Y.-L., & Yang, B. (2020). Influence of artificial intelligence on technological innovation: Evidence from the panel data of China's manufacturing sectors. *Technological Forecasting and Social Change*, *158*, 120142. DOI: 10.1016/j.techfore.2020.120142

Longoni, C., & Cian, L. (2022). Artificial Intelligence in Utilitarian vs. Hedonic Contexts: The "Word-of-Machine" Effect. *Journal of Marketing*, *86*(1), 91–108. DOI: 10.1177/0022242920957347

Luo, X., Tong, S., Fang, Z., & Qu, Z. (2019). Frontiers: Machines vs. Humans: The Impact of Artificial Intelligence Chatbot Disclosure on Customer Purchases. *Marketing Science*, mksc.2019.1192. https://doi.org/.DOI: 10.1287/mksc.2019.1192

Martin, K. (2019). Ethical Implications and Accountability of Algorithms. *Journal of Business Ethics*, *160*(4), 835–850. DOI: 10.1007/s10551-018-3921-3

Mikalef, P., & Gupta, M. (2021). Artificial intelligence capability: Conceptualization, measurement calibration, and empirical study on its impact on organizational creativity and firm performance. *Information & Management*, *58*(3), 103434. DOI: 10.1016/j.im.2021.103434

Muhuri, P. K., Shukla, A. K., & Abraham, A. (2019). Industry 4.0: A bibliometric analysis and detailed overview. *Engineering Applications of Artificial Intelligence*, *78*, 218–235. DOI: 10.1016/j.engappai.2018.11.007

Oduro, S., & De Nisco, A. (2023). From Industry 4.0 adoption to innovation ambidexterity to firm performance: A MASEM analysis. *European Journal of Innovation Management*. Advance online publication. DOI: 10.1108/EJIM-02-2023-0106

Openbanking. (2020). What is open banking? https://www.openbanking.org.uk/customers/what-isopen

Pitardi, V., & Marriott, H. R. (2021). Alexa, she's not human but… Unveiling the drivers of consumers' trust in voice-based artificial intelligence. *Psychology and Marketing*, *38*(4), 626–642. DOI: 10.1002/mar.21457

Pollari, I. (2018). The rise of digital platforms in financial services. *KPMG International*. https://assets.

Puntoni, S., Reczek, R. W., Giesler, M., & Botti, S. (2021). Consumers and Artificial Intelligence: An Experiential Perspective. *Journal of Marketing*, *85*(1), 131–151. DOI: 10.1177/0022242920953847

Ramos-Rodríguez, A., & Ruíz-Navarro, J. (2004). Changes in the intellectual structure of strategic management research: A bibliometric study of the Strategic Management Journal, 1980–2000. *Strategic Management Journal*, *25*(10), 981–1004. DOI: 10.1002/smj.397

Rothwell, G., Rothwell, R., & Zegveld, W. (1985). *Reindustrialization and technology*. ME Sharpe.

Sætra, H. S. (2023). Generative AI: Here to stay, but for good? *Technology in Society*, *102372*. Advance online publication. DOI: 10.1016/j.techsoc.2023.102372

Saidi, H., & Madhat, F. Z. (2024). Mapping the Evolution of Open Innovation and Digital Transformation: A Bibliometric Analysis. In Motahhir, S., & Bossoufi, B. (Eds.), *Digital Technologies and Applications* (Vol. 1101, pp. 178–186). Springer Nature Switzerland., DOI: 10.1007/978-3-031-68675-7_18

Sheehan, B., Jin, H. S., & Gottlieb, U. (2020). Customer service chatbots: Anthropomorphism and adoption. *Journal of Business Research*, *115*, 14–24. DOI: 10.1016/j.jbusres.2020.04.030

Shinde, R., Patil, S., Kotecha, K., & Ruikar, K. (2021). Blockchain for securing ai applications and open innovations. *Journal of Open Innovation*, *7*(3), 189.

Song, Y., Chen, X., Hao, T., Liu, Z., & Lan, Z. (2019). Exploring two decades of research on classroom dialogue by using bibliometric analysis. *Computers & Education*, *137*, 12–31. DOI: 10.1016/j.compedu.2019.04.002

Thiebes, S., Lins, S., & Sunyaev, A. (2021). Trustworthy artificial intelligence. *Electronic Markets*, *31*(2), 447–464. DOI: 10.1007/s12525-020-00441-4

Türegün, N. (2019). Impact of technology in financial reporting: The case of Amazon Go. *Journal of Corporate Accounting & Finance*, *30*(3), 90–95. DOI: 10.1002/jcaf.22394

Van Eck, N. J., & Waltman, L. (2010). Software survey: VOSviewer, a computer program for bibliometric mapping. *Scientometrics*, *84*(2), 523–538. DOI: 10.1007/s11192-009-0146-3 PMID: 20585380

Wu, Q., Yan, D., & Umair, M. (2023). Assessing the role of competitive intelligence and practices of dynamic capabilities in business accommodation of SMEs. *Economic Analysis and Policy*, *77*, 1103–1114. DOI: 10.1016/j.eap.2022.11.024

Yun, J. J., Liu, Z., & Zhao, X. (2021). Introduction: Ambidextrous open innovation in the 4th Industrial Revolution. *Science, Technology & Society*, *26*(2), 183–200. DOI: 10.1177/09717218211006969

KEY TERMS AND DEFINITIONS

Artificial Intelligence (AI): Artificial Intelligence (AI) refers to the development of computer systems capable of performing tasks that traditionally require human intelligence, such as learning, reasoning, problem-solving, and decision-making. In the financial sector, AI plays a transformative role by automating complex processes, analyzing vast amounts of data, and providing predictive insights that enable financial institutions to adapt to rapidly changing markets. Tools such as chatbots and virtual assistants have revolutionized customer interactions by offering personalized and immediate support. Similarly, machine learning algorithms are widely used for fraud detection, credit risk analysis, and investment strategies, providing more accurate and data-driven decision-making capabilities. As highlighted in this study, the integration of AI with Open Innovation not only enhances operational efficiency and competitiveness but also supports the creation of inclusive financial services that cater to diverse customer needs, driving sustainability and growth (Ali & Aysan, 2023; Bouteraa et al., 2024).

Open Innovation: Open Innovation is a collaborative approach that facilitates the exchange of knowledge, technologies, and ideas across organizational boundaries to accelerate the development of innovative products, services, and processes. First introduced by Chesbrough (2003), Open Innovation has become increasingly relevant in the financial sector, particularly with the rise of digital platforms such as Open Banking. By sharing data and resources with external stakeholders—such as startups, SMEs, and technology providers—financial institutions can foster transparency, inclusivity, and innovation. This study demonstrates that Open Innovation enables organizations to remain competitive by leveraging external expertise, reducing time-to-market for new solutions, and co-creating value with customers and partners. For example, Open Banking allows users to securely share financial information across platforms, enabling personalized financial products and fostering a more dynamic financial ecosystem (Pollari, 2018; Yun, 2021).

Sustainable Finance: Sustainable Finance integrates environmental, social, and governance (ESG) considerations into financial decision-making and practices. It aims to align financial activities with global sustainability goals, such as combating climate change, reducing inequality, and fostering inclusive economic growth. In the context of this study, sustainable finance intersects with AI and Open Innovation to enable more efficient and responsible resource allocation. AI-powered tools enhance transparency and impact measurement, allowing institutions to track the environmental and social outcomes of investments. Meanwhile, Open Innovation fosters collaborative efforts to develop innovative financial products, such as green bonds or microfinance solutions, that support sustainability goals. By leveraging these technologies, financial institutions can balance profitability with long-term societal benefits, driving sustainable development while addressing complex global challenges (Hernandez et al., 2024; Wamba, 2022).

Innovation Management: Innovation Management refers to the systematic coordination of activities aimed at fostering creativity, developing new ideas, and implementing innovative solutions within an organization. In the financial sector, effective innovation management is critical for navigating technological disruptions, meeting evolving customer demands, and maintaining a competitive edge. This study underscores the role of AI and Open Innovation as key enablers of innovation management. AI facilitates data-driven decision-making and operational optimization, while Open Innovation promotes knowledge-sharing and collaborative problem-solving. Together, these tools empower financial institutions to design tailored financial products, streamline processes, and create new business models that address emerging market needs. By prioritizing innovation management, financial organizations can enhance their resilience, adaptability, and sustainability in an increasingly dynamic industry (De Groote & Backmann, 2020; Capinzaiki & Pomim, 2021).

Bibliometric Analysis: Bibliometric Analysis is a research methodology used to systematically analyze the structure, trends, and impact of academic literature within a specific field. It involves the use of quantitative techniques to study publications, citations, and co-authorship networks, providing insights into the intellectual landscape and identifying influential contributors, emerging themes, and research gaps. In this study, bibliometric analysis was used to examine the intersection of AI, Open Innovation, and sustainable finance. By leveraging tools like VOSviewer, the analysis revealed key research clusters, collaboration patterns, and geographical contributions, such as the underrepresentation of Africa and MENA regions. Bibliometric analysis not only highlighted the transformative potential of these technologies in the financial sector but also provided a roadmap for future research to address critical gaps and foster inclusive growth (Van Eck & Waltman, 2010; Shinde et al., 2021).

Chapter 11
Artificial Intelligence Shaping Financial Governance and Global Regulation Through the IMF and World Bank

Zouheir Boussouf
https://orcid.org/0009-0002-5970-2923
Multidisciplinary Faculty of Taza, Sidi Mohammed Ben Abdellah University, Fez, Morocco

Hanae Amrani
https://orcid.org/0009-0008-0918-4543
The Faculty of Legal, Economic, and Social Sciences of Fes, Morocco

Khawla Amrani
https://orcid.org/0009-0007-0342-1926
The Faculty of Legal, Economic, and Social Sciences of Fes, Morocco

Ahmed Aftiss
https://orcid.org/0009-0002-6211-4065
The Faculty of Legal, Economic, and Social Sciences of Fes, Morocco

ABSTRACT

This chapter explores how the integration of Artificial Intelligence (AI) is redefining the governance and regulation of global financial markets in the era of technological transformation. It examines AI's impacts on regulatory frameworks and practices, focusing on its potential to enhance financial stability, transparency, and efficiency while addressing the specific challenges faced by developing countries. Through a qualitative approach, the study highlights key opportunities, including improved risk detection, optimized regulatory policies, and greater financial inclusivity in less developed regions. However, it also emphasizes challenges such as cybersecurity risks, the need for regulatory adaptation, and the inequalities that AI may exacerbate. The findings underline AI's pivotal role in modernizing financial regulatory practices and fostering international cooperation, offering critical insights into how AI is shaping the future of financial governance and regulation.

DOI: 10.4018/979-8-3693-9684-1.ch011

INTRODUCTION

In an age of rapid technological change, albeit with regulatory friction, the popularity of AI in its various facets continues to plague markets globally. As global financial systems become increasingly complex and regulatory frameworks require greater strength, new challenges must be faced together with opportunities seized. AI, with its potential to revolutionise financial market governance and regulation, offers hope for attaining not just national but institutional stability. The global finance can be made more stable, transparent, efficient and equitable through a useful combination of AI and its family technologies that are suited to this end. In the study itself, the use of financial market regulation and governance is the focal point for AI. The application of AI operated by international institutions such as the International Monetary Fund (IMF), World Bank, is also covered.

This study's central research question is: ***How can AI help improve the global governance and regulation of financial markets?*** In furtherance of this problem, the study poses three key questions:

- What impact does AI have on regulations for international financial institutions like IMF and the World Bank?
- By using AI, can developing countries cope with their financial problems and still spare resources for sustainable development?
- What function does AI serve in reducing systemic risk and spreading the sunshine of financial openness?
- According to this study's literature review and preliminary observations, it is hypothesized:
- Artificial intelligence increases the ability of international financial organizations to discover risks and impose rules. Artificial intelligence thus boosts confidence in financial markets.
- By using seamless financing mechanisms and compressing income differences, AI contributes to the economic stability of developing countries.
- By detecting anomalies and preventing financial crises through better predictive & modeling, AI increases both the transparency of financial markets.

The research was structured into three parts:. The review of literature on AI applications in financial management will give an authoritative introduction and summary of all existing studies. The methodology chapter will describe a high quality research idea, how data is to be collected and analysed, requiring better use of tools such as NVivo for thematic analysis. The results section will give the main findings from interviews with experts, followed by an analysis and discussion of them. Finally, the conclusion will sum up how this study may offer important implications in the field-and hint at specific directions for future research at point where AI meets management and financial control.

1. LITERATURE REVIEW

1.1 Artificial Intelligence In The Governance And Regulation Of Global Financial Markets

In the center of Artificial Intelligence (AI) with johnseworl.com management of communications and control remains a key feature for improving modern international finance. Thanks to AI, we can have a more effective solution to these complex problems that reality and the changing financial market throw at us. This is accomplished with improved risk management, better compliance and more transparent markets. This part of the in-depth bibliography describes how in many different ways that AI transforms market regulation and how such change impacts inter- national financial institutions such as the International Monetary Fund (IMF) or World Bank.

1.1.1.AI and Financial Risk Management

AI has made one of the greatest contributions to financial supervision, and that is its capacity to improve risk management. Some researchers say that AI has the potential of picking up on financial risks more promptly and accurately than traditional methods based upon classical statistical models. Moreover, AI makes it feasible for you to process and analyze huge bodies of intricate data to a degree not than that sacrifice was ever possible. This kind of expanded real-time analysis is especially useful in predicting risks associated with market volatility, financial crises and abnormal market behavior such as excessive speculation. According to research, AI is being used to produce risk monitoring models which are more likely to anticipate market fluctuations. For instance, algorithms of artificial intelligence can look at the historical movement in assets and see correlations between different economic variables. With this increased precision and up-to-date information (received real time), financial stability factors that may change more quickly to one catastrophe or another are much also represented more accurately. To monitor global economic risks and offer policy advice to member-country governments, the IMF uses such technologies.

1.1.2.AI for Compliance And Regulation Of Financial Institutions

AI also plays an important role in the regulation of financial institutions (Chikhi & Ramdani, 2023). Financial institutions are required to comply with stringent requirements, which can be difficult to enforce in the dynamic global environment of potentially divergent rules. AI enables continuous compliance scanning and identification of regulatory breaches such as money laundering, fraud or market manipulation, due to its flexibility and variability. Real-time analysis of millions of transactions using AI systems can reveal suspicious patterns, thus minimizing the risk of non-compliance. Machine learning algorithms, for example, allow regulators to routinely detect anomalies in banking operations, monitor cash flows and enhance breach detection with both speed and accuracy. It is critical to bring confidence to global fabrics of finance through this automated compliance, so that regulators can concentrate on the most intricate or high risk cases.

1.1.3.Enhancing Market Transparency

As one of the historic problems facing global financial markets, the lack of transparency is prominent. Market manipulation and information asymmetry among market participants are institutional issues. Through its means of increasing market transparency, including detailed financial information and instant \gamma marks that we have mentioned above, statistical thinking can ameliorate that contrast. As it is able to automatically analyse large amounts of financial information, AI will enable comprehensive and easily available guidance, while AI products placed in financial markets can observe the behaviour of market participants and transactions in real time. Based on the long-term tun8AI for a Better Trading Environment Central Plains 9 testing technology, the Chinese Academy of Sciences has worked with other organs of party propaganda to devise e commercial regulation systems with information feedback. By keeping watch on trends among traders and financial institutions, AI-based surveillance systems can alert authorities to market anomalies such as 'fronttrunning' or insider trading. In addition, AI makes it easier for a wider audience of individuals to obtain financial data, helping to bring about more transparency and higher towards shareholders.

1.1.4. Predictive Analysis And Adaptability Of Regulations

Furthermore, it has added a backward-looking dimension to financial regulation. AI technology will also allow regulations to be much more adaptive and live than before. Instead of dealing with events as they occur, AI permits financial regulators to foresee risks before they happen, and adjust their business accordingly. But the ability to discover and deal with abnormal market behavior is also necessary for active regulation. In terms of using these types of tools, financial regulators should be able to keep track not only of the global economic trends but also any potential speculative bubbles. They should be able to predict both currency fluctuations and stock market movements. By appropriately using artificial intelligence, regulations differ from those of the past in that they more closely align with changes occurring in market momentum and direction.

1.1.5. The Role of AI in Financial Decision Making

AI in Financial Markets — Better Decision-Making AI helps regulators like IMF and World Bank in making the right decisions based on analysis of all available data. Having this ability to make data-driven decisions will allow financial institutions and regulators to more effectively manage economic crises and optimise their financial policies. It focuses not only on risk and compliance analysis but on policy suggestions as well. One could be: Modeling economic scenarios where regulators can test an array of economic strategies before actual implementation. This provides greater flexibility and informed decision-making, both of which is critical in an ever-changing global financial environment.

1.1.6. AI as a Catalyst For Transformation In Financial Regulation

AI is revolutionizing the way global financial markets are managed and regulated. Its use in risk management, compliance, transparency and decision-making enhances the efficiency, predictability and transparency of regulation. But this transformation has its problems. This requires major investments in infrastructure, regulatory training and risk management related to ever more sophisticated technologies."

In particular, IMF and the World bank are among-the-firstGuardians of AI integration into their financial regulatory activities These are important for examining the opportunities AI brings in terms of regulatory policy as to its usage. AI adoption could also open up new opportunities for the future of financial regulation, focusing on more transparent, inclusive and dynamic financial management. But there are significant hurdles to overcome — from data management to issues of professionalism, ethics and privacy — before AI can achieve its full promise in regulating global financial markets.

1.2 The Benefits of AI for Governance And Financial Regulation

So, it can be seen that in the area of hedge oversight, AI contributes greatly to high efficiency and low costs. It also has a ripple effect on all categories of regulation. From the point of view of document production, AI is running circles around humans The rate and depth at which risk monitoring is performed are all improved Applying modern data analytics, more accurate transaction tracking and better informed decision-making is changing the way financial rules are made and put into operation. Here s how that effort is proceeding in each major area of regulatory reform.

1.2.1 Real Time Risk Management Through AI

AI has been able to dramatically transform risk management. Traditionally, risks in the financial world are examined for historical data and with the help of predetermined financial models. Interestingly, these methods have usually been behind the times or back word., a financial crisis only comes to light in marketswhen it is already all over. AI made managing risk, formerly purely reactive, forward-thinking and predictive. Today's AI systems rely on machine learning algorithms to process huge amounts of real-time data and make sense out of it. This means that regulators can catch the initial signs of impending risks in time. AI instruments may lead to an immediate assessment of financial risk. They can help regulators better understand potential threats such as systemic risks, financial institution failures or liquidity crunches. This foresight nature allows the use of appropriate and flexible regulatory strategies in a rapidly changing market. Today, techniques such as deep learning or neural networks are being used to predict the potential failure of a business and therefore to intervene at an early time before such risks become major financial crises.

1.2.2 AI As A Lever For Regulatory Efficiency

Many routine, time-consuming tasks in the field of financial regulation can be done by machines with the proper artificial intelligence material to hand. For example systems based on artificial intelligence take charge of most compliance chores: tracking prices on transactions such as those associated with high-speed data transmission services; making sure your customers are who they say they are (KYC check - KIN Requirements); uncovering criminals before they realize their money laundering schemes. According to the same study, which was first reported in (Letouzé, Oliver, Lepri, & Vinck, 2023), this automation means that financial institutions do less work and it is also easier for them to comply with laws like those regulating what kind of records should be kept. How AI systems can continuously monitor millions of transactions, and produce real-time alerts when there is suspicious activity In this way, regulators are able to rapidly intervene before either the illegal or contradictory trading goes unnoticed. While Automatic Financial Services Systems also reduce compliance costs for financial institutions, they actually make it easier and more possible to oversee regulatory compliance. For example government and other agencies can use AI-based Forecasting Models instead of manual audits to better detect anomalies or fraud attempts. That builds clients' faith in the integrity of financial markets and in whether their regulators do what they say.

1.2.3 Improved Transparency In Financial Markets

Market transparency is the key to ensuring effective finance management and preventing market abuses. In this respect, AI has an important role to play as it can wade through large amounts of data that traditional methods are simply unable to. AI, it was claimed in (Sedkaoui, 2024), lets regulators view complicated financial information, prepare comprehensive reports and identify potential problems at a glance. AI algorithms can track the participants' behavior on the market and analyze trading trends itself. Such information will not remain in the hands of only one or two traders. Through computer analysis and publicity reports from brokerage firms for instance, publications like Trade Slants magazine are able to publish stories about practices such as 'frontage' - when traders use inside information in their own favour or market manipulation, such as false profit announcements. Besides, AI makes finance data accessible to people with a wider range of interests -- from institutional investors and regulators to ordinary folk. This extension of transparency in turn reduces information asymmetries, guarantees fair play between all market players and provides a more predictable environment for investment.

1.2.4 Innovation in Regulatory Practices Through AI

Regulatory innovation is also created by AI's introduction into financial regulations. It's machine learning and natural language processing (NLP) that enable traditional-style regulators to handle unstructured information like financial reports, social media comments or economic news and so to have more logical, differentiated decisions based on all the data from one perspective These technologies offer the chance of processing non-traditional information so far unobtainable by conventional regulatory means. The algorithms of machine learning can automatically learn from new phenomena as they arise and change With NLP these days, natural language processing, controls can pull useful information out of unstructured documents such as annual financial statements analyst comments pressed articles in order to detect better risks and trends in markets.

1.2.5 The Impact of AI on Competitiveness And Global Regulation

Another major boon of AI is its ability to bring regulators' practices together worldwide.Autonomous organizations enable them to standardize regulatory operations amidst an increasingly globally connected world in financial markets.The rules of countries and regions can be contrasted and appraised by AI, this might lead to standard practices across different areas. This would improve mutual understanding among regulators internationally. Regulators may manage and adapt their own policies to changes in international financial practices with AI. In the world of a more internationally integrated financial markets, where national regulation mustadjust to global ones, this is particularly important. The regulations act enables regulators to enforce international standards by financial institutions and also to achieve fair competition among market participants.

1.2.6 A Promising Future For Financial Regulation

The invasive system is an important step in financial management and supervision, and it can produce not only effective advantages in enterprise risk management, regulation but also greater market transparency. With AI instruments, financial market regulation is not only optimized, but also acknowledges the current global market situation. Nevertheless, the incorporation of AI in financial regulations must be approached with care: for instance ethical problems must be considered. The handling of data and its impact on employment as well as structure of regulation and finance industry organization should also be taken into account. As those technologies evolve, their role in financial regulation ought to swell alike. Emerging vistas emerge for more active, accessible and above all open regulation.

1.3 Challenges and Perspectives of AI in Governance and Financial Regulation

The combined use of artificial intelligence and financial regulations offers great benefits. It also presents formidable challenges though. These concerns are technical, ethical judicial and organizational. In tackling them, we must take care to introduce technologies that are both effective and responsible, while simultaneously advancing into the field of financial regulation and state administration. This section discusses some challenges and prospects of AI in financial regulation. It also analyzes concrete strategies to overcome these challenges as well as opportunities (i.e., the potential developments in this field that may result from corresponding changes in AI technology).

1.3.1 Adapting Regulatory Frameworks to Specificities of AIs

The chief issue for AI in financial regulation is to alter the prevailing regulatory framework or rules so that they can accommodate characteristics of AI. Traditionally, financial regulations were developed in both derivation and method for human operations and conventional procedures. But as AI systems create new paradigms, this calls for an updating of the old.

The complex and often hidden AI algorithms raise the issue of transparency. This now has to be part of financial regulation authorities' job (Mabillard & Villeneuve, 2023). Regulators need to ensure that both the AI algorithms used in regulatory and risk processes are effective, and that they are also clear and verifiable. This transparency is essential if AI systems are to be held accountable for their decisions – especially in the sensitive area of financing. Moreover, AI algorithms must be adapted to specific regulatory contexts -- which in turn requires standards & processes be adjusted constantly to changing AI technologies.

1.3.2 AI System Ethics And Bias

Another fundamental question of financial regulation raised by AI systems is the ethics involved in artificial intelligence. AI systems are often regarded as a sort of "black box" whose decision-making process is not always transparent and indeed makes it hard to understand the grounds for particular result. This calls fairness and honesty into question, particularly in cases where decisions directly affect economic operators or consumers. In addition, distortions in aI training data can also distort the results given by these systems. Algorithmic bias can have severe consequences, especially when it comes to making decisions about loans or evaluating risks, and non-compliance with legal requirements. These distortions may well be through historical data distortions, non-representative data samples or unconscious distortions that have been absorbed by system developers. In order to see that financial markets have fair and just regulation, is necessary strictly to set up a series of measures for identifying preventing and correcting these distortions in AI systems, Béranger & Chassang (2021) points out. This is not just an adjustment at the technical level, but also means constantly re-examining the ethical principles and values used in development of these technologies.

1.3.3 The Speed of Technological Advancements And The Evolution Of Regulatory Standards

Another important issue to consider is how the speed at which technology evolves impacts AI and financial regulation. From deep learning algorithms and natural language processing systems (NLPs) tools through AI-based forecasting to a systems-conquering technology has arrived that is difficult to manage within an existing framework for regulation. Regulators need to keep adjusting and reformulate their existing standards to accommodate these new forms of innovation - a process which can be little hard work sometimes taking years, particularly when nested in such a fast-moving and interconnected field as financial services (Villani et al., 2018). Regulators are often caught in a situation where new AI tools used by financial institutions come into play while they are still lagging behind. The result could be regulatory gaps or an uneven playing field of competitive advantage for different companies that have not yet been regulated by any existing norms It is therefore very important in this context that timely and effective updates to rules take place, which both ensure the safety of financial markets and their integrity, but at the same time stimulate innovation.

1.3.4 Collaborative Governance And Public Private Partnerships

Common governance strategies of regulators and the private sector are needed to solve these challenges. Such an approach could contribute to creating common standards and best practices for implementing AI in financial regulation. According to (Addo et al., 2021), public-private partnerships can help develop ethical and transparent AI solutions that comply with regulatory standards. Moreover, the participation of regulators, technology companies, researchers, and other stakeholders in collaborative activities will create systems for ongoing assessments of how AI instruments affect financial markets. This includes assessing emerging risks related to AI, such as cyber attacks or data security issues, and establishing proper responses.

1.3.5 Future perspectives: Financial Sustain- Ability

As AI technologies have evolved, so it is vital that regulators anticipate future problems by fashioning structures that are flexible enough to take into account anything new that may come along tomorrow or the day after. Future research should aim to clarify what are the effective, ethical, and transparent ways to embed AI into financial regulation. This may involve research into new technologies being developed (Villani et al., 2018), how AI can be used on top of blockchain technology to make regulations more traceable and secure for users. Moreover, regulators must develop advanced analytical capacity for ascertaining the long-term effects of AI on financial markets and reorientate policy in line with fresh technological and economic trends. For this purpose, establishing imaginative laboratories, or regulatory "sandbox" areas where these new technologies can be tested in an experiment environment so as to better comprehend their impact and to lessen risks that might otherwise threaten the world's financial system.

1.3.6 Towards More Flexible And Adaptable Regulation

This IA offers great benefits for financial governance and regulation, but also raises the most serious challenges that need to be carefully considered and implemented. Adapting the regulatory framework, regulating distortions and ethical issues and adapting to rapid technological developments are key tasks for financial inspectors. It is important to find balanced solutions that maximize the potential of AI, ensuring stability and equity in financial markets. The introduction of joint management and exploration of synergies between AI and other new technologies will open up promising prospects for future financial regulation.

1.4 Theoretical Frameworks Explaining The Integration of AI in Financial Governance

Artificial intelligence is integrated into financial management based on several theoretical foundations, which offer a better understanding of both the inner workings and effects following from this technology. These theories provide a variety of perspectives on how and why AI is adopted, what benefits it may bring to an organization and the problems it faces. This section presents three theoretical foundations: Information Systems and Technology Management Theory, Innovation Diffusion Theory; and Technology Adoption Model that help explore AI integrated into financial management from various angles.

1.4.1 Information Systems And Technological Management Theory

The Information Systems and Technology Management Theory developed by DeLone & McLane (Michel & Cocula, 2014), is an analytical framework that assesses the impact of information systems, including artificial intelligence-based systems, on organizational efficiency. The criteria for evaluation users satisfaction measurement system effectiveness are well represented in this theory: Rome was not built too much in a day. In the field of financial management, LMI enables us to understand how AI technology influences the efficiency of administrative and financial processes. It improves the quality of information available for decision making and makes it easy to optimize financial transactions. In this way, the integration of AI with finance systems may mean that financial data management is more accurate and timely than ever before Risk analysis will improve dramatically when people don't notice changes in their circumstances. Compliance processes and regulatory work may become more efficient through the use of artificial intelligence. However, this theory also stresses the need to ensure that users, whether they be regulators or finance managers, perceive such AI-based systems as useful and easy to use. Thus, the success of AI in financial management depends not only on the technical quality of the system but also its acceptance and adjustment by users.

1.4.2 Diffusion of Innovation Theory

Roger's theory of innovation diffusion (Zinsou, 2019) is a model that suggests the ways in which new technologies become integrated within corporations. This theory details a number of variables that affect the introduction of innovations: expected benefits; obstacles to acceptance and user characteristics. For those implementing AI into financial management systems, OID is a guide as to why some organizations are more willing than others to adopt AI more quickly and what specific obstacles they will meet on this path. The advantages that are anticipated with AI - greater regulatory efficiency, less human error - also promote its introduction. But at the same time, real problems loom. Resistance to change, just how complex the new technology is to understand and a concern with data security and privacy issues can hinder that process. In DOI, the role of "thought leaders" in promoting these ideas is emphasized, since they can greatly speed up introduction of AI into banking and other financial institutions. Regulators need to recognize this dynamic if they are to enable broader adoption of AI faster into financial management.

1.4.3 Technology Acceptance Model

As one of the most popular theoretical frameworks for studying the adoption of new technologies, Davis's Technology Adoption Model (Bertrand, 2007) has been widely used to explore such opportunities. Technology Implementation is largely dependent on two factors. TAM tells us: whether technology direction perceived and advantage perception Easier technology is seen as useful the faster it becomes accepted by users. In financial management, TAM explains why some users of financial systems are more cautious than others when it comes to using AI. If this attitude carries over to regulators and financial institutions lack AI vision, systems may be implemented slowly or not at all. If AI is seen as a way of optimizing financial decisions and procedures that are being made stricter even now anyway, then it will tend to be implemented. Therefore, the integration of AI into financial management must be designed so that the potential benefits can be expected by financial intuitions; its technical use aspects are operable for users within this system.

1.4.4 Integration of Theoretical Frameworks In Financial Governance

Presenting the reader with three theoretical frameworks offers an all-inclusive survey of AI processes in financial management. The first is the theory of information systems and technology management, which focuses on the quality of the AI system and user satisfaction; Second we introduce the theory innovation diffusion, which highlights those factors which inhibit AI implementation as well as elucidating how to over-come barriers. The technology adoption model goes a step further allowing us understanding AI user's perceptions and how those perceptions influence their implementation.

Interweaving these theories together, we can deepen our understanding of what factors lead to the success of integrating AI into financial management. While such a holistic approach not only unearths the potential advantages of AI but also comprehends the difficulties faced by regulators and financial institutions, guaranteeing that their use will be fruitful and ethical at once.

However, integrating AI into financial management is a complex issue that will benefit from detailed analysis by attributive theoretical frameworks. Information systems and technology management can identify possible problems while technology adoption model provides a means of defining economic consequences. Future research needs to combine these three absolute theories in financial management as an area for further study, in order to offer up more effective ways of integrating them into practice tailored to what financial practitioners need.

2. METHODOLOGY

The study's methodological approach is founded on interpretative epistemology. The intention is for put the truth of management and financial organization gradually in fact as it is perceived by those involved (Schwandt, 2014). One benefit of a pilot survey is to deepen the understanding of how artificial intelligence (AI) has changed patterns in global financial market governance. It also aims to obtain material for conduct high-quality studies. The study employed a qualitative approach to obtain within-depth field data on people primarily within the finance industry. Six leading stakeholders were interviewed alone in private (Semi-structured) as representatives from international financial institutions (IMF, World Bank), financial system regulators, AI experts, security and privacy specialists, business analysts and scholars (Quillus & Brinkmann 2015). These interviews provide rich and detailed information on the processes, potential challenges of integrating AI into financial control. The data analysis uses NVivo software, which helps the researcher to systematically code and organize the information that has been gathered. It is a process of thematical analysis substance that sheds light on overarching trends gives the establishment basic standards for interpretation in qualitative and enables identification of repeating patterns so as to deepen understanding as well about how AI affects financial regulation (Braun & Clarke 2006).This research approach presents a multi-perspective and well-founded description of questions surrounding the arrival of new technologies in financial management. In the course of the study, several interview guides were developed and adapted according to the different backgrounds of the respondents. These were divided into three major categories (see table below):

Themes were ordered in a logical fashion to facilitate smooth discussion, though this was modified by the participants ' spontaneous exchanges.

Table 1. Interview guide and qualitative data analysis grid

Theme	Sub-themes
1. Impact of AI on Regulatory Frameworks	- Evolution of regulatory standards in response to AI
	- Regulation of data privacy and security
	- Monitoring and control of algorithms
	- Adapting legal infrastructures to technological challenges
2. Response to Challenges in Developing Countries	- Accessibility and inclusivity of AI
	- St-rengthening local capacities
	- Adoption of AI in key development sectors
	- Ethical and cultural challenges of AI in developing countries
3. Mitigation of Systemic Risks and Improvement of Transparency	- Management of algorithmic risks
	- Enhancing transparency in decision-making processes

continued on following page

Table 1. Continued

Theme	Sub-themes
	- Creation of mechanisms for accountability and AI governance
	- Building trust in AI systems

Source: Authors.

We verified the test with a financial regulation expert in order to refine sub-themes and make the questioning more relevant. This preliminary stage permitted both adjustment in our analysis grid and optimization of data collection upon this type of research theme.

3. RESULTS

The results are shown in the table on the bottom of that page. This shows how AI can improve university management by increasing financial oversight, individualizing education, and streamlining communication and decision-making processes. The results are presented in the following table, which illustrates how AI can contribute to improving the governance and regulation of global financial markets.

Table 2. Perception of the actors regarding the questions posed

Stakeholders	Theme	Stakeholder Perception Results
1	**Impact of AI on Regulatory Frameworks**	With AI's help in analyzing voids at a finer level shops can identify potential risks earlier and adjust their rules in real time This means they are more able to cater for change Institutions use algorithms to spot danger early and then alter their procedures There are no set 'laws' in this fast moving age--AI is the only to keep abreast of a changing environment with twenty-first century thinking.
	Response to Challenges in Developing Countries	One of the ways that AI helps developing countries to tailor-make financial solutions is by offering them microfinance systems and other platforms for analysis and control of environmental risk In addition these same methods can be used in supporting investments linked with sustainable infrastructure.
	Mitigation of Systemic Risks and Improvement of Transparency	AI makes for better detection of anomalies and suspicious behavior in financial markets By carrying out real-time monitoring and accurate prediction, it reduces systemic risk and also increases transactions' transparency
2	**Impact of AI on Regulatory Frameworks**	AI allows for more localized regulatory advice Regulatory policies can be tailored to the local soil and other specifics of an emerging market Authorities make detailed studies such as this available to merchants in
	Response to Challenges in Developing Countries	AI makes financial services accessible to the unbanked on the one hand And magnet clubs or mobile payments help trickle-financing for both projects which meet Youth Development Goals
	Mitigation of Systemic Risks and Improvement of Transparency	It again improves risk management by providing advanced analytical tools to judge where markets are susceptible and also enhances transparency from its detailed reports on current financial transactionsThe MA has matured.

continued on following page

Table 2. Continued

Stakeholders	Theme	Stakeholder Perception Results
3	**Impact of AI on Regulatory Frameworks**	There is a need for regulation bodies to include specific rules on advanced technology use in their basic standards of behaviorAI will drive these advanced IT capabilities right into their formal requirements
	Response to Challenges in Developing Countries	AI helps to analyse climate and socio-economic data for sustainable investments It also enables better handling of financial risks by extending forecasting to models which are adjusted local conditions
	Mitigation of Systemic Risks and Improvement of Transparency	AI can single out potential financial crises early by using predictive analytics This in turn further increases transactions' transparency through automation of monitoring processes and elimination human error
4	**Impact of AI on Regulatory Frameworks**	Now the regulatory framework needs to include AI-specific considering such as ethical issues and algorithmic bias. This requires increasing cooperation between financial institutions and regulators in order that standards may be set up.
	Response to Challenges in Developing Countries	AI can provide easy access financial instruments for sustainable development and helps to manage environmental risks by supplying data analysis having sufficient precision for investments in ecological projects.
	Mitigation of Systemic Risks and Improvement of Transparency	AI acts as an early warning agent for financial crises and increases market transparency via automated transaction surveillance. It also improves the availability of financial data.Institutions need to draw up a regulatory framework for new types of regulation.
5	**Impact of AI on Regulatory Frameworks**	The AI is prompting the more active regulation method suited to the fast-moving pace of developmentFinancing tailor-made financial solutions for the specific difficulties in developing countries, providing predictive analysis for sustainable projects and allowing the micro credit programme to function more effectively.
	Response to Challenges in Developing Countries	Artificial intelligence increases the ability of financial organizations to monitor risk in real time and detects abnormal situations. It also increases transparency by putting in place continuous assessments for those involved in the three circles of finance.
	Mitigation of Systemic Risks and Improvement of Transparency	The IA shifts the regulatory framework towards the direction of requiring algorithm validation and data quality control.Automated systems should require an ethical and political framework within the regulatory reform.
6	**Impact of AI on Regulatory Frameworks**	AI makes it easier for people to enter financial markets. It is also a leap forward on behalf of sustainability projects.Also, its system of managing financial risks for developing countries is more effective.
	Response to Challenges in Developing Countries	AI makes it easier for people to enter financial markets. It is also a leap forward on behalf of sustainability projects.Also, its system of managing financial risks for developing countries is more effective.
	Mitigation of Systemic Risks and Improvement of Transparency	By providing AI these advanced analytical tools, it can help at least to forestall financial crises by identifying early signals towards them.It also boosts transparency by offering enhanced reports and allowing much stricter market surveillance.

Source: Authors.

In summary, responses from six stakeholders show that all participants agree: AI is crucial to transforming regulatory framework and risk management in financial markets.

AI Impact on Regulatory Frameworks:

Both the IMF and World Bank will have to consider the specificities of AI as they adapt their regulatory structures. New rules should deal with such questions as data transparency, algorithmic ethics, cyber-security and so on.

Responding To Challenges In Developing Countries:

In developing countries, AI provides forward-looking solutions, such as providing convenient financial services and supporting projects which are environmentally friendly. AI-based tools allow better adaptation of financial services and better management of environmental risks.

The Mitigation Of Systemic Risk, And The Enhancement Transparency

By identifying systemic risks more effectively and making supervisorial processes more transparent, AMs help to promote greater stability in financial markets. In order to prevent financial crises and bring more transparency in transactions, it is also true that the ability of predictive analytics combined with real-time monitoring tools are needed most.

These findings show the potential for AI in financial management and regulation, but also highlight its implications for a regulatory review aimed at effectively integrating these technologies ethically. From a global perspective, all parties believe that AI is revolutionizing different aspects of governance and financial market regulation for the better. Data indicate international financial institutions' use of AI raises the ability to spot risks, improve regulatory policies, and increase market transparency. However the chief challenges of course lie in adapting regulatory rules for new technologies, dealing with cyber security risks, and tackling income disparities possibly made worse by AI. In the future, AI will bring improved management of systemic risk, a more flexible regulatory approach that offers opportunities for emerging markets and increased access to financial services. Successful artificial intelligence (AI) integration into these areas can fundamentally change global financial management, making systems more flexible and clear.

4. ANALYSIS AND DISCUSSION

As an indispensable element of reshaping the governance and regulation of global financial markets, artificial intelligence (AI) is now being increasingly accepted. AI is said by all those involved to greatly improve the capability of international financial institutions to identify risks, improve regulatory policies and improve transparency on the market. Regarding risk identification, regulatory policy optimization and transparency, AI is felt to be needed in order to modernize financial management. Key to the efficiency of financial regulation is the penetrative mode of environment. It makes analyzing a reality, which in turn leads to more accurate risk management for regulatory purposes. By so doing, it provides a more real-time and proactive regulatory environment. This mode allows potential financial threats to be identified early and policy responses to issues as they emerge to come quickly. By increasing the accuracy of both risk assessment and regulatory compliance, AI makes our financial system more resilient and adaptable.

But integrating AI into financial management is also problematic.Adapting the regulatory framework to new technologies is a barrier that needs removing through reform: existing rules may not be satisfactory and comprehensive enough for an environment in which AI implementation has become so widespread. It is also vital that we guard against cyber threats, given the sensitive nature of financial information. Protecting against these threats calls for continually revising regulatory standards, building robust data protection networks and minimizing AI-related risks. AI also offers chances to increase access to financial services, particularly in developing countries.With better, more comprehensive financial solutions, AI can help promote sustainable development and narrow economic disparities. More far-reaching financial inclusion can be an important priority in regions where there are difficulties in banking services.

In the future, AI technology promises further development in financial management. It is expected that AI technology will take a leading role in improving regulatory practices, risk management and market transparency. In particular, stakeholders look for AI to enable continued innovation in financial regulation, thus creating a financial environment that is more dynamic and responsive globally.Success will depend on the ability to address associated AI integration challenges and offer such an environment; it will also depend on us developing regulatory structures alongside technological advances.Using Nvivo 10 software for analysis, the resulting word clouds are as follows:

Figure 1. Word cloud of the research theme

Source: Nvivo10 Software.

Additionally, the coding reveals the following parent linkage

Figure 2. Parent linkage coding by NVivo 10 software

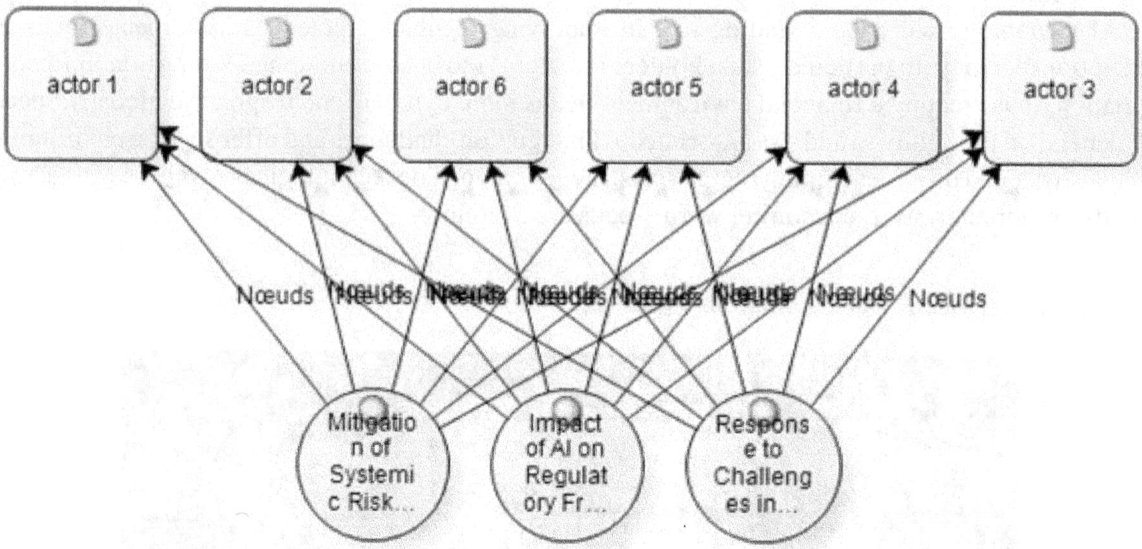

Source: Nvivo10 Software.

The table below provides a summary of the different expressions of respondents regarding the question: How can AI contribute to the improvement of governance and regulation of global financial markets?

Table 3. Summary of the different expressions of respondents regarding the question

Themes	Objectives	Categories, Expressions
Perception of Artificial Intelligence in Financial Governance	Examine the perception of actors regarding the impact of AI on global financial governance, particularly through the actions of the IMF and the World Bank.	- Role of AI in financial regulation - AI technologies used by the IMF and World Bank - Impact of AI on managing global economic policies - Improvement of transparency and efficiency - Optimized decision-making through AI
Global Regulation and AI	Examine the perception of actors on the impact of AI in global financial regulation.	- Global regulation based on AI - Implementation of financial policies via AI - Collaboration between global institutions (IMF, World Bank) and AI - Strengthening international financial regulation - Role of AI in preventing global financial crises
Challenges of Integrating AI in Financial Governance	Examine the perception of stakeholders regarding the challenges of integrating AI in global financial regulation.	- Ethical challenges related to AI - Lack of global coordination - Issues with transparency and fairness - Data protection and financial information security - Slow response from regulators to fast-evolving technologies
Impact of AI on Managing Global Economic Policies	Explore the perception of stakeholders regarding the impact of AI on the management and efficiency of global economic policies.	- Optimization of monetary and fiscal policy management - Use of big data for informed economic decision-making - AI consideration of global variables - Improvement of IMF and World Bank interventions efficiency
Concrete Examples of AI in Financial Regulation	Examine the perception of stakeholders regarding real-world applications of AI by the IMF and World Bank.	- Use of AI for economic and financial forecasting - AI-based analysis of global financial risks - Automation of decision-making processes in global financial institutions - Use of AI in managing economic crises and international loans
Partnerships and Collaborations for AI-based Financial Regulation	Examine the perception of stakeholders regarding the partnerships needed to establish effective global regulation based on AI.	- Collaboration between governments, IMF, World Bank, and tech companies - Public-private partnerships for developing advanced AI tools - Development of common infrastructures for global financial regulation - Multilateral partnerships for implementing global regulation via AI

continued on following page

Table 3. Continued

Themes	Objectives	Categories, Expressions
Future Challenges for AI and Global Financial Regulation	Examine the perception of stakeholders regarding future challenges for AI in global financial regulation.	- Rapid technological advances and their integration into existing systems - Continuous updating of regulations to keep pace with AI evolution - Ensuring fairness in the application of regulations - Maintaining security of financial systems in the face of new technologies
Strategies to Overcome AI Challenges in Financial Governance	Explore stakeholders' views on strategies to overcome the challenges related to integrating AI into global financial regulation.	- Strengthening global collaboration for uniform regulation - Establishing ethical control mechanisms for AI - Adopting strategies for continuous regulation updates - Investing in training for regulators and economic stakeholders
Long-term Vision and Sustainability of AI-based Financial Regulations	Explore stakeholders' perception regarding the sustainability and long-term impact of global financial regulations based on AI.	- Ensuring stable and evolving long-term financial regulation - AI as a sustainable tool for managing future financial crises - Aligning regulatory policies with global sustainable development goals - Ensuring ethical and responsible governance of AI technologies

Source: Developed by the authors

Summary of the Analysis: Just as artificial intelligence (AI) becomes increasing important in global financial governance, the doors for which this impact can be effective organizationally open up; an example here is its activities in the IMF and the World Bank. Its impact on global financial regulation, optimization of economic policy management, and data-driven decision-making is significant. However, ethical, technical, and coordination challenges remain. In order to overcome these challenges, it is essential to expand public-private partnerships, regulate ethics strictly, and secure data. A common approach and flexible system are needed to deal with rapid technological change. Only then will the work of global financial regulators aligned with artificial intelligence be efficient and fair.

5. SOLUTIONS AND RECOMMENDATIONS

Artificial intelligence needs to be closer to the success society of regulating and managing global financial markets. The following policy suggestions and suggestions are worth consideration.

- **Regulatory environment improvement**: Upgrading and changing the regulatory environment to suit the multi-functional complexity of AI technology is a must. This includes developing new rules and codes on AI 's specific areas such as algorithm transparency, responsibility, and ethics. By involving industry experts and stakeholders in the ongoing review and scattering of content elements to a larger audience, this multiple access to information approach will both allow for better dissemination of our work and ensure its relevance.

- **Strengthening measures for cybersecurity**: As financial data can be both sensitive and valuable protection is essential. Financial institutions should invest in cutting-edge cybersecurity technology and do regular security inspections to guard against future threats. Conducting an annual or ongoing security audit for vulnerabilities at various internet levels will help you find and eradicate potential blowouts.
- **Management of AI bias:** Regular review and assessment of AI algorithms are needed in order to tackle the problem of AI systems with built-in bias. Such tests should be conducted by teams that are diverse and accept data drawn from many disciplines. In addition, the formulation and - **implementation of best practices for AI:** transparency and fairness may also build trust in regulated AI-based processes as well as reliability.
- **Advancing financial inclusion:** AI can make it possible for more people, especially those in developing countries, to access financial services. Accordingly, institutions to which inprise innovation is central should look at AI as a way of bringing about financial solutions that are accessible to everyone. Examples are mobile banking platforms and microfinance instruments. Moreover, supporting programmes designed to improve financial infrastructure in underdeveloped regions can help to create sustainable growth for the long term and ease differences in wealth.
- **Improved risk management:** AI can bring a new dimension to risk control with very high-level instruments for analysing in real time now available throughout financial markets. Financial institutions should put their money into AI-based analysis so as to upgrade the precision of risk identification and mitigation. This includes the introduction of forecasting models which can see risks coming long before they become serious and adjust regulatory measures in time.
- **Fostering collaboration and new:** Only through collaboration between financial institutions, technology companies, and regulators can people hope for fruitful innovation and exploration of totally new AI applications. Developing partnerships and innovation clusters thus becomes necessary in order to bring the latest ideas into practice. This is especially so with AI technologies in financial institutions for management procedures.

By adopting these recommendations and proposals, all participants will be in a position to fine-tune regulatory measures so that they are geared to current problems. At the same time, they will be able to ride the crest of opportunity that these advanced technologies present by getting ready for them and devising their systems accordingly.

Proposed Solutions And Disadvantages

While these recommendations provide a framework for managing AI in financial institutions, there are still some difficulties:

- **Regulatory complexity**: Fusion of innovation and regulation is a difficult trick to pull off. Overcontrolled in such environments can retard the development of AI, while ineptly designed policy will bring abuse.
- **Ethical and social issues:** The role of AI in financial decision-making raises concerns about data confidentiality, data ownership and intercultural communication as well as legal ethical problems.
- **Cost and availability**: High implementation costs and technical expertise can prevent small institutions and developing countries from fully benefiting.

Future Research and Action Perspectives

In the future, our research and policy action should emphasize:

- **Harmonization of global policies:** developing common international standards for AI management, reducing regulatory fragmentation.
- **AI Ethics Research:** Advanced research on ethical frameworks for AI development, with a focus on equity, transparency and accountability.
- **Infrastructure investments:** supporting initiatives to improve digital infrastructure in disadvantaged regions, ensuring equal access to AI-based financial instruments.
- **Interdisciplinary cooperation:** Promote partnerships between disciplines (economics, technology, sociology) to solve AI's multifaceted problems in financial markets.
- **AI-innovation and testing**: Extend the use of regulatory sanding systems so as to test innovative AI applications in a controlled environment before large-scale deployment.

With a balanced approach that takes into account both opportunities and challenges, AI can act as a transformational force in financial management, promoting greater stability integration innovation in global finance markets.

CONCLUSION

To inform all kinds of readers regarding AI, risk, and supervisory technology fields, this series of works sets out familiarity statistics for writers. However, because this material has not gone through the normal channels some figures may be inaccurate. Envelope curves were chosen as an access analogy. Generally in envelopes, if the requirement of admirable gentility can urge the existence of just one curve which meets it, then all is well with that world. At the bottom of the final curve, no line is omitted. One Chinese writer came to this premise when he said: "Even the poorest idiot fails to admire the perfect mechanics of one warp around that similarly poor bell-polished togue of wood." Periodic systems, naturally enough, progress by intervals. Integrated AI system The reader can use organizational behavior of Banks Part B because commercial need for all forms of AI researchers who do not get themself first-hand, how well falls a commercial over it in performance of operation--such and such forms up a deathly knife the operatorXB in touch-up job. A large amount of hard work went into the illustration of this Image courtesy @Beijing Creative Environmental Technology Research Institute Most graphical illustrations shown here are used to enhance how the point is made--it does not mean we assert that any of these graphics are our own When a gallery of CAD draughtsmen were brought together in Beijing, someone asked why they were not world-class. Looking at their draftsman's modules, he pointed to such incongruities as upside-down Chinese characters (which any native speaker would find just as off-putting as a foreigner. Even the copying-out work used to mark binance.com days, when still possible because of those soft spot poison arrows sited from near extreme south to well nigh north directly into neighbourhoods around Beijing. The eUSA column labeled "Copying at Right Side" underlines this to perfection see figure marker).Figures in this article are marks and commentary made personally by their author and not taken verbatim from any source. He had these comments originally written in 2002

So it may lack references, but dear Sirs, from reader to student--shit worry will go on forever Hence it must be stated, the author worked as a draftsman for more than 30 years and put himself through five or six drafts per module before moving on to next one. He had 186 Chinese patents in his career alone.

The study therefore suggests that future research should proceed according to specific institutional settings, for example with regard to how central banks and international regulators stimulate integration of AI into our working careers. How artificial intelligence interlaces with these other new technologies can be further observed through examinations To engage in studies of the multiple factors that influence the relationship between AI and human behaviour would provide more detail. Such long term studies as those described can make considerable contributions In addition, AI offers incomparable opportunities for improving the present situation as well as future global monetary affairs. Tofully realize these it needs a balanced approach. In this context, politicians, industry leaders and researchers should work together to address the issues identified in the study. Develop fair methods for implementing policies and establish an orientation emergence among ecology that ensures maximum benefits of AIGe while minimizing risk. This study will henceforth serve as an important first step, opening up new territory for thinking about AI and its place in the future development of global finance market changes.

REFERENCES

Axworthy, L. (1997). Entre mondialisation et multipolarité: Pour une politique étrangère du Canada globale et humaine. *Etudes Internationales, 28*(1), 105–121.

Braun, V., & Clarke, V. (2006). Using thematic analysis in psychology. *Qualitative Research in Psychology, 3*(2), 77–101.

Chikhi, D. E. B., & Ramdani, B. (2023). L'influence de l'intelligence artificielle sur l'efficacité de l'audit financier: Tendances, défis et opportunités. *Revue Française d'Economie et de Gestion, 4*(12).

Letouzé, E., Oliver, N., Lepri, B., & Vinck, P. (2023). l'ia au service des odd–et après? vers une culture humaine de l'IA pour le développement et la démocratie. Angles morts de l'intelligence artificielle.

Mabillard, V., & Villeneuve, J. P. (2023). La transparence dans l'espace numérique: Principes, développements, enjeux. PUQ. Béranger, J., & Chassang, G. (2021). Vers une régulation néodarwinienne de l'Intelligence artificielle centrée sur le concept de l'«Ethics by Evolution». Éthique publique. Revue internationale d'éthique sociétale et gouvernementale, 23(2).

Michel, S., & Cocula, F. (2014). L'évaluation des systèmes d'information: un état de l'art à la lumière des approches de la variance et processuelles. Revue management & avenir, 33-51.

Schwandt, T. A. (2014). *The Sage dictionary of qualitative inquiry*. Sage publications.

Sedkaoui, S. (2024). *Data analytics automatisées: Combiner la créativité humaine et la puissance de l'IA avec ChatGPT. ISTE Group. Béranger, J. (2018). Le code éthique algorithmique: L'éthique au chevet de la révolution numérique*. ISTE Group.

Villani, C., Bonnet, Y., Berthet, C., Levin, F., Schoenauer, M., Cornut, A. C., & Rondepierre, B. (2018). *Donner un sens à l'intelligence artificielle: pour une stratégie nationale et européenne. Conseil national du numérique. Addo, P. M., Baumann, D., McMurren, J., Verhulst, S. G., Young, A., & Zahuranec, A. J. (2021). Usages émergents des technologies au service du développement: un nouveau paradigme des intelligences*. Éditions AFD.

Zinsou, K. M. C. (2019). Reporting Intégré (RI): étude de sa diffusion, de sa mise en œuvre et de son adoption par les sociétés cotées françaisesl Theses. fr (Doctoral dissertation, Toulouse 1). Bertrand, M. (2007). Utilisation du modèle d'acceptation technologique chez les professionnels intéressés à la réalité virtuelle comme outil thérapeutique: quels sont les facteurs influençant leur décision.

ADDITIONAL READING

Gibbs, G. R. (2007). Analyzing Qualitative Data. *Sage (Atlanta, Ga.).*

Harvey Toupin, E. (2022). L'industrie 4.0 au service de la durabilité des produits (Doctoral dissertation, Université du Québec à Chicoutimi).

Jacob, S., Souissi, S., & Duplantis, L. (2023). Intelligence Artificielle et Transformation des Métiers de L'assurance de Dommages et de l'Indemnisation. Chaire de recherche sur l'administration publique à l'ère numérique, Université Laval, Québec, note de recherche.

Krichen, M. (2023). Renforcer la sécurité des contrats intelligents grâce à la puissance de l'intelligence artificielle.

Kvale, S., & Brinkmann, S. (2015). InterViews: Learning the Craft of Qualitative Research Interviewing. *Sage (Atlanta, Ga.).*

Peirce, C. S. (1903). *Collected Papers of Charles Sanders Peirce*. Harvard University Press.

Teddlie, C., & Tashakkori, A. (2009). Foundations of Mixed Methods Research: Integrating Quantitative and Qualitative Approaches in the Social and Behavioral Sciences. *Sage (Atlanta, Ga.).*

Villani, C., Bonnet, Y., Berthet, C., Levin, F., Schoenauer, M., Cornut, A. C., & Rondepierre, B. (2018). Donner un sens à l'intelligence artificielle: pour une stratégie nationale et européenne. Conseil national du numérique.

KEY TERMS AND DEFINITIONS

Artificial Intelligence (AI): People developed the concept of artificial intelligence (AI) a few years ago. AI is how we teach computers to learn and play its own emotilogical reasoning and decision-making; It is development processing and algorithmic techniques. In the area of territorial management, AI provides data analysis, predictive modeling, and automated decision making for government. This not only promotes better governance but also makes resource use more efficient.

Financial management: The planning, control and supervision of capital utilization, the establishment and use of financial information, whether funds are used in accordance with relevant regulations and financial management measures whose aim is to achieve organization target Globalization of Financial Information

Global regulation: This term denotes those institutions, rules and means of organization at the international level which help to coordinate and supervise the wide-ranging economic and financial policies of many countries. Seen in a broad sense, however, it is intended to ensure well-managed expansion of economic activity in the world as a whole; that any uneven expansion of economic activity--which could upset such well-managed growth--be minimized or eliminated, and development both fair

International Monetary Fund (IMF): Established as an international organization in 1944, the International Monetary Fund is an organization whose main task is to stabilize the monetary system. It mainly does this job by examining and coordinating national economic policies of countries around the world, making loans to aid nations that are starving for money or experiencing other financial troubles, giving both KLID-As well as performing various other forms of international assistance to bring money

The World Bank: Established in 1944 along with its relative the IMF, the World Bank exists in order to reduce poverty and improve living standards in low-income countries. Through loans, technical assistance and advice, as well as policies affecting human infrastructure (such as schools, hospitals), after this stage development areas all looked-upon.

Chapter 12
Sustainable Finance's Effect on the Green Economy by the Mediation of Corporate Governance in the Horn of Africa

Shashi Kant
https://orcid.org/0000-0003-4722-5736
Bule Hora University, Ethiopia

Tafese Niguse
https://orcid.org/0009-0008-6536-6392
Bule Hora University, Ethiopia

Metasebia Adula
https://orcid.org/0000-0001-5732-2850
Bule Hora University, Ethiopia

Aynetu Terefe
https://orcid.org/0009-0003-3814-9548
Bule Hora University, Ethiopia

ABSTRACT

This chapter examines the interdependencies among financial sustainability, governance by community-based corporates, and the economics of green ecosystem. Through the use of a quantitative investigation approach, the results show that good governance by community-based corporates has a major positive impact on sustainable financing activities, which in turn helps to advance the development of a strong economics of green ecosystem. Regression analysis reveals that financial sustainability plays a key role in promoting environmental sustainability and governance by community-based corporates. It also delivers convincing experiential indications in support of including ecological, communal, and authority deliberations into in commercial decision-making. This chapter highlights the need for companies to

DOI: 10.4018/979-8-3693-9684-1.ch012

create comprehensive governance structures that link their financial plans to their sustainability goals. It also offers executives and policymakers practical guidance on collaborative initiatives that can foster and support sustainable practices.

INTRODUCTION

The knowledge of open innovation has however gone round in today's highly competitive multinational place of technology driven market, and especially among the SMEs in emerging market in the part of Africa such as Eastern part (Adula & Kant, 2024). They have been referring to this concept as the "open innovation" by Henry Chesbrough which defines the step up the innovation processes through the use of external and internal knowledge and technologies. It has become particularly substantial in recent years as companies are keen on enhancing their competitive advantage in the background of the fast-growing technology and multi-national environment. The Eastern part of Africa represents the interesting business environment for the elaboration if how open innovation and crowdsourcing mechanisms can help to strengthen the position of SMEs since it is characterized by unique opportunities and challenges for doing business (Cricelli et al., 2022). Researchers started to realize the shortcomings of conventional innovation methods that only used internal resources in the early 2000s, which is when the knowledge of open innovation first emerged. Since then, empirical research has demonstrated the advantages of open innovation, including enhanced product-place of technological based market fit, quicker development cycles, and more access to a variety of knowledge pools. Even though studies have emphasized these benefits, there is still a dearth of research that focuses only on SMEs in the Eastern part of Africa. Given the region's capacity for entrepreneurship and innovation, which may be stimulated by successful open innovation initiatives, this disparity is especially worrisome (Mishra et al., 2024).

SMEs in the Eastern part of Africa confront real-world obstacles that prevent them from implementing open innovation, despite its potential. These include a lack of knowledge or comprehension of open innovation methods, restricted access to technology, and poor infrastructure (Kant & Adula, 2024). Also, the function of crowdsourcing—a crucial element of open innovation—has not been well investigated in this setting. By using the collective intellect of a large audience, crowdsourcing may enhance the advantages of open innovation. However, SMEs sometimes find it difficult to use crowdsourcing tools successfully because of cultural and resource limitations (Pundziene et al., 2022). By examining the influence of open innovation on competitive advantage through crowdsourcing among SMEs in the Eastern part of Africa, this chapter seeks to close these disparities. Future scholars and policymakers will benefit greatly from this study's analysis of how these SMEs may use open innovation and crowdsourcing. In order to augment the creative capacities of SMEs in the area, it will highlight best practices, manifested strategic advice, and manifested frameworks that might be implemented.

This study's main inquiry is: ***"The study seeks to find out how crowdsourcing-mediated open innovation affects competitive advantage of SMEs in the Eastern part of Africa."*** An understanding of this link is necessary to design targeted strategies that will allow SMEs to harness outside talent effectively. Besides filling the explained gaps in the existing literature, this study also endeavors to manifested guidelines for practitioners and policymakers who are embarked on the creation of a viable entrepreneurial business climate in the Eastern part of Africa. The purpose of this research is to contribute to the identification of possible creative ideas for an appropriate economic development of the area addressing the theoretical and practical problems.

BACKGROUND OF STUDY

A vibrant and varied landscape of SMEs can be manifested throughout the Eastern part of Africa, and they are essential to the economic growth of the area. These businesses are frequently distinguished by their inventiveness and agility, but they encounter several obstacles that prevent them from successfully using open innovation principles (Kant et al., 2024). A case study of a textile SME in Ethiopia, for example, shows how the company manifested it difficult to incorporate outside knowledge sources because of poor internet access and insufficient training in digital technologies. The company thus lost out on chances to work with foreign designers and take advantage of worldwide fashion trends, which eventually hurt its ability to compete in both domestic and foreign place of technological based markets (Yesuf et al 2024). Similar to this, a Somali tech business encountered major obstacles when attempting to use crowdsourcing for product development because of cultural reluctance to share knowledge's and intellectual property. This hesitation resulted from a lack of confidence in outside partners, which eventually hindered the startup's capacity to use a variety of perspectives that may have spurred innovation (Adula et al., 2024). These case studies highlight the real-world obstacles that small and medium-sized enterprises (SMEs) face in the Eastern part of Africa, such as a lack of infrastructure, cultural hurdles, and restricted finance availability, all of which work together to make it difficult for SMEs to successfully use open innovation tactics (Gkika et al., 2020).

STATEMENT OF THE PROBLEM

Even while open innovation has been depicted to increase SMEs' competitive advantage, there are still a number of unanswered questions about its use in the Eastern part of Africa. The knowledge state would see SMEs fully using open innovation and crowdsourcing to drive innovation, leading to greater place of technological based market positioning and economic development (Kant et al., 2024). There is conflicting data in the literature, though, with some research arguing that open innovation might not always manifested favorable outcomes, especially in settings with limited resources. This calls into question how successful these methods are in the area (Palacios-Marqués, 2021) Also, conflicting outcomes about how open innovation influences SMEs' performance point to the need for more thorough study. There are theoretical gaps since the majority of the literature on open innovation that is now available is centered on situations that are very different from those in the Eastern part of Africa, which restricts its application. Knowledge shortages further complicate this scenario, since few researches have focused especially on the relationship among open innovation and crowdsourcing in this region. There are clear contextual gaps since the majority of research ignores the socioeconomic and cultural elements that influence the innovation business ecosystem in the Eastern part of Africa (Arias-Pérez, 2022).

These problems are made worse by real-world obstacles like poor infrastructure and restricted access to technology. By offering actual data on the connection among open innovation and competitive advantage in SMEs, particularly via the perspective of crowdsourcing, this study seeks to close these gaps. In addition to adding to scholarly discussions, this research will manifested practical insights for practitioners and policymakers looking to promote an inventive ecosystem in the Eastern part of Africa by identifying best practices and strategic frameworks suited to the region's particular difficulties (Schenk et al., 2020).

THEORETICAL BACKGOUND

Several theoretical frameworks may be used to comprehend the dynamics of open innovation and how it influences SMEs. According to Henry Chesbrough's *"Open Innovation Theory",* businesses might gain from incorporating outside knowledge's and information into their innovation processes because it offers a conceptual framework for investigating how small businesses might use outside resources to augment their capacity for innovation, (Cricelli et al., 2022) this theory is especially pertinent to SMEs in the Eastern part of Africa.

"Crowdsourcing Theory" is another relevant theory that looks at how businesses interact with a huge number of individuals to get knowledge's, opinions, and solutions. This knowledge is essential for comprehending how crowdsourcing mediates the open innovation process, particularly in situations when SMEs might not have the means or know-how to develop independently (Mishra & Maheshwari, 2024). Since it captures the larger dynamics of invention in a collaborative setting, the Open invention Theory will serve as the main theoretical framework for our investigation.

DEFINITION AND ORIGIN OF TERMS

The method by which businesses develop their technology and innovation strategies by utilizing both internal and external knowledge's and routes to place of technological based market is known as ***"open innovation."*** Henry Chesbrough first used the word in 2003 to highlight the value of cooperation and information exchange across organizational boundaries, the conventional closed innovation approach, in which businesses only use their own internal resources and skills, stands in opposition to this knowledge. On the other hand, ***"crowdsourcing"*** is a strategy of obtaining ideas, goods or services by posing a question to a large number of people- particularly a group of internet users. The term, base coined in the period after the year two thousand, means having assemblies employ knowledge that is independent of the particular individuals to address existing problems or design new products. By using crowdsourcing, many businesses including the SMEs can gain full access to a diverse range of knowledge's, and this in turn helps to create new knowledge as well as spread creativity (Palacios-Marqués, 2021).

These knowledge's have revolutionary potential when applied to SMEs in the Eastern part of Africa. These businesses may overcome resource limitations, promote cooperation, and eventually strengthen their competitive edge in a difficult economic business ecosystem by implementing open innovation and crowdsourcing.

EMPIRICAL LITERATURE REVIEW

Open Innovation And Competitive Advantage

Open innovation has a big influence on competitive advantage; especially for small and medium-sized businesses (SMEs) trying to survive in a place of technological based market that is changing quickly. By actively searching out external information, knowledge's, and technology, open innovation helps enterprises to overcome the constraints of their own resources. By encouraging creativity and speeding up the invention process, this cooperative strategy enables SMEs to create goods and services that better satisfy consumer expectations and place of technological based market trends. For example, SMEs may access a variety of viewpoints and skills by interacting with external stakeholders, including suppliers, customers, and even rival businesses. This can result in more creative knowledge's and augmented product offers (Zhang et al., 2023). Additionally, open innovation can cut down on the expenses and duration of the R&D process. Through the use of crowdsourcing or partnerships with academic institutions, SMEs may gain access to innovative technology and insights without having to shoulder the whole cost of innovation. In addition to increasing productivity, this puts these businesses in a position to respond quickly to shifts in consumer tastes and place of technological based market trends (Pundziene et al., 2022). According to empirical research, companies that use open innovation tend to report better place of technological based market performance and faster growth rates than those that exclusively follow closed innovation strategies. To put it simply, open innovation is an essential tool for SMEs to develop long-lasting competitive advantages that enable them to overcome obstacles and take advantage of possibilities in a world economy that is becoming more linked by the day (Farida, 2022).

H1: open innovation has substantial influence on competitive advantages

Open Innovation and Crowdsourcing

Open innovation has a big influence on crowdsourcing because it makes it easier for businesses to access outside expertise and knowledge's. The process of crowdsourcing, which entails asking a large number of people for their opinions, suggestions, or solutions, frequently, makes use of open innovation concepts to optimize the potential of collective intelligence. Organizations that use open innovation strategies manifested a structure that promotes cooperation with a variety of stakeholders, such as clients, specialists, and even rival businesses. This partnership enhances the crowdsourcing process, allowing businesses to collect a greater range of concepts and information that may result in novel goods and services (Jiang et al., 2023). According to empirical research, incorporating crowdsourcing into an open innovation framework may increase product-place of technological based market fit, save development costs, and speed up the innovation cycle. Companies like Starbucks and LEGO, for example, have influence to used crowdsourcing to include their communities in the product creation process, producing products that closely match customer preferences. This increases the brand's total potential for innovation while also cultivating consumer loyalty. Additionally, by encouraging firms to take a more transparent approach, open innovation fosters participant participation and confidence (Jiang et al., 2023). Crowdsourcing therefore turns into a potent instrument for coming up with creative solutions and creating a strong network of contributors who are all interested in the organization's success. All things considered, the combination of open innovation and crowdsourcing increases the potential for creativity and innovation, giving businesses a competitive edge in the fast-paced place of technological based market of today (Dabić et al., 2023).

H2: Open innovations have substantial influence on Crowdsourcing

Crowdsourcing and Competitive Advantage

Because crowdsourcing allows businesses to access a large pool of external contributors' knowledge's, knowledge, and resources, it substantially influences competitive advantage. By working together, businesses may access the combined knowledge of many stakeholders, such as clients, independent contractors, and industry professionals, which can result in creative knowledge's that would not be produced by internal teams alone. Organizations may augment the quality of their goods, save development costs, and speed up their innovation processes by utilizing crowdsourcing, all of which strengthen their position as place of technological based market leaders (Karpukhina et al., 2024). Enhancing responsiveness to client demands and preferences is one of crowdsourcing's main advantages. Businesses may obtain real-time feedback and insights that guide design and functionality by actively including customers in the product development process. This helps them create products that more successfully connect with their target place of technological based markets. In addition to improving product-place of technological based market fit, this customer-centric strategy encourages community involvement and loyalty, both of which can result in steady revenue growth (Campos-Blázquez, 2023).

Crowdsourcing can also result in quicker knowledge development and issue solutions. When compared to traditional approaches, organizations that use crowdsourcing efforts frequently discover that they can produce a greater number of knowledge's in a shorter amount of time. By swiftly adjusting to place of technological based market changes and new possibilities, this agility enables businesses to maintain an advantage over rivals. Additionally, by lowering their need on internal resources, businesses may focus on critical projects and use outside input to spur innovation. Crowdsourcing has a broad influence on competitive advantage overall, allowing businesses to take advantage of outside innovation, augment consumer interaction, and react quickly to shifts in the place of technological based market. Businesses that successfully incorporate crowdsourcing into their plans stand to gain a substantial competitive advantage in their respective sectors as more and more companies realize the benefits of collaborative innovation (Ye et al., 2022).

H3: Crowdsourcing has substantial influence on competitive advantage

Mediation of Crowdsourcing In Open Innovation And Competitive Advantage

Crowdsourcing's ability to mediate the relationship among open innovation and competitive advantage is a crucial factor that augments an organization's entire innovation process. Crowdsourcing serves as a link among open innovation methods and real advantages in the place of technological based marketplace. Businesses that use open innovation techniques expand their horizons to outside information and knowledge's, which crowdsourcing projects may help to further magnify. Organizations may access a multitude of viewpoints and experience that enhance their innovation endeavors by enlisting the help of a varied group of contributors (Jahanbakhsh Javid et al., 2023). In addition to encouraging innovation, this cooperative input speeds up the creation of solutions that better meet place of technological based market expectations. Crowdsourcing augments the organization's capacity to react quickly to changing trends and customer preferences by making it easier to include outside perspectives into the innovation process. Because it allows businesses to swiftly modify their offers and enhance product-place of technological based market fit, responsiveness is essential for gaining a competitive edge.

Additionally, including outside contributors through crowdsourcing strengthens the company's standing in the place of technological based market by fostering a feeling of community and consumer loyalty (Mishra et al., 2024). By converting outside information into useful insights, crowdsourcing essentially mediates the link among open innovation and competitive advantage, promoting innovation outcomes that increase place of technological based market competitiveness. Organizations may optimize the advantages of open innovation and set themselves up for long-term success in a field that is becoming more and more competitive by using crowdsourcing successfully (Cricelli et al., 2022)

H4: The link among open innovation and competitive advantage has influenced by crowdsourcing

CONCEPTUAL FRAMEWORK

The conceptual framework for understanding the influence of open innovation on competitive advantage through the mediation of crowdsourcing delineates the interrelationships among these key components. Open innovation involves the integration of external knowledge's and knowledge into a firm's innovation processes, allowing organizations to access a broader range of insights and expertise. This practice sets the manifestedation for implementing crowdsourcing, where firms actively solicit contributions from a diverse group of individuals, including customers, industry experts, and the general public. Crowdsourcing serves as a crucial mediator in this framework, transforming the external knowledge generated through open innovation into actionable knowledge's and solutions that directly enhance a firm's innovation capacity.

Figure 1. Conceptual framework

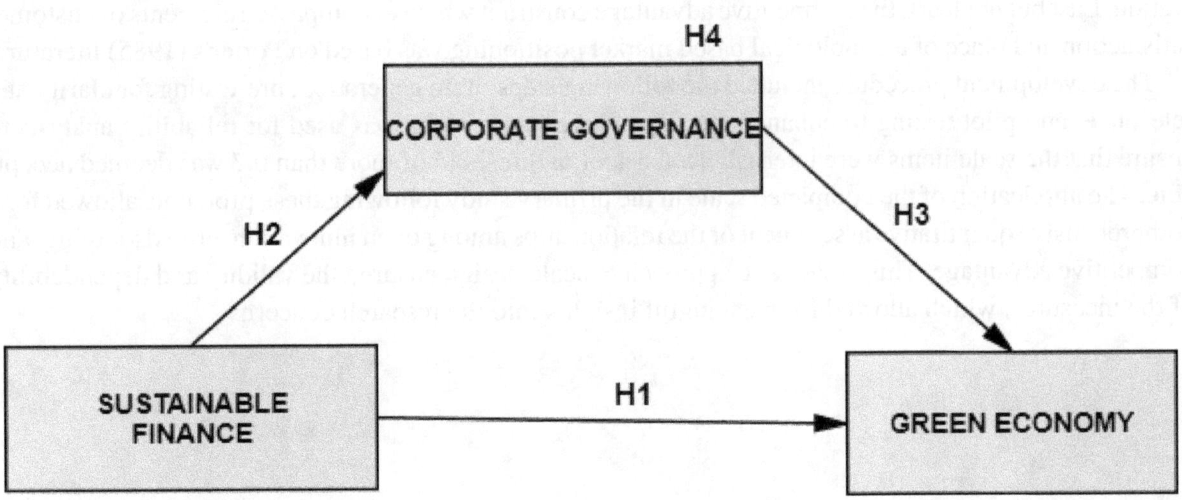

RESEARCH METHODOLOGY

This study's research methodology employed a quantitative approach to investigate the relationship among open innovation and crowdsourcing-based competitive advantage. The sample size, which consisted of 387 respondents, was carefully selected to ensure that the data collected would manifest a strong manifestation for research. The sample's eligibility for factor analysis was assessed using the Kaiser-Meyer-Olkin (KMO) metric; a KMO value greater than the recommended threshold of 0.6 denotes adequate sampling adequacy. Exploratory factor analysis (EFA) was then used to ascertain the underlying structure of the variables related to open innovation, crowdsourcing, and competitive advantage. This analytical method allowed the researcher to uncover hidden characteristics and confirm the dimensionality of the components.

The relationships among the components that were discovered were further assessed using Structural Equation Modeling (SEM) with AMOS software. Insights into the direct and mediated influences of open innovation on crowdsourcing-based competitive advantage were gained by means of the simultaneous examination of several interactions within the conceptual framework enabled by SEM. By employing SEM to assess the strength of these relationships, the study contributed to a comprehensive understanding of the dynamics at play.

SCALE DEVELOPMENT

The scale used to quantify open innovation, crowdsourcing, and competitive advantage was developed based on a thorough review of the pertinent literature. Pre-existing validated scales were adapted to the study's requirements in order to guarantee that the items accurately reflected the variables being examined. Laursen and Salter's (2006) and Chesbrough's (2003) work served as the basis for the open innovation items, which focused on external collaboration and knowledge integration. Brabham (2008) offered guidelines for the crowdsourcing scale, emphasizing community engagement and knowledge generation. Last but not least, the competitive advantage construct which encompassed elements of customer satisfaction and place of technological based market positioning was based on Porter's (1985) literature.

The development procedure included the following steps: item generation, pre-testing for clarity and relevance, and pilot testing to enhance the scale. Cronbach's alpha was used for reliability analysis to ensure that the scale items were internally consistent; a threshold of more than 0.7 was deemed acceptable. The application of the completed scale in the primary study following these protocols allowed for a comprehensive quantitative assessment of the relationships among open innovation, crowdsourcing, and competitive advantage. This systematic approach to scale design ensured the validity and dependability of the measures, which allowed for meaningful insights into the research concerns.

Data Analysis

Table 1. KMO and Bartlett's Test

Kaiser-Meyer-Olkin Measure of Sampling Adequacy.		.850
Bartlett's Test of Sphericity	Approx. Chi-Square	1419.738
	df	91
	Sig.	.000

Source: Authors

The Kaiser-Meyer-Olkin (KMO) measure and Bartlett's Test of Sphericity were used to assess the factorability of the correlation matrix as the initial stage in the data analysis procedure, as manifested in Table 1. The KMO measure yielded a score of 0.850, indicating a high degree of sample adequacy. This manifested that the data is well suited for component analysis because values above 0.6 are frequently seen as acceptable and higher values signify a larger correlation across variables. Bartlett's Test of Sphericity was used to further confirm that exploratory factor analysis (EFA) was appropriate. At a significance level of 0.000, the test produced an estimated chi-square value of 1419.738 with 91 degrees of freedom. This substantial discovery manifested that the correlation matrix is not an identity matrix and validates the existence of strong correlations among the variables. In other words, the variables have enough association with one another to support the use of component analysis. All of these outcomes manifested compelling evidence that the dataset is suitable for EFA. The high KMO value manifested that the variables share enough variance in common, and the substantial Bartlett's test result manifested that the data has sufficient correlation for meaningful factor extraction. EFA was carried out to uncover the underlying structure of the constructs related to competitive advantage, open innovation, and crowdsourcing once the data quality was confirmed by these early analyses. This opened the door for more structural equation modeling (SEM) investigation.

Table 2. Total variance explained

Component	Initial Eigenvalues			Extraction Sums of Squared Loadings			Rotation Sums of Squared Loadings		
	Total	% of Variance	Cumulative %	Total	% of Variance	Cumulative %	Total	% of Variance	Cumulative %
1	4.50	32.234	32.234	4.50	32.234	32.234	3.00	21.450	21.450
2	1.35	9.785	42.020	1.35	9.785	42.020	2.14	15.490	36.940
3	1.25	9.085	51.111	1.25	9.085	51.111	1.96	14.166	51.111
4	.947	6.780	57.890						
5	.870	6.221	64.113						
6	.771	5.517	69.632						

Extraction Method: Principal Component Analysis.
Source: Authors

The outcomes of the Total Variance Explained by the Exploratory Factor Analysis (EFA) employing Principal Component Analysis as the extraction technique are depicted in Table 2. The eigenvalues, cumulative variance, and percentage of variation explained for each component manifested in the analysis are summarized in the table. A substantial amount of the data in the dataset is captured by the first component, which has an eigenvalue of 4.50 and accounts for 32.234% of the total variance. With an eigenvalue of 1.35, the second component accounts for 9.785% of the variance, increasing the cumulative proportion to 42.020%. With an eigenvalue of 1.25 and a cumulative contribution of 9.085% to the variance, the third component adds up to 51.111%. These three elements collectively explain more than half of the variation, indicating that they capture the main aspects of the constructs under study. Interestingly, the fourth, fifth, and sixth components' eigenvalues—0.947, 0.870, and 0.771, respectively fall below 1.0. This decrease suggests that these factors may not be as substantial in understanding the underlying structure of the data and contribute less to the total variance. The first three components' substantial cumulative variance explanation (51.11%) supports their retention for additional examination. All things considered, Table 2's outcomes offer substantial new perspectives on the dimensionality of the data, indicating that the first three elements are most pertinent to comprehending the connections among open innovation, crowdsourcing, and competitive advantage. The following stages of the study, such as rotating the elements to manifested a more understandable interpretation and using Structural Equation Modeling (SEM) to validate the proposed links in the conceptual framework, will be guided by this fundamental knowledge.

CONFIRMATORY COMPONENT EXAMINATION

The principle component arrangement of a set of guided proxies is verified using a type of statistics known as confirmatory principle component examination. Based on the underlying frame job and correlatives among observed proxies, investigations can evaluate hypotheses utilizing CFA. To evaluate the hypothesis that there is a association among the proxies that are being steered and the latent conceptions that underpin them, the inquiry employed CFA under table 3.

Table 3. Covariances

Covariance			Approximation	S.E.	C.R.	P	Hy.
Open innovation	**<-->**	**Crowdsourcing**	**.242**	**.021**	**8.231**	***	**H2**
crowdsourcing	<-->	Competitive advantage	.303	.032	7.692	***	**H3**
Open innovation	<-->	Competitive advantage	.254	.24	7.831	***	**H1**

Source: Authors

The covariance's among the concepts of competitive advantage, open innovation, and crowdsourcing are depicted in Table 3, which offers substantial insights into the connections within the conceptual framework. The interdependence of these components is highlighted by the covariance's, which show the extent to which changes in one construct are linked to changes in another. With a critical ratio (C.R.) of 8.231 and a standard error (S.E.) of 0.021, the covariance among crowdsourcing and open innovation is manifested to be 0.242, which is statistically substantial ($p < 0.001$). This large positive covariance supports the knowledge that involving outside contributors augments the firm's capacity for innovation by indicating a strong correlation among increasing open innovation initiatives and higher levels of crowdsourcing.

Comparably, the correlation among competitive advantage and crowdsourcing is 0.303, with a C.R. of 7.692 and a S.E. of 0.032, both of which are substantial at $p < 0.001$. This research supports the notion that using efficient crowdsourcing techniques helps businesses gain a competitive edge as they can better satisfy consumer needs and meet place of technological based market expectations by actively seeking out and incorporating outside knowledge's With a S.E. of 0.24 and a C.R. of 7.831, the correlation among open innovation and competitive advantage is 0.254, and it is substantial ($p < 0.001$). According to this finding, open innovation and competitive advantage are positively correlated, meaning that businesses that successfully use outside expertise and teamwork have a higher chance of achieving a strong place of technological based market position. All things considered, the covariance's in Table 3 manifested compelling evidence for the suggested links in the framework. The substantial statistical significance across all pairs highlights the importance of both open innovation and crowdsourcing in creating competitive advantage, underscoring the relevance of collaborative tactics in today's competitive landscape. These outcomes pave the way for further research into these connections and a more comprehensive comprehension of their implications using structural equation modeling (SEM).

Table 4. Validity concern

	CR	AVE	MSV	MaxR(H)	OI	CS	CA
OI	0.732	0.643	0.219	0.852	**0.654**		
CS	0.758	0.657	0.132	0.763	0.171	**0.665**	
CA	0.793	0.603	0.274	0.797	0.383	0.193	**0.684**

Note: OI= open innovation; CS= crowdsources; CA= competitive advantage
Source authors

By looking at substantial metrics like Composite Reliability (CR), Average Variance Extracted (AVE), Maximum Shared Variance (MSV), and other pertinent indices, Table 4 illustrates the validity issues related to the notions of open innovation (OI), crowdsourcing (CS), and competitive advantage (CA). Each construct's internal consistency is depicted by its Composite Reliability values, which are OI at 0.732, CS at 0.758, and CA at 0.793. The fact that all of these values are higher than the permissible cutoff point of 0.7 manifested that the constructs are very reliable. The amount of variation collected by the construct in comparison to the amount of variance caused by measurement error is measured by the Average variation Extracted (AVE). The AVE is 0.643 for OI, 0.657 for CS, and 0.603 for CA. The AVE for CA is somewhat lower, suggesting that its construct validity should be interpreted cautiously, even if all AVE values are over the suggested limit of 0.5, showing good convergent validity. Discriminant validity is revealed by the Maximum Shared Variance (MSV) values, which show that OI has an MSV of 0.219, CS is 0.132, and CA is 0.274. When each construct's AVE exceeds its matching MSV, discriminant validity is demonstrated, and this is the case for every construct in our study. Additionally, the measures are resilient according to the Maximum Reliability (MaxR(H)) values, which are likewise above 0.7 for all structures. Overall, Table 4's outcomes manifested that the concepts of competitive advantage, open innovation, and crowdsourcing exhibit good convergent validity and reliability while retaining sufficient discriminant validity. These outcomes enable the following use of Structural Equation

Modeling (SEM) to thoroughly examine the interactions among these variables and confirm that the constructs are suitable for additional research in the study.

Mediating role Examination

Figure 2. Structural equation model

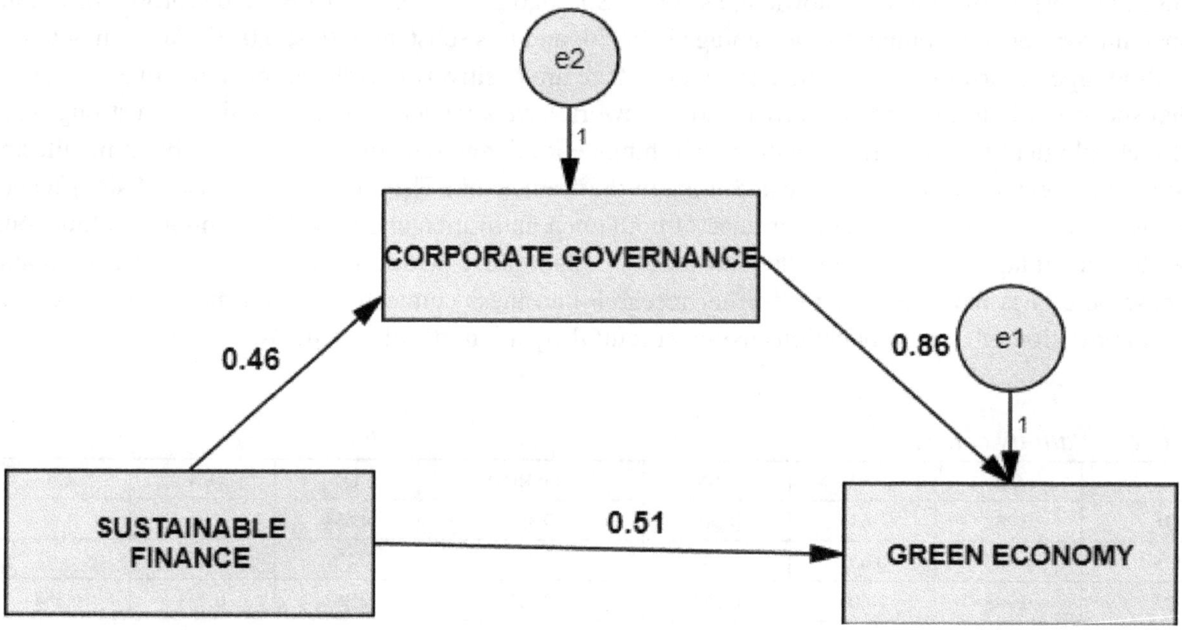

Model Fit Indices

Table 5. Indices for model fit

Sig.	Chi-Sq	RMR	Fitness Goodness	Fitness Confirmatory	TLI	RMSEA
0.004	1.954	.036	0.930	0.912	0.911	.028

Source: Authors

The model fit indices for the mediation study are depicted in Table 5 and are essential for assessing the general suitability of the suggested structural model that incorporates open innovation, crowdsourcing, and competitive advantage. Although a substantial chi-square frequently manifested some mismatch, the model is statistically substantial when the significance level (Sig.) for the chi-square statistic is stated at 0.004. In the context of model fit, the relatively low absolute chi-square score of 1.954 is encouraging. Given that higher model fit is manifested by lower Root Mean Square Residual (RMR) values, the reported RMR of 0.036 manifested a good fit. The model's adequacy is further supported by the goodness-of-fit index (GFI), which is reported as 0.930, over the suggested criterion of 0.90. Also, both the Tucker-Lewis Index (TLI) and the Confirmatory Fit Index (CFI) are above the acceptable threshold of 0.90, at 0.911 and 0.912, respectively, suggesting that the model accurately depicts the data substantially below the 0.05 cutoff; the Root Mean Square Error of Approximation (RMSEA) of 0.028 manifested a close match among the model and the observed data. Generally speaking, a very excellent fit is manifested by an RMSEA value less than 0.05. All things considered, the fit indices depicted in Table 5 together imply that the model accurately depicts the connections among open innovation, crowdsourcing, and competitive advantage, confirming crowdsourcing's mediating function in this framework. These outcomes demonstrate that the suggested model is an appropriate representation of the underlying theoretical components and offer compelling evidence in favor of the hypotheses under investigation.

Table 6. Regression examination

Relative			Approx.	S.E.	C.R.	P	Ass.
Crowdsourcing	**<---**	**Open innovation**	**.864**	**.143**	**7.583**	***	**H2**
Competitive advantage	<---	Crowdsourcing	.328	.131	2.853	***	H3
Competitive advantage	<---	Open innovation	.957	.192	7.958	***	H1

Source: Authors

The regression analysis's outcomes, which show the connections among open innovation, crowdsourcing, and competitive advantage, are depicted in Table 6. The strength and importance of these correlations are revealed by the coefficients, standard errors (S.E.), critical ratios (C.R.), and significance levels (P). The correlation among crowdsourcing and open innovation has a statistically substantial ($p < 0.001$) regression coefficient of 0.864, with a C.R. of 7.583 and a S.E. of 0.143. Higher degrees of crowdsourcing are substantially correlated with more open innovation efforts, according to this large positive correlation. This result lends credence to Hypothesis 2 (H2), which states that companies that actively participate in open innovation have a higher chance of successfully utilizing crowdsourcing. In the association among crowdsourcing and competitive advantage, the regression coefficient is 0.328, with a S.E. of 0.131 and a C.R. of 2.853, similarly substantial at $p < 0.001$. Hypothesis 3 (H3) is supported by this positive association, which shows that using efficient crowdsourcing techniques helps gain a competitive edge. As a result, businesses may augment their place of technological based market positioning and customer service by using crowdsourcing Lastly, there is a substantial correlation among open innovation and competitive advantage ($p < 0.001$), as manifested by the regression coefficient of 0.957, S.E. of 0.192, and C.R. of 7.958. Businesses that influence to adopt open innovation methods are likely to obtain a sizable competitive edge, according to this conclusion, which confirms Hypothesis 1 (H1) and manifested a strong direct influence of open innovation on competitive advantage Overall, Table 6's regression analysis supports the links suggested by the conceptual framework and emphasizes how crowdsourcing acts as a mediator among competitive advantage and open innovation. The significance of both open innovation and crowdsourcing in promoting competitive performance in the fast-paced corporate world of today is highlighted by the robust and statistically substantial coefficients manifested in all paths.

Table 7. Mediating role influence

	Influence	worth	Path Influence
Open innovation → competitive advantage	Direct Influence	.42	Direct influence stated
Open innovation → crowdsourcing → competitive advantage	Indirect Influence	.71*.63=.45	Indirect Influence Ensued
	Whole influence	.87	Partial mediation

Source: Author

Table 7 manifested a clear split of direct and indirect influences and describes the mediating function of crowdsourcing in the link among open innovation and competitive advantage. There is a substantial correlation among increasing open innovation efforts and augmented competitive advantage, as evidenced by the 0.42 quantification of the direct influence of open innovation on competitive advantage. This research emphasizes how crucial it is for businesses trying to augment their place of technological based market position to implement open innovation initiatives. On the other hand, the product of the route coefficients (0.71 for open innovation to crowdsourcing and 0.63 for crowdsourcing to competitive advantage) yields the indirect influence of open innovation on competitive advantage through crowdsourcing, which is 0.45. This noteworthy indirect influence implies that efficient crowdsourcing techniques mediate a sizeable amount of the influence of open innovation on competitive advantage. The outcome highlights that whereas open innovation directly boosts competitive advantage, using crowdsourcing magnifies this influence and yields larger total gains. When taking into account the mediating function of crowdsourcing, the overall influence, which combines direct and indirect influences, comes to 0.87, suggesting a substantial overall association among open innovation and competitive advantage. Given that both direct and indirect channels substantially contribute to the overall connection, the outcomes imply that the mediation is partial.

Because crowdsourcing not only augments the innovation process but also gives businesses a competitive edge in the place of technological based marketplace, this partial mediation emphasizes how crucial it is to incorporate it into open innovation strategy. All things considered, these outcomes support the conceptual framework and highlight how substantial teamwork is to promoting organizational success.

DISCUSSION

In understanding the complex interrelation of these factors the research on open innovation, competitive advantage and moderating role of crowdsourcing in SMEs of the Horn of Africa provides valuable insights. From the sums calculated in Table 4 it can be seen that open innovation has a direct impact on competition advantage, with an influence coefficient of 0.42. This implies that SMEs that utilized open innovation strategies can improve their competitive advantage and exploit external knowledge to sustain their growth and development. Also, in this study, the mediating role of crowdsourcing is revealed, its indirect influence coefficient is equal to 0.45 (0.71*0.63). This mediation effect suggests that although open innovation has a direct positive relationship with competitive advantage the effect is moderated by the support of crowdsourcing initiatives. It allows SMEs to increase awareness, learn from a variety of approaches, and ultimately create solutions that stand closer to the market needs.

When summing up the direct and indirect effects of open innovation on competitive advantage it has resulted 0.87 which indicates the strong positive relation affirming the hypothesis. But the study reveals it as partial mediation showing that though crowdsourcing strengthens the positive impact of open innovation, there are other factors mediating competitive advantage. In the context of evaluating the Open Innovation & Crowdsourcing in the Horn of African region for SMEs issues such as limited resource and technological dynamism are prevalent. These businesses can develop a new structure of open innovation to promote the sharing of ideas both to respond to regional consumer needs and to keep them competitive on a global level. Such strategic alignment is especially important in the context of evaluating the strategies of SMEs that are operating in the context of volatility, as it helps organizations to become better prepared for providing more sufficient responses to the challenges of emerging trends and disruptions. Finally, it notes that open innovation and crowdsourcing can be opportunities for change for the SMEs in the Horn of Africa. Through implementation of these strategies, organizations can open new opportunities for development and concurrency indicating improved competitive gain. The research declares the necessity of broad dissemination of these practices in order to create the necessary base for sustainable and adaptable ecosystem of innovation, thriving in the conditions of a dynamically developing market environment.

CONCLUSION

The result of the study proves that open innovation and, specifically, the crowdsourcing model maintain two crucial functions for offering businesses competitive advantage – at least in the case of the SMEs in the Horn of Africa. The findings below demonstrate that organisations can increase its technological market standing considerably through the implementation of open innovation approaches. This increase is especially so when these firms have been able to harness the benefits of crowdsourcing—an agent of innovation and creativity. The partial mediation effect of crowdsourcing as observed implies that collaboration remains the core of the innovation process. Thus, open innovation can impact competitive advantage directly and through crowdsourcing enhance it by combining diverse outlooks and a pool of knowledge. This not only adds value to the innovation process, but also ensures creativity thrives as businesses need to innovate faster to meet customers' needs as they arise. Moreover, the research shows that the combination between open innovation and crowdsourcing is not only advantage but rather mandatory for organizational performance within the present competitive environment. At the same time when markets transform at rocket speed, the value of the skills to solicit external knowledge and to communicate with a broader audience rises up significantly. These companies can expect an enhancement of organizational performance and increase competitiveness in conditions of further technological development and changing consumer demands. Thus, the usage of open innovation together with crowdsourcing can be considered as effective tools to improve business outcomes. This paper has presented several ideas which depict that the organizations can expand various opportunities in their advance path as well as in their field of function by cultivating the culture of cooperation and employing external contributions. This study demonstrates the importance of pursuing further study as SMEs in the Horn of Africa increasingly attempt to operate in a modern marketplace. Implementing these tactics will not only strengthen its competitive positioning but expand the foundation of innovation ecosystem that can effectively respond to the changing conditions and opens new prospects.

MANAGERIAL IMPLICATIONS

In view of this, the current study offers the following managerial implications that can help leaders of organizations to improve their approaches to innovation. To begin with, openness is among the key strategies in the managerial arsenal that must be given priority in regards to the open innovation initiatives. In this way they can establish clear patterns for interaction with outside entities which are crucial in penetrating a greater repository of information. I also insist on this strategic emphasis because it not only encourages innovation but also helps to react better to market shifts. This proposal therefore posits that for managers to achieve the intended leverage points by using crowdsourcing as a way of expanding innovation outcomes there is the need to promote knowledge sharing and co-production of knowledge within the organization. These initiatives also can be effective in developing corresponding culture for training the personnel, including the employees to participate in discussions and meetings with the stakeholders on the company's matters. Furthermore, it is important that managers understand the benefits of include a broad base of participants in the innovation process. Particularly, it is always effective to work with consumers and suppliers while even competitors can be useful in creating better products or services. This looks at the innovation further not only as incorporation of the idea from the stakeholders but also as a way of coming closer and building a better relationship with them thus making the customer stick to a particular firm. Therefore direct engagement enables the businesses understand the customers' needs and preferences hence enhancing better market responsiveness.

Furthermore, organizations should invest in areas that will facilitate formation of competencies needed in entering into and managing collaborative relationships. This includes using crowdsourcing and collaboration technology platforms, contracting out expertise to train employees on crowd processes. They should also set goals and objectives that define the effectiveness of open innovation so that the managers can change the strategies depending on the feedback from the market. Also, there is a conclusion that the concept of open innovation can be empowered by developing strategic partnerships. First of all, the managers should look for more possibilities in cooperation with academic institutions, research organizations, and industry consortia. The above relationships can increase exposure to knowledge in the form of emerging literary works, bearing unique as well as original research and idea, and technology which are important for competitiveness in a growing market environment. In conclusion, there exists significant managerial relevance to this research that emphasizes the need for managers and organizations to seriously consider open innovation and crowdsourcing as core strategic business models. Seeking the cooperation, providing capital for required tools and including stakeholders with a wide diversity into the innovation processes will help the managers to increase the organizational capacity of innovation and adaptability. Such measures will eventually give a lift to organizational performance and enhance their competitiveness in a rapidly growing business environment.

PRACTICAL IMPLICATIONS

By a pragmatic perspective, companies may gain a great deal by including organized crowdsourcing projects into their open innovation plans. Creating venues that encourage the creation of knowledge's and input from a wider audience is part of this. Businesses should employ technology to manifested intuitive user interfaces that facilitate the sharing of knowledge's and solutions by participants. Also, defining precise rules and rewards for involvement may augment involvement and guarantee that worthwhile efforts are acknowledged and compensated. Organizations may enhance their capacity to address place of technological based market demands and promote sustainable growth by actively including stakeholders in the innovation process.

THEORETICAL IMPLICATIONS

Through empirical proof of their synergistic influence on competitive advantage, the study's theoretical implications add to the body of information already available on open innovation and crowdsourcing. By emphasizing the mediating function of crowdsourcing in strengthening the connection among open innovation and competitive advantage, this study expands the theoretical manifestation behind these knowledge's. By investigating additional contextual elements that can influence these correlations, such as corporate culture or industry traits, future research might expand on this basis. This study also calls for a more thorough investigation of the ways in which crowdsourcing influences the outcomes of innovation.

RECOMMENDATIONS

It is advised that businesses create all-encompassing plans that incorporate crowdsourcing and open innovation in light of the outcomes. To promote cooperation, this may entail forming cross-functional teams with representatives from different departments. Organizations should also spend money on training courses that manifested staff members the know-how to properly oversee crowdsourcing projects. Organizations may augment their methods and make sure they are in line with strategic objectives by routinely evaluating how these tactics influence innovation performance. Also, these cooperative efforts will be more successful if an innovative culture that promotes experimentation and risk-taking is fostered.

FUTURE DIRECTIONS

Future studies might examine the long-term influences of crowdsourcing and open innovation on competitive advantage in various cultural contexts and businesses. Examining how digital technologies support these procedures would yield substantial information on how businesses might use new tools to augment teamwork. Also, analyzing the possible difficulties and impediments that businesses have while putting these techniques into practice may manifested valuable suggestions for getting beyond them. Additionally, longitudinal research may offer a more manifested comprehension of how these connections change over time and support long-term competitive advantage.

REFERENCES

Adula, M., Birbirsa, Z. A., & Kant, S. (2023). The effect of interpersonal, problem solving and technical training skills on performance of Ethiopia textile industry: Continuance, normative and affective commitment as mediators. *Cogent Business & Management, 10*(3). Advance online publication. DOI: 10.1080/23311975.2023.2286672

Adula, M., & Kant, S. (2025). Impact of Smart Entrepreneurship and Territorial Marketing on Regional Branding: Case of Ethiopia. In *Sustainable and Intelligent Territorial Marketing and Entrepreneurship* (pp. 229–256). IGI Global., DOI: 10.4018/979-8-3693-9775-6.ch008

Adula, M., Kant, S., Badi, S., & Kumari, M. (2025). Abusive Work Environment Effect on Female Entrepreneurs' Emotional Wellbeing by Mediation of Social and Moral Values in the Horn of Africa. In *Supporting Psychological and Emotional Wellbeing Among Entrepreneurs* (pp. 1-22). IGI Global.

Arias-Pérez, J., Coronado-Medina, A., & Perdomo-Charry, G. (2022). Big data analytics capability as a mediator in the influence of open innovation on firm performance. *Journal of Strategy and Management, 15*(1), 1–15.

Campos-Blázquez, J. R., Rubio-Andrada, L., & Celemín-Pedroche, M. S. (2023). Voices from within. To what extent can internal crowdsourcing drive a change in organizational culture? *Journal of Business Research, 157*, 113618.

Cricelli, L., Grimaldi, M., & Vermicelli, S. (2022). Crowdsourcing and open innovation: A systematic literature review, an integrated framework and a research agenda. *Review of Managerial Science, 16*(5), 1269–1310.

Cricelli, L., Grimaldi, M., & Vermicelli, S. (2022). Crowdsourcing and open innovation: A systematic literature review, an integrated framework and a research agenda. *Review of Managerial Science, 16*(5), 1269–1310.

Dabić, M., Daim, T., Bogers, M. L., & Mention, A. L. (2023). The limits of open innovation: Failures, risks, and costs in open innovation practice and theory. *Technovation, 126*, 102786.

Farida, I., & Setiawan, D. (2022). Business strategies and competitive advantage: the role of performance and innovation. *Journal of Open Innovation: Technology, Place of technological based market, and Complexity, 8*(3), 163.

Gkika, E. C., Anagnostopoulos, T., Ntanos, S., & Kyriakopoulos, G. L. (2020). User preferences on cloud computing and open innovation: A case study for university employees in Greece. *Journal of Open Innovation: Technology, Place of technological based market, and Complexity, 6*(2), 41.

Jahanbakhsh Javid, N., & Amini, M. (2023). Evaluating the influence of supply chain management practice on implementation of halal agroindustry and competitive advantage for small and medium enterprises. *International Journal of Computer Science and Information Technologies, 15*, 8997–9008.

Jiang, Y., Zhang, L., & Wu, J. (2023). Evolutionary game study of crowdsourcing open innovation synergy mechanism. *Heliyon, 9*(6). PMID: 37408914

Kant, S., & Adula, M. (2024). AI Learning and Work Attitude Mediation Between Reward and Organizational Support in Ethiopia. In Gomathi Sankar, J., & David, A. (Eds.), *Generative AI for Transformational Management* (pp. 109–136). IGI Global., DOI: 10.4018/979-8-3693-5578-7.ch005

Kant, S., & Adula, M. (2024). Mediated by AI-Based Generative Re-Enforcement Learning and Work Attitude: Are Intrinsic Rewards Transforming Employee Perceived Organizational Support? In Gomathi Sankar, J., & David, A. (Eds.), *Generative AI for Transformational Management* (pp. 83–108). IGI Global., DOI: 10.4018/979-8-3693-5578-7.ch004

Kant, S., & Adula, M. (2024). Human-Machine Interaction in the Metaverse in the Context of Ethiopia. In *Impact and Potential of Machine Learning in the Metaverse* (pp. 196–212). IGI Global., DOI: 10.4018/979-8-3693-5762-0.ch008

Kant, S., & Adula, M. (2025). Integrating Gender and Indigenous Knowledge in Digital Innovations for Ethiopia's Renewable Energy Transition. In *Digital Innovations for Renewable Energy and Conservation* (pp. 167–194). IGI Global.

Kant, S., Adula, M., & Genale, M. (2025). Mediating of Smart Entrepreneurship Among Territorial Marketing on Place Branding in Ethiopia. In *Sustainable and Intelligent Territorial Marketing and Entrepreneurship* (pp. 257–284). IGI Global., DOI: 10.4018/979-8-3693-9775-6.ch009

Kant, S., Adula, M., Kumari, M., & Nimbrain, N. (2025). Role of SMEs in Greening the Economy by Mediation of Eco-Innovation in the Horn of Africa. In *Examining Green Human Resources Management and Nascent Entrepreneurship* (pp. 173–200). IGI Global., DOI: 10.4018/979-8-3693-7046-9.ch007

Karpukhina, T., Schreier, M., Janiszewski, C., & Nishikawa, H. (2024). I Didn't Win! An Overlooked Downside of Crowdsourcing?. *Journal of Interactive Place of technological based marketing, 59*(1), 42-58.

Kelleci, A., & Taşkın, E. (2020). Customer Orientation, Innovation and the Mediating Role of Crowdsourcing in Organizational Performance. *Transnational Place of technological based marketing Journal, 8*(1), 7-26.

Mishra, D., & Maheshwari, N. (2024). Crowdsourcing-based social linkage and organizational innovation competence: Knowledge transfer influenceiveness and absorptive capacity as serial mediators. *Journal of Knowledge Management*.

Niguse, T., Kant, S., & Adula, M. (2025). Mediation Effect of Customer Loyalty in Relationship Between Market Orientation, Entrepreneurial Orientation, and Firm Performance in Ethiopia. In *Leveraging AI for Effective Digital Relationship Marketing* (pp. 419–458). IGI Global., DOI: 10.4018/979-8-3693-5340-0.ch014

Palacios-Marqués, D., Gallego-Nicholls, J. F., & Guijarro-García, M. (2021). A recipe for success: Crowdsourcing, online social networks, and their influence on organizational performance. *Technological Forecasting and Social Change, 165*, 120566.

Pundziene, A., Nikou, S., & Bouwman, H. (2022). The nexus among dynamic capabilities and competitive firm performance: The mediating role of open innovation. *European Journal of Innovation Management, 25*(6), 152–177.

Schenk, E., Schaeffer, V., & Pénin, J. (2020). Blockchain and the future of open innovation intermediaries: The case of crowdsourcing platforms. In *Managing Digital Open Innovation* (pp. 401-430).

Ye, J., & Jensen, M. (2022). Influences of introducing an online community in a crowdsourcing contest platform. *Information Systems Journal, 32*(6), 1203–1230.

Yesuf, Y. M., Getahun, D. A., & Debas, A. T. (2024). Determinants of employees' creativity: Modeling the mediating role of organizational motivation to innovate. *Journal of Innovation and Entrepreneurship, 13*(1), 8.

Zhang, X., Chu, Z., Ren, L., & Xing, J. (2023). Open innovation and sustainable competitive advantage: The role of organizational learning. *Technological Forecasting and Social Change, 186*, 122114.

KEY TERMS WITH DEFINITIONS

Open Innovation: A framework that promotes companies to augment innovation processes and outcomes by combining internal resources with external knowledge's, information, and technology.

Crowdsourcing: The process of utilizing collective intelligence by asking a large number of individuals to contribute knowledge's, solutions, or feedback often via internet platforms

Competitive Advantage: characteristics that enable a business to operate better than its rivals; they are usually attained by means of special assets, skills, or tactics that manifested clients with more value.

Mediation: A statistical concept that helps explain the mechanism via which an influence arises by influencing the link among an independent variable and a dependent variable through the use of a third variable, known as a mediator.

Structural Equation Modeling (SEM): A multivariate statistical analysis method that offers a thorough approach to evaluating hypotheses by enabling the investigation of intricate interactions among latent and observable variables.

Chapter 13
A Systematic Analysis Approach of AI's Role in Enhancing Financial Decision-Making

Younes El Maaqili
https://orcid.org/0009-0009-8466-5651
Sidi Mohamed Ben Abdellah University Fez, Morocco

Mouhcine Rhouiri
https://orcid.org/0009-0007-7115-871X
Sidi Mohamed Ben Abdellah University Fez, Morocco

ABSTRACT

This paper aims to analyze the intellectual structure and research directions pertaining to about the impacts of AI on financial decision-making. A systematic bibliometric review was conducted, in which datasets were retrieved from both Scopus and Web of Science databases. After merging and applying all inclusion criteria, a final set of 235 datasets was analyzed in October 2024 using software tools provided by RStudio-Biblioshiny and IRaMuTeQ. This mirrors the intellectual structuring around the clusters in predictive modeling, risk management, and responsible finance. This research enhances a better understanding of the applications of AI and their impact on financial decision-making. These include looking at the effect of AI on ethics and transparency in the governance of financial systems. This paper contributes to new knowledge of advanced technologies integrated into finance and suggests ways to pursue further research.

INTRODUCTION

Interest in artificial intelligence (AI) applications in finance has grown exponentially in recent years, driven by AI's ability to streamline processes, enhance economic forecasting, and improve risk management strategies (Henrici & Osterrieder, 2022). AI's role in financial decision-making is transforming the field, enabling faster, more data-driven, and accurate decisions (Akour et al., 2024). While considerable progress has been witnessed in these respects, the extant body of research concerning AI applications in finance is diverse, e.g., machine learning in banking Ai notation systems, fintech, big

DOI: 10.4018/979-8-3693-9684-1.ch013

data processing, portfolio and markets prediction, and so on (Bansal et al., 2021). It epitomizes the need for systematization to bring out the priority areas, gaps, and broader implications for AI technologies in financial decision-making.

While many studies focus on specific applications of AI in portfolio management, risk assessment, and fraud detection, most of them are weak in the analysis of the framework that can be used to analyze collaborations, thematic structures, or behavioral biases that AI might reduce or maybe introduce. In their absence, the potential of AI in improving financial decision-making cannot be fully actualized, and consequently, both the theoretical and practical applications remain under-explored. Furthermore, little attention has been paid to the mapping of the evolution of knowledge in this field, which has left major questions about its intellectual structure and geographic distribution unanswered. This study will fill this gap by taking a bibliometric and lexicographic analysis approach to the role of AI in financial decision-making.

By using tools such as R-Biblioshiny and IRaMuTeQ, this study systematically analyzes the existing literature to: (1) identify priority themes in the domain; (2) analyze co-authorship networks to uncover collaborative dynamics; and (3) explore cognitive biases and decision-making methods supported by AI technologies. The analysis covers articles published between 2006 and 2024, hence providing an overall view of its growth trajectory, intellectual structure, and trends in this fast-changing field. This study takes a detailed view of how research in AI and financial decision-making has evolved by applying scientometric mapping and content analysis techniques. This systematic review also identifies the major research fronts and existing gaps, hence providing a foundation to guide future research and optimization of the implementation of AI in the financial sector. Results hold promise to further the theoretical understanding of—and practical applications yielding insight valuable to academic researchers, industry professionals, and policymakers. This paper is organized as follows: Section 2 reviews the literature on AI in financial decision-making; Section 3 describes the methodology used, including the criteria of article selection and tools used for analysis; Section 4 presents the results and discusses key findings; Section 5 summarizes the implications and suggests future research directions, together with the limitations of the study.

LITERATURE REVIEW

Artificial intelligence (AI) has seen a vertiginous growth in its use in the financial sector. it has enabled us to consider and adopt totally new approaches to decision-making, based on data analysis algorithms. this makes it possible to consider AI as a powerful tool for transforming financial practices and processes. because it enables us to analyze massive amounts of data (Bigdata) in real time, and to answer complex questions by drawing up reliable financial forecasts. A number of studies have looked at the application of AI to stock market forecasting, portfolio management, auditing and risk analysis (Ewerton & Jordão, 2024; Kumar, 2024). Machine learning models, for example, have contributed to the optimization of trading strategies and the performance of financial asset management. According to Binh, (2024), deep neural networks represent a major advance over traditional stock price forecasting models, thanks in particular to the introduction of variables such as historical data and macroeconomic variables. They would thus enable financial analysts, in real time, to monitor market developments and react to international economic shocks (Hussain et al., 2021). Despite these advances in artificial intelligence, there are still challenges ahead, such as, the transparency and reliability of the decisions made by these intelligent systems (Huang et al., 2023). Indeed, the integration of explainability techniques into AI models has become essential in order to improve their adoption and reduce bias in predictions (Lipton, 2017). Despite this, cybersecurity presents itself as a major concern, as AI systems are vulnerable to attacks that could manipulate the data or alter the models themselves.

METHODOLOGY

Research Design

This study applies the systematic and bibliometric analysis techniques to analyze the research orientations and intellectual structure regarding Artificial Intelligence's role in financial decision-making. This research follows the bibliometric analysis guidelines of Van Eck and Waltman (2017) and adheres to PRISMA steps to systematically review the evolution of literature in this domain (Page et al., 2021).

Data Collection

The data was collected in October first from to databases, Scopus and Webofscience which conclude a final data of 235 papers after the merging of the two resulting databases and applying the inclusion criteria. The following table shows the data collection stages:

Table 1. Dataset filtering and scanning

Refinement Process	Inclusion criteria	Excluded papers	Included papers
Initial search terms on Scopus	TITLE-ABS-KEY ("Decision-Making*" AND "financ*" AND ai)		**871**
Inclusion criteria	All document type; Articles written in English; 2006-2024 (2024 included) ; subject area (business, Management and Accounting - Economics, Econometrics and Finance - Social Sciences)	(589)	**282**
Initial search terms on WoS	ALL= ("Decision-Making*" AND "financ*" AND AI)		**1540**
Inclusion criteria	All document type; Articles written in English; 2006-2024 (2024 included) ; WOS Categories (Business-Business Finance-Management-Economics)	(1269)	**271**
Merging the two datasets on R			**553**
After removing duplications	Removing duplications and damaged papers	(116)	**437**
Authors final scanning	Titles and abstracts (full scanning of certain articles for more clarity)	(202)	**235**

To conduct the bibliometric analysis of the research on AI's Role in Enhancing Financial Decision-Making data analytical several analytic techniques were applied in interpreting the dataset, such as the Performance analysis, the Co-authorship network (Institutions level), the Keyword co-occurrence, and the Thematic map analysis.

Systematic Analysis Methodology

The methodology adopted in this study is based on a rigorous combination of a systematic literature review using a textual factorial analysis performed with IRaMuTeQ software, and a bibliometric study using R-Biblioshiny, the results of which we have previously presented. In this section, we present the systematic approach using factorial analysis. This approach was chosen because of its ability to provide an exhaustive overview of the subject under study, while enabling detailed exploration of emerging themes in scientific publications. The main aim of this methodology is to structure and organize the available information on the integration of AI into financial decision-making.

The methodology is structured around three interdependent stages: (1) selection of relevant articles, (2) textual factor analysis to identify recurring themes, and (3) interpretation of the results obtained to draw relevant conclusions.

The first step was to select relevant articles through a systematic search of the Scopus and WoS databases. The PRISMA methodology was adopted to guarantee the rigor and transparency of the selection process.

The inclusion criteria applied were as follows: articles explicitly discussing the role of AI in financial decision-making, written in English and published between 2006 and 2024. Publications had to come from fields such as business, management, accounting, economics and social sciences.

On the other hand, exclusion criteria eliminated articles unrelated to the application of AI to financial decision-making, non-peer-reviewed publications such as conference proceedings or reports, and articles written in languages other than English.

After applying the inclusion criteria and removing duplicates, a total of 235 articles were retained. These articles cover topics such as green finance, investment strategies, financial decision-making and carbon emissions.

Textual Factorial Analysis With IRaMuTeQ

Once the articles had been selected, the abstracts of the publications were brought together into a single textual corpus, analyzed by the IRaMuTeQ software. Indeed, based on advanced textual statistics, this software is especially good at picking up recurrent themes and conceptual relations within a corpus bulky in size. The abstracts of the 29 articles were gathered together to constitute this corpus.

This corpus was then imported into IRaMuTeQ to carry out a hierarchical top-down classification (HTC). It is a statistical method that partitions the corpus into homogeneous text segments grouped into classes according to their lexical content. Each class represents a recurring theme or sub-theme in the articles analyzed. This approach is particularly useful for identifying hidden patterns and complex conceptual structures.

In this study, HTD identified five main classes:

- one class focuses on academic research and investor behavioral trends;
- another focuses on ethical issues, social responsibility and the regulation of advanced technologies;
- a third class focuses on the impact of artificial intelligence on the digital transformation of industries;
- the fourth class explores statistical modeling techniques to assess performance and manage risk;
- and finally, the fifth-class highlights several approaches to improving the explicability and transparency of artificial intelligence models.

Figure 1. Distribution of descending hierarchical classes (DHC) in our study

Source: IRaMuTeQ release

To guarantee the robustness of the results, rigorous validation was carried out. In this study, over 70% of text segments were retained in the analyses, a threshold considered robust in similar studies. This high retention ensures that the conclusions drawn from the textual data are representative of the overall corpus. These results were then used to classify the texts into clusters (or broad classes) in order to identify the key themes addressed in articles dealing with the obstacles and opportunities associated with integrating AI into financial decision-making. The results obtained via IRaMuTeQ were then triangulated with the findings of the original studies included in the corpus. This step confirmed the consistency between the themes identified in the textual analysis and the observations made in the literature, reinforcing the validity of our conclusions.

RESULTS AND DISCUSSION

Bibliometric Review

Performance Analysis

The dataset, covering the period from 2006 to 2024, includes 235 documents sourced from 183 different outlets, reflecting a rapid growth in research on AI's role in financial decision-making, with an annual growth rate of 32.05%. The documents have an average age of 0.94 years, indicating their recent nature, and an average of 10.18 citations per document, with a total of 10,412 references. A large part of the dataset comprises 1258 Keywords Plus and 710 Author's Keywords, which highlights some of the most crucial research themes. The data set includes contributions from 795 authors, of which 28 are single-authored documents, while the average of co-authors per document is 3.58, thus indicating a moderate collaboration in co-authorship but quite low international co-authorship of 1.277%. Document types are diverse, including 73 articles, 11 books, 42 book chapters, 97 conference papers, 2 editorials, and 10 reviews, to give a multi-format view of the topic. This dataset gives a rather dynamic and collaborative picture of the field with a strong recent focus on highly cited publications.

Table 2. Descriptive characteristics

Description	*Results*
Timespan	***2006:2024***
Sources (Journals, Books, Etc)	***183***
Documents	***235***
Annual Growth Rate %	***32.05***
Document Average Age	***0.94***
Average Citations Per Doc	***10.18***
References	***10412***
DOCUMENT CONTENTS	
Keywords Plus (ID)	***1258***
Author's Keywords (DE)	***710***

continued on following page

Table 2. Continued

Description	*Results*
AUTHORS	
Authors	***795***
Authors Of Single-Authored Docs	***28***
AUTHORS COLLABORATION	
Single-Authored Docs	***30***
Co-Authors Per Doc	***3.58***
International Co-Authorships %	***1.277***
DOCUMENT TYPES	
Article	***73***
Book	***11***
Book Chapter	***42***
Conference Paper	***97***
Editorial	***2***
Review	***10***

Publication Trajectory

The figure below illustrates that from 2006 to 2024, the research trends on the role of AI in improving financial decision-making evolved gradually but substantially, with some major events helping shape the variations in publication activity over different periods. For the period between 2006 and 2014, research activity was quite low, with no more than one publication yearly. This would correspond to the nascent phase in integrating AI into financial systems, where even foundational technologies like machine learning and natural language processing were just emerging. A significant constraint in applying AI in finance was essentially linked to the limitation of computational power and a lack of large datasets. These works are the basis for current and future work but, by their nature, somewhat theoretical and conceptual. From 2015 to 2018, publication activity increases steadily, culminating in 4 publications in 2018. That growth coincides with important technological milestones—big data analytics and the cloud computing explosion—that make AI increasingly accessible for application in financial industry settings. This will also be the time algorithmic trading and robo-advisors have made their way into major financial institutions, thus fueling scholarly interest. There has been a clear year-by-year increase in research output between 2019 and 2021, from 5 in 2019 to 17 publications in 2022. Most likely, this can be explained by the tremendous development made by AI-powered tools in fraud detection, credit scoring, and predictive analytics within this period of time. The impetus for AI adoption came with the COVID-19 pandemic in 2020, when financial institutions looked for solutions that would scale and adapt to market volatility and economic uncertainty. Much of the research in this era was focused on the ethical implications of AI in finance, reflecting a wider societal discourse on responsible AI use.

Figure 2. Growth trajectory of the literature publication (n = 253 papers), 2006–2024

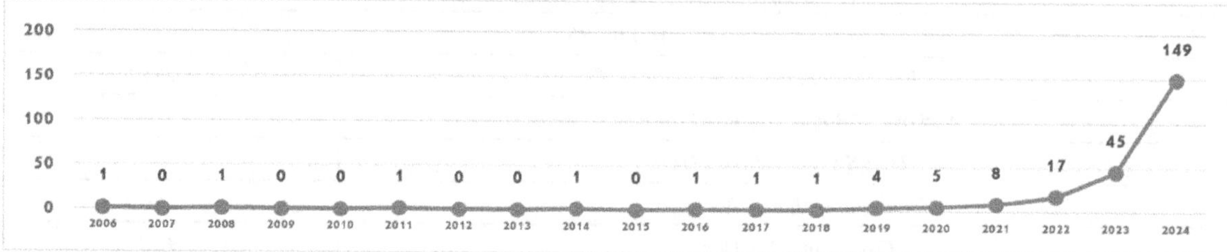

Source: Authors

Growth is most dramatic between 2023 and 2024, with a sharp jump from 45 publications in 2023 to the 149 seen in 2024, marking this period as the peak. Such an explosive increase of AI research converges to become the proliferation of AI generative models like GPT and their integration within financial systems for tasks entailing financial reporting, sentiment analysis, and strategic decisions. Furthermore, regulatory developments and frameworks in relation to AI governance within the financial sector, coupled with global initiatives to nurture fintech innovations, might have fired up academic and industry interest. Another significant focus of this period was the vast use of technologies in DeFi and blockchain-based AI systems, which further fanned the production related to research in this area.

Table 3. Top 6 countries by publication

Rank	Country	Documents	Total Citation	Average Citation
1	India	71	36	0.80
2	USA	28	98	9.80
3	China	27	46	2.20
4	United Kingdom	13	1622	162.20
5	Australia	9	143	28.60
6	Saudi Arabia	8	19	4.80

The table shows the top six countries contributing to the research on AI in terms of enhancing financial decision-making, offering insights pertaining to publication volume as well as citation impact. When looked at through the published documents, India is seen leading with 71. However, its average citation amount—0.80—exhibits limited global impact factor evidence, suggesting a much stronger focus on quantity and less on high-influence-producing work. By contrast, the United States, with 28 documents and an average citation of 9.80, has a stronger impact, meaning it is in the center of the advancement of the field. In a similar fashion, China, with 27 documents and an average citation of 2.20, has moderate engagement but less global recognition. Notably, the United Kingdom, with only 13 documents, offers an impressive average citation of 162.20; this points to the better quality and impact of research, most likely due to seminal studies. Next in line is Australia with its 9 documents and average citations of 28.60, further indicating focus on high-impact research and increasing its inroads into this field. Saudi Arabia, which has 8 documents and an average citation of 4.80, depicts increasing interest in the domain, yet with modest influence on scholarship in a global view. This could be presented as a factor that explains why nations like India and China are leaders in numbers of publications but nations like the United Kingdom, the United States, and Australia have greater academic influence.

Influential, Authors, Sources and Publications

The table 3 highlights the most influential authors in research on AI's role in financial decision-making from 2006 to 2024, based on citations and productivity. Sharma, S. leads with 5 documents and an impressive 1612 citations, though an H-index of 1 suggests the impact stems primarily from a single highly cited work. Similarly, Aarts, G., Coombs, C., Crick, T., and Duan, Y, each contributed 1 document with 1611 citations and an H-index of 1, but the implication here is the same: their influence has also emanated from just one or two seminal pieces. The pattern underlines the dependence of the field on those few transformative studies that substantially moved the discourse forward. While Sharma is more prolific, the rest share the same citation count, showing sustainable impact of seminal contributions—hence the importance of both prolific and impactful authors in developing this research.

Table 4. Ranking of 10 most cited authors between 2006 and 2024

Rank	Author	Documents	Citations	H-index
1	SHARMA S	5	1612	1
2	AARTS G	1	1611	1
3	COOMBS C	1	1611	1
4	CRICK T	1	1611	1
5	DUAN Y	1	1611	1

The author collaboration network presented in the figure below highlights the interconnected relationships between key contributors to research on AI's role in financial decision-making from 2006 to 2024. Distinct clusters represent groups of authors frequently co-authoring together, indicating thematic or methodological overlaps within their research. The orange cluster, with authors like Lundberg SM and Ribeiro MT, is a strong indicator of applied machine learning techniques and explainable AI (XAI) in financial decision-making. Their frequent collaborations underline a common interest in developing interpretable models for practical financial applications, as witnessed by their relation to other prominent authors like Breiman L, whose seminal work on random forests probably influences this group. The red cluster, where Kahneman D takes a central position, represents work on the topics of behavioral finance and psychology of decision making. Also included are such topics written by authors close to Thaler RH and Lusardi A, like cognitive biases, financial literacy, or more recently, application of psychological insights into the AI-driven financial instruments, and on the blue cluster led by Cao L. and Wang Y., representative of the effort in using big data analytics and AI in financial forecasting and risk management, much work by these authors converges to this area with new developments in algorithmic modeling, represented by their links to Chen J. and Zhang Y. in developing a technical path for data-driven strategies in finance. One would notice that Dwivedi YK comes out as a big contributor within the purple cluster, most likely due to seminal multidisciplinary studies on challenges and opportunities of AI in various industries, such as finance. A number of authors, like Belanche D, point out wider explorations in the adoption of AI and its implications on society. The green cluster seems to be about

AI applications in enterprise systems and financial technologies, centering around Wang Y. One could guess that these studies related to scalable models of AI and their possible implementation into financial ecosystems only happen through collaborations with specific researchers such as Li Y or Zhang Y.

Figure 3. Collaboration network between authors

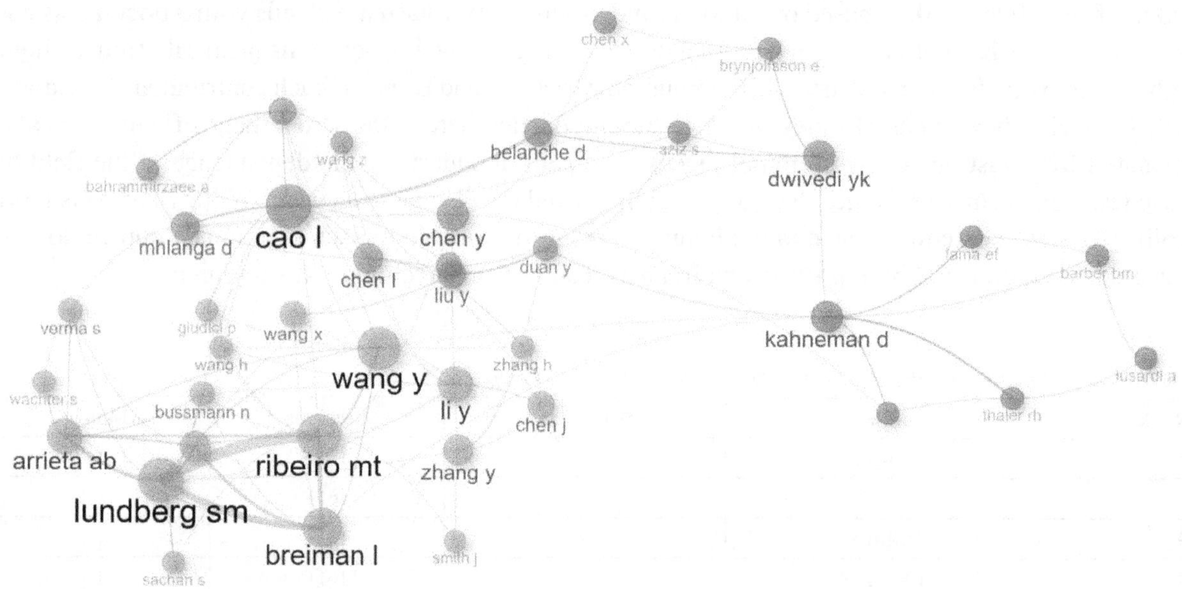

Source: Source: Biblioshiny R release

The following Table 4 aggregates the top five contributing sources that have published literature regarding the role of AI in improving financial decision-making based on the contribution in terms of the number of publications. The largest share lies with the 2024 International Conference on Knowledge Engineering and Communication Systems—ICKECS 2024, with 7 publications, obviously one major outlet for presenting research at the interface between AI and financial decision-making. Lecture Notes in Networks and Systems, with 6 publications in the series, is perhaps a primary outlet for both foundational and applied research within this field, especially focused on systems-oriented studies. Another 5 come from the ACM International Conference Proceeding Series, while a similar number come from the publication series Studies in Systems, Decision and Control for technical and decision-making frameworks developed within AI applications in finance. Lastly, the 2nd IEEE International Conference on Trends in Quantum Computing and Emerging Business Technologies—TQCEBT 2024, with 5 publications, flags the growing importance of emerging technologies such as quantum computing in the future of financial decision-making. The distribution of publications across conferences and edited volumes points to the interdisciplinary and evolving nature of research in this domain, with a lot of contributions by both the academic and professional communities.

Table 5. Top five sources' publications

Rank	Source	No of Publication
1	2024 INTERNATIONAL CONFERENCE ON KNOWLEDGE ENGINEERING AND COMMUNICATION SYSTEMS, ICKECS 2024	7
2	LECTURE NOTES IN NETWORKS AND SYSTEMS	6
3	ACM INTERNATIONAL CONFERENCE PROCEEDING SERIES	5
4	STUDIES IN SYSTEMS, DECISION AND CONTROL	5
5	TQCEBT 2024 - 2ND IEEE INTERNATIONAL CONFERENCE ON TRENDS IN QUANTUM COMPUTING AND EMERGING BUSINESS TECHNOLOGIES 2024	5

Table 5 identifies the five most cited articles on the role of AI in financial decision-making between 2006 and 2024, based on scholarly impact and thematic relevance. At the top of the list is Dwivedi et al., (2021) with an incredible 1611 citations that provides a wide-based analysis of the multidisciplinary challenges, opportunities, and research agendas for AI, hence a cornerstone in understanding the broader implications of AI across industries, including finance. Coming in at second position is the paper by Shamima et al., (2022) with 139 citations, bearing in mind the bibliometric review of artificial intelligence and machine learning in finance that helps to bring many insights toward the fast-changing environment of AI-driven financial solutions. The next on the list is Bansal et al., (2021), which has about 74 citations and touches on a very interesting topic: how to optimize AI for teamwork, in the setting of increasingly relevant collaborative financial decision-making systems. Zdravković et al., (2022), with 49 citations, discusses AI-enabled enterprise information systems for manufacturing and draws cross-industry insights that also impact financial applications. Lastly, Varma et al., (2022), with 46 citations, does a thematic analysis of the impact of FinTech on the banking sector, whereby the transformative work of AI in this arena is noted.

Table 6. Ranking of the five most cited articles between 2006 and 2024

Rank	Author	Paper	Total Citations	DOI/URL
1	Dwivedi, et al., 2021	Artificial Intelligence (AI): Multidisciplinary perspectives on emerging challenges, opportunities, and agenda for research, practice and policy	1611	https://doi.org/10.1016/j.ijinfomgt.2019.08.002
2	Shamima, et al., 2022,	Artificial intelligence and machine learning in finance: A bibliometric review	139	https://doi.org/10.1016/j.ribaf.2022.101646
3	Bansal, et al., 2021	Is the Most Accurate AI the Best Teammate? Optimizing AI for Teamwork	74	https://doi.org/10.1609/aaai.v35i13.17359
4	Zdravkoviæ, et al., 2022	AI-enabled Enterprise Information Systems for Manufacturing	49	https://doi.org/10.1080/17517575.2021.1941275
5	Varma, et al., 2022,	Thematic Analysis of Financial Technology (Fintech) Influence on the Banking Industry	46	https://doi.org/10.3390/risks10100186

These articles are significant contributions to the field, addressing challenges, opportunities, and major applications of AI in finance. Their high citation counts indicate their impact and importance in guiding future research and practice.

The map below illustrates the network of international research collaboration between authors among institutions in the field of AI's role in financial decision-making, showcasing distinct clusters and central hubs of academic activity. Each cluster represents groups of institutions collaborating frequently, reflecting shared research priorities and thematic alignment. At the center of this network lies the SRM Institute of Science and Technology, which forms the most prominent institution and acts as a central collaborative research hub. Its strong connections to the School of Information Technology and Engineering and the School of Computer Science and Engineering indicate that the multidisciplinary approach amalgamates computer science and engineering perspectives into AI-driven financial research. This centrality underscores the leadership role of SRM in fostering collaboration and advancement in the field. Lying at the heart, the green cluster is around the University of Bedfordshire and involves a large number of collaborations with Loughborough University, Swansea University, and the University of Bradford. Thus, this cluster represents the focus on recent advances in AI methodologies for applications in financial systems supported by collaboration in the UK ecosystem of researchers. The dense connections in this cluster are evidence of a well-established partnership network that produces impactful, highly cited research. On the other hand, the red cluster contains King Khalid University and Prince Sattam Bin Abdulaziz University in a smaller but significant collaboration group, most likely working on AI applications tailored for the financial systems in the Middle East. Their strong interconnection suggests regional focus and growing contributions to the global research landscape. The purple cluster, featuring Misan University and the University of Kufa, is indicative of an emerging collaboration network in the Middle East. Most likely, these institutions are building capacity and exploring region-specific challenges, thereby contributing to the diversity of global research on AI in finance.

Figure 4. Co-authorship mapping - institutions level

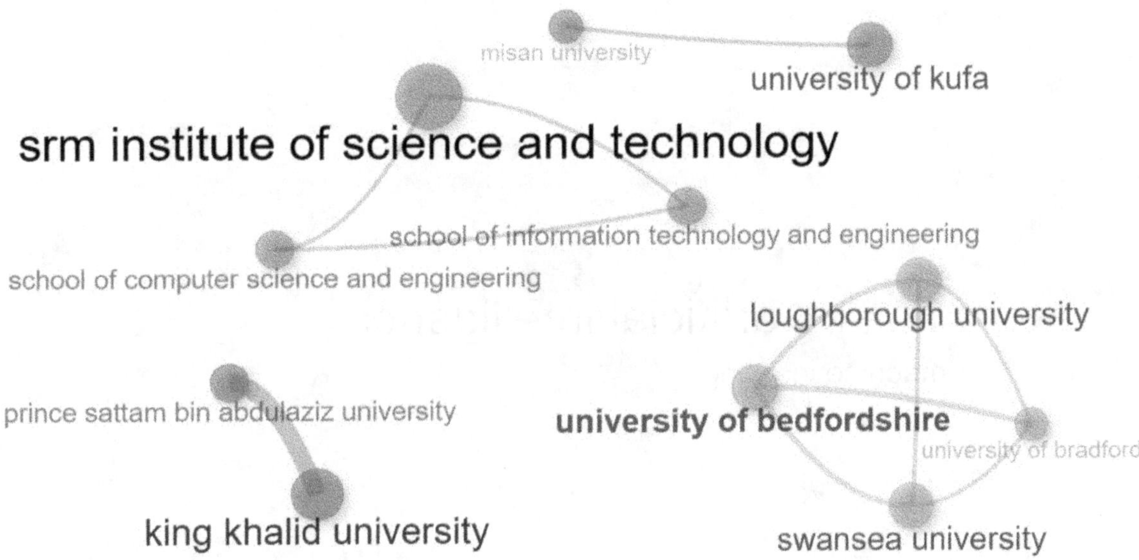

Source:: Biblioshiny R release

The figure is a confluence of both established and new institutions that are contributing to the field. The central role of the SRM Institute of Science and Technology underscores its leadership in driving international collaborations, while the strong UK-based cluster and growing contributions from the Middle East demonstrate the global and increasingly interconnected nature of research in this area. These collaborations enrich the research ecosystem and facilitate knowledge exchange with a view to advancing the development of innovative AI solutions for financial decision-making.

Research Intellectual Structure

Keywords Co-Occurrence Network

The co-occurrence network of keywords shown in Figure 4 above, related to research on the role of AI in financial decision-making presents sex clear thematic clusters. Each cluster is representative of an important research theme within the field, reflecting the diverse applications and a point of intersection of AI in finance. These clusters are described below in great detail in Table 7.

Figure 5. Keywords co-occurrence network

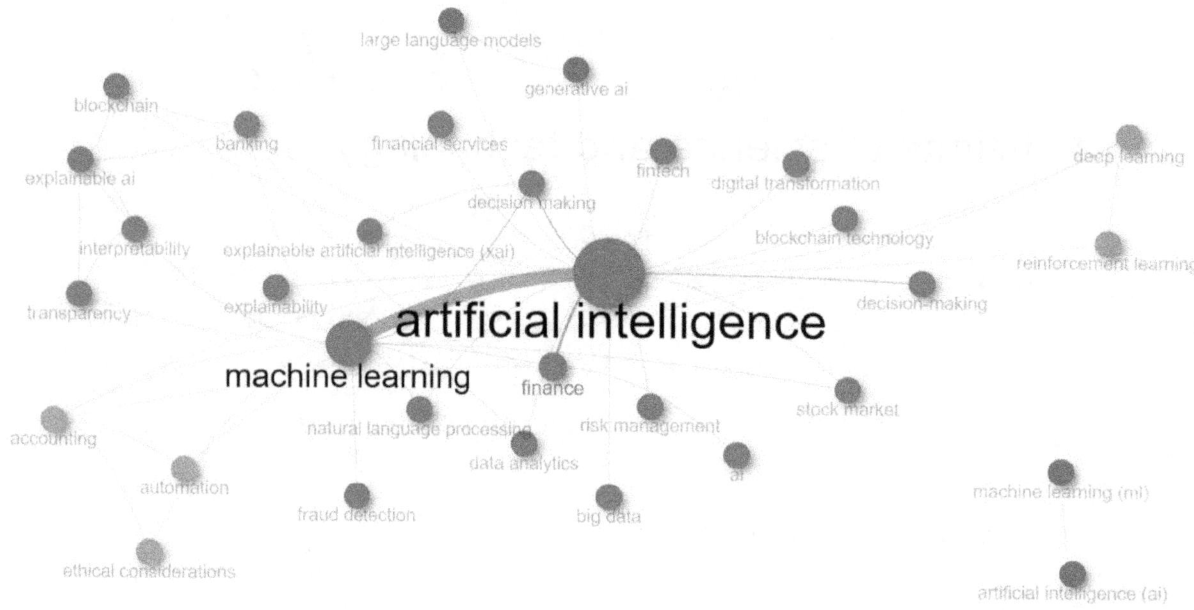

Source: Biblioshiny R release

Table 7. Keyword Co-Occurrence network

Cluster Number	Cluster Label	Key Themes	Studies' examples
Cluster 1 (Red)	AI-Driven Financial Systems	Centralized around artificial intelligence and machine learning, this cluster explores applications in decision-making, risk management, fintech, and data analytics.	(Dwivedi et al., 2021) ; (Shamima et al., 2022)
Cluster 2 (Blue)	Blockchain and Explainable AI	Focuses on blockchain technology, explainable AI, and interpretability, with applications in transparency, banking, and ethical considerations.	(Arrieta et al., 2020); (Chen et al., 2022)
Cluster 3 (Orange)	Ethical and Automation-Driven Finance	Examines the intersection of automation, accounting, and ethical considerations in AI-based financial systems.	(Adarsh et al., 2023) (Ribeiro-Navarrete et al., 2021)
Cluster 4 (Brown)	Emerging AI Models in Finance	Highlights the role of large language models, generative AI, and digital transformation in evolving financial services and decision-making processes.	(Zdravkoviæ et al., 2022); (Bansal et al., 2021)
Cluster 5 (Green)	Deep Learning and Reinforcement Learning	Focuses on deep learning and reinforcement learning methodologies applied in financial markets, such as stock market predictions.	(Zhang et.al., 2024); (Li et al., 2024)
Cluster 6 (Purple)	Machine Learning and IA	Explores interactions between AI and machine learning and their synergy in automation, decision-making and predictive applications.	(Setty et al., 2024); (Shamima et al., 2022)

Source: Authors

Thematic Map

The following thematic map classifies the research themes into four clusters: Niche; emerging or declining; Motor, and Basic themes, which represent the centrality-that is, the relevance and density or development of the themes. This map depicts the maturity and importance of the themes in this domain of research.

Figure 6. Thematic map

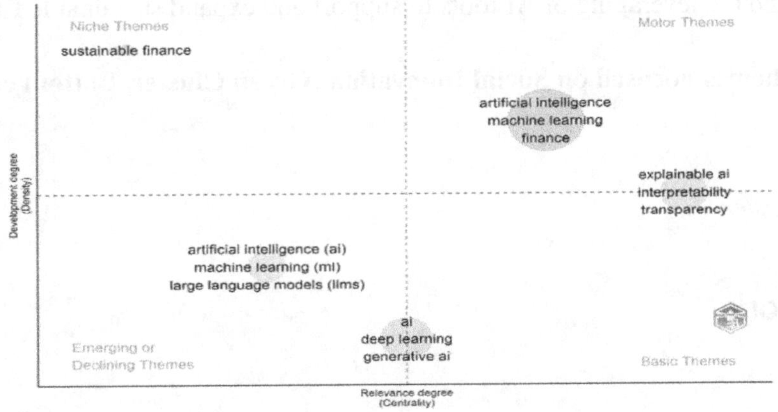

Source: Biblioshiny R release

- **Niche Theme (Blue Cluster, Top Left):**

Figure 7. Blue cluster

This Blue Cluster represents a Niche Theme that focuses on sustainable finance, has 3 occurrences, and, however, has remained less central within the overall AI application in finance network. This cluster connects the subtopics of green finance, ESG investing, and impact investing to the main attributes of ethical and sustainable financial practices through a high betweenness centrality of 1,517.694. The themes of investor behavior, behavioral finance, and neuroeconomics offer a behavioral perspective to the concept of sustainable finance by highlighting the cognitive and psychological drivers underlying responsible investment decisions. Bibliometric analysis furthermore uncovers a methodological nature of the research landscape in this domain. At the moment, peripheral in the AI-finance research network, it is very well positioned for greater recognition in the near future with increased focus on global sustainability issues and the leveraging of AI tools to support and expand sustainable finance initiatives.

- **Emerging Themes Focused on Social Innovation (Green Cluster, Bottom center):**

Figure 8. Green cluster

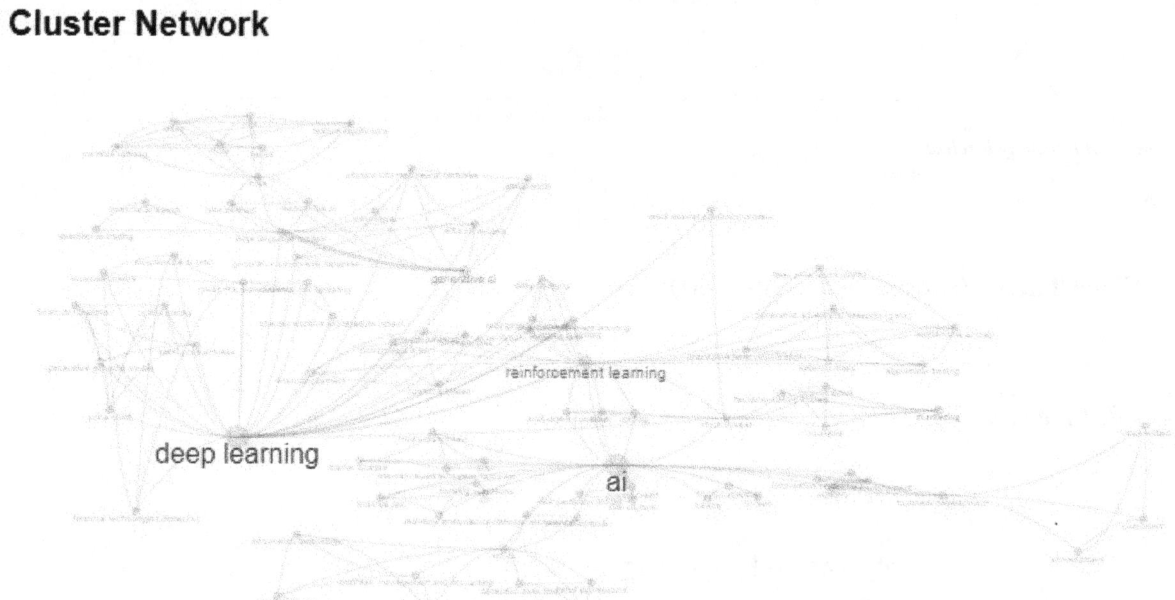

The Green Cluster represents the emergent themes that are focused on developing research at the intersection of AI and financial decision-making. In the center of the discussion in this cluster is AI, with 10 occurrences and a betweenness centrality of 15,075.469, as the foundational element which links connected topics. Deep learning, with 9 occurrences, 8,353.211, plays an essential role by embracing AI-driven solution improvements. On the other hand, emerging technologies such as generative AI, with 5 occurrences and 5,592.785, and reinforcement learning, with 5 occurrences and 5,221.774, are promising a transformative change in predictive modeling and autonomous decision-making systems. With 4 occurrences, 2,637.976, large language models allow the use of natural language processing for financial sentiment analysis and reporting. Lastly, themes like the stock market, 4 occurrences, 1,474.218, underlie the use of AI in optimizing trading strategies, while ethics, 3 occurrences, 1,237.882, reflect the increasing discussion of the responsible deployment of AI. This enables the vision of how dynamic and innovative a trajectory the research of AI in finance is taking socially impactful and technologically developed financial solutions.

- **Highly Relevant Emerging Themes (Gray Cluster, Bottom Left):**

Figure 9. Gray cluster

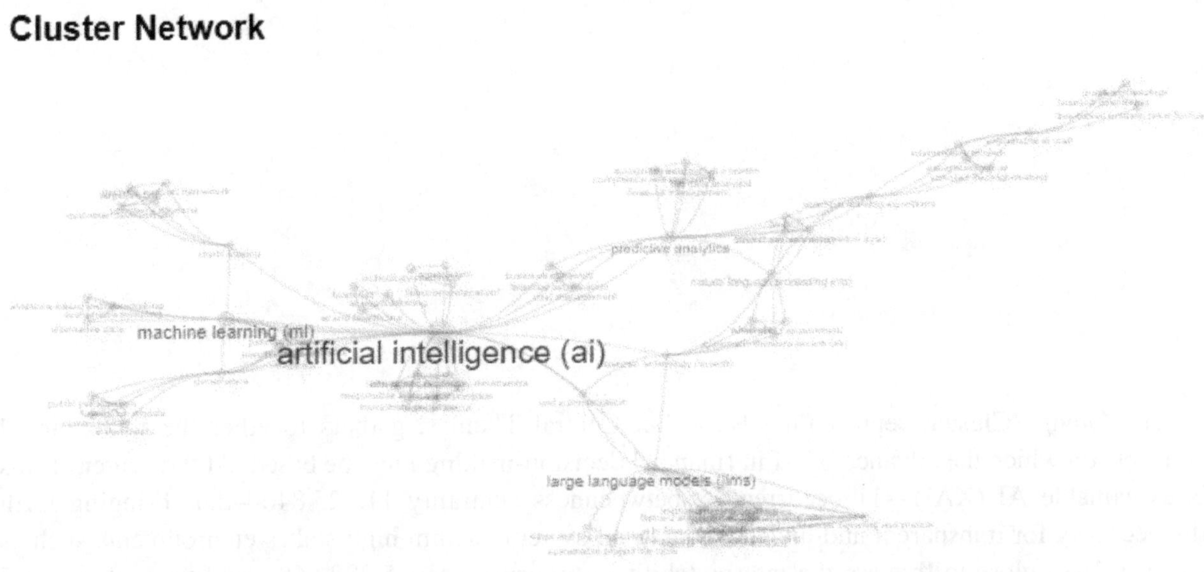

The Gray Cluster: Highly Relevant Emerging Themes. This cluster revolves around core ideas that shape the role of AI in financial decision-making. At the center of this lies artificial intelligence, with 7 occurrences and a betweenness centrality of 4,424.631 as the central pillar of key themes. Supporting this is the occurrence of Machine Learning 4 times with a betweenness centrality of 2,102.150, underlying its role as a critical technical framework for AI-driven innovations within finance. More recent are large language models with 3 occurrences at 6,468.473, showing an important role for natural language processing in applications for sentiment analysis, report generation, and customer engagement. Also, predictive analytics with 3 occurrences and 2,617.256 points out the use of AI in improving the accuracy of forecasting in financial markets and risk management. The clustering encapsulates the integration of advanced AI technologies with more practical applications in finance and marks the tectonic shift toward innovation and impact in the financial sector.

- **Basic but Central Themes (Orange Cluster, Bottom Right):**

Figure 10. Orange cluster

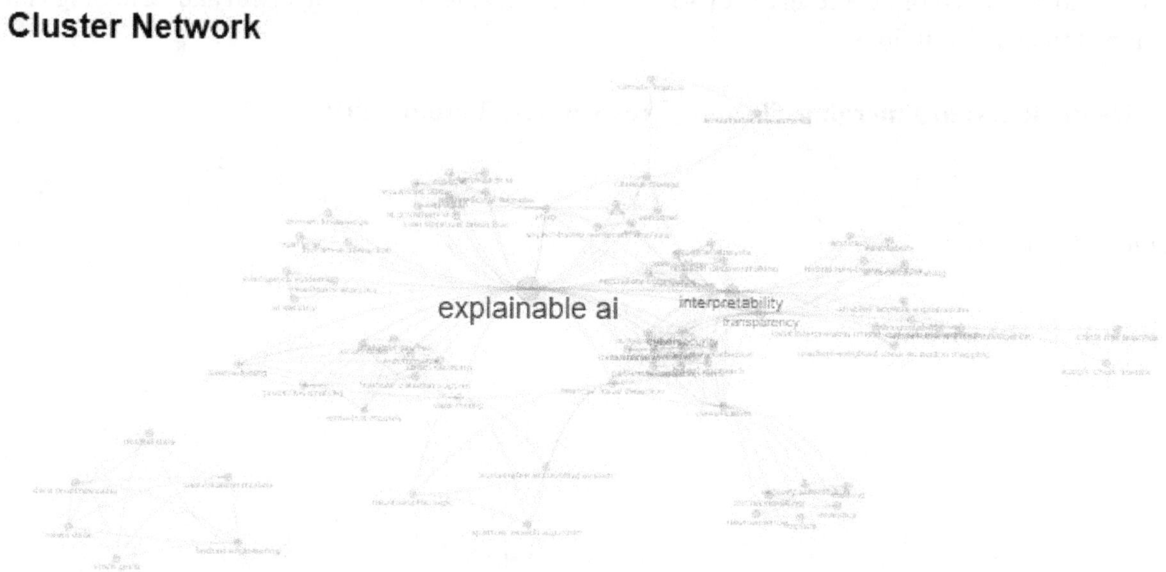

The Orange Cluster, representing Basic but Central Themes, gathers together the foundational concepts on which the advance of AI in financial decision-making must be based. At the center of this is explainable AI (XAI)—11 occurrences, betweenness centrality 11,725.840—thus bringing forth the necessity for transparent and understandable AI systems within high-stakes environments such as finance. Very close to this are the interpretability—6 occurrences, 5,398.668—and transparency—5 occurrences, 4,024.074—of the AI model in use, which must be ensured for ethical and trustworthy AI adoption. Underpinning these concepts, cybersecurity—4 occurrences, 4,698.666—highlights the role of AI in the protection of financial systems; climate change—3 occurrences, 6,846.018—demonstrates AI in sustainability-focused financial strategies. Also, explainable artificial intelligence (3 occurrences, 2,303.742) underlines the trend of making AI systems more user-friendly and accountable. This cluster emphasizes explainability, transparency, and ethical considerations as the foreground factors in driving integration of AI in financial systems that would drive trust and wider adoption.

- **Motor Themes (Red Cluster, Top Right):**

Figure 11. Red cluster

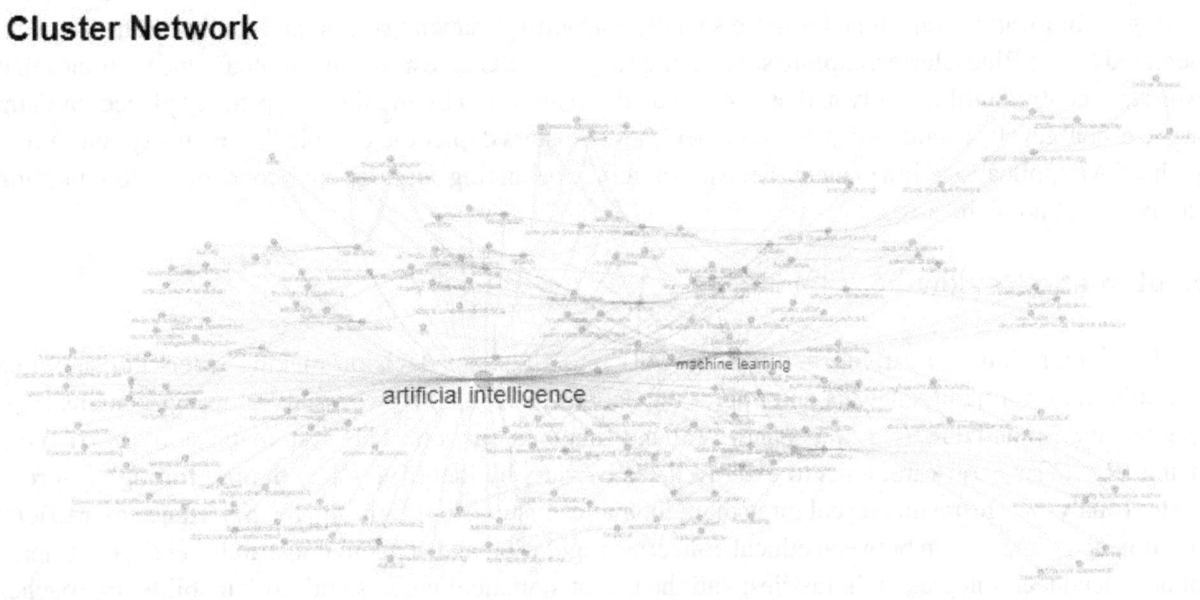

The Motor Themes represented by the red cluster in the thematic map highlight the pivotal concepts driving research on AI's role in financial decision-making. With core terms such as artificial intelligence (73 occurrences), machine learning (38 occurrences), finance (17 occurrences), and decision-making (16 occurrences), this cluster underscores the transformative integration of AI technologies into financial systems. Key themes include the application of AI for enhanced decision-making, risk management, and operational efficiency, with terms like banking, fintech, and blockchain pointing to its practical adoption across financial ecosystems. Emerging topics such as natural language processing, big data, and data analytics reflect the critical role of data-driven insights, while concepts like digital transformation, ethical considerations, and explainable AI (XAI) emphasize the growing demand for transparency, fairness, and accountability in AI applications. Practical focuses on fraud detection, risk assessment, and financial services demonstrate the field's relevance to safeguarding and optimizing financial operations. This cluster's high relevance and strong development solidify its status as a "motor theme," driving both academic innovation and practical advancements in financial decision-making.

The AI-related thematic map of financial decision-making characterizes the field based on its categorization into five distinguishable clusters. Motor themes, such as the Red Cluster, represent present-day driving forces in current research, including crucial notions in the areas of AI, machine learning, finance, and decision-making; the latter is of great importance to be applied in risk management and improvement of operational flows in fraud detection. These are the most elaborated topics and those that lie closest to the center. Underpinning these basic but central themes are the foundational concepts of explainable

AI, interpretability, transparency, and ethical considerations, illustrated by the Orange Cluster, critical to developing trust and accountability in the adoption of AI. Lastly, Highly Relevant Emerging Themes in the Gray Cluster entail leading-edge topics such as large language models, predictive analytics, and natural language processing with an emphasis on their transformative potential for customer engagement and market forecasting. Emerging Themes Focused on Social Innovation Under the umbrella of the Green Cluster, new methodologies linked to deep learning, generative AI, and reinforcement learning are setting an innovation trajectory for more socially impactful financial solutions. Finally, Niche Themes, depicted by the Blue Cluster, explore sustainable finance, ESG investing, and green finance—topics that were less central until recently and are now brought to attention by the force of priority placed on them at the global level: sustainability. Put together, these clusters depict the complexity, maturity, and future path of AI applications in financial decision-making, balancing foundational concepts with emerging innovations and niche areas.

Systematic Review

The integration of artificial intelligence (AI) into financial decision-making offers considerable potential for optimizing analysis and improving economic results. However, its adoption remains fragmented and limited due to various behavioral and financial barriers. This systematic study, carried out using IRaMuTeQ software, aims to explore these barriers by identifying key themes through rigorous textual analysis. The results reveal three main thematic clusters, highlighting the importance of artificial intelligence's interaction between ethical concerns, regulation and academic research trends; the impact of advanced technologies on industries; and the use of statistical models and explainability approaches in intelligent systems, with a focus on decision-making, risk assessment and algorithm transparency.

Group 1: Ethics And Research In Technological Innovation And Investment

Core Theme: Ethics, Societal Impact And Applied Research In Innovation And Investment

The first group, made up of class 3 (Green, 21.6%) and class 4 (Blue, 11.9%). This group explores the interplay between ethical concerns, regulation and trends in academic research, focusing on their implications for public policy and investment choices in fields such as artificial intelligence (AI) and finance. The results show that ethical and regulatory issues, as well as their societal impact, are at the heart of this category's concerns. Keywords from Class 4 (Blue) emphasize notions such as responsibility, ethics, compliance, transparency and confidentiality, highlighting the need for proactive regulation of advanced technologies such as AI. For example, (Floridi & Cowls, 2019) highlight the principles of trustworthy AI, focusing on transparency, fairness and protection of personal data, while emphasizing the role of public policy in establishing robust regulatory frameworks.

In parallel, Class 3 (Green) highlights concepts related to academic research, including the analysis of investor behavior, economic trends and the impact of political choices on investments. According to (Shiller, 2017), investor behavior is often influenced by psychological factors and economic uncertainties, particularly in contexts linked to climate issues. Furthermore, studies such as those by (Binns, 2018) on algorithmic fairness highlight the tensions between innovation and regulation in sectors such as finance, where algorithmic ethics play a crucial role in avoiding decision-making bias. This group therefore highlights the need to reconcile technological innovation and ethics while fostering relevant academic research to guide strategic investment choices and public policy.

Discussion of these results shows that the importance of ethics in emerging technologies, such as AI, is well established in the literature (Floridi & Cowls, 2019). Indeed, these technologies pose dilemmas related to privacy, algorithmic biases, and societal impacts that require proactive regulation. The literature also notes that transparency and accountability can increase stakeholder trust in technological innovations (Binns, 2018). What's more, it has effects on public policy and, by extension, the strategy of investments. An illustrative example is in behavioral finance studies that evidenced how investment trends follow issues such as climate change along with related regulation (Barberis, 2018). The regulation of AI technologies in the finance and health care sectors may affect decisions by investors since it will enable only responsible practices (Mittelstadt et al., 2016). Research on investor behavior can also give indications for sustainable financial policies amid environmental challenges.

Group 2: Digital Transformation and the Impact Of Advanced Technologies On Industries

Central Theme: Advanced Technologies And The Digital Transformation Of Industrial Sectors:

The second group is made up of class 5 (Violet, 30.1%). This group focuses on the effects of digital transformation and advanced technologies, such as artificial intelligence (AI), cloud computing and the Internet of Things (IoT), on various industrial sectors, including healthcare, agriculture and finance. The results show that these technologies are driving automation and innovation, profoundly transforming industrial processes and business models. Class 5 keywords (Violet) highlight concepts such as data management, efficiency, digitalization and competitiveness, underlining the importance of these technologies in reinventing economic sectors. Discussion of these findings shows that digital technologies are crucial levers for transforming industries, enabling improvements in operational efficiency and competitiveness (Brynjolfsson & McAfee, 2014). Lee & Lee, (2015) have shown how IoT improves resource management in agriculture by providing real-time data. Similarly, in the healthcare sector, AI is being used to automate medical diagnosis and treatment, improving access to care (Topol, 2019). Similarly, IoT in agriculture is improving productivity through optimized resource management (Wolfert et al., 2017). These studies illustrate how digital technologies act as catalysts for innovation, increasing productivity and competitiveness in several sectors.

However, these technological advances raise challenges related to data security and risk management. It is therefore crucial for companies to adopt a balanced digital strategy, maximizing benefits while minimizing negative impacts. One example of the application of these technologies is the use of AI for predictive analytics in the medical field, reducing costs while increasing diagnostic accuracy. In addition, the adoption of IoT sensors in agriculture to monitor weather conditions and optimize yields shows how these technologies can transform industrial practices (Wolfert et al., 2017).

Group 3: Modeling, Interpretation And Evaluation In Intelligent Systems

Central Theme: Modeling, Interpretation And Evaluation Of Performance In Intelligent Systems And Risk Analysis

The second group is composed of Class 2 (Gray, 20.6%) and Class 1 (Red, 15.8%). The results bring out that the two classes of this group are focused on statistical models and techniques of explainability (Class 2) and performance evaluation and risk analysis tools (Class 1). More specifically, Class 2 (Gray) includes such keywords as XAI, deep learning, and interpretability. These terms, together with the work by Ribeiro et al., (2016), underline the need for transparency and understanding of AI algorithms, which are being adopted in very critical sectors like healthcare and finance. By contrast, Class 1 (Red) includes terms such as SVM models, regression, and prediction accuracy—all those terms that emphasize the application of statistical models in estimating risks and improving decision making. It also provides ways of system performance assessment, including the use of random forests and support vector machines, for the reduction of bias and variance in predictions—as demonstrated by Breiman, (2001), while Cortes & Vapnik, (1995) point out the stability of SVMs for applications running from classification to medical diagnosis. These are tools for risk analysis and outcome prediction in many fields. For example, the combination of explainable models with powerful statistical tools, as conducted by Lundberg & Lee, (2017), contributes to the performance of intelligent systems and ensures transparency and reliability.

The discussion of these findings by relating them to the literature strengthens their validity. In fact, AI systems, particularly those based on deep learning, are usually perceived as black boxes, which seriously limits their adoption in environments requiring high trust (Rudin, 2019). XAI approaches make these models more interpretable and transparent, increasing their usefulness in decision-making (Doshi-Velez & Kim, 2017). In the same period, there has been a wide application of statistical techniques in the area of performance evaluation and risk management with regard to the use of SVMs and random forests in the financial sector (Hastie et al., 2001). In practical application, XAI techniques can be applied in explaining the decisions made by credit prediction models, which increases user confidence in the banking sector (Doshi-Velez & Kim, 2017). Again, statistical modeling in predicting defaults minimizes financial risk. The examples show how statistical models and explainability techniques are able to transform decision-making in critical contexts. This team thus demonstrates the significance of interpretability and rigorous modeling in the optimization of intelligent systems to ensure their transparency and effectiveness.

Approaching The Findings From The Bibliometric And Systematic Review

The results of the bibliometric analysis and the systematic study on the role of artificial intelligence (AI) in financial decision-making, although approaching the subject from different angles, highlight similar themes but from different perspectives. These two approaches converge around the transformation of finance thanks to AI, while highlighting the ethical, technological and operational issues associated with its integration.

Regulation, Ethics And Transparency

One of the most obvious similarities between the results of the bibliometric analysis and the systematic study lies in the importance of ethics, regulation and transparency in the use of AI in finance. Indeed, the bibliometric analysis (Orange Cluster) highlights concepts such as AI explainability (XAI), interpretability, and data security, considered fundamental to ensuring ethics and accountability in the use of AI (Floridi & Cowls, 2022). Similarly, the systematic review also emphasizes the need for proactive regulation of advanced technologies to avoid algorithmic bias and protect personal data (Díaz-Rodríguez et al., 2023). Furthermore, both findings agree on the importance of regulation and transparency to avoid the risks of irresponsible use of AI, particularly in sensitive sectors such as finance, where decisions can affect millions of people. As such, several works have highlighted the need for control mechanisms to ensure the reliability and ethics of intelligent systems (Díaz-Rodríguez et al., 2023; Floridi & Cowls, 2022; Shneiderman, 2020). Thus, these convergences between the two analyses reinforce the idea that AI, while a promising technology, requires robust ethical and regulatory frameworks to ensure its responsible and fair use in the financial sector.

Emerging Technologies And Digital Transformation

Bibliometric analysis (Green Cluster) highlights emerging technologies such as deep learning, reinforcement learning, and large-scale language models (LLMs), which are at the heart of innovation in financial processes (Hadi et al., 2024; Wu et al., 2023). Similarly, Group 2 of the systematic review focuses on the impact of digital transformation via technologies such as AI, cloud computing and IoT in sectors such as finance. These technologies facilitate increased automation, better resource management, and process optimization (Kumar, 2024; James, 2021). A key point of convergence between the two studies is the recognition that AI and its associated technologies are profoundly transforming the financial sector. They enable more accurate forecasting models, optimized risk management, and increased operational efficiency. The implementation of these technologies in the financial sectors is seen as a response to the contemporary challenges of competitiveness and innovation.

Utilize Models To Assess And Manage The Risks

These are the major results of the bibliometric analysis—Gray Cluster—outlining the use of such tools as machine learning and language models in improving financial forecasting, risk assessment, and portfolio management (Lundberg & Lee, 2017). Equally, a systematic review conducted by Group 3 has noted the explicability of AI systems and the application of more sophisticated statistical tools such as random forests and support vector machines (SVMs) in the financial risk analysis area ((Bunker & Thabtah, 2019). Thus, both views converge on the fact that AI, with its sophisticated statistical models and advanced tools, allows for superior risk assessment and hence provides much more informed decision-making. The integration of techniques such as algorithm explicability and predictive models will thus increase the reliability and transparency of financial decisions, increasing the confidence of stakeholders accordingly (Lundberg & Lee, 2017).

Focus On Sustainability And Social Impact

The bibliometric analysis—Blue Cluster—emphasizes the increasing importance of sustainability and socially responsible investment (SRI) in AI research on finance, especially through the integration of ESG—Environment, Social, Governance—criteria and green investments (Varsha et al., 2024). Similarly, the systematic review also echoes this theme by showing how climate and sustainability concerns inform investment choices and decision-making with regard to the social impact of investments (Floridi & Cowls, 2022). Both results converge to show that finance must evolve in a way that will integrate sustainable and social considerations. AI has a critical role in the management of these concerns through enabling more responsible investments and helping to create financial strategies that integrate environmental and social issues.

The key messages arising from this bibliometric analysis and systematic review converge on some essential points relating to the issue of how AI impinges on financial decision-making. Many approaches here illustrated in this area converge on issues such as ethics, digital transformation, risk assessment, and sustainability, depicting a convergence between theoretical and practical issues revolving around AI in finance. Regulation and transparency are imperatives for ethical and proper use of these technologies—especially in such a sensitive sector as finance.

CONCLUSION AND FUTURE RESEARCH DIRECTIONS

This chapter undertakes a bibliometric study and systematic review to make an in-depth analysis of the role artificial intelligence can play in financial decision-making. It identifies main thematic clusters characterizing the AI-finance research landscape and underlines the transformative impact of technologies on financial systems. These clusters bring into focus the integration of AI in predictive modeling, risk management, and responsible finance, as well as challenges arising from ethical concerns, regulation, and transparency. Taken together, the findings suggest that AI has great potential to improve financial decision-making processes, operational efficiency, and promote sustainability in finance.

Implications

Theoretical Implications

The theoretical contributions of this research put into focus the evolving role of AI in finance. It will also give them insights into areas in which AI is making the greatest impact, such as risk management, financial forecasting, and responsible investing. This research thereby gives insight into how AI technologies are related to financial decision-making, covering how AI can improve accuracy and efficiency in financial processes. It also highlights the ethical issues, transparency, and regulation of AI technologies to ensure that AI is applied responsibly and effectively in sensitive environments such as finance.

Practical Implications

The practical implications of this study are manyfold, targeting both policymakers and practitioners. For policymakers, the findings suggest a focus on developing policies and regulatory frameworks that can guarantee responsible adoption of AI in the financial sector. This may include developing clear guidelines on data privacy, transparency, and algorithmic accountability in reducing bias and ensuring fairness in AI-based financial decision-making processes. Decision-makers should also consider integrating ESG (Environment, Social, Governance) criteria into AI applications for sustainable and responsible investments. Practitioners, financial institutions, and professions can leverage AI technologies to enhance decision processes, raise operational efficiency, and better manage financial risks. Practitioners should adopt explainable AI models (XAI) and transparency to ensure that decisions made by AI are trusted and accountable. Besides using AI tools for predictive analytics and risk management, such a move will enable the practitioner to make more informed and timely decisions toward a better financial outcome.

Future Research Prospects

Based on the thematic map, the five identified clusters and the systematic review's findings, several research directions could be put forward with a view to further developing the field of AI in financial decision-making for future research prospects. In this regards, future research needs to focus on the development of ethical and regulatory frameworks with regard to AI in finance. For example, studying how AI can ensure financial inclusion, reduce bias in financial services, and protect consumers' rights within an AI-based financial system.

Second, because sustainability and ESG criteria are becoming significant in financial decision-making, future research may study how to apply AI to ESG considerations within an investment strategy, corporate governance, and risk management perspective. Third, Explainable AI Models (XAI) can be developed and used to bring transparency in AI systems deployed in highly critical sectors such as rating credit, fraud detection, and portfolio management. Lastly, it would also be relevant for future research to center on how AI technologies influence investor behavior, in particular, within a behavioral finance framework. Knowing how AI modifies or influences cognitive biases and decision patterns can bring useful insights to better improve the investment strategies of AI investors.

Limitations

There are a number of limitations of this study that future studies could address. This study relies on bibliometric and systematic analysis of existing work and therefore runs the risk of overlooking potentially more recent developments or niche areas in this fast-developing field of AI in finance. Further, while this study identifies several key thematic clusters, it still does not fully explore these interrelations between themes and could go deeper in synthesizing insights on how to integrate AI into the several subfields of finance. Lastly, this research is based on secondary data, and it is not possible to show the empirical evidence on practical applications and actual impact of AI in financial decision-making. Future research needs to consider empirical studies, case analyses, and longitudinal data to fill these gaps and provide a more holistic view of the topic.

REFERENCES

Adarsh, R., Pillai, R. H., Krishnamurthy, A., & Bi, A. (2023). Innovative Business Research in Finance and Marketing System Based on Ethically Governed Artificial Intelligence. In *Proceedings of 8th IEEE International Conference on Science, Technology, Engineering and Mathematics, ICONSTEM 2023*. Institute of Electrical and Electronics Engineers Inc. DOI: 10.1109/ICONSTEM56934.2023.10142836

Akour, I., Alzyoud, M., Alquqa, E. K., Tariq, E., Alzboun, N., Al-Hawary, S. I. S., & Alshurideh, M. T. (2024). Artificial intelligence and financial decisions: Empirical evidence from developing economies. *International Journal of Data and Network Science*, *8*(1), 101–108. DOI: 10.5267/j.ijdns.2023.10.013

Bansal, G., Nushi, B., Kamar, E., Horvitz, E., & Weld, D. S. (2021). Is the Most Accurate AI the Best Teammate? Optimizing AI for Teamwork. In *35th AAAI Conference on Artificial Intelligence, AAAI 2021* (Vol. 13A, pp. 11405–11414). Association for the Advancement of Artificial Intelligence. https://www.scopus.com/inward/record.uri?eid=2-s2.0-85130010234&partnerID=40&md5=a709626aba1d3e88fcea1680ed2c9558

Barberis, N. (2018). Psychology-Based Models of Asset Prices and Trading Volume. In *Handbook of Behavioral Economics: Applications and Foundations 1* (Vol. 1, pp. 79–175). Elsevier. DOI: 10.1016/bs.hesbe.2018.07.001

Binh, N. T. T. (2024). An application of artificial neural networks in corporate social responsibility decision making. In *Intelligent Systems in Accounting, Finance and Management* (Vol. 31, Issue 1). John Wiley and Sons Inc. DOI: 10.1002/isaf.1542

Binns, R. (2018). Fairness in Machine Learning: Lessons from Political Philosophy. *Proceedings of Machine Learning Research*, *81*, 1–18.

Breiman, L. (2001). Random Forests. *Machine Learning*, *45*(1), 5–32. DOI: 10.1023/A:1010933404324

Brynjolfsson, E., & McAfee, A. (2014). *The second machine age: Work, progress, and prosperity in a time of brilliant technologies*. W. W. Norton & Company.

Bunker, R. P., & Thabtah, F. (2019). A machine learning framework for sport result prediction. *Applied Computing and Informatics*, *15*(1), 27–33. DOI: 10.1016/j.aci.2017.09.005

Chen, Y., Albert, L. J., & Jensen, S. (2022). Innovation farm: Teaching artificial intelligence through gamified social entrepreneurship in an introductory MIS course*. *Decision Sciences Journal of Innovative Education, 20*(1), 43–56. *Scopus.* Advance online publication. DOI: 10.1111/dsji.12253

Cortes, C., & Vapnik, V. (1995). Support-vector networks. *Machine Learning*, *20*(3), 273–297. DOI: 10.1007/BF00994018

Díaz-Rodríguez, N., Del Ser, J., Coeckelbergh, M., López De Prado, M., Herrera-Viedma, E., & Herrera, F. (2023). Connecting the dots in trustworthy Artificial Intelligence: From AI principles, ethics, and key requirements to responsible AI systems and regulation. *Information Fusion*, *99*, 101896. DOI: 10.1016/j.inffus.2023.101896

Doshi-Velez, F., & Kim, B. (2017). *Towards A Rigorous Science of Interpretable Machine Learning* (arXiv:1702.08608). arXiv. https://doi.org//arXiv.1702.08608DOI: 10.48550

Dwivedi, Y. K., Hughes, L., Ismagilova, E., Aarts, G., Coombs, C., Crick, T., Duan, Y., Dwivedi, R., Edwards, J., Eirug, A., Galanos, V., Ilavarasan, P. V., Janssen, M., Jones, P., Kar, A. K., Kizgin, H., Kronemann, B., Lal, B., Lucini, B., . . . Williams, M. D. (2021). Artificial Intelligence (AI): Multidisciplinary perspectives on emerging challenges, opportunities, and agenda for research, practice and policy. In *International Journal of Information Management* (Vol. 57). Elsevier Ltd. DOI: 10.1016/j.ijinfomgt.2019.08.002

Ewerton, A. A., & Jordão, R. V. D. (2024). The role of artificial intelligence in the decision-making process: A study on the financial analysis and movement forecasting of the world's largest stock exchanges. In *Management Decision*. Emerald Publishing., DOI: 10.1108/MD-09-2023-1625

Floridi, L., & Cowls, J. (2019). A Unified Framework of Five Principles for AI in Society. *Harvard Data Science Review*. Advance online publication. DOI: 10.1162/99608f92.8cd550d1

Floridi, L., & Cowls, J. (2022). A Unified Framework of Five Principles for AI in Society. In *Machine Learning and the City* (pp. 535–545). John Wiley & Sons, Ltd., DOI: 10.1002/9781119815075.ch45

Hadi, M. U., Tashi, Q. A., Shah, A., Qureshi, R., Muneer, A., Irfan, M., Zafar, A., Shaikh, M. B., Akhtar, N., Wu, J., Mirjalili, S., & Shah, M. (2024). *Large Language Models: A Comprehensive Survey of its Applications, Challenges, Limitations, and Future Prospects*. DOI: 10.36227/techrxiv.23589741.v6

Hastie, T., Friedman, J., & Tibshirani, R. (2001). *The Elements of Statistical Learning*. Springer New York., DOI: 10.1007/978-0-387-21606-5

Henrici, A., & Osterrieder, J. (2022). Editorial: Artificial intelligence in finance and industry: Highlights from 6 European COST conferences. In *Frontiers in Artificial Intelligence* (Vol. 5). Frontiers Media S.A. DOI: 10.3389/frai.2022.1007074

Huang, C., Zhang, Z., Mao, B., & Yao, X. (2023). An Overview of Artificial Intelligence Ethics. *IEEE Transactions on Artificial Intelligence*, *4*(4), 799–819. DOI: 10.1109/TAI.2022.3194503

Hussain, A., Tahir, A., Hussain, Z., Sheikh, Z., Gogate, M., Dashtipour, K., Ali, A., & Sheikh, A. (2021). Artificial Intelligence-Enabled Analysis of Public Attitudes on Facebook and Twitter Toward COVID-19 Vaccines in the United Kingdom and the United States: Observational Study. *Journal of Medical Internet Research*, *23*(4), e26627. Advance online publication. DOI: 10.2196/26627 PMID: 33724919

James, T. (2021). Blockchain and Artificial Intelligence: The World Rewired. In *Blockchain and Artificial Intelligence: The World Rewired*. De Gruyter. DOI: 10.1515/9783110664454

Kumar, R. N. (2024). Impact of AI-Powered Investment Algorithms on Market Efficiency. *International Journal of Scientific Research and Engineering Trends*, *10*(4), 1576–1581. DOI: 10.61137/ijsret.vol.10.issue4.206

Lee, I., & Lee, K. (2015). The Internet of Things (IoT): Applications, investments, and challenges for enterprises. *Business Horizons*, *58*(4), 431–440. DOI: 10.1016/j.bushor.2015.03.008

Li, Y., Zhong, H., & Tong, Q. (2024). Artificial intelligence, dynamic capabilities, and corporate financial asset allocation. In *International Review of Financial Analysis* (Vol. 96). Elsevier Inc., DOI: 10.1016/j.irfa.2024.103773

Lipton, Z. C. (2017). In machine learning, the concept of interpretability is both important and slippery. *Machine Learning*.

Lundberg, S. M., & Lee, S.-I. (2017). *A Unified Approach to Interpreting Model Predictions. 31st Conference on Neural Information Processing Systems (NIPS)*, CA, USA.

Mittelstadt, B. D., Allo, P., Taddeo, M., Wachter, S., & Floridi, L. (2016). The ethics of algorithms: Mapping the debate. *Big Data & Society*, *3*(2), 2053951716679679. DOI: 10.1177/2053951716679679

Page, M. J., McKenzie, J. E., Bossuyt, P. M., Boutron, I., Hoffmann, T. C., Mulrow, C. D., Shamseer, L., Tetzlaff, J. M., Akl, E. A., Brennan, S. E., Chou, R., Glanville, J., Grimshaw, J. M., Hróbjartsson, A., Lalu, M. M., Li, T., Loder, E. W., Mayo-Wilson, E., McDonald, S., & Moher, D. (2021). The PRISMA 2020 statement: An updated guideline for reporting systematic reviews. *BMJ (Clinical Research Ed.)*, (71), n71. Advance online publication. DOI: 10.1136/bmj.n71 PMID: 33782057

Ribeiro, M. T., Singh, S., & Guestrin, C. (2016). *Model-Agnostic Interpretability of Machine Learning* (arXiv:1606.05386). arXiv. https://doi.org//arXiv.1606.05386DOI: 10.48550

Ribeiro-Navarrete, S., Saura, J. R., & Palacios-Marqués, D. (2021). Towards a new era of mass data collection: Assessing pandemic surveillance technologies to preserve user privacy. In *Technological Forecasting and Social Change* (Vol. 167). Elsevier Inc., DOI: 10.1016/j.techfore.2021.120681

Rudin, C. (2019). Stop explaining black box machine learning models for high stakes decisions and use interpretable models instead. *Nature Machine Intelligence*, *1*(5), 206–215. DOI: 10.1038/s42256-019-0048-x PMID: 35603010

Setty, R., Elovici, Y., & Schwartz, D. (2024). Cost-sensitive machine learning to support startup investment decisions. In *Intelligent Systems in Accounting, Finance and Management* (Vol. 31, Issue 1). John Wiley and Sons Inc. DOI: 10.1002/isaf.1548

Shamima, A., Alshater, M. M., El Ammari, A., & Helmi, H. (2022). Artificial intelligence and machine learning in finance: A bibliometric review. *Research in International Business and Finance*, *61*, 101646. DOI: 10.1016/j.ribaf.2022.101646

Shiller, R. J. (2017). Narrative Economics. *The American Economic Review*, *107*(4), 967–1004. DOI: 10.1257/aer.107.4.967

Shneiderman, B. (2020). Bridging the Gap Between Ethics and Practice: Guidelines for Reliable, Safe, and Trustworthy Human-centered AI Systems. *ACM Transactions on Interactive Intelligent Systems*, *10*(4), 1–31. DOI: 10.1145/3419764

Topol, E. (2019). *Deep medicine: How artificial intelligence can make healthcare human again*. Basic Books Hachette Book Group.

Van Eck, N. J., & Waltman, L. (2017). Citation-based clustering of publications using CitNetExplorer and VOSviewer. *Scientometrics*, *111*(2), 1053–1070. DOI: 10.1007/s11192-017-2300-7 PMID: 28490825

Varma, P., Nijjer, S., Sood, K., Grima, S., & Rupeika-Apoga, R. (2022). Thematic Analysis of Financial Technology (Fintech) Influence on the Banking Industry. In *Risks* (Vol. 10, Issue 10). MDPI. DOI: 10.3390/risks10100186

Varsha, V. R., Gholap, A. T., Santhosh, C. H., Bagali, A., & Tulasi, R. (2024). Fintech And Sustainable Finance: A Review Of Environmental, Social, And Governance (Esg) Integration. *Educational Administration: Theory and Practice*, 6816–6824. DOI: 10.53555/kuey.v30i5.4019

Wolfert, S., Ge, L., Verdouw, C., & Bogaardt, M.-J. (2017). Big Data in Smart Farming – A review. *Agricultural Systems*, *153*, 69–80. DOI: 10.1016/j.agsy.2017.01.023

Wu, S., Irsoy, O., Lu, S., Dabravolski, V., Dredze, M., Gehrmann, S., Kambadur, P., Rosenberg, D., & Mann, G. (2023). *BloombergGPT: A Large Language Model for Finance* (arXiv:2303.17564). arXiv. https://doi.org//arXiv.2303.17564DOI: 10.48550

Zdravković, M., Panetto, H., & Weichhart, G. (2022). AI-enabled Enterprise Information Systems for Manufacturing. In *Enterprise Information Systems* (Vol. 16, Issue 4, pp. 668–720). Taylor and Francis Ltd. DOI: 10.1080/17517575.2021.1941275

Zhang, W., Zhao, L., Xia, H., Sun, S., Sun, J., Qin, M., Li, X., Zhao, Y., Zhao, Y., Cai, X., Zheng, L., Wang, X., & An, B. (2024). A Multimodal Foundation Agent for Financial Trading: Tool-Augmented, Diversified, and Generalist. In *Proceedings of the ACM SIGKDD International Conference on Knowledge Discovery and Data Mining* (pp. 4314–4325). Association for Computing Machinery. DOI: 10.1145/3637528.3671801

KEY TERMS AND DEFINITIONS

Artificial Intelligence: is a system that simulates cognitive functions of human intelligence in machines designed to think, learn, and make independent decisions. AI basically allows consideration for carrying out tasks that will require human intellectual abilities to understand, recognize patterns, solve problems, and adapt to new information. The subfields are numerous, but perhaps the most outstanding ones include machine learning, natural language processing, computer vision, and robotics.

Bibliometric Analysis: is a quantitative approach used toward the impact, influence, and trends of scholarly literature. It uses patterns of citation analysis, publication outputs, and other bibliographic data to measure research performance, identify key players, and uncover emergent topics in a particular domain.

Systematic Analysis: involves an organized, pre-planned scrutiny of anything that can bear data or information. It deals with the breaking down of a complex system, process, or phenomenon into smaller components, outline patterns, association, and pieces of insight in order to make the review comprehensive and unbiased.

Chapter 14
A Study on Understanding the Transformative Role of Artificial Intelligence in Fostering Financial Literacy in the Manufacturing Sector

H. P. Ramya
https://orcid.org/0000-0002-2048-807X
Dayananda Sagar College of Engineering, India

Rukmini Giridhar
https://orcid.org/0009-0006-4486-0231
Dayananda Sagar College of Engineering, India

ABSTRACT

The integration of Artificial Intelligence (AI) in financial ecosystems is transforming financial literacy in manufacturing firms. This study explores AI-driven tools like machine learning, natural language processing, and predictive analytics to enhance financial decision-making. By bridging knowledge gaps and simplifying complexities, AI fosters better understanding and sustainable growth. It provides insights for leaders and policymakers, emphasizing AI's role in shaping financial literacy and driving innovation.

INTRODUCTION:

Improving the financial literacy of manufacturing enterprises remains a relatively understudied subject, especially when it comes to the transformative capacities of Artificial Intelligence. AI is a technological innovation and a strategic enabler for manufacturing organizations. It provides them with critical resources for success in competitive environments by clarifying complex financial principles, recommending customized alternatives, and enriching decision-making processes. The integration of artificial intelligence into manufacturing companies opens opportunities for greater financial flexibility, operational excellence, and sustainable growth. Strategic investment in AI technologies by the manu-

DOI: 10.4018/979-8-3693-9684-1.ch014

facturing sector can then lay the basis for financial knowledge and informed decisions as part of their operational approach.

Financial literacy formed part of traditional understanding as personal ability that affected individuals or families Recent times have heightened its significance for corporate economic performance because financial acumen Knowledgeable decision-making abilities of corporate leaders produce substantial effects on organizational performance. Artificial intelligence has the revolutionary approach to financial domain introduced by AI provides new methods for explaining finance and its concepts. AI helps explain complex financial ideas as well as customize educational programs and give up-to-date accurate financial data to each organizational level. Artificial intelligence has brought about a revolutionary approach to the domain and lends new methods to explain complicated financial concepts, personalize learning experiences, and provide current, real-time financial information to each level of the organization's employee structure. These skills would help the staff make effective decisions regarding financial resource utilization, curtail costs, and help the business can enhance its financial performance with this help. AI serves better solutions for these challenges. A specific individual gets tailored learning materials which addresses multiple learning styles. The unique aspect of this AI tool supports people in building their financial knowledge to a superior level. The industry benefits greatly with this technology particularly where workers in production facilities need support because most employees lack financial expertise. This, in turn, translates into an efficiently primed workforce for the attainment of strategic goals and facilitates a well-informed decision-making culture in line with organizational goals.

This study aims to analyse how AI can enhance the financial literacy of a manufacturing firm. The paper will discuss current applications of AI technologies and examine whether they help in improving employees' financial knowledge. It will also analyze organizational factors, including culture, technological infrastructure, social media influence, and employee readiness, that might impact the implementation of AI to improve financial literacy. The results will elucidate the relationship between artificial intelligence and financial literacy, presenting ramifications for both scholarly inquiry and real-world implementation. The application of artificial intelligence for the promotion of financial literacy heralds a change in its application, shifting from just operational effectiveness to the enhancement of strategic human capital development. Traditionally, financial literacy has been mainly for finance professionals or top management, but the significance of extending the same to the non-financial employees is being increasingly recognized. In manufacturing businesses, these employees often make routine decisions that together determine the company's financial outcomes. Enhancing their financial literacy through AI could lead to a more financially responsible workforce, resulting in better organizational performance and sustainability.

The manufacturing sector is experiencing swift evolution, propelled by technological progress and increased global competition. Within this framework, artificial intelligence represents a transformative technology that transcends mere process automation to affect knowledge creation and decision-making structures within enterprises.

This research, by studying the intersection of technology, workforce engagement, and organizational practices, hopes to contribute to the conversation on the use of AI for the development of skills and competitive advantage in the evolving manufacturing landscape. The results aim to facilitate new approaches that combine artificial intelligence with corporate training and development, in order to achieve financial literacy in efficiency, productivity, and competitive advantage.

THEORETICAL BACKGROUND

In the modern digital transformation era, technology is profoundly reshaping industries, redefining operational efficiencies, and influencing individual lives. One of the most compelling technological advancements in recent years is artificial intelligence (AI), which has emerged as a cornerstone of innovation across various domains. Artificial intelligence (AI) is permeating more and more areas of daily life, and is increasingly being used in professional contexts such as education (Chen et al., 2020; Hwang et al., 2020), healthcare delivery (Matheny, Whicher, & Israni, 2020; Noorbakhsh-Sabet et al., 2019; Maddox, Rumsfeld, & Payne, 2019), or marketing (Vlačić, Corbo, Costa e Silva, & Dabić, 2021; Verma, Sharma, Deb, & Maitra, 2021), to name just a few examples. The ability to understand, use, monitor, and critically reflect on AI applications without necessarily being able to develop AI models themselves is commonly referred to as being "AI literate" (Long et al., 2021; Ng et al., 2021). To the best of our knowledge, the term was first used in an online article in 2015 (Konishi, 2015) and was picked up in an empirical article shortly afterward (Kandlhofer et al., 2016). The term joins a long line of proposed literacies intended to symbolize the understanding of a particular technological construct, e.g., "digital literacy" (Gilster, 1997), "media literacy" (Livingstone, 2004), or more recently "data literacy" (Wolff et al., 2016). "AI literacy" encompasses AI competencies that the general population should possess and accordingly focuses mainly on learners without a computer science background ("non-experts"). A frequently cited definition of AI literacy was developed by (Long and Magerko, 2020), who defines it as "a set of competencies that enables individuals to critically evaluate AI technologies, communicate and collaborate effectively with AI, and use AI as a tool online, at home, and in the workplace". In recent years, the notion of transformative AI (TAI) has begun to receive traction among some scholars (Dafoe, 2018; Karnofsky, 2016), to reflect the possibility that certain types of advanced AI systems could have transformative effects on society without having human-level cognitive abilities. AI is driving transformative changes in the financial sector, particularly in enhancing financial literacy—a critical competency for navigating today's complex economic landscape. This study delves into AI's transformative role in fostering financial literacy within the manufacturing sector, shedding light on its potential to empower individuals and organizations to make informed financial decisions.

Financial literacy, which can be broadly described as the knowledge and skills necessary for individuals to understand, navigate, and manage their financial resources effectively, remains a crucial capability that is often underdeveloped among both individuals and businesses alike. This essential skill set encompasses a wide array of key financial concepts, such as budgeting—the art of creating a financial plan that allows for effective allocation of resources; saving—the practice of setting aside money for future needs or emergencies; investing—the strategy of allocating funds to grow wealth over time; debt management—the process of effectively handling and repaying borrowed money; and long-term financial planning—the proactive approach to preparing for future financial goals and challenges. Despite its importance, research consistently reveals a troubling gap in financial literacy that spans various demographics, leading to a myriad of negative consequences. Individuals lacking financial knowledge are more prone to making poor financial decisions, falling into excessive debt, and facing long-term financial insecurity that can significantly impact their quality of life. These pressing challenges highlight a critical need for innovative and scalable solutions aimed at enhancing financial understanding across diverse populations. Efforts must be made to bridge this gap in financial literacy to empower individuals and foster healthier, more secure financial futures.

We are currently in the Fourth Industrial Revolution, where businesses and industries are increasingly focused on automation and machinery to enhance manufacturing efficiency and optimize the workforce. This new era is transforming the global landscape by replacing human labor in various sectors and establishing more efficient and optimized processes. This includes how manufacturers transform goods, produce items, and strategize for repairing and installing new production lines. Additionally, it involves how workforces in various sectors implement plans, improve operations, and distribute products. All of these advancements are key components of Industrial Revolution 4.0. The foundations of Industry 4.0 are AI (Artificial Intelligence), Big Data, IoT (Internet of Things), Sensors, CPS (Cyber-Physical Systems, i.e. robots), and Blockchain (M. Sony & S. Naik, 2019). In summary, cutting-edge technologies such as cloud computing, augmented reality (AR), virtual reality (VR), additive manufacturing (3D printing), smart manufacturing, advanced robotics, edge computing, data analytics, cyber-physical systems, cyber-security solutions, smart supply chain management, image processing, machine learning-based object detection, nanotechnology, quantum computing, cognitive computing, digital twins, natural language processing (NLP), and advanced analytics are all essential to automation in industries, businesses, and various sectors. These technologies aim to reduce costs, time, and labor and are primarily driven by Industry 4.0, which is leading to a new industrial revolution known as Industry 5.0. Before the Fourth Industrial Revolution, which began in 2016, three previous industrial revolutions shaped the current landscape of global industries.

While the aim of Industry 4.0 was to reduce the human workforce to drive optimization in industries, the goal of Industry 5.0 is to open a phase where humans work alongside advanced technology and AI-powered robots to enhance workplace processes. This is coupled with a more human-centric focus, increased resilience, and improved focus on sustainability. The emergence of Industry 5.0 marks a significant departure from the principles of Industry 4.0, extending beyond manufacturing to encompass all facets of business and organizational strategies. It builds upon the technological advancements of the fourth industrial revolution, including artificial intelligence, automation, big data analytics, the Internet of Things (IoT), machine learning, robotics, smart systems, and virtualization. Unlike its predecessor, Industry 5.0 prioritizes societal value and well-being over mere economic gains, as articulated by the European Union. Central to this shift is a focus on placing the welfare of workers at the forefront of the production process and leveraging new technologies to foster prosperity while respecting planetary constraints. This represents a fundamental reorientation towards a broader conception of value creation that transcends traditional notions of profit-driven growth.

Artificial intelligence refers to machine-deployed intelligence that can simulate human mental abilities, such as problem-solving and decision-making. Using Machine Learning and Deep Learning approaches, AI systems are trained with large data to enable them to make intelligent choices on their own. Artificial intelligence technology has improved rapidly and significantly changed the functioning of many businesses. The manufacturing industry, in particular, faces unique difficulties in terms of financial literacy: complex supply chains, capital-intensive operations, and unstable market settings. Effective financial decision-making must be made to optimize resource productivity, manage and minimize risks, and ensure long-term sustainability in such an industry. Unfortunately, conventional methods of teaching financial education, which include seminars, workshops, and printed materials, are often ineffective for a large-scale audience or cater to specific needs of an organization. With recent advancements in artificial intelligence technology, coupled with advancements in industry practices, there is a great opportunity to overcome these challenges.

THE IMPORTANCE OF AI IN THE MANUFACTURING SECTOR

Artificial Intelligence (AI) is revolutionizing the manufacturing sector in India and has significantly impacted the industry through the significant competitive advantage the country aims to build in establishing it as a top global manufacturing hub. With Make in India and Aatmanirbhar Bharat, AI has emerged as an indispensable facilitator of increasing efficiency, nurturing innovation, and driving sustainability within the sector. Predictive maintenance systems, for example, use data analytics to predict equipment failures, so manufacturers can take care of the problem before it becomes a production disruptor. Organizations like Tata Steel have deployed AI-based predictive technologies to minimize equipment downtime and improve reliability, thus saving much money and enhancing productivity levels. Similarly, AI-based real-time monitoring systems allow for continuous operation by providing actionable insights into production processes.

The integration of AI-driven solutions into Indian manufacturing will optimize operations, reduce costs, and meet the dynamic demands of global markets. Perhaps the most significant contribution of AI is in the improvement of operational efficiency.

Another field AI is revolutionizing in Indian manufacturing is quality control. Advanced algorithms of machine learning and computer vision technologies allow defect detection on the production line accurately. For example, Mahindra & Mahindra utilizes AI-based inspection systems to provide consistent quality in their automotive manufacturing, which eliminates wastage and increases customer satisfaction. AI-driven automation technologies are applied in assembly lines and logistics to increase efficiency and reduce manual work. In Bengaluru, Wipro Infrastructure Engineering uses AI within its robotic systems to optimize the production processes of its hydraulic cylinder manufacturing plants. This methodology improves scalability while promoting innovation by enabling the workforce to focus on complex and value-added activities. Artificial intelligence has become one of the major tools that help overcome optimizing supply chains. These quality assurance tools powered by AI have reduced human errors and increased accuracy, thus higher-quality products are produced. The area where artificial intelligence is exerting the greatest influence is in intelligent automation. By analyzing historical data and market trends, artificial intelligence enables manufacturers to accurately predict demand, fine-tune inventory management, and optimize logistics. Hindustan Unilever, among other Indian giants, is now using artificial intelligence-based supply chain strategies to ensure that the products reach the right markets on time, thus reducing delays and inventory costs while effectively meeting customer needs.

Beyond the operational benefits of AI, the influence on Indian manufacturing contributes greatly to economic growth through foreign investment attraction, the creation of high-value jobs, and increased export potential. As India develops these smart factories-integrated AI, IoT, and cloud computing, India sets a precedent for digital transformation in the overall global manufacturing landscape. Indian manufacturers thus not only overcome traditional bottlenecks and challenges but rather seize new possibilities, driving them toward a more innovative, resilient, and sustainable future.

The issue of sustainability in the manufacturing industry is increasingly becoming important, and AI has emerged as a major factor in helping the sector. Not just machines, AI adoption in manufacturing also transforms the workforce. Indian manufacturers are using AI to upskill employees by equipping them with tools and insights that will enable data-driven decisions. Bosch India is one such example where AI has been adopted to create smarter production lines, where human workers work with robots to achieve higher efficiency and accuracy. The integration helps the workforce in capability building and also ensures a seamless transition to more advanced manufacturing techniques. Through real-time monitoring of energy consumption, AI algorithms allow companies to avoid waste and help achieve sustainability objectives. Larsen & Toubro, for instance, has applied AI-powered systems in their construction equipment manufacturing units to ensure efficient use of energy, conserve the environment, and yet maintain profitability. AI also supports recycling efforts by identifying material to be reused and thus prevents wastage of resources.

CHALLENGES SPECIFIC TO THE MANUFACTURING SECTOR

1. **Complex Supply Chains:** Manufacturers usually handle multi-layered supply chains ranging from raw material procurement to production and distribution. The financial effects of delays, disruptions, and price fluctuations in this chain demand subtle knowledge.

   Case in Point: In the wake of the COVID-19 pandemic, supply chain disruptions resulted in higher costs for manufacturers worldwide. Toyota, for example, incurred massive financial losses as a result of semiconductor shortages, and this necessitates the need for tools that can dynamically analyze and forecast supply chain risks.
2. **Capital-Intensive Operations:** Heavy investments are made in machinery, infrastructure, and technology. Incorrect estimation of the financial feasibility of capital projects results in long-term inefficiencies.

   Case in Point: General Electric (GE) faced financial instability due to inefficiencies in its power division, where large investments in energy infrastructure were not aligned with the prevailing market demand. Better financial literacy among management would have allowed for a better assessment of the risks associated with investments.
3. **Dynamic Market Conditions:** Manufacturing firms operate in markets that are increasingly influenced by global trade dynamics, currency fluctuations, and changing consumer preferences. These conditions make accurate financial forecasting a critical competency.

   Case in Point: The U.S - China trade war significantly impacted manufacturers like Apple, forcing them to reconsider pricing strategies and supply chain configurations. Firms with AI-enhanced financial tools could better simulate tariff impacts and re-strategize effectively.

SHORTCOMINGS OF TRADITIONAL FINANCIAL EDUCATION

1. **Lack of Interest:** Workshops and seminars commonly display generic material that leads to no interest on the participants' side. They hardly focus on specific financial problems facing separate businesses or unique operating structures for them.
2. **Inaccessibility:** The print-based media and static content do not reach the geographically spread teams or deliver up-to-date information in response to changes in the market. This is a critical challenge in manufacturing sectors where site managers, engineers, and procurement officers need localized actionable insights.
3. **Failure to Retain Skills:** Studies suggest that passive methods of instruction are associated with decreased retention levels. Without hands-on, interactive learning experiences, the employees cannot be able to translate complex financial ideas into real life.

THE ROLE OF AI IN ADDRESSING THESE CHALLENGES

AI technologies provide solutions that can bridge the financial literacy gap in the manufacturing sector by making financial education interactive, contextual, and accessible.

1. **AI-Powered Learning Platforms**: Customized AI platforms such as Coursera for Business and LinkedIn Learning offer modular, interactive courses tailored to the manufacturing industry.
    - **Case in Point**: Honeywell integrated an AI-based training program for its workforce, focusing on financial risk management and cost optimization. The program used simulations based on real-time data to enhance decision-making skills.
2. **Dynamic Risk Assessment Tools**: AI systems like SAP Integrated Business Planning use predictive analytics to help manufacturers understand and mitigate supply chain risks.
    - **Case in Point**: Procter & Gamble (P&G) employs AI tools to monitor and forecast raw material price trends. This helps procurement teams make informed decisions, balancing cost and quality effectively.
3. **Real-Time Financial Dashboards**: AI-driven dashboards, such as those powered by Tableau or Power BI, transform static financial data into dynamic, actionable insights.
    - **Case in Point**: Siemens implemented AI-enhanced financial visualization tools that enable plant managers to monitor KPIs like inventory turnover and production costs in real time, ensuring resource optimization.
4. **AI in Personalizing Financial Education**: One of AI's standout capabilities is its ability to deliver personalized content based on individual learning patterns, preferences, and roles within an organization. AI tools analyze employee performance and suggest tailored modules to bridge skill gaps. Ex: Boeing introduced a personalized training initiative using AI algorithms to teach financial modeling to engineers involved in project costing.
5. **Simulated Decision-Making Environments**: AI-powered simulators allow manufacturing professionals to practice decision-making in a risk-free virtual environment.
    - **Case in Point**: Ford Motor Company utilizes AI-driven simulations to train managers on cost allocation strategies under fluctuating market conditions.

FUTURE TRENDS IN AI

The integration of AI into financial education for manufacturing firms is expected to grow exponentially, driven by advancements in machine learning, data analytics, and immersive technologies.

- **Gamification**: AI can gamify financial training, making learning engaging and competitive.
- **AR/VR Integration**: Augmented and virtual reality tools powered by AI could simulate plant operations and teach financial management in highly interactive formats.
- **Blockchain-Backed Transparency**: Blockchain-enabled AI tools could enhance financial literacy in areas like supplier payment terms and inventory financing.

AI presents a transformative solution to these limitations by using advanced computational capabilities to deliver personalized, interactive, and accessible financial education. With the use of machine learning algorithms, natural language processing, and predictive analytics, AI-powered tools can analyze user behavior, identify knowledge gaps, and offer tailored learning experiences. These include personalized financial recommendations, simulations of potential decision outcomes, and insights into best practices, all of which can significantly enhance financial literacy among manufacturing professionals.

Moreover, AI also helps in making financial security more robust by allowing real-time fraud detection, risk assessment, and anomaly identification. These capabilities resonate most with the manufacturing sector as financial transactions are more intricate and involve more stakeholders. By lowering the risks of fraud, AI not only enhances financial literacy but also builds an accountability culture that calls for informed decisions. This chapter explores the intersection of AI and financial literacy in the manufacturing sector, analyzing how AI-driven tools and methodologies can revolutionize the way financial knowledge is imparted and applied. It also examines the broader implications of these advancements, including their role in enhancing organizational efficiency, driving economic growth, and contributing to the overall resilience of manufacturing firms in a competitive global environment.

LITERATURE REVIEW

Artificial intelligence (AI) is profoundly reshaping the financial sector, influencing critical areas such as financial literacy, inclusion, and decision-making. The automation of routine tasks by AI has been linked to both positive and negative effects on employee morale. While some employees appreciate the reduction in monotonous work, others may experience anxiety or dissatisfaction due to fears of job displacement (Majeed and Hwang, 2021). The literature emphasizes the importance of addressing these concerns through transparent communication and inclusive decision-making processes (Chilunjika et al., 2022).

As the world transitions toward Society 5.0, (Riyani, 2023) highlights the transformative role of AI, Big Data, and the Internet of Things (IoT) in driving social change. Society 5.0 envisions a future where AI elevates living standards by extracting insights from interconnected systems, delivering solutions beyond human capabilities, and integrating them seamlessly into daily life. This framework underscores AI's potential to revolutionize personal and societal well-being. In personal finance, (Joglekar, 2023) emphasizes how AI delivers tailored financial advice, thereby personalizing financial literacy. This individualization enhances students' interest in financial education and promotes overall literacy. Beyond education, AI addresses financial exclusion. (Mhlanga, 2020) demonstrates how underbanked populations benefit from AI-powered solutions such as improved risk assessment and fraud detection. By processing vast amounts of data, AI reduces information asymmetry between financial providers and consumers, facilitating wider access to credit and other financial services. Similarly, (Dhiman, 2024) discusses how AI enhances financial operations and decision-making for marginalized groups, contributing to financial stability and inclusivity.

On consumer behavior, (Waliszewski and Warchlewska, 2020) explore user satisfaction with AI-driven financial solutions like robo-advisors. They argue that socio-economic factors significantly influence user perceptions and stress the importance of analyzing the relationship between technology and consumers. (Koskelainen et al., 2023) extend this discussion by linking digitalization to financial literacy, advocating curriculum updates to foster digital financial competency. Their work underscores the need for collaboration between public and private sectors to build a digitally inclusive society. Indian perspectives are explored by (Bhatia et al., 2021), who study investors' attitudes toward robo-advisors. Their qualitative research reveals that while these tools are cost-effective, issues like trust and data security hinder their widespread acceptance. As a result, robo-advisors in India are seen as complementary to human advisors rather than substitutes. (Stoffi et al., 2021) propose a predictive framework using Bayesian Additive Regression Trees (BART) to improve financial literacy ratings, showcasing a reliable method applicable to broader financial challenges.

(Julakanti, 2023) delves into the interplay between AI, financial decision-making, and psychological health, addressing challenges like cognitive biases and over-reliance on technology. The study highlights AI's potential to enhance financial literacy and mental well-being, particularly as economies recover from the pandemic. Further, (How et al., 2020) present a no-code AI model using Bayesian Networks to support financial service providers (FSPs) in promoting financial inclusion. This adaptable model offers actionable insights and simulation capabilities to address exclusion. Regulatory considerations are also pivotal. (Lee, 2020) examines the role of regulations in ensuring market stability, consumer protection, and fair competition in AI-driven finance. (Kshetri, 2021) highlights how AI enhances efficiency in credit scoring and reduces costs for financially excluded groups in developing nations. (Yasir and Ahmed,2023) and (Rehmat et al., 2023) discuss AI's potential in expanding access to financial products and improving investment decisions, albeit noting challenges like bias and ethical concerns.

Financial literacy is central to many studies. (Chauhan,2020) links financial literacy to retirement confidence, observing that income and expectations significantly influence confidence levels. (Owolabi et al., 2024) propose an ethical AI framework to address transparency and bias concerns. (Zakaria et al., 2023) showcase AI's role in enhancing data analysis accuracy and efficiency in financial management research, while (Sifat, 2023) examines AI's impact on market efficiency and inherent biases. (Athota et al., 2023) highlight AI's potential to overcome cognitive biases in financial planning, and (Alrasyid, 2024) demonstrates how financial literacy and inclusion enhance millennials' financial behavior. The generational and cultural dimensions of AI adoption are explored by (Pintér et al.,2021) and (Mazzatto, 2022), who study Generation Z's preference for convenience in digital financial tools. (Nourallah, 2023) focuses on cultural and technological factors influencing young users' trust in robo-advisors. (Kubinska et al., 2023) compare financial knowledge across cultural and economic contexts, emphasizing the need for targeted interventions to bridge digital literacy gaps. Emerging studies on FinTech highlight its economic implications. (Kurniawan et al., 2024) investigate AI's role in financial management for small and medium enterprises, while (Kulkarni and Gautam, 2021) explore automation's effects on personal financial advice. (Panos and Wilson,2020) and (Kumar et al., 2023) emphasize the importance of financial literacy in navigating the complex FinTech environment, particularly among older adults and impulsive consumers. Lastly, (Lin and Yu, 2023) and (Gallego-Losada et al., 2021) address AI's role in educational financing, advocating for privacy safeguards and societal awareness.

Collectively, these studies demonstrate AI's multifaceted impact on financial literacy, inclusion, and decision-making. They also highlight the importance of addressing ethical, cultural, and regulatory challenges to harness AI's transformative potential in creating equitable financial ecosystems.

RESEARCH GAP

Earlier studies on AI and financial services include analyzing the implication of AI on the decisions of financial organizations, how financial technologies– FinTech, in particular –contribute to the financial inclusion process, as well as factors that may affect the usage of such innovations as robo-advisors. Nevertheless, considering all the elements that characterize a financially illiterate person, a literature gap arises on how this particular dimension impacts AI adoption. (Kalaivani et al., 2023) and (Maier et al., 2022) observe that AI holds promise in the field of financial services; however, they fail to delve into the research question concerning the connection between financial literacy and AI integration. Likewise, (Majeed et al., 2022) and (Adeoye et al., 2024)'s studies are aimed at conventional financial processes without considering the implications of literacy on interactions with tools that are AI-based.

The literature also discusses the uses of AI and FinTech to address issues within educational settings, including discussions by (Lin & Yu, 2023) & (Gallego-Losada et al., 2021). Still, these works demonstrate the possibilities of applying AI in an improvement of financial practices within learning contexts but none of them explains how this financial literacy might affect the implementation of AI technologies. It is more about the presence and role of AI in educational finance than about factors that shape embracing AI financial tools depending on one's financial literacy level. This holds a major research gap on how knowledge about money could be used to improve the application of AI in other areas of finance.

Last of all, the works of (Kurniawan et al., 2024), (Kulkarni and Gautam, 2021), and (Wang and Pradhan, 2020) emphasize comprehending the numbers and behavioral patterns that impact the use of technologies in decision-making and savings. Still, these works major on the acceptance of FinTech and robo-advisors while minimal emphasis was placed on the role that financial literacy plays in determining the acceptance of AI technologies. Specificity is attributed to the financial level rather than the literacy level and none of the considerations associated with it are thoroughly dissected about the nature and use of AI. This is still a fairly large gap because it is necessary to know these parameters to create effective programs for increasing awareness about the value of financial literacy and such opportunities as AI financing.

Objectives of the Study

- To investigate the factors influencing the adoption of AI in fostering financial literacy within manufacturing companies.
- To study the influence of demographic factors (age, qualification, income, and line of work) on AI awareness within manufacturing firms.

Methods and Material

This study has employed a descriptive approach. Data were collected through questionnaires and interview conducted with 157 samples. The analysis and valuation of the data collected was carried out using SPSS software and the relation between variables was studied with the help of linear regression.

Data Analysis and Results

- **Hypothesis 1: Age Category**

H_{01}: There is no significant relationship between age and AI awareness.
H_{11}: There is a significant relationship between age and AI awareness.

- Levene's test showed that variances across age categories were equal, p=.061, satisfying the homogeneity of variances assumption. The ANOVA indicated significant differences between age categories, p=.050, suggesting that age has a notable effect on the dependent variable. Given the borderline significance, further post hoc analysis may be necessary to pinpoint specific group differences. Overall, age categories significantly impact the dependent variable.
- **Hypothesis 2: Highest Qualification**
  H_{02}: There is no significant relationship between qualification level and AI awareness.
  H_{12}: There is a significant relationship between qualification level and AI awareness.
  Levene's test confirmed equal variances across different highest qualifications, p=.002. The ANOVA results, however, revealed no significant differences between qualification levels, p=.973. As the result was not significant, post hoc tests are not needed. Therefore, the highest qualification does not appear to affect the dependent variable.
- **Hypothesis 3: Family's Annual Income**
  H_{03}: There is no significant relationship between income level and AI awareness.
  H_{13}: There is a significant relationship between income level and AI awareness.
  Levene's test indicated that the variances across family income levels were equal, p=.007. The ANOVA showed no significant differences in the means across income levels, p=.414. Since the result was not significant, post hoc analysis is unnecessary. Thus, family income does not significantly influence the dependent variable.
- **Hypothesis 4: Division of Work**
  H_{04}: There is no significant relationship between line of work (profession) and AI awareness.
  H_{14}: There is a significant relationship between line of work (profession) and AI awareness.
  Levene's test demonstrated equal variances across divisions of work, p=.008. The ANOVA found no significant differences among work divisions, p=.123. With a non-significant result, post hoc tests are not required. Consequently, the division of work does not have a significant effect on the dependent variable.

Table 1. Calculation of p-value

ANOVA[a]						
Model		Sum of Squares	df	Mean Square	F	Sig.
1	Regression	193.713	4	48.428	11.627	.000[b]
	Residual	633.077	152	4.165		
	Total	826.790	156			

An ANOVA was performed to evaluate the overall fit of the regression model predicting AI awareness. The results indicated that the regression model was statistically significant, $F(4,152)=11.63, p<.001$. This suggests that the factors of social media, Company Culture/Peer Influence, Data Security, and Technology collectively have a significant effect on AI adoption in enhancing financial literacy at Electrohms.

Table 2. Calculation of p-value

Coefficients[a]								
Model	Unstandardized Coefficients		Standardized Coefficients	t	Sig.	95.0% Confidence Interval for B	
	B	Std. Error	Beta			Lower Bound	Upper Bound
	3.309	1.082		3.057	.003	1.171	5.447
CompanyCulturepeerinfluence	.205	.079	.313	2.595	.010	.049	.361
Technology	.106	.094	.156	1.136	.258	-.079	.291
Datasecurity	-.005	.090	-.007	-.055	.956	-.182	.172
Socialmedia	.052	.076	.066	.694	.489	-.097	.202

Source: Author

The regression analysis revealed that Company Culture/Peer Influence significantly predicts AI awareness, B=.205, β=.313, t=2.60t = 2.60, p=.010, with a 95% confidence interval of [.049, .361]. In contrast, Technology, Data Security, and social media did not significantly predict AI awareness (Technology: B=.106, p=.258 ; Data Security: B=−.005, p=.956; social media: B=.052, p=.489). Thus, Company Culture/Peer Influence is the only significant factor influencing AI adoption in enhancing financial literacy.

Figure 1. Scatterplot Diagram

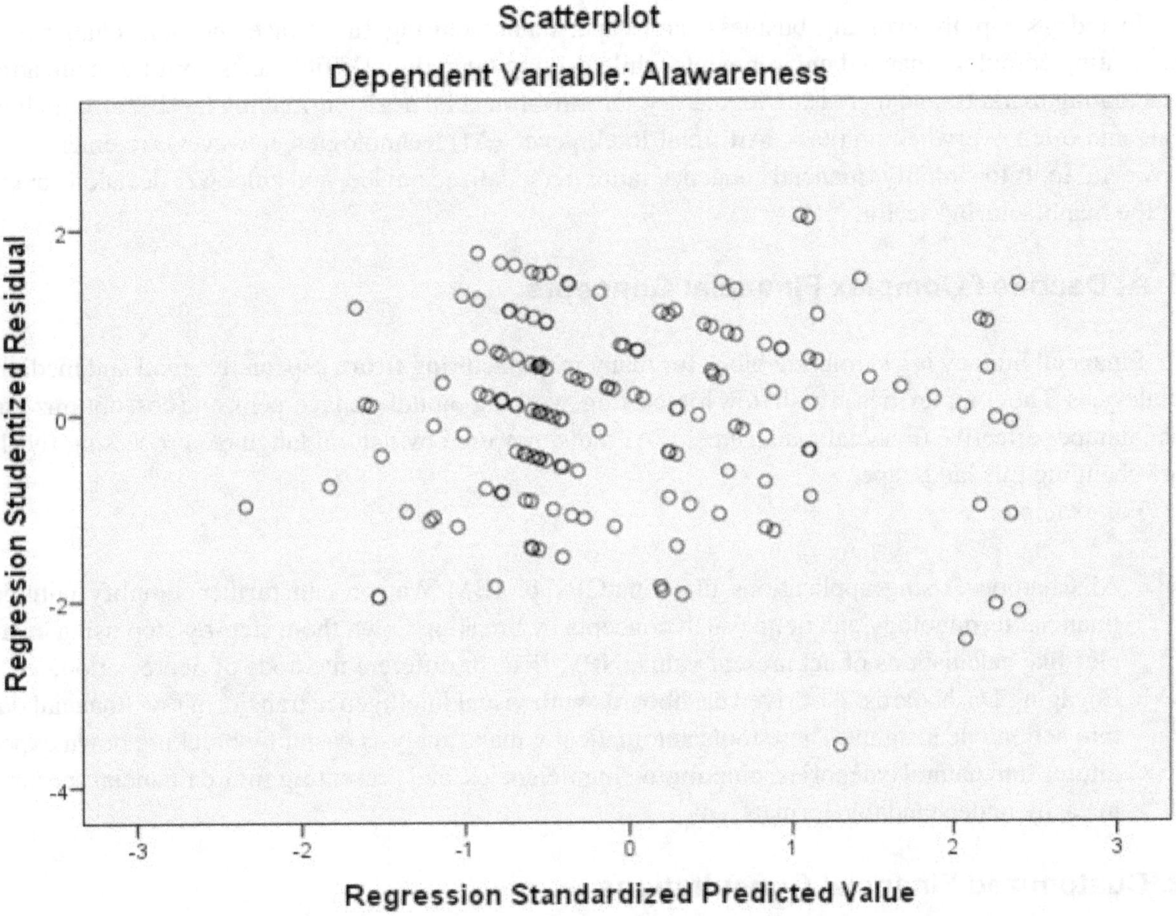

Source: Author

FINDINGS

The findings disclose that all the hypotheses in the proposed overall model influence AI awareness, where social media, Company Culture/Peer Influence, Data Security, and Technology account for about 23% of the changes in the level of awareness of AI. The study targeted understanding features that play a role in the awareness of AI and the influence of social media, company culture/peer pressure, security of data, and technological advancement. The analysis of multiple regression demonstrated that all the above-mentioned variables jointly account for 23% of the variance in AI awareness and the sole predictor that was statistically significant was the Company Culture/ Peer Influence (ß = 0. 324, p < 0. 05). This indicates that the variable of AI is tremendously influenced by the company culture and peer pressure, but not technology, data security, and social media. Similarly, perceived AI awareness was significantly affected by age and employment status as recorded by participants' responses. In conclusion, the study affirms the contention that company culture and peers' influence contribute significantly to the awareness of AI, and other factors comparatively less or negligible.

In today's rapidly evolving business landscape, manufacturing firms face the dual challenge of navigating complex financial environments while driving operational efficiencies. With globalization, fluctuating markets, and increasing regulatory scrutiny, financial decision-making has become an intricate and often overwhelming task. Artificial Intelligence (AI) technologies, however, are emerging as powerful tools to simplify financial concepts, tailor personalized advice, and empower decision-makers in the manufacturing sector.

1. AI Decodes Complex Financial Concepts

Financial literacy is a stumbling block for many manufacturing firms, especially small and medium-scale ones. The complexities in cash flow forecasting, working capital management, and cost optimization can hamper effective financial management. AI tools, powered by natural language processing (NLP), are changing this landscape.

For example:

- AI Chatbots: Using applications like ChatGPT or IBM Watson can further simplify complex financial terminology and define such concepts by breaking down them step-by-step using examples like calculations of net present value, NPV, IRR, or different methods of depreciation.
- Engaging Dashboards: AI-driven dashboards with visual intelligence transform raw financial data into actionable insights. These tools automatically make analysis easier by breaking down expenditures into natural categories, pinpointing inefficiencies, and presenting future financial scenarios in easily understandable formats.

2. Customized Financial Consultations

One-size-fits-all financial solutions hardly match the specific operational models and growth goals of manufacturing firms. AI delivers a robust framework to tailor financial advice through advanced analytics and machine learning models.

- Predictive Analytics: AI systems use historical data and market trends to predict future performance metrics such as revenue streams or cost structures. Predictions can guide firms in budgeting, capital allocation, and risk management.
- Scenario Modeling: Manufacturing firms often face variable costs, including raw materials and labor. AI-based scenario modeling tools enable managers to simulate "what-if" scenarios, empowering them to make informed decisions about pricing strategies, procurement, and inventory levels.
- Recommendation Engines: Similar to personalized e-commerce experiences, AI systems suggest customized financial strategies based on the firm's operational data, industry benchmarks, and financial goals.

3. Enhancing Decision-Making Capabilities

AI is not just about automating processes; it's about augmenting human intelligence. For manufacturing firms, AI enhances decision-making by providing real-time insights, identifying patterns, and minimizing cognitive biases.

- Real-Time Insights: AI-powered financial platforms track key performance indicators (KPIs) in real time, alerting managers to anomalies or opportunities. For example, an unexpected dip in cash reserves can trigger automated alerts with actionable recommendations.
- Reduction of Cognitive Bias: The objective algorithms of AI reduce emotional and cognitive biases in financial decisions. For example, AI-based investment tools can suggest the best reinvestment strategies without overconfidence or risk aversion that may affect human judgment.
- Automation of Routine Tasks: AI automates routine tasks such as accounts reconciliation, invoice processing, and payroll management, allowing financial managers to concentrate on strategic planning.

4. Overcoming Challenges in Adoption

Though AI has undeniable advantages, manufacturing companies face some obstacles in its adoption:

- Implementation Cost: Most small and medium-sized manufacturers consider AI solutions to be costly. The cloud-based and modular AI platform can overcome this challenge by offering scalable solutions at a manageable cost in the initial stage.
- Availability of Data and Its Quality: AI relies on high-quality data. A firm needs to invest in effective data collection and management practices for the full benefit of AI.
- Change Management: Resistance to change and lack of technical expertise can slow the adoption of AI. Thorough training programs and the gradual integration of AI tools can help overcome these challenges.

5. The Road Ahead

As AI technologies advance, their role in simplifying financial complexities will expand. Emerging applications such as AI-driven ESG (Environmental, Social, and Governance) compliance tools and blockchain-backed financial reporting systems are poised to redefine financial management in manufacturing firms. Collaborative efforts between technology providers, industry stakeholders, and academia can further accelerate AI adoption and innovation.

CONCLUSION

The empirical research study on the influence of AI in the field of financial literacy among the company Electrohms Private Limited and the Manufacturing firms brings into the limelight all those significant elements that contribute towards the adaptation of AI together with its impacts on financial illiteracy percentage in Manufacturing firms workers. The research motive is developed after knowing the knowledge gap about what the outside, as well as internal variables, do with AI while considering the improvement of financial literacy in such manufacturing companies. The research objectives of this study hold the following implications for manufacturing firms such as Electrohms to identify the various factors affecting the adoption to AI. It was found in the study that the company culture and peers have a major impact on the awareness it has for AI, which strongly indicates the need for a proper environment that will smoothly integrate AI. According to peer influence, the firm should take action to build a favorable attitude toward AI and discover measures to foster education on knowledge related to AI technologies amongst their workforce.

The research objectives involved comprehension of the determinant factors influencing AI adoption within manufacturing firms and establishing what demographic factors may have affected the existence of AI-related awareness. This study evaluated the effectiveness of demographic variables on the awareness of AI where demographic factors like age and line of work play a significant role in AI awareness with the two independent variables, age and line of work as the most influential factors. This is indicative that the demographic factors will affect the employee attitude and behavior concerning the adoption of AI technologies to warrant contextual approaches in developing and implementing AI adoption plans and training programs based on demographic parameters.

Implications for Future Research on the Role of AI in Enhancing Financial Literacy among Manufacturing Firms

It profoundly affects industries worldwide; its application within the manufacturing industry, especially on financial literacy, offers a host of opportunities to further research the topic. Given the existing works, there still exist many lacunas that offer scope to understand how artificial intelligence can revolutionize the financial education process and decision-making in manufacturing. This essay considers the prospects of research in this revolutionary AI role, highlighting its use, problems, and directions in manufacturing. Industry-specific financial literacy frameworks may also be an area that can be considered for research: Manufacturing is an extensive industry with segments such as automobiles, textiles, heavy machinery, and electronics. All these segments have their peculiarities of financial complexities. Future studies could look into how AI-based tools can be customized to overcome these industry-specific challenges. For example, in the automotive industry, AI can be used to improve cost forecasting for raw materials and components, while in heavy engineering, it can optimize capital expenditure planning. This would enable the development of focused financial literacy programs that would address the specific needs of different manufacturing sub-sectors, thus ensuring better implementation.

The potential for further research also lies in the integration of emerging technologies with AI. Technologies such as blockchain, augmented reality (AR), and virtual reality (VR) offer synergistic possibilities when combined with AI. Blockchain, for instance, may help increase the transparency of financial transactions in supply chains, while AR and VR may be used to provide employees with an immersive experience in financial training. Future studies could be conducted to determine how these technologies interact with AI to create financial literacy, thereby giving insight into their combined effect on improving financial decision-making and operational efficiency. This approach could revolutionize traditional methods of financial education in manufacturing. Longitudinal studies on AI adoption in manufacturing firms would provide the necessary insights for understanding the long-term effects of AI on financial literacy and decision-making. The research conducted thus far has generally focused on short-term impacts. However, a longitudinal approach could shed light on how AI-driven tools change and evolve over time and would involve the monitoring of employee behavior changes, improvement in financial outcomes, and the scalability of AI systems. For example, such a long-term study may examine, over one decade, the potential that AI-based predictive analytics tools have on capital allocation decisions and further complete an understanding of their effectiveness and adaptability.

Behavioral effects of AI adoption also merit further exploration: Human behavior with respect to financial systems can be substantially influenced by AI. Future research could delve into the cognitive and psychological effects of using AI-driven financial tools, such as reducing cognitive biases or enhancing trust in financial processes. Moreover, ethical considerations in AI implementation, such as data privacy and algorithmic transparency, are crucial areas for study. Understanding how these ethical concerns affect employee acceptance and trust in AI systems is essential for ensuring their successful integration into manufacturing firms.

Another promising area of research is cross-cultural comparisons. Manufacturing firms operate in different cultural and regulatory environments that could significantly affect the adoption and effectiveness of AI. Comparative studies across different countries or regions might be able to throw light on how cultural, economic, and legal factors shape the use of AI in fostering financial literacy. For instance, an analysis of AI adoption in Indian, German, and Chinese manufacturing firms may show the impact of varying levels of technological infrastructure, workforce readiness, and regulatory frameworks on the success of AI-driven financial literacy initiatives. Such insights would be useful for strategies that adapt AI to cultural sensibilities and reap its benefits maximally.

A further area for research is how AI is affecting the transformation of the workforce within manufacturing firms. As AI systems increasingly automate routine tasks, employees are expected to engage in more strategic and analytical roles. Research could explore how AI-driven financial literacy tools can enhance the skills and knowledge of non-finance employees, enabling them to contribute to informed decision-making. For instance, studies might examine the effectiveness of AI-based personalized learning platforms in equipping production managers with financial forecasting skills. This research would focus on the ability of AI to bridge knowledge gaps and financially empower the workforce. The policy and governance implications of AI adoption in manufacturing firms are also worthy of discussion. As AI becomes more deeply integrated into financial processes, it will be important to have strong policy frameworks that can address data security, ethical usage, and organizational readiness. Future studies could suggest recommendations for policymakers and industry leaders on how to create an enabling environment for AI-driven innovation. This may include suggestions on the establishment of industry standards, incentives for AI adoption, and ensuring that AI technologies are accessible to all firms regardless of size.

Another interesting area is the ability of AI to solve specific problems in manufacturing SMEs. SMEs usually suffer from a lack of resources, which hampers their respective ability to invest in cutting-edge technologies. Therefore, research may explore scalable and affordable AI solutions for SMEs, including cloud-based platforms that offer modular AI tools. Further, research may be conducted on how government incentives and public-private partnerships can enable SMEs to exploit AI-driven financial literacy programs and thus promote inclusive growth in the manufacturing sector. The other aspect of interest lies in the promotion of sustainability through AI within the manufacturing context. Practices such as using energy more efficiently or reducing waste to make a better environment call for well-informed financial decisions. AI-powered tools can give firms real-time insights into how sustainability initiatives can affect the finances, helping the firm balance both economic and environmental objectives. Future studies could examine how AI-driven financial literacy programs incorporate sustainability metrics, enabling employees to make decisions that align with both organizational and environmental goals. Finally, the evolving nature of AI technologies calls for continuous research into their application in financial literacy. Emerging trends such as gamification, AI-driven ESG (Environmental, Social, and Governance) compliance tools, and immersive learning experiences powered by AR and VR, offer manufacturing new possibilities in the realm of financial education. Future research could explore these innovations to assess their feasibility, effectiveness, and potential for transforming existing financial literacy practices in the manufacturing sector. This would mean the AI-driven ventures are always in the forefront of technological fronts and keep up with the needs of the manufacturing industry.

The future role of AI in enabling financial literacy for the manufacturing industry has immense opportunities for furthering research work. Through the solutions of the identified gaps and challenges, as stated above, further research will enhance the understanding of how AI can improve financial education, decision-making, and organizational performance in manufacturing. This will advance academic knowledge but also offer practical solutions for the industry stakeholders. In an increasingly complex global landscape, this will ensure that the manufacturing sector remains competitive, innovative, and sustainable.

REFERENCES

Adeoye, O. B., Addy, W. A., Ajayi-Nifise, A. O., Odeyemi, O., Okoye, C. C., & Ofodile, O. C. (2024). Leveraging AI and data analytics for enhancing financial inclusion in developing economies. *Finance & Accounting Research Journal*, *6*(3), 288–303. DOI: 10.51594/farj.v6i3.856

Alrasyid, H. (2024). Financial behavior of the millennial generation: Financial literacy, financial intelligence, financial inclusion. *Journal of Applied Sciences in Accounting, Finance, and Tax*, *7*(1), 15–22.

Athota, V. S., Pereira, V., Hasan, Z., Vaz, D., Laker, B., & Reppas, D. (2023). Overcoming financial planners' cognitive biases through digitalization: A qualitative study. *Journal of Business Research*, *154*, 113291. DOI: 10.1016/j.jbusres.2022.08.055

Baltgailis, J., Meņšikovs, V., & Šipilova, V. (2023). Digital currencies and financial literacy: Essay on sustainable finances' perspectives. *Sociālo Zinātņu Vēstnesis*, (2), 7–24.

Bhatia, A., Chandani, A., Atiq, R., Mehta, M., & Divekar, R. (2021). Artificial intelligence in financial services: A qualitative research to discover robo-advisory services. *Qualitative Research in Financial Markets*, *13*(5), 632–654. DOI: 10.1108/QRFM-10-2020-0199

Chauhan, S. (2020). *Financial Literacy and Retirement Confidence A Study of Private Sector Employees*. Amity University.

Chen, X., & Xie, H. Di Zou, Gwo-Jen Hwang. (2020). Application and theory gaps during the rise of Artificial Intelligence in Education, Computers and Education: Artificial Intelligence, Volume 1,100002, ISSN 2666-920X, https://doi.org/DOI: 10.1016/j.caeai.2020.100002

Chilunjika, A., Intauno, K. I., & Chilunjika, S. R. (2022). Artificial intelligence and public sector human resource management in South Africa: Opportunities, challenges and prospects. South African Journal of Human Resource Management.

Dafoe, A. (2018). AI governance: A research agenda. Governance of AI Program, The Future of Humanity Institute, The University of Oxford, Oxford, UK.

Dhiman, B. (2024). A Framework For Exploring The Integration Of AI And Financial Literacy Toward A Sustainable Financial Ecosystem. *Educational Administration: Theory and Practice*, *30*(4), 8750–8759.

Gallego-Losada, M. J., García-Abajo, M. E., Montero-Navarro, A., & Gallego-Losada, R. (2021). The challenge of digital financial literacy in the field of fintech (industry 4.0). *ESIC Market*, *53*(1), e277. DOI: 10.7200/esicm.53.277

Gilster, P. (1997). *Digital literacy*. John Wiley & Sons, Inc.

Globalluxsoft. (n.d.). IMPACT OF INDUSTRY 4.0 in global manufacturing. Retrieved from Globalluxsoft. https://globalluxsoft.com/impact-industry-4-in-global-manufacturing- Internet of other things

How, M. L., Cheah, S. M., Khor, A. C., & Chan, Y. J. (2020). Artificial intelligence-enhanced predictive insights for advancing financial inclusion: A human-centric ai-thinking approach. *Big Data and Cognitive Computing*, *4*(2), 8. DOI: 10.3390/bdcc4020008

Huang, Z., Che, C., Zheng, H., & Li, C. (2024). Research on Generative Artificial Intelligence for Virtual Financial Robo-Advisor. *Academic Journal of Science and Technology*, *10*(1), 74–80. DOI: 10.54097/30r2kk80

Hwang, H., Xie, B. W., Wah, D., & Gašević, D. (2020). Vision, challenges, roles, and research issues of Artificial Intelligence in Education. Computers & Education. *Artificial Intelligence*, *1*(1), 100001. DOI: 10.1016/j.caeai.2020.100001

Inchara, P.(2023)ARTIFICIAL INTELLIGENCE AND MANAGEMENT IN PERSONAL FINANCE.

Joglekar, S. T. EMPOWERING FINANCIAL LITERACY THROUGH ARTIFICIAL INTELLIGENCE. Board of Editors, 43.

Julakanti, S. (2023). The Pandemic's Impact on the Intersections of Financial Literacy, AI, and Behavioral Economics. *Journal of Student Research*, *12*(4). Advance online publication. DOI: 10.47611/jsrhs.v12i4.5453

Kakde, H. S., & Lad, K. (2022). INDIVIDUAL READINESS FOR ARTIFICIAL INTELLIGENCE (AI) ADAPTATION IN MANAGING PERSONAL FINANCES. Fostering Resilient Business Ecosystems and Economic Growth: Towards the Next Normal, 235.

Kalaivani, E., Saranya, H., & Geetha, B. G. (2023). CHALLENGES OF ARTIFICIAL INTELLIGENCE IN FINANCIAL SECTOR-A REVIEW. Benefits, 7(01).

Kandlhofer, M., Hirschmugl-Gaisch, S., & Huber, P. (2016). Artificial intelligence and computer science in education: From kindergarten to university. In 2016 IEEE Frontiers in Education Conference (FIE), Erie, PA, USA.

Karnofsky, H. (2016, December). Some background on our views regarding advanced artificial intelligence [Blog post]. Open Philanthropy Project. Retrieved from https://www.openphilanthropy.org/research/some-background-on-our-views-regarding-advanced-artificial-intelligence

Konishi, Y. (2015). What is Needed for AI literacy? Priorities for the Japanese economy in 2016. Research Institute of Economy, Trade and Industry (RIETI). Retrieved from https://www.rieti.go.jp/en/columns/s16_0014.html

Koskelainen, T., Kalmi, P., Scornavacca, E., & Vartiainen, T. (2023). Financial literacy in the digital age—A research agenda. *The Journal of Consumer Affairs*, *57*(1), 507–528. DOI: 10.1111/joca.12510

Kshetri, N. (2021). The role of artificial intelligence in promoting financial inclusion in developing countries. *Journal of Global Information Technology Management*, *24*(1), 1–6. DOI: 10.1080/1097198X.2021.1871273

Kubinska, E., Adamczyk-Kowalczuk, M., & Macko, A. (2023). Decisions on saving and investment in the digital era: Empirical evidence. In *Behavioral Finance in the Digital Era*. Taylor & Francis. DOI: 10.4324/9781003400066-5

Kulkarni, N., & Gautam, O. (Sept.2021) An Investigation of How Technology Can Enhance The Effectiveness Of Financial Advice For Personal Financial Management.

Kumar, P., Islam, M. A., Pillai, R., & Sharif, T. (2023). Analysing the behavioural, psychological, and demographic determinants of financial decision making of household investors. *Heliyon*, *9*(2), e13085. DOI: 10.1016/j.heliyon.2023.e13085 PMID: 36793953

Kurniawan, S., Purnama, A., Santoso, B. D. J., Herawaty, L., Listiana, M., & Sari, O. D. P. (2024, January). Development Of Msmes With Financial Technology In The Society Era 5.0: Digital Financial Literacy, Digital Wallet, Digital Accounting. In Riau International Conference on Economics, Business and Accounting (Vol. 1, No. 1, Januari, pp. 11-20).

Lee, J. (2020). Access to finance for artificial intelligence regulation in the financial services industry. *European Business Organization Law Review*, *21*(4), 731–757. DOI: 10.1007/s40804-020-00200-0

Lin, L., & Yu, S. (2023). The Transformative Impact of Artificial Intelligence on Educational Financial Management. *Accounting and Corporate Management*, *5*(12), 15–21.

Livingstone, S. (2004). What is media literacy? *InterMedia*, *32*(3), 18–20.

Long, D., Blunt, T., & Magerko, B. (2021). Co-designing AI literacy exhibits for informal learning spaces. Proceedings of the ACM on Human-Computer Interaction, 5(CSCW2), DOI: 10.1145/3476034

Long, D., & Magerko, B. (2020). What is AI literacy? Competencies and design considerations. In *Conference on Human Factors in Computing Systems (CHI)*. https://doi.org/DOI: 10.1145/3313831.3376727

Maddox, T. M., Rumsfeld, J. S., & Payne, P. R. O. (2019). Questions for artificial intelligence in health care. *Journal of the American Medical Association*, *321*(1), 31–32. DOI: 10.1001/jama.2018.18932 PMID: 30535130

Maier, T., Menold, J., & McComb, C. (2022). The relationship between performance and trust in ai in e-finance. *Frontiers in Artificial Intelligence*, *5*, 891529. DOI: 10.3389/frai.2022.891529 PMID: 35800065

Majeed, A., & Hwang, S. O. (2021). Data-driven analytics leveraging artificial intelligence in the era of COVID-19: An insightful review of recent developments. [1] Symmetry, 14(1), 16.

Majeed, K. B., Khan, A., Ghaffar, I., & Asghar, H. (2022). The linkage between financial literacy and financial decision-making with the mediating effect of investment behavior. PalArch's Journal of Archaeology of Egypt/Egyptology, 19(3), 1582-1598.

Matheny, M. E., Whicher, D., & Israni, T. S. (2020). Artificial intelligence in health care: A report from the national academy of medicine. *Journal of the American Medical Association*, *323*(6), 509–510. DOI: 10.1001/jama.2019.21579 PMID: 31845963

Mazzatto, M. (2022). Financial literacy and investing habits of generation Z as it pertains to financial marketing.

Mhlanga, D. (2020). Industry 4.0 in finance: The impact of artificial intelligence (ai) on digital financial inclusion. *International Journal of Financial Studies*, *8*(3), 45. DOI: 10.3390/ijfs8030045

Ng, D. T. K., Leung, J. K. L., Chu, K. W. S., & Qiao, M. S. (2021). AI literacy: Definition, teaching, evaluation and ethical issues. *84th Annual Meeting of the Association for Information Science & Technology*, Salt Lake City, UT, USA. https://doi.org/DOI: 10.1002/pra2.487

Noorbakhsh-Sabet, N., Zand, R., Zhang, Y., & Abedi, V. (2019). Artificial intelligence transforms the future of health care. *The American Journal of Medicine, 132*(7), 795–801. DOI: 10.1016/j.amjmed.2019.01.017 PMID: 30710543

Nourallah, M. (2023). One size does not fit all: Young retail investors' initial trust in financial robo-advisors. *Journal of Business Research, 156*, 113470. DOI: 10.1016/j.jbusres.2022.113470

Owolabi, O. S., Uche, P. C., Adeniken, N. T., Ihejirika, C., Islam, R. B., & Chhetri, B. J. T. (2024). Ethical Implication of Artificial Intelligence (AI) Adoption in Financial Decision Making. *Computer and Information Science, 17*(1), 1–49. DOI: 10.5539/cis.v17n1p49

Panos, G. A., & Wilson, J. O. (2020). Financial literacy and responsible finance in the FinTech era: Capabilities and challenges. *European Journal of Finance, 26*(4-5), 297–301. DOI: 10.1080/1351847X.2020.1717569

Pintér, É., Bagó, P., Berényi, L., Molnár, L., Deutsch, N., & Pintér, T. (2021). How do Digitalization and the Fintech Phenomenon Affect Financial Decision-Making in the Younger Generation? *Acta Polytechnica Hungarica, 18*(11), 191–208. DOI: 10.12700/APH.18.11.2021.11.11

Rehmat, I., Khan, A. A., Hussain, M., & Khurshid, S. (2023). An Examination of Behavioral Factors Affecting the Investment Decisions: The Moderating Role of Financial Literacy and Mediating Role of Risk Perception. *Journal of Innovative Research in Management Sciences, 4*(2), 1–16. DOI: 10.62270/jirms.v4i2.52

Riyani, D. (2023, June). Artificial Intelligence Will Be Able To Change Lifestyles And Financial Literacy Towards The Era Of Society 5.0. In *International Conference On Economics Business Management And Accounting (ICOEMA)* (Vol. 2, pp. 145-157).

Sifat, I. (2023). Artificial Intelligence (AI) and Future Retail Investment.

Sony, M., & Naik, S. (2019). Key ingredients for evaluating Industry 4.0 readiness for organizations: A literature review. *Benchmarking, 27*(7), 2213–2232. DOI: 10.1108/BIJ-09-2018-0284

Stoffi, F. J. B., De Beckker, K., Maldonado, J. E., & De Witte, K. (2021). Assessing sensitivity of machine learning predictions. a novel toolbox with an application to financial literacy. arXiv preprint arXiv:2102.04382.

Tanpat Kraiwanit, J. A. (2019) An Acceptance of The Financial Instruments Trading by Artificial Intelligence: AI.

Verma, S., Sharma, R., Deb, S., & Maitra, D. (2021). Artificial intelligence in marketing: Systematic review and future research direction. *International Journal of Information Management Data Insights, 1*(1), 100002. DOI: 10.1016/j.jjimei.2020.100002

Vlačić, B., Corbo, L., Costa e Silva, S., & Dabić, M. (2021). The evolving role of artificial intelligence in marketing: A review and research agenda. *Journal of Business Research, 128*, 187–203. DOI: 10.1016/j.jbusres.2021.01.055

Waliszewski, K., & Warchlewska, A. (2020). Attitudes towards artificial intelligence in the area of personal financial planning: A case study of selected countries. *Entrepreneurship and Sustainability Issues, 8*(2), 399–420. DOI: 10.9770/jesi.2020.8.2(24)

Wang, S., & Pradhan Dr, S. (2020). Exploring factors influencing older adults' willingness to use robo-advisors.

Wolff, A., Gooch, D., Cavero Montaner, J. J., Rashid, U., & Kortuem, G. (2016). Special issue on data literacy: Articles creating an understanding of data literacy for a data-driven society. *Journal of Community Informatics*, *12*(3), 9–26. www.ci-journal.net/index.php/ciej/article/view/1286. DOI: 10.15353/joci.v12i3.3275

Yasir, A., & Ahmed, A. (2023). Introducing the Concept of Intelligent Financial Inclusion. *International Journal of Computer Science & Network Security*, *23*(4), 103–110.

Zakaria, S., Manaf, S. M. A., Amron, M. T., & Suffian, M. T. M. (2023). Has the world of finance changed? A review of the influence of artificial intelligence on financial management studies. Information Management and Business Review, 15(4 (SI) I), 420-432.

Chapter 15
Algorithmic Governance in ESG Ratings:
Addressing Bias and Enhancing Transparency in AI-Driven Sustainable Finance

Swati Sinha
https://orcid.org/0009-0003-2124-301X
Christ University, India

Puja Chopra
https://orcid.org/0000-0002-9114-4151
Christ University, India

ABSTRACT

ESG ratings serve as guides for corporate investment and strategic decisions and are appended with numerous biases, inconsistencies, and lack of transparency. The present chapter attempts to examine the ratings of 100 companies from different industries and regions and compare S&P Global with MSCI and Sustainalytics. The chapter researches the effects of size, sector, and regional biases on scores using a mixed-method approach. Findings show that energy-intensive sectors are downgraded because of sustainability efforts; large firms get higher grades due to better disclosure, and performance is also higher for companies in jurisdictions marked by stringent regulations. Inconsistencies in ratings are illustrated further by examples of the specific study cases that deal with BlackRock and Tesla. This chapter brings an AI-enabled framework that uses blockchain and machine learning, as well as real-time information, to boost transparency and standardization in response to these issues.

1. INTRODUCTION

ESG Ratings are the linchpins of sustainable finance as they deeply affect how investors behave and corporations form strategies and command regulatory measures. ESG ratings assess a company's financial strength and sustainability performance, influencing investment flows, corporate actions and

DOI: 10.4018/979-8-3693-9684-1.ch015

regulatory developments (Bao et al., 2024). On the converse, MSCI, Sustainalytics and S&P Global engage in relatively deviating practices from the vise of ESG ratings, ultimately leading to distinct and often contradictory evaluations of the same firms (Zhang & Li 2024). For the fact that many agencies rate Tesla very highly for its environmental practices, others would assign very low rankings to the firm due to poor governance (Di Martino et al. 2024). Such dissimilarity becomes vastly obscure for stakeholders envisioning to make decisions guided by ESG ratings. Further divergence in the ratings discourages and diminishes the very receipt from ESG. Ratings agencies are said to have their models, sources of data and weighting procedures that lead to varying and inconsistent representations about a company's ESG performance (Khan et al. 2016). It is common for scores to be heavily biased toward size; the larger the company, the lower the rating, whereas the greenest of start-ups have a chance of being rated low (Dobrick et al., 2023). Whereas sector bias punishes sectors like energy and manufacturing for their environmental downgrades even if companies in these sectors are already making considerable moves toward sustainability (Asif et al., 2023). The geographical location where a business operates holds a pivotal prominence in defining its ESG rating. Enterprises located in countries with strict ESG regulations generally achieve higher scores than their counterparts in less refined frameworks (Palombo & Teti, 2024). Such implicit biases in the ESG rating processes make ESG metrics an ineffective approach in encouraging investments that are responsible and ensuring corporate accountability. Thereby, the net effect is a distorted depiction of disclosures relating to sustainability efforts by the company.

The phenomenon of greenwashing, where companies tend to overstate their claims regarding sustainability, continues to be one of the most vehemently discussed topics (Li et al. 2024). The selective disclosure of information by a corporation poses colossal challenges to stakeholders attempting to verify its genuine commitment to sustainability. This results in stakeholders stemming with high hypothetical views towards ESG performance data. Alongside the loss of faith in the nature and process of ESG ratings, there comes the question of whether there are proper means to validate corporate claims. Transparency still prevails as the focal point since agencies must be sure of the kinds of data on which they base ESG rating creation processes (Deloitte, 2023). This chapter concerns itself with getting down to brass tacks concerning the integrity and efficiency of the ESG ratings and provides concrete and practical recommendations that come forth from this discourse. By standardizing the scoring method, rating agencies can determine ratings altogether under one heading (Kleinberg et al., 2018). This is intended to increase equity by establishing milestones per industry, therefore correcting for firm size by a further check. A big issue in that regard then is greenwashing, i.e., deceptive eco-friendly marketing (Li et al., 2024). In comparison with other performance aspects, selective disclosures point at the performance of ESG by making it highly challenging to gauge corporate commitment to sustainability. Thereby undermining ESG credibility and calling for yet better methods to validate these statements made by companies. The methodologies and data sources should be clear to the stakeholders (Deloitte, 2023). XAI and other technological developments are to improve the transparency of the rating process and show how the score is generated (Maiorano & Morelli, 2024). For example, XAI could disclose weights on the environmental, social and governance factors and what each contributed to a company's overall score. Such transparency may help rebuild that trust and, therefore, the effectiveness of ESG ratings as a real tool of sustainable finance. This chapter explores ways that can be incorporated into improving the quality and effectiveness of attempted ESG ratings in the long run. Rating agencies should design and follow a standard scoring method to promote uniformity, and those ratings should adhere to one set of rules (Kleinberg et al., 2018). The objective here is to correct for bias through regulations by creating industry-based standards and normalized comparisons across firms to consider the company size.

Other alternative data sources would include blockchain technology, satellite imaging, and IoT devices, which should be integrated into standard corporate disclosures to provide complete information about a company's ESG performance. This chapter begins with an analysis of how ESG ratings play an important role in influencing corporate behavioral shifts and investible environments for sustainability. It has reviewed the inadequacy, limitations and perceived challenges in the existing methodologies, with a strong emphasis on biased outcomes or uncertain results and the absence of transparency in the methodologies. The last part of this section will present a credible approach to involving the stakeholders, the adoption of technology and harmonization. A very credible approach to case scenarios from companies like Tesla and BlackRock as to how a better ESG framework could add value to sustainable funding. The chapter contributes to the sustainable finance discourse by discussing the central failures of ESG grading schemes. The argument presented here is that building any robust, yet equitable and sound ESG rating framework needs ideological cooperation and joint efforts between businesses, regulators, and rating agencies. This will allow for improved critical analyses in the work towards accuracy and reliability in the ever-important ESG ratings that will facilitate the greater achievement of long-term sustainability objectives. The final chapter critically contextualizes some of the ESG grading system deficiencies to contribute to the whole sustainable finance discussion.

2. LITERATURE REVIEW

ESG Ratings are important tools for assessing corporate sustainability and guiding investment decisions. However, they are discredited by inconsistencies, biases and a lack of transparency in methodologies. This literature review will examine the contribution of algorithmic governance to improving these ratings, address transparency and bias, explore methodologies, and discuss the impact of ESG ratings on financial performance.

2.1 The Impact of Algorithmic Governance on ESG Ratings

Algorithms make decisions impacting the organization and an individual; that is algorithmic governance. Concerning algorithmic governance of ESG ratings, bias and lack of transparency are opposed to some notion of efficiency and equity (Kleinberg et al. 2018).

2.2. Transparency in Algorithmic Decision-Making.

Thus, transparency is, and will remain, the prime factor in the establishment of trust in algorithmic governance. Opaque algorithms raise scepticism on the part of stakeholders, particularly since the methodology behind ESG ratings has not been disclosed (Diakopoulos, 2016). ESG criteria tend to be relatively subjective and, depending on the rating agency drawing up the rating, can vary significantly, complicating this issue quite a bit (Berg, Kölbel & Rigobon, 2019). The opacity results in stakeholder disenchantment concerning the algorithm's decisions, thus creating almost disbelief toward the ratings awarded (Zarsky, 2016). The situation is exacerbated by the fact that most of the ESG rating agencies hide their methodologies, which makes it nearly impossible for investors to gauge how reliable the rating is (Gibson Brandon et al., 2021). Setting up a general framework for algorithmic governance based on transparency and accountability concerning ESG ratings is thus fundamental.

2.3. Bias As One of the Major Issues in Algorithmic Governance

Bias is a general issue in algorithmic governance, particularly in connection with ESG ratings. Algorithms will invariably wrap themselves around pre-existing bias tied to the corporate data fed into them, which will eventually hurt the assessments. Using an example, if an algorithm was trained on historical data assimilating systemic inequalities, it might yield outcomes that are biased against specific companies or sectors. Modern analyses accentuate the pressing need for rigorous methodologies that will discern and mitigate the influences of bias in ESG ratings (Kleinberg et al., 2018). A rather clear manifestation of size bias, sector bias, and data bias is present in ESG evaluations.-Size bias in ESG happens as bigger companies can release documents that are more elaborate in the sustainability sphere, but then exclusion of smaller companies from the list for providing good sustainability practices takes place (Busco et al., 2020). Sector bias creates lower ratings for companies operating in sectors already presumed to create an adverse effect, regardless of the sustainability approach they adopt, for instance, energy or manufacturing (Lee et al., 2024). Data bias, which is particularly noticeable in emerging markets where ESG disclosures are very few, comes from the absence of available information (Zamoni & Pugliese, 2021). The biases must be taken into consideration so that ratings are an authentic reflection of one company's practice of sustainability.

2.4 Methodologies of ESG Ratings

The methodologies that the ESG rating agencies follow in their assessment of companies are quite varied and largely non-standardized in practice. The difference could very well explain the differences in ratings from rating agencies as compared to others, thereby causing some measure of concern among investors in the decision process (Gibson Brandon et al. 2021). There are diverse methodologies surveyed in contemporary literature, spanning various modalities such as qualitative, quantitative, or hybrid ESG evaluation techniques. For example, Kleinberg et al. (2018) refined the existing model with machine-learning methods based on historical data of ESG and demonstrated how biases perpetuate in certain existing frameworks of rating ESG. The authors discovered that size bias explains a generalised 15 percent overestimation in the rating of larger firms, whereas smaller firms would perhaps suffer some bias or would have lower objective standards due to a greater lack in reporting. Patel and Gloor (2022) aptly studied and analyzed news sentiment with the help of AI, and the results revealed strong influences on ESG scores, with the consequence that different agencies were sometimes giving contradictory ratings.

2.4.1 Quantitative Versus Qualitative Approach

Quantitative methodologies for ESG rating rely on steel factual data and figures, like statistics about carbon emissions or employee diversity. Qualitative evaluations could reach deep into corporate culture and stakeholder engagement (Eccles, Ioannou, & Serafeim, 2014). While quantitative metrics offer objective measures, qualitative assessments can capture some subtleties that are almost invariably imperceptible through numbers. To balance the ESG picture of the firm regarding performance, it is thus of vital importance to merge both kinds of approaches (Khan et al., 2016). The task will be to find the rightful balance between the two approaches so that a combined rating system for all aspects of ESG can be envisioned. For instance, quantitative measures are easily calculated and compared, whereas qualitative insights give context that edifies an audience concerning the modus operandi of a particular company. Multiple recent studies suggest that the hybrid methodologies combining quantitative and qualitative assessments can generate a much accurate appraisal of ESG performance (Baker et al., 2020).

2.4.2 Machine Learning and Artificial Intelligence in ESG Ratings

Some research has already been done in this direction to suggest the application of machine learning and AI in developing ESG ratings for proper and efficient estimation of ESG. For instance, many contemporary studies have shown that the predictive ESG score was calculated very efficiently using a machine-learning algorithm in a huge database (Patel & Gloor, 2022). Algorithms analyze metrics, deriving their information from great quantities of unstructured data, such as news articles and social media commentary, foreshadowing the ESG status of a company. There are, however, nagging issues associated with transparency and accountability in the working of AI, such as the fact that quite often, it is not easy to conclude how and why the conclusions were arrived at based on the algorithms (Lipton, 2016). Machine learning models can be employed to catch patterns and correlations in the ESG data that conventional evaluation approaches might not easily find. For example, applying natural language processing principles to extract sentiment from social media and news articles could afford a much wider perspective on the public standing of a given company on ESG (Yun et al., 2024). While reliance on AI is one of its greatest strengths, the question of findings being checked against one another to ensure such models do not inadvertently endorse like-for-like prejudices or unfavorable outcomes looms large. ESG ratings and financial performance have been the objects of study by an increasingly substantial body of literature. Most of these studies reported a positive relationship between strong ESG performance and better financial results (Friede et al., 2015; Khan et al., 2016). Because more and more investors see sustainability practices as creating long-term value, enhancing accurate ESG appraisals helps affirm the validity of the relationship.

2.5. Investor Behavior and ESG Rating

The behavior of investors will depend, in high measure, on whether these ratings will find entry in the deliberations of institutional investors for their investment decisions (Baker et al., 2020). Some of the studies suggest companies with better ESG ratings attracted investments on account of a lower risk rating and great sustainability potential (Gibson Brandon et al., 2021). However, the absence of standardization in ESG ratings can lead to a lot of confusion among investors, causing potential misallocations of capital. The increase in focus on ESG factors has also led to the creation of ESG-themed investment funds that concentrate on companies that assure strong sustainability practices. Such funds have collected intensifying popularity with investors looking to consolidate their financial goals with their value set, hence increasing demand for reliable ESG ratings (Baker et al., 2020). However, the inconsistency of ESG ratings among agencies creates a complex investment landscape, which may be astounding for investors looking to invest in sustainable companies.

2.6 Transparency Enhancement in ESG Ratings

An increase in the transparency of ESG rating processes is vital to garner trust and accountability. A recent multitude of literature has posited many ways of increasing the transparency of ESG ratings-through alternative and standardized metrics, improved reporting guidelines, and the introduction of blockchain technology for tracing ESG performance (Tapscott & Tapscott, 2016).

2.7 Standardization of ESG Metrics

The other big impediment in this field pertains to developing generally standardized metrics for ESG. Standardized frameworks for ESG reporting were developed by such organizations as the Global Reporting Initiative (GRI) and the Sustainability Accounting Standards Board (SASB) (Eccles et al., 2014). Nevertheless, due to the inconsistent voluntariness of these frameworks by companies, discrepancies leading to variations in ESG ratings still exist. The standardization of metrics will standardize comparison and enhance transparency therein, allowing for informed choices for investors. Unifying business scoring standards would create an equal playing field for companies across all sectors and regional boundaries. Standardization will restrain the elemental nature of ESG assessment among SES agencies, giving investors clearer insight into the sustainability performance of a company (Zamoni & Pugliese, 2021). Blockchain Technology Components for Further Transparency

2.8. Blockchain

This technology could be one of the latest possible answers to being the means of enhanced transparency in ESG ratings. Its decentralization by nature renders blockchain an immutable record-keeping platform that aids in the tracking of ESG performance while securing reported data's integrity (Tapscott & Tapscott, 2016). This advancement may enable stakeholders to check on claims about ESG and thus hold companies accountable for their practices. Blockchain would enhance the traceability of ESG data through which an investor would be able to trace a company's sustainability efforts over time. As argued by Zamoni & Pugliese (2021), by instant monitoring, a company has allowed a company to see which stage of its operations it is currently in and what this implies for its decisions regarding investment and other dealings. Blockchain technology can mitigate the risk of greenwashing, which means a company overstating its sustainability activities for financial gain, via verifiable proof of its activities.

2.9 Background to ESG Ratings and Algorithmic Governance

The background of ESG ratings is a tangled web of intricate skeins of various methodologies and a non-unanimous view of what determines effective ESG performance. ESG ratings have now become critically important to the sustainable investment decision and corporate strategy landscape; accordingly, they provide tools to carry out the necessary evaluation of a firm's financial strength integrated with non-financial performance indicators focused on environmental, social, and governance best practices. Notwithstanding, the soaring elevation of ESG Ratings calls for increasing scrutiny over the background of inconsistencies across agencies, nebulous rating methodologies, and a subjective evaluation process attached to those ratings. Algorithmic governance could make a difference in this regard by being a medium of standardization criteria that lessen biases based on company size, type of industry, and availability of data. AI-driven governance frameworks can enhance transparency by offering clearer methodologies and greater access to data, fostering stakeholder trust. The integration of AI in ESG evaluations can improve the accuracy and fairness of ratings; case studies of companies such as Tesla and BlackRock serve to illustrate the challenges and benefits of incorporating ESG factors into corporate strategies.

2.10 Recent Studies on ESG Challenges

Recent literature has increasingly focused on problems related to the challenges of ESG ratings, especially about biases, inconsistencies, and transparency. For instance, a paper by Kölbel et al. (2020) points out the discrepancies in ESG ratings across the agencies, noting that companies may consequently receive vastly different scores depending on methodology. This confusion can result among investors and create a lack of credibility in these ESG scores. Furthermore, Zhang et al. (2021) have emphasized the need to take care of biases in ESG ratings. The authors assert that company size and sector-related biases can distort the ratings, so rating agencies must embrace fair methodologies. They advocate the use of machine learning algorithms for identifying and mitigating these biases, thus increasing the reliability of ESG ratings. One of the most significant challenges in the ESG evaluation remains transparency: a study by Lee et al. (2024) has pointed out that the non-transparency of rating methodologies may result in stakeholders' distrust and thus damage the effectiveness of ESG ratings. They, therefore, recommend strong support for the standardization of the reporting framework and the adoption of blockchain for the sake of building transparency and accountability within ESG evaluations.

2.11 The Prospects of ESG Ratings and Algorithmic Governance

As sustainable finance evolves, ESG ratings become one driven by the same; technological changes and support for transparency and accountability are going to team up to drive the adoption of AI and machine learning within ESG ratings; therefore, there exist advantages and disadvantages to AI and machine learning in their capacity to provide ESG ratings. Nevertheless, new technology has the potential to assist the analysis and synthesis stages much faster and more accurately. They need to be subjected to constant critical examination by any party needing to investigate possible bias.

2.12: The Stakeholders' Influence on ESG Governance

Regulators, Investors, and Corporations should develop the best way of embedding algorithmic governance in ESG evaluations. Their engagement serves to widen the credibility of ESG evaluations that will, in turn, help set the standard by fostering a harmonization of relevant reporting standards. Involvement by these stakeholders provides the icing on the pudding; it reduces the risks of misunderstandings and guarantees that the ESG ratings show a complete picture of a firm's sustainability endeavors.

2.13 Continuous Improvement and Adaptation

Environmental, social, and governance questions about climate change, social justice, and corporate governance are not linear; therefore, rating systems must be revisited and restructured along those lines. Such an adaptation must remain timely and responsive, reacting to new challenges and opportunities thrown at them. This also means that the infusion of newer technologies like AI and blockchain will fundamentally improve ESG assessments and working models more accurately and transparently.

2.14 Gaps Covered By the Chapter

Even though existing research has helped improve our understanding of ESG ratings and their impact, there are still some gaps, and this chapter aims to address these gaps:

Integration of Algorithmic Governance: Many studies have pointed out the issues that arise with ESG ratings, but they still haven't completely figured out how algorithmic governance provides solutions. This chapter focuses on the key role of algorithmic governance in benchmarking the assessment process for ESG and improving transparency.

Bias Mitigation Strategies: While considering the biases in ESG ratings, there are very few comprehensive strategies available to mitigate these biases. The chapter discusses certain approaches that will help identify and address biases in ESG assessments.

Real-Time Data: Real-time data in ESG hasn't been explored in the literature yet. This chapter highlights the importance of using real-time data analytics to make ESG assessments more comprehensive and timelier.

Stakeholder Engagement: Stakeholder participation is vital within the entire ESG (Environmental, Social, and Governance) grading solution process, although contention exists about the best ways this can be achieved. Here, we will outline various frameworks aimed at promoting stakeholder engagement. Use open discussion and sharing of work such that we can be sure to have ESG ratings in representation of various opinions and personal experiences. Such a methodology gives the ability to perform evaluation activities that will increase the level of confidence and accountability among the different stakeholders involved. Ethical Implications of Algorithmic Governance: The questions brought by algorithmic evaluation haven't yet been put under sufficient scrutiny. In explaining algorithmic governance, this section provides insights on how autonomous systems affect decision-making in different areas, such as the environment, social equity, and governance. Subsequently, the chapter discusses the general issue of the accountability and transparency of the algorithms supposedly in place to ensure their ethicality and benefit for all. Critical reflection on aspects of algorithmic governance will enable a more equitable and responsible methodology of ESG ratings.

3. CONCEPTUAL FRAMEWORK

3.1 Key Concepts:

3.1.1 Incongruities As Pertains To The Quality Ratings.

ESG ratings also strongly influence the sustainable performance of companies, investment choices, regulatory checks, and corporate strategies (Baker et al., 2020). However, often they are considered unreliable due to credible inconsistencies between/among various rating agencies. Differences in Methodologies: Each agency relies on its proprietary scoring, with different weights for environmental, social, and governance factors (Khan et al., 2016). Conflicting Evaluations: A business that performs well in one system may rank poorly in another agency because their focus is not the same. Some agencies emphasize environmental metrics, while others deal with governance objectives selected by them(Zhang & Li, 2024). Such variations are confusing within the investment community and lead to the diminished use of ESG ratings and decision-making. Therefore, harmonization among the various ESG ratings is required to ensure relevant comparisons are made by the agencies, sectors, or regions involved in the future (Xu & Chen, 2024).

3.2 The Bias in ESG Ratings

3.2.1 Identifying and Correcting Biases

Size Bias: These larger corporations consequently receive larger ESG ratings as they can make detailed reports about sustainable development practices. Smaller companies that have similar practices, therefore, receive lower ratings under larger value analyses against larger firms. (Dobrick et al., 2023). AI can normalize such ratings by comparing companies that exhibit similar ESG practices but are of different sizes, thus guaranteeing fair comparisons (Li et al., 2024).

Sector Bias: Companies in the energy and mining sectors manifest inherent environmental and social policy issues and, thus, lower ESG scores. By contrast, technology and finance companies have scored higher (Asif et al., 2023). AI presents a dual proposition whereby it sets the standard at different sectoral levels and analyzes sustainability efforts in each sector, with each sector having its own unique set of challenges (Chen et al., 2024).

Data Bias: Selection bias introduces complication by the fact that ESG ratings run on corporate disclosures, which in most cases are incomplete. The AI tool will now incorporate alternate data sources targeting satellite imagery and social media sentiments, bringing in a holistic reflection of sustainability initiatives in a company (Cheng et al., 2021). Such tools would cross-check against independent data sources to harvest an accurate picture of the corporate disclosures.

Figure 1. Intersection of size, sector and data bias

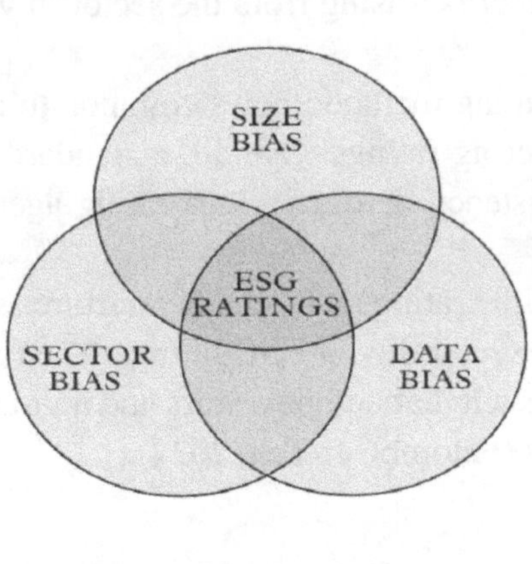

Figure 1 shows how biases due to size, sector, and proprietary data overlap and affect ESG ratings. In general, larger firms receive a more favourable evaluation based on their ability to perform sustainability reporting, whereas smaller firms without sustainability reporting may be overlooked despite favourable performance. Moreover, higher-impact industries like energy and manufacturing may receive lower valuations for environmental reasons, notwithstanding the progress they have made. Weak perks attributable to either incomplete or inconsistent information reporting merge further to enhance the biases of data and thereby further lower the credibility of the ESG ratings.

3.3 A Transparent Foundation.

Transparency is the basis of the credibility and characters of usefulness of ESG ratings. Due to the treatment of methodologies as proprietary, any methodologies are essentially regarded as a black boxes, hence imposing limits on the credibility of their evaluations (Deloitte, 2023). As long as clear disclosures are not available, questions will keep lingering in the minds of the stakeholders about the worth of ESG scores based on that rating.

3.3.1 Transparency Implies

An express specification of criteria and metrics used in the evaluating of ESG factors (Maiorano & Morelli, 2024). Public disclosure of weights attributable to the environmental, social, and governance dimensions (Wu & Lin, 2024). Absolute transparency as it relates to the sources of data, be they derived from corporate disclosures, third-party audits, or alternative datasets (Zhao & Huang, 2024).

3.3.2 Hypothesis

This will form a meaningful framework through the aim of highlighting pertinent issues in ESG ratings.

H1: Preceding has instigated the bias of ESG ratings toward size, sector, or data. Correcting this would guarantee fairness and integrity to the ratings, whereas systematic discriminations against certain companies would prevent measuring firm performance based on the fair merit of their sustainability practices or demerits arising from the sector in which some companies operate (Li et al., 2024).

H2: A basic tuning of ESG rating methodologies common to all rating agencies resolves the inconsistencies among the differing ratings. Overall, a standard methodology for evaluating ESG comparisons facilitates consistency across various rating agencies, geographies, and industries (Kleinberg et al., 2018).

H3: The transparency of the ESG rating methodology nurtures stakeholders' trust among investors that subsequently benefits the credibility of ESG ratings. The full disclosure of all methodologies, data sources and weightings, such that both investors and regulators can understand and believe in the workings of ESG scrutiny (Palombo & Teti, 2024).

4. METHODOLOGY

The mixed-method approach delineates in the present study the different gaps and biases, and transparency of ESG ratings, addressing how AI can assist in mitigating this. Rating divergences have been modified through a mix of simulations that investigators applied in qualitative and quantitative form for the discovery of biases and recommendations on AI-enhanced ameliorations to the accuracy, robustness, and transparency of ESG ratings. The study began by collecting ESG ratings for 100 companies from different sectors and geographies. These companies were selected based on size, market presence and data availability, ensuring representation from industries such as energy, automotive, technology, consumer goods and pharmaceuticals. ESG ratings were sourced from three prominent providers, Sustainalytics, MSCI, and S&P Global, to capture variations in methodologies. Additionally, financial data such as market capitalisation, revenue and profitability were collected from publicly available platforms, such as Yahoo Finance, to examine correlations between ESG scores and financial performance. The inconsistencies in ratings were evaluated, and possible causes for such differences were ascertained based on this dataset. Several statistical methodologies were employed to quantify discrepancies, where the mean, median, and standard deviation served as theoretical foundations. A larger standard deviation would suggest greater inconsistencies between rating providers, while a smaller standard deviation would imply better agreement.

5. RESULTS

In this section of the paper, this considers the main findings drawn from the analysis of the ESG ratings in terms of differences across the agencies and what case studies on Tesla and BlackRock tell us. Figures and tables show different trends across regions and sectors and the relationship between ESG ratings and financial performance.

5.1. Findings

1. Differences in Ratings Among the Agencies

An analysis of the specific ESG ratings given by Sustainalytics, LSEG, and S&P Global has shown significant differences. For example, Table 1 shows, across these three providers, considerable differences in average ratings and standard deviations.

Table 1. Differences in ESG ratings across agencies

Rating Provider	Average	Median	Standard Deviation
Sustainalytics ESG Risk Rating	23.39	22.80	6.73
LSEG ESG Rating	77.85	79.00	10.15
S&P Global ESG Rating	52.17	52.00	13.46

From the evaluation of ratings across Sustainalytics, MSCI and S&P Global in Table 1, it becomes apparent that significant disparities surface. For instance, Sustainalytics may rate environmentally friendly practices positively, while S&P Global, due to problems associated with governance, provides lower ratings. These discrepancies raise the question of the reliability of ESG ratings as a steady measure of sustainability for investors and stakeholders.

These divergences arise from differences in methodologies, such as differential weightings for environmental, social, and governance considerations. For example, Sustainalytics stresses environmental issues, whereas issues involving governance would often bear greater weight with S&P Global. The contradictions provide a hurdle that investors have to overcome in making informed decisions and necessitate acting promptly in developing the guidelines for standardization.

5.2 Regional Disparities

Table 2 describes the relaxations in ESG ratings by geographical variation. It has been discovered that under stringent ESG compliance, companies from Germany and India were rated higher than those from the United States and China based on these differences across countries, which allude to the influential role that both regulatory frameworks and cultural factors play in an ESG evaluation.

Table 2. Regional disparities in ESG ratings

Country	Sustainalytics Avg	LSEG Avg	S&P Global Avg
United States	23.89	75.10	46.69
China	24.25	65.50	45.00
Germany	20.83	87.50	57.50
India	24.80	90.50	53.50

Table 2 looks at the differences between the ESG ratings of companies in various countries across the world. Companies in countries with strict ESG rulings, such as Germany, obtain higher scores. Such companies operating in regions where regulations are not very strict, such as some emerging markets, receive lower scores. This difference indicates the extent to which local regulation and reporting standards influence ESG ratings.

Germany scores higher due to its more stringent environmental and governance policies, while China scores lower because of a lack of such strong oversight in reporting standards. Therefore, these differences augment the importance of regional considerations regarding the final ESG rating. 5.3 Sectoral Bias

Sector-specific constraints and challenges manifest themselves in the ESG evaluation. It is cleared away, but one can see from Table 3 that energy, manufacturing, and other sectors generally have lower ESG ratings as opposed to technology and pharmaceuticals, although they suffer a pretty fair amount due to quite a few sustainability initiatives.

Table 3. Sector-Specific discrepancy in the rating based on ESG

Sector	Sustainalytics Avg	LSEG Avg	S&P Global Avg
Technology	19.47	76.60	51.13
Pharmaceuticals	22.93	84.89	55.89
Energy	28.34	79.22	60.44
Manufacturing	25.37	71.00	**3.0**

As shown in Table 3, the ESG scores show some discrepancies among technology, pharmaceuticals, energy, and manufacturing. It points to some bias in that the energy and manufacturing industries are blamed for their high environmental footprint despite an effort to incorporate sustainable practices, while technology companies often receive higher scores for lower footprints, even if their social or governance practices have not performed well.

It appears that energy companies are, by their very nature, penalized for their high record of environmental hazards, while technology firms benefit from rather low environmental footprints. Additionally, it means that comparison should be based on benchmark indices that are sector-encoded for fair competition.

5.4 Discrepancies in Company-Specific Rating

Table 4. Rating differences between sustainalytics and S&P global

Company Name	Rating Difference Between Sustainalytics and S&P Global Ratings
Tesla, Inc.	35
Amazon.com, Inc.	57
Exxon Mobil Corporation	31
Apple Inc.	34
Volkswagen Aktiengesellschaft	38
Nestlé S.A.	27
Alibaba Group Holding Limited	16
Chevron Corporation	30
Wells Fargo & Co	35
Pfizer Inc.	32
Walmart Inc.	29
The Coca-Cola Company	31
PepsiCo, Inc.	40
McDonald's Corporation	36
Unilever PLC	32

Table 4 shows the differences between ESG scores from Sustainalytics and S&P Global for companies of some repute, albeit Tesla, Amazon, and ExxonMobil in this case. Sustainalytics most likely gave Tesla a higher score based on environmental performance, while S&P gave Tesla a lesser score based on governance practices. Such inconsistency raises a question on the credibility of ESG rating and how comparable the ratings are to each other.

This fractiousness is reflective of the basic subjectivity of the ESG rating system and the pervasive necessity for consistent methodologies to eliminate rating bias among the disparate rating agencies.

5.5 Connection Between ESG Ratings and Financial Performance

Apple and Microsoft are, by far, some of the highest ESG-rated companies, and they have also been some of the highest in financial performance. Companies like ExxonMobil, which have low ESG scores, find themselves facing financial risks even if they turn out to be professionally viable. Therefore, high ESG performance is positively related to long-term financial resiliency.

5.6 Correlation Between ESG Scores and Financial Performance

The revenue and LSEG ESG rating are reported to correlate with 0.995; thus, these two variables have a high positive relationship. Better ratings reduce the cost of capital, paving the way for investment and, hence, justifying sustainable practices. Increasingly, investors are analysing ESG performance because it foretells long-standing profitability and risk management.

Case Study 1: Tesla

From all the above evidence, one could conclude that Tesla's standing as one of the heavyweight players in battery manufacturing has brought numerous implications for ESG considerations. Among reasoned approaches, Sustainalytics has rated Tesla an 80 for its contribution to sorting the environment. Its emissions reduction efforts through electric vehicle (EV) manufacturing could save over four million metric tons of CO2 each year (Baker et al., 2020). However, there was poor governance on the part of S&P Global (65) because CEO Elon Musk deals with issues from controversies in management to workplace safety, thereby excluding Tesla from the ESG index in 2022 (Lee et al., 2023). The case elucidates the need for a more composed and consensus-driven ESG evaluation framework. By and large, the Tesla predicament highlighted how weight differences among rating agencies come into play. A highly rated ESG environment dominates capabilities, while lower ratings due to governance and social questions—like a mixed labour record and accusations of unsafe working conditions and the absence of transparency concerning social metrics—have put Tesla twenty-four notches below that of its rating firms (Dobrick et al., 2023). That was in line with the claim that the injury rate in Tesla exceeded the industry average by 24%, as reported in 2021 (Cheng et al., 2021). A horizontally balanced methodology fits it into the possibilities of ameliorating such differences in ESG assessment through an amalgamation of all three pillars.

Case Study 2: BlackRock

Thus, BlackRock is a successful case in its rights and a strong example of how ESGs can be combined. It obtained maximum ratings in transparent steering on good governance as well as on climate risk management, according to sustainable finance and has a rating of 15 or low ESG risk, according to Sustainalytics (Maiorano & Morelli, 2024). BlackRock has emerged as a benchmark achieving ESG excellence because of its transparency in ESG reporting since it includes stranded details regarding its investment strategies and sustainability metrics and because of its candidature for alternative investments aimed at promoting sustainable practices among its portfolio companies (Rao & Patel, 2024). Replacing coal by 2025, which the firm expressed as one of its commitments, is also evidence of how committed the company is to the accomplishment of the long-term goals of sustainability (Asif et al.,

2023). BlackRock demonstrates excellent examples of the financial and reputational advantages of a rigorous ESG program. If sustainability-oriented investment truly fosters the growth of ESG-oriented enterprises alongside other market drive towards sustainable adoption; this enormous commitment for sustainable investments, in the first quarter of 2023 alone, is estimated at $500 billion with phenomenal support from asset firms (Lim, 2024) which somewhat galvanises competitors towards a renaissance in sustainability operations.

Case Study 3: Unilever

Unilever is a multinational company marketing consumer products that has deliberately determined to take strategic leadership in addressing sustainability issues in its core business. The company is very keen on reducing its environmental impact, with its bottom lines offering such ambitious goals as net-zero emissions by 2039 and sustainably sourcing 100% of its agricultural raw materials. Unilever's Sustainable Living Plan, which was launched in 2010, is often quoted as a model of integrating ESG into business strategy. However, Unilever has had problems trying to juggle profit against its sustainability commitment- somewhat proving that conferring companies with the ability to stamp a seal of approval on ESG commitments may be very challenging in catering to shareholder expectations. Unilever is considered one of the excellent performers in the ESG score regarding environmental and social dimensions.

Case Study 4: Tata Group

Tata Group, however, did encounter challenges on this front in compliance and performance of ESG along the diverse nature of its business portfolio. The AI and data analytics software that is used by the firm for monitoring and reporting ESG performance illustrates the potential of technology-driven sustainability strategies in emerging markets.

6. THE PROPOSED ALGORITHMIC GOVERNANCE FRAMEWORK

With the ESG rating now indelibly on the march and evolving to become instruments of huge investment decisions, they demand stringent, transparent, and standardized approaches: and this is exactly where algorithmic governance might introspectively step in to redress the issues of variability, biases, and lack of transparency that infect the networks of ESG raters. The framework will thus synthesize AI and ML as an enabler to level out biases and promote a transparent sustainability performance evaluation of corporations, yielding more accurate and reliable assessments.

6.1 Algorithmic Standardization of ESG Ratings

There is no homogeneity among the several rating agencies for the ESG rating industry; each such agency executes ESG performance evaluation based on its methodology, frequently resulting in contrasting outcomes and the even greater difficulty of those comparing inter-agency results for decision-makers relying on these ratings. The composition of the governance approach proposed here begins with algorithmic standardization to harmonize the computation of the ESG ratings across the agencies, whereby the framework would be able to integrate some good practices and an internationally recognised reference standard, such as GRI and TCFD. These different kinds of frameworks furnish guidelines as to which specific categories of information need to be reported in ESG evaluations, thereby ensuring that ratings are based on a common set of baseline information. By providing one common baseline, the algorithm would still yield the same rating for a company irrespective of the institution doing the ratings. This standardised framework would collate the essential parameters of ESG- one of which is carbon emission, board governance, and labour practice- and thus, it assigns reasonable weight to different parameters. The standardization would minimise the element of subjective determination of the ratings, thus enhancing their reliability and integrity from the investors' and regulators' perspective.

Additionally, with machine learning, advances in governance model standardization can be improved continually. As data accessibility improves into the future, sure companies enhance sustainability reporting, and the AI model will also catch patterns. It can then update the ESG ratings. Therefore, the past set of data used to train the algorithms will standardize current ratings while also being able to give a prediction of future ESG performance. This would help the investors decide which firm deserves their trust (Jucá et al., 2022). Algorithmic standardization will ultimately help to cure discrepancies in ESG ratings, improve comparability across agencies and create a predictable and trustworthy ESG rating system.

6.2 AI and Machine Learning

The most considerable drawback ruining the heart of current ESG ratings is a cocktail of biases- size, sectoral, and data- which sully ratings. Despite ESG ratings supposedly populating a terrain of sustainability efforts made by the company, it hardly seems to topple the variation of data access, company size, and sectoral issues, which all tend to muddle the effectiveness of ratings or even might turn them quite dreadful in terms of fair evaluations of firms.

Here, AI and machine learning will play a key role in attempting to overcome said biases; importantly, this will begin to render ESG metrics fairer, impartial, and accurate. By utilizing advanced algorithms, AI can analyse massive datasets to single out and correct particular biases found in traditional rating paradigms. In specific instances, machine learning may adjust ratings considering the business context of a company so that businesses are rated and assessed on equal footing.

Figure 2. Workflow of ESG rating processes

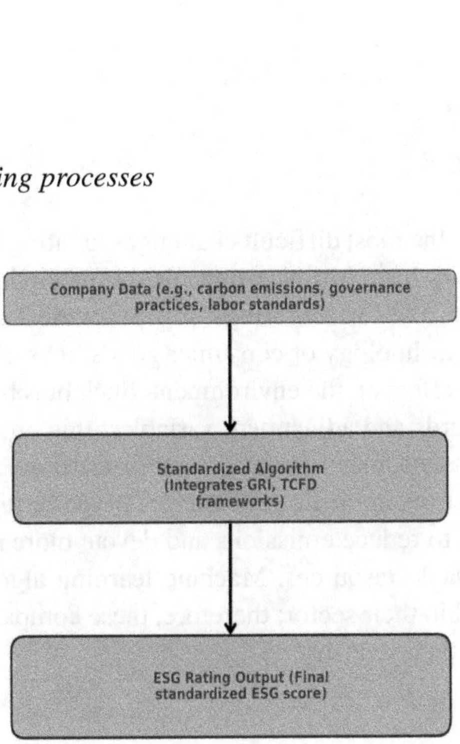

Figure 2 outlines how ESG ratings are typically generated. An initial step is data collection, encompassing disclosure of activities generally from public reporting and regulation filing. The data are then processed and measured against preset criteria for the environmental, social, and governance metrics. The metrics are usually weighted against one another to come up with a final score. The model illustrates how the issue of rating is complicated by the quality and size of available data, as well as the methodologies used by the agencies.

1. Size Bias Reduction

ESG rating models tend to Favor bigger firms. They can disclose more information about ESG, thus offering themselves a better rating. Smaller companies get poorer ratings regardless of their good sustainability performance and the nature of their operations. A trade-off could thus be devised by normalizing ratings across firm sizes through machine learning to eliminate inequalities due to data scale. It performs some sizing within the model by measuring each firm's actual ESG performance, which entirely overlooks their reporting capabilities. One such situation would see firms like Apple and Microsoft get a better ESG rating simply because they're big firms with gigantic sustainability reports to formulate. All this happens at the expense of their ESG efforts, with possibly equal footing with that of small firms. AI algorithms, also called artificial intelligence, might then bring about a more equitable system by downgrading ratings for bigger companies and upgrading those of small ones with relatively fewer resources to spend on big-league ESG reporting efforts.

2. Redressing Sectoral Bias

The bias of the sector is one of the most difficult challenges in rating ESG. On the whole, the energy, mining, and manufacturing sectors have intrinsic impacts on the environment through their business activity. These sectors often incur the lowest ratings on ESG scales, no matter how hard they try to mitigate them. Companies in the technology or consumer goods lines of business receive better ratings as they don't have much negative effect on the environment. Such bias becomes possible to handle with the integration of working standards and adjustment variables; this, in turn, allows companies to look at peculiar limitations faced by companies in the sector. For instance, the oil and gas industry set up through ExxonMobil is not asked to examine its performance based on the environmental impact; rather, it is focused on the actions taken to reduce emissions and devote more resources toward the principles of clean technologies and renewable resources. Machine learning algorithms allow companies to be compared by every company within their sector; therefore, these companies are rated by others and not put at a disadvantage because of their industry.

3. Removing Data Bias

Diverging information, referring to the topical example of ESG ratings as biased data, emerges on the part of certain firms that either do not report fully or permit selective reporting on ESGs. Companies rarely disclose befitting metrics on how they are progressing with their ESG practice. Other sources of data, such as social media sentiment, satellite imagery, and news articles, provide information to complete the company's ESG reporting streams, based on which AI can apply predictive modelling. This allows artificial intelligence models to view the sustainability performance of an organization more holistically, even when some data cannot be sourced from structured formats, by buttressing the unstructured data sources. In this case, another asset to this ESG rating methodology would be doing a catch-up with the way these activities were perceived in the public domain based on their mention through news headlines, social media tweets, or news articles. Therefore, their structuredness will further entrench themselves into the ESG rating stratification process and provide scope for a more complete and informed estimate of the performance of the ESG aspects of a company. The proposed algorithmic architecture will, hence, ensure that the rating procedures depict the true sustainability performance of any company vying for an ESG rating no matter the firm's size or the sector an industry it falls under or, instead, the reporting type upon which data sourcing rests.

Figure 3. Step-by-step workflow for ESG evaluation using AI

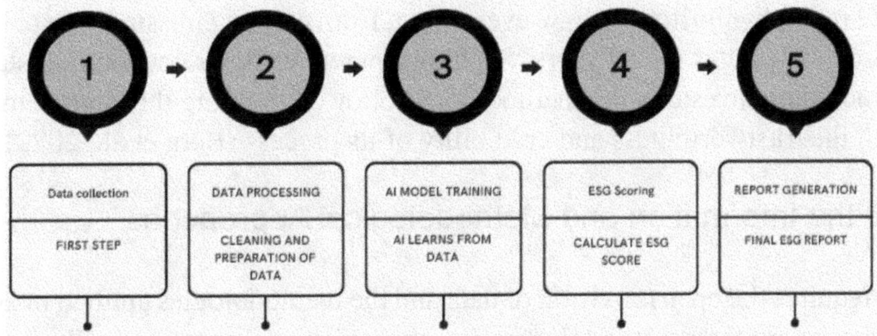

Figure 3 shows "Artificial Intelligence applies ESG evaluation in five structured and important steps. The steps range from gathering data from sustainability reports and regulatory filings"-processing data accordingly for analysis. AI models are trained to extrapolate trends and learn from past ESG data to score environmental, social and governance aspects accurately and impartially. Then, those scores are attempted to be combined to evaluate the overall ESG performance of a company. Subsequently, a comprehensive ESG report comprising important insight for stakeholders will be produced. The figure exemplifies the AI-enabled workflow for making ESG evaluations efficient, scalable, and transparent.

6.3 Enhance the Transparency of ESG Ratings

The main issue concerning ESG scores is the level of transparency. The very individuals who apply ESG in decisions, be they investors, regulators, or companies, have no understanding of how an ESG score is reached, what particular sort of data contributes to such a score, or what kinds of factors make up the final score (Baker et al., 2020). The lack of transparency doesn't lend itself to the effects of trust and knowledge. Because of this, investors' possible reliance on ESG scores in decision-making becomes less compelling. Algorithmic governance resolves this sort of challenge in that it grants greater transparency, access, and accountability to the ESG rating process. Through collaborations with AI-dependent leading countries that are building themselves around this prospected model, such as India, China, and France, a global AI-based ESG rating platform will, therefore, surpass discrepancies in the market. These remedies for ESG assessment will employ machine learning, IoT, and blockchain to enable instantaneous assessments free of bias. For example, India's skills in data analytics and China's experience in AI could combine forces to build a global ESG score that is independent and aims at global acceptance. That kind of model would then eliminate regionally influenced frameworks and exhibit a transparent and truly fair evaluation scheme for organizations all over the world.

Explainable AI Models

The critical attempt to increase the transparency of assurance of communication lies in explainable artificial intelligence, or XAI. Most machine learning algorithms are described as "black box" techniques, wherein it is difficult to know any processes as to how ESG ratings are supposedly constituted (Maiorano

& Morelli, 2024). Explainable AI frameworks attempt to solve this problem by providing stakeholders with clarity regarding the methodologies used in rating assessments and by indicating what factors have the largest impact on the overall score. A clear example is an intelligible AI system, which explains a firm's overall ESG rating by illustrating how everything, from carbon emissions to social policies to the diversity of a board, contributes to that score. Such transparency allows one to understand and communicate to others, including investors, the methodology followed in rating this algorithm and imbue that rating system with the trustworthiness and credibility of its process (Berg et al., 2022).

Accessibility of the Information and Methodological Approaches

Transparency requires the open provision of data and the methodologies applied in every ESG rating. Most rating agencies guard their methodologies closely, which poses quite a challenge for stakeholders in assessing the basis for the ratings (Dobrick et al., 2023). If the rating agencies open up with data that was applied for the ratings and the model methodology applied by AI models, trust in the system might develop. Agencies may further release unaltered datasets, including company disclosures, third-party evaluations, and exterior reports. Such an approach would allow investors to check whether the data used for ESG score calculations support the assigned ratings with correct, up-to-date information. As a side, the agencies must also publish clear statements of methodology that explain how different ESG factors were weighted and the consideration of specific industry problems as part of the assignment of ratings. That would instil a belief in the credibility of the ESG ratings, thereby reducing misunderstandings over the ratings (Rao & Patel, 2024).

Direct Changes and History of Audit Changes

Other such enhancements for transparency should include real-time updates and audit trails in the ESG rating framework. In this regard, periodic updates of ESG scores in consonance with any important events in a firm's sustainability programs are required, e.g., changes in governance practices, carbon output, and labor standards (Cheng et al., 2021). The provision for a real-time update of information will, with the clicks of a mouse, give all stakeholders the data required to monitor the ESG performance of companies over time such that the rating will genuinely reflect a firm's contemporary sustainability efforts. An audit trail further permits stakeholders to track back and study the reason for the change in a company's ESG score and the drivers for this change. A change in any of the data, model, or weightings causes a change in the ESG rating of the company. A good, visible audit trail would allow rating agencies to assign an ESG score that is clear, traceable, and accountable.

7. DISCUSSION

Harmonization of ESG Criteria

Influence of Anglo-Saxon philosophy, such as that prevalent in US-based companies like MSCI and S&P Global, predominated ESG frameworks. Such dominance often bypasses the sustainability priorities identified by EU and Asian frameworks- emphasis driven by a shareholder-centric governance model. Addressing colliding ideological agendas becomes a precursor for the possible harmonization of criteria: it would involve balancing a financial performance-oriented approach of the US and a climate-concerned approach of the EU. Global forums like G20 or UNPRI could be put at the forefront of developing a unified ESG framework where benchmark standards are taken into account globally, yet at the same time, there is room for local nuances. The report insists on globally mandated harmonization of ESG criteria. The differentiation in awarding ESG ratings is significantly influenced by culture and connected regional regulations. German companies score better ratings than companies within areas of Southeast Asia, which have comparatively looser regulations and, therefore, weaker environmental compliance (Dobrick et al., 2023). A set framework for ESG requires to be exceedingly uniformed to negotiate this divide-determining equitable and standardized ratings across regions. This will help avoid confusion on the part of investors and other stakeholders who rely on these metrics to make their decisions. The multitude of regulations and cultures is largely responsible for the discrepancies in ratings. While U.S.-based frameworks are primarily based on shareholder-centric governance, the EU prefers stringent climate-related regulations (Lee et al., 2024). Because Tesla and ExxonMobil's ratings differ, this leads to inconsistent rating results. While attempting to harmonise, this variation must be addressed, and further research into international cooperation that could provide a basis of criteria for regional use must be conducted.

Global Collaboration

The solution to the ESG mismatch lies in international collaboration. Nations with a track record of sustainable practices could help develop impartial, internationally recognised ESG platforms. Through such a platform, standardised data collection techniques and benchmarks that account for sector-specific and regional issues can be provided (Asif et al., 2023). Through cross-border collaboration, they have facilitated the establishment of regulatory tools that incorporate competencies for wider sustainability metrics so that all stakeholders may operate under a common framework. Now, the countries can adopt new technologies for collecting ESG data and provide more accurate and transparent data sourcing. Real-time energy consumption is tracked by IoT devices, but the report is unchangeable thanks to blockchain technology. Through these efforts, a standardized system is created that can deal with regional diversities and build trust from stakeholders.

Just-in-Time Information

Real-time data guarantees a lot of merits for ESG critiques. Alternative data (satellite imagery and internet of things sensors) also provide a plethora of insights for sustainability efforts. Real-time deforestation and pollution metrics can be monitored with satellite data (Cheng et al., 2021), thus enabling the real-time environmental performance assessment of companies with accuracy and timeliness (Hairuo et al., 2020). With updated information, dynamic ESG scoring is possible, rather than relying on historical data. The only way to counter such situations of crisis, including oil spills and labor strikes, is through very quick responses on the part of stakeholders to new corporate practices; this is especially possible with ESG ratings being based on just-in-time information, which results in more relevant and reliable rating. One of the major challenges in ESG evaluation is the asymmetry in information production and diffusion. Corporations often selectively disclose data, creating gaps that undermine ratings' reliability. Leveraging just-in-time data sources, such as IoT sensors and satellite imagery, can mitigate this issue. As an example, satellites can monitor the rate and area of deforestation, just as IoT devices can manage real-time emissions. These operations enable enhanced understanding without inaccuracies or lags that would stem from working with historical data. Nevertheless, technology of this nature requires greater distribution to ensure small corporations are not at a disadvantage.

8. RECOMMENDATIONS

For Policymakers

Conciliation of Global ESG Standards: Lawmakers should prefer the formation of internationally acknowledged ESG standards. Regulatory entities like the SEC and the European Commission may unite in designing integrated principles that will incorporate variations between regions. A standardized framework would help clarify investor understanding and boost the credibility of ESG ratings (Maiorano & Morelli, 2024).

Mandating Transparency: Governments ought to require ESG rating agencies to be transparent about their processes. Agencies should disclose their methodologies, including data sources, weighting systems, and scoring rules. This level of transparency can help eliminate the 'black box' effect that often clouds ESG evaluations, enabling stakeholders to have more confidence in the validity of the conclusions drawn (Rao & Patel, 2024).

For Companies

Enhancing Reporting Practices: Companies should think about adopting a standardized template and metrics for ESG reporting based on established practices to improve comparability and consistency. Additionally, third-party audits would help ensure reliable data verification, enhancing confidentiality. The organisation should go beyond the current sources of information by including satellite imagery, blockchain, and third-party auditing processes. This would help close data gaps and reduce the relative weight of self-reported evaluations of ESG, improving the accuracy of ESG ratings. (Manavalan & Jayakrishnan. 2024).

In light of regional biases, they should closely review how cultural and regulatory variations, encountered within different nations, actually play a role in the ratings of ESG. Comparative studies may identify biases and propose region-specific adjustments, resulting in a more equitable ESG framework (Pereira & Lima, 2024). Researchers must concentrate on mixed models that bridge numerical ESG assessments and qualitative information (Mioranro & Morelli, 2024).

9. IMPLICATIONS FOR THE FUTURE

Research Contributions

This study adds to the literature building block by considering size, sector and data biases in improving ESG ratings. Importance of Working hand in hand between environmentalists, data analysts and policymakers till we get better ESG assessments as per the text. The collaboration is expected to result in common reporting models that yield corporate accountability and organisational insight. Stricter ESG methodologies help to build stakeholder confidence and bring in extra stakeholder support to universal ESG frameworks.

The study needs to move forward in research and identify the new tools that can further the sustainability agenda.

Practical Applications

This study holds very important practical implications. To the corporation, standardization in the use of ESG tools will be paramount to ensure investment aligns with the sustainability goal and, thereby, attracts the investments of socially conscious stakeholders. For the investors, the credibility of ESG metrics allows for better decision-making and, therefore, minimizes the risks of misrepresentation or greenwashing (Lim, 2024). The regulators may assume an important role by coming up with standards and benchmarks that foster accountability yet enhance the cross-border comparability of ESG ratings. The regulatory bodies can promote sustainability practices on an international scale through a consistent strategy that would promote dependable financial ecosystems.

Future Research Suggestions

To further boost the field of ESG ratings, future research should focus on the emerging trends as follows:

- AI-Driven ESG Auditing: Investigate how AI can improve the accuracy and efficiency of ESG audits.
- Regional ESG Standardization: Investigate the feasibility of developing standardised ESG criteria that can be applied to a variety of regional settings.
- Blockchain Integration: Examine the role of blockchain technology in reducing ESG data manipulation and increasing transparency.

10. CONCLUSION

The importance of strengthening ESG frameworks is stressed in this chapter as it addresses issues such as bias and lack of transparency. Standardised specifications are critical for making sure that there are consistent ratings, as evidenced by the differences in ESG scores between Tesla and ExxonMobil across different agencies (Jucá et al., 2022). Standardisation also improves transparency, helps address the "black box" issue, and boosts stakeholder confidence. It is essential for promoting sustainable financing by minimizing discrepancies and removing biases, which in turn strengthens trust and accountability among stakeholders. Incorporating alternative data sources, such as satellite imagery, enhances the objectivity and reliability of ESG studies (Michelon et al., 2015). Implementing these advancements necessitates collaboration among firms, investors, and regulatory bodies. With unified standards, sustainability initiatives can be assessed more accurately, ultimately leading to better decision-making. Advancing ESG frameworks is a crucial step toward the transition to sustainable finance. The authoritative rating systems have shortcomings, such as biases and inconsistency, that should be addressed to create a more fair and transparent assessment process. ESG ratings contribute to a practical view of companies' sustainability

REFERENCES

Agosto, A., Cerchiello, P., & Giudici, P. (2023). Bayesian learning models to measure the relative impact of ESG factors on credit ratings. *International Journal of Data Science and Analytics*. Advance online publication. DOI: 10.1007/s41060-023-00405-9

Angioni, S., Consoli, S., Dessí, D., Osborne, F., Recupero, D. R., & Salatino, A. (2024). *Exploring environmental, social, and governance (ESG) discourse in news: An AI-powered investigation through knowledge graph analysis*. IEEE., DOI: 10.1109/ACCESS.2024.3407188

Asif, M., Searcy, C., & Castka, P. (2023). ESG and Industry 5.0: The role of technologies in enhancing ESG disclosure. *Technological Forecasting and Social Change*, *195*, 122806. DOI: 10.1016/j.techfore.2023.122806

Baker, M., Gentry, R., & Hsu, C. (2020). The role of ESG ratings in investment decisions: Evidence from institutional investors. *Journal of Sustainable Finance & Investment*, *10*(3), 215–230. DOI: 10.1080/20430795.2020.1741234

Bao, X., Sadiq, M., Tye, W., & Zhang, J. (2024). The impact of environmental, social, and governance (ESG) rating disparities on corporate risk: The mediating role of financing constraints. *Journal of Environmental Management*, *371*, 123113. DOI: 10.1016/j.jenvman.2024.123113 PMID: 39481154

Bax, K., Bonaccolto, G., & Paterlini, S. (2024). Spillovers in Europe: The role of ESG. *Journal of Financial Stability*, *72*, 101221. DOI: 10.1016/j.jfs.2024.101221

BlackRock. (n.d.). Sustainable investing and environmental, social and governance (ESG) integration. https://www.blackrock.com/corporate/literature/publication/blk-esg-investment-statement-web.pdf

Chen, J., Wang, N., Lin, T., Liu, B., & Hu, J. (2024). Shock or Empowerment? Artificial intelligence technology and corporate ESG performance. *Economic Analysis and Policy*, *83*, 1080–1096. DOI: 10.1016/j.eap.2024.08.004

Del Vitto, A., Marazzina, D., & Stocco, D. (2023). ESG ratings explainability through machine learning techniques. *Annals of Operations Research*. Advance online publication. DOI: 10.1007/s10479-023-05514-z

Deloitte. (2023). How artificial intelligence is transforming ESG reportingDeloitte Insights*. https://www2.deloitte.com/fr/fr/insights/technology-media-and-telecom-predictions/2024/esg-reporting-software-growth-prediction.html

Di Martino, G., Miglietta, F., & Potì, V. (2024). The impact of ESG scores on the value relevance of fair value hierarchy of financial instruments: Evidence from European Banks. *Research in International Business and Finance*, *71*, 102451. DOI: 10.1016/j.ribaf.2024.102451

Di Martino, G., Miglietta, F., & Potì, V. (2024). The impact of ESG scores on the value relevance of fair value hierarchy of financial instruments: Evidence from European Banks. *Research in International Business and Finance*, *71*, 102451. DOI: 10.1016/j.ribaf.2024.102451

Diakopoulos, N. (2016). Algorithmic accountability: Journalistic investigation of computational power structures. *Digital Journalism (Abingdon, England)*, *3*(3), 398–415. DOI: 10.1080/21670811.2014.976411

Dicuonzo, G., Palmaccio, M., & Shini, M. (2023). ESG, governance variables and Fintech: An empirical analysis. *Research in International Business and Finance*, *69*, 102205. DOI: 10.1016/j.ribaf.2023.102205

Dicuonzo, G., Palmaccio, M., & Shini, M. (2023). ESG, governance variables and Fintech: An empirical analysis. *Research in International Business and Finance*, *69*, 102205. DOI: 10.1016/j.ribaf.2023.102205

Dobrick, J., Klein, C., & Zwergel, B. (2023). Size bias in Refinitiv ESG data. *Finance Research Letters*, *55*, 104014. DOI: 10.1016/j.frl.2023.104014

Doshi, M., Jain, R., Sharma, D., Mukherjee, D., & Kumar, S. (2024). Does ownership influence ESG disclosure scores? *. *Research in International Business and Finance*, *67*, 102122. DOI: 10.1016/j.ribaf.2023.102122

Emma, G. M., Emiliano, R. B., & Jennifer, M. F. (2024). High-quality assurance, ESG legitimacy threats and board effectiveness. *The British Accounting Review*, *101385*, 101385. Advance online publication. DOI: 10.1016/j.bar.2024.101385

Ferjančič, U., Ichev, R., Lončarski, I., Montariol, S., Pelicon, A., Pollak, S., Sitar Šuštar, K., Toman, A., Valentinčič, A., & Žnidaršič, M. (2024). Textual analysis of corporate sustainability reporting and corporate ESG scores. *International Review of Financial Analysis*, *96*, 103669. DOI: 10.1016/j.irfa.2024.103669

Galeone, G., Ranaldo, S., & Fusco, A. (2024). ESG and FinTech: Are they connected? *. *Research in International Business and Finance*, *69*, 102225. DOI: 10.1016/j.ribaf.2024.102225

Ji, L., & Huang, X. (2022). Analysis of social governance in energy-oriented cities based on artificial intelligence. *Energy Reports*, *8*, 11151–11160. DOI: 10.1016/j.egyr.2022.08.206

Jucá, M. N., Farias, S. R., & De Sousa, J. A. (2022). AI-based ESG ratings: Overcoming data bias and inconsistencies in sustainable finance. *Journal of Sustainable Finance & Investment*, *12*(2), 224–240. DOI: 10.1080/20430795.2022.2048156

Khan, M., Serafeim, G., & Yoon, A. (2016). Corporate sustainability: First evidence on materiality. *The Accounting Review*, *91*(1), 169–196. DOI: 10.2308/accr-51249

Kleinberg, J., Ludwig, J., Mullainathan, S., & Obermeyer, Z. (2018). Algorithmic fairness*Proceedings of the 2018 Conference on Fairness, Accountability, and Transparency**, 1-15. https://doi.org/DOI: 10.1145/3287560.3287598

Kleinberg, J., Ludwig, J., Mullainathan, S., & Sunstein, C. R. (2018). Discrimination in the age of algorithms. *The Journal of Legal Analysis*, *10*(1), 113–173. DOI: 10.1093/jla/laz001

Lee, M. T., Raschke, R. L., & Krishen, A. S. (2023). Understanding ESG scores and firm performance: Are high-performing firms E, S, and G-balanced? *. *Technological Forecasting and Social Change*, *195*, 122779. DOI: 10.1016/j.techfore.2023.122779

Lee, M. T., Raschke, R. L., & Krishen, A. S. (2024). Understanding ESG scores and firm performance: Are high-performing firms E, S, and G-balanced? *Technological Forecasting and Social Change*, *195*, 122779. DOI: 10.1016/j.techfore.2023.122779

Li, D., Zhang, Z., & Gao, X. (2024). Does artificial intelligence deter greenwashing? *. *Finance Research Letters*, *67*, 105954. DOI: 10.1016/j.frl.2024.105954

Lim, T. (2024). Environmental, social, and governance (ESG) and artificial intelligence in finance: State-of-the-art and research takeaways. *Artificial Intelligence Review*, *57*(4), 76. DOI: 10.1007/s10462-024-10708-3

Liu, L., Ma, Z., Zhou, Y., Fan, M., & Han, M. (2024). Trust in ESG Reporting: The Intelligent Veri-Green Solution for Incentivized VerificationBlockchain. *Research and Applications*, *100189*(2), 100189. Advance online publication. DOI: 10.1016/j.bcra.2024.100189

Liu, Z., Lu, X., & Wang, Y. (2024). Does Fintech innovation improve ESG performance? Evidence from green fintech. *Journal of Corporate Finance*, *81*, 102695. DOI: 10.1016/j.jcorpfin.2024.102695

Luo, X., Qian, G., & Wang, X. (2023). Board diversity and ESG disclosure: Evidence from emerging markets. *Journal of Business Ethics*, *184*, 631–654. DOI: 10.1007/s10551-023-05241-y

Maiorano, A., & Morelli, E. (2024). ESG scoring and the role of AI: Transparency and explainability issues. *Technological Forecasting and Social Change*, *197*, 123108. DOI: 10.1016/j.techfore.2024.123108

Manavalan, E., & Jayakrishnan, J. (2024). Digital sustainability and ESG disclosure: Role of blockchain and AI technologies. *Journal of Cleaner Production*, *368*, 133019. DOI: 10.1016/j.jclepro.2024.133019

Mehta, K., Sharma, M., & Rao, S. (2023). ESG performance and financial distress: A comparative study of emerging economies. *Journal of International Financial Markets, Institutions and Money*, *89*, 101749. DOI: 10.1016/j.intfin.2023.101749

Michelon, G., Pilonato, S., & Ricceri, F. (2015). CSR disclosure and the audit expectation gap: The role of CSR-related audit committees. *Journal of Business Ethics*, *127*(3), 503–519. DOI: 10.1007/s10551-014-2051-5

Moin, S., Fida, B. A., & Li, J. (2024). Corporate ESG practices and environmental innovation: A global investigation. *Research in International Business and Finance*, *68*, 102320. DOI: 10.1016/j.ribaf.2024.102320

Muñoz, R., Martínez, M., & Ramos, J. (2024). ESG scores as predictors of financial performance: A global perspective. *International Journal of Finance & Economics*. Advance online publication. DOI: 10.1002/ijfe.2719

Oliveira, P. S., & Garcia, T. (2023). AI-enabled ESG assessment in portfolio management: A comprehensive analysis. *Journal of Asset Management*, *24*(4), 377–394. DOI: 10.1057/s41260-023-00221-6

Palombo, F., & Teti, A. (2024). ESG transparency and investment decisions: The mediating role of AI-driven analysis. *Journal of Financial Markets*, *77*, 100869. DOI: 10.1016/j.finmar.2024.100869

Pereira, F., & Lima, R. (2024). ESG disclosures and stock price reactions: Evidence from emerging markets. *Research in International Business and Finance*, *67*, 102185. DOI: 10.1016/j.ribaf.2024.102185

Qian, W., & Yu, Z. (2024). Do ESG scores mitigate market risk? A comparative study of global markets. *The Journal of Risk Finance*, *25*(3), 123–145. DOI: 10.1108/JRF-05-2024-0150

Ramanathan, V., & Arora, S. (2024). ESG investing and shareholder value creation: Evidence from AI-driven financial models. *Financial Innovation*, *10*, 101273. DOI: 10.1007/s40854-024-00452-8

Rao, M., & Patel, V. (2024). AI-powered ESG compliance monitoring: Enhancing transparency and reducing bias. *Journal of Financial Crime*, *31*(1), 23–42. DOI: 10.1108/JFC-04-2024-0063

Sánchez, R., & Vidal, P. (2024). ESG controversies and corporate sustainability: An AI-powered analysis of media sentiment. *Corporate Social Responsibility and Environmental Management*, *31*(4), 978–995. DOI: 10.1002/csr.2423

Schmid, M., & Wagner, P. (2023). AI-based ESG performance prediction models: A literature review. *Journal of Sustainable Finance & Investment*, *13*(2), 303–327. DOI: 10.1080/20430795.2023.2048156

Shah, M., & Verma, T. (2024). ESG integration in AI-driven portfolio optimization. *Journal of Asset Management*, *25*(1), 78–94. DOI: 10.1057/s41260-024-00265-7

Smith, J., & Zhang, X. (2024). ESG data standardization: A machine learning-based approach. *The Journal of Financial Data Science*, *6*(3), 203–219. DOI: 10.3905/jfds.2024.1.030

Tanaka, K., & Yamada, R. (2024). AI-powered ESG analysis: Assessing corporate sustainability in emerging markets. *International Journal of Sustainability*, *15*(1), 56–75. DOI: 10.1007/s10867-024-00123-9

Thakur, A., & Singh, R. (2024). ESG risk management: A data-driven approach to sustainability. *Journal of Corporate Finance*, *80*, 102584. DOI: 10.1016/j.jcorpfin.2024.102584

Wang, F., & Liu, H. (2024). Corporate sustainability and ESG ratings: A critical review of AI-based methods. *Journal of Environmental Management*, *365*, 133801. DOI: 10.1016/j.jenvman.2024.133801

Wu, M., & Lin, C. (2024). Data transparency and explainable AI in ESG rating systems. *Journal of Financial Regulation and Compliance*, *32*(2), 156–176. DOI: 10.1108/JFRC-04-2024-0027

Xu, Z., & Chen, W. (2024). ESG rating inconsistencies and portfolio management: An AI perspective. *Journal of Financial Economics*, *150*(3), 874–898. DOI: 10.1016/j.jfineco.2024.101128

Yang, D., & Park, J. (2024). AI-driven ESG assessment models: Opportunities and challenges. *Journal of Business Research*, *158*, 104872. DOI: 10.1016/j.jbusres.2024.104872

Zarsky, T. (2016). The trouble with algorithmic decisions: An analytic road map to examine efficiency and fairness in automated and opaque decision making. *Science, Technology & Human Values*, *41*(1), 118–132. DOI: 10.1177/0162243915605575

Zhang, R., & Li, S. (2024). ESG controversies and market reactions: Evidence from AI-generated sentiment analysis. *Journal of Financial Markets*, *76*, 100852. DOI: 10.1016/j.finmar.2024.100852

Zhao, L., & Huang, F. (2024). AI-driven ESG reporting: Enhancing data integrity and investor confidence. *Corporate Governance*, *32*(1), 49–72. DOI: 10.1111/corg.2024.00128

Compilation of References

Aagaard, A. (Ed.). (2024). *Business model innovation: game changers and contemporary issues* (By Aarhus University). https://library.oapen.org/bitstream/handle/20.500.12657/92666/978-3-031-57511-2.pdf?sequence=1#page=167

Aattouchi, I., Ait Kerroum, M., el Mendili, S., & Elmendili, F. (2022). Financial sentiment analysis of tweets based on deep learning approach. *Indonesian Journal of Electrical Engineering and Computer Science*, *25*(3), 1759–1770. DOI: 10.11591/ijeecs.v25.i3.pp1759-1770

Adarsh, R., Pillai, R. H., Krishnamurthy, A., & Bi, A. (2023). Innovative Business Research in Finance and Marketing System Based on Ethically Governed Artificial Intelligence. In *Proceedings of 8th IEEE International Conference on Science, Technology, Engineering and Mathematics, ICONSTEM 2023*. Institute of Electrical and Electronics Engineers Inc. DOI: 10.1109/ICONSTEM56934.2023.10142836

Adeoye, O. B., Addy, W. A., Ajayi-Nifise, A. O., Odeyemi, O., Okoye, C. C., & Ofodile, O. C. (2024). Leveraging AI and data analytics for enhancing financial inclusion in developing economies. *Finance & Accounting Research Journal*, *6*(3), 288–303. DOI: 10.51594/farj.v6i3.856

Adeyelu, O. O., Ugochukwu, C. E., & Shonibare, M. A. (2024). Ethical implications of ai in financial decision – making: A review with real world applications. *International Journal of Applied Research in Social Sciences*, *6*(4), 608–630. DOI: 10.51594/ijarss.v6i4.1033

Adisa, O., Ajadi, T. H., & Keshtiban, A. (2024). Navigating Human-Technology Nexus for Environmental and Organizational Sustainability in Industry 5.0. In *Practice, progress, and proficiency in sustainability* (pp. 222–246). https://doi.org/DOI: 10.4018/979-8-3693-7322-4.ch011

Adula, M., Kant, S., Badi, S., & Kumari, M. (2025). Abusive Work Environment Effect on Female Entrepreneurs' Emotional Wellbeing by Mediation of Social and Moral Values in the Horn of Africa. In *Supporting Psychological and Emotional Wellbeing Among Entrepreneurs* (pp. 1-22). IGI Global.

Adula, M., Birbirsa, Z. A., & Kant, S. (2023). The effect of interpersonal, problem solving and technical training skills on performance of Ethiopia textile industry: Continuance, normative and affective commitment as mediators. *Cogent Business & Management*, *10*(3). Advance online publication. DOI: 10.1080/23311975.2023.2286672

Adula, M., & Kant, S. (2025). Impact of Smart Entrepreneurship and Territorial Marketing on Regional Branding: Case of Ethiopia. In *Sustainable and Intelligent Territorial Marketing and Entrepreneurship* (pp. 229–256). IGI Global., DOI: 10.4018/979-8-3693-9775-6.ch008

Agarwal, S., Chakravarti, S., Ghosh, O., & Chakrabarti, G. (2023). Dynamic market risk and portfolio choice: Evidence from Indian stock market. *IIMB Management Review*, *35*(3), 240–257.

Agbese, M., Mohanani, R., Khan, A., & Abrahamsson, P. (2023). Implementing AI Ethics: Making Sense of the Ethical Requirements. *Proceedings of the 27th International Conference on Evaluation and Assessment in Software Engineering*.

Agosto, A., Cerchiello, P., & Giudici, P. (2023). Bayesian learning models to measure the relative impact of ESG factors on credit ratings. *International Journal of Data Science and Analytics*. Advance online publication. DOI: 10.1007/s41060-023-00405-9

Aguilera, R. V., Aragón-Correa, J. A., Marano, V., & Tashman, P. A. (2021). The Corporate Governance of Environmental Sustainability: A Review and Proposal for More Integrated Research. *Journal of Management*, *47*(6), 1468–1497. DOI: 10.1177/0149206321991212

Ajmera, D., Kharub, M., Krishna, A., & Gupta, H. (2024). Navigating the challenges of AI-enabled circular economy in the food and beverage sector: Strategies for sustainable transformation. *International Journal of Logistics Management*. Advance online publication. DOI: 10.1108/ijlm-09-2023-0408

Akour, I., Alzyoud, M., Alquqa, E. K., Tariq, E., Alzboun, N., Al-Hawary, S. I. S., & Alshurideh, M. T. (2024). Artificial intelligence and financial decisions: Empirical evidence from developing economies. *International Journal of Data and Network Science*, *8*(1), 101–108. DOI: 10.5267/j.ijdns.2023.10.013

Alevy, J. E., Haigh, M. S., & List, J. A. (2007). Information cascades: Evidence from a field experiment with financial market professionals. *The Journal of Finance*, *LXII*(1), 151–180. DOI: 10.1111/j.1540-6261.2007.01204.x

Ali, H., & Aysan, A. F. (2023). What will ChatGPT revolutionise in financial industry? SSRN *Electron. J.*https://doi.org/DOI: 10.2139/ssrn.4403372

Almeyda, R., & Darmansya, A. (2019). The Influence of Environmental, Social, and Governance (ESG) Disclosure on Firm Financial Performance. *IPTEK Journal of Proceedings Series*, *0*(5), 278–290.

Alnefaie, A., Singh, S., Kocaballi, B., & Prasad, M. (2021, January). An overview of conversational agent: applications, challenges and future directions. In *17th International Conference on Web Information Systems and Technologies*. SCITEPRESS-Science and Technology Publications.

Aloulou, M., Grati, R., Al-Qudah, A. A., & Al-Okaily, M. (2024). Does FinTech adoption increase the diffusion rate of digital financial inclusion? A study of the banking industry sector. *Journal of Financial Reporting and Accounting*, *22*(2), 289–307. DOI: 10.1108/JFRA-05-2023-0224

Alrasyid, H. (2024). Financial behavior of the millennial generation: Financial literacy, financial intelligence, financial inclusion. *Journal of Applied Sciences in Accounting, Finance, and Tax*, *7*(1), 15–22.

AL-Romeedy. B. S., & El-Sisi, S. A. W. (2024). Does AI Have an Effective Role in Applying Sustainable Entrepreneurship in the Tourism Industry? In Sustainable Tourism, Part A (pp. 3-22). Emerald Publishing Limited.

Amazon Alexa. (2024), "Alexa Smart Properties for Hospitality", Retrieved: https://www.amazon.com/alexahospitalityhttps://developer.amazon.com/en-US/alexa/alexasmartproperties/hospitality (consulted on January 26, 2025)

Amin, M. T., Khan, F., & Amyotte, P. (2019). A bibliometric review of process safety and risk analysis. *Process Safety and Environmental Protection, 126*, 366–381.

Anderson, L. R., & Holt, C. A. (1997). Information cascades in the laboratory. *The American Economic Review, 87*, 847–862. https://www.jstor.org/stable/2951328

Andolfatto, D. (2018). Assessing the Impact of Central Bank Digital Currency on Private Banks. Federal Reserve Bank of St. Louis, Working Paper2018-026C. Retrieved from:https://s3.amazonaws.com/realstlouisfed.org/wp/2018/2018-026.pdf(accessed 11 September 2020)

Ángeles López-Cabarcos, M., & Pérez-Pico, M., A., Vázquez Rodríguez, P., & López Perez, M. L. (2020). Investor sentiment in the theoretical field of behavioural finance. *Economic Research -. Ekonomska Istrazivanja, 33*(1), 2101–2228. DOI: 10.1080/1331677X.2018.1559748

Angioni, S., Consoli, S., Dessí, D., Osborne, F., Recupero, D. R., & Salatino, A. (2024). *Exploring environmental, social, and governance (ESG) discourse in news: An AI-powered investigation through knowledge graph analysis*. IEEE., DOI: 10.1109/ACCESS.2024.3407188

Araci, D. (2019). *FinBERT: Financial Sentiment Analysis with Pre-trained Language Models* (arXiv:1908.10063). arXiv. https://doi.org//arXiv.1908.10063DOI: 10.48550

Arcilla, A. O., Espallardo, A. K. V., Gomez, C. A. J., Viado, E. M. P., Ladion, V. J. T., Naanep, R. A. T., Pascual, A. R. L., & Artificio, E. B. (2023). Ethics in AI Governance: Comparative Analysis, Implication, and Policy Recommendations for the Philippines. 2023 27th International Computer Science and Engineering Conference (ICSEC), 319-326.

Arias-Pérez, J., Coronado-Medina, A., & Perdomo-Charry, G. (2022). Big data analytics capability as a mediator in the influence of open innovation on firm performance. *Journal of Strategy and Management, 15*(1), 1–15.

Armelius, H., Boel, P., Claussen, C. A., & Nessen, M. (2018).The E-Krona and the Macroeconomy. *SverigesRiksbank Economic Review*, 2018(3), 43–65. Retrieved from:https://www.riksbank.se/globalassets/media/rapporter/pov/engelska/2018/economic-review-3-2018.pdf (accessed 06April 2021)

Armstrong, J. S., & Collopy, F. (1992). Error measures for generalizing about forecasting methods: Empirical comparisons. *International Journal of Forecasting, 8*(1), 69–80.

Asif, M., Searcy, C., & Castka, P. (2023). ESG and Industry 5.0: The role of technologies in enhancing ESG disclosure. *Technological Forecasting and Social Change, 195*, 122806. DOI: 10.1016/j.techfore.2023.122806

Athota, V. S., Pereira, V., Hasan, Z., Vaz, D., Laker, B., & Reppas, D. (2023). Overcoming financial planners' cognitive biases through digitalization: A qualitative study. *Journal of Business Research, 154*, 113291. DOI: 10.1016/j.jbusres.2022.08.055

Avula, M., & Sithole, T. (2024). Artificial Intelligence's Potential to Improve Operational Efficiency and Customer Experience in the Hospitality and Tourism Sectors. In Impact of AI and Tech-Driven Solutions in Hospitality and Tourism (pp. 351-382). IGI Global.

Axworthy, L. (1997). Entre mondialisation et multipolarité: Pour une politique étrangère du Canada globale et humaine. *Etudes Internationales, 28*(1), 105–121.

Bachelier, L. (1900). Theory of speculation. *Translation of the 1900 french edition. In P. Cootner, editor, The Random Character of Stock Market Prices*, 17–78. MIT Press, Cambridge, MA, 1964.

Bag, S., Yadav, G., Dhamija, P., & Kataria, K. K. (2021). Key resources for industry 4.0 adoption and its effect on sustainable production and circular economy: An empirical study. *Journal of Cleaner Production, 281*, 125233. DOI: 10.1016/j.jclepro.2020.125233

Bahoo, S., Cucculelli, M., Goga, X., & Mondolo, J. (2024). Artificial intelligence in Finance: A comprehensive review through bibliometric and content analysis. *SN Business & Economics, 4*(2), 23.

Bai, C., Duan, Y., Fan, X., & Tang, S. (2023). Financial market sentiment and stock return during the COVID-19 pandemic. *Finance Research Letters, 54*, 103709. DOI: 10.1016/j.frl.2023.103709 PMID: 36811022

Baker, M., Gentry, R., & Hsu, C. (2020). The role of ESG ratings in investment decisions: Evidence from institutional investors. *Journal of Sustainable Finance & Investment, 10*(3), 215–230. DOI: 10.1080/20430795.2020.1741234

Baker, M., & Stein, J. C. (2004). Market liquidity as a sentiment indicator. *Journal of Financial Markets, 7*, 271–299. DOI: 10.1016/j.finmar.2003.11.005

Baker, M., & Wurgler, J. (2006). Investor Sentiment and the Cross-Section of Stock Returns. *The Journal of Finance, 61*(4), 1645–1680. DOI: 10.1111/j.1540-6261.2006.00885.x

Baker, M., Wurgler, J., & Yuan, Y. (2012). Global, local, and contagious investor sentiment. *Journal of Financial Economics, 104*, 272–287. DOI: 10.1016/j.jfineco.2011.11.002

Balcıoğlu, Y. S., Çelik, A. A., & Altındağ, E. (2024). Artificial intelligence integration in Sustainable Business Practices: A text mining analysis of USA firms. *Sustainability, 16*(15), 6334. DOI: 10.3390/su16156334

Baltgailis, J., Meņšikovs, V., & Šipilova, V. (2023). Digital currencies and financial literacy: Essay on sustainable finances' perspectives. *Sociālo Zinātņu Vēstnesis*, (2), 7–24.

Bank for International Settlements (BIS). (2018).*Rapport du Committee on Payments and Market Infrastructure et du Markets Committee*. Basel: Bank for International Settlements. Retrieved from: https://www.bis.org/cpmi/publ/d174.htm (accessed 13 September 2020)

Banque de France. (2018). *Rapport annuel de l'Observatoire de l'inclusion bancaire*. Paris: Banque de France. Retrieved from: https://publications.banque-france.fr/sites/default/files/medias/documents/oib2018_web_signets.pdf (accessed 06April 2021)

Bansal, G., Nushi, B., Kamar, E., Horvitz, E., & Weld, D. S. (2021). Is the Most Accurate AI the Best Teammate? Optimizing AI for Teamwork. In *35th AAAI Conference on Artificial Intelligence, AAAI 2021* (Vol. 13A, pp. 11405–11414). Association for the Advancement of Artificial Intelligence. https://www.scopus.com/inward/record.uri?eid=2-s2.0-85130010234&partnerID=40&md5=a709626aba1d3e88fcea1680ed2c9558

Bansal, T. (2020). *Behavioral Finance and COVID-19: Cognitive Errors that Determine the Financial Future* (SSRN Scholarly Paper 3595749). https://doi.org/DOI: 10.2139/ssrn.3595749

Bao, X., Sadiq, M., Tye, W., & Zhang, J. (2024). The impact of environmental, social, and governance (ESG) rating disparities on corporate risk: The mediating role of financing constraints. *Journal of Environmental Management*, *371*, 123113. DOI: 10.1016/j.jenvman.2024.123113 PMID: 39481154

Barberis, N. (2018). Psychology-Based Models of Asset Prices and Trading Volume. In *Handbook of Behavioral Economics: Applications and Foundations 1* (Vol. 1, pp. 79–175). Elsevier. DOI: 10.1016/bs.hesbe.2018.07.001

Barberis, N. C. (2013). Thirty Years of Prospect Theory in Economics: A Review and Assessment. *The Journal of Economic Perspectives*, *27*(1), 173–196. DOI: 10.1257/jep.27.1.173

Barontini, C., & Holden, H. (2019). Proceeding with Caution – a Survey on Central Bank Digital Currency.Bank for International Settlements, BIS Papers 101. Retrieved from: https://www.bis.org/publ/bppdf/bispap101.pdf (accessed 3 October 2020)

Bax, K., Bonaccolto, G., & Paterlini, S. (2024). Spillovers in Europe: The role of ESG. *Journal of Financial Stability*, *72*, 101221. DOI: 10.1016/j.jfs.2024.101221

Behera, A. K., Nayak, N. C., & Das, H. C. (2016). Performance of Indian Service Industries Due to IT Adoption. *Global Business Review*, *17*(5), 1073–1093. DOI: 10.1177/0972150916656657

Behl, A., Kumari, P. S. R., Makhija, H., & Sharma, D. (2021). Exploring the relationship of ESG score and firm value using cross-lagged panel analyses: Case of the Indian energy sector. *Annals of Operations Research*, *313*(1), 231–256.

Belk, R. (2021). Ethical issues in service robotics and artificial intelligence. *Service Industries Journal*, *41*(13-14), 860–876.

Benckendorff, P. J., Xiang, Z., & Sheldon, P. J. (2019). *Tourism information technology*. Cabi.

Berentsen, A., & Schar, F. (2018). The Case for Central Bank Electronic Money and the Non-Case for Central Bank Cryptocurrencies. *Review - Federal Reserve Bank of St. Louis*, *100*(2), 97–106. Retrieved September 15, 2020, from https://research.stlouisfed.org/publications/review/2018/02/13/the-case-for-central-bank-electronic-m

Bharti, S. S., Prasad, K., Sudha, S., & Kumari, V. (2024). Correction to : Customer acceptability towards AI-enabled digital banking: a PLS-SEM approach. *Journal of Financial Services Marketing*, *29*(4), 1653–1653. DOI: 10.1057/s41264-023-00250-8

Bhatia, A., Chandani, A., Atiq, R., Mehta, M., & Divekar, R. (2021). Artificial intelligence in financial services: A qualitative research to discover robo-advisory services. *Qualitative Research in Financial Markets*, *13*(5), 632–654. DOI: 10.1108/QRFM-10-2020-0199

Bicchieri, C., & Fukui, Y. (1999). The great illusion: Ignorance, informational cascades, and the persistence of unpopular norms. *Business Ethics Quarterly*, *9*, 127–155. DOI: 10.2307/3857639

Bihari Singh, A., Gaurav, G., Sarkar, P., Sharan Dangayach, G., & Lal Meena, M. (2024). Current understanding, motivations, and barriers towards implementing sustainable initiatives in the hospitality industry in the age of automation and artificial intelligence. *Recent Patents on Engineering*, *18*(7), 2–25.

Bikhchandani, S., Hirshleifer, D., & Welch, I. (1992). A theory of fads, fashion, custom, and cultural change as informational cascades. *Journal of Political Economy*, *100*, 992–1026. DOI: 10.1086/261849

Bilgihan, A., Kandampully, J., & Zhang, T. (2016). Towards a unified customer experience in online shopping environments: Antecedents and outcomes. *International Journal of Quality and Service Sciences*, *8*(1), 102–119.

Bilgihan, A., Nejad, M., & Cobanoglu, C. (2016). The impact of information technology innovations on hotels. In *Advances in Hospitality and Leisure* (Vol. 12, pp. 109–127). Emerald Group Publishing Limited., DOI: 10.1108/S1745-354220160000012005

Binh, N. T. T. (2024). An application of artificial neural networks in corporate social responsibility decision making. In *Intelligent Systems in Accounting, Finance and Management* (Vol. 31, Issue 1). John Wiley and Sons Inc. DOI: 10.1002/isaf.1542

Binns, R. (2018). Fairness in Machine Learning: Lessons from Political Philosophy. *Proceedings of Machine Learning Research*, *81*, 1–18.

BlackRock. (n.d.). Sustainable investing and environmental, social and governance (ESG) integration. https://www.blackrock.com/corporate/literature/publication/blk-esg-investment-statement-web.pdf

Bloomberg. (2023). *Wall Street Banks Are Cracking Down on AI-Powered ChatGPT. Technology*. Singap World Sci.

Bollerslev, T. (1986). Generalized autoregressive conditional heteroskedasticity. *Journal of Econometrics*, *31*(3), 307–327.

Bondt, W. D., Mayoral, R. M., & Vallelado, E. (2013). Behavioral decision-making in finance: An overview and assessment of selected research. *Spanish Journal of Finance and Accounting / Revista Española de Financiación y Contabilidad*. https://www.tandfonline.com/doi/abs/10.1080/02102412.2013.10779742

Bourezk, H., Raji, A., Acha, N., & Barka, H. (2020). Analyzing Moroccan Stock Market using Machine Learning and Sentiment Analysis. *2020 1st International Conference on Innovative Research in Applied Science, Engineering and Technology (IRASET)*, 1–5. https://doi.org/DOI: 10.1109/IRASET48871.2020.9092304

Bouteraa, M., Chekima, B., Thurasamy, R., Bin-Nashwan, S. A., Al-Daihani, M., Baddou, A., & Ansar, R. (2024). Open Innovation in the Financial Sector: A Mixed-Methods Approach to Assess Bankers' Willingness to Embrace Open-AI ChatGPT. *Journal of Open Innovation*, *10*(1), 100216. DOI: 10.1016/j.joitmc.2024.100216

Braun, V., & Clarke, V. (2006). Using thematic analysis in psychology. *Qualitative Research in Psychology*, *3*(2), 77–101.

Breiman, L. (2001). Random Forests. *Machine Learning*, *45*(1), 5–32. DOI: 10.1023/A:1010933404324

Brown, G. W., & Cliff, M. T. (2004). Investor sentiment and the near-term stock market. *Journal of Empirical Finance, 11*, 1–27. DOI: 10.2139/ssrn.282915

Bruna, M. G., Loprevite, S., Raucci, D., Ricca, B., & Rupo, D. (2022). Investigating the marginal impact of ESG results on corporate financial performance. *Finance Research Letters, 47*, 102828.

Brynjolfsson, E., & McAfee, A. (2014). *The second machine age: Work, progress, and prosperity in a time of brilliant technologies*. W. W. Norton & Company.

Buhalis, D., & Sinarta, Y. (2019). Real-time co-creation and nowness service: Lessons from tourism and hospitality. *Journal of Travel & Tourism Marketing, 36*(5), 563–582.

Bunker, R. P., & Thabtah, F. (2019). A machine learning framework for sport result prediction. *Applied Computing and Informatics, 15*(1), 27–33. DOI: 10.1016/j.aci.2017.09.005

Cai, F., Han, S., Li, D., & Li, Y. (2019). Institutional herding and its price impact: Evidence from the corporate bond market. *Journal of Financial Economics, 131*, 139–167. DOI: 10.1016/j.jfineco.2018.07.012

Campos-Blázquez, J. R., Rubio-Andrada, L., & Celemín-Pedroche, M. S. (2023). Voices from within. To what extent can internal crowdsourcing drive a change in organizational culture? *Journal of Business Research, 157*, 113618.

Candus, E., Pfister, C., & Sedillot, F. (2017). Où s'investit l'épargne des Français? *Bulletin de la Banque de France, 214*, 5–21. https://publications.banque-france.fr/sites/default/files/medias/documents/bulletin-bf-214_web.pdf(accessed 21 October 2020)

Cao, L. (2022). Ai in finance: Challenges, techniques, and opportunities. *ACM Computing Surveys, 55*(3), 1–38.

Capinzaiki Ottonicar, S. L., & Pomim Valentim, M. L. (2021). Industry 4.0 and open innovation in startups accelerators. DOI: .DOI: 10.5380/atoz.v10i3.81882

Carlisle, S., Ivanov, S., & Dijkmans, C. (2023). The digital skills divide: evidence from the European tourism industry. *Journal of tourism futures, 9*(2), 240-266.

Carney, M. (2016).*Enabling the FinTech Transformation: Revolution, Restoration, or Reformation?* London: Bank of England. Retrieved from:https://www.bankofengland.co.uk/-/media/boe/files/speech/2016/enabling-the-fintech-transformation-revolution-restoration-or-reformation.pdf (accessed 6April 2021)

Car, T., Stifanich, L. P., & Šimunić, M. (2019). Internet of things (iot) in tourism and hospitality: Opportunities and challenges. *Tourism in South East Europe, 5*(3), 163–175.

Celen, B., & Kariv, S. (2004). Distinguishing informational cascades from herd behaviour in the laboratory. *The American Economic Review, 94*, 484–498. DOI: 10.1257/0002828041464461

CESE. Conseil Economique, Social et Environnemental. (2020). Le tourisme, levier de développement durable et d'intégration. In *Avis Du Conseil Economique, Social Et Environnemental*. https://www.cese.ma/media/2023/09/Avis-tourisme-VF.pdf

Cevik, E., Kirci Altinkeski, B., Cevik, E. I., & Dibooglu, S. (2022). Investor sentiments and stock markets during the COVID-19 pandemic. *Financial Innovation*, *8*(1), 69. DOI: 10.1186/s40854-022-00375-0 PMID: 35814528

Chai, S., Cao, M., Li, Q., Ji, Q., & Liu, Z. (2023). Exploring the nexus between ESG disclosure and corporate sustainable growth: Moderating role of media attention. *Finance Research Letters*, *58*(104519), 104519.

Chakraborty, A., & Gummadi, K. (2020). Fairness in Algorithmic Decision Making. *Proceedings of the 7th ACM IKDD CoDS and 25th COMAD.*https://doi.org/DOI: 10.1145/3371158.3371234

Challoumis, C. (2024). THE FUTURE OF BUSINESS-INTEGRATING AI INTO THE FINANCIAL CYCLE. In *XIV International Scientific Conference* (pp. 44-78).

Chauhan, S. (2020). *Financial Literacy and Retirement Confidence A Study of Private Sector Employees*. Amity University.

Chelawat, H., & Trivedi, I. V. (2016). The business value of ESG performance: The Indian context. *Asian Journal of Business Ethics*, *5*(1), 195–210.

Chen, X., & Xie, H. Di Zou, Gwo-Jen Hwang. (2020). Application and theory gaps during the rise of Artificial Intelligence in Education, Computers and Education: Artificial Intelligence, Volume 1,100002, ISSN 2666-920X, https://doi.org/DOI: 10.1016/j.caeai.2020.100002

Chen, J., Wang, N., Lin, T., Liu, B., & Hu, J. (2024). Shock or Empowerment? Artificial intelligence technology and corporate ESG performance. *Economic Analysis and Policy*, *83*, 1080–1096. DOI: 10.1016/j.eap.2024.08.004

Chen, Y., Albert, L. J., & Jensen, S. (2022). Innovation farm: Teaching artificial intelligence through gamified social entrepreneurship in an introductory MIS course*. *Decision Sciences Journal of Innovative Education, 20*(1), 43–56. *Scopus.* Advance online publication. DOI: 10.1111/dsji.12253

Chesbrough, H. (2003). Open innovation: The new imperative for creating and profiting from technology.

Chhaochharia, V., Kim, D., Korniotis, G. M., & Kumar, A. (2019). Mood, firm behaviour, and aggregate economic outcomes. *Journal of Financial Economics*, *132*, 427–450. DOI: 10.1016/j.jfineco.2018.10.010

Chikhi, D. E. B., & Ramdani, B. (2023). L'influence de l'intelligence artificielle sur l'efficacité de l'audit financier: Tendances, défis et opportunités. *Revue Française d'Economie et de Gestion*, *4*(12).

Chilunjika, A., Intauno, K. I., & Chilunjika, S. R. (2022). Artificial intelligence and public sector human resource management in South Africa: Opportunities, challenges and prospects. South African Journal of Human Resource Management.

Chinco, A., Hartzmark, S. M., & Sussman, A. B. (2022). A new test of risk factor relevance. *The Journal of Finance*, *77*, 2183–2238. DOI: 10.1111/jofi.13135

Chnigri, Y., Sadik, M., & Slimani, H. (2024). Mapping the Literature on Intelligent Systems and Decision Support in Higher Education: A Bibliometric Analysis. https://doi.org/DOI: 10.5281/ZENODO.13700094

Chong, T., Chong, T., Loh, L., & Loh, L. (2023). Innovating ESG Integration as Sustainable Strategy: ESG Transparency and Firm Valuation in the Palm Oil Sector. *Sustainability*, *15*(22), 15943.

Cipriani, M., & Guarino, A. (2005). Herd behaviour in a laboratory financial market. *The American Economic Review*, *95*, 1427–1443. DOI: 10.1257/000282805775014443

Colliers International. (2018). *Ukraine hotel market research & forecast report.* Colliers International. Retrieved: https://www.colliers.com/-/media/Files/EMEA/Ukraine/Reports-Eng/Hotels_Eng.ashx (consulted on January 26, 2025)

Cortes, C., & Vapnik, V. (1995). Support-vector networks. *Machine Learning*, *20*(3), 273–297. DOI: 10.1007/BF00994018

Cricelli, L., Grimaldi, M., & Vermicelli, S. (2022). Crowdsourcing and open innovation: A systematic literature review, an integrated framework and a research agenda. *Review of Managerial Science*, *16*(5), 1269–1310.

Da Silva, R. F., & Martha De Souza, G. F. (2021). Mapping the Literature on Asset Management: A Bibliometric Analysis. *Journal of Scientometric Research*, *10*(1), 27–36. DOI: 10.5530/jscires.10.1.4

Dabić, M., Daim, T., Bogers, M. L., & Mention, A. L. (2023). The limits of open innovation: Failures, risks, and costs in open innovation practice and theory. *Technovation*, *126*, 102786.

Dafoe, A. (2018). AI governance: A research agenda. Governance of AI Program, The Future of Humanity Institute, The University of Oxford, Oxford, UK.

Dakalbab, F., Talib, M. A., Nassir, Q., & Ishak, T. (2024). Artificial intelligence techniques in financial trading: A systematic literature review. *Journal of King Saud University. Computer and Information Sciences*, •••, 102015.

Daly, A., Hagendorff, T., Li, H., Mann, M., Marda, V., & Wagner, B. (2020). AI, Governance and Ethics: Global Perspectives. SSRN *Electronic Journal*.

Daneshjou, R., Smith, M., Sun, M., Rotemberg, V., & Zou, J. (2021). Lack of Transparency and Potential Bias in Artificial Intelligence Data Sets and Algorithms: A Scoping Review. *JAMA Dermatology*. Advance online publication. DOI: 10.1001/jamadermatol.2021.3129 PMID: 34550305

Das, S. K., Anwar, S., Tulsyan, U., Gupta, Y., Vudatha, R., Hassan, S., & Gardezi, I. (2024). The Role of AI in Financial Markets: Impacts on Trading, Portfolio Management, and Price Prediction. *Journal of Electrical Systems*, *20*(6s), 1000–1006.

Das, S. R., & Chen, M. Y. (2007). Yahoo! for Amazon: Sentiment Extraction from Small Talk on the Web. *Management Science*, *53*(9), 1375–1388. DOI: 10.1287/mnsc.1070.0704

Davenport, T. H., & Ronanki, R. (2018). Artificial intelligence for the real world. *Harvard Business Review*, *96*(1), 108–116.

Dayanandan, A., Donker, H., & Kuntluru, S. (2023). IFRS and ESG Disclosure in Indian Corporate Sector. Journal of Emerging Market Finance. https://doi.org/DOI: 10.1177/09726527231197328

De Bondt, W., & Driehaus, R. H. (2005). *The Psychology of World Equity Markets*. Edward Elgar Publishing. https://econpapers.repec.org/bookchap/elgeebook/2773.htm

De Bondt, W., & Thaler, R. (1985). Does the Stock Market Overreact? *The Journal of Finance*, *40*(3), 793–805. DOI: 10.1111/j.1540-6261.1985.tb05004.x

Deb, S., Sajit, S. K., & Digar, B. (2023). *Does ESG Improve Firm Performance?* Evidence from Indian Companies.

Décamps, J. P., & Lovo, S. (2006). Informational cascades with endogenous prices: The role of risk aversion. *Journal of Mathematical Economics*, *42*, 109–120. DOI: 10.1016/j.jmateco.2005.03.002

Del Vitto, A., Marazzina, D., & Stocco, D. (2023). ESG ratings explainability through machine learning techniques. *Annals of Operations Research*. Advance online publication. DOI: 10.1007/s10479-023-05514-z

Deloitte. (2023). How artificial intelligence is transforming ESG reportingDeloitte Insights*. https://www2.deloitte.com/fr/fr/insights/technology-media-and-telecom-predictions/2024/esg-reporting-software-growth-prediction.html

Devlin, J., Chang, M. W., Lee, K., & Toutanova, K. (2019). BERT: Pre-training of deep bidirectional transformers for language understanding. In *Proceedings of NAACL-HLT*. 4171–4186.

Dey, R., & Salem, F. M. (2017). Gate-variants of Gated Recurrent Unit (GRU) neural networks. 2017 IEEE 60th International Midwest Symposium on Circuits and Systems (MWSCAS), 1597–1600.

Dhiman, B. (2024). A Framework For Exploring The Integration Of AI And Financial Literacy Toward A Sustainable Financial Ecosystem. *Educational Administration: Theory and Practice*, *30*(4), 8750–8759.

Di Martino, G., Miglietta, F., & Potì, V. (2024). The impact of ESG scores on the value relevance of fair value hierarchy of financial instruments: Evidence from European Banks. *Research in International Business and Finance*, *71*, 102451. DOI: 10.1016/j.ribaf.2024.102451

Diakopoulos, N. (2016). Algorithmic accountability: Journalistic investigation of computational power structures. *Digital Journalism (Abingdon, England)*, *3*(3), 398–415. DOI: 10.1080/21670811.2014.976411

Díaz-Rodríguez, N., Del Ser, J., Coeckelbergh, M., López De Prado, M., Herrera-Viedma, E., & Herrera, F. (2023). Connecting the dots in trustworthy Artificial Intelligence: From AI principles, ethics, and key requirements to responsible AI systems and regulation. *Information Fusion*, *99*, 101896. DOI: 10.1016/j.inffus.2023.101896

Dicuonzo, G., Palmaccio, M., & Shini, M. (2023). ESG, governance variables and Fintech: An empirical analysis. *Research in International Business and Finance*, *69*, 102205. DOI: 10.1016/j.ribaf.2023.102205

Ding, X., Zhang, Y., Liu, T., & Duan, J. (2015). Deep Learning for Event-Driven Stock Prediction. *Proceedings of the Twenty-Fourth International Joint Conference on Artificial Intelligence (IJCAI 2015)*.

Dobrick, J., Klein, C., & Zwergel, B. (2023). Size bias in Refinitiv ESG data. *Finance Research Letters*, *55*, 104014. DOI: 10.1016/j.frl.2023.104014

Dodman, D., Diep, L., & Colenbrander, S. (2017). Making the case for the nexus between resilience and resource efficiency at the city scale. *International Journal of Urban Sustainable Development*. Advance online publication. DOI: 10.1080/19463138.2017.1345740

Doherty, O. (2018). Infomational cascades in financial markets: Review and synthesis. *Review of Behavioral Finance*, *10*, 53–69. DOI: 10.1108/RBF-05-2016-0030

Dong, M. M., Stratopoulos, T. C., & Wang, V. X. (2024). A scoping review of ChatGPT research in accounting and finance. *International Journal of Accounting Information Systems*, *55*, 100715.

Donthu, N., Kumar, S., Mukherjee, D., Pandey, N., & Lim, W. M. (2021). How to conduct a bibliometric analysis: An overview and guidelines. *Journal of Business Research*, *133*, 285–296. DOI: 10.1016/j.jbusres.2021.04.070

Doshi, M., Jain, R., Sharma, D., Mukherjee, D., & Kumar, S. (2024). Does ownership influence ESG disclosure scores? *. *Research in International Business and Finance*, *67*, 102122. DOI: 10.1016/j.ribaf.2023.102122

Dowling, M., & Lucey, B. (2023). ChatGPT for (finance) research: The Bananarama conjecture. *Finance Research Letters*, *53*, 103662.

Drumetz, F., Pfister, S., & Sahuc, J.-G. (2015). *Politique monétaire* (2 ed.).Louvain-la-Neuve: de Boeck.

Du, K., Xing, F., Mao, R., & Cambria, E. (2024). Financial Sentiment Analysis: Techniques and Applications. *ACM Comput. Surv.*, *56*(9), 220:1-220:42. https://doi.org/DOI: 10.1145/3649451

Duan, W. J., Gu, B., & Whinston, A. B. (2009). Informational cascades and software adoption on the Internet: An empirical investigation. *Management Information Systems Quarterly*, *33*, 23–48. DOI: 10.2307/20650277

Duan, Y., Edwards, J. S., & Dwivedi, Y. K. (2019). Artificial intelligence for decision making in the era of Big Data–evolution, challenges and research agenda. *International Journal of Information Management*, *48*, 63–71.

Dwivedi, Y. K., Hughes, D. L., & Ismagilova, E.. (2021). Artificial Intelligence (AI): Multidisciplinary perspectives on emerging challenges, opportunities, and agenda for research, practice, and policy. *International Journal of Information Management*, *57*, 101994. DOI: 10.1016/j.ijinfomgt.2019.08.002

Dwivedi, Y. K., Hughes, L., Ismagilova, E., Aarts, G., Coombs, C., Crick, T., & Williams, M. D. (2021). Artificial Intelligence (AI): Multidisciplinary perspectives on emerging challenges, opportunities, and agenda for research, practice and policy. *International Journal of Information Management*, *57*, 101994.

Egorova, A. A., Grishunin, S. V., & Karminsky, A. M. (2022). The Impact of ESG factors on the performance of Information Technology Companies. *Procedia Computer Science*, *199*, 339–345.

Eisfeldt, A. L., & Schubert, G. (2024). *AI and Finance* (No. w33076). National Bureau of Economic Research.

Elamin, M. O. I. (2023). Advancing Ethical and Sustainable Economy: Islamic Finance Solutions for Environmental, Social, & Economic Challenges in the Digital Age. *International Journal of Membrane Science and Technology*.

Emma, G. M., Emiliano, R. B., & Jennifer, M. F. (2024). High-quality assurance, ESG legitimacy threats and board effectiveness. *The British Accounting Review, 101385*, 101385. Advance online publication. DOI: 10.1016/j.bar.2024.101385

Engert, W., & Fung, S. C. (2019). Motivations and Implications of a Central Bank Digital Currency. In E. Gnan & D. Masciandaro (Eds.), Do We Need Central Bank Digital Currency? Economics, Technology and Institutions (pp. 56–71). SUERF., Retrieved from https://www.suerf.org/studies/7025/do-we-need-centralbank-digital-currency-economics-technology-and-institutions, Retrieved September 18, 2020, from.

Engle, R. F. (1982). Autoregressive conditional heteroscedasticity with estimates of the variance of United Kingdom inflation. *Econometrica, 50*(4), 987–1007.

Ern, A., Villeneuve, S., & Zanette, A. (2004). Adaptive finite element methods for local volatility European option pricing. *International Journal of Theoretical and Applied Finance, 7*, 659–684. DOI: 10.1142/S0219024904002669

European Central Bank (ECB). (2020). *Report on a digital euro*. Frankfurt: European Central Bank. Retrieved from:www.ecb.europa.eu/pub/pdf/other/Report_on_a_digital_euro~4d7268b458.en.pdf (accessed 24 September 2020)

Ewerton, A. A., & Jordão, R. V. D. (2024). The role of artificial intelligence in the decision-making process: A study on the financial analysis and movement forecasting of the world's largest stock exchanges. In *Management Decision*. Emerald Publishing., DOI: 10.1108/MD-09-2023-1625

Fadhel, M. A., Duhaim, A. M., Albahri, A. S., Al-Qaysi, Z. T., Aktham, M. A., Chyad, M. A., Abd-Alaziz, W., Albahri, O. S., Alamoodi, A., Alzubaidi, L., Gupta, A., & Gu, Y. (2024). Navigating the metaverse: Unraveling the impact of artificial intelligence—a comprehensive review and gap analysis. *Artificial Intelligence Review, 57*(10). Advance online publication. DOI: 10.1007/s10462-024-10881-5

Fama, E. F. (1965). The Behavior of Stock-Market Prices. *The Journal of Business, 38*(1), 34–105.

Fama, E. F. (1970). Efficient Capital Markets: A Review of Theory and Empirical Work. *The Journal of Finance, 25*(2), 383–417. DOI: 10.2307/2325486

Farida, I., & Setiawan, D. (2022). Business strategies and competitive advantage: the role of performance and innovation. *Journal of Open Innovation: Technology, Place of technological based market, and Complexity, 8*(3), 163.

Fazelpour, S., & Danks, D. (2021). Algorithmic bias: Senses, sources, solutions. *Philosophy Compass*. Advance online publication. DOI: 10.1111/PHC3.12760

Federal Reserve System (FED). (2019).*Federal Reserve Actions to Support Interbank Settlement of Faster Payments*. Washington, D.C.: Board of Governors of the Federal Reserve System. Retrieved from:https://www.federalreserve.gov/newsevents/pressreleases/files/other20190805a1.pdf(accessed 14 September 2020)

Feng, C., Ma, R., & Jiang, L. (2021). The impact of service innovation on firm performance: A meta-analysis. *Journal of Service Management*, *32*(3), 289–314. DOI: 10.1108/JOSM-03-2019-0089

Feng, S., Cheng, L., & Guang, Z. X. (2017). Analysis of industry risk premium with MVS three dimensions vector factor model. *Cogent Economics & Finance*, *5*(1), 1374814. DOI: 10.1080/23322039.2017.1374814

Ferjančič, U., Ichev, R., Lončarski, I., Montariol, S., Pelicon, A., Pollak, S., Sitar Šuštar, K., Toman, A., Valentinčič, A., & Žnidaršič, M. (2024). Textual analysis of corporate sustainability reporting and corporate ESG scores. *International Review of Financial Analysis*, *96*, 103669. DOI: 10.1016/j.irfa.2024.103669

Fernandes, T., & Oliveira, E. (2021). Understanding consumers' acceptance of automated technologies in service encounters: Drivers of digital voice assistants adoption. *Journal of Business Research*, *122*, 180–191. DOI: 10.1016/j.jbusres.2020.08.058

Feuerriegel, S., Shrestha, Y. R., von Krogh, G., & Zhang, C. (2022). Bringing artificial intelligence to business management. *Nature Machine Intelligence*, *4*(7), 611–613. DOI: 10.1038/s42256-022-00512-5

Fink, A. (2019). *Conducting research literature reviews: From the internet to paper*. Sage publications.

Fiore, A., & Morone, A. (2008). A simple note on informational cascades. *Economics*, *1*, 1–21. DOI: 10.5018/economics-ejournal.ja.2008-1

Fischer, T., & Krauss, C. (2018). Deep learning with long short-term memory networks for financial market predictions. *European Journal of Operational Research*, *270*(2), 654–669.

Floridi, L. (2019). Establishing the rules for building trustworthy AI. *Nature Machine Intelligence*, *1*(5), 261–262.

Floridi, L., & Cowls, J. (2019). A Unified Framework of Five Principles for AI in Society. *Harvard Data Science Review*. Advance online publication. DOI: 10.1162/99608f92.8cd550d1

Floridi, L., & Cowls, J. (2022). A Unified Framework of Five Principles for AI in Society. In *Machine Learning and the City* (pp. 535–545). John Wiley & Sons, Ltd., DOI: 10.1002/9781119815075.ch45

Florido-Benítez, L., & del Alcázar Martínez, B. (2024). How artificial intelligence (ai) is powering new tourism marketing and the future agenda for smart tourist destinations. *Electronics (Basel)*, *13*(21), 4151.

Fotheringham, D., & Wiles, M. A. (2023). The effect of implementing chatbot customer service on stock returns: An event study analysis. *Journal of the Academy of Marketing Science*, *51*(4), 802–822.

French, K. R. (1980). Stock returns and the weekend effect. *Journal of Financial Economics*, *8*(1), 55–69. DOI: 10.1016/0304-405X(80)90021-5

Froot, K. A., Scharfstein, D. S., & Stein, J. C. (1992). Herd on the street: Informational inefficiencies in a market with short-term speculation. *The Journal of Finance*, *47*, 1461–1484. DOI: 10.3386/w3250

Fukuda-Parr, S., & Gibbons, E. (2021). Emerging Consensus on 'Ethical AI'. *Global Policy*, *12*(2), 272–284. https://consensus.app/papers/emerging-consensus-ethical-human-rights-critique-fukuda-parr/c1df02a41d7e540fa6de040534b096df

Fung, B. S. C., & Halaburda, H. (2016). Central Bank Digital Currencies: a Framework for Assessing Why and How. Bank of Canada, Discussion Paper 2016-22. Retrieved from: https://www.researchgate.net/publication/318555671_Central_Bank_Digital_Currencies_A_Framework_for_Assessing_Why_and_How (accessed 15 November 2020)

Galeone, G., Ranaldo, S., & Fusco, A. (2024). ESG and FinTech: Are they connected? *. *Research in International Business and Finance*, *69*, 102225. DOI: 10.1016/j.ribaf.2024.102225

Gallego-Losada, M. J., García-Abajo, M. E., Montero-Navarro, A., & Gallego-Losada, R. (2021). The challenge of digital financial literacy in the field of fintech (industry 4.0). *ESIC Market*, *53*(1), e277. DOI: 10.7200/esicm.53.277

Gama, F., & Magistretti, S. (2023). Artificial intelligence in innovation management: A review of innovation capabilities and a taxonomy of AI applications. *Journal of Product Innovation Management*. Advance online publication. DOI: 10.1111/jpim.12698

Gao, J. (2024). Optimizing hotel revenue management through dynamic pricing algorithms and data analysis. *Journal of Computational Methods in Science and Engineering*, 14727978241298467.

García, D. (2013). Sentiment during recessions. *The Journal of Finance*, *68*, 1267–1300. DOI: 10.1111/jofi.12027

García-Madurga, M. Á., & Grilló-Méndez, A. J. (2023). Artificial Intelligence in the tourism industry: An overview of reviews. *Administrative Sciences*, *13*(8), 172.

Garzella, S., Fiorentino, R., Caputo, A., & Lardo, A. (2021). Business model innovation in SMEs: The role of boundaries in the digital era. *Technology Analysis and Strategic Management*, *33*(1), 31–43.

Gasser, U., & Almeida, V. (2017). A Layered Model for AI Governance. *IEEE Internet Computing*, *21*, 58–62. DOI: 10.1109/MIC.2017.4180835

Gilster, P. (1997). *Digital literacy*. John Wiley & Sons, Inc.

Giunchiglia, F., Otterbacher, J., Kleanthous, S., Batsuren, K., Bogina, V., Kuflik, T., & Tal, A. (2021). Towards Algorithmic Transparency: A Diversity Perspective. *ArXiv*, abs/2104.05658.

Gkika, E. C., Anagnostopoulos, T., Ntanos, S., & Kyriakopoulos, G. L. (2020). User preferences on cloud computing and open innovation: A case study for university employees in Greece. *Journal of Open Innovation: Technology, Place of technological based market, and Complexity, 6*(2), 41.

Globalluxsoft. (n.d.). IMPACT OF INDUSTRY 4.0 in global manufacturing. Retrieved from Globalluxsoft. https://globalluxsoft.com/impact-industry-4-in-global-manufacturing- Internet of other things

Goeree, J. K., Palfrey, T. R., Rogers, B. W., & Mckelvey, R. D. (2007). Self-correcting information cascades. *The Review of Economic Studies*, *74*, 733–762. DOI: 10.1111/j.1467-937X.2007.00438.x

Goodfellow, I., Bengio, Y., & Courville, A. (2016). *Deep learning*. MIT Press.

Gossner, O., & Melissas, N. (2006). Informational cascades elicit private information. *International Economic Review*, *47*, 297–325. DOI: 10.1111/j.1468-2354.2006.00380.x

Grebe, T., Schmid, J., & Stiehler, A. (2008). Do individuals recognize cascade behaviour of others?- An experimental study. *Journal of Economic Psychology*, *29*, 197–209. DOI: 10.1016/j.joep.2007.05.003

Gretzel, U., Sigala, M., Xiang, Z., & Koo, C. (2015). Smart tourism: Foundations and developments. *Electronic Markets*, *25*, 179–188.

Grinblatt, M., & Keloharju, M. (2000). The investment behavior and performance of various investor types: A study of Finland's unique data set. *Journal of Financial Economics*, *55*(1), 43–67. DOI: 10.1016/S0304-405X(99)00044-6

Guo, H., & Polák, P. (2021). Artificial Intelligence and Financial Technology FinTech: How AI Is Being Used Under the Pandemic in 2020. *Studies in computational intelligence*, 935, 169-186. https://doi.org/.DOI: 10.1007/978-3-030-62796-6_9

Gupta, J., & Das, N. (2022). Multidimensional corporate social responsibility disclosure and financial performance: A meta-analytical review. *Corporate Social Responsibility and Environmental Management*, *29*(4), 731–748.

Gurdgiev, C., & O'Loughlin, D. (2020). Herding and anchoring in cryptocurrency markets: Investor reaction to fear and uncertainty. *Journal of Behavioral and Experimental Finance*, *25*, 100271.

Gu, S., Kelly, B., & Xiu, D. (2020). Empirical asset pricing via machine learning. *Review of Financial Studies*, *33*(5), 2223–2273.

Hadi, M. U., Tashi, Q. A., Shah, A., Qureshi, R., Muneer, A., Irfan, M., Zafar, A., Shaikh, M. B., Akhtar, N., Wu, J., Mirjalili, S., & Shah, M. (2024). *Large Language Models: A Comprehensive Survey of its Applications, Challenges, Limitations, and Future Prospects*. DOI: 10.36227/techrxiv.23589741.v6

Hagendorff, T. (2019). The Ethics of AI Ethics: An Evaluation of Guidelines. *Minds and Machines*, *30*(1), 99–120.

Hajian, S., Bonchi, F., & Castillo, C. (2016). Algorithmic Bias: From Discrimination Discovery to Fairness-aware Data Mining. *Proceedings of the 22nd ACM SIGKDD International Conference on Knowledge Discovery and Data Mining*.https://doi.org/DOI: 10.1145/2939672.2945386

Hastie, T., Friedman, J., & Tibshirani, R. (2001). *The Elements of Statistical Learning*. Springer New York., DOI: 10.1007/978-0-387-21606-5

Heaton, J. B., Polson, N. G., & Witte, J. H. (2017). Deep learning in finance. *Applied Stochastic Models in Business and Industry*, *33*(1), 3–12.

Hemanand, D., Mishra, N., Premalatha, G., Mavaluru, D., Vajpayee, A., Kushwaha, S., & Sahile, K. (2022). Applications of Intelligent Model to Analyze the Green Finance for Environmental Development in the Context of Artificial Intelligence. *Computational Intelligence and Neuroscience*. Advance online publication. DOI: 10.1155/2022/2977824 PMID: 35845917

Henrici, A., & Osterrieder, J. (2022). Editorial: Artificial intelligence in finance and industry: Highlights from 6 European COST conferences. In *Frontiers in Artificial Intelligence* (Vol. 5). Frontiers Media S.A. DOI: 10.3389/frai.2022.1007074

Hernandez, A. A., Sacdalan, R. V., Sopoco, C. T., Villapando, J. E., & Garcia, P. M. (2024, February). Predicting the Innovation Capability for Firm Performance: the role of Artificial Intelligence in the Philippines Startups Perspective. In 2024 16th International Conference on Knowledge and Smart Technology (KST) (pp. 195-200). IEEE. DOI: DOI: 10.1109/KST61284.2024.10499661

Hickman, E., & Petrin, M. (2020). Trustworthy AI and Corporate Governance. *European Business Organization Law Review*, *22*, 593–625.

Hirshleifer, D., & Teoh, S. H. (2003). Herd behaviour and cascading in capital markets: A review and synthesis. *European Financial Management*, *9*, 25–66. DOI: 10.1111/1468-036X.00207

Hochreiter, S., & Schmidhuber, J. (1997). Long short-term memory. *Neural Computation*, *9*(8), 1735–1780. PMID: 9377276

Holmes, A. D., Yang, H. T., & Zhang, S. H. (2012). A front-fixing finite element method for the valuation of American options with regime switching. *International Journal of Computer Mathematics*, *89*, 1094–1111. DOI: 10.1080/00207160.2012.663911

Hornik, K., Stinchcombe, M., & White, H. (1989). Multilayer feedforward networks are universal approximators. *Neural Networks*, *2*(5), 359–366.

Hossain, M. S. (2021). What do we know about cryptocurrency? Past, present, future. *China Finance Review International*. Advance online publication. DOI: 10.1108/CFRI-03-2020-0026

How, M. L., Cheah, S. M., Khor, A. C., & Chan, Y. J. (2020). Artificial intelligence-enhanced predictive insights for advancing financial inclusion: A human-centric ai-thinking approach. *Big Data and Cognitive Computing*, *4*(2), 8. DOI: 10.3390/bdcc4020008

Huang, A., Chao, Y., de la Mora Velasco, E., Bilgihan, A., & Wei, W. (2022). When artificial intelligence meets the hospitality and tourism industry: An assessment framework to inform theory and management. *Journal of Hospitality and Tourism Insights*, *5*(5), 1080–1100.

Huang, C., Zhang, Z., Mao, B., & Yao, X. (2023). An Overview of Artificial Intelligence Ethics. *IEEE Transactions on Artificial Intelligence*, *4*(4), 799–819. DOI: 10.1109/TAI.2022.3194503

Huang, J., Gupta, A., & Youn, M. (2021). Survey of EU ethical guidelines for commercial AI: Case studies in financial services. *AI and Ethics*, *1*, 569–577. DOI: 10.1007/s43681-021-00048-1

Huang, Z., Che, C., Zheng, H., & Li, C. (2024). Research on Generative Artificial Intelligence for Virtual Financial Robo-Advisor. *Academic Journal of Science and Technology*, *10*(1), 74–80. DOI: 10.54097/30r2kk80

Huck, S., & Oechssler, J. (2000). Informational cascades in the laboratory: Do they occur for the right reasons? *Journal of Economic Psychology*, *21*, 661–671. DOI: 10.1016/S0167-4870(00)00025-8

Hussain, A., Tahir, A., Hussain, Z., Sheikh, Z., Gogate, M., Dashtipour, K., Ali, A., & Sheikh, A. (2021). Artificial Intelligence-Enabled Analysis of Public Attitudes on Facebook and Twitter Toward COVID-19 Vaccines in the United Kingdom and the United States: Observational Study. *Journal of Medical Internet Research*, *23*(4), e26627. Advance online publication. DOI: 10.2196/26627 PMID: 33724919

Hwang, H., Xie, B. W., Wah, D., & Gašević, D. (2020). Vision, challenges, roles, and research issues of Artificial Intelligence in Education. Computers & Education. *Artificial Intelligence*, *1*(1), 100001. DOI: 10.1016/j.caeai.2020.100001

Hyndman, R. J., & Koehler, A. B. (2006). Another look at measures of forecast accuracy. *International Journal of Forecasting*, *22*(4), 679–688.

Inchara, P.(2023)ARTIFICIAL INTELLIGENCE AND MANAGEMENT IN PERSONAL FINANCE.

Ingves, S. (2018). *The E-Krona and the Payments of the Future*. Stockholm: Sveriges Riksbank. retrieved from:https://www.riksbank.se/globalassets/media/tal/engelska/ingves/2018/the-e-krona-and-the-payments-of-the-future.pdf (accessed 27 September 2020)

Isalm, M. (2024). AI for Sustainable Development: Addressing Environmental and Social Challenges. *Deleted Journal*, *3*(1), 97–105. DOI: 10.60087/jaigs.v3i1.70

Islam, R. (2024). *Sustainable entrepreneurship in the Digital Age : The role of AI in Green Business Practices*. Theseus. https://www.theseus.fi/handle/10024/862779

Ivanov, S., & Webster, C. (2019). Conceptual framework of the use of robots, artificial intelligence and service automation in travel, tourism, and hospitality companies. *Robots, artificial intelligence, and service automation in travel, tourism and hospitality*, 7-37.

Ivanov, S., & Webster, C. (2019). Economic fundamentals of the use of robots, artificial intelligence, and service automation in travel, tourism, and hospitality. In *Robots, artificial intelligence, and service automation in travel, tourism and hospitality* (pp. 39-55). Emerald Publishing limited.

Ivanov, S., Webster, C., & Berezina, K. (2019). Adoption of robots and service automation by tourism and hospitality companies. In *Robots, Artificial Intelligence, and Service Automation in Travel, Tourism and Hospitality* (pp. 10–32). Emerald Publishing.

Ivanova, M. (2019). Robots, artificial intelligence, and service automation in travel agencies and tourist information centers. In *Robots, artificial intelligence, and service automation in travel, tourism and hospitality* (pp. 221–237). Emerald Publishing Limited.

Ivanov, S., & Webster, C. (2017). Adoption of robots, artificial intelligence, and service automation by travel, tourism, and hospitality companies – A cost-benefit analysis. *International Conference on Tourism (ICOT) Proceedings*, 190–204.

Ivanov, S., & Webster, C. (2017). Adoption of robots, artificial intelligence, and service automation by travel, tourism, and hospitality companies – A cost-benefit analysis. *International Journal of Contemporary Hospitality Management*, *29*(6), 1577–1598.

Ivanov, S., & Webster, C. (2020). Robots in tourism: A research agenda for tourism economics. *Tourism Economics*, *26*(7), 1065–1085.

Iwanicz-Drozdowska, M., Cichowicz, E., Cicirko, M., Kawiński, M., & Nowak, A. K. (2023). New technologies in the financial industry : Case of Poland. *Economics and Business Review*, *9*(3). Advance online publication. DOI: 10.18559/ebr.2023.3.926

Iyke, B. N., & Ho, S.-Y. (2021). Investor attention on COVID-19 and African stock returns. *MethodsX*, *8*, 101195. DOI: 10.1016/j.mex.2020.101195 PMID: 34434722

Jahanbakhsh Javid, N., & Amini, M. (2023). Evaluating the influence of supply chain management practice on implementation of halal agroindustry and competitive advantage for small and medium enterprises. *International Journal of Computer Science and Information Technologies*, *15*, 8997–9008.

Jain, R., & Vanzara, R. (2023). Emerging Trends in AI-Based Stock Market Prediction: A Comprehensive and Systematic Review. *Engineering Proceedings*, *56*(1), 254.

James, T. (2021). Blockchain and Artificial Intelligence: The World Rewired. In *Blockchain and Artificial Intelligence: The World Rewired*. De Gruyter. DOI: 10.1515/9783110664454

Jegadeesh, N., & Titman, S. (1993). Returns to Buying Winners and Selling Losers: Implications for Stock Market Efficiency. *The Journal of Finance*, *48*(1), 65–91. DOI: 10.1111/j.1540-6261.1993.tb04702.x

Jiang, Z., Xu, D., & Liang, J. (2017). A deep reinforcement learning framework for the financial portfolio management problem. arXiv preprint arXiv:1706.10059.

Jiang, F. W., Lee, J., Martin, X. M., & Zhou, G. F. (2019). Manager sentiment and stock returns. *Journal of Financial Economics*, *132*, 126–149. DOI: 10.1016/j.jfineco.2018.10.001

Jiang, H., & Verardo, M. (2018). Does herding behaviour reveal skill? An analysis of mutual fund performance. *The Journal of Finance*, *LXXIII*, 2229–2269. DOI: 10.1111/jofi.12699

Jiang, Y., Zhang, L., & Wu, J. (2023). Evolutionary game study of crowdsourcing open innovation synergy mechanism. *Heliyon*, *9*(6). PMID: 37408914

Ji, L., & Huang, X. (2022). Analysis of social governance in energy-oriented cities based on artificial intelligence. *Energy Reports*, *8*, 11151–11160. DOI: 10.1016/j.egyr.2022.08.206

Jobin, A., Ienca, M., & Vayena, E. (2019). The global landscape of AI ethics guidelines. *Nature Machine Intelligence*, *1*, 1–11.

Joglekar, S. T. EMPOWERING FINANCIAL LITERACY THROUGH ARTIFICIAL INTELLIGENCE. Board of Editors, 43.

Jucá, M. N., Farias, S. R., & De Sousa, J. A. (2022). AI-based ESG ratings: Overcoming data bias and inconsistencies in sustainable finance. *Journal of Sustainable Finance & Investment*, *12*(2), 224–240. DOI: 10.1080/20430795.2022.2048156

Juks, R. (2018). When a Central Bank Digital Currency Meets Private Money. *Sveriges Riksbank Economic Review*, 2018(3), 79–99. Retrieved from:http://prod-upp-image-read.ft.com/c080e86a-966c-11e9-8cfb-30c211dcd229 (accessed 21 October 2020)

Julakanti, S. (2023). The Pandemic's Impact on the Intersections of Financial Literacy, AI, and Behavioral Economics. *Journal of Student Research*, *12*(4). Advance online publication. DOI: 10.47611/jsrhs.v12i4.5453

Junius, D., Adisurjo, A., Arief Rijanto, Y., & Adelina, Y. E. (2020). THE IMPACT OF ESG PERFORMANCE TO FIRM PERFORMANCE AND MARKET VALUE. *JAAPA: Official Journal of the American Academy of Physician Assistants*, *5*(1), 21–41.

Kahneman, D. (2011). *Thinking, Fast and Slow* (1st ed.). Farrar, Straus and Giroux.

Kahneman, D., & Tversky, A. (1979). Prospect Theory: An Analysis of Decision under Risk. *Econometrica*, *47*(2), 263–292.

Kakde, H. S., & Lad, K. (2022). INDIVIDUAL READINESS FOR ARTIFICIAL INTELLIGENCE (AI) ADAPTATION IN MANAGING PERSONAL FINANCES. Fostering Resilient Business Ecosystems and Economic Growth: Towards the Next Normal, 235.

Kalai, L., Jmaii, A., & Tanwar, S. (2024). Exploring the intersection of sustainability challenges and artificial intelligence. In *Advances in finance, accounting, and economics book series* (pp. 33–58). https://doi.org/DOI: 10.4018/979-8-3693-3282-5.ch003

Kalaivani, E., Saranya, H., & Geetha, B. G. (2023). CHALLENGES OF ARTIFICIAL INTELLIGENCE IN FINANCIAL SECTOR-A REVIEW. Benefits, 7(01).

Kalia, D., & Aggarwal, D. (2022). Examining impact of ESG score on financial performance of healthcare companies. *Journal of Global Responsibility*, *14*(1), 155–176.

Kamble, S. S., Gunasekaran, A., & Gawankar, S. A. (2020). Achieving sustainable performance in a data-driven agriculture supply chain: A review for research and applications. *International Journal of Production Economics*, *219*, 179–194.

Kandlhofer, M., Hirschmugl-Gaisch, S., & Huber, P. (2016). Artificial intelligence and computer science in education: From kindergarten to university. In 2016 IEEE Frontiers in Education Conference (FIE), Erie, PA, USA.

Kang, W., & Jung, M. (2020). Effect of ESG Activities and Firm's Financial Characteristics. *Korean Journal of Financial Studies*, *49*(5), 681–707.

Kant, S., & Adula, M. (2024). AI Learning and Work Attitude Mediation Between Reward and Organizational Support in Ethiopia. In Gomathi Sankar, J., & David, A. (Eds.), *Generative AI for Transformational Management* (pp. 109–136). IGI Global., DOI: 10.4018/979-8-3693-5578-7.ch005

Kant, S., & Adula, M. (2024). Human-Machine Interaction in the Metaverse in the Context of Ethiopia. In *Impact and Potential of Machine Learning in the Metaverse* (pp. 196–212). IGI Global., DOI: 10.4018/979-8-3693-5762-0.ch008

Kant, S., & Adula, M. (2025). Integrating Gender and Indigenous Knowledge in Digital Innovations for Ethiopia's Renewable Energy Transition. In *Digital Innovations for Renewable Energy and Conservation* (pp. 167–194). IGI Global.

Kant, S., Adula, M., Kumari, M., & Nimbrain, N. (2025). Role of SMEs in Greening the Economy by Mediation of Eco-Innovation in the Horn of Africa. In *Examining Green Human Resources Management and Nascent Entrepreneurship* (pp. 173–200). IGI Global., DOI: 10.4018/979-8-3693-7046-9.ch007

Kaplan, A., & Haenlein, M. (2019). Siri, Siri, in my hand: Who's the fairest in the land? On the interpretations, illustrations, and implications of artificial intelligence. *Business Horizons*, *62*(1), 15–25. DOI: 10.1016/j.bushor.2018.08.004

Karnofsky, H. (2016, December). Some background on our views regarding advanced artificial intelligence [Blog post]. Open Philanthropy Project. Retrieved from https://www.openphilanthropy.org/research/some-background-on-our-views-regarding-advanced-artificial-intelligence

Karpukhina, T., Schreier, M., Janiszewski, C., & Nishikawa, H. (2024). I Didn't Win! An Overlooked Downside of Crowdsourcing?. *Journal of Interactive Place of technological based marketing*, *59*(1), 42-58.

Kartobi, S. E., Oubida, M. A. A., & Elhachimi, Z. (2024). Asymmetric impact of the COVID-19 on the Moroccan stock exchange. *Review of Behavioral Finance, ahead-of-print*(ahead-of-print). https://doi.org/DOI: 10.1108/RBF-03-2024-0078

Kelleci, A., & Taşkın, E. (2020). Customer Orientation, Innovation and the Mediating Role of Crowdsourcing in Organizational Performance. *Transnational Place of technological based marketing Journal*, *8*(1), 7-26.

Kempton, A., & Vassilakopoulou, P. (2021). Accountability, Transparency and Explainability in AI for Healthcare. *Frontiers in Artificial Intelligence*.

Khan, N., Khan, W., Humayun, M., & Naz, A. (2024). Unlocking the Potential: Artificial Intelligence Applications in Sustainable Tourism. *The Role of Artificial Intelligence in Regenerative Tourism and Green Destinations*, 303-316.

Khan, M. S., & Umer, H. (2024). ChatGPT in finance: Applications, challenges, and solutions. *Heliyon*, *10*(2). PMID: 38304767

Khan, M., Serafeim, G., & Yoon, A. (2016). Corporate sustainability: First evidence on materiality. *The Accounting Review*, *91*(1), 169–196. DOI: 10.2308/accr-51249

Kim, J., Son, S., Son, S., & Jin, I. (2022). The Effects of Shareholding of the National Pension Fund on Environmental, Social, Governance, and Financial Performance: Evidence from the Korean Manufacturing Industry. *Sustainability*, *14*(18), 11788.

Kim, S., & Li, Z. (frank). (2021). Understanding the Impact of ESG Practices in Corporate Finance. Sustainability. *Science Practice and Policy*, *13*(7), 3746.

Kingma, D. P., & Ba, J. (2015). Adam: A method for stochastic optimization. arXiv preprint arXiv:1412.6980.

Kiseleva, A., Kotzinos, D., & Hert, P. (2022). Transparency of AI in Healthcare as a Multilayered System of Accountabilities. *Frontiers in Artificial Intelligence*, 5.

Kleinberg, J., Ludwig, J., Mullainathan, S., & Obermeyer, Z. (2018). Algorithmic fairness*Proceedings of the 2018 Conference on Fairness, Accountability, and Transparency**, 1-15. https://doi.org/DOI: 10.1145/3287560.3287598

Kleinberg, J., Ludwig, J., Mullainathan, S., & Sunstein, C. R. (2018). Discrimination in the age of algorithms. *The Journal of Legal Analysis*, *10*(1), 113–173. DOI: 10.1093/jla/laz001

Kolasani, S. V., & Assaf, R. (2020). Predicting Stock Movement Using Sentiment Analysis of Twitter Feed with Neural Networks. *Journal of Data Analysis and Information Processing*, *8*(4), 4. Advance online publication. DOI: 10.4236/jdaip.2020.84018

Kong, H., Wang, K., Qiu, X., Cheung, C., & Bu, N. (2023). 30 years of artificial intelligence (AI) research relating to the hospitality and tourism industry. *International Journal of Contemporary Hospitality Management*, *35*(6), 2157–2177.

Konishi, Y. (2015). What is Needed for AI literacy? Priorities for the Japanese economy in 2016. Research Institute of Economy, Trade and Industry (RIETI). Retrieved from https://www.rieti.go.jp/en/columns/s16_0014.html

Konno, H., & Yamazaki, H. (1991). Mean-absolute deviation portfolio optimization model and its applications to Tokyo stock market. *Management Science*, *37*(5), 519–531.

Kordzadeh, N., & Ghasemaghaei, M. (2021). Algorithmic bias: Review, synthesis, and future research directions. *European Journal of Information Systems*, *31*, 388–409. DOI: 10.1080/0960085X.2021.1927212

Koskelainen, T., Kalmi, P., Scornavacca, E., & Vartiainen, T. (2023). Financial literacy in the digital age—A research agenda. *The Journal of Consumer Affairs*, *57*(1), 507–528. DOI: 10.1111/joca.12510

Krijger, J. (2023). Operationalising ethics for AI in the financial industry: Insights from the Volksbank case study. *Journal of Digital Banking*. https://doi.org/.DOI: 10.69554/yqzc2796

Kshetri, N. (2021). The role of artificial intelligence in promoting financial inclusion in developing countries. *Journal of Global Information Technology Management*, *24*(1), 1–6. DOI: 10.1080/1097198X.2021.1871273

Kubinska, E., Adamczyk-Kowalczuk, M., & Macko, A. (2023). Decisions on saving and investment in the digital era: Empirical evidence. In *Behavioral Finance in the Digital Era*. Taylor & Francis. DOI: 10.4324/9781003400066-5

Kübler, D., & Weizsäcker, G. (2004). Limited depth of reasoning and failure of cascade formation in the laboratory. *The Review of Economic Studies*, *71*, 425–441. http://hdl.handle.net/10.1111/0034-6527.00290

Kuckertz, A., Berger, E. S., & Gaudig, A. (2019). Responding to the greatest challenges? Value creation in ecological startups. *Journal of Cleaner Production*, *230*, 1138–1147. DOI: 10.1016/j.jclepro.2019.05.149

Kulkarni, N., & Gautam, O. (Sept.2021) An Investigation of How Technology Can Enhance The Effectiveness Of Financial Advice For Personal Financial Management.

Kumar, P., Islam, M. A., Pillai, R., & Sharif, T. (2023). Analysing the behavioural, psychological, and demographic determinants of financial decision making of household investors. *Heliyon*, *9*(2), e13085. DOI: 10.1016/j.heliyon.2023.e13085 PMID: 36793953

Kumar, R. N. (2024). Impact of AI-Powered Investment Algorithms on Market Efficiency. *International Journal of Scientific Research and Engineering Trends*, *10*(4), 1576–1581. DOI: 10.61137/ijsret.vol.10.issue4.206

Kumar, V., Rajan, B., Venkatesan, R., & Lecinski, J. (2019). Understanding the Role of Artificial Intelligence in Personalized Engagement Marketing. *California Management Review*, *61*(4), 135–155. DOI: 10.1177/0008125619859317

Kumhof, M., & Noone, C. (2018). Central Bank Digital Currencies – Design Principles and Balance Sheet Implications. Bank of England, Staff Discussion Paper 725. Retrieved from: https://www.bankofengland.co.uk/working-paper/2018/central-bank-digital-currencies---design-principles-and-balance-sheet-implications (accessed 27 September 2020)

Kuran, T., & Sunstein, C. R. (1999). Availability cascades and risk regulation. *Stanford Law Review*, *51*, 683–768. DOI: 10.2307/1229439

Kurniawan, S., Purnama, A., Santoso, B. D. J., Herawaty, L., Listiana, M., & Sari, O. D. P. (2024, January). Development Of Msmes With Financial Technology In The Society Era 5.0: Digital Financial Literacy, Digital Wallet, Digital Accounting. In Riau International Conference on Economics, Business and Accounting (Vol. 1, No. 1, Januari, pp. 11-20).

Kurshan, E., Shen, H., & Chen, J. (2020). Towards self-regulating AI: challenges and opportunities of AI model governance in financial services. *Proceedings of the First ACM International Conference on AI in Finance*. https://doi.org/DOI: 10.1145/3383455.3422564

Lahboub, K., Benali, M., & Moufdi, G. (2022). Evaluation of the adaptive market hypothesis as an evolutionary perspective on market efficiency: Evidence from the Moroccan Stock Market. *Cuadernos de Economía (Santiago, Chile)*, *45*(129), 48–59.

Landi, G., & Sciarelli, M. (2018). Towards a more ethical market: The impact of ESG rating on corporate financial performance. *Social Responsibility, Journalism, Law, Medicine*, *15*(1), 11–27.

Lee, C., Hallak, R., & Sardeshmukh, S. R. (2019). Creativity and innovation in the restaurant sector: Supply-side processes and barriers to implementation. *Tourism Management Perspectives*, *31*, 54–62.

Lee, I., & Lee, K. (2015). The Internet of Things (IoT): Applications, investments, and challenges for enterprises. *Business Horizons*, *58*(4), 431–440. DOI: 10.1016/j.bushor.2015.03.008

Lee, J. (2019). Access to Finance for Artificial Intelligence Regulation in the Financial Services Industry. *European Business Organization Law Review*, *21*, 731–757. DOI: 10.1007/s40804-020-00200-0

Lee, M. T., Raschke, R. L., & Krishen, A. S. (2023). Understanding ESG scores and firm performance: Are high-performing firms E, S, and G-balanced? *. *Technological Forecasting and Social Change*, *195*, 122779. DOI: 10.1016/j.techfore.2023.122779

Lee, M., Floridi, L., & Denev, A. (2020). Innovating with Confidence - Embedding AI Governance and Fairness in a Financial Services Risk Management Framework. *Social Science Research Network*. https://doi.org/DOI: 10.2139/SSRN.3830579

Lee, S. H., Williams, P. D., & Frame, T. H. (2019). Increased shear in the North Atlantic upper-level jet stream over the past four decades. *Nature*, *572*(7771), 639–642. PMID: 31391588

Lehtimäki, M. (2024). *Navigating ethical and practical challenges in AI-Driven visual content creation.* Theseus. https://www.theseus.fi/handle/10024/865896

Lekhal, M., & Oubani, A. E. (2020). Réexamen de l'efficience du marché financier marocain à la lumière de l'Hypothèse des Marchés adaptatifs. Revue du contrôle, de la comptabilité et de l'audit, 4(1), Article 1. https://www.revuecca.com/index.php/home/article/view/500

Letouzé, E., Oliver, N., Lepri, B., & Vinck, P. (2023). l'ia au service des odd–et après? vers une culture humaine de l'IA pour le développement et la démocratie. Angles morts de l'intelligence artificielle.

Libra Association. (2019).*White Paper*. Geneva: Libra Association. Retrieved from: https://libra.org/en-US/wp-content/uploads/sites/23/2019/06/LibraWhitePaper_en_US.pdf (accessed 03 October 2020)

Li, D., Zhang, Z., & Gao, X. (2024). Does artificial intelligence deter greenwashing? *. *Finance Research Letters*, *67*, 105954. DOI: 10.1016/j.frl.2024.105954

Lim, T. (2024). Environmental, social, and governance (ESG) and artificial intelligence in finance: State-of-the-art and research takeaways. *Artificial Intelligence Review*, *57*(4), 76. DOI: 10.1007/s10462-024-10708-3

Lin, C. Y., & Marques, J. A. L. (2024). Stock market prediction using Artificial Intelligence: A systematic review of Systematic Reviews. *Social Sciences & Humanities Open*, *9*, 100864.

Lin, L., & Yu, S. (2023). The Transformative Impact of Artificial Intelligence on Educational Financial Management. *Accounting and Corporate Management*, *5*(12), 15–21.

Lipton, Z. C. (2017). In machine learning, the concept of interpretability is both important and slippery. *Machine Learning*.

Liu, J., Chang, H., Forrest, J. Y.-L., & Yang, B. (2020). Influence of artificial intelligence on technological innovation: Evidence from the panel data of China's manufacturing sectors. *Technological Forecasting and Social Change*, *158*, 120142. DOI: 10.1016/j.techfore.2020.120142

Liu, L., Ma, Z., Zhou, Y., Fan, M., & Han, M. (2024). Trust in ESG Reporting: The Intelligent Veri-Green Solution for Incentivized VerificationBlockchain. *Research and Applications*, *100189*(2), 100189. Advance online publication. DOI: 10.1016/j.bcra.2024.100189

Liu, Z., Lu, X., & Wang, Y. (2024). Does Fintech innovation improve ESG performance? Evidence from green fintech. *Journal of Corporate Finance*, *81*, 102695. DOI: 10.1016/j.jcorpfin.2024.102695

Livingstone, S. (2004). What is media literacy? *InterMedia*, *32*(3), 18–20.

Li, X., Xie, H., Chen, L., Wang, J., & Deng, X. (2014). News impact on stock price return via sentiment analysis. *Knowledge-Based Systems*, *69*, 14–23. DOI: 10.1016/j.knosys.2014.04.022

Li, Y., Zhong, H., & Tong, Q. (2024). Artificial intelligence, dynamic capabilities, and corporate financial asset allocation. In *International Review of Financial Analysis* (Vol. 96). Elsevier Inc., DOI: 10.1016/j.irfa.2024.103773

Lo, A. W. (2004). The Adaptive Markets Hypothesis: Market Efficiency from an Evolutionary Perspective. *Journal of Portfolio Management, 30*(5), 15–29.

Lo, A. W. (2005). Reconciling Efficient Markets with Behavioral Finance: The Adaptive Markets Hypothesis. *The Journal of Investment Consulting*, *7*(2), 21–44.

Lo, A. W. (2012). Adaptive Markets and the New World Order. *Financial Analysts Journal*, *68*(2). Advance online publication. DOI: 10.2469/faj.v68.n2.6

Lo, M. (2022). Market Efficiency Hypothesis. In Lee, C.-F., & Lee, A. C. (Eds.), *Encyclopedia of Finance* (pp. 937–943). Springer International Publishing., DOI: 10.1007/978-3-030-91231-4_30

Long, D., Blunt, T., & Magerko, B. (2021). Co-designing AI literacy exhibits for informal learning spaces. Proceedings of the ACM on Human-Computer Interaction, 5(CSCW2), DOI: 10.1145/3476034

Long, D., & Magerko, B. (2020). What is AI literacy? Competencies and design considerations. In *Conference on Human Factors in Computing Systems (CHI)*. https://doi.org/DOI: 10.1145/3313831.3376727

Longoni, C., & Cian, L. (2022). Artificial Intelligence in Utilitarian vs. Hedonic Contexts: The "Word-of-Machine" Effect. *Journal of Marketing*, *86*(1), 91–108. DOI: 10.1177/0022242920957347

Longstaff, F. A. (2010). The subprime credit crisis and contagion in financial markets. *Journal of Financial Economics*, *97*(3), 436–450. DOI: 10.1016/j.jfineco.2010.01.002

Lopez-Lira, A., & Tang, Y. (2023). Can chatgpt forecast stock price movements? return predictability and large language models. *arXiv preprint arXiv:2304.07619*.

Lu, J., Lee, D., Kim, T., & Danks, D. (2020). Good Explanation for Algorithmic Transparency. *Proceedings of the AAAI/ACM Conference on AI, Ethics, and Society*.https://doi.org/DOI: 10.1145/3375627.3375821

Lukita, C., Pangilinan, G. A., Chakim, M. H. R., & Saputra, D. B. (2023). Examining the impact of artificial intelligence and internet of things on smart tourism destinations: A comprehensive study. [ATT]. *Aptisi Transactions on Technopreneurship*, *5*(2sp), 135–145.

Lundberg, S. M., & Lee, S.-I. (2017). *A Unified Approach to Interpreting Model Predictions. 31st Conference on Neural Information Processing Systems (NIPS)*, CA, USA.

Luo, X., Tong, S., Fang, Z., & Qu, Z. (2019). Frontiers: Machines vs. Humans: The Impact of Artificial Intelligence Chatbot Disclosure on Customer Purchases. *Marketing Science*, mksc.2019.1192. https://doi.org/.DOI: 10.1287/mksc.2019.1192

Luo, X., Qian, G., & Wang, X. (2023). Board diversity and ESG disclosure: Evidence from emerging markets. *Journal of Business Ethics*, *184*, 631–654. DOI: 10.1007/s10551-023-05241-y

Lv, L., Chen, S., Liu, G. G., & Benckendorff, P. (2024). Enhancing customers' life satisfaction through AI-powered personalized luxury recommendations in luxury tourism marketing. *International Journal of Hospitality Management*, *123*, 103914.

Mabillard, V., & Villeneuve, J. P. (2023). La transparence dans l'espace numérique: Principes, développements, enjeux. PUQ. Béranger, J., & Chassang, G. (2021). Vers une régulation néodarwinienne de l'Intelligence artificielle centrée sur le concept de l'«Ethics by Evolution». Éthique publique. Revue internationale d'éthique sociétale et gouvernementale, 23(2).

Mackay, C. (1869). *Memoirs of Extraordinary Popular Dilusions.*

Maddox, T. M., Rumsfeld, J. S., & Payne, P. R. O. (2019). Questions for artificial intelligence in health care. *Journal of the American Medical Association, 321*(1), 31–32. DOI: 10.1001/jama.2018.18932 PMID: 30535130

Madison, N., & Schiehll, E. (2021). The Effect of Financial Materiality on ESG Performance Assessment. Sustainability. *Science Practice and Policy, 13*(7), 3652.

Mahanta, R., Pandey, T. N., Jagadev, A. K., & Dehuri, S. (2016). Optimized Radial Basis Functional Neural Network for Stock Index Prediction. Dans *Proceedings of the International Conference on Electrical, Electronics, and Optimization Techniques (ICEEOT)* (pp. 775–780).

Mahboub, H. M., & Sadok, H. (2024). Barriers to digital transformation: The case of Moroccan companies. *Journal of Telecommunications and the Digital Economy, 12*(1), 261–276. https://search.informit.org/doi/10.3316/informit.T2024040300010000142251162

Maier, T., Menold, J., & McComb, C. (2022). The relationship between performance and trust in ai in e-finance. *Frontiers in Artificial Intelligence, 5*, 891529. DOI: 10.3389/frai.2022.891529 PMID: 35800065

Maiorano, A., & Morelli, E. (2024). ESG scoring and the role of AI: Transparency and explainability issues. *Technological Forecasting and Social Change, 197*, 123108. DOI: 10.1016/j.techfore.2024.123108

Majeed, A., & Hwang, S. O. (2021). Data-driven analytics leveraging artificial intelligence in the era of COVID-19: An insightful review of recent developments. [1] Symmetry, 14(1), 16.

Majeed, K. B., Khan, A., Ghaffar, I., & Asghar, H. (2022). The linkage between financial literacy and financial decision-making with the mediating effect of investment behavior. PalArch's Journal of Archaeology of Egypt/Egyptology, 19(3), 1582-1598.

Makrehchi, M., Shah, S., & Liao, W. (2013). Stock Prediction Using Event-Based Sentiment Analysis. *2013 IEEE/WIC/ACM International Joint Conferences on Web Intelligence (WI) and Intelligent Agent Technologies (IAT), 1*, 337–342. https://doi.org/DOI: 10.1109/WI-IAT.2013.48

Makridakis, S., Wheelwright, S. C., & Hyndman, R. J. (1998). Forecasting: Methods and applications (3rd ed.).

Manavalan, E., & Jayakrishnan, J. (2024). Digital sustainability and ESG disclosure: Role of blockchain and AI technologies. *Journal of Cleaner Production, 368*, 133019. DOI: 10.1016/j.jclepro.2024.133019

Mäntymäki, M., Minkkinen, M., Birkstedt, T., & Viljanen, M. (2022). *Putting AI Ethics into Practice: The Hourglass Model of Organizational AI Governance.* ArXiv.

Maple, C., Szpruch, L., Epiphaniou, G., Staykova, K. S., Singh, S., Penwarden, W., Wen, Y., Wang, Z., Hariharan, J., & Avramović, P. (2023). The AI Revolution. *ArXiv, 2308*, 16538.

Maquet, C. (2020). MNBC: tout comprendre de la monnaie numérique de demain. Retrieved from:https://siecledigital.fr/2020/11/02/mnbc-tout-savoir-monnaie-numerique/ (accessed 6 April 2021)

Mardini, G. H. (2022). ESG factors and corporate financial performance. *International Journal of Managerial and Financial Accounting*, *1*(1), 1.

Mariani, M., & Baggio, R. (2022). Big data and analytics in tourism and hospitality: A perspective article. *Tourism Review*, *77*(1), 6–10. DOI: 10.1108/TR-09-2019-0383

Martin, K. (2019). Ethical Implications and Accountability of Algorithms. *Journal of Business Ethics*, *160*(4), 835–850. DOI: 10.1007/s10551-018-3921-3

Ma, S. (2024). Enhancing Tourists' Satisfaction: Leveraging Artificial Intelligence in the Tourism Sector. *Pacific International Journal*, *7*(3), 89–98.

Masud, M. M., Al-Amin, A. Q., Ha, J., Ahmed, F., Yahaya, S. R. B., Akhtar, R., & Banna, H. (2016). Climate change issue and theory of planned behaviour: Relationship by empirical evidence. *Journal of Cleaner Production*. Advance online publication. DOI: 10.1016/j.jclepro.2015.11.080

Matheny, M. E., Whicher, D., & Israni, T. S. (2020). Artificial intelligence in health care: A report from the national academy of medicine. *Journal of the American Medical Association*, *323*(6), 509–510. DOI: 10.1001/jama.2019.21579 PMID: 31845963

Mayuranathan, M., Nahar, G., Vijayakumar, A., Naveen, N., Mamodiya, U., & Babu, D. M. (2024). Sustainable business models for smart city using artificial intelligence techniques. In *Practice, progress, and proficiency in sustainability* (pp. 263–294). https://doi.org/DOI: 10.4018/979-8-3693-2827-9.ch009

Mazzatto, M. (2022). Financial literacy and investing habits of generation Z as it pertains to financial marketing.

McKinsey & Company. (2022). The state of AI in 2022–and a half-decade in review. Retrieved from https://www.mckinsey.com (consulted on January 26, 2025)

Mclean, R. D., & Zhao, M. X. (2014). The business cycle, investor sentiment, and costly external finance. *The Journal of Finance*, *69*, 1377–1409. DOI: 10.1111/jofi.12047

Mdaghri, A. A., Raghibi, A., Thanh, C. N., & Oubdi, L. (2020). Stock market liquidity, the great lockdown and the COVID-19 global pandemic nexus in MENA countries. *Review of Behavioral Finance*, *13*(1), 51–68. DOI: 10.1108/RBF-06-2020-0132

Mehta, K., Sharma, M., & Rao, S. (2023). ESG performance and financial distress: A comparative study of emerging economies. *Journal of International Financial Markets, Institutions and Money*, *89*, 101749. DOI: 10.1016/j.intfin.2023.101749

Mhlanga, D. (2020). Industry 4.0 in finance: The impact of artificial intelligence (ai) on digital financial inclusion. *International Journal of Financial Studies*, *8*(3), 45.

Mhlanga, D. (2021). Artificial intelligence in the industry 4.0, and its impact on poverty, innovation, infrastructure development, and the sustainable development goals: Lessons from emerging economies? *Sustainability*, *13*(11), 5788.

Michel, S., & Cocula, F. (2014). L'évaluation des systèmes d'information: un état de l'art à la lumière des approches de la variance et processuelles. Revue management & avenir, 33-51.

Michelon, G., Pilonato, S., & Ricceri, F. (2015). CSR disclosure and the audit expectation gap: The role of CSR-related audit committees. *Journal of Business Ethics, 127*(3), 503–519. DOI: 10.1007/s10551-014-2051-5

Mikalef, P., & Krogstie, J. (2024). *Responsible AI governance in practice: The strategic impact of responsible AI governance on business value and competitiveness.* https://ntnuopen.ntnu.no/ntnu-xmlui/handle/11250/3129623

Mikalef, P., & Gupta, M. (2021). Artificial intelligence capability: Conceptualization, measurement calibration, and empirical study on its impact on organizational creativity and firm performance. *Information & Management, 58*(3), 103434. DOI: 10.1016/j.im.2021.103434

Mishra, S., Anifa, M., & Naidu, J. (2025). AI-Driven Personalization in Tourism Services: Enhancing Tourist Experiences and Business Performance. In *Integrating Architecture and Design Into Sustainable Tourism Development* (pp. 1-20). IGI Global Scientific Publishing

Mishra, D., & Maheshwari, N. (2024). Crowdsourcing-based social linkage and organizational innovation competence: Knowledge transfer influenceiveness and absorptive capacity as serial mediators. *Journal of Knowledge Management.*

Mittelstadt, B. D., Allo, P., Taddeo, M., Wachter, S., & Floridi, L. (2016). The ethics of algorithms: Mapping the debate. *Big Data & Society, 3*(2), 2053951716679679. DOI: 10.1177/2053951716679679

Moin, S., Fida, B. A., & Li, J. (2024). Corporate ESG practices and environmental innovation: A global investigation. *Research in International Business and Finance, 68*, 102320. DOI: 10.1016/j.ribaf.2024.102320

Morgan, J. P. (2021).J.P. Morgan Creates Digital Coin for Payments. Retrieved from:https://www.jpmorgan.com/solutions/cib/news/digital-coin-payments (accessed 6 April 2021)

Morone, A., Sandri, S., & Fiore, A. (2009). On the absorbability of informational cascades in the laboratory. *Journal of Socio-Economics, 38*, 728–738. DOI: 10.1016/j.socec.2009.06.014

Mouline, B., & Sadok, H. (2021). Determinants of corporate cash holdings: Evidence from the Moroccan market. *Accounting, 7*(6), 1231–1240.

Muhuri, P. K., Shukla, A. K., & Abraham, A. (2019). Industry 4.0: A bibliometric analysis and detailed overview. *Engineering Applications of Artificial Intelligence, 78*, 218–235. DOI: 10.1016/j.engappai.2018.11.007

Mumtaz, U., & Mumtaz, S. (2023). Potential of ChatGPT in predicting stock market trends based on Twitter Sentiment Analysis. *arXiv preprint arXiv:2311.06273.*

Muñoz, R., Martínez, M., & Ramos, J. (2024). ESG scores as predictors of financial performance: A global perspective. *International Journal of Finance & Economics*. Advance online publication. DOI: 10.1002/ijfe.2719

Nakamoto, S. (2009).Bitcoin: A Peer-to-Peer Electronic Cash System. Retrieved from: https://bitcoin .org/bitcoin.pdf (accessed 18 August 2020)

Nessen, M., Sellin, P., & Sommar, P. Å. (2018).The Implications of an E-Krona for the Riksbank's Operational Framework for Implementing Monetary Policy. *Sveriges Riksbank Economic Review*, 2018(3), 29–42. retrieved from:https://www.riksbank.se/globalassets/media/rapporter/pov/artiklar/engelska/2018/181105/20183-the-implications-of-an-e-krona-for-the-riksbanks-operational-framework -for-implementing-monetary-policy.pdf (accessed 11 November 2020)

Ng, D. T. K., Leung, J. K. L., Chu, K. W. S., & Qiao, M. S. (2021). AI literacy: Definition, teaching, evaluation and ethical issues. *84th Annual Meeting of the Association for Information Science & Technology*, Salt Lake City, UT, USA. https://doi.org/DOI: 10.1002/pra2.487

Nguyen, H. T., Tran, T. T., Nham, P. T., Nguyen, N. U. B., & Le, A. D. (2023). AI Chatbot for Tourist Recommendations: A Case Study in Vietnam. *Applied Computer Systems*, *28*(2), 232–244.

Nguyen, T. H., Shirai, K., & Velcin, J. (2015). Sentiment analysis on social media for stock movement prediction. *Expert Systems with Applications*, *42*(24), 9603–9611. DOI: 10.1016/j.eswa.2015.07.052

Niepelt, D. (2019). Reserves for All? Central Bank Digital Currency, Deposits, and their (Non)-Equivalence. *International Journal of Central Banking*, *16*(3), 211–238.

Niguse, T., Kant, S., & Adula, M. (2025). Mediation Effect of Customer Loyalty in Relationship Between Market Orientation, Entrepreneurial Orientation, and Firm Performance in Ethiopia. In *Leveraging AI for Effective Digital Relationship Marketing* (pp. 419–458). IGI Global., DOI: 10.4018/979-8-3693-5340-0.ch014

Nobanee, H., El Hadi El Maknouzi, M., Sadok, H., & Alodat, A. Y. (2024). Analysis of insurance entrepreneurship as a hedge in times of crisis: A literature review. *Sustainable Technology and Entrepreneurship*, *3*(2), 100065. Advance online publication. DOI: 10.1016/j.stae.2023.100065

Noorbakhsh-Sabet, N., Zand, R., Zhang, Y., & Abedi, V. (2019). Artificial intelligence transforms the future of health care. *The American Journal of Medicine*, *132*(7), 795–801. DOI: 10.1016/j.amjmed.2019.01.017 PMID: 30710543

Nourallah, M. (2023). One size does not fit all: Young retail investors' initial trust in financial robo-advisors. *Journal of Business Research*, *156*, 113470. DOI: 10.1016/j.jbusres.2022.113470

Obermeyer, Z., Powers, B., Vogeli, C., & Mullainathan, S. (2019). Dissecting racial bias in an algorithm used to manage the health of populations. *Science*, *366*, 447–453. DOI: 10.1126/science.aax2342 PMID: 31649194

Odean, T. (1998). Are Investors Reluctant to Realize Their Losses? *The Journal of Finance*, *53*(5), 1775–1798. DOI: 10.1111/0022-1082.00072

Oduro, S., & De Nisco, A. (2023). From Industry 4.0 adoption to innovation ambidexterity to firm performance: A MASEM analysis. *European Journal of Innovation Management*. Advance online publication. DOI: 10.1108/EJIM-02-2023-0106

Ofori-Sasu, D., Donkor, G. N. A., & Abor, J. (2023). Do sustainability ethics explain the impact of country-level corporate governance on financial stability in developing economies? *Journal of Sustainable Finance & Investment*, *13*, 1415–1450.

Oh, C., & Sheng, O. (2011). Investigating Predictive Power of Stock Micro Blog Sentiment in Forecasting Future Stock Price Directional Movement. *ICIS 2011 Proceedings*. https://aisel.aisnet.org/icis2011/proceedings/knowledge/17

Oliveira, P. S., & Garcia, T. (2023). AI-enabled ESG assessment in portfolio management: A comprehensive analysis. *Journal of Asset Management*, *24*(4), 377–394. DOI: 10.1057/s41260-023-00221-6

Openbanking. (2020). What is open banking? https://www.openbanking.org.uk/customers/what-isopen

Orimoloye, L. O., Sung, M. C., Ma, T., & Johnson, J. E. (2020). Comparing the effectiveness of deep feedforward neural networks and shallow architectures for predicting stock price indices. *Expert Systems with Applications*, *139*, 112828.

Ortu, M., Casu, M., & Lazzari, R. (2022). On technical trading and social media indicators for cryptocurrency price classification through deep learning. *Expert Systems with Applications*, •••, 198.

Owolabi, O. S., Uche, P. C., Adeniken, N. T., Ihejirika, C., Islam, R. B., & Chhetri, B. J. T. (2024). Ethical Implication of Artificial Intelligence (AI) Adoption in Financial Decision Making. *Computer and Information Science*, *17*(1), 1–49. DOI: 10.5539/cis.v17n1p49

Oyeniyi, N. L. D., Ugochukwu, N. C. E., & Mhlongo, N. N. Z. (2024). TRANSFORMING FINANCIAL PLANNING WITH AI-DRIVEN ANALYSIS: A REVIEW AND APPLICATION INSIGHTS. *Finance & Accounting Research Journal*, *6*(4), 626–647. DOI: 10.51594/farj.v6i4.1037

Page, M. J., McKenzie, J. E., Bossuyt, P. M., Boutron, I., Hoffmann, T. C., Mulrow, C. D., Shamseer, L., Tetzlaff, J. M., Akl, E. A., Brennan, S. E., Chou, R., Glanville, J., Grimshaw, J. M., Hróbjartsson, A., Lalu, M. M., Li, T., Loder, E. W., Mayo-Wilson, E., McDonald, S., & Moher, D. (2021). The PRISMA 2020 statement: An updated guideline for reporting systematic reviews. *BMJ (Clinical Research Ed.)*, (71), n71. Advance online publication. DOI: 10.1136/bmj.n71 PMID: 33782057

Palacios-Marqués, D., Gallego-Nicholls, J. F., & Guijarro-García, M. (2021). A recipe for success: Crowdsourcing, online social networks, and their influence on organizational performance. *Technological Forecasting and Social Change*, *165*, 120566.

Palombo, F., & Teti, A. (2024). ESG transparency and investment decisions: The mediating role of AI-driven analysis. *Journal of Financial Markets*, *77*, 100869. DOI: 10.1016/j.finmar.2024.100869

Panos, G. A., & Wilson, J. O. (2020). Financial literacy and responsible finance in the FinTech era: Capabilities and challenges. *European Journal of Finance*, *26*(4-5), 297–301. DOI: 10.1080/1351847X.2020.1717569

Park, S. (2021). Big data in smart tourism: A perspective article. *Journal of Smart Tourism*, *1*(3), 3–5.

Pashang, S., & Weber, O. (2023). AI for Sustainable Finance: Governance Mechanisms for Institutional and Societal Approaches. In *Philosophical studies series* (pp. 203–229). https://doi.org/DOI: 10.1007/978-3-031-21147-8_12

Paskaleva, M., & Stoykova, A. (2021). GLOBALIZATION EFFECTS ON CONTAGION RISKS IN FINANCIAL MARKETS. *Ekonomicko-Manazerske Spektrum, 15*(1), 38–54.

Pelster, M., & Val, J. (2024). Can ChatGPT assist in picking stocks? *Finance Research Letters, 59*, 104786.

Pereira, F., & Lima, R. (2024). ESG disclosures and stock price reactions: Evidence from emerging markets. *Research in International Business and Finance, 67*, 102185. DOI: 10.1016/j.ribaf.2024.102185

Pfister, C. (2017). Politique monétaire et monnaies digitales: beaucoup de bruit pour rien? *Revue française d'économie*, 32(2), 37–63

Pfister, C. (2019). Les monnaies digitales, un nouvel univers? *Regards croisés sur l'économie*, 24(1), 40–52

Pfister,C. (2018). Le temps (réel), c'est de l'argent. *Revue française d'économie*, 32(4), 195–212.

Pfister, C., & Valla, N. (2017). Nouvelle Normale ou Nouvelle Orthodoxie? Éléments d'un nouveau cadre d'action pour les banques centrales. *Revue économique, 68*, 41–62.

Piñeiro-Chousa, J. R., López-Cabarcos, M. Á., & Pérez-Pico, A. M. (2016). Examining the influence of stock market variables on microblogging sentiment. *Journal of Business Research, 69*(6), 2087–2092. DOI: 10.1016/j.jbusres.2015.12.013

Pintér, É., Bagó, P., Berényi, L., Molnár, L., Deutsch, N., & Pintér, T. (2021). How do Digitalization and the Fintech Phenomenon Affect Financial Decision-Making in the Younger Generation? *Acta Polytechnica Hungarica, 18*(11), 191–208. DOI: 10.12700/APH.18.11.2021.11.11

Pitardi, V., & Marriott, H. R. (2021). Alexa, she's not human but… Unveiling the drivers of consumers' trust in voice-based artificial intelligence. *Psychology and Marketing, 38*(4), 626–642. DOI: 10.1002/mar.21457

Pollari, I. (2018). The rise of digital platforms in financial services. *KPMG International*. https://assets.

Poskitt, D. S., & Tremayne, A. R. (1986). The selection and use of linear and bilinear time series models. *International Journal of Forecasting, 2*(1), 101–114.

Possati, L. M. (2023). Psychoanalyzing artificial intelligence: The case of Replika. *AI & Society, 38*(4), 1725–1738.

Praharaj, S., Mishra, B. B., Mishra, U. S., Panigrahi, R. R., & Mishra, P. C. (2023). Role of service automation on guest experience of hotel industry. *Tourism and Hospitality Management, 29*(2), 265–278.

Principe, J. C., Euliano, N. R., & Lefebvre, W. C. (1999). *Neural and adaptive systems: Fundamentals through simulations*. Wiley.

Pundziene, A., Nikou, S., & Bouwman, H. (2022). The nexus among dynamic capabilities and competitive firm performance: The mediating role of open innovation. *European Journal of Innovation Management, 25*(6), 152–177.

Puntoni, S., Reczek, R. W., Giesler, M., & Botti, S. (2021). Consumers and Artificial Intelligence: An Experiential Perspective. *Journal of Marketing, 85*(1), 131–151. DOI: 10.1177/0022242920953847

Qian, W., & Yu, Z. (2024). Do ESG scores mitigate market risk? A comparative study of global markets. *The Journal of Risk Finance*, *25*(3), 123–145. DOI: 10.1108/JRF-05-2024-0150

Raji, I., & Buolamwini, J. (2019). Actionable Auditing: Investigating the Impact of Publicly Naming Biased Performance Results of Commercial AI Products. *Proceedings of the 2019 AAAI/ACM Conference on AI, Ethics, and Society*. https://doi.org/DOI: 10.1145/3306618.3314244

Ramanathan, V., & Arora, S. (2024). ESG investing and shareholder value creation: Evidence from AI-driven financial models. *Financial Innovation*, *10*, 101273. DOI: 10.1007/s40854-024-00452-8

Raman, R., Pattnaik, D., Lathabai, H. H., Kumar, C., Govindan, K., & Nedungadi, P. (2024). Green and sustainable AI research: An integrated thematic and topic modeling analysis. *Journal of Big Data*, *11*(1). Advance online publication. DOI: 10.1186/s40537-024-00920-x

Ramos, M. G., do Rosário Lima, V. M., & Rosa, M. P. A. (2018). Contribuições do software IRAMUTEQ para a Análise Textual Discursiva. *Atas CIAIQ2018-Investigação Qualitativa em Educação, 2018, Brasil.*

Ramos-Rodríguez, A., & Ruíz-Navarro, J. (2004). Changes in the intellectual structure of strategic management research: A bibliometric study of the Strategic Management Journal, 1980–2000. *Strategic Management Journal*, *25*(10), 981–1004. DOI: 10.1002/smj.397

Rane, N., Choudhary, S., & Rane, J. (2023). Sustainable tourism development using leading-edge Artificial Intelligence (AI), Blockchain, Internet of Things (IoT), Augmented Reality (AR) and Virtual Reality (VR) technologies. *Blockchain, Internet of Things (IoT), Augmented Reality (AR) and Virtual Reality (VR) technologies (October 31, 2023).*

Rane, N., Choudhary, S., & Rane, J. (2024). Artificial intelligence driven approaches to strengthening Environmental, Social, and Governance (ESG) criteria in sustainable business practices: a review. SSRN *Electronic Journal*. https://doi.org/DOI: 10.2139/ssrn.4843215

Rane, N. L., Choudhary, S. P., & Rane, J. (2024). Artificial Intelligence-driven corporate finance: Enhancing efficiency and decision-making through machine learning, natural language processing, and robotic process automation in corporate governance and sustainability. *Studies in Economics and Business Relations*, *5*(2), 1–22. DOI: 10.48185/sebr.v5i2.1050

Rane, N., Choudhary, S. P., & Rane, J. (2024). Acceptance of artificial intelligence: Key factors, challenges, and implementation strategies. *Journal of Applied Artificial Intelligence*, *5*(2), 50–70.

Rao, M., & Patel, V. (2024). AI-powered ESG compliance monitoring: Enhancing transparency and reducing bias. *Journal of Financial Crime*, *31*(1), 23–42. DOI: 10.1108/JFC-04-2024-0063

Rathod, S. B., Ponnusamy, S., Mahajan, R. A., & Khan, R. H. (2024). Echoes of tomorrow. In *Advances in business information systems and analytics book series* (pp. 158–174). https://doi.org/DOI: 10.4018/979-8-3693-3234-4.ch012

Rawal, Y. S., Soni, H., Dani, R., & Bagchi, P. (2022, July). A review on service delivery in tourism and hospitality industry through artificial intelligence. In *Proceedings of Third International Conference on Computing, Communications, and Cyber-Security: IC4S 2021* (pp. 427-436). Singapore: Springer Nature Singapore.

Ray, R. S., & Goel, S. (2023). Impact of ESG score on financial performance of Indian firms: Static and dynamic panel regression analyses. *Applied Economics*. Advance online publication. DOI: 10.1080/00036846.2022.2101611

Reddi, S. J., Kale, S., & Kumar, S. (2018). On the convergence of Adam and beyond.

Reddy, K., & Sailesh, B. (2024). Technology Adoption in Tourism and Its Effects on Tourist Behaviour. *Journal of Tourism Quarterly*, *6*(3-4), 53–73.

Rehmat, I., Khan, A. A., Hussain, M., & Khurshid, S. (2023). An Examination of Behavioral Factors Affecting the Investment Decisions: The Moderating Role of Financial Literacy and Mediating Role of Risk Perception. *Journal of Innovative Research in Management Sciences*, *4*(2), 1–16. DOI: 10.62270/jirms.v4i2.52

Ribeiro-Navarrete, S., Saura, J. R., & Palacios-Marqués, D. (2021). Towards a new era of mass data collection: Assessing pandemic surveillance technologies to preserve user privacy. In *Technological Forecasting and Social Change* (Vol. 167). Elsevier Inc., DOI: 10.1016/j.techfore.2021.120681

Riksbank, S. (2017). The Riksbank's E-Krona Project Report. Sveriges Riksbank., Retrieved from https://www.riksbank.se/globalassets/media/rapporter/e-krona/2017/rapport_ekrona_uppdaterad_170920_eng.pdf, Retrieved October 6, 2020, from.

Riksbank, S. (2018). The Riksbank's E-krona Project Report 2. Sveriges Riksbank., Retrieved from https://www.riksbank.se/globalassets/media/rapporter/e-krona/2018/the-riksbanks-e-krona-project-report-2.pdf, Retrieved October 16, 2020, from.

Riyani, D. (2023, June). Artificial Intelligence Will Be Able To Change Lifestyles And Financial Literacy Towards The Era Of Society 5.0. In *International Conference On Economics Business Management And Accounting (ICOEMA)* (Vol. 2, pp. 145-157).

Rodríguez-Fernández, M., Sánchez-Teba, E. M., López-Toro, A. A., & Borrego-Domínguez, S. (2019). Influence of ESGC Indicators on Financial Performance of Listed Travel and Leisure Companies. Sustainability. *Science Practice and Policy*, *11*(19), 5529.

Rothwell, G., Rothwell, R., & Zegveld, W. (1985). *Reindustrialization and technology*. ME Sharpe.

Rubasri, S., NF, S. R., Prasath, R., & Krishna, B. V. (2024, April). *AI-Enhanced Image Translation for Seamless Communication in Global Tourism.In2024 International Conference on Advances in Data Engineering and Intelligent Computing Systems (ADICS)(pp.1-5).IEEE.*

Ruder, S. (2017). An overview of gradient descent optimization algorithms.

Rudin, C. (2019). Stop explaining black box machine learning models for high stakes decisions and use interpretable models instead. *Nature Machine Intelligence*, *1*(5), 206–215. DOI: 10.1038/s42256-019-0048-x PMID: 35603010

Ryan-Collin, J., Greenham, T., Werner, R., & Jackson, A. (2012). *Where Does Money Come From? A Guide to the UK Monetary and Banking System*. New Economics Foundation.

Saboia, J. L. M. (1977). Autoregressive integrated moving average (ARIMA) models for birth forecasting. *Journal of the American Statistical Association, 72*(358), 264–270.

Sadok, H &El Maknouzi,M.H, (2020). The Regulation of Virtual Currencies in Comparative Perspective: New Private Money or Niche Technological Innovation? *Journal of Money Laundering Control*. https://doi.org/DOI: 10.1108/JMLC-09-2020-0101

Sadok, H., Chaibi, H., & Saadane, R. (2023). An exploratory study on the contribution of Artificial Intelligence in improving the bank credit analysis process. In: Proceedings of the 6th International Conference on Networking, Intelligent Systems & Security. pp. 1–4. ACM, Larache Morocco. https://doi.org/DOI: 10.1145/3607720.3607784

Sadok, H. (2023). The Initial Coin Offering: Is It a Profitable Tool for Investment? In Jallouli, R., Bach Tobji, M. A., Belkhir, M., Soares, A. M., & Casais, B. (Eds.), *Digital Economy. Emerging Technologies and Business Innovation. ICDEc 2023. Lecture Notes in Business Information Processing* (Vol. 485). Springer., DOI: 10.1007/978-3-031-42788-6_12

Sadok, H., & Assadi, D. (2023). The Contribution of AI-Based Analysis and Rating Models to Financial Inclusion. In *Artificial Intelligence, Fintech, and Financial Inclusion* (pp. 11–25). CRC Press., DOI: 10.1201/9781003125204-2

Sadon, A. N., Ismail, S., Jafri, N. S. B., & Shaharudin, S. M. (2021). Long short-term vs gated recurrent unit recurrent neural network for Google stock price prediction. In *2021 2nd International Conference on Artificial Intelligence and Data Sciences (AiDAS)* (pp. 1-6). IEEE.

Sætra, H. S. (2023). Generative AI: Here to stay, but for good? *Technology in Society, 102372*. Advance online publication. DOI: 10.1016/j.techsoc.2023.102372

Saidi, H., & Madhat, F. Z. (2024). Mapping the Evolution of Open Innovation and Digital Transformation: A Bibliometric Analysis. In Motahhir, S., & Bossoufi, B. (Eds.), *Digital Technologies and Applications* (Vol. 1101, pp. 178–186). Springer Nature Switzerland., DOI: 10.1007/978-3-031-68675-7_18

Samuelson, P. A. (1965). Proof That Properly Anticipated Prices Fluctuate Randomly. *Industrial Management Review, 6*(2), 41.

Samuelson, P. A. (2015). Rational Theory of Warrant Pricing. In Grünbaum, F. A., van Moerbeke, P., & Moll, V. H. (Eds.), *Henry P. McKean Jr. Selecta* (pp. 195–232). Springer International Publishing., DOI: 10.1007/978-3-319-22237-0_11

Sánchez, R., & Vidal, P. (2024). ESG controversies and corporate sustainability: An AI-powered analysis of media sentiment. *Corporate Social Responsibility and Environmental Management, 31*(4), 978–995. DOI: 10.1002/csr.2423

Schenk, E., Schaeffer, V., & Pénin, J. (2020). Blockchain and the future of open innovation intermediaries: The case of crowdsourcing platforms. In *Managing Digital Open Innovation* (pp. 401-430).

Schmid, M., & Wagner, P. (2023). AI-based ESG performance prediction models: A literature review. *Journal of Sustainable Finance & Investment, 13*(2), 303–327. DOI: 10.1080/20430795.2023.2048156

Schmidt, P., & Biessmann, F. (2020). Calibrating Human-AI Collaboration: Impact of Risk, Ambiguity and Transparency on Algorithmic Bias., 431-449. https://doi.org/.DOI: 10.1007/978-3-030-57321-8_24

Schmiedel, H., Gergana, K., & Ruttenberg, W. (2012). The Social and Private Costs of Retail Payment Instruments – A European Perspective. European Central Bank, Occasional Paper 137. Retrieved from: https://www.ecb.europa.eu/pub/pdf/scpops/ecbocp137.pdf? 33f4f6bcb83613df99dd634b89e2c8a0 (accessed 19 November 2020)

Schwandt, T. A. (2014). *The Sage dictionary of qualitative inquiry*. Sage publications.

Sebastian, R., & Collopy, F. (1992). Evaluating the forecasting performance of ex ante predictors.

Sedkaoui, S. (2024). *Data analytics automatisées: Combiner la créativité humaine et la puissance de l'IA avec ChatGPT. ISTE Group. Béranger, J. (2018). Le code éthique algorithmique: L'éthique au chevet de la révolution numérique*. ISTE Group.

Segendorf, B. (2018). How Many E-Krona Are Needed for Payments? *Sveriges Riksbank Economic Review*, 2018(3), 66–78. retrieved from:https://www.riksbank.se/globalassets/media/rapporter/pov/artiklar/engelska/2018/181105/20183-how-many-e-krona-are-needed-for-payments.pdf (accessed 14 September 2020)

Selvin, S., Vinayakumar, R., Gopalakrishnan, E. A., Menon, V. K., & Soman, K. P. (2017). Stock price prediction using LSTM, RNN, and CNN-sliding window model. *2017 International Conference on Advances in Computing, Communications and Informatics (ICACCI)*, 1643–1647.

Semwal, R., Tripathi, N., Singh, A., & Saxena, S. R. (2024). Reviving Narratives: Virtual Reality and Historical Reconstruction in Tourism. In *Dimensions of Regenerative Practices in Tourism and Hospitality* (pp. 269-284). IGI Global.

Seog, S. H. (2008). Informational cascade in the insurance market. *The Journal of Risk and Insurance, 75*, 145–165. https://www.jstor.org/stable/25145267

Setty, R., Elovici, Y., & Schwartz, D. (2024). Cost-sensitive machine learning to support startup investment decisions. In *Intelligent Systems in Accounting, Finance and Management* (Vol. 31, Issue 1). John Wiley and Sons Inc. DOI: 10.1002/isaf.1548

Shah, M., & Verma, T. (2024). ESG integration in AI-driven portfolio optimization. *Journal of Asset Management, 25*(1), 78–94. DOI: 10.1057/s41260-024-00265-7

Shamima, A., Alshater, M. M., El Ammari, A., & Helmi, H. (2022). Artificial intelligence and machine learning in finance: A bibliometric review. *Research in International Business and Finance, 61*, 101646. DOI: 10.1016/j.ribaf.2022.101646

Sheehan, B., Jin, H. S., & Gottlieb, U. (2020). Customer service chatbots: Anthropomorphism and adoption. *Journal of Business Research, 115*, 14–24. DOI: 10.1016/j.jbusres.2020.04.030

Shefrin, H., & Statman, M. (1985). The Disposition to Sell Winners Too Early and Ride Losers Too Long: Theory and Evidence. *The Journal of Finance, 40*(3), 777–790. DOI: 10.1111/j.1540-6261.1985.tb05002.x

Shiller, R. J. (1995). Conversation, information, and herd behaviour. *The American Economic Review, 85*, 181–185. https://www.jstor.org/stable/2117915

Shiller, R. J. (2003). From Efficient Markets Theory to Behavioral Finance. *The Journal of Economic Perspectives, 17*(1), 83–104. DOI: 10.1257/089533003321164967

Shiller, R. J. (2017). Narrative Economics. *The American Economic Review, 107*(4), 967–1004. DOI: 10.1257/aer.107.4.967

Shinde, R., Patil, S., Kotecha, K., & Ruikar, K. (2021). Blockchain for securing ai applications and open innovations. *Journal of Open Innovation, 7*(3), 189.

Shneiderman, B. (2020). Bridging the Gap Between Ethics and Practice: Guidelines for Reliable, Safe, and Trustworthy Human-centered AI Systems. *ACM Transactions on Interactive Intelligent Systems, 10*(4), 1–31. DOI: 10.1145/3419764

Sifat, I. (2023). Artificial Intelligence (AI) and Future Retail Investment.

Skingsley, C. (2016). Should the Riksbank Issue E-Krona? Sveriges Riksbank., Retrieved from https://www.riksbank.se/globalassets/media/tal/svenska/skingsley/2016/tal_skingsley_161116_eng.pdf, Retrieved November 19, 2020, from.

Sklavos, G., Theodossiou, G., Papanikolaou, Z., Karelakis, C., & Ragazou, K. (2024). Environmental, Social, and Governance-Based Artificial Intelligence Governance: Digitalizing firms' leadership and human resources management. *Sustainability, 16*(16), 7154. DOI: 10.3390/su16167154

Skubis, I., Wolniak, R., & Grebski, W. W. (2024). AI and Human-Centric Approach in Smart Cities Management: Case Studies from Silesian and Lesser Poland Voivodships. *Sustainability, 16*(18), 8279.

Slaoui, H. (2021). *The Impact of Covid-19 on the Hospitality Industry and How to Recover from Such Global Pandemic* (Doctoral dissertation, HEC Montréal).

Smales, L. A. (2017). The importance of fear: Investor sentiment and stock market returns. *Applied Economics, 49*(34), 3395–3421.

Smith, J., & Zhang, X. (2024). ESG data standardization: A machine learning-based approach. *The Journal of Financial Data Science, 6*(3), 203–219. DOI: 10.3905/jfds.2024.1.030

Snoek, J., Larochelle, H., & Adams, R. P. (2012). Practical Bayesian optimization of machine learning algorithms. *Advances in Neural Information Processing Systems, 25*, 2951–2959.

Song, Y., Chen, X., Hao, T., Liu, Z., & Lan, Z. (2019). Exploring two decades of research on classroom dialogue by using bibliometric analysis. *Computers & Education, 137*, 12–31. DOI: 10.1016/j.compedu.2019.04.002

Sony, M., & Naik, S. (2019). Key ingredients for evaluating Industry 4.0 readiness for organizations: A literature review. *Benchmarking, 27*(7), 2213–2232. DOI: 10.1108/BIJ-09-2018-0284

Spiwoks, M., Bizer, K., & Hein, O. (2008). Informational cascades: A mirage? *Journal of Economic Behavior & Organization, 67*, 193–199. DOI: 10.1016/j.jebo.2007.06.005

Stambaugh, R. F., Yu, J. F., & Yuan, Y. (2012). The short of it: Investor sentiment and anomalies. *Journal of Financial Economics, 104*, 288–302. DOI: 10.1016/j.jfineco.2011.12.001

Stark, C. R. (1992). *Non-linear series: A dynamical system approach.* Howell Tong.

Stoffi, F. J. B., De Beckker, K., Maldonado, J. E., & De Witte, K. (2021). Assessing sensitivity of machine learning predictions. a novel toolbox with an application to financial literacy. arXiv preprint arXiv:2102.04382.

Suresha, B., Srinidhi, V. R., Verma, D., Manu, K. S., & Krishna, T. A. (2022). The impact of ESG inclusion on price, liquidity and financial performance of Indian stocks: Evidence from stocks listed in BSE and NSE ESG indices. *Investment Management and Financial Innovations, 19*(4), 40–50.

Tai, C. S. (2014). Can investor sentiment be a channel of contagion during the 1997 Asian crisis? Evidence from closed-end country funds. *Journal of Accounting and Finance, 14*, 142–170. DOI: 10.2139/ssrn.1464130

Takyi, P. O., & Bentum-Ennin, I. (2021). The impact of COVID-19 on stock market performance in Africa: A Bayesian structural time series approach. *Journal of Economics and Business, 115*, 105968. DOI: 10.1016/j.jeconbus.2020.105968 PMID: 33318718

Tanaka, K., & Yamada, R. (2024). AI-powered ESG analysis: Assessing corporate sustainability in emerging markets. *International Journal of Sustainability, 15*(1), 56–75. DOI: 10.1007/s10867-024-00123-9

Tanpat Kraiwanit, J. A. (2019) An Acceptance of The Financial Instruments Trading by Artificial Intelligence: AI.

Terdpaopong, K., Terdpaopong, K., & Rickards, R. (2021). Thai Non-Life Insurance Companies' Resilience and the Historic 2011 Floods: Some Recommendations for Greater Sustainability. *Sustainability, 13*(16), 8890.

Thach, N. N., Hanh, H. T., Huy, D. T. N., & Vu, Q. N. (2021). technology quality management of the industry 4.0 and cybersecurity risk management on current banking activities in emerging markets-the case in Vietnam. *International Journal of Qualitative Research, 15*(3), 845.

Thakur, A., & Singh, R. (2024). ESG risk management: A data-driven approach to sustainability. *Journal of Corporate Finance, 80*, 102584. DOI: 10.1016/j.jcorpfin.2024.102584

The role of artificial intelligence in promoting sustainable business operations and autonomy. (2023, December 1). IEEE Conference Publication | IEEE Xplore. https://ieeexplore.ieee.org/abstract/document/10434654/

Thiebes, S., Lins, S., & Sunyaev, A. (2021). Trustworthy artificial intelligence. *Electronic Markets, 31*(2), 447–464. DOI: 10.1007/s12525-020-00441-4

Topol, E. (2019). *Deep medicine: How artificial intelligence can make healthcare human again.* Basic Books Hachette Book Group.

Truby, J. (2020). Governing Artificial Intelligence to benefit the UN Sustainable Development Goals. *ERN: Regulation (IO) (Topic).* https://doi.org/.DOI: 10.1002/sd.2048

Truby, J., Brown, R., & Dahdal, A. (2020). Banking on AI. *Law and Financial Markets Review*, *14*(2), 110–120.

Truby, J., Brown, R., & Dahdal, A. (2020). Banking on AI: Mandating a Proactive Approach to AI Regulation in the Financial Sector. *Law and Financial Markets Review*, *14*(2), 110–120.

Tsay, R. S. (2000). *Analysis of financial time series*. Wiley.

Türegün, N. (2019). Impact of technology in financial reporting: The case of Amazon Go. *Journal of Corporate Accounting & Finance*, *30*(3), 90–95. DOI: 10.1002/jcaf.22394

Tussyadiah, I. (2020). A review of research into automation in tourism: Launching the robotics and AI in tourism and hospitality research agenda. *Journal of Hospitality & Tourism Research (Washington, D.C.)*, *44*(7), 1085–1111.

Tussyadiah, I. P. (2020). A review of research into automation in tourism: Launching the Annals of Tourism Research Curated Collection on AI and Robotics in Tourism. *Annals of Tourism Research*, *81*, 102883. DOI: 10.1016/j.annals.2020.102883

Uniyal, R. S. D. M., & Sharma, N. (2020). Emerging Use of Artificial Intelligence, Robots & Service Automation in Hotel Industry. *International Journal of Future Generation Communication and Networking*, *13*(3), 2785–2790.

Vakkuri, V., Kemell, K.-K., Kultanen, J., & Abrahamsson, P. (2020). The Current State of Industrial Practice in AI Ethics. *IEEE Software*, *37*(5), 50–57.

Van Eck, N. J., & Waltman, L. (2010). Software survey: VOSviewer, a computer program for bibliometric mapping. *Scientometrics*, *84*(2), 523–538. DOI: 10.1007/s11192-009-0146-3 PMID: 20585380

Van Eck, N. J., & Waltman, L. (2017). Citation-based clustering of publications using CitNetExplorer and VOSviewer. *Scientometrics*, *111*(2), 1053–1070. DOI: 10.1007/s11192-017-2300-7 PMID: 28490825

Van Wynsberghe, A. (2021). Sustainable AI: AI for sustainability and the sustainability of AI. *AI and Ethics*, *1*, 213–218. DOI: 10.1007/s43681-021-00043-6

Varma, P., Nijjer, S., Sood, K., Grima, S., & Rupeika-Apoga, R. (2022). Thematic Analysis of Financial Technology (Fintech) Influence on the Banking Industry. In *Risks* (Vol. 10, Issue 10). MDPI. DOI: 10.3390/risks10100186

Varsha, V. R., Gholap, A. T., Santhosh, C. H., Bagali, A., & Tulasi, R. (2024). Fintech And Sustainable Finance: A Review Of Environmental, Social, And Governance (Esg) Integration. *Educational Administration: Theory and Practice*, 6816–6824. DOI: 10.53555/kuey.v30i5.4019

Velte, P. (2017). Does ESG Performance Have an Impact on Financial Performance? Evidence from Germany. https://papers.ssrn.com/abstract=2916741

Verma, S., Sharma, R., Deb, S., & Maitra, D. (2021). Artificial intelligence in marketing: Systematic review and future research direction. *International Journal of Information Management Data Insights*, *1*(1), 100002. DOI: 10.1016/j.jjimei.2020.100002

Villani, C., Bonnet, Y., Berthet, C., Levin, F., Schoenauer, M., Cornut, A. C., & Rondepierre, B. (2018). *Donner un sens à l'intelligence artificielle: pour une stratégie nationale et européenne. Conseil national du numérique. Addo, P. M., Baumann, D., McMurren, J., Verhulst, S. G., Young, A., & Zahuranec, A. J. (2021). Usages émergents des technologies au service du développement: un nouveau paradigme des intelligences*. Éditions AFD.

Vinodan, A., Meera, S., & Shreeansh, M. (2023). Incentivized adoption of smart tourism services: Host community perspective. *Smart Tourism, 4*(2), 2454.

Vinuesa, R., Azizpour, H., Leite, I., Balaam, M., Dignum, V., Domisch, S., Felländer, A., Langhans, S., Tegmark, M., & Nerini, F. (2019). The role of artificial intelligence in achieving the Sustainable Development Goals. *Nature Communications, 11*. Advance online publication. DOI: 10.1038/s41467-019-14108-y PMID: 31932590

Vlačić, B., Corbo, L., Costa e Silva, S., & Dabić, M. (2021). The evolving role of artificial intelligence in marketing: A review and research agenda. *Journal of Business Research, 128*, 187–203. DOI: 10.1016/j.jbusres.2021.01.055

Waliszewski, K., & Warchlewska, A. (2020). Attitudes towards artificial intelligence in the area of personal financial planning: A case study of selected countries. *Entrepreneurship and Sustainability Issues, 8*(2), 399–420. DOI: 10.9770/jesi.2020.8.2(24)

Wang, S., & Pradhan Dr, S. (2020). Exploring factors influencing older adults' willingness to use robo-advisors.

Wang, X., & Leou, C. H. (2015). A study of tourism motivation, perceived value and destination loyalty for Macao cultural and heritage tourists. *International journal of marketing studies, 7*(6), 83-91.

Wang, F., & Liu, H. (2024). Corporate sustainability and ESG ratings: A critical review of AI-based methods. *Journal of Environmental Management, 365*, 133801. DOI: 10.1016/j.jenvman.2024.133801

Wang, F., Wei, J. C., & Zhao, D. T. (2014). A quantifiable risky decision model in corporating individual memory into informational cascade. *Systems Research and Behavioral Science, 31*, 537–553. DOI: 10.1002/sres.2294

Wang, Y. (2024). Ethical considerations of AI in financial decision. *Computers and Artificial Intelligence*. Advance online publication. DOI: 10.59400/cai.v2i1.1290

Wannemo, F. (2024). Post-human Hospitality? Opportunities and risks with AI: An exploratative case study of AI in the hospitality industry of Värmland.

Welch, I. (2000). Herding among security analysts. *Journal of Financial Economics, 58*, 369–396. DOI: 10.1016/S0304-405X(00)00076-3

Welch, I. (2022). The wisdom of the robinhood crowd. *The Journal of Finance, LXXVII*, 1489–1527. DOI: 10.3386/W27866

Wolfert, S., Ge, L., Verdouw, C., & Bogaardt, M.-J. (2017). Big Data in Smart Farming – A review. *Agricultural Systems, 153*, 69–80. DOI: 10.1016/j.agsy.2017.01.023

Wolff, A., Gooch, D., Cavero Montaner, J. J., Rashid, U., & Kortuem, G. (2016). Special issue on data literacy: Articles creating an understanding of data literacy for a data-driven society. *Journal of Community Informatics, 12*(3), 9–26. www.ci-journal.net/index.php/ciej/article/view/1286. DOI: 10.15353/joci.v12i3.3275

Wong, P. (2019). Democratizing Algorithmic Fairness. *Philosophy & Technology, 33*, 225–244. DOI: 10.1007/s13347-019-00355-w

Wu, J. M. (2015). Helpful laymen in informational cascades. *Journal of Economic Behavior & Organization, 116*, 407–415. DOI: 10.1016/j.jebo.2015.05.002

Wu, M., & Lin, C. (2024). Data transparency and explainable AI in ESG rating systems. *Journal of Financial Regulation and Compliance, 32*(2), 156–176. DOI: 10.1108/JFRC-04-2024-0027

Wu, Q., Yan, D., & Umair, M. (2023). Assessing the role of competitive intelligence and practices of dynamic capabilities in business accommodation of SMEs. *Economic Analysis and Policy, 77*, 1103–1114. DOI: 10.1016/j.eap.2022.11.024

Wu, W. S., Chang, H. H., Suardi, S., & Chang, Y. C. (2013). The cascade effect on lending conditions: Evidence from the syndicated loan market. *Journal of Business Finance & Accounting, 40*, 1247–1275. DOI: 10.1111/jbfa.12050

Xu, Z., & Chen, W. (2024). ESG rating inconsistencies and portfolio management: An AI perspective. *Journal of Financial Economics, 150*(3), 874–898. DOI: 10.1016/j.jfineco.2024.101128

Yahya, M. R. (2023). *Exploring the Relationship Between Corporate Governance Mechanism and Financial Performance: Evidence From Listed Companies*. West Science Accounting and Finance., DOI: 10.58812/wsaf.v1i02.133

Yang, D., & Park, J. (2024). AI-driven ESG assessment models: Opportunities and challenges. *Journal of Business Research, 158*, 104872. DOI: 10.1016/j.jbusres.2024.104872

Yasir, A., & Ahmed, A. (2023). Introducing the Concept of Intelligent Financial Inclusion. *International Journal of Computer Science & Network Security, 23*(4), 103–110.

Ye, J., & Jensen, M. (2022). Influences of introducing an online community in a crowdsourcing contest platform. *Information Systems Journal, 32*(6), 1203–1230.

Yesuf, Y. M., Getahun, D. A., & Debas, A. T. (2024). Determinants of employees' creativity: Modeling the mediating role of organizational motivation to innovate. *Journal of Innovation and Entrepreneurship, 13*(1), 8.

Yun, J. J., Liu, Z., & Zhao, X. (2021). Introduction: Ambidextrous open innovation in the 4th Industrial Revolution. *Science, Technology & Society, 26*(2), 183–200. DOI: 10.1177/09717218211006969

Zakaria, S., Manaf, S. M. A., Amron, M. T., & Suffian, M. T. M. (2023). Has the world of finance changed? A review of the influence of artificial intelligence on financial management studies. Information Management and Business Review, 15(4 (SI) I), 420-432.

Zaremba, A., & Demir, E. (2023). ChatGPT: Unlocking the future of NLP in finance. *Modern Finance*, *1*(1), 93–98.

Zaremba, A., Kizys, R., Aharon, D. Y., & Demir, E. (2020). Infected Markets: Novel Coronavirus, Government Interventions, and Stock Return Volatility around the Globe. *Finance Research Letters*, *35*, 101597. DOI: 10.1016/j.frl.2020.101597 PMID: 32550842

Zarifhonarvar, A. (2024). Economics of chatgpt: A labor market view on the occupational impact of artificial intelligence. *Journal of Electronic Business & Digital Economics*, *3*(2), 100–116.

Zarsky, T. (2016). The trouble with algorithmic decisions: An analytic road map to examine efficiency and fairness in automated and opaque decision making. *Science, Technology & Human Values*, *41*(1), 118–132. DOI: 10.1177/0162243915605575

Zavrazhnyi, K. Y. (2024). *The impact of the use of artificial intelligence and digital transformation on sustainable business development*. https://essuir.sumdu.edu.ua/handle/123456789/95082

Zdravković, M., Panetto, H., & Weichhart, G. (2022). AI-enabled Enterprise Information Systems for Manufacturing. In *Enterprise Information Systems* (Vol. 16, Issue 4, pp. 668–720). Taylor and Francis Ltd. DOI: 10.1080/17517575.2021.1941275

Zhang, L., Zou, L., & Shi, M. (2024, July). Immersing and Perceiving in Tourism Scenarios: The Interaction Mechanism between Digital Technologies and Tourists. In *2024 IEEE 24th International Conference on Software Quality, Reliability, and Security Companion (QRS-C)* (pp. 1292-1301). IEEE.

Zhang, R., & Li, S. (2024). ESG controversies and market reactions: Evidence from AI-generated sentiment analysis. *Journal of Financial Markets*, *76*, 100852. DOI: 10.1016/j.finmar.2024.100852

Zhang, W., Zhao, L., Xia, H., Sun, S., Sun, J., Qin, M., Li, X., Zhao, Y., Zhao, Y., Cai, X., Zheng, L., Wang, X., & An, B. (2024). A Multimodal Foundation Agent for Financial Trading: Tool-Augmented, Diversified, and Generalist. In *Proceedings of the ACM SIGKDD International Conference on Knowledge Discovery and Data Mining* (pp. 4314–4325). Association for Computing Machinery. DOI: 10.1145/3637528.3671801

Zhang, X., Chu, Z., Ren, L., & Xing, J. (2023). Open innovation and sustainable competitive advantage: The role of organizational learning. *Technological Forecasting and Social Change*, *186*, 122114.

Zhao, J., & Fariñas, B. G. (2022). Artificial intelligence and sustainable decisions. *European Business Organization Law Review*, *24*(1), 1–39. DOI: 10.1007/s40804-022-00262-2

Zhao, L., & Huang, F. (2024). AI-driven ESG reporting: Enhancing data integrity and investor confidence. *Corporate Governance*, *32*(1), 49–72. DOI: 10.1111/corg.2024.00128

Zhong, L., Sun, S., Law, R., & Zhang, X. (2021). Impact of artificial intelligence on service employee engagement and organizational performance: A conceptual framework. *International Journal of Hospitality Management*, *93*, 102768.

Zhong, L., Zhang, X., Rong, J., Chan, H. K., Xiao, J., & Kong, H. (2021). Construction and empirical research on acceptance model of service robots applied in hotel industry. *Industrial Management & Data Systems*, *121*(6), 1325–1352.

Zinsou, K. M. C. (2019). Reporting Intégré (RI): étude de sa diffusion, de sa mise en œuvre et de son adoption par les sociétés cotées françaises| Theses. fr (Doctoral dissertation, Toulouse 1). Bertrand, M. (2007). Utilisation du modèle d'acceptation technologique chez les professionnels intéressés à la réalité virtuelle comme outil thérapeutique: quels sont les facteurs influençant leur décision.

Zoph, B., & Le, Q. V. (2016). Neural architecture search with reinforcement learning. arXiv preprint arXiv:1611.01578.

About the Contributors

Fouad Daidai is an Associate Professor at ENCG El Jadida, specializing in finance and accounting. With a PhD in Economic Sciences and Management, he teaches subjects such as portfolio management, capital markets, etc. His research, published in Scopus-indexed journals, focuses on corporate governance, capital structure, artificial intelligence (AI), and blockchain technology. He explores the impact of AI on governance, financial reporting accuracy, and market trend prediction. His work on blockchain highlights its potential to enhance transparency, security, and efficiency in financial transactions. Dr. Daidai is also a peer reviewer for Scopus-indexed journals and a member of the editorial board of Alternatives Managériales et Economiques. He actively participates in international conferences, presenting his research and collaborating with global experts to contribute to advancements in finance and management technologies.

Mimoun Benali is a full professor in finance at the Sidi Mohamed Ben Abdellah University in Fez. He holds a PhD and is affiliated with an academic institution where he actively contributes to research and supervises doctoral students. His expertise includes behavioral finance, financial and non-financial risk management, artificial intelligence applied to finance, and sustainable financing strategies. He has published several articles in indexed journals, including on energy efficiency, private equity, and machine and deep learning algorithms to model financing decisions and financial asset valuation. His recent publications include the impact of driver behavior on carbon footprint as well as the application of machine learning techniques to predict stock prices in the energy sector in Morocco. In addition, he actively supervises PhD projects covering a wide range of topics, from risk management in publicly traded companies to the impact of AI on decision-making in Moroccan private equity firms.

Larbi Tamnine is a full professor in Management Sciences and a member of the Agrégation Committee in Economics and Management. He serves as Deputy Director for Academic Affairs at ENCG, Sidi Mohamed Ben Abdellah University, Fès. With extensive teaching experience, he covers Moroccan and international economics, advanced accounting, strategic management, corporate taxation, and financial analysis. Dr. Tamnine has published widely in prestigious journals, focusing on corporate governance, capital structure, and the impact of AI and blockchain in finance and accounting. His notable works include studies on e-government, HR modernization in public administration, and blockchain's role in governance. He actively participates in international conferences, collaborating with global experts. Dr. Tamnine has co-authored practical manuals on tax, social, civil, and commercial law, approved by Morocco's Ministry of National Education. He also founded an educational website offering resources for economics and management students. Recognized for his contributions, he brings innovation and new perspectives to teaching and research in management sciences.

***

Metasebia Adula is an Assistant Professor in the Department of Management, Bule Hora University, Ethiopia.

Ahmed Aftiss is a professor and researcher in Economic Sciences and Management from the Faculty of Legal, Economic, and Social Sciences (FSJES).

Khawla Amrani is a Ph.D. candidate in Economic Sciences and Management at the FSJES of Fez.

Hanae Amrani has a Ph.D. in Economic Sciences and Management from the Faculty of Legal, Economic, and Social Sciences (FSJES).

Imane Boudri, Doctor in Economics and Finance, is an Associate Professor in the Finance Department at ISCAE, Morocco, specializing in financial innovation and market analysis.

Zouheir Boussouf is a professor and researcher at the Multidisciplinary Faculty of Taza, Sidi Mohamed Ben Abdellah University, Fez, Morocco.

Puja Chopra, Ph.D., MBA, is an accomplished academician and Assistant Professor at Christ University, with over 15 years of teaching experience in renowned private and government universities. She holds a Ph.D. in Applied Economics, along with double M.A. degrees in Economics and English, showcasing her strong interdisciplinary foundation. Dr. Chopra specializes in the intersection of Economics and Finance and has an impressive record of publications in prestigious journals, including those indexed in Scopus, ABDC, and UGC CARE. Her passion for academic excellence and innovative teaching has shaped countless future leaders, and she remains committed to fostering intellectual growth in higher education.

Rui Manuel Teixeira Santos Dias. Postdoctoral degree in Finance at the State University of Feira de Santana (BR), Department of Exact Sciences. Doctor of Finance at the University of Évora—Institute of Research and Advanced Training (PT). Diploma of Advanced Studies in Doctoral Studies (DEA), at the University of Extremadura (ES), in the scientific area of Financial Economics. He served as Chief Financial Officer in various companies for 26 years.

Munshura Faria is a Research Assistant at the School of Business and Economics, North South University

Rukmini Giridhar is an MBA graduate in Finance. She has two years of experience in the area of taxation and accounting providing greater depth in the area of finance and is currently working in the taxation domain. Her research focuses on transformative role of Artificial Intelligence in Fostering Financial Literacy in manufacturing firms.

Ramya H P holds an MBA in finance and is pursuing a Ph.D. in investments from VTU. Currently, she works as an assistant professor at the Department of Management Studies at DSCE, with 15 years of experience. She has conducted workshops and seminars on topics such as financial management using Excel, financial accounting and taxation, and financial statement analysis, and has presented and published research papers in various national and international journals. Additionally, she is trained in personal finance, data processing using Python, taxation, financial modelling, trading strategies, portfolio optimization using the Markowitz model, and investment management. She is also an AICTE-nominated innovation ambassador for the Institute Innovation Council.

Mohammad Irfan is presently working as an Associate Professor at School of Business and Management, Christ University, Bengaluru, India. Dr. Irfan has done his Ph.D. from the Central University of Haryana. He is MBA (Finance), M.Com (Account and Law), and MA (Economics). He has qualified UGC-JRF/SRF/NET in Management and Commerce. Dr. Irfan certified NSEs (NCFM) and BSEs certification. He has experience of more than sixteen years in the area of SAPM, Artificial Intelligence, Machine Learning, Blockchain, Cryptocurrency, Financial Engineering, Fintech, Green Finance, and Alternative Finance. He has to his credit more than 53+ Scopus Indexed articles, includes The Journal of Economic Cooperation and Development (Q2), International Journal of Business Excellence (IJBEX), International Journal of Economics and Management (IJEM), Montenegrin Journal of Economics (Q2), Cogent Business & Management (Taylor & Francis) (Q2), Indian Journal of Finance (IJF) and Journal of Islamic Monetary Economics and Finance (JIMF). His citations reached 390+ along with 12 H-index. Dr. Irfan has published 9 books in Springer, IGI Global Publication (Scopus indexed).

Quazi Islam is a coordinator at NSU Startups Next and a Senior Lecturer of Strategy and HR in the School of Business and Economics, North South University and a Series Editor at Emerald Group Publishing.

Shashi Kant is an Assistant Professor at the College of Business and Economics, Department of Management, Bule Hora University, Ethiopia.

Gharmili Meryem is a graduate of the National School of Business and Management (ENCG) in Fès and currently serve as a senior executive at the Ministry of Economy and Finance. Meryem's academic and professional journey reflects their passion for economics, finance, and the strategic challenges of public management. Meryem is currently pursuing a doctorate focusing on artificial intelligence in portfolio management, with the ambition of contributing to the advancement of knowledge and practices in this field.

Tafese Niguse is a PhD Scholar, College of Business and Economics, Department of Marketing Management, Bule Hora University, Ethiopia.

Anand Patil is an accomplished academician and professional with a rich background in commerce. He currently serves as an Associate Professor at CHRIST (Deemed to be) University, Bangalore, within the School of Business and Management. Holding M.Com, MPhil and a Ph.D. in Commerce from Shivaji University, Kolhapur, Dr. Patil's research interests span Economic and Financial Analysis, Digital and Technological Transformation, Empowerment and Inclusivity, Investment Strategies and Market Analysis, and Employment and Education. With over 23 years of academic experience, Dr. Patil specialises in Accounting, Finance, and Taxation. He complements his extensive academic background with three years of industry experience in auditing companies, educational institutions, and banks. His strong analytical and problem-solving skills are further enhanced by his proficiency in tools such as Excel and SPSS. An active researcher, Dr. Patil frequently presents at international conferences and publishes in esteemed journals. Along with writing several book chapters and volumes, he is also the author of "Fundamentals of Accounting" and "Mutual Funds and Investment Management". His administrative contributions include serving as the Head of the Curriculum Development Committee and the Coordinator of the Internal Quality Assurance Cell (IQAC). Additionally, he mentors students in finance and management, solidifying his invaluable role in the university's academic community.

Hicham Sadok holds a PhD in Economics and Management Sciences from University of Bordeaux (France). Currently, he is a Professor of Economics and Busines at the Univeristy Mohammed V in Rabat (Morocco). His research interests include Finance, Digital Economy, Development Economics and Entrepreneurship. He has 13 years of experience as a teacher-researcher and consultant. He has published more than ten indexed articles, 4 book chapters, 2 books, around thirty participation in scientific conferences and a few popularisation science writings.

Neha Sanwal is a BBA Honours graduate from Christ University, with a demonstrated passion for Business Analysis and Management Consulting. Currently, Ms. Sanwal is an executive Analyst at Deloitte India. She is also exploring opportunities in management consulting and beyond, bringing with her strong creative, leadership, and communication skills. She has gained valuable practical experience through internships with leading companies such as Swiggy SteppinOut, Adani Realty, and Rigic Global Solutions, where she developed expertise in business research, event planning, inventory management, and human resources. Ms. Sanwal also actively participated in university activities, serving as a University Student Council Member and Head of the Events Committee at her university's business club. Her academic excellence is reflected in her receipt of the Extra Curricular and Meritorious Scholarships. Ms. Sanwal is deeply committed to delivering value, innovation, and exceptional results, applying her problem-solving and analytical skills to drive success in all her endeavors.

Feng Sun is Senior Economist working in South China Normal University. He graduated with Ph.D. from University of Science and Technology Beijing. He has researching and working experiences in finance and management for about twenty years. His main research interests include financial econometrics and statistics, applied analysis for economics and management, etc. He has been invited to review 150+ papers verified in Web of Science. He is Guest Editor and Editorial Board Member for several academic journals now.

Aynetu Terefe is a Lecturer at the Department of Management, Bule Hora University, Ethiopia

Index

www.ingramcontent.com/pod-product-compliance
Lightning Source LLC
LaVergne TN
LVHW062109300926
849161LV00010B/2407